Claude-Nicolas

L E D O U X

The MIT Press

Cambridge, Massachusetts

London, England

Claude-Nicolas

L E D O U X

*Architecture and
Social Reform at the
End of the
Ancien Régime*

ANTHONY VIDLER

This book was set in Bembo by Graphic Composition and printed and bound by Halliday Lithograph in the United States of America.

Library of Congress Cataloging-in-Publication Data

Vidler, Anthony.
Claude-Nicolas Ledoux : architecture and social reform at the end of the Ancien Régime / Anthony Vidler.
    p. cm.
Bibliography: p.
Includes index.
ISBN 0-262-22032-6
1. Ledoux, Claude Nicolas, 1736–1806—Criticism and interpreta-
tion. 2. Architecture and society—France—History—18th cen-
tury. 3. Neoclassicism (Architecture)—France. I. Title.
NA1053.L4V5   1990
720′.92—dc20   89-30482
                                          CIP

For Emily

CONTENTS

Frontispiece: Marguerite Gér-
ard, *Portrait of Claude-Nicolas
Ledoux*. Painting from the
Musée Cognacq-Jay, Paris.
The drawing on the table
shows the Barrière de Reuilly.

My interest in the work of Ledoux was stimulated by Colin Rowe in Cambridge nearly thirty years ago; it has been sustained by the curiosity of colleagues and students in Princeton and encouraged by architects and scholars both in the United States and Europe. During this long period many have contributed in different ways to my understanding of the subject and the furthering of my research, and I here gratefully acknowledge those whom I am unable to mention by name. I have been especially indebted to successive classes of undergraduate and graduate students, whose architectural analyses have each year revealed new aspects of Ledoux's formal imagination. My doctoral students have been both receptive and patient as the study was developed and revised, generously offering time and expertise to the reading of partial drafts. Three in particular, who have become valued friends and colleagues, have had a formative influence on the work: Demetri Porphyrios, Mary McLeod, and Richard Etlin. Richard Etlin's own study of the social and architectural history of the cemetery in late-eighteenth-century France provided, so to speak, a test case in the elaboration of a social history of architecture at a time when such studies were rare. A number of individuals have contributed analytical drawings to the book, among whom Deborah Oliver, who spent an entire summer reconstructing the workings of the *saline,* and Malvina Lampietti and Lorissa Kimm, who developed the comparative studies of the *barrières,* must be singled out.

Earlier versions of this book, some considerably different in approach and length than the present monograph, were read by George Collins, Giorgio Ciucci, Robin Middleton, Robin Evans, Bruno Fortier, Françoise Choay, Alan Colquhoun, Antoine Picon, Joseph Rykwert, and Georges Teyssot, all of whom have offered substantial commentary and advice important for the revision of the manuscript. Mona Ozouf, Monique Mosser, Daniel Rabreau, Wolfgang Herrmann, Robert Darnton, Michael Fried, Werner Szambien, David van Zanten, Stanford Anderson, Kurt Forster, Ignasi Solà Morales, and Manfredo Tafuri have responded to portions of the work presented as papers or published essays, and have been extremely generous with the results of their own research. Before his death, Donald Drew Egbert was an enthusiastic listener and often passed on information culled from the archives of the Ecole des Beaux-Arts; Ira O. Wade made his research notes on Voltaire and the foundations of Versoix freely available.

My scholarly interest in Ledoux has always been complemented by my interest in contemporary architecture, itself shaped by critics and architects who have looked to the work of the eighteenth century with more than academic curiosity. Among numerous friends whose theory and design have been committed to a conscious rereading of eighteenth-century typologies and languages, I have to mention Aldo Rossi, Leon Krier, Maurice Culot, Antoine Grumbach, Diana Agrest, Mario Gandelsonas, and, above all, Peter Eisenman, who has never ceased to wonder at the stubbornness with which I have followed historical as well as critical concerns. The scholarly example and friendship of Carl Schorske has, more than he knows, sustained my work throughout.

Initial research in Besançon and Paris in 1969 and 1970 was partially financed by grants from the Committee on Research in the Humanities and Social Sciences of Princeton University. Paid leaves of absence from Princeton allowed for long periods of work in Paris and the archives of the Salines de l'Est at Lons-le-Saunier. The librarians and staffs of the Firestone and Marquand libraries in Princeton, the Clark Art Institute in Williamstown, Massachusetts, the Bibliothèque Nationale, the Archives Nationales, and the Ecole des Beaux-Arts in Paris, and the departmental archives in Lons-le-Saunier, Besançon, and Aix-en-Provence have been receptive and helpful. The School of Architecture in Princeton, the Dipartimento di storia dell'architettura in Venice, the Architectural Association School of Architecture in London, and the former Institute for Architecture and Urban Studies in New York have provided lively contexts for discussion of work in progress. Richard Edwards, Director of the Fondation Claude-Nicolas Ledoux, Arc-et-Senans, and his staff have been unfailingly supportive throughout. Finally, I must pay homage to the calm and forceful way in which my successive editors, Georges Teyssot and Mark Rakatansky, helped to bring the book to a conclusion, and to the skills of Alicia Kennedy for her long-drawn-out struggle to unify a heterogeneous manuscript.

The architecture of Claude-Nicolas Ledoux, from well before the French Revolution until the present, has proved to be a fertile ground for critical battles and mythical interpretations, even as it has stubbornly resisted historical exegesis. A history of attitudes toward Ledoux would, indeed, furnish a well-illustrated account of the most extreme political and aesthetic positions in architectural criticism, theory, and history over the last two centuries, without, at the same time, revealing more than a caricature of his life and professional activity. The history of these admittedly creative misinterpretations began in his own lifetime. Ledoux, at first recognized as a brilliant but wayward designer, was quickly attacked as an architect ruinous for his patrons, a dangerous megalomaniac, and an enemy of the classical tradition. The staunch neoclassicist Quatremère de Quincy accused him of having submitted architecture to "kinds of torture,"[1] and this aesthetic disapproval was soon reinforced by Ledoux's political disgrace after 1789. The former architect of Madame du Barry and faithful servant of the Crown, designer of the monumental tollgates of Paris erected by the hated Ferme Générale, found little sympathy either for his buildings or for his ideal projects of rural and social reform during the last years of his life.

Quatremère de Quincy's verdict was, for different reasons, echoed by the generation of the 1830s. Accusing the architects of the late eighteenth century of having reduced architecture to mere geometry, "the bony skeleton of an emaciated invalid," Victor Hugo counted the *barrières* of Paris among the worst examples of modern architecture: "Are we fallen to such a degree of misery that we should be forced to admire the *barrières* of Paris?" he asked in his celebrated declaration of "War on the Demolishers," in 1832.[2] Hugo's was only one of the voices condemning Ledoux's architecture under the July Monarchy and Empire. Léon Vaudoyer, the architect son of one of Ledoux's younger contemporaries and emulators, Antoine-Laurent-Thomas Vaudoyer, invented the caustic epithet *architecture parlante* to characterize the most pictogrammatic of his designs.[3] Only Haussmann's demolition of the remaining *barrières* in conjunction with the expansion of Paris in 1859 renewed interest in these survivals of an *ancien régime* already being nostalgically remembered by the brothers Goncourt in their studies of the lives of Madame du Barry and Mlle Guimard.

The commonplaces fixed earlier in the century were repeated with few exceptions until the late 1920s, when a modernist sensibility, appreciative of abstraction, allowed Emil Kaufmann to invent a new myth: Ledoux as the forerunner of Le Corbusier, as he expressed it in the tantalizing if historically fallacious characterization of his *Von Ledoux bis Le Corbusier*, published in 1933.[4] Ledoux was now presented as an eponymous hero of modernism, a "revolutionary" avant-garde architect before the fact. Certainly, as Kaufmann himself recognized, Ledoux was no political revolutionary; but his formal transformations and utopian aspirations seemed, in retrospect, to anticipate those of the emerging bourgeois state. Like Ernst Cassirer, preoccupied at the same time with the resolution of problems of individuality (Rousseau) and objectivity (Kant), Kaufmann found in Ledoux a rich subject for study at a moment when the rational ideals of the *neue Sachlichkeit* were being attacked by the nostalgic and emotive appeals of the Third Reich. That Hitler's architects would themselves find inspiration in the archaistic monumentality of neoclassicism, while denouncing modernism as Bolshevik; that the socialist architect Hannes Meyer would, on his part, claim Ledoux as a forerunner of the social architect; that, in opposition to both Meyer and Kaufmann, Hans Sedlmayr, a conservative and former Nazi sympathizer, would rejoin the attack on Ledoux, this time as the evil, rationalist genius of a "loss of center"; these turns of interpretation only reinforced the mystique surrounding his architecture.[5]

The record was further confused by the sociopolitical debates of the late 1960s in which Ledoux was variously hailed as anticipating the communal architecture of utopian socialism, preparing the way for the garden-city movement, inventing the formal vocabulary of Russian constructivism, and even exploring in advance the visual symbolism of surrealism. Underlying many of these positions was the belief that his inventive forms and evident utopianism indicated a "visionary" power that stemmed from his involvement with late-eighteenth-century mysticism, reinforcing the idea that Ledoux was an architect above and beyond history. The confusion has been further encouraged during the last twenty years by Ledoux's adoption by two, not entirely synonymous, architectural movements: "neorationalism" has claimed his legacy of formal "reduction" and typological invention, while "postmodernism" has unmercifully ransacked his imagery as a so-called palliative to the very abstract modernism he was, half a century ago, seen as inspiring.

Over fifty years ago, Meyer Schapiro, in an incisive review of the publications of the "New Viennese School" of art history, set out the main outlines of the kind of study that was needed.[6] Assessing Emil Kaufmann's article "The City of the Architect Ledoux" and the later *Von Ledoux bis Le Corbusier*, Schapiro, while recognizing the merit of Kaufmann's rescue of Ledoux, pointed to the limitations of the formal approach in relating architecture to its social context. Kaufmann had attempted to join what he called Ledoux's principle of architectural "autonomy"—the derivation of an architectural aesthetic from internal requirements of construction and use rather than from any external, imposed artistic conception—to a similar characteristic of emerging bourgeois society, "which thinks of itself as composed of isolated, equally free individuals."[7] Schapiro argued that Kaufmann, in fact, had succeeded only in joining an architectural principle to a social principle, one found indeed in Ledoux's writings: "The correlation," Schapiro wrote, "is with bourgeois ideology, not with the actual class structure and conditions of bourgeois society, and depends more on quotations than on a study of social and economic history."[8] Schapiro's conclusion was that Ledoux's apparent modernity had blinded Kaufmann to the specifically eighteenth-century character of his architecture. He noted Ledoux's reliance on symmetry, on massiveness, his lack of interest in new materials, his "encyclopaedist temper," and his close relation to English architects of the period. And in his refusal of ornament and interest in geometry, he was after all equally of his time: "Ledoux," Schapiro hazarded, in a nice comparison, "is, in a sense, the David of the French architecture of his age; he might have constructed the setting of the 'Horatii' or the box and bathtub of 'Marat.'"[9] Schapiro concluded that "Dr. Kaufmann has not yet located Ledoux clearly within his own time," a criticism that has posed a challenge to historians and one that has been answered only partially.

The groundwork for such a social and cultural history of his career has, however, been laid by a number of historians who, working against these "ideologies of reception," have recently tried to resituate Ledoux within the complex conditions of his eighteenth-century practice. Following the lead provided by Geneviève Levallet-Haug in the early 1930s, Wolfgang Herrmann and Johannes Langner have questioned the dating of Ledoux's ideal projects, finding them less precocious than Ledoux or previous historians had claimed; the painstaking research of Michel Gallet has uncovered the archival sources of his biography and work; Bruno Fortier, Monique Mosser, Serge Conard, and Daniel Rabreau have placed his projects in the context of those of his contemporaries and the institutions he served; Mona Ozouf, Beatrice Didier, and Hubert Damisch have reread his "unreadable" text with reference to other, equally difficult pre- or protoromantic writing.[10] A number of monographic studies of other important eighteenth-century architects, including Germain Boffrand, Jacques Soufflot, Etienne-Louis Boullée, Alexandre-Théodore Brongniart, Jean-Laurent Legeay, Charles De Wailly, and Jean-Nicolas-Louis Durand have deepened our knowledge of Ledoux's contemporaries and the conditions of their practice.[11] From these studies it has become clear that, while he certainly cannot be divested of paradox or uniqueness, Ledoux was evidently more typically an architect of the late Enlightenment than many have wished to admit.

The long resistance to a historical consideration of Ledoux's career is, nevertheless, puzzling. For Ledoux, more than many of his architectural contemporaries, was connected through personal relationships and institutional commitments to the highest levels of political administration in the last years of the *ancien régime,* and thereby, by implication at least, must be closely associated with the circumstances of its demise. His works were, by virtue of the rank and notoriety of his patrons, highly visible symbols of *ancien régime* mores and policies. His public service, framed by the end of the Seven Years' War in 1763 and the Revolutionary events of 1789–99, has to be seen in the context of the long-drawn-out financial and political crisis precipitated by foreign wars, domestic debt, and agricultural dearth before 1789; his fortunes were intimately joined to those of the treasury, and to successive ministers of finance. His private practice, sustained by patrons themselves tied to the big fiscal institutions of the regime, was set in the context of the last urban economic boom of the *ancien régime*. In this crisis Ledoux, together with his supporters, attempted to resolve its contradictions by a combination of economic opportunism and an idealistic faith in progressive reform.

Ledoux was noticed very early in his career by the court of Louis XV and adopted by Madame du Barry as an agent of her cultural battle against the supporters of her predecessor, Madame de Pompadour. His elevation to the Académie Royale d'Architecture was forced by du Barry, as was his appointment to the saltworks of eastern France as an architect-inspector. Thence taken up by Parisian society, he received commissions for *hôtels,* country houses, and decorative pavilions from some of the more celebrated courtesans, connoisseurs, and bankers of the day. Moving easily in theatrical, artistic, and literary circles, Ledoux developed lasting friendships with painters such as Hubert Robert and Joseph Vernet and poets such as the Abbé Delille and Jean-Charles-Julien Luce de Lancival together with musicians associated with his father-in-law, the first oboist at the court of Versailles.

For much of this period Ledoux's livelihood was in large part derived from commissions awarded by the richest, most generally hated semiprivate corporation in the realm, the Ferme Générale, or royal general tax farm, composed of a tightly restricted group of *fermiers* earning fixed but considerable profits on sales taxes levied on behalf of the state. Unified by Jean-Baptiste Colbert in 1669 and formally incorporated in 1726, the Ferme had grown by the 1770s to become one of the most important fiscal institutions of the regime. The *fermiers* themselves were immensely rich, guarding their privileges and passing on their offices from father to son to create whole dynasties. Many of Ledoux's private commissions and his two largest public works, the Saline de Chaux and the *barrières* of Paris, stemmed from the patronage of the Ferme.

At the same time, while deeply committed to a society of estates and rapidly disappearing traditional interests, Ledoux was equally firm in his rejection of the "false masks" of luxury denounced by the *philosophes* since Rousseau. His consciousness of the need for an enlightened administration to address problems of rural and urban poverty at their roots was derived from and supported by the laissez-faire economic theories of François Quesnay, the Comte de Mirabeau, and the Abbé Baudeau; his understanding of the crucial role of industry and manufacturing, at first embedded in the "naturalist" theories of these economists, was quickly expanded to embrace a general theory of progress through industry of all kinds. Building on the detailed analyses of *arts et métiers* in Diderot's *Encyclopédie,* Ledoux was quick to register the competition posed by England's increasing industrialization. A new professional, trained at a time when the ideas of the Enlightenment were gaining wide acceptance in the administration, Ledoux was a believer in the technological and aesthetic solution of social problems. In the circle of Physiocratic reformers such as Jean-Charles-Philibert Trudaine de Montigny, Jacques Turgot, and Chrétien-Guillaume de Lamoignon de Malesherbes, Ledoux found an appreciative, if sometimes skeptical, audience for his attempt to invent an appropriate architecture for an agricultural revolution modeled on that of England. With the appointment of Charles-Alexandre de Calonne as Finance Minister after 1783, he found a patron willing to support his ideas for the replanning of Paris in practice.

These ideological affiliations are more or less decipherable in the text of his treatise, entitled, significantly enough, *L'architecture considérée sous le rapport de l'art, des moeurs et de la législation;* published in 1804, two years before his death, it stands, despite its fragmentary qualities, as the architectural equivalent of many reformist programs from the last years of the monarchy. His designs for the ideal city of Chaux, conceived as an extension of the earlier *saline* built for the Ferme Générale in Franche-Comté, attempted to weld rural reform

and industrial progress together in a veritably encyclopedic vision of the aspirations of the Enlightenment. In this, again, Ledoux was less the victim of an untrammeled imagination than he was a proponent of the realistic programs for regional development advanced by engineers and administrators since Colbert—development premised on the extension of the road and canal network, the opening up of mines and quarries, the support of new industries, and the economic benefits of a renewed agriculture.

If his social and ideological leanings were, in this context, easily explicable, his designs, from the beginning, resisted assimilation into the acknowledged currents of taste. While Ledoux shared the reaction of many of his contemporaries to the vegetal excesses of the rococo, his particular version of that "return to antiquity" noted by historians from Louis Hautecoeur to Gallet avoided the eclectic play of an older generation of "Piranesians" like Jean-Laurent Legeay and the scaleless sublime of Etienne-Louis Boullée even as it refused the increasing historicism of younger Greek revivalists following David Le Roy. Similarly, while his Palladianism, like that of his contemporaries Alexandre-Théodore Brongniart, François-Joseph Bélanger, and Jean-François-Thérèse Chalgrin, had its roots in England, his effortless absorption of forms and motifs from the English baroque—Wren, Vanbrugh, and Hawksmoor—demonstrated little strict allegiance to Venetian mannerism.

These peculiarities may, on one level, be explained by the circumstances of Ledoux's education. With no independent means or rich patron, he was unable to follow the traditional route to Rome; his "antiquity" as far as it existed was confined to books and to French examples, and his classicism looked to seventeenth-century France as much as to Italy or Greece. If indeed he ever visited England, it was no doubt late in his career, a confirmation of sources already tapped. Trained as an engraver, his architectural knowledge was derived almost entirely from engravings, from Colin Campbell's *Vitruvius Britannicus,* Jacques-François Blondel's *Architecture française,* and the plates of the *Encyclopédie.* This is perhaps why his architecture, more than that of Blondel's other students, seems at once abstract and theoretical: freely assembled out of representations and images of other buildings, its geometrical reduction is both a product of engraving technique and a means toward aesthetic unity. Ledoux's work is didactic in the same way as Denis Diderot's plates, analytical and synthetic at the same time. This was where Kaufmann sensed the essentially modernizing character of Ledoux's work, an architecture formed not so much out of the combination of ready-made elements, nor out of a replication of historical precedent, nor again with any neoclassical ideal in mind of the sort proposed by Quatremère de Quincy, but rather out of the transformational properties of three-dimensional geometry. Before the standardization of geometric method and stereotomy introduced by the technical schools after the Revolution, Ledoux's geometry produced a rich variety of effects, with solid massing on the exterior and complex interpenetrations of volumes in the interior. Here Ledoux registered the influence of the civil engineers trained in the Ecole des Ponts et Chaussées by Jean-Rodolphe Perronet, many of whom he worked with as architect to the Département des Eaux et Forêts in Burgundy and as Commissaire des Salines in Franche-Comté. Their unique synthesis of mathematical calculation and aesthetic representation became a model for Ledoux's individual public style, one that he himself recognized was a hybrid genre, difficult to accept within the traditional canons of high classicism.

Ledoux's professional career falls into four more or less clearly defined phases, which themselves correspond roughly to changes in the political and financial administration. In his period of apprenticeship, from the early 1760s to 1771, he refurbished a number of *hôtels* and *châteaux* for a patronage circle that included Fermiers Généraux and Parlementaires. These years saw the conclusion of the Seven Years' War (1763) in a peace negotiated by the Duc de Choiseul, the increasing ascendancy of the Parlements, the developing influence of the Physiocrats in economic policy, and a series of reform initiatives in agriculture and commerce instigated by Daniel Trudaine, Intendant du Commerce since 1743, and his son Trudaine de Montigny. The rise to power of René-Nicolas de Maupeou, appointed Chancellor in 1768, and the Abbé Terray, appointed Contrôleur Général in 1769, was consolidated

by the exile of Choiseul in 1770 and his replacement by the Comte de Vergennes as Secretary of State for Foreign Affairs, a triumvirate supported by the new royal favorite, Madame du Barry. Maupeou succeeded in 1771 in breaking, for an instant, the resistance of the Parlements, dismissing the traditional regional courts of justice and fiscal administration in favor of new courts composed of appointed judges responsible to the king. It was in this year that Ledoux, under the protection of Madame du Barry, was appointed to the Salines de l'Est, as architect-engineer assisting Perronet.

During the second period, that of the planning and building of the Saline de Chaux from 1771 to 1779, Ledoux expanded his patronage circle to include the Ferme Générale and the mondaine of Paris. He built the pavilions for Madame du Barry and Mlle Guimard; the new theater for Besançon was commissioned in 1785 by the progressive Intendant of Franche-Comté, Charles-André de Lacoré. The building campaign of the *saline* was punctuated by the death of Louis XV in May 1774 and the fall from power of the triumvirate in favor of a reform ministry appointed by Louis XVI on the advice of the elderly Comte de Maurepas, his so-called mentor. The old Parlements were recalled and a new ministry formed that included Jacques Turgot, the former energetic Intendant of Limousin, a *philosophe* and Physiocrat, who became Contrôleur Général in 1774; Lamoignon de Malesherbes, friend of Diderot and the *philosophes* and protector of the *Encyclopédie,* who became Royal Censor; and a number of administrators in the Intendency of Commerce, including Trudaine de Montigny, a loyal supporter of Ledoux until his resignation with Turgot in 1776. Between 1776 and 1781, the Swiss banker Jacques Necker took over the Ministry of Finances and Ledoux found fewer supporters; his commissions during these years stemmed from recommendations received from Trudaine and from certain of the Fermiers Généraux involved in the building of the Saline de Chaux. A letter from Trudaine to the Intendant of Provence began the long process of planning the new quarters for the reestablished Parlement of Provence; one from an administrator of *salines* in the Ferme gained him the project for the Hôtel Thélusson in Paris.

The third period, spanning the ten years from 1779 to the Revolution, saw the construction of the Hôtel Thélusson and the *barrières* of Paris and the beginning of building work on the Palais de Justice and prisons at Aix-en-Provence as well as the first projects for the expansion of the Saline de Chaux into the ideal city of Chaux. This was the moment of Ledoux's greatest success and influence in government, supported by the Finance Minister Calonne. Calonne's fall in 1787, with the refusal of the First Estate to accept his fiscal reforms, anticipated and largely determined that of Ledoux. The final stage in Ledoux's career, the seventeen years of semiretirement after 1789, was almost entirely without building activity. Following his imprisonment under the Terror, Ledoux was almost solely concerned with the writing and engraving of his treatise and the elaboration of projects for the ideal city.

The chapters of this book follow this rough periodization, examining Ledoux's designs, built and unbuilt, in their cultural, social, and institutional context and attempting to draw a picture of the complexities, aesthetic and political, of professional practice toward the end of the *ancien régime*. Each chapter is built around certain problems of architectural representation and institutional formation. Beginning with an account of his educational formation, in college and professional apprenticeship, I go on, in chapter 2, to consider Ledoux's private practice before the Revolution. Here I examine his designs for *hôtels* and *châteaux* in Paris and the countryside as they exemplify his developing ideas of character and representation in response to individual clients of differing social status and his transformation of the traditional typologies of urban *hôtel* and *maison de campagne* in a unique synthesis of antique reference and neo-Palladianism.

The question of character in its emerging role as a generator of institutional form became of central significance to Ledoux in his design for the Saline de Chaux, where the question of the propriety of applying the motifs and plan forms of high architecture to the functions of a rural factory threw into relief Ledoux's ambitions for the modern architect. In chapter 3, on the *saline,* I trace the way in which Ledoux joined architectural inventiveness to a real knowledge of production techniques and managerial problems to create a model factory town.

Ledoux's projects for urban institutions, developed in the 1780s, in which he attempted to resolve the question of character with respect to programs that demanded a complex mixture of utilitarian planning and representation, are the subject of chapter 4. Buildings for Paris and the provinces, the Theater of Besançon, the Palais de Justice and prisons of Aix-en-Provence, and the *barrières* of Paris are discussed as stages in Ledoux's elaboration of a public, institutional manner informed at once by classical precedent and by post-Burkean theories of the sublime.

I then study, in chapter 5, the way in which Ledoux's later architectural utopianism grew out of a consistent attempt to address the economic and social problems of the countryside, in a mingling of agronomic reformism, Physiocratic economics, and picturesque landscape vision. The ideal city of Chaux, an apparently continuous extension of the seminal commission for the Saline de Chaux, is analyzed in the light of these rural concerns as well as in the context of the social idealism and formal symbolism of the Freemasonic lodges, the milieu of Ledoux's urban sociability. I conclude with a chapter on the last seventeen years of Ledoux's life during the Revolution, Consulate, and Empire, when he was forced into semiretirement, concentrating on the writing and publication of his treatise. This difficult text and its accompanying engravings is explicated as a heterogeneous assemblage of fragments of different genres, a self-conscious attempt to bring all political, social, cultural, and aesthetic concerns into the architect's domain at a time when the ideology of the modern architect was only partially developed.

Ledoux did not in his lifetime have the reputation of an *érudit*—an impression that has to be somewhat modified in the light of the extensive references to literature, ancient and modern, in his own text. But it is true that his active professional practice, his deep involvement with the practical and social demands of an architect-builder, allowed him less of an opportunity for theoretical speculation than many of his contemporaries. His treatise had a high moral tone, but without the philosophical or aesthetic sophistication of Boullée or Le

Camus de Mézières; he certainly displayed none of the archaeological or antiquarian sensibility of Le Roy or the polemical consistency of Quatremère.

This said, however, the nonsystematic nature of *L'architecture* and its fragmentary allusions to conceptual problems should not be taken as an indication that Ledoux was in any way ignorant of the philosophical discussions and historical sensibilities of the Enlightenment. He was educated in Paris at a moment of intense activity on the part of the *philosophes:* between 1749 and 1753, the period of his residence at the Collège de Beauvais, some of the most seminal works of the Enlightenment were published, many concerned with rethinking the art of architecture, from the first volume of Diderot's *Encyclopédie* (1751), with its essay on architecture by Jacques-François Blondel, to the Abbé Laugier's *Essai sur l'architecture* (1753). In social and moral philosophy, Montesquieu's *Esprit des lois* had appeared in 1748; Turgot's discourse on the progress of humanity had been delivered at the Sorbonne in 1750, the same year that Rousseau had published the first of his attacks on "civilization" in the *Discours sur les sciences et les arts.* While Ledoux, at the age of fourteen and cloistered in college, would have registered little of this debate at the time, his writing and, more important, his architecture, were to show a continuous involvement with the premises and problems of "progress" and its social effects. Ledoux consistently joined questions of "origin," "type," and "language" in architecture to their counterparts in society, nature, and religion. Boullée was perhaps to phrase his aesthetic response to social ideals more elegantly; Durand was to incorporate logical thought more systematically into his theories of design; Quatremère was to show a more historically correct adherence to the Greek rediscoveries of Le Roy; but Ledoux, of all his contemporaries, was to register the message of the *Encyclopédie* in all its aspects, from the productive to the aesthetic. In this sense we might reformulate Meyer Schapiro's comparison of Ledoux to David, proposing, in its stead, a Ledoux as the Diderot of the French architecture of his age.

In tracing the historical Ledoux, I have at the same time remained conscious of his formal inventiveness as an architect and have tried to bring more than an account of sources and styles to the interpretation of his compositional techniques. This is where I remain convinced by Kaufmann's formal insights, as he sensed a Ledoux whose approach anticipated the elementarism of a later period. And while it may be historically risky to compare Ledoux to Le Corbusier once again, it is nevertheless true that both architects, relying on the firm precedent of Palladian classicism, developed their formal systems out of the interplay of narrative and structure, movement and volume, as they, in different ways, transgressed their model. Le Corbusier's interweaving of the *promenade architecturale* and the primary solids produced an inversion and decentering of Palladian space; Ledoux's exploitation of movement, literal and figural, marked by routes emblematically defined, was combined with a systematic exploration of the cube divided into thirty-six cubes—the nine-square Palladian grid projected into three dimensions. A less anachronistic analogy, and one that would have been understood by Ledoux, would be to the intersection of the ritual movements of Gluck's operatic narratives and the symmetrical elegance of Mozart's symphonies.

Claude-Nicolas

L E D O U X

Detail of engraving entitled
"The Shelter of the Poor,"
showing the gods and the
muses assembled in the clouds,
prepared to shower their benefits on the poor inhabitant of
the earth: a visual allegory of
the powers of architecture and
a demonstration of the domi-
nance of the classical tradition
in Ledoux's theory. From
Claude-Nicolas Ledoux, *L'architecture considérée sous le rapport de l'art, des moeurs et de la
législation* (Paris, 1804), pl. 33.

Architectural Education
1749 – 1762

For the moralists you should open up Cicero's dialogues on old age, friendship, and the nature of

the gods; in this way you will substitute the real for the false and encourage the practice of all the

virtues. For the farmer you should open up the treasures of Columella, the *Works and Days* of

Hesiod, and the *Georgics* of the poet of Mantua, already gal-

licized by our own Virgil [the Abbé Delille]. But where will

all these efforts lead? Where indeed! They will familiarize you

with the famous men of letters, and those divine minds who

guide my own audacity.

◆

Claude-Nicolas Ledoux, *L'architecture,* 1 8 0 4.[1]

CLASSICAL MAXIMS

Architectural education in the second half of the eighteenth century was as little standardized as the exercise of the profession itself, which lacked any uniform regulatory code. Neither fully professional in the modern sense, nor entirely bound by the apprenticeship system of the Middle Ages and Renaissance, the liberal practice of architecture took its place within a variety of roles, ranging from the Architecte du Roi, member of the exclusive Académie d'Architecture, to the differing professions of *architecte, architecte juré expert* (or juridical assessor), and *entrepreneur des bâtiments* (often a master mason or carpenter).[2] Many professionals, like Jean-Rodolphe Perronet (1708–94), Director of the Ponts et Chaussées and member of the Académie, or Emiliand Gauthey (1732–1806), combined the expertises of architect and civil engineer. Most practitioners, including members of the Académie, would engage in more than one role and would often invest and speculate in property and development. Many, too, would engage in both design and construction, although the mixing of roles between architect and contractor was forbidden to members of the First Class in the Académie in an attempt to preserve the distinction between commerce and the liberal art of architecture.[3]

The family origins of architects were equally various. Of the older generation, born in the late seventeenth or early eighteenth century, some architects, like Ange-Jacques Gabriel (1698–1782), the Premier Architecte du Roi from 1742, or Pierre-Louis Moreau-Desproux (1727–94), later Maître des Bâtiments of Paris, were descended from generations of architects; others, like Etienne-Louis Boullée (1728–99), were the sons of architects expected to follow the profession. Many more, however, came from the professional classes: Jacques-

Germain Soufflot (1713–80), the architect of Sainte Gene-viève, was the son of a lawyer; Julien-David Le Roy (1724–1806), the antiquarian and professor of architectural history, was the son of the royal clockmaker. Some came from the poorer artisan or merchant classes, such as Jacques-Denis Antoine (1733–1801), the son of a carpenter.

The most important school of architecture was that of the Académie Royale d'Architecture, established by Jean-Baptiste Colbert in 1671, which combined an education in theory with an apprenticeship in ateliers. It also provided the possibility of competing for the monthly and yearly prizes, the highest of which was the Prix de Rome.⁴ Winning the Rome prize ensured the journey to Rome as a *pensionnaire* under the auspices of the Académie. In turn, many architects of Ledoux's generation, Le Roy, Moreau-Desproux, Charles De Wailly, Marie-Joseph Peyre, Jean-François-Thérèse Chalgrin, Victor Louis, and Jacques Gondouin, among many others, followed Soufflot and Jean-Laurent Legeay to Italy, learning draftsmanship and composition in the circle of Piranesi and extending the classical vocabulary through their archaeological campaigns and travels to Paestum and Agrigentum.⁵ In the context of the resulting "Piranesian" school in France, with its generalized fascination with ruins and complicated compositional articulation, the exceptions to the rule of the Grand Tour were themselves noteworthy: among those who did not for various reasons study in Italy, including Antoine and Nicolas Le Camus de Mézières, were Boullée and Ledoux. Perhaps because of their distance from the sources, they demonstrated a general freedom from antiquarian or archaeological constraint.

Those denied entry to the restricted numbers of the Académie school learned the profession by apprenticeship to artists or architects. Many, indeed, would work as architects with little or no professional training: Le Camus de Mézières (1721–92), architect of the new Halle au Blé in Paris, practiced under the appelation of *architecte expert bourgeois*. The traditional guild formation still afforded a route to architecture: Antoine, architect of the Mint, or Hôtel des Monnaies, was trained as a mason. Early patronage played an important role, as in the case of Victor Louis (1731–1800), son of a mas-ter mason and architect of the new theater of Bordeaux, which was built under the protection of the Duc de Richelieu. Such patronage afforded the means for travel and for participation in the Académie competitions, and included sponsorship for the Académie as well as public and private offices.

After 1743, a younger generation of architects had the opportunity to attend lectures and classes at the Ecole des Arts, the new school of architecture founded by Jacques-François Blondel (1705–74) in competition with the moribund Académie school. Blondel's lectures were soon officially recognized by the royal administration as a supplementary course for the Ecole des Ponts et Chaussées founded in the same year. Boullée and Pierre Patte (1723–1814), two of Blondel's first students, soon followed his example in offering private lessons, and were joined by other architects such as Pierre Panseron. For artisans and the poorer students "free drawing schools" were established, the first of which dated from the 1760s.⁶ Jean-Jacques Lequeu (1757–1825) studied in such a school in his home town of Rouen before joining Soufflot's atelier in Paris.⁷

Not all of Blondel's students had previous formal education. Boullée entered his school after having worked as an apprentice painter; De Wailly (1730–98), son of a shopkeeper, seems to have been apprenticed to Blondel or Legeay at the early age of thirteen; Gondouin (1737–1818) son of the Jardinier du Roi and future architect of the Ecole de Chirurgie, was sent directly to Blondel's school; Chalgrin (1739–1811) worked for the painter and stage designer Giovanni Niccolò Servandoni before studying with Boullée. Increasingly, however, aspiring students of architecture were sent for a few years to a college prior to professional training. Soufflot, as an intending student of law, had already begun his courses in Paris when he left for his formative journey to Rome; Alexandre-Théodore Brongniart (1739–1813) studied at the Parisian Collège de Beauvais as an intending medical student before turning to architecture and the lessons of Boullée and Blondel; François-Joseph Bélanger (1744–1818) also attended the Collège de Beauvais and later studied experimental physics before working with David Le Roy and Pierre Contant d'Ivry; the engineer Claude-Antoine Garnier de la Sablonnière, too, studied at the Collège de Beauvais before being admitted to the Ecole des Ponts et Chaussées in 1751.[8]

In many respects, the education and professional formation of Claude-Nicolas Ledoux were similar to those of his contemporaries, combining a Parisian college education, attendance at Blondel's school, and a number of apprenticeships, first to an engraver, then to at least one architect, finally for a period in the public office of the Département des Eaux et Forêts. Yet in at least two important ways, Ledoux's early life differed from those of his peers: he was brought up not in Paris but in the country, and he never traveled to Italy.

Born on 27 March 1736 in the village of Dormans, Champagne, Ledoux came from a relatively modest family— his father, Claude Ledoux, was described as a *marchand* (shopkeeper or tradesman)—and he therefore lacked the supports of birth, patronage, or urban experience that commonly led to a career in architecture.[9] Having distinguished himself as a student in the parish school, he was fortunate to receive a scholarship to the Collège de Dormans-Beauvais in Paris, where he studied for three years before beginning his work in architecture. Thus, while he was unable to claim descent from a dynasty of architects, like the Mansarts or the Gabriels, or profit from an apprenticeship in the traditional building trades, he followed a route that was becoming increasingly common in the mid-eighteenth century: a professional career opened by talent.

Ledoux was to look back on his first thirteen years in the countryside of Champagne with a certain nostalgia. Some of his earliest commissions were to come from the region and his professional career was always to be linked to the reform of agriculture. This preoccupation was to culminate in the utopia he imagined for Franche-Comté, an ideal society pervaded with images of his lost childhood: the seasonal changes, rustic festivals, and artisan practices of village life. In a sentimental tone that betrayed his reading of Rousseau, Ledoux remembered his maternal upbringing: "The caresses received in childhood, your sharpening of my first pencils, the first impressions and precepts you instilled, my happy outbursts of feeling, my successes, the prize that crowned them; none of this can be forgotten."[10] Also registering the

influence of Rousseau, Ledoux was to conflate his own experience as a child with the general search for natural origins: "The calmness of the day," he wrote on a spring morning in Franche-Comté, "reminded me of the first moments of life; then pleasures were pure, hardships light, and the soul, still in its innocent sleep, disdained all vanities" (129).

The move to Paris and the experience of the Collège de Beauvais was decisive for Ledoux's career on a number of levels. It effected a rupture with his country roots and family— "The father," he later noted, "looking at his son, can hardly recognize him" (123). It gave him a lifelong taste for classical literature, and its modern imitations, that marked all his designs and pervaded the text of his treatise. It provided him with an approach to architectural design derived more expressly than that of many of his contemporaries from the methods of textual study and rhetorical exposition learned in these first classes. Perhaps most important, the experience gave him an intimate sense of belonging to a group of administrative reformers, *philosophes,* and writers who considered themselves heirs to the principles of the Enlightenment, many of whom, including Ledoux's future friends and mentors, Charles-Alexandre de Calonne and the Abbé Delille, also studied at the Collège de Beauvais.

Between 1 December 1749 and 5 February 1753, Ledoux followed the regular course of studies at the college, living in common with the masters and other *boursiers,* wearing the obligatory blue and white robes, and acquiring a lifelong taste for Greek and Latin rhetoric.[11] Measured according to the rigorous standards of the *philosophes,* the curriculum of the University of Paris seemed to hold few advantages; as Jean le Rond d'Alembert observed in his article "Collège" for the *Encyclopédie,* the first effect of such a cloistered education was the artificial separation between the world of words inside and reality outside,[12] a double enclosure, as the historian Jean-Claude Chevalier has noted: "The child was confined equally in the circle of words as in the encircling walls."[13] This "ghostly universe of words" would certainly influence Ledoux, as would that other exercise condemned by d'Alembert, the little theatrical presentations encouraged by the teachers. But the Jansenist curriculum of the Collège de

Beauvais was perhaps not as limiting as those of the Jesuit foundations—the Collèges Louis le Grand or d'Harcourt, for example—to which, indeed, many of the *philosophes* owed their own education and which were the main objects of their criticism.

Founded in 1370 by Jean, Cardinal of Dormans and Bishop of Beauvais, the college had established its reputation for the teaching of rhetoric in the seventeenth century under the leadership of Jean Vitement, Rector of the University of Paris, before being entirely reformed by the Jansenist educator Charles Rollin.[14] Adding two professors of philosophy, introducing the study of the "Moderns," and expanding the treatment of ancient and modern history, Rollin framed a more liberal course of studies than that professed by his Jesuit rivals.[15] Rollin's successor, also a Jansenist, was Charles Coffin, who, presiding over the Collège until his death in 1749, attracted a faculty of recognized quality in each subject: Jean-Baptiste-Louis Crevier, later to write the history of the University of Paris, taught rhetoric; Paul Hamelin, who succeeded Coffin as director in 1749, lectured in the humanities; Dominique-François Rivard and Jean Vauvilliers firmly established the teaching of mathematics and geometry within the division of philosophy.

The organization of the courses was traditional enough: subjects were ranged according to the division between the so-called *trivium*—grammar, dialectics, and Latin rhetoric—and the *quadrivium*—geometry, arithmetic, astronomy, and music. Classes were, for the most part, conducted in Latin.[16] Even in the mid-eighteenth century the *trivium* dominated, emphasizing the reading of a limited list of classical texts.[17] Despite Rollin's avowed enthusiasm for the Greeks, their culture and literature was still understood almost uniquely from Roman sources—Cicero, Horace, Virgil, Tacitus, Livy, Sallust, Plutarch, and Ovid—and there was little evidence of that dedicated return to Greek originals characteristic of the late eighteenth century.

For Ledoux, this list of set books left its trace in his inveterate sciolism, and his writing, like that of many of his contemporaries, was full of half-digested classical references and inaccurately remembered quotations. In keeping with this sensibility for the patina, if not the substance, of erudition, the text of Ledoux's *L'architecture* opens with a Latin epigraph, *Omnia vincit amor*, and closes with an allegorical account of a descent into Hades that doubles as a conducted tour of his design for a cannon foundry. As exhibited in this work, his comprehension of the classics was nothing if not conventional: "blind Homer," "charming Virgil," "erotic Ovid," "pompous Horace" were all secure in his pantheon, as were the historians and chroniclers Plutarch, Pliny, Tacitus, and Caesar. Among the orators he most admired Cicero and Aristotle; he quoted from the letters of the statesman Cassiodorus (42) and cited Hesiod, Xenophon, Columella, and Pliny for their teachings on rural life and agriculture: "read Columella, read Pliny," he exhorted, in the context of a description of his designs for the director's stables in the Saline de Chaux (145). Ledoux also mentioned lesser-known Roman writers, including Catullus, Propertius, the "wise" soldier-poet Gallus, "tender" Tibullus, Petronius (especially signaled for the "lascivious scenes" of the *Satyricon*), and Lactantius, whom he lauded for his legal wisdom. Among the Greeks, Ledoux cited Anacreon for the gaiety of his memorials of old age and the grammarian and poet Philitas, who, as Ledoux noted, "invented the elegaic style," as a forerunner of Virgil (148). Others he branded as pedants, "falsifying, self-interested rhetoricians" (141): Demosthenes, Sallust, Titus-Livy, Diodorus of Sicily, Paterculus, and Quintus-Curtius were, especially as repeated by rote in the schoolroom, to be viewed with suspicion as guides to the past. As rhetoricians they "represented men as they ought to be and not as they were" (141), warned Ledoux with almost Jansenist rigor.

Some of the Moderns introduced by the Jansenists also became Ledoux's favorites and the foundations of his general nostalgia for the golden age of Louis XIV. Racine and Pascal he considered the twin supports of classicism and rationalism. He cited Fénelon's *Les aventures de Télémaque* (1699) as a precedent for his own attempt to act as "Mentor" to government administrators, and his ideal city owed much to Fénelon's descriptions of Salentum as rebuilt by Idomeneus. Fontenelle's *Entretiens sur la pluralité des mondes* (1686) provided a model for the dream narratives that punctuate the text of *L'architecture;* La Fontaine's *Fables* (1668–94), La Bruyère's *Caractères* (1688), and La Rochefoucauld's *Maximes* (1665–78) supplied moral anecdotes and physiognomical portraits.[18]

The method by which these "classics" were introduced to the students of the college was itself eclectic, piecemeal, and susceptible to misuse.[19] Forced to overlook the still embarrassing question of paganism, the teachers adopted the solution, proposed by Rollin, of extracting from each work a kind of repertoire of quotations suitable for all occasions, an anthology of passages for memorization and stylistic exercises, each illustrating a moral attribute or heroic act. Rollin had emphasized that "if we would make an impression, our precepts should be short and lively and pointed as a needle," and his treatise demonstrated how to plunder texts for such examples.[20] Thus Homer was combed for stories that reinforced the human virtues—love of piety and justice, prudence, wisdom, hospitality, princely conduct, respect for the gods. In this way all the dubious aspects of the classics might be avoided, and an artificial world of morality built up out of the fragments. This education by means of what Rollin called *morceaux choisies* (selected pieces) would, he hoped, act to "transport the students into other countries and other times, thus opposing the torrent of false maxims and bad examples that sweeps away almost the whole world, and replacing them by the maxims and examples of the great men of antiquity."[21] Historical events thus became so many rhetorical figures of good conduct; lifted out of time and place, they were no more than the commonplaces of classroom exercises. Time, similarly, became an endless repetition of the same; as in Bishop Bossuet's *Discours sur l'histoire universelle* (1681), Rollin's idea of history was essentially cyclical: "There one sees all the kingdoms of the world emerge like the earth itself; raise themselves little by little by insensible degrees; extend their conquests on all sides, and, suffering revolutions, fall suddenly from this height, losing themselves, buried in the same void whence they came."[22] Ledoux was often to be comforted in administrative and personal defeat by such a vision of an eternal return.

The effect of this mode of study was, as d'Alembert had

recognized, to substitute rhetorical statement for real experience. For many students, the outside world would always be seen through this idealizing filter, as analogy, maxim, and citation took the place of observation and induction. The historian Pierre Goubert has commented on this instruction that prepared the professional and the bureaucrat in the second half of the century, creating "a sort of privileged milieu," with its own "cultural code of references, tags and allusions." To the members of this new elite it became second nature to refer to present and future through the "past" figured in their schoolbooks, "to cram their tracts and correspondence with classical references lovingly larded with pedantic commentaries."[23] Ledoux, it is clear, entered this culture eagerly and assimilated its best and worst aspects; it determined not only the allusive and often obscure character of his writing, but also, and fundamentally, his approach to architecture and his personal form of *visual* rhetoric.

Indeed, in one sense, as the text of *L'architecture* suggests, Ledoux was never to leave the borders of this utopia of the schoolroom, where history was taught "without tears" and where the golden sun of antiquity colored nature and art alike. The classical authors he cited were inevitably used less for their contents than for their "authority" that legitimized personal inventions, rather as a later generation of Revolutionaries would adopt the clothing and forms of classical Republicanism.[24] Whenever Ledoux contemplated the unprecedented, a classical reference was always at hand. He imagined himself struggling against tradition like Apollo combating Marsyas; or, comparing himself to Racine, he waited for history to take its own revenge: "Pradon was applauded for a day, and Racine, hissed, gained immortality" (138). The example of "Roman Charity" was evoked to justify a new system of poor relief for the town of Chaux (165); Plato, by way of Horace, was cited to authorize a shocking sexual license (202). Ledoux selected appropriate allegories to characterize existing and invented building types; he engraved maxims on the walls of ideal designs or used them to dignify lowly occupations. Thus he assigned the collectors of wood taxes, as he designed their offices outside the Saline de Chaux, a tag from Ovid, *ut ameris amabilis esto* (121); and the clerk-overseers of the *saline* were given the motto *grandiaque effosis mirabatur ossa sepulchris* (128).

In the same way, Ledoux's somewhat idiosyncratic understanding of etymology allowed him to name the *barrières,* or tollgates, that he designed for Paris after the Propylaea of the Acropolis: "*Propylaea,*" he wrote, "comes from προ, πυλη, front gate, or from προ, πυλοσ, pile, pillar, structure, construction" [16]. Similarly he adduced Roman foundation rites to dignify the building of the Saline de Chaux: "The Capitol takes its name from the Latin word *caput* because of the horse's head found there when the foundations were dug" (131). Etymology also allowed for the creation of neologisms, which, invented to characterize ideal institutions of Ledoux's imagination, became the verbal counterparts of his utopian designs. Thus the "Oikéma," from the Greek ὀικημα meaning variously "house," "dwelling," "temple," "prison," or more significantly, as used by Herodotus, Plato, and Xenophon, "place of debauchery," was the name Ledoux gave to his imaginary house of pleasure, the ideal brothel of Chaux (199–204). The word "Panarèthéon," from the Greek παυοιρετος, meaning "accomplished virtue," after the philosopher and member of the Academy of Athens, Panaretos, denoted a monument designed to reward good social conduct, its walls to be inscribed with texts from Socrates, Polyclitus, and Lactantius, the "Christian" Cicero. The "Pacifère," or "House of Peace," ("Pacifère or the Conciliator," noted Ledoux, "One says *morbifère, sommifère, mortifère,* thus one can say *pacifère*" (113)) was Ledoux's utopian answer to courts of law; its description was preceded by an epigraph from Virgil's *Georgics:*

Non mihi, si linguae centum sint oraque centum,
Ferrea vox, omnes scelerum comprendere formas,
Omnia paenarum percurrere nomina possim. (113)[25]

Similar neologisms were to be used by other social reformers—notably Nicolas-Edme Rétif de la Bretonne and Charles Fourier—to confirm the nature and express the special character of their own invented institutions: Rétif was to call his regulated house of prostitution a "Parthénion"; Fourier, like Ledoux, played with Greek roots for his "Phalanstère." [26]

Such lexical tactics were supported by the rhetorical exercises of the college, which, following tradition, employed fragments of classical and religious discourse to give life to the different literary figures and genres.[27] According to preselected models, the students composed epigrams, epitaphs, elegies, eclogues, satires, odes, hymns, epistles, and fables, learning the commonplaces and the topics by working in different styles and according to the proprieties. Technical exercises in rhetoric varied greatly in kind: constructing *periods* and *discourse,* including considerations of rhythm, balance, harmony, and cadence; practicing *transposition* by applying a passage from a classical author to another contemporary subject, using the same figures while changing only the words and ideas; memorizing every figure of speech, every *trope* listed in the manuals with their already "classical" citations; learning the art of *précis,* or abbreviation, and, especially important for Ledoux, that of *amplification,* or, as one pedagogue put it, "the art by means of which small things become large." [28]

Sustaining this didactic roster was a system of teaching that organized the classroom into a "theater of rivalry," and divided up the students' roles according to the hierarchies of ancient Roman society. Each pupil took a part, as emperor, consul, tribune, censor, or senator, in an exercise of emulation, which, the teachers hoped, would stimulate both oratory and high-minded social conduct. Punishments, rewards, and, above all, incessant debates were administered in this way: camps of warring armies were set up, treaties negotiated, eulogies and elegies delivered, senates sat in deliberation, poets appealed to centurions for justice and mercy.[29] It was no doubt through these exercises that Ledoux was introduced to the power of theatricality.

The influence of these *exercices du style* on Ledoux's writing was marked. Indeed, the text of *L'architecture* might be read as a collection of Rollin's models, each on a set theme, each following a set form. In describing his designs Ledoux commonly resorts to *amplification:* lowly topics are raised to dramatic levels, small subjects are enlarged, microcosms are transformed into macrocosms. This approach, Ledoux noted, is fundamental for an architect who, at every scale, tried "to offer to the smallest object whatever is permissible for the largest" (16). Passages of *transposition* also abound, as conventional descriptions of arcadian landscapes are applied to contemporary observations on the countryside of Franche-Comté.[30] In this vein, almost all of Ledoux's descriptions of towns and landscapes take on the aspect of a guidebook to an ideal classical world. Stylistic *periods* are assayed in long and rambling sentences. *Commonplaces* for every topic are routinely trotted out.

None of this was especially novel; a host of minor writers of the period composed their texts in similar ways. But Ledoux, as an architect, insisted on transposing the approach to architectural design. Treating the classical tradition in architecture as a kind of language, he almost literally cut it into its constituent parts, formulating and reformulating its elements as if they were so many words. Later, as his imagination turned to ideal projects, he found ways to construct *figures* and *tropes* in architecture much as he did in writing, the three-dimensional equivalents of rhetorical devices. In these designs, Ledoux conceived of buildings as so many visual *maxims,* the permanent preceptors of morality, exhibiting for literate and illiterate alike what Ledoux and his peers had learned in school. "Example," he emphasized, paraphrasing Rollin, "is the most powerful of lessons" (2).

But Ledoux, even as he later reacted against the pedantry of his architectural professors, was aware of the dangers in the blind acceptance of what he termed "inculcated ideas" (141). Despite his yearning for the "consoling chimeras of the school" and his understanding that "it was only there that the imagination was not chained" (129), he continuously warned against the "illusions" fostered by rhetoric, the sterility of knowledge learned by rote, and its lack of vital "enthusiasm" (141).

The classically static world of the *trivium* was in the 1750s beginning to be countered by the expanding range of topics covered by the *quadrivium,* including a greater concentration in mathematics, astronomy, and the physical and natural sciences. The secularizing, rationalist tenor of Jansenist education, inherited from the schools of Port Royal, had always stressed logic and mathematics; Rollin himself had introduced physics, although he had been careful to distinguish between what he called *la physique des savants* and his preferred *physique des enfants* that looked to the cultivation of gardens rather than to astronomy. His successors had worked toward a stronger scientific curriculum: Kepler, Descartes, and Newton were added, joining Ptolemy, Copernicus, and Tycho Brahe. Ledoux cited these, together with the more recent Herschel (196), as evidence of his interest in astronomical discoveries, one that was to be dramatically illustrated in his engraving of the earth surrounded by the planets, the allegorical "Elevation of the Cemetery of Chaux."

The Collège de Beauvais also had a reputation for studies in the natural sciences: J.-F. Demachy, the future director of the Pharmacie Centrale, and Jean-Charles Desessarts, the future Dean of the Faculty of Medicine, were only two of the distinguished doctors to graduate after 1755.[31] Ledoux learned of the therapeutic values of ventilation, of the composition of the air and the noxious effects of its impurities, and would demonstrate his concern with health in planning the *saline* and town of Chaux. Perhaps it was a gentle tribute to Rollin's heritage that Ledoux throughout his life retained a hatred of cruelty to animals and an opposition to blood sports.

Equally important for the formation of architects, engineers, and scientists were the classes in mathematics and geometry conducted by Rivard, author of the influential *Eléments de géometrie* of 1732, followed by the complementary *Abrégé des éléments de mathématiques* and the evocative dissertation *Traité de la sphère,* works that no doubt encouraged the play of geometry in Ledoux's designs both as elements of composition and as symbolic forms.[32]

Ledoux's *bourse* expired early in 1753 and almost no record exists of his activities during the next decade before his first recorded independent commission in 1762. The architect Jacques Cellérier (1742–1814), Ledoux's friend and first biographer, noted only that "his first experiments were in engraving; he engraved battle scenes in order to defray his expenses."[33] This initial training as an engraver, however, seems to have been more influential than has generally been recognized. As an architect-engraver, Ledoux evolved a style of representation and a method of design markedly different from those of other architect-artists of the period—Boullée or De Wailly, for example—whose tastes were more painterly. Thus Boullée, who attached the epigraph *Ed io anche son pittore* (an echo of Correggio's profession of faith on discovering the painting of Raphael) to the manuscript of his treatise, was clearly interested in developing an architecture derived from the laws of the pictorial sublime.[34] His almost monochromatic wash drawings, depicting an architecture subjected to all the forces and atmospheres of nature and aspiring to the grandeur and scale of natural phenomena, describe the effects of nature on architecture more than they convey the inner construction of the designs. Equally, the elegant and almost baroque renderings of De Wailly, who was influenced by Legeay and Servandoni, register a desire, noted by his contemporary Bélanger, "to abandon the compass in order to compose architecture more freely with his brushes."[35] His designs, both decorative and architectural, show his fondness for dramatic scenes, rich textures, and the subtle but variegated play of shadows. By contrast, Ledoux, rather than following the previous generation of architect-engravers trained in the manner of Piranesi—Gabriel-Pierre-Martin Dumont, Jean-Michel Moreau le Jeune—developed a graphic style that owed much to the processes and graphic conventions of technical engraving.[36] His insistence on the continual revision of his designs on the copperplates themselves, sometimes several times; the specific qualities of line, light, and shade and their combination to produce the effect of a simple and almost abstract sublime; his reliance on primary geometrical forms and their rendering as so many illustrations in a textbook of solid geometry were all strongly influenced by his training with the burin rather than the brush. No doubt his experience with the engraving of battle scenes also gave him a taste for heraldic display, later to be evinced in the façades of his hunting lodges and palaces. An echo of this early training is found in Ledoux's self-conscious emulation of the layout of the plates of the *Encyclopédie* in the presentation of his projects in *L'architecture*. The framed perspective view of a building placed above its plans, elevations, and sections is almost unique to Ledoux, and directly refers to Diderot's systematic presentation of a perspective vignette illustrating a manufacturing process in operation above an analytical breakdown of tools, machines, and processes.[37]

Ledoux's architectural education was, according to Cellérier, begun in Blondel's school and completed in the atelier of Louis-François Trouard (1729–94). This would indicate that Ledoux attended lectures at the Ecole des Arts between 1754, when Blondel reopened his public lecture series, and 1758, when Trouard returned from Rome. Certainly it was from Blondel that he derived his sense of the high professional role of the architect, his rudimentary understanding of architectural history, his taste for seventeenth-century classicism, his concepts of planning and aesthetic expression, and his vision of himself as an *architecte-philosophe*, heir to the reforming idealism of the midcentury.

PROFESSIONAL DOCTRINES

Before 1740, there was no school in Paris where a young architect could form himself and learn everything he should know about the design of architecture, ornament and figures, perspective, mathematics, stone cutting, surveying, and finally all the innumerable details concerning the construction of buildings. He had to go successively to different masters to instruct himself in each of these subjects, which lengthened his studies a great deal and made him, after having mastered drawing, often neglect everything else. Such were the reasons that led M. Blondel to establish an Ecole des Arts.

Pierre Patte, *Cours d'architecture*, 1 7 7 7.[38]

The Ecole des Arts on the rue de la Harpe, where Blondel had first opened his lectures to the public on 6 May 1743, with the agreement of the Académie d'Architecture, had by the mid-1750s gained a reputation as an enlightened and open alternative to the Académie school.[39] Signaled by d'Alembert in 1751 in the "Discours préliminaire" to the *Encyclopédie*, it had already started a generation of architects in professional careers, even drawing students from abroad, among whom William Chambers was perhaps the most influenced by French developments.[40] The Ecole des Arts had been subsequently recognized by the Intendant de Commerce, Daniel Trudaine, as a necessary complement to the Bureau de Dessinateurs-géographes (later formally constituted as the Ecole des Ponts et Chaussées), a school that he had founded in 1747, appointing the chief engineer of the Ponts et Chaussées, Perronet, as its first director. By 1753 the Royal administration was contributing six scholarships for students of the Ponts et Chaussées to study *architecture civile* and drawing in Blondel's school, while Blondel himself offered twelve free places.[41]

The success of the school was no doubt based on the emerging need for a broadly defined education in architecture that coincided with the expansion in middle-class and aristocratic building activity toward the end of the *ancien régime*. Certainly Blondel himself stressed the public nature of his enterprise, hoping, as he announced in the introductory discourse of 1754, to draw amateurs as well as intending professionals to his lectures:

We recognize that the greater number of those whose birth constrains them to apply themselves to many kinds of studies neglect absolutely the first principles of architecture; that those who wish to make it their profession still need to be presented with a theory that is consistent, analytical, and demonstrated in a clear and convincing manner; finally that it is necessary that those who devote themselves by their estate to the practice of building should find in our public lessons principles that are proportioned and conformed to their needs.[42]

Future clients and administrators would thereby be introduced to architectural taste, professional students might undertake a comprehensive course that joined technical and theoretical instruction, and entrepreneurs would find the abstruse rules of classicism simply explained. Whether Blondel's desired mix was ever attained is uncertain—the evidence points to a preponderance of architects—but the triple appeal demonstrates his understanding of the crucial role to be played by an educated patronage in a period characterized by an increase in the size and function of public bureaucracy. For architects his success was legendary; scarcely a single important architect failed to pass through his courses after the 1740s, including, among others, Boullée, Patte, Trouard, De Wailly, Antoine, de Neufforge, Peyre, Desprez, Brongniart,

Rondelet, Legrand, Molinos, Huvé, Potain, Gondouin, and, of course, Ledoux.

For these students the order of lessons was strict and occupied every day of the week from seven in the morning to seven at night. Each day, save for Monday, Blondel himself lectured on "the principles of design as they concern architecture and ornament, interior and exterior decoration, gardening, joinery, metal work, etc."[43] On Wednesdays and Fridays between three and six in the afternoon, he also taught the classes on theory—"on suitability, harmony, proportion, siting, etc."[44] Every Monday from Whitsun to All Saints' Day, Blondel conducted visits to important buildings in Paris and the surrounding region; one day a week he would also take his students to different construction sites. These guided tours served as lessons in practical criticism, and the memory of Blondel's trenchant assessments is conserved in *Les amours rivaux ou l'homme du monde éclairé par les arts,* edited and published posthumously by the novelist Jean-François Bastide, in which many of Blondel's former students, including Ledoux, were subjected to mixed reviews.[45]

On Wednesday, Friday, and Saturday from nine in the morning to midday, mathematicians and engineers taught classes in calculation, geometry, mensuration, stereotomy, hydraulics, and mechanics. Life drawing classes were held on the same days from three to eight in the afternoon, supplemented by lectures in "those aspects of history necessary to select correctly the attributes and allegories suitable for Royal palaces, sacred buildings, country houses, public buildings, fêtes, etc."[46] These classes were overseen by one of the three Saint-Aubin brothers; other artists taught perspective drawing and proportional theory, relief modeling in clay and wax, and decoration in bas-relief. On-site instruction in masonry, carpentry, and joinery completed the technical curriculum.[47]

On one level, this course of study systematized the classical tradition as established by François Blondel, the first director of the Académie, in the 1670s; at the same time, it opened this tradition to the shifts in taste of the mid-eighteenth century. Diderot and d'Alembert had recognized this mixture of conservatism and judicious innovation in selecting Blondel as architectural contributor to the *Encyclopé-*

die. Neither a staunch believer in the unmediated imitation of the Ancients, nor a follower of rococo ornamentalism, Blondel nevertheless appreciated the rational, theoretical approach of the Encyclopedists; his self-appointed role as a public lecturer and his knowledge of every aspect of the craft of building appealed equally to Diderot. Blondel wrote over five hundred articles for the *Encyclopédie* on theoretical, antiquarian, and technical subjects, from "Abajour" to "Palette," before his death prevented further contributions.[48] In these brief pieces he demonstrated his affection for what he termed "the style of definition" precisely suited to the Encyclopedic project.[49] Incorporating them into his lectures given at the Ecole des Arts from 1750 and at the Académie from 1762, Blondel fashioned his magisterial *Cours d'architecture,* the first four volumes of which were published before 1774. The *Cours,* completed by Pierre Patte, remained the basic reference work of the Académie and later of the Ecole des Beaux-Arts for more than a century. Boullée's *Architecture* and, more self-consciously, Ledoux's *L'architecture* were in part written as elaborate glosses on and revisions of their master's text, copies of which were listed in the inventories of both their libraries after their deaths.[50]

Ledoux's theoretical debts to Blondel were many. From him he took the standard list of architectural concepts, represented by academic key words, and repeated them with significant variations in the introduction to *L'architecture* nearly fifty years later. Some of these were commonplaces of classicism, inherited from Vitruvius and interpreted by François Blondel and Claude Perrault in the seventeenth century. These included "health" (*salubrité*), propriety (*bienséance*), order (*ordonnance*), fitness or suitability (*convenance*), symmetry, and proportion. Others had been given special meaning by artistic and literary theories of academic classicism from Poussin to Boileau: ideas of unity, severity, judgment, method, and reasoning. Others again were drawn from classical aesthetic doctrine but as endowed with connotations of empiricism and sensationism under the influence of Locke and his followers in France; the most important of these were character, contrast, and variety. Concepts of necessity (*besoin*) and of planning or distribution were similarly qualified by the materialism of the Enlightenment.[51]

Ledoux was to follow Blondel not only in his repetition of these categories, but also in his emphasis on the classification of building types according to their distribution and architectural expression. The first two volumes of the *Cours* had distinguished among what Blondel termed the "genres" of architecture and had applied them to the description of the architect's repertory of building types; Ledoux's own list of types, which was to be longer and more inclusive of every social occupation than Blondel's, would be similarly accompanied by injunctions to the effect that, as Blondel demanded, "All the different kinds of works belonging to architecture must bear the imprint of the particular purpose of each building; all must have a *character* that determines their general form and that announces the building for what it is."[52]

This call for characterization, which was evidently a repeated leitmotiv of Blondel's teaching, emerged as a central preoccupation for his students: Patte called for the exterior of a building to exhibit "le caractère qui lui convient"; Gondouin spoke of his design for the Ecole de Chirurgie as possessing "le caractère convenable"; Le Camus de Mézières noted that in nature every object had a "caractère" of its own, often delineated by a few expressive lines, that should be emulated in architecture; Boullée elaborated an entire poetics of architecture on the idea of the "caractère qui est propre" to each kind of building; Quatremère de Quincy, rivaling Blondel in his love of "definition," devoted over forty pages to the word "caractère" in his dictionary.[53] Ledoux, who in the eyes of his contemporaries always seemed a little overenthusiastic, explored the idea to its expressive, and sometimes caricatured, limits.

The idea of character was closely linked in Blondel's theory and design method with that of the "program," the oral or written statement of a design problem, whether as a class exercise or as an announcement of a prize competition. In Blondel's treatment this traditionally brief text became itself a teaching instrument, implying the definition of the problem and the steps necessary for its solution:

By program we understand the statement of a project, with few details, that the professor gives to his students to make them understand his intentions, and the route [la marche] they must follow in the composition of the sketch they have to undertake.[54]

The stages of design were specified in detail, and after the 1760s they became common practice in the Académie and later in the Ecole des Beaux-Arts. The first task of the professor was to explain, clearly and concisely, the "conditions" of the program—the site and its contours together with any foreseeable pitfalls for the student. Blondel recommended that the design instructor should try out the problem prior to analyzing the program before the students. He should "extend and develop speculatively the kind of project with which he is concerned, give references and call the attention of the students to buildings of the same kind built by the great masters."[55] This talk would include advice as to the proper style and ordering of the building, the special requirements of its character, and the best management of the twelve hours or so allotted for the design; the students would then be enjoined to work "in the greatest silence." Each of Blondel's programs was conceived to exercise a particular aspect of design: some for practice in exterior proportions and *ordonnance,* some for complicated problems in distribution, some for interior decoration. Ledoux followed Blondel's advice as to working method, speaking often of the need for silence and isolation in designing. On a more general level, his theory and practice was to be governed by the twin demand for programmatic definition and characteristic form; this was to an almost systematic degree illustrated by the final conception of *L'architecture* as an encyclopedic compendium of programs, at once a rewriting of Blondel's *Cours* and an homage to Diderot's *Encyclopédie.*

Ledoux was less willing to accept the often acerbic criticism of his former master; as Cellérier observed, he possessed "a fiery spirit, a passionate love of glory," and "could not for long subject himself to the principles of these schools." Even at the end of his life, Ledoux was to remember Blondel's strictures against the giant orders of the Hôtel d'Uzès with anger and in his imagination would hear his for-

mer teacher's fulminations against the rusticated orders of the Saline de Chaux:

I hear the professor, circumscribed by the five Orders, cry out against their abuse; perplexed, he opens his textbook, turning over every page; he sees nothing in the established rules to justify the error. The rules of grammar have been violated! All is lost! . . . The doctrine has been attacked, he defends the ramparts; in vain he displays his insignificant manifestoes; on all sides his thunderclaps reverberate from the stubborn walls of the Gymnasium. (135)

PUBLIC APPRENTICESHIP

In those days, architects built bridges. (45)

Ledoux undertook his architectural apprenticeship in the atelier of Louis-François Trouard, who had returned to Paris after three years in Rome to build his house at 9 Faubourg Poissonnière in 1758. In the early 1760s Trouard joined the royal works at Versailles, designing and building the church of Saint-Symphorien de Montreuil and the barracks in the Place d'Armes between 1765 and 1770. Trouard's house of 1758 with its neo-Greek frieze and absence of orders seems to have contributed little to Ledoux's first exercises in domestic architecture after 1762;[56] the plan, massing, and style of the church of Saint-Symphorien, however, would seem to have been more influential.[57] Ledoux would repeat its basilical form—often claimed, together with the church of Saint-Louis at Saint-Germain-en-Laye by Nicholas-Maris Potain (1765) and that of Saint-Philippe-du-Roule by Chalgrin (1768), as one of the earliest revivals of the Roman type—adopting the coffered barrel vault and the semicircular vaulted apse in many of his works.[58] The entrance portico with its giant order of four plain Tuscan columns and pediment; the rear entrance into the bell tower, flanked by recessed Tuscan columns; the tower itself, topped with a four-sided dome reminiscent of many traditional parish churches in the region; the interior colonnade of partially fluted Doric columns supporting a horizontal architrave were motifs that would likewise reappear in Ledoux's early designs.

Ledoux, Church of Saint-Pierre, Rolampont, Haute-Marne, 1764. *Above,* entrance and bell tower; *right,* bell tower. Photographs by A. Vidler.

Ledoux, Church of Saint-Barthélémy, Cruzy-le-Châtel, Yonne, 1764. *Above,* bell tower; *below,* porch. Photographs by A. Vidler.

Trouard's Saint-Symphorien was indeed designed at the same moment when Ledoux, newly appointed to the Département des Eaux et Forêts, was beginning his own practice in church design, supervising the construction of a series of additions, restorations, and new structures in rural parishes scattered through the Haute-Marne, Haute-Saône, Yonne, and Aube.[59] The administration of Eaux et Forêts, overseeing all matters concerning the waters and forests in the royal domain, including construction timber, had general control of certain parish works. Ledoux worked under the direction of Louis-François Du Vaucel, Grand Maître des Eaux et Forêts for Paris, perhaps acting as a replacement to Claude-Louis Daviler, architect of Eaux et Forêts, who had fallen ill in 1763. He prepared plans and estimates, decided on necessary repairs, and designed new constructions for sacristies, presbyteries, schoolhouses, cemeteries, roads, river quays, wells, drinking fountains, and washing places, as well as larger structures such as churches and bridges.[60] In their range these buildings must be seen as the foundation of Ledoux's growing preoccupation with the reform of rural architecture; in their style they anticipate his later experiments in a reduced classicism suitable for public works.

Four of the many churches to which repairs were carried out show substantial work that may be attributed directly to Ledoux. In 1764 and 1765 Ledoux designed the nave and belfry of Saint-Pierre-aux-liens, Rolampont, some five miles to the north of Langres; reconstructed the church of the Assumption, Fouvent-le-Haut, to the northeast of Gray; built the new church of Saint-Didier at Roche-et-Raucourt close to Fouvent-le-Haut; and rebuilt the nave, aisles, and porch of Saint-Barthélémy at Cruzy-le-Châtel, near Tonnerre. The earliest building, at Rolampont, established the basic elements of Ledoux's style: the nave and aisles are vaulted with flattened segmental arches carried on plain, square piers, with elongated corbels fashioned out of Doric triglyphs; the porch is entered through an arched doorway recessed in a cut-stone façade surmounted by a pediment; the bell tower is topped by the bell-shaped roof typical of Franche-Comté. Fouvent-le-Haut is similar, though without aisles, and its belfry is decorated with Doric triglyphs; Roche-et-Raucourt is less ornate again, with the pattern of a porch pediment marked in flat relief. The most elaborate design was that for Cruzy-le-Châtel, where the nave and aisles are vaulted by semicircular arches on square piers, again in simple Doric, while the porch, flanked by double Doric pilasters, is crowned by a pediment in full relief with triglyphs and metopes. In each of these buildings, the simple geometries and massing of the cut stone and the diagrammatic treatment of the orders anticipated Ledoux's more mature "public" style in, for example, the *barrières* of Paris. Other commissions for religious structures showed equal signs of Ledoux's emerging individual style. At the Cathedral of Notre-Dame d'Auxerre in 1767, Ledoux prepared designs for the remodeling of the choir and its chapels, proposing to "classicize" the Gothic pillars with Doric fluting and to recarve the capitals accordingly. At the cathedral of Sens, he designed a chapter house that he described in 1767 as an oval room in "the form of a circus," surrounded by steps and decorated with eight Ionic columns framing statues of the Evangelists in semicircular niches. This project, only the foundations of which were completed, was to be the first of many centralized, top-lit chapels in Ledoux's *oeuvre*.[61] No doubt Ledoux's work at Sens and Auxerre led to further commissions: the Cardinal de Luynes's Château de Brinon, where Ledoux simply refurnished the existing building; and the cloister and front courtyard of the Abbey of Echalis, near Sens, which was still unfinished in 1767.[62]

Equally portentous, however, were the forms of the bridges that Ledoux designed, especially the single-arched bridge at Marac over the river Suize and the larger, three-arched Pont Prégibert across the Marne near Rolampont, which seem to register his understanding of the reform of bridge design initiated by Perronet and taught at the Ponts et Chaussées.[63] Following Perronet, Ledoux studied the dangers of erosion, citing the bridges of Saumur, Courseau, and Moulins, which had all suffered damage to their piers, and argued for stonework shaped to the flow of water. Aesthetically, Ledoux preferred simple arches cut cleanly out of smooth stone: "The principal beauty of a bridge consists in the purity of its lines," he wrote much later, attacking the

traditional ornamental cornices and balustrades as "details that break up the principle object" (47). These arches revealed his predilection for visual framing, to be exploited in the proscenium of the Theater of Besançon and in the engraved view of the Rural School of Meillant; few monuments were susceptible, he found, "to more variety in relation to their slopes, their sites, and the distance from which they are viewed" (47). In the construction of these bridges Ledoux was no doubt brought into contact with young engineers in the Ponts et Chaussées, like Philippe Bertrand, professor under Perronet since 1748, or Emiliand Gauthey, student of Gabriel-Pierre Dumont and Perronet, both of whom would be active in developing bridges, roads, and canals in Franche-Comté and Burgundy in the 1760s, and 1770s.

Such work in the regions of Franche-Comté and Burgundy prepared Ledoux for a career that encompassed more than the traditional programs of a society architect: the reform and maintenance of the forests, the social conditions of their population, the development of road and river transport, the construction of bridges and canals, the revolution of agrarian practices, and the encouragement of rural industry would all prove central to Ledoux's theory and design. More practically, his appointment to the Eaux et Forêts brought him into contact for the first time with a patronage circle that

was to support him throughout his career: the administrators of the Ferme Générale. Du Vaucel himself was the son of a powerful Fermier and was related by marriage to the Parseval family, another dynasty of Fermiers Généraux, a member of which was to be closely involved with the building of the Saline de Chaux.[64]

These socially important connections had been reinforced in 1764 by Ledoux's marriage to the daughter of a prominent musician at the court, Joseph-Gaspard Bureau, first oboist of the Bedchamber and a member of the orchestra of the Versailles opera.[65] Profiting from his introduction to the Eaux et Forêts, Ledoux also began to make connections at court, in the world of music, theater, and salons. From the mid-1760s Ledoux used such advantages to good effect, building himself a private practice that soon outstripped his administrative work. Cellérier, always admiring, noted, "Endowed with good looks and a fine mind, his manners were relaxed, with a tone of assurance that seduced and inspired confidence; he was shortly to be successfully launched in the world."[66] Perhaps more important still was the quality also noted by Cellérier that "he loved society in general, but he preferred the company of artists and of women, where he found more charm and instruction for his art."[67]

Ledoux, Bridge at Marac,
Haute-Marne, 1764.

Hôtels *and* Châteaux
1765–1780

███████████████████████

Hôtels are buildings erected in capital cities where the great noblemen normally take up their

residence; the character of their decoration requires a beauty matched to the origins of the titled

persons who live in them. The different characters that it is suitable to give to each of these

buildings must necessarily spring from the diversity of the

ranks and the dignity of these subjects of the King. The rank

of the proprietor is thus the source from which the architect

should draw the elements of his decoration.

◆

Jacques-François Blondel, *Cours d'architecture,* 1 7 7 1[1]

CHARACTER AND SOCIETY

The idea of character as inherited from Blondel by Ledoux and his peers was essentially a social construct, joining decoration to rank and to use.[2] As such, in the new academic orthodoxy that Blondel had wished to create, it reinforced social hierarchy by aesthetic hierarchy, by means of a code of graduated luxury and appropriate decoration. The pyramid of society based on birth and talent was thereby ideally mirrored by a pyramid of embellishment legislated by the academic architect. As a concept that was both constitutive and communicative, "character" subsumed all notions of propriety, suitability, and fitness in plan and decoration, at the same time as it prescribed codes of representation and rhetorical expression. Blondel insisted that architectural characterization embrace not only appropriate sculptural decoration but also the "disposition of the general masses, the choice of forms, and a sustained style," that is, the calculated effect of the entire building, inside and out.[3] The determination and the representation of character controlled the use of the different orders, the nature of all applied emblems and attributes, the "movement of the plan," and the massing of the building in three dimensions, together with the associated programs of decoration, sculptural and painterly. Calculated, as he wrote, according to "the diversity of buildings and their different uses," character was to be compared to the various literary genres, heroic, lyrical, or pastoral; to the images of passions presented by the painter; or to the evocative signs of music that expressed "in turn, terror or mercy, heroism or delight."[4]

Similarly, Germain Boffrand, writing in the 1740s and deriving his architectural principles from Horace's *Ars Poetica,* had called for buildings to inspire appropriate moods of joy, seriousness, and sadness by their characterization: "one who does not know these different characters and who does not make them felt in his works is not an architect," he concluded.[5] The equally didactic Blondel drew up a list of possible genres in relation to their appropriate subjects and guided his students in finding the proper means of expression. These included what he called "male, or strong and virile," "light, elegant, or delicate," "rustic," "naive," "feminine," "mysterious," "grand," "bold," "terrible," "stunted," "frivolous," "licentious," "differentiated," "amphibological," "vague," "barbarous," "slavish," "cold," "sterile," "thin," "futile," and "poor." Such categories, besides setting the tone for the design of each building type in the architect's repertory, also established the rudiments of a critical vocabulary.[6] Blondel's explicit aim was both to widen the potential gamut of expressions available to architects faced with a rapidly expanding set of tasks and to fix these languages of character in a hierarchy that approximated that of the traditional classical system of genres and their suitability.

This hierarchy of characters thus corresponded to the hierarchy of programs, which, in turn, was set by a sense of their place in the social order. Blondel divided them into four broad groups: dwellings in the city and the country; buildings dedicated to magnificence, including monuments, theaters, and all festival structures; buildings for public utility, including churches and other religious foundations such as colleges, hospitals, and cemeteries, together with mints, stock exchanges, libraries, academies, factories, fountains, baths, reservoirs, aqueducts, ports, quays, bridges, markets, fairs, slaughterhouses, barracks, town halls, observatories, and basilicas; and, finally, buildings for public security, comprising arsenals, prisons, city gates, and lighthouses.[7] Within each of these divisions a hierarchy of its own was evident, and, of course, in the domain of a single type many further subdivisions of propriety had to be made: dwellings, for example, were ranged in order of importance from the palace (royal, electoral, ducal, pontifical, cardinal, episcopal, etc.), the *hôtel,* the town house for rich individuals, the house for merchants and shopkeepers, to the various country houses, which were similarly ranked—royal seats, *châteaux, maisons de plaisance,*

maisons de campagne, and so on. Each was carefully described, its appropriate orders fixed, and its levels of decoration and quality of mood delineated. Blondel then suggested appropriate genres for each of these types: the *genre champêtre* for agricultural, rural, and garden structures; the *genre féminin* for *maisons de plaisance;* the *genre grand* for high public buildings; the *genre hardie* for utilitarian public buildings; the *genre mystérieuse* for the lighting of sacred structures; the *genre terrible* for prisons. Blondel's design exercises, set for his students in the rue de La Harpe, reiterated these rules, and the master was outspoken in his criticism of historical and contemporary works that seemed to him to ignore the codes of what he called *convenance* and *caractère.*

In theory, as we have noted, most of Blondel's students subscribed to his enthusiasm for proper characterization; their differences stemmed more from shifts in the nature of taste and social demands than from any deep theoretical disagreement. Certainly when Quatremère de Quincy came to elaborate the theory in the long article on "Caractère" in his *Encyclopédie méthodique,* he found little to quarrel with in the academic precepts of his Encyclopedist predecessor.[8]

In practice, however, gradual changes became evident in the strict hierarchical system insisted on by Blondel. The need to accommodate new building types in the architect's repertory; the demands of newly rich and fashion-conscious clients for a rhetoric of representation equivalent to their hard-won status; these concerns supported an emerging taste for aesthetic criteria based on the effect of forms on the sensations rather than on the absolute norms of proportion or beauty. The demand, stemming from the linguistic enquiries of the Encyclopedists, that all buildings should unambiguously demonstrate their purpose further encouraged architects to experiment with new formal combinations and historical borrowings.

Ledoux's own practice—beginning in the early 1760s with the design of interiors and the remodeling of existing houses for private clients—only gradually responded to these changes in the idea of characterization; not until the mid-1770s, with his design for the Saline de Chaux would his work exhibit that radical break with academic conventions that formed the basis of his reputation for both brilliance and unorthodoxy. But from the start, his treatment of these conventions showed an originality, recognized by Blondel himself, that anticipated his more dramatic experiments in the character of public monuments. In this respect, the *hôtels* and *châteaux* of his early career acted as a kind of laboratory in which he was able to define an entirely personal style while building a patronage circle that would support him in larger undertakings through to the Revolution.

EMBLEMS OF SOCIABILITY

Ledoux's early commissions were therefore designed and judged under Blondel's criteria of late academic classicism, which attempted to accommodate, on the one hand, a new climate of rational classification and, on the other, changing social tastes. Blondel himself, together with members of his circle, was quick to praise or criticize the efforts of this obviously talented pupil, who, while "not lacking in genius, allows himself to be carried along by the tide and neglects the proprieties."[9] Ledoux's first recorded design, however, received only eulogies. This, the *salle de café* of the Café Godeau, more familiarly called the Café Militaire after its clientele of veterans and officers, was built in 1762, in the rue Saint-Honoré, and is presently reinstalled in the Musée Carnavalet.[10] As if to create a textbook illustration of his classical education and lessons in characterization, Ledoux invented a fictional program, perhaps adapted from Caesar's *Commentaries,* as a device to unify the decoration. Blondel's friend, the critic Elie Fréron, writing in his journal, the *Année littéraire,* approved of this literary conceit as at once ingenius and evoking the sense of what he called "a noble and sound antiquity":

The author imagines that the soldiers, having left the battle, find a place to rest, and, bundling their spears together, they bind them with the laurels of victory and top them picturesquely with their helmets. This gives the effect, around the entire room, of twelve triumphal columns, which are then repeated to infinity by the magic of the mirrors. The helmets are well chosen and contrasted; they characterize with different emblems the heroes and gods of antiquity.[11]

Ledoux's visual expression of this literary allusion clearly followed Blondel's rules of characterization to the letter: the old soldiers, taking their coffee and reminiscing over past triumphs and present defeats, were surrounded by an elegant mise-en-scène comprised of alternating mirrored and wooden panels, separated by vertical fasces that rose the whole height of the room like some primitive giant order, crowned by plumed helmets. The wooden panels were carved with trophies and shields in strong relief. In Ledoux's imagination, these surroundings would no doubt remind the café goers of their Gallo-Roman ancestors resting beneath a temporary shelter set up in a forest clearing, a tent built out of their spears and festooned with their shields and helmets. This emblematic program was conceived, as Daniel Rabreau has pointed out, toward the end of the Seven Years' War with England, a year after the French peace initiative of 31 March 1761.[12] It no doubt symbolized hopes for an honorable settlement despite a series of punishing defeats, an optimism that was to be foreclosed by the humiliating terms of the Treaty of Paris in 1763.

In this design, Ledoux also seemed to imply a specifically architectural commentary on what had become a lively debate since the mid-1750s: the "search for origins," epitomized by the Abbé Laugier's description of a paradigmatic primitive hut in his *Essai sur l'architecture* of 1753.[13] Ledoux's own primitivism was evident in the carved attributues, with their grotesque boars' heads and intertwined snakes surmounting the helmets, in the "original" heraldry of the gods' shields, in the fasces-columns, and, finally, in the allusion to a primitive shelter formed out of freestanding posts, certainly a version of an original architectural type. But whereas Laugier, as illustrated in the celebrated frontispiece to the second edition of his *Essai* in 1755, had proposed a *natural* origin for each of the three principal elements of architectural structure—the tree for the column, the branch for the architrave, and the roof of inclined members for the pediment—Ledoux, by contrast, preferred an origin rooted not in nature but in *symbolic form.* Ledoux's columns owed nothing to trees but were rather the signs of warrior life, and, in representing the moment when weapons were transformed into the symbols

of unity—the fasces—they also stood as emblems of an original sociability. In this ascription, the origins of architecture were to be found less in the natural development of the orders out of primitive wooden supports than in the history of cultural expression, less in the structural rigorism of a proto-Greek model than in the visual conventions of a developed society. Here Ledoux showed a predilection for rhetorical motifs, rooted in the expressive language of a culture, that was to inform his mature work in a gamut of different ways. In the light of contemporary interpretations of the tent as an original model for architecture, a type identified by Quatremère de Quincy with the transitory life of the hunter, perhaps Ledoux found its impermanence and flexibility appropriate to the origins of a warrior class descended from the first lineages of France.

In his description of the café, Fréron had noted not only the reference to classical tradition and the rugged simplicity of the decor, but also its "imprint of true taste," which he saw as a model of a "rich, grand, and simple style," one that he posed against the excesses of the rococo, with its "ornaments unhappily too analogous to the spirit of the century." [14] Here Fréron was entirely in agreement with Blondel and others nostalgic for the clarity and order of the classical tradition. And indeed the style of Ledoux's motifs, carved in bold relief on plain surfaces, echoed that of the French Renaissance or the classicism of Louis XIV's reign perhaps more than it referred directly to antique sources.

In sum, the café advanced a number of themes that would characterize Ledoux's designs before the Revolution: the idea of the origins of architecture in visual rhetoric; the need for a suitable literary allusion to act as a programmatic text that would provide social and aesthetic support for his architecture; the attempt to imagine the activities of daily life transformed according to a utopian vision; the dramatic illusionism, here sustained by the play of mirrors, that sustained such a social fiction; and, finally, the attempt to develop a new and purer form of classicism out of a selective lexicon of antique and seventeenth-century French precedent.

PATRONAGE CIRCLES

Ledoux's patrons during the late 1760s were to prove especially receptive to such an aesthetic, combining as it did the attributes of nobility with a simplified and historicized classicism. [15] Composed for the most part of members of the nobility of the robe or the sword, parliamentarians, soldiers, and Fermiers Généraux, supported by new sources of revenue—commercial and bureaucratic—interlinked by marriage and social circles, by military or court service, his patrons shared a common aspiration to trace their pedigrees, confirm their titles, and reconsolidate their position in Paris or the provinces after the cessation of hostilities with England in 1763. [16] Ledoux displayed a talent for flattering the aspirations of this failing noble class by the art of dramatizing their qualities in emblems, attributes, and giant orders. His taste for military exploits and nostalgia for a golden age of chivalry and heroism was also shared by his patrons, similarly nostalgic for a France where order and privilege had seemed to count for more than commercial or educational success. [17]

After the Revolution, despite his own imprisonment and the execution or exile of many of these early clients, Ledoux was to reaffirm his allegiance to the nobility in unambiguous terms: "When I speak of the nobility, I wish to recall that indefeasible value handed down by the descendents of Ceasar to the heroes of this country, a value that the hand of time cannot efface." (212). During his first years of practice, Ledoux, with the instinct of an upwardly mobile professional and with some of the innocence of the arriviste, sought out his patrons as if in pursuit of that most elusive of eighteenth-century fables, an *original* nobility, entering a circle wedded to what a contemporary observer dubbed the *titromanie,* or genealogical fervor. [18] Ledoux himself never hid his own ambitions to be received at court, elected to the Académie, and, above all, ennobled; and he reserved his first affection for those families, like the de Montesquious and the de Bauffremonts, who pretended to direct descent from Clovis—a return to origins entirely sympathetic with Ledoux's architectural version. But the elaborate genealogies commissioned by the Montmorency family from the historian Désormeaux in

1764 or by the Marquis de Montesquiou from Gaillard in 1784 or earlier by the Fermiers Généraux Du Vaucel and Haudry de Soucy, were only the most evident of the links that joined an architect desirous of ennobling his art and clients defensive of their birthrights and privileges.[19] For Ledoux's hyperbolic instinct with regard to what he considered "architectural power" found in the nobility its social and political equivalent, as if the art of building, by renewing its sources of representation, might consolidate the second estate and, in turn, receive its own title as the founding art of culture.

Like many other architects of his generation—Chalgrin, Bélanger, Brongniart, De Wailly—Ledoux was forced to piece together his clientele by recommendations within overlapping social circles. In this, at least until the Revolution, he was extremely successful. Thus the Fermier Général and Président of the Parlement of Metz Jean-Hyacinthe Hocquart, no doubt introduced to Ledoux by Blondel, who had earlier proposed a plan for the redevelopment of Metz, called Ledoux to his family estate at Montfermeil in order to reconstruct the old *château* and at the same time commissioned him to build his Parisian residence in the Chaussée d'Antin in 1765.[20] Hocquart's brother-in-law, the Marquis de Montesquiou, brought Ledoux to Maupertuis in the early 1760s to rebuild the old house and extend the park.[21] Hocquart also seems to have introduced Ledoux to the Duc d'Uzès when the latter rejected the designs of Mathurin Cherpitel and Pierre-Noël Rousset for remodeling his *hôtel* in Paris.[22] Hocquart's parliamentary circle further included the Président de Sénozan, married to a Lamoignon, who introduced Ledoux to another branch of the family, Chrétien-François II de Lamoignon, and thence to his sister, the Présidente de Gourgues (whose frustrating demands caused the architect to launch a protracted lawsuit for fees).[23] De Senozan's wife was the sister of the *philosophe* and *censeur royale,* Chrétien-Guillaume Lamoignon de Malesherbes, friend and protector of Diderot and himself an agrarian reformer, who no doubt brought Ledoux into contact with the group of economic reformers around Jean-Charles-Philibert Trudaine de Montigny and Jacques Turgot. Both Madame de Gourgues and the Marquis de Montesquiou were intimates of Madame de Montesson, mis-

tress and later wife of the Duc d'Orléans, brother of Louis XV. De Montesson's close friend the Marquis de Livry contracted with Ledoux to rebuild his *château* at Bénouville in Normandy between 1769 and 1771.[24] Ledoux's connections to the Fermiers Généraux led to commissions from the rich Fermier François Fontaine de Cramayel and the Marquise de Foucault.[25] De Cramayel himself was married to a member of the powerful de La Borde family, financiers, art collectors, and *fermiers.* Madame de Cramayel's brother, Jean-Benjamin de la Borde, was Premier Valet de Chambre to the king; he was also a dramatist and stage director of some distinction, producing plays first at Cramayel and then in the private theater of Mlle Guimard, for whom Ledoux built a residence and *salle de spectacle* after 1770. Many of these clients were also military officers, socializing in the clubs of the capital and notably in the Café Militaire close to the Palais Royal. From them Ledoux attracted other work. In 1766 he reconstructed an *hôtel* in the Marias for Franz-Joseph d'Hallwyl, colonel of the Swiss Guard. D'Hallwyl was linked by business interests to the Swiss Protestant banking firm of Thélusson and Necker, his neighbors in the rue Michel le Comte. Ledoux profited from these connections both in the commission for Madame Thélusson's *hôtel* in 1778, and in his widening circle of friends in the arts, many of whom gathered in the salon of Madame Necker: the final title of *L'architecture* testified to his respect for Necker's daughter, the later Madame de Staël, echoing that of her treatise on literature. Ledoux's position as architect to the nobility was, finally, confirmed by his introduction to the Baron Crozat de Thiers, a rich collector and antiquarian, whose apartment in the Place Vendôme he refurbished before 1767, and to one of the first families of France, the Montmorency-Luxembourgs, as architect for the Prince and Princesse de Montmorency building their *hôtel* on the Boulevard between 1769 and 1771.[26]

At least in the initial years of his practice Ledoux was attentive to the often imperious demands of these patrons; he was to compare his unsuccessful negotiations with Madame de Gourgues to the demanding relationship between doctor and patient: "A new request from Madame de la Présidente, new errands for me, as if I were a doctor from whom one expects a cure when one is very ill." [27] But his willingness to please was matched, as Michel Gallet has shown, by a readiness to defend and define his professional interests by rhetoric and litigation when respect for his rights and role as a liberal architect were ignored by clients more used to absolute servitude. In his disputes with clients—with the Présidente de Gourgues, Mlle Saint-Germain, M. de Witt, and others who thought they had been overcharged or ruined by their architect—Ledoux, in retrospect, seems less arrogant than he was principled, concerned to define a boundary of respect between client and professional not yet clearly drawn. His day-to-day struggle to invent a moral, aesthetic, and social code no doubt laid the groundwork for his reputation for exaggeration, as he inflated his claims for the architect's powers sometimes beyond merely professional dimensions.

ANTIQUE MODELS

The monuments of antiquity, their fragments, such as they are, bear a character that commands our respect. Those of modern architects could help to fix the bases of instruction if they adapted whatever was good in antique buildings to our usages. (109)

The style of Ledoux's first *hôtels* has been identified with a general rejection of the rococo in favor of a "new classicism." In Blondel's terms, however, this had represented less a "return to antiquity" in general than a restitution of the sober forms of the French classical tradition, judiciously modified to accommodate contemporary needs: that is, the creation of a modern French architecture. Such a new academicism was recognized in the designs of Jacques-Ange Gabriel and his followers. Writing in 1777, three years after Blondel's death, Pierre Patte noted this stylistic turn with approval. [28] Summarizing the history of taste in interior decoration over the previous century, he identified three so-called revolutions. First there appeared the "grave and serious style" of Louis XIV, with its severity, proscription of irregular forms, noble and strong proportions, its decorations in the "male genre"; then occurred a subsequent period of decline in taste with the rococo, the "extraordinary contours," "the confused assem-

blage of attributes placed without thought" joined to "ornaments of a bizarre imagination," that "ridiculous mass of bent cartouches, shells, dragons, reeds, palm trees, and all sorts of imaginary plants," which had led to a "kind of unreason in architecture"; finally there emerged a "return of good taste." This last stage, inspired by the work of Germain Boffrand and Giovanni Niccolò Servandoni who, "little by little . . . returned to wiser and less bizarre forms," Patte dated from the end of the Seven Years' War in 1763: it was characterized by a mingling of the "good genre of decoration" from the time of Louis XIV with more modern qualities—less severity, more delicacy, and, above all, more variety in form. [29] By the late 1770s, indeed, Patte was prepared to admit the emergence of what he called a new art, *un art nouveau.*

This return to good taste was, in Patte's description, sustained by another return, what he saw as a "return of the taste for antiquity," a development more evident to the generation of Blondel's students after the 1760s than to Blondel himself. Marked by a series of publications dedicated to the illustration of sites no longer confined to the Italian peninsula, beginning with Robert Wood's and James Dawkins's engravings of Palmyra and Balbec published between 1753 and 1757, this passion for new sources had been popularized in France by the well-publicized journey of Soufflot, the engraver Charles-Nicolas Cochin, and the Marquis Marigny, brother of Madame de Pompadour, to Italy in 1753, followed by Gabriel Dumont's publication of their views of the temples of Paestum. [30] The already strong influence of Johann Bernhard Fischer von Erlach's historical fantasies of the 1720s—still the only source for depictions of "Egyptian" architecture—was complemented, after 1758, by Julien-David Le Roy's report of Greek architecture and the ensuing battle for veracity between the young academician and his British rivals, James Stuart and Nicholas Revett. The competition for "authentic" historical origins of architectural style was made fiercer by Piranesi's espousal of Etruscan beginnings, based on his reading of Vico's cultural history of institutions.

In this light, the "return" identified by Patte should be seen as multiple in nature, divided between an allegiance to French and to antique precedent, then again between diverse

theories of origins, and, increasingly, between different antiquities, Greek and Roman, Etruscan and Egyptian. Ledoux,
who would seize on this tension as the source of some of his
most successful combinatory exercises in the 1780s, revealed
a more tentative stance in the 1760s, moving from direct quotation to allusion and abstraction, and from French to Roman
models. These marks of attachment to the teachings of Blondel were, of course, equally signs of an architect trained exclusively in France; they would be supplemented in the later
1770s by a turn toward an anglicized Palladianism and then to
Greek models. Unifying this otherwise eclectic stance was an
uncompromising boldness in the application of motifs, a so-
phisticated sense of interior decor supported by an ability to
manage the relations among the different crafts to brilliant
effect, and an almost systematic control of plan and section
by geometry, much of which met with even Blondel's
approval.[31]

Ledoux's contribution to this "return to antiquity" was
confined at first to the façades and interior decoration of *hôtels*
and *châteaux*, constrained by the traditional plans of the existing buildings he was asked to remodel. Thus the Hôtel
d'Hallwyl, like the Hôtel d'Uzès two years later, was entirely
conventional in plan, with its *corps de logis*, or main block, set
back from the street, stretching between the side walls of its
narrow urban sites, and set between front courtyards and rear
gardens. Ledoux seems not to have altered the interior distributions of either house to any great extent, devoting his attention to new programs for the interior decor and to the
exterior effect of the building masses. In this task, however—
the remodeling of the façades, courts, *communs* or outbuildings, and suites of semipublic and semiprivate rooms—Ledoux successfully created the illusion of *hôtels* that, as he
described the Hôtel d'Hallwyl, appeared to be "constructed
almost entirely anew."[32]

Of the two, the earlier *hôtel*, belonging to Franz-Joseph
d'Hallwyl (extant today, although in a much degraded state),
was the smaller. In the restricted context of the Marais, Ledoux was forced to divide the *communs* in two, surrounding
the small front courtyard on three sides with kitchens, offices,
and a tiny carriage house. The stables themselves were

stretched longitudinally along the eastern party wall and were
entered not from the rue Michel le Comte, but from the rear
along the rue de Montmorency. The *hôtel* proper was entered
from a grand triple-height stair hall opening onto the *cour
d'honneur,* or forecourt; this led to the main apartments on the
second floor—the grand salon, dining room, and *salle de compagnie*. The bedrooms, together with their *cabinets de toilette,*
bathrooms, wardrobes, and *lieux anglaises* or water closets,
were distributed around the *cour d'honneur* on the same floor.
Below, opening into the garden court, was another salon with
its attendant studies and bedroom, while on the third floor
were three more bedroom suites and servants' quarters.

On the exterior, Ledoux unified all of the façades with
a consistent use of horizontally channeled rustication, fashioned over the windows into subtly dropped keystones, flush
with the smooth surface, and horizontal architraves and dentils on two floors. The entry façade on the rue Michel le
Comte was slightly set back in the center, framing a round-
arched doorway that rose above the first floor architrave, its
tympanum holding a bas-relief of two seated winged figures
holding scrolls—no doubt famæ—originally placed on either
side of a shield bearing the double eagle of the Swiss Guards,
d'Hallwyl's regiment. Bas-reliefs of coats of arms and lions
inside the entry passage repeated the military motifs of the
façade. To either side of this door, supporting the architrave
and set into the entry façade, were two fluted Doric columns.
The same order, unfluted, appeared on the first floor of the
entry block on the courtyard side, opening onto the gallery
that led at second-floor level onto the gallery joining one side
of the bedroom wing to the other. The *cour d'honneur* itself
was small and marked only by the alternately triangular and
round pediments over the second-floor windows to the grand
apartments.

Ledoux, while treating these front blocks with some re-
serve, if not strictness, conserved his architectural inventiveness for the rear garden court. In emulation of a Roman
atrium house, the courtyard was flanked on either side by arcades of unfluted Doric columns—*Dorique composée,* as Ledoux called them—covering a walk raised a few steps above
the level of the court. Conceived some years before the pub-

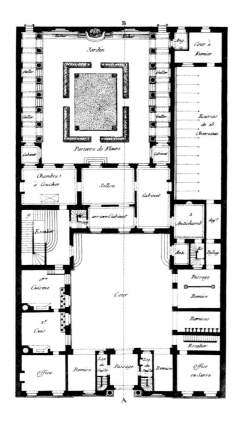

Ledoux, Hôtel d'Hallwyl, rue
Michel le Comte, Paris, 1766.
Top, plan of first floor show–
ing front and rear courtyards;
middle, elevation of entry
façade, rue Michel le Comte;
bottom, sculptured group above
street entrance. Engravings
from Daniel Ramée, *L'architecture de C.-N. Ledoux* (Paris,
1847), pls. 156, 158;
photograph by F. Contet.

lication of the domestic courtyards of Pompeii, this architectural set piece reinforced the theme of a return to Rome, envisaged on a domestic scale precisely calculated to the program. Further developing the theme of a Roman country villa, Ledoux closed the court with an elaborately worked back wall, rusticated in a Serlian manner, with a central arched fountain niche surrounded by a border of carved droplets and framed by rusticated pilasters down which cascaded stone torrents pouring from overturned urns that surmounted the heavy capitals. The engraved version was even more rustic, with horizontally banded rustication and three arched niches, each containing nymphs and satyrs bathing in the fountain that played into a continuous trough, or *thalus*, running across the front. These motifs, while they evidently prefigure the more celebrated urns and waterspouts, rustication, and Serlian echoes of the Saline de Chaux, also look back to the decorative and genuinely Serlian treatment of the seventeenth-century Fontaine des Medicis in the Luxembourg gardens, attributed to Solomon de Brosse.

Extending the view from this garden court was an even bolder gesture of architectural trompe l'oeil, where Ledoux, to compensate for the restricted depth of the garden and *parterre*, designed a painted landscape to be rendered at second-floor level on the blank wall of the Carmelite monastery across the rue de Montmorency. This depicted a double, open arcade of Doric columns that disclosed a fictitious garden beyond, with the tips of its poplars and fountains appearing above the balustrade. To either side stood statuary groups that mimicked the horse tamers of Versailles. Writing in 1767, Ledoux noted that this decorative gesture was still not realized: "Next year there should be, on the wall of the Carmelite monastery, a backdrop of painted decoration that will relate to the real colonnade of the garden. I have adopted this *parti* because the garden was dominated by very high walls on every side; any planting at all would have destroyed the healthiness of the dwelling."[33]

In the Hôtel d'Uzès, such scenic dissimulation was not necessary. The house was approached by a long and narrow tree-lined *allée;* there was ample space along its sides and around its large *cour d'honneur* to accommodate stables, carriage houses, and offices. At the rear, the *hôtel* gave onto a garden of equal length. Profiting from this site, Ledoux was concerned to exploit the drama of entry. For this he designed a triumphal gateway, reminiscent of Marie-Joseph Peyre's entrance for the Château de Neubourg in 1765, flanked by freestanding Doric columns that were topped by antique torsos bearing shields, helmets, and arms and hung with trophies, shields, swords, and lion skins, honoring the military exploits of the Duc d'Uzès. The entry to the *corps de logis* was marked by a colossal order of four Corinthian columns supporting a heavy architrave, reminiscent of Robert Wood's engravings of Balbec and self-consciously competing with the contemporary portico designed by Gabriel for the Ecole Militaire. To the rear, Ledoux decorated the garden façade with another giant order, of six Ionic pilasters, their capitals festooned, above which stood an equal number of life-size sculptures of

Ledoux, Hôtel d'Hallwyl, colonnade of garden court. Photograph from Marcel Raval and J.-Ch. Moreux, *Claude-Nicolas Ledoux, 1756–1806* (Paris, 1945), pl. 6.

Ledoux, Hôtel d'Hallwyl, rear wall of garden courtyard. Photograph by F. Contet.

Ledoux, Hôtel d'Hallwyl, detail of rear courtyard showing fountain and mural on wall of the Carmelite monastery facing onto the rue de Montmorency. Engraving from Ramée, *Ledoux,* pl. 158.

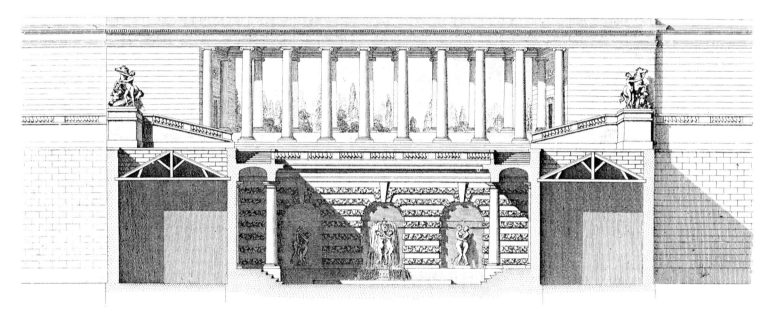

ancient heroes by the academic sculptor Félix Lecomte. Beyond this, the symmetrical garden terminated in a raised exedra, anticipating the more theatrical layouts of many of Ledoux's gardens in the 1780s.

For both of these bold gestures—the *porte d'entrée* and the colossal order of the entry façade—Ledoux received criticism that bordered on accusations of plagiarism. Jean-Louis Viel de Saint-Maux recorded that his friend Legeay, on returning to Paris from Prussia in the 1760s was

astonished to see that his students had put columns everywhere. "This was good," he said, "in the designs of decorations or of feux d'artifices that I gave them to copy." He showed us in effect many magnificent drawings where we recognized, among others, the columns built at the gate of the Hôtel d'Uzès, rue Montmartre."[34]

The second criticism was more serious, coming from his former teacher Blondel just before his death. In *Les amours rivaux,* the old academician described a visit to the *hôtel;* he claimed that the portico was plagiarized not from Legeay, but from Pierre Contant d'Ivry—with whom Ledoux had per-

haps served a period of apprenticeship—and that the plan of the house itself was taken from Alexandre Le Blond, architect of the Hôtel de Vendôme. On this evidence, Blondel agreed with the rumor that Ledoux was "more imitator than inventor." Blondel's aesthetic reservations were even more serious, however, and went to the heart of the emerging dispute over the notion of character between the generations of Boffrand and Blondel, on the one hand, and his students, Boullée, De Wailly, and Ledoux, on the other. Ledoux, Blondel stated, had neglected "the *convenances,* the proportions, and that sustained style that should show itself in all the products of art." His principal objection was to the colossal order of the front—"ridiculously colossal," he noted—which was crowded into far too small a space to be properly seen. Such columns, he held, should be criticized on two counts: first, for the unwieldy contrast of their "gigantic size" with the other decorative elements and with the very proportions of the human figure—an especially necessary relation to observe in a dwelling—and, secondly, for their complete lack of harmony with the character of the program:

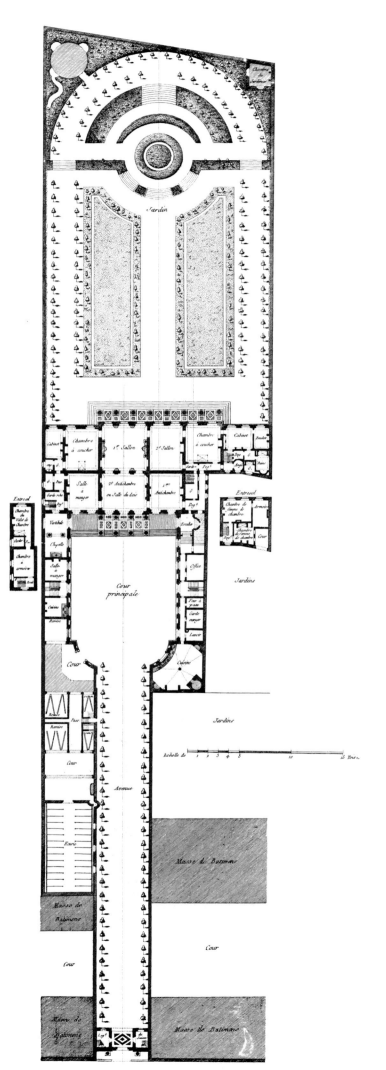

Ledoux, Hôtel d'Uzès, rue Montmartre, Paris, 1768. *Left to right:* plan of first floor and site, showing entrance avenue, front court, and garden; front elevation of entrance gate; plans and section of entrance gate; detail of façade to front court. Engravings from Ramée, *Ledoux,* pls. 153, 152, 202, 154 (pl. 154 by François-Noël Sellier).

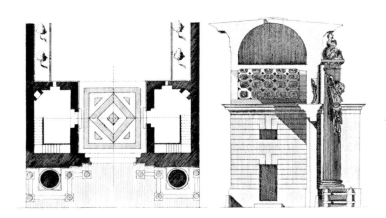

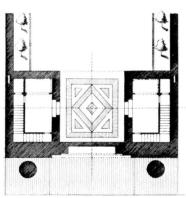

Ledoux, Hôtel d'Uzès: entry
façade (*above*) and garden
façade (*below*), before 1870.
Photographs from Raval and
Moreux, *Ledoux*, pls. 13, 15.

The size of the order infallibly repulses you. It is not only vicious in itself for its exaggeration, but it becomes almost impossible to consider it in the façade as a whole because of the lack of space and the organization of the site. . . . There you see the effect of an unruly imagination that gives to a bourgeois house the air of an hôtel *and to this* hôtel *the aura of a palace. How can one forget, or help feeling that there exists a character suitable for every building? I have discussed the matter a hundred times with a gentlemen celebrated for this art, and I agree with him when he agrees with Mansart. The most essential object in architecture is to know how to assign to the ordering of façades a character that relates to the subject one wishes to express. A giant order should only be applied to a sacred building or a public monument.*[35]

Ledoux had thereby broken the careful hierarchical structure of orders and genres assembled by Blondel to counter the new taste and to sustain, if not return to, the classical values of *convenance* and the codes of sumptuary embellishment operative in the previous century.

In both of these early works Ledoux developed a scheme of interior decoration that, following the model of the Café Militaire, responded emblematically to the nature of his clients. The main salon of the Hôtel d'Hallwyl was embellished with motifs drawn from classical iconography—chimeras holding lyres—as well as from French classicism, mingling what one historian, Daniel Rabreau, has seen as motifs of peace with the marks of d'Hallwyl's affiliation to the monarchy as a member of the Swiss Guard. Michel Gallet has hazarded that this decorative program must count as "one of the first French examples of the neoclassical arabesque."[36] In the even more elaborate *salon de compagnie* or second salon of the Hôtel d'Uzès, carved by two craftsmen who would often collaborate with Ledoux, Jean-Baptiste Boiston and Joseph Métivier, he returned to the metaphors of the café by creating the illusion of a gilded forest with its trees rising from floor to ceiling and hung with trophies and emblems of the arts of war and peace. Gallet has claimed an apparent similarity of aesthetic purpose between these trees and Laugier's tree-columns, but in this instance Ledoux's entirely naturalistic versions, slender and elegant, bound with laurels and rib-

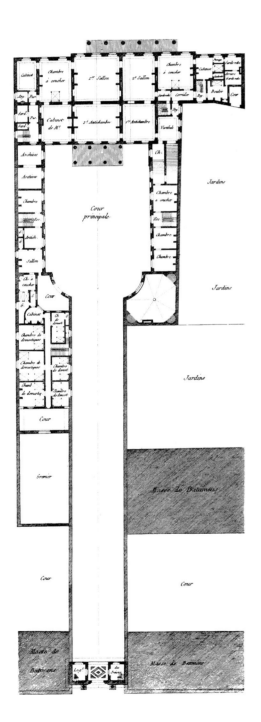

Ledoux, Hôtel d'Uzès, plan of second floor. The salon to the right of the central first salon is the *salon de compagnie*. Engraving from Ramée, *Ledoux*, pl. 153.

bons, seem more concerned with the theatricality of the setting as a highly wrought allegory of a forest grove than with any structural model for architecture. Blondel once more was critical, finding fault with the break in convention that had established a dado at sofa height in domestic decoration: he noted that "the designer, solely preoccupied in dedicating his decoration to the art of war, has suspended trophies of weapons from the branches of palms that seem to take root in the parquet," confusing in this way allegory and naturalism.[37] Ledoux further decorated the four main doors of this salon with attributes symbolizing the four quarters of the globe: crocodiles for America, dromedaries for Asia, elephants for Africa, and horses for Europe—an allegory of world unity also present in some Masonic lodges of the period. The possibility of a Masonic connection is here supported by the allegorical figure of the four Masonic virtues, Wisdom, Strength, Justice, and Truth, carved in the shields hung from the trees. These iconographic suggestions are, in turn, reinforced by the high office held in the Grand Orient by François-Emmanuel's son in the late 1780s.[38]

PALLADIAN TRANSFORMATIONS

Although he never, like so many of his contemporaries, undertook a voyage to Italy, Ledoux, as he later confirmed, "traveled for two years for [his] education" (43), most probably between the late 1760s and 1774. Historians have surmised that this tour included some time in England after 1763: Cellérier mentions Ledoux's work for Lord Clive of Plassey, Viceroy of India, who passed through France in 1768 and 1769, and who was occupied in developing his family estates in England with the aid of architects, such as William Chambers, who were themselves strongly connected with France.[39] Ledoux himself mentions a stay in Lyons (43), leading to speculation that another English tie was there formed at the invitation of the Pitt family, whose French villa had been envisaged since 1763.[40] Neither of these two fragments of evidence, however, would necessarily point to a visit to England at this time; both, in fact, seem predicated on meetings in France, and the hypothesis of a later journey to En-

Ledoux, Hôtel d'Uzès, *salon de compagnie,* details of door paneling, showing emblems of "America," "Asia," "Africa," and "Europe" (*left to right*). Photographs by Giraudon from the Musée Carnavalet.

gland (perhaps following the exile of Ledoux's mentor Charles-Alexandre Calonne in 1787), seems more tenable. This notwithstanding, in the late 1760s Ledoux's designs undoubtedly began to reflect an increasing influence from English neo-Palladianism.[41] Certainly his first domestic commission in Paris, the pavilion for Président Hocquart begun in 1765, was distinctly Palladian in derivation; from the later, and obviously idealized, engraving this appears to have been a semifreestanding block with a centralized plan loosely based on the Villa Rotonda.

Centralized pavilions, with what Louis Hautecoeur has termed a *plan masse,* were not new in French architecture: Boffrand had used an octagonal rotunda for his hunting pavilion at Bouchefort, while Mansart had earlier referred directly to Palladian precedent in his pavilions at Marly; Gabriel had followed with the Petit Trianon, and de Neufforge would publish an octagonal house in 1767. Ledoux, however, seems precocious in bringing this essentially country-house type to the city, where in the ensuing decades he made it a leit motiv of his domestic architecture. Hence his desire to illustrate the pavilion Hocquart at the first and purest example of the type. Ionic, pedimented porticoes to front and rear gave onto a formal garden and created an axis on the interior that passed through the central dining room. This took the shape of a double-height rotunda, with a coffered dome lit through graduated openings in its shell; surrounded by a colossal order of Corinthian pilasters and overlooked by a second-story gallery leading to the bedroom suites, this room formed a link to the *chambres de parade* and private apartments on the main floor. These were planned in suites of three around this common center: the antechamber, dining room, and *salon de compagnie* on the main axis, flanked by a bedroom, library, and study suite for the president on one side and a bedroom, *cabinet de toilette,* boudoir, and *anglaise* for Madame Hocquart on the other.

Nevertheless, Ledoux's Palladianism emerged fully developed only with the commission for the Hôtel Montmorency between 1769 and 1771. Here an unambiguously square, centralized plan was ingeniously inflected to receive a corner entrance, thus recognizing its position on two major

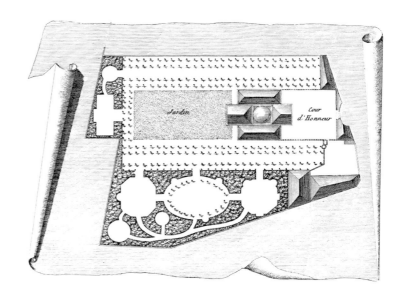

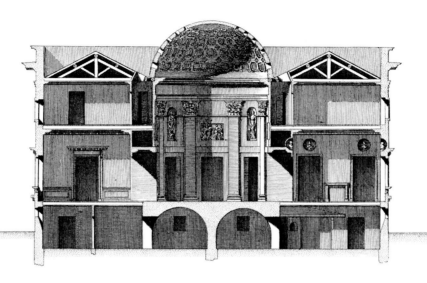

Ledoux, House for Président Hocquart, rue Saint-Lazare, Paris, 1765. *Above,* section; *below,* plan of first floor; *opposite,* site plan. Engravings from Ramée, *Ledoux,* pls. 197, 198.

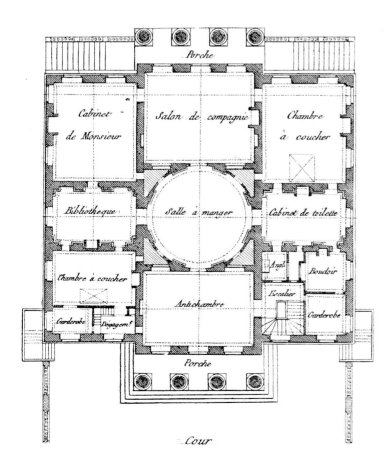

Porche

Cabinet de Monsieur

Salon de compagnie

Chambre à coucher

Bibliotheque

Salle à manger

Cabinet de toilette

Chambre à coucher

Angl.

Boudoir

Escalier

Antichambre

Garderobe

Dégagem.t

Garderobe

Porche

Cour

streets, the Boulevard Montmartre and the newly cut Chaussée d'Antin, to each of which it presented equal façades. The entrance led to a major suite of rooms planned along the diagonal of the square. On the first floor, a circular porch at the corner gave onto an oval vestibule encircled by baseless Doric columns at the center of the plan, from which the main stair, split on either side of the kitchen at the rear corner, made a magnificent double sweep to the rear corner of the next floor and the *chambres de parade;* the stair, again reflecting Ledoux's interest in French classical examples, seems to echo one of Girard Desargues's perspective inventions. On the second floor, from the first antechamber the movement doubled back along the diagonal toward the outer corner, through an oval, double-height second antechamber, subtly top-lit and decorated with a painted sky, to the circular grand salon immediately above the entrance vestibule. To either side of the grand salon the orthogonal axes were taken up by a second salon and a bedroom respectively. In his later, revised version of this design, Ledoux replaced the colossal Ionic pilasters that marked these last rooms on the exterior by columns enclosing terraces that overlooked the street. On the third floor, a gallery around the second antechamber led to a more private salon at the corner, an oval room with its long axis at right angles to the main diagonal, and to suites of bedrooms on either side.

On the outside, the Palladian effect was reinforced by the straight architrave and balustrade that was topped by eight statues representing, in Ledoux's words, "the eight constables of Montmorency," a reference to the (more precisely six) members of the family who had in preceding centuries been dignified with the title of *connétable,* or first soldier of France. Ledoux was later to recall the criticism evoked by this quasihistorical invention:

In 1770, the statues of eight constables placed on the palace of the Prince de Montmorency were criticized by those of both low and high birth, the former out of ignorance, the latter from jealousy. Heroic virtues, destroyed by vandalism! Profound impressions that time cannot efface! . . . The constables, founders of an immortal glory, have left us with heroes. (176)

A series of panels carved with trophies, set between the Ionic pilasters on the façades, and a figure of Fame holding the arms of Montmorency above the corner entrance completed the external iconography.

Inside, the paneling of the grand salon, sketched by Ledoux and carved by Métivier, showed muses, alternating with cupids and vases, displaying attributes of the arts and sciences. Reflecting the strong adherence of the Montmorency family to Freemasonry—the Montmorency-Luxembourgs had founded their own lodge in the early 1760s, and the Duc de Luxembourg acted as general administrator of the Grand Orient from 1771 to the Revolution—the symbolism was here overt, including the compasses, squares, globes, and staff of Mercury.

Ledoux's predilection for the pavilion form was confirmed in the early 1770s by a house built on a site adjacent to the Hôtel Hocquart for Mlle Saint-Germain. The original

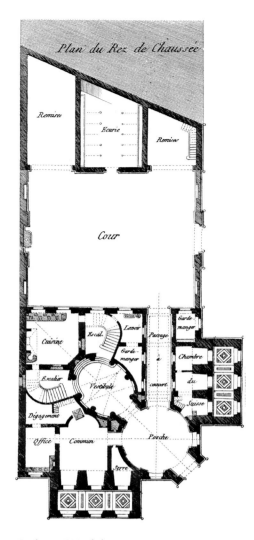

Ledoux, Hôtel de Montmorency, Chaussée d'Antin, Paris, 1769. *Clockwise from upper left:* plan of first floor (reversed), plan of second floor, section, plan of third floor, elevation.

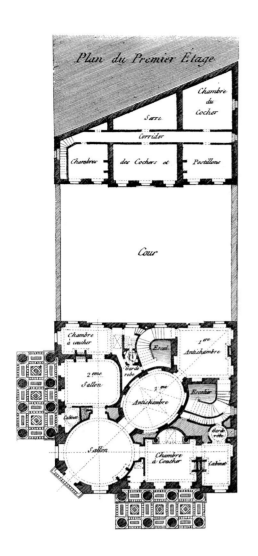

Plan du Premier Étage

Chambre du Cocher

Sare

Corridor

Chambres des Cochers et Postillons

Cour

Chambre à coucher

1.ere Antichambre

Escal

Garde robe

2.me Sallon

Cabinet

2.me Antichambre

2.me Escalier

Garde robe

Sallon

Chambre à Coucher

Cabinet

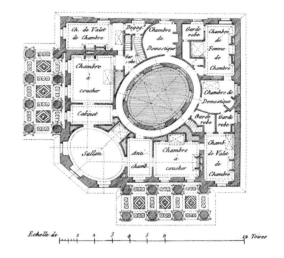

Ch. de Valet de Chambre

Dégag.

Chambre de Domestique

Garde robe

Chambre de Femme de Chambre

Chambre à coucher

Gar robe

Chambre de Domestique & Garde robe

Garde robe

Cabinet

Chamb. de Valet de Chambre

Sallon

Anti chamb.

Chambre à coucher

Echelle de   1   2   3   4   5   6   12 Toises

Echelle de   1   2   3   4   5   10 Toises

Ledoux, House for Mlle Saint-
Germain, idealized perspective
view. Engraving from Ramée.
Ledoux, pl. 201.

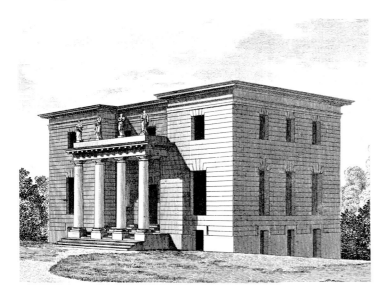

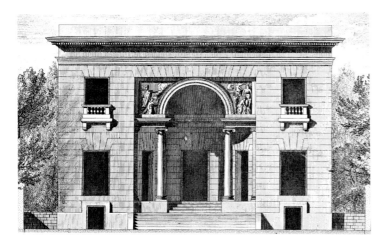

Ledoux, House for M. Tabary,
rue du Faubourg Poissonnière,
1771, elevation. Engraving
from Ramée, *Ledoux*, pl. 201.

project published by Gallet shows a villalike design that seems
directly influenced by Peyre's *château* for the Comte de Neubourg (1765): a central block, with a Doric portico and
straight entablature topped by statues, was recessed between
two end blocks in typical Italian fashion.[42] Inside, a circular
salon behind the vestibule and antechamber projected into the
garden—an echo of Le Vau's Vaux-le-Vicomte, or perhaps of
De Wailly's Château de Montmusard (1764–69). In the later
engravings of the front façade and perspective view, Ledoux
removed the unifying pitched roof, thus emphasizing still
more the pavilionate scheme.

Completing this series of pavilions for the Parisian high
bourgeoisie was that designed for Pierre-René de Tabary in
1771. This pavilion introduced, for the first time in Ledoux's
work, another Palladian motif, later to become ubiquitous,
the Palladian opening, or Serliana, here probably derived
from Soufflot's house for the Marquis de Marigny of 1766,
but transplanted from the upper-story balcony to the entry.
Ledoux created a screen with bas-reliefs in the spandrels
standing in front of a semicircular porch. The *porte cochère,*
was depicted in a drawing by William Chambers as if both
entry and house were *fabriques* in a park: an intimation of Ledoux's own taste for the isolated, freestanding block.

GIANT ORDERS

As in his early *hôtels,* Ledoux was forced to contend with existing structures in his commissions for country houses and
châteaux between 1765 and 1770: at Montfermeil for Président
Hocquart, at Maupertuis for the Marquis de Montesquiou,
and at Bénouville for the Marquis de Livry, Ledoux remodeled old family seats, extending the *corps de logis,* embellishing
them with giant orders and porticoes, adding *communs,* and
laying out new gardens. At Montfermeil two wings were
added to the main house and the entry and garden façades
refashioned by the addition of pediments carried on four colossal Doric pilasters. With customary exaggeration, Ledoux
described them as "columns" in his application for membership to the Académie in 1767. At Maupertuis, the existing
pavilion was, as Ledoux noted, "without form" and easily

subsumed within a new plan. The thirteenth-century fortified farmhouse, altered in the seventeenth century, was thus incorporated into Ledoux's first grand plan for a country house. The central block itself was over three hundred feet long, decorated with a colossal Ionic order; the wings, each over a hundred feet in length, enclosed the two sides of the front court and housed respectively the stables and carriage houses to the left of the entry and the orangery, later used by de Montesquiou as a theater, to the right. The main building, with its single bank of rooms overlooking both entry court and garden, accommodated the vestibule, in which a screen of Ionic columns enclosed the stair; the *salle de compagnie* leading to the private bedroom suite; and the first and second antechambers before the buffet and dining room. To either side of this central block, corridors along the courtyard served the wings, giving access to a second salon in the orangery wing and a chapel adjacent to the *communs*. An imaginary restoration of the house as built, hazarded by the local historian C. Rivière and based on a survey conducted in 1776, shows a more modest building in elevation than that depicted in Ledoux's later engraving of the mid-1780s. Certainly the original roofs, as at Montfermeil, would have been mansarded, and the columns carrying the pediments of the main block would have been pilasters. But a comparison of Ledoux's ground plan with that shown in estate maps indicates that in size and grandeur Ledoux's final engraving in fact differed little from the *château* as completed. A frequent visitor in the eighties, Madame Vigée-Lebrun, remembered that during the continuous round of house parties it had accommodated up to thirty households at a time.[43]

The real design problem for Ledoux was not, however, in the relatively traditional layout of the *château* itself but in the site that sloped steeply from the main entrance of the park toward the river Aubetin. Ledoux planned the approach with skill; as he wrote in 1767:

Until then a central entry seemed impracticable because of the huge rocks buried in the ground and the level of the land, which sloped up to the first floor of the château. *I created a horseshoe some 952 feet in circumference, ringed with balustrades pierced with niches alter-*

nately round and square, thus arriving by means of a gentle slope at the door of the vestibule. As the stone of the region, because of its random forms and color, lent itself to decoration, I used it as it was to terminate the center of the horseshoe by a fountain and sculpted naïades set on pedestals that distributed water to the whole château.[44]

To complete the composition Ledoux placed a statue on a base at the foot of each of the ramps. "The view terminates by a colossal figure holding a reversed urn," wrote the critic Villiers in the year of Ledoux's death, lauding the talent shown in "creating a site, animating it, joining the useful to the agreeable, populating it, and giving life to ten leagues of mountainous and difficult terrain."[45] In the park itself, Ledoux built other *fabriques,* including what he described as a pheasantry, "decorated with an Ionic order and forming a small temple in the midst of the woods," and a pavilion for the estate guards; the forerunners of many of his more idealized designs, both buildings would themselves be redesigned idealistically in the 1780s.

Ledoux's work at Maupertuis was important for his career on at least two levels. In the first place, the patronage of the Marquis de Montesquiou was, and remained throughout two decades, effective in introducing the architect to a wider intellectual and social circle. A prominent member of the court, a distinguished soldier, and an aspiring industrial and commercial investor, de Montesquiou was also a passionate literary adventurer. His plays, none of which were published in his lifetime, were noticed somewhat favorably by Frederick Melchior Grimm; he directed them in the private theater of Madame de Montesson. For little more than perseverance and a few memorable aphorisms he was finally elected to the Académie des Inscriptions et Belles-Lettres in 1784; the Abbé Suard's discourse of reception strained to delineate his qualities, which might equally have been applicable to Ledoux: "you have written comedies where you have depicted the mores of society with the fine gaze of an observer and the art of a poet." "Men of letters," concluded Suard, "are the preceptors of peoples"; Ledoux was to apply similar standards to the architect.[46] In the gatherings at Maupertuis, from 1765 to

Ledoux, Château de Maupertuis, Brie, 1765, plan of first
floor as redrawn by Ledoux in
the early 1780s. Engraving
from Ramée, *Ledoux,* pl. 251.

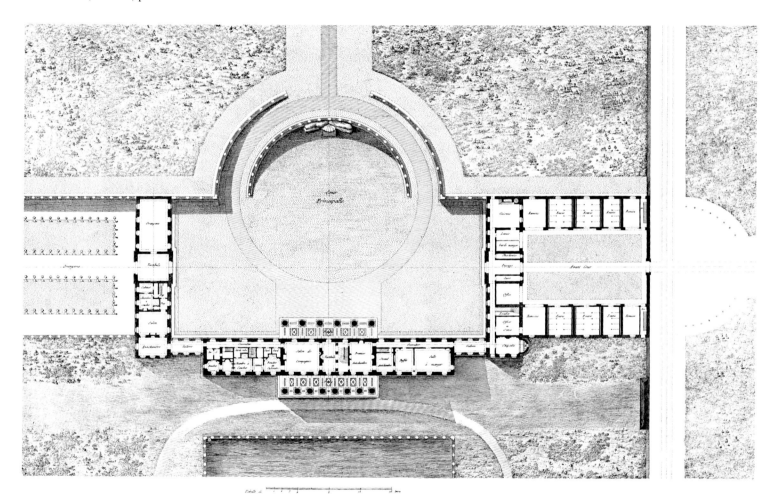

Coupe.

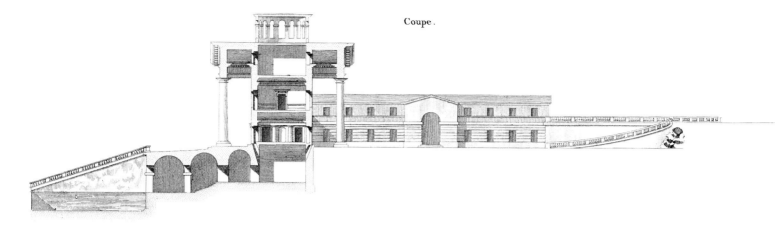

Elévation sur le Jardin.

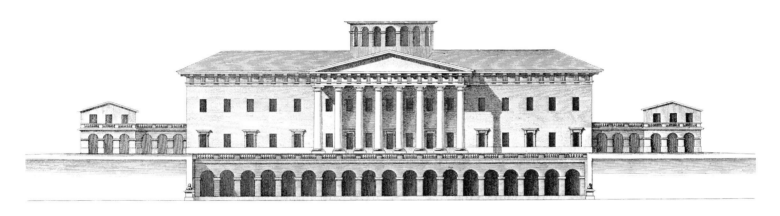

Elévation sur la Cour.

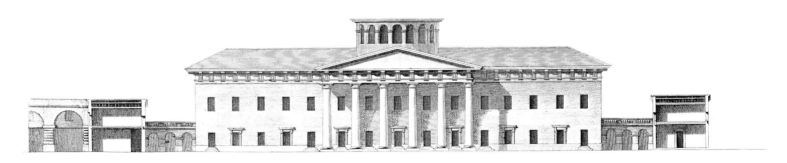

Echelle de   1   2   3   4   5   6   12 Toises .

Ledoux, Château de Maupertuis, section and elevations as
redrawn by Ledoux in the
early 1780s. Engraving from
Ramée, *Ledoux*, pl. 252.

Ledoux, Château de Maupertuis, pheasant house; perspective view, plan, and section.
Engraving from Ramée, *Ledoux,* pl. 253.

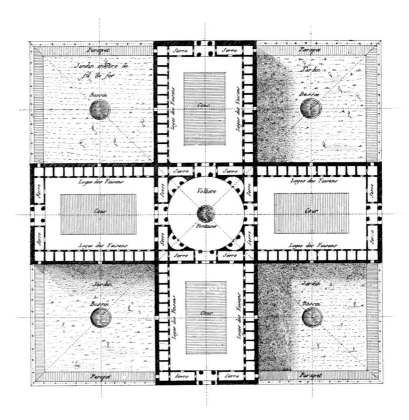

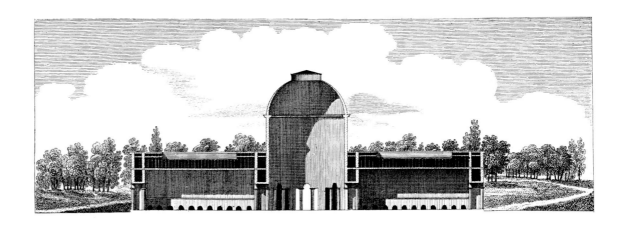

Ledoux, Château de Bénouville, Normandy, 1769, entrance façade. Photograph by Georges Fessy.

the Revolution, Ledoux must have encountered a number of the important artists and poets of the day: the painter Hubert Robert whose depictions of picturesque gardens and classical ruins were formative for Ledoux's aesthetic; the Abbé Delille, poet and translator of Virgil; the architect Alexandre-Théodore Brongniart, with whom Ledoux unsuccessfully competed in 1784 to complete the gardens of Maupertuis; the art dealer Jean–Baptiste Lebrun and his wife, the painter Madame Vigée-Lebrun. Ledoux found a confidante in Madame de Montesquiou, née Hocquart, and felt at home in her salon. Ledoux's views on agriculture, landscape aesthetics, social mores, and painting can all be traced to this circle. Commissions, too, stemmed from Maupertuis, including an unbuilt Parisian *hôtel* for de Montesquiou, the Hôtel d'Artagnan-Fezensac, and a house for the Abbé Delille, who would dedicate a long *éloge* to Ledoux in his poem "L'imagination" just before the architect's death;[97] Ledoux would also collaborate with Robert in the decoration of later houses. Uniting this circle was the Parisian lodge, Saint-Jean d'Ecosse du Contrat Social—to which belonged not only de Montesquiou from 1778, but also Brongniart, the painter J.-M. Moreau jeune, and the composer Antonio Sacchini. Perhaps it was in their assemblies that Ledoux was introduced to the ideology and symbolism of the Freemasons, important influences in his later utopian work.

Ledoux's third major commission for a country house, the Marquis de Livry's *château* at Bénouville in Normandy, begun in 1769 and presenting fewer restrictions in its already remodeled form, demonstrated his aspirations for country

Ledoux, Château de Bénouville. *Above,* entrance portico (photograph by M. Nahmias); *below,* garden façade (photograph by Georges Fessy).

domestic architecture in an advanced form. Ledoux conceived the *château* as a freestanding block, its roof no longer mansarded but hidden behind a tall attic story with a horizontal cornice. To the front was a portico with an entablature supported by four colossal Ionic columns, their capitals festooned, standing free of the façade, their bays marked on the wall behind by six attached columns of the same order. To the rear of the house was a corresponding giant order of six Ionic pilasters framing the central bays. Unlike Maupertuis, the *corps de logis* was doubled in depth, with dining room, buffet, anteroom, and salon on the entrance side, and a grand central stair flanked by two bedroom suites on the garden side. The two upper floors and attic were occupied by bedrooms and servants' quarters.

Following the example of the Hôtel d'Uzès, Ledoux's sculptural program emphasized the military rank and naval interests of the owner: the Marquis de Livry's armorial bearings, supported by helmeted goddesses and framed by banners and fasces, stood over the entry, while, on the garden façade, six trophy groups with ships' prows and torsos carved in deep bas-relief, each the entire height of the attic story, were placed above the Ionic pilasters.

But the architectural tour de force of this building, with its uneasy vertical proportions, was the grand stairway. A high, square volume, surrounded by attached Ionic columns and pilasters that framed pedimented niches and doors and supported a cornice with dentils, mutules, and semicircular arches above, this space was vaulted by a coffered *calotte* open at the summit and surrounded by a balustrade that revealed a painted sky. The stair itself, built entirely out of stone with balusters decorated with the marquis's insignia, comprised a single flight from the first floor, splitting on either side to the bedroom level. This evocation of Mansart's style has been justly described by Michel Gallet as "the most beautiful space by Ledoux still in existence."[48] Its central position, taking up the place normally occupied by the salon and preventing direct access to the garden, not only gave emphasis to the major suite of rooms to the front, as Alan Braham has remarked, but also allowed Ledoux a symmetrical distribution of bedrooms for the marquis and his wife to either side.

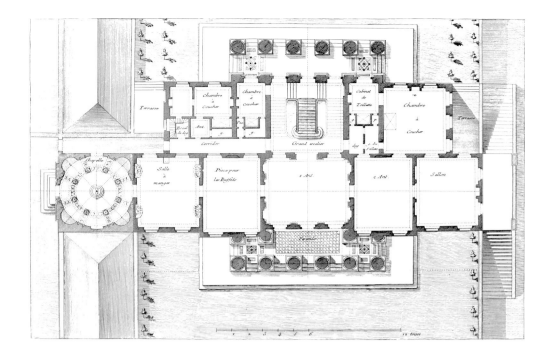

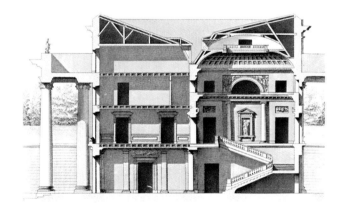

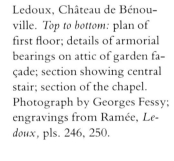

Ledoux, Château de Bénou-
ville. *Top to bottom:* plan of
first floor; details of armorial
bearings on attic of garden façade; section showing central
stair; section of the chapel.
Photograph by Georges Fessy;
engravings from Ramée, *Ledoux,* pls. 246, 250.

In a later modification of the design, Ledoux replaced the existing chapel, which still stands in front of the *château,* with a square pavilion adjoining the dining room and *communs.* Within this cube, Ledoux planned a circular space with coffered corner niches and a centrally placed altar; an upper tribune was supported on a circular colonnade. This chapel was the first of a series of centrally planned sacred spaces, domed and top-lit, that proliferated in his work of the 1780s.

IDEALIZING THE TYPE

Each of these designs, as a remodeling of an earlier structure, inevitably displayed the compromises forced on a beginning architect. Mansards instead of flat roofs or slopes hidden behind attics, pilasters economically substituted for freestanding columns, irregularities in plan and elevation obscuring the pure play of geometrical combinations, all interfered with what for Ledoux was becoming an evident taste for regular, rectilinear, isolated blocks of building, with simplified neo-Palladian plans and exterior orderings of colossal columns, extending the model of Gabriel's Petit Trianon. Not surprisingly, scholars have found multiple discrepancies between what is known of the commissions as built or remaining today and Ledoux's engraved representations, themselves often surviving in several different states. At first wrongly interpreted by Emil Kaufmann and others as evidence of Ledoux's neoclassical, if not modernist, precociousness, these differences, following the careful studies of Herrmann, Langner, and Gallet, now reveal a continuous revision and reinvention of previously built schemes.[49]

This process went far beyond the tradition of subtle changes made to designs by architects before publishing their works in a quasi-theoretical guise. Taking his cue from Palladio, Ledoux reworked almost all of his early domestic commissions before final engraving for his *recueil* in the mid- and late 1780s. In his imagination, the Hôtel Hocquart gained colossal Ionic columns instead of pilasters and became a freestanding pavilion in centralized isolation from its *communs.* Inside, the dining room was enriched by a giant Corinthian order and the obviously rococo style of the paneling, which Ledoux had been forced to reuse from the demolished Châ-

teau de Gagny, was suppressed in favor of a simplified antique decor. The cornice of the Hôtel d'Hallwyl's street façade was straightened and its vertical articulations subordinated to horizontal emphases; flutings were removed from the Doric columns in the doorway to correspond to the primitive order of the garden court, the rear façade of which was redesigned, in turn, to subdue the French classical references of the 1760s. The gateway of the Hôtel d'Uzès was simplified by the removal of the central coat of arms and its doorway elaborated to form a coffered arch similar to that later used by Ledoux in his unrealized project for the Hôtel d'Artagnan de Fesenzac (de Montesquiou) and for the Hôtel Thélusson. The colossal columns and pilasters to the front and rear of the *corps de logis* were extended from the façades to form deep porticoes; an even later perspective rendering probably from the 1790s showed the *hôtel* entirely freestanding, a pavilion in a park with all surrounding service structures and party walls stripped away. The Hôtel Montmorency, likewise, was redrawn to remove its mansards, extend its giant orders from the façades, light its upper rooms at the center from a cylindrical lantern, and regularize its *communs.* Bénouville itself, as Wolfgang Herrmann has demonstrated, was submitted to at least five states of redesign that progressively altered the façades, though not the interior distribution, toward simpler and simpler massing, leading to a strange conflict between the stair, retained in its original form, and the new fenestration. In a final, perspective view, Ledoux reduced the attic to a square block over the center, giving the composition the air of an exercise in combinatory geometry. In all these late revisions, the festoons and garlands on the columns, perhaps too reminiscent of Vignola, have been removed.

Ledoux's insistence on continuous modification might, on one level, be interpreted as the "evolution" of a design sensibility ever attentive to the presentation of an entire body of work within a single aesthetic. On another level, it seems to point to a characteristic of these first works often overlooked: that Ledoux considered them to be "origins" or prototypes for his later work and, thereby, to require "perfection" in representation.

Above: Ledoux, Project for the Hôtel d'Artagnan de Fesenzac. Drawing from the Musée Carnavalet. Photograph from Michel Gallet, *Claude-Nicolas Ledoux, 1736–1806* (Paris, 1980), pl. 357.

Below: Ledoux, Hôtel d'Uzès, perspective view as freestanding pavilion, c. 1785. Engraving from Ramée, *Ledoux,* pl. 204.

THE DISTRIBUTION OF PLEASURES

The house of a dancer suggests the idea of the Temple of Terpsicore.
(16)

In 1770 Ledoux's ascending reputation as an architect of fashion was sealed by two commissions, readily associated in the public imagination not only for the elegance of their design but also for the notoriety of their clients, two of the most celebrated courtesans of the day. The one, Mlle Guimard, a dancer at the Opéra, and under the "protection" of numerous powerful admirers, was, at twenty-seven, at the height of her career; for her Ledoux built a pavilion and private theater in the rapidly expanding quarter of the Chaussée d'Antin.[50] The other, Madame du Barry, was the same age, and recently installed at Versailles as the favorite of the aging Louis XV. Emulating her predecessor, Madame de Pompadour, in her patronage of the arts, she selected Ledoux to build a luxurious pavilion on her new estate at Louveciennes, a retreat for royal receptions.[51]

The aura of delicious scandal surrounding these commissions, exaggerated no doubt by the nostalgic voyeurism of Edmond de Goncourt, whose studies of Guimard and du Barry titillated the sensibilities of Proust's generation, has tended to obscure their architectural interest and their place in Ledoux's aesthetic development: as mature formulations of the pavilion type, as synthetic experiments in the combination of the decorative arts, as exercises in the organization of complex plans within simple envelopes, and as essays in the theatrical illusionism later to be exploited at Besançon and in projects for Marseilles. In both designs Ledoux confirmed what had already been evident in the Hôtel Montmorency, his talent for characterization and *distribution:* the art of planning each room and suite of rooms to meet the often conflicting requirements of display and comfort.

Blondel had already heralded *distribution* as a "new art" that recognized the proper needs of contemporary life, that in mid-eighteenth-century France had finally succeeded in accommodating the differences between the mores, religions, climates, and materials of antiquity and those of the present. Pierre Patte, following Blondel, had equally stressed the "ver-

itable revolution" in architecture that had been accomplished by architects concerned with comfort and convenience as well as with display. In 1780 Nicolas Le Camus de Mézières, summarizing in *Le génie de l'architecture* two decades of gradual improvement in domestic planning, spoke of the "progress" in architecture that had led to the triumph of modernity over antique precedent: "Our mores are not the the same [as those of antiquity] even as our customs are different."[52] In these terms, *distribution* reinforced characterization by determining the variety of forms and connections between rooms, each room designed to evoke a mood appropriate to its function and each sequence of rooms reflecting the shifting interplay of public and private activities in the house as a whole. Le Camus, taking his analogy from the theater, compared the rooms of a house to a sequence of scenes, each dedicated to generating appropriate sensations in their occupants; he devoted the major part of his work to the detailed description of every space in the house, from the salon to the stables, discussing suitable plan forms and decoration as well as services and furnishing. When, in his title, he referred to "the genius of architecture, or the analogy of this art with our sensations," he was responding to a late-eighteenth-century sensibility preoccupied with the psychological effects of surroundings on social and individual life; in his text he elaborated the doctrine, specifying the necessary *character* of vestibules, antechambers, salons, dining rooms, bedrooms, boudoirs, and bathrooms, as well as that of their service quarters. Blondel, in his *Cours d'architecture,* had attempted a similar catalogue; but Le Camus infused the exercise with a new sense of pleasure in luxury, sensuousness, and even exoticism. The moods of his ideal house shifted from seriousness to gaiety, calm to excitement, reverie to voluptuousness, with the movement from room to room.

Blondel's editor, Jean-François de Bastide, had already described the prototype for such an architecture of domestic sensation in his novel of manners, *La petite maison,* first published in 1753.[53] Here the house was depicted as both the setting and the instrument of an elaborate seduction. A freestanding pavilion on the banks of the Seine, set amid variegated gardens, Bastide's *petite maison* contained rooms of increasing beauty, each differentiated from the next by decorative motifs and color scheme: the circular, domed garden salon surrounded by mirrors; the dining room and buffet, with tables that dropped down to the kitchens below; the bedroom, square in plan, decorated in yellow and blue; its associated bathrooms embellished with pagodas, seashells, and grottos; and the boudoir, the inner sanctuary of this "temple of genius and taste," "asylum of love."[54] The walls of this boudoir were, Bastide recounted, entirely covered by mirrors,

the joints of which were hidden by the trunks of artificial trees, carved, composed, and foliaged with admirable skill. These trees are arranged to form a quinconce; they are strewn with flowers and festooned with chandeliers whose candles throw a subtle light onto the mirrors by means of the care taken to stretch thicker or thinner gauzes over these transparent forms at the end of the room; a magic touch that so harmonizes with the optical effects of the mirrors that one thinks one is standing in a natural forest grove lit with the help of art.[55]

Similar decorative effects would be used by Boullée and Ledoux and embodied as doctrine in Le Camus's treatise. Each space described by Le Camus seemed to offer a gamut of comforts and delights for the senses as well as for the mind, elaborate allegories setting the tone for each decorative program. Le Camus conducted his reader through the progressively ornate anterooms to the grand salon, with its decoration expressive of opulence and pleasure, and thence to the more private rooms: the bedroom, an "asylum of sleep," its walls painted in green tones to imitate the foliage of a bower and its bed, no longer withdrawn in an alcove but freestanding "at the end of the room as in the sanctuary of a temple"; beyond the bedroom, the boudoir, dedicated to Venus and described as "the dwelling place of voluptuousness," to be decorated as if it were "the retreat of Flora," surrounded by mirrors framed in imitation tree trunks to provide the illusion of a wooded grove (a direct borrowing from Bastide); behind this, the bathroom, perhaps conceived as a Turkish baldachino, a grotto of Amphitrite, a room in Neptune's palace, or a clearing by a pool suitable for Diana at her bath, in

each case—whether the bath was Neptune's chariot or a marble pool set amidst trompe l'oeil trellises—reinforcing the illusion with all "the magic of optics." Dining rooms, buffets, studies, libraries, private museums were described with equal attention to the character of the place and its occupants.[56]

Such scenes of domestic pleasure, as suited to the elegant life of the salons as to the more intimate licentiousness of *Les liaisons dangereuses* of Choderlos de Laclos or the *Philosophie dans le boudoir* of the Marquis de Sade, were, as Le Camus described them in 1780, already present in the new *hôtels* and pavilions of the capital.[57] Boullée had set the tone in the early 1760s in his *hôtel* for Racine de Monville, with its *salon turc,* imitating, according to a contemporary description, "a pavilion overlooking Asiatic gardens, from which one sees the tops of the trees between the columns that hold up the tent"; or in the mirrored salon of the Hôtel d'Evreux, now the Elysée Palace, where the framing of the mirrors was carved to represent tree trunks, in the manner described by Bastide. In both instances, Boullée blurred the distinction between reality and dream, architecture and nature by optical and theatrical illusion.[58] Here, as Pérouse de Montclos has pointed out, Boullée was exploiting the ambiguity present in the name *folie,* that "enjoyable uncertainty of etymology, evoking at once extravagant expenses and a frame of foliage."[59] In this context, Ledoux's *folies* for Mlle Guimard and Madame du Barry were paradigmatic, achieving a perfect equivalence between the character of their owners and that of the architecture, and an ingenious balance between the demands of characterization and distribution.

Marie-Madeleine Guimard, former first dancer at the Comédie-Française and from 1762 dancer at the Opéra, protected by, among others, the Bishop of Orleans, the Maréchal de Soubise, and Jean-Benjamin de La Borde, commissioned Ledoux's design for a new house and private theater toward the end of 1769; approved for construction the next year, the theater and pavilion were inaugurated in December 1772. The plan submitted for the building permit showed Ledoux's strategy for using the long, narrow site facing onto the Chaussée d'Antin: an entry pavilion whose angled façade followed the street, stables, and carriage house below and the

Ledoux, House for Mlle Guimard, Chaussée d'Antin, Paris, 1770, site plan and front elevation. Engravings from Ramée, *Ledoux*, pls. 175, 176.

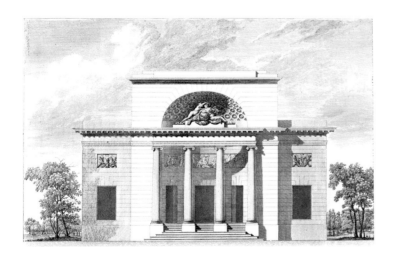

theater above, elegantly filling the trapezoidal plan; beyond this a square front court, then the cubic block of the main house, and behind a formal garden. Contemporary depictions of the pavilion emphasize its virtually freestanding character set among trees, the result of Ledoux's self-conscious attempt to replicate the form of a country retreat in the more open western quarters of the city.

The house was entered through a peristyle of four Ionic columns that gave onto a semicircular porch with a covered and coffered ceiling. Above the colonnade, Ledoux preserved the architrave to act as a freestanding base for a sculptured group depicting the crowning of Terpsichore, muse of the dance; the theme was repeated in the frieze above the doorway behind, which illustrated a festive procession where Terpsichore was drawn on a chariot by cupids and bacchantes and followed by the Graces and dancing fauns. Both sculpture and frieze were executed by Félix Lecomte, who had previously worked at the Hôtel d'Uzès. This unusual porch, reminiscent of Piranesi's etching of the ruined apse of the Temple of Venus at Rome, with some allusion to its previous use by Robert Adam, provided a symmetrical vestibule to an otherwise entirely asymmetrical plan. The main door, to the right of the central porch, led into an oval antechamber with its long axis diagonally across the path of entry; this in turn led, on axis with the side wall of the pavilion, into the main suites of rooms, at the same time providing access to bathrooms and a *cabinet de toilette* that took up the remainder of the front portion of the house to the left of the entrance. From a square second antechamber, immediately after the oval vestibule, one might pass either directly into the *salle de compagnie,* a rectangular salon overlooking the rear garden, and thence to the bedroom and boudoir, likewise with windows to the garden, or, to the left, into the dining room, otherwise known as the winter garden. In section, Ledoux reinforced this tripartite division of the plan, between front anterooms, winter garden, and rear salon and bedrooms, by treating the central bay as a single-story, top-lit *passage,* or gallery, and carrying front and rear portions to the full two stories, with bedrooms, private salon, and servants' quarters above. This gallery, divided between the second antechamber and the dining room, was dec-

Ledoux, House for Mlle Guimard, plan of first floor and section through second antechamber and dining room. Engraving from Ramée, *Ledoux,* pl. 175.

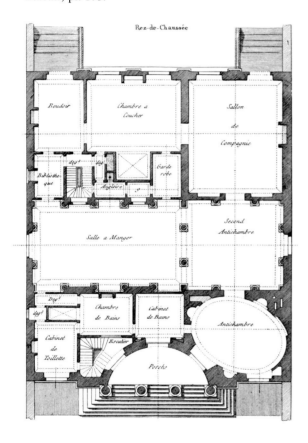

orated with attached Ionic columns that framed continuous mirrored panels with lifelike trees, trellises, and fountains painted directly onto the glass.

This Temple of Terpsichore delighted Blondel, or perhaps more properly his editor Bastide, who recognized its affinities with his own "petite maison":

The apartments seem to owe their different pleasures to magic; rich without confusion and galant without indecency, they present the interiors of a Palace of Love, embellished by the Graces. The bedroom invites one to rest, the salon to pleasure, the dining room to gaiety. . . . A hothouse incorporated into the interior of the apartment joins it to the garden: it is decorated in the very style of winter. The [painted] landscape is soft without destroying the effect. The trellises are subordinated to the rule of good architecture; the arabesques have nothing chimerical about them, and, (something I should not forget) the execution of all these different marvels seems to be the work of the same hand.[60]

Bastide's appreciation of the way in which Ledoux had assembled and coordinated a team of the best craftsmen, many already employed on the decorations of the Hôtels d'Uzès and de Montmorency and to be used again at Louveciennes, pointed to an often overlooked aspect of Ledoux's professional skill, one that was a result of his easy relations with artists and craftsmen and of his ability to sketch outline designs for every detail, from cornices to furniture, in a style that allowed latitude for each craftsman while harmonizing with the whole. For the Maison Guimard, Ledoux directed the celebrated cabinetmaker Jean-François Leleu, a favorite of Madame du Barry, together with Jean-Baptiste Feuillet for sculptural and stucco reliefs. The painted panels for the *salle de compagnie* were begun by Jean-Honoré Fragonard, who outlined four allegories of Terpsichore, and the ceiling was completed by the young Jacques-Louis David, whose uncle had worked with Ledoux in the administration of the Eaux et Forêts.[61]

Equally important for Ledoux's later career was the small theater built over the *porte cochère.* Its oval auditorium, a miniature version of that completed for the opera at Versailles by Gabriel at the end of 1769, accommodated an audience of some five hundred guests in a seated *parterre* and four rows of gallery seating, divided, in homage to Palladio at Vicenza, by an Ionic colonnade topped by architrave and balustrade. Royal boxes were inserted into the proscenium arch. The stage itself, framed by two colossal Corinthian columns completing the oval of the *salle,* deployed its scene in deep one-point perspective. In many respects, the Guimard theater anticipated Ledoux's design for the Theater of Besançon after 1776; in the context of a private house it was recognized, in Bastide's words, as "a masterpiece of its kind," especially for the intimate relationship it forged between spectators and performers. The lavish productions, parties, and quasi-pornographic performances staged by Mlle Guimard introduced Ledoux to an expanded patronage circle. There he met the Duc de Chartres, later his client for one of the *barrières* in the park of Monceau; the designer of this new park in the picturesque English style with its *fabriques* and mock ruins, Louis de Carmontelle, provided sets for Guimard's performances, combining theatrical illusion and landscape aesthetic in a way that was to be influential for Ledoux. Among Guimard's visitors were also Frederick II, Landgrave of Hesse-Cassel, who was to call Ledoux to Cassel in 1776, and Joseph II, brother of Marie-Antoinette, an early subscriber to the collection of engravings that would eventually become *L'architecture.*

If the Guimard house sealed Ledoux's professional reputation, the pavilion for du Barry consolidated his patronage under the aegis of the court. Presented at Versailles for the first time in 1769, Madame du Barry had installed her private apartments above those of the sixty-year-old king the following year, employing Leleu to design furniture in the new taste and insisting on a new bathroom suite, work superintended by Jacques-Ange Gabriel.[62] The Château de Louveciennes, originally the dwelling of the controller of the Machine de Marly, had been transferred to du Barry for life in 1769, and it was in the grounds of this refurbished house that she planned a pavilion rivaling the Petit Trianon; both Charles De Wailly and Ledoux submitted designs, of which Ledoux's was the preferred solution. His project started construction at the end of 1770 and was completed a year later, inaugurated by a

reception in the presence of the king on 2 September 1771.

Du Barry's pavilion seemed to echo Wren's Queen's House at Greenwich, geometrically pure, or, more immediately, Gabriel's Petit Trianon; the horizontal cornice and balustrade, the banded rustication, and the framing of its windows in clearly defined panels also recalled Gabriel's earlier Pavillon Français also at the Trianon. But in contrast to the four-sided block of the Petit Trianon, with its vertical proportions emphasized by colossal pilasters and attached Corinthian columns, Ledoux designed a more horizontal composition, without a high rusticated base, its front and rear façades marked respectively by four freestanding and four attached Ionic columns. The main entrance, like that of the Guimard house, used the columns with their architrave as a screen in front of a semicircular, nichelike porch. Unlike the Guimard entrance, the coffered ceiling was hidden behind the architrave so as not to disturb the regular line of the roof. A bas-relief, sculptured by Lecomte, depicting what Edmond de Goncourt termed a "bacchanal with children," took the place of Mlle Guimard's triumph of Terpsichore, while to the rear, on the riverfront, relief panels were set between the columns. The peristyle and porch opened directly onto the grand dining room, denoting the building's major function. An oval space of Adam-like proportions, its main axis lay horizontal to the entry. Surrounding the room which was furnished to the designs of Ledoux, were Corinthian pilasters in white marble with decorative motifs in gold. Two tribunes for the court musicians reached by stairs on either side of the porch were opened in the semicircular apses above the side doors to the buffet and the cloakrooms. Beyond the dining room and overlooking the river was the square, central *salon du roi,* decorated with mirrors and sculpted groups of nymphs; to its left was a second, elliptical salon and to the right a third salon, apsidal at one end. For this last room Fragonard was commissioned to paint a sequence of four episodes in the life of an allegorical Madame du Barry: *The Meeting, The Pursuit, The Declaration of Love,* and *The Lover Crowned;* these were, according to legend, considered too explicit even for du Barry's taste, and Fragonard was replaced by Joseph-Marie Vien, whose "symbolic history of Love"

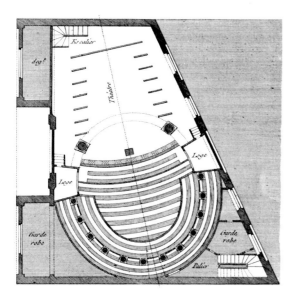

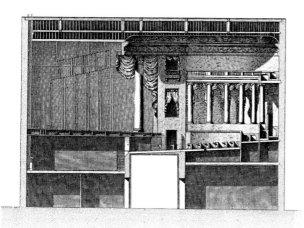

Ledoux, Theater for Mlle Guimard. *Above,* plan of first level; *below,* section. Engraving from Ramée, *Ledoux,* pl. 177.

Jean-Michel Moreau le Jeune, "Fête at Louveciennes," 2 September 1771, depicting the opening celebration for Madame du Barry's pavilion at Louveciennes attended by Louis XV. Watercolor from the Musée du Louvre, Paris; photograph from Arch. Phot. Paris/SPADEM.

Ledoux, Pavilion for Madame du Barry, Louveciennes, 1770. *Top to bottom:* elevation of garden façade; plan of first floor; section through dining room and king's salon. Engravings from Ramée, *Ledoux,* pls. 270, 271.

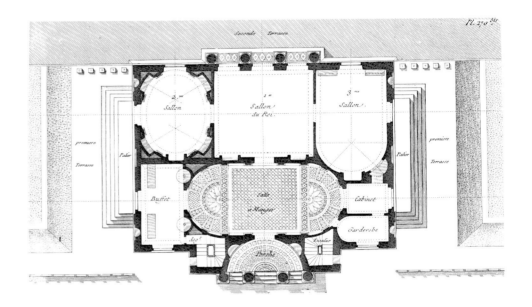

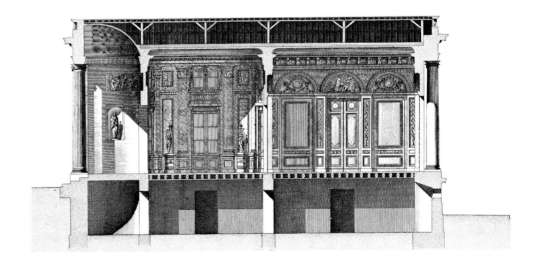

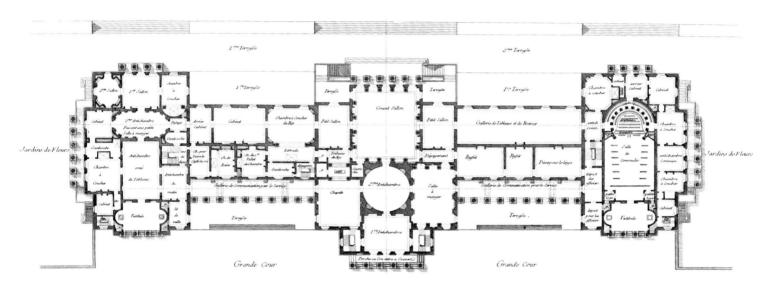

found few objectors.[63] To these artists Ledoux joined another group of craftsmen, including the bronze chaser Pierre Gouthière and the sculptors Boiston, Feuillet, and Métivier. More sober in its distribution than the Hôtel de Montmorency or the Pavillon Guimard, this semiprivate rendezvous nevertheless incorporated its different salons, each with dissimilar plans, into a regular block with considerable ingenuity.

Equally ingenious was the place Ledoux reserved for this pavilion in the larger-scale plans he drew up for a new *château* at Louveciennes, the foundations of which were laid in 1773. Madame du Barry's new palace was to have retained the earlier pavilion as a small part of one of its flanking pavilions, its salons becoming antechambers to a large picture gallery; the second of these larger pavilions was intended to house a theater rivaling the Versailles opera in size, while the central *corps de logis* would have entered its grand salon through two antechambers, one of which was circular. The projects for "le grand Louveciennes," suspended in 1774 with the death of Louis XV, were drawn by Ledoux in three different states: the original with high proportions and the pavilions articulated by separate mansard roofs; the second with

the mansards removed and the attic of the central block raised around the circular antechamber; and the third, still later, with the basement story removed and continuous Corinthian colonnades joining the side wings to the center.

Ledoux prepared another, more modest design for Madame du Barry's Château de Saint-Vrain at Arpajon on her exile in 1775. Here a pedimented porch on four Tuscan columns opened into the vestibule and thence to a domed, elliptical salon that projected into the garden, in a plan that was otherwise conventional. A third project for Madame du Barry, no doubt proposed before 1774 but probably not engraved until the mid-1780s, was for a vast town house to be sited between the rue d'Artois and the Chaussée d'Antin. Ledoux created two front courts surrounded by services and connected to the main building by side pavilions containing a chapel, a theater, a greenhouse, a tennis court, a billiard room, and an orangery. Sixteen-column Ionic porticoes flanked the entrance passage and ran across the front and rear façades, all of which were terminated by horizontal architraves. The spatial sequence from the first antechamber through the great circular second antechamber to the first salon was perhaps the most dramatic envisaged by Ledoux in

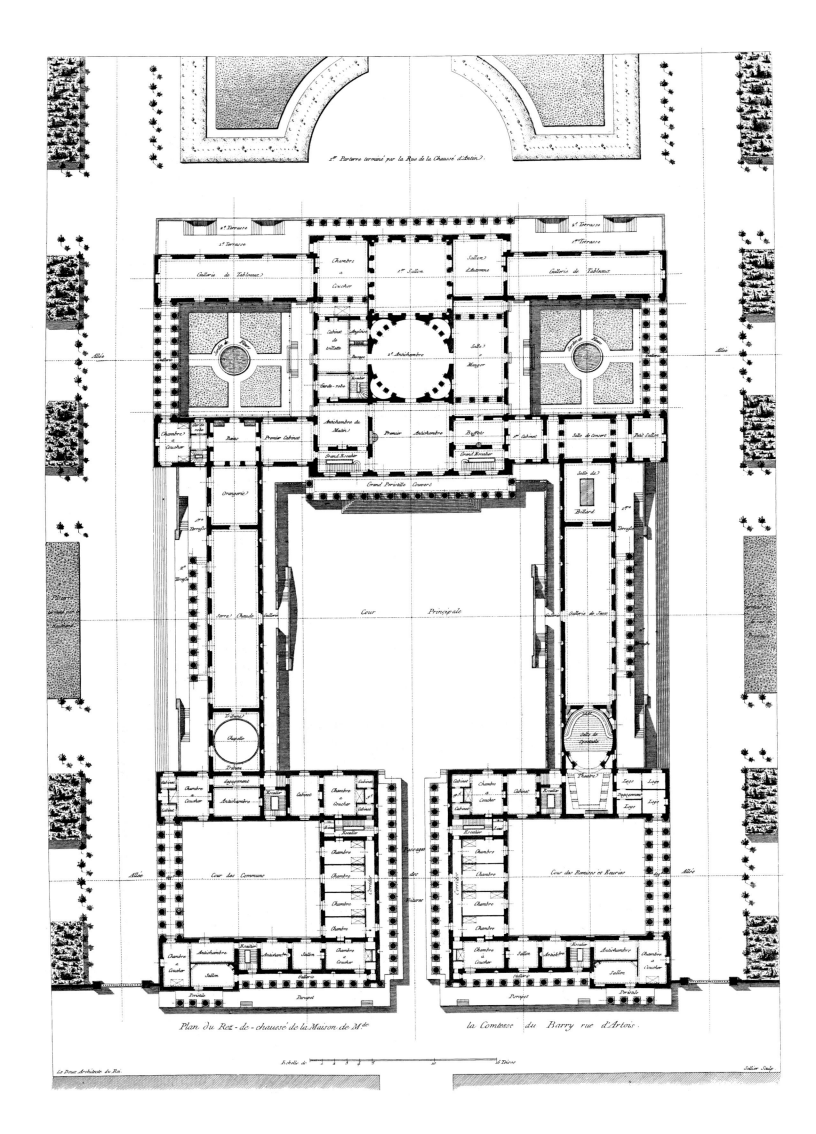

1.er Parterre terminé par la Rue de la Chaussé d'Antin.

Galerie de Tableaux

Chambre
a
Coucher

1.er Sallon

Sallon
d'Automne

Galerie de Tableaux

2.e Terrasse

1.er Terrasse

1.er Terrasse

2.e Terrasse

Jardin de Fleurs

Cabinet
de
toillette

2.e Antichambre

Salle
a
Manger

Jardin de Fleurs

Passage

Escalier

Garde-robe

Chambre
a
Coucher

Garde
robe

Bains

Premier Cabinet

Antichambre
du
Matin

Premier Antichambre

Buffets

1.er Cabinet

Salle de Concert

Petit Sallon

Grand Escalier

Grand Escalier

Orangerie

Grand Peristille Couvert

Sallon de
Billard

1.er
Terrasse

2.e
Terrasse

Serre Chaude

Galerie

Cour Principale

Galerie

Galerie de Jeux

Tribune

Chapelle

Tribune

Salle de
Spectacle

Theatre

Chambre
a
Coucher

Cabinet

degagement

Antichambre

Escalier

Cabinet

Cabinet

Chambre
a
Coucher

Cabinet

Cabinet

Cabinet

Chambre
a
Coucher

Cabinet

Escalier

Loge

Loge

degagement

Loge

Loge

Escalier

Chambre

Cabinet

Escalier

Chambre

Passage
des

Corridor

Chambre

Chambre

Voitures

Corridor

Chambre

Cour des Communes

Cour des Remises et Ecuries

Allée

Allée

Chambre

Chambre

Chambre
a
Coucher

Antichambre

Escalier

Antichambre

Sallon

Chambre
a
Coucher

Chambre
a
Coucher

Sallon

Antich.

Antichambre

Chambre
a
Coucher

Sallon

Galerie

Sallon

Galerie

Sallon

Peristile

Parapet

Parapet

Peristile

Allée

Allée

Plan du Rez - de - chaussé de la Maison de M.de   la Comtesse du Barry rue d'Artois.

Le Doux Architecte du Roi.

Echelle de

15 Toises

Sellier Sculp.

his domestic projects, a palatial suite that rivaled Pierre Rousseau's Hôtel du Salm, also built in the early 1780s.

A final, and realized, scheme for du Barry was for her
carriage house and stables in Versailles. Its monumental gateway, reminiscent of the entry to the Hôtel d'Hallwyl, was
formed by an arch carried on inset Doric columns and framed
by spandrels with bas-reliefs of centaurs; inside, two courtyards, one a carriage court, the other a stable court, led to a
projected menagerie, unbuilt but prophetic in its circular
Doric colonnade, open to the sky, surrounding a central fountain and court.[64] Here, in 1772, Ledoux clearly anticipated the
robust and almost agricultural style of the Saline de Chaux,
even in the stone waterspouts serving the drinking troughs.

THE URBAN LANDSCAPE

*Over the last twenty years, Paris, despite the wall that appears to
circumscribe its extension, has been considerably enlarged. A new
town has been formed in a quarter that previously had only a few
scattered houses in the midst of vast gardens or marshes. Now elegant
and comfortable dwellings have attracted numerous inhabitants to the
district. After a series of rapid transformations, the Chaussée
d'Antin has witnessed luxury establishing its brilliant domicile in its
center*

Jean-Jacques Menuret, *Essais sur l'histoire médico-topographique de Paris,* 1 8 0 4.[65]

From the beginning of his private practice in Paris, Ledoux had built in an area of the city—surrounding the Chaussée d'Antin—that, from the mid-1760s, had been rapidly laid
open for the development of fashionable residences. Released
for speculation by the demolition of the wall of Louis XIII
and by the building of the new boulevards, this land originally outside the boundaries of Paris had attained new value.
Named after the Duc d'Antin, former director of the king's
buildings, who had, in the 1720s, prolonged the Champs
Elysées to the site of the present Etoile, thus opening up the
area between the Place Louis XV (the present Place de la Concorde) and the village of Neuilly, the Chaussée d'Antin was a
quarter that, after 1770, became a favored site for investment.
The banker Jean-Joseph de La Borde, the Comte d'Artois,

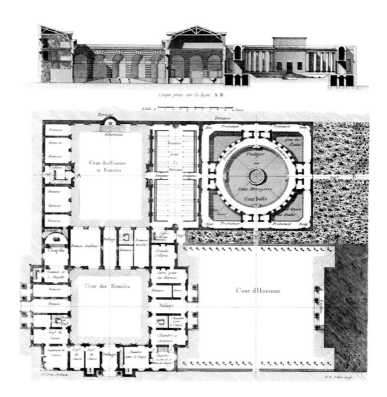

Ledoux, Carriage house and
stables for Madame du Barry,
Versailles, 1772, section and
plan of first floor showing unbuilt menagerie. Engraving by
Sellier from Ramée, *Ledoux,*
pl. 173.

Ledoux, Hôtel Thélusson, rue de Provence, Paris, 1778, perspective view of house seen through entrance gateway. Engraving from Ramée, *Ledoux,* pl. 165.

Ledoux, Hôtel Thélusson, perspective view of garden from beneath arch of rocks looking toward entrance. Engraving from F. de Nobelle, *L'architecture de Ledoux* (Paris, 1962).

and the Comte de Provence were among many of the high nobility and the rich Fermiers Généraux who built speculatively in the new quarters to the northwest. In a recent study, the historian Pierre Pinon has analyzed the financial activities of de La Borde, the Baron de Thun, Bouret de Vézalay, Marin de La Haye, and others in the development of this district, and has shown that architects—Brongniart, Bélanger, De Wailly, Aubert, and Ledoux—were interested in investment.[66] Development had taken off in 1769, stimulated by the low price of land and by the practice of large landowners—such as the religious order of the Mathurins, whose holdings included much of the Chaussée d'Antin area—to grant ninety-nine-year leases in order to gain immediate revenue. The Baron de Thun leased two parcels, on one of which he built an *hôtel* designed by Boullée, which he then sold in 1771, conserving for himself a lifelong interest in the house and grounds; de Vézalay and de La Borde bought, again from the Mathurins, much larger tracts, which they then developed with *hôtels* or divided into lots for resale. Brongniart took part in at least six financial operations between 1769 and 1783, including property that was then sold to Madame de Montesson and the Duc d'Orléans for their *hôtel* and theater, not surprisingly designed by Brongniart; similar dealings led to his construction of the Hôtels Bourbon-Condé and de Montesquiou after 1779.[67] The interlinked interests of financiers, architects, and would-be residents were evident, and readily exploited.

Ledoux, who had already engaged in modest speculation, building an apartment house in the rue de l'Université on land sold to him by de Montesquiou in 1772, had also been involved in two similar ventures in the Chaussée d'Antin: the building of the Hôtel Montmorency, on land owned by the investor, Lenormand de Mézières, and leased to the prince and princess for life; and that of the Pavillon Guimard, part of the subdivision developed in 1770 by the financier and entrepreneur of the king's buildings, Jean-François Le Tellier, who also acted as contractor for the work. At least before 1778, Ledoux had refrained from blatantly commercial ventures such as those of Brongniart. In that year, however, profiting from his friendship with the Fermier Général André Haudry de Soucy, who had supervised and supported the building of the Saline de Chaux, Ledoux joined a profit-making association for the development of land north of the rue de Provence, a street created in 1769 by de Vézalay in closing an open sewer. This site, bought from de La Borde, was destined for the new residence of Madame Thélusson, widow of the banker and a close friend of Haudry.[68] Together with Haudry and Thélusson's bailiff, Rumel, Ledoux drew up a plan for the large parcel that included the Thélusson house at the center and two subsidiary lots for sale to either side, adjacent to the two new streets cut by de la Borde, the rue Neuve St. Georges and the rue Chauchat. The prospectus advertised these "plots for sale . . . according to the subdivisions indicated by lines traced on the plan, by advance, for life, or for rent," and listed Ledoux and Rumel as agents.[69] The accompanying plan showed that, like Brongniart on the nearby site of the Convent des Capucines, Ledoux had been able to design his own site within the larger parcel provided by the speculation. Thus, rather than following the grid of the rue de Provence, in the otherwise rectangular block, he had chosen to place his house and dependencies on the axis of the rue d'Artois, which mounted at an angle to the site from the south. The entry gate as well as the entire *hôtel* and its lot lines were disposed as if they were a triumphal conclusion to this street, while two smaller and flanking sites, advertised for sale, adopted the same angle and were themselves restricted so that any buildings erected on them would not stand in front of the Thélusson house. The remainder of the lots followed the more logical lines of the enclosing streets. In this way Ledoux, as Pierre Pinon has noted, used the freedom afforded by a large initial lot to raise its value by a grand aesthetic gesture, a pitch for the desirability of the terrain, otherwise known as marshy, unstable, and difficult to build on.

The Hôtel Thélusson, built between 1778 and 1781, was the largest of Ledoux's private commissions to be realized and it was certainly the most celebrated in Paris for its unorthodox composition and dramatic presentation to the street. A combination of pavilion and palace, it represented the late-eighteenth-century *folie* in its most elaborate form. At once a picturesque assemblage of set pieces derived from antique,

Ledoux, Hôtel Thélusson, plan of first floor and gardens. Engraving from Ramée, *Ledoux*, pl. 161.

Italian Renaissance, and French classical architecture welded into a neo-Palladian whole, it was also a huge *fabrique* in a park, a picturesque setting contrived with brilliant artifice as a miniature landscape garden. Designed after Ledoux's experience with the Saline de Chaux, the palace was self-consciously a kind of city in miniature: with external boulevards, with different levels of natural scenery, from savage grottoes to elegant *parterres,* crossed by bridges and viaducts and tunnels, with separate public and private circulation inside. A virtual forum of antique fragments and quasi-Piranesian quotations in its parts, the *hôtel* even incorporated an allusion to the plan of the Saline de Chaux in the form of its rear courtyard, a reference to the overtly theatrical nature of the entire composition; both *Saline* and *hôtel* in turn echoed the equally theatrical hemicycle of Vignola's Villa Madama.

This theatricality was evident from the first approach. What struck passersby, and continued to amaze Parisians until the moment of its demolition in 1824, was the form of the entry gate, which seemed to emulate in its wide semicircular arch and truncated proportions some half-buried antique ruin, such as the Arch of Theseus in Athens as depicted by David Le Roy or any one of Piranesi's views of Roman arches like that of the Circus of Maxentius, fantasies on Ledoux's favorite theme of architecture viewed from beneath an arch or bridge.[70] Certainly the coffering resembled that of the entrance to the Italian engraver's "Entrance to an ancient gymnasium," thus adding another possible significance to the already multiple levels of meaning visible in the *hôtel*. Ledoux had, indeed, used a similar device on a reduced scale in the revised design for the portico of the Hôtel d'Uzès and in the rusticated and coffered *porte cochère* to the unbuilt project for the de Montesquiou *hôtel* in Paris, the Hôtel d'Artagnan-Fezensac.[71] More immediately, Ledoux's own architecture provides a source linked directly to the theater: the proscenium arch of the Theater of Besançon, itself derived from the double idea of the shape of the eye and the framing of a view by a bridge. In any event, Ledoux's intention was clear: to construct an architectural lesson in the correct way to view a landscape or a city. "The picture must be confined within the frame that suits it in order to avoid its dispersal," he wrote in

1804, speaking of the loss of detail that stems from too great a viewing distance, that "decomposes the most sensitive and concentrated appraisals" (134). He added a note: "See the house of Madame Thélusson . . . [where] these means have been used with success."

Sustaining this drama the house appeared beyond the gate, rising above a picturesque garden, approached across bridges along the sides of the site that sloped toward a carriage entrance beneath the main floor and passed under the house to the rear, semicircular carriage court. In a bold reversal of eighteenth-century practice, Ledoux had placed the rear of the house together with its garden at the front, pushing the forecourt, *communs,* and services behind. At first sight the "front" façade thus presented the traditional finale of the procession from vestibule through antechambers to grand salon. This salon, elliptical in form and extended half out of the main block with a peristyle of eight Corinthian columns, seemed like a reincarnation of the Temple of Vesta at Tivoli, leading engravers like Krafft to depict it from the angle chosen by Piranesi in his view of that monument.

At the first-floor level, the covered passage and entry for carriages gave into the "grand peristyle" beneath the salon and terrace, which in turn led to the major stair. Two straight, monumental flights, on the right of the central axis, brought the visitor to the rear of the building, overlooking the *cour d'honneur,* before the turn into the first antechamber on the piano nobile. From there, the *route de parade* led back through the central, octagonal second antechamber, lit from above through a circular *calotte,* and to the grand salon at the front, similarly lit from an oval semidome. The sequence of geometrically varied spaces, from a square through an octagon to an ellipse, thus culminated triumphally in the sight of the entry arch through the Corinthian peristyle. The rectangular dining room, with a screen of columns at each end, was reached from the second antechamber through an intervening buffet. The front corners of the plan were taken up with square rooms opening onto the terrace and occupied by a *salon de musique* and principal bedroom, both connecting to the grand salon through, respectively, the library and a *salon d'automne.* The private apartments of Madame Thélusson, with

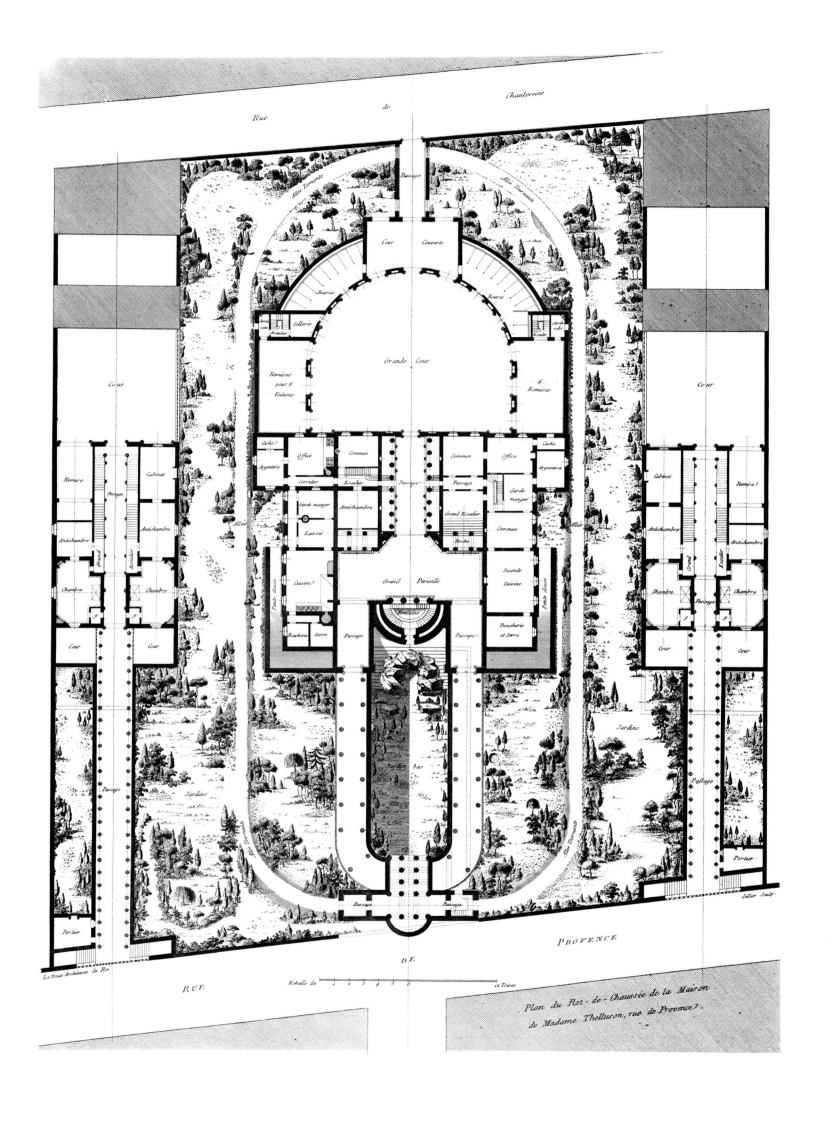

Plan du Rez-de-Chaussée de la Maison
de Madame Thellusson, rue de Provence.

Ledoux, Hôtel Thélusson,
section through grand salon,
first and second antechambers,
gardens, and rear courtyard.
Engraving from Ramée,
Ledoux, pl. 166.

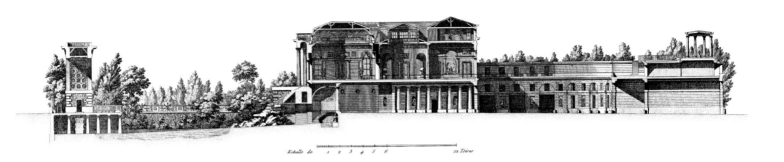

Ledoux, Hôtel Thélusson, sec-
tion. Drawing by Armand-
Parfait Prieur for Pierre-Louis
Van Cléemputte and Armand-
Parfait Prieur, *Petites maisons de
Paris* (Paris, 1796).

Sale plan for property surrounding the Hôtel Thélusson,
Paris, 1778. Engraving by Sellier from the Bibliothèque
Historique de la Ville de Paris,
Cartes et plans, B.782. Photograph from Gallet, *Ledoux,*
pl. 343.

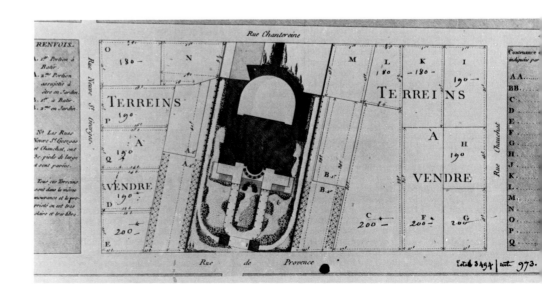

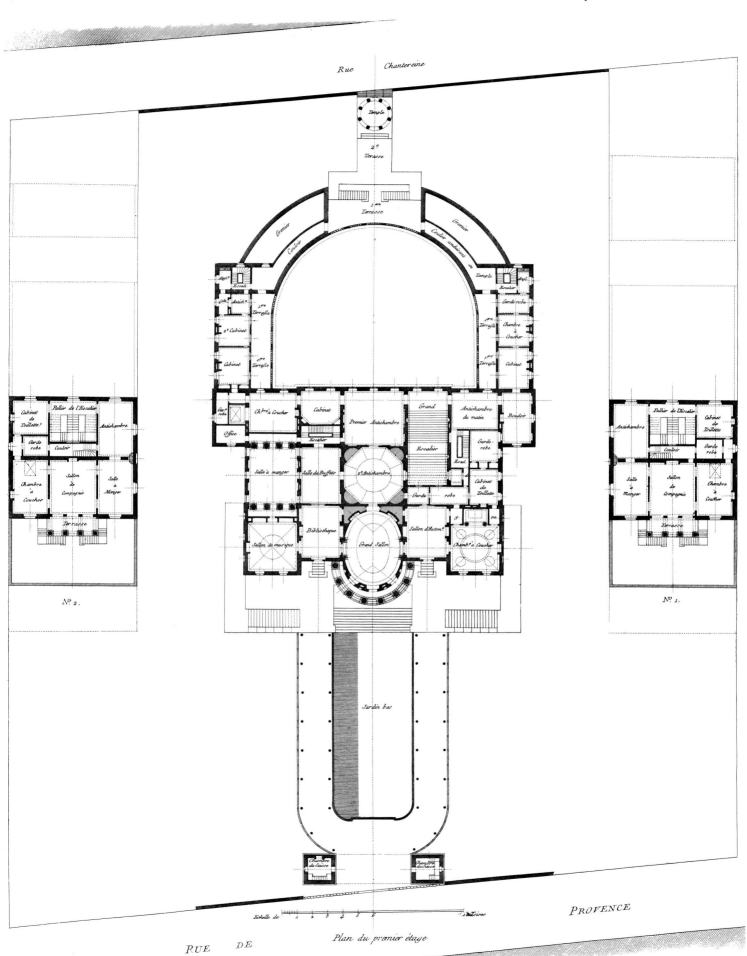

Ledoux, Hôtel Thélusson,
plan of second floor. Engraving from Ramée, *Ledoux,*
pl. 163.

antechambers, boudoir, and dressing rooms, were accommodated to the right of the main stair leading from the bedroom at the front to the morning room or *antichambre du matin* at the rear.

The interior decoration of the house was sumptuous, although, as Gallet has argued, not as luxurious as was rumored at the time. The first antechamber, decorated by the sculptor Audry with bas-reliefs of "Love," "Friendship," "Pleasure," and "Liberty;" the second, octagonal antechamber, again by Audry, with a painted sky above the *calotte* and lit through a glass lantern; the grand salon, entirely surrounded by mirrors and crowned by a painted ascent of Apollo—a favorite subject for Ledoux—were perhaps less luxurious than their counterparts in the Guimard or du Barry houses. But so "Roman" did the exterior appear to Parisians newly sensitive to the *vedute* of the *campagna* that many imagined the motifs of the interior to be grander than they actually were; thus A.-P. Prieur, drawing the sections for Van Cléemputte's collection of engravings, showed the second antechamber and the *salon de musique* domed and coffered like miniature pantheons, and the grand salon with an even higher, equally pure, dome, painted like the sky and lit from a single central opening.

The garden level, strewn with huge rocks, was watered by a fountain beneath the front terrace; from this source, a mock cave much like that in the entrance to the Saline de Chaux, ran a river along the central axis toward the entry. From within this grotto, the entrance arch appeared rising above a primitive Doric peristyle, as though the natural arch and the architectural arch were reflected in each other. In plan, the garden, with Doric passages, hemicycles, and niches, terminating at the very rear of the *cour d'honneur* in a circular Ionic temple, carried further echoes of Piranesian fora.[72]

This idiosyncratic mingling of Roman motifs, Palladian plan, and English landscape garden aesthetic was perhaps Ledoux's greatest private building. It set the tone for a number of huge palaces, projected but not built, for Paris and its environs. After the palace for Madame du Barry, planned for a large site between the rue d'Artois and the Chaussée d'Antin, Ledoux drew up a scheme, probably not engraved until after the Revolution, for a terraced *château* for the Princesse de Conti at Louveciennes; here the Palladian plan is exploded to provide an open courtyard in the center surrounded by a colonnaded rotunda. An equally theatrical composition, for a town house on the rue Neuve de Berry, presented an Ionic temple pavilion overlooking a stepped hemicycle in the form of an open-air theater that covered underground grottoes entered through baseless Doric porticoes. Set in a landscape of rocky outcrops, this mansion seems to have been destined for a lover of the revived Greek theater, responding no doubt to the fashion for neo-Greek costumes, banquets, and furniture that swept Paris in the late 1780s. Madame Vigée-Lebrun's celebrated *souper grec,* staged according to the descriptions provided in the Abbé Barthélemy's *Voyage du jeune Anacharsis* of 1788, to which the architect Jean-François Chalgrin was invited, would have found its proper surroundings in this late historical conceit by Ledoux.[73]

CHIVALRIC NOSTALGIA

The complex amalgam of Roman allusions and picturesque landscape aesthetics that characterized the Hôtel Thélusson was, in the same year, 1778, paralleled by another exercise in antique nostalgia, the design of a hunting lodge in Franche-Comté for the Prince de Bauffremont.

The Prince Charles-Roger de Bauffremont (1713–95) had retired from the army in 1773, after long service in the courts of Stanislas, duc de Lorraine, and the armies of the King of France; having served in eight campaigns during the Seven Years' War, he had reached the rank of Maréchal de Camp. Like the Marquis de Montesquiou, he was not only a military man but also an enlightened *homme-de-lettres*. A friend of the poet Saint Lambert as well as of Voltaire, the Marquise Du Châtelet, the Comte de Tressan, and the Marquise de Boufflers, he was held by his intimates—notably Madame du Deffand—as "le prince incomparable." The Bauffremonts were powerful nobility of Franche-Comté: Charles-Roger's father, Louis-Bénigne de Bauffremont, was Marquis de Listenois, a lieutenant general in the royal service; his elder brother Louis was Gouverneur de Seyssel; his

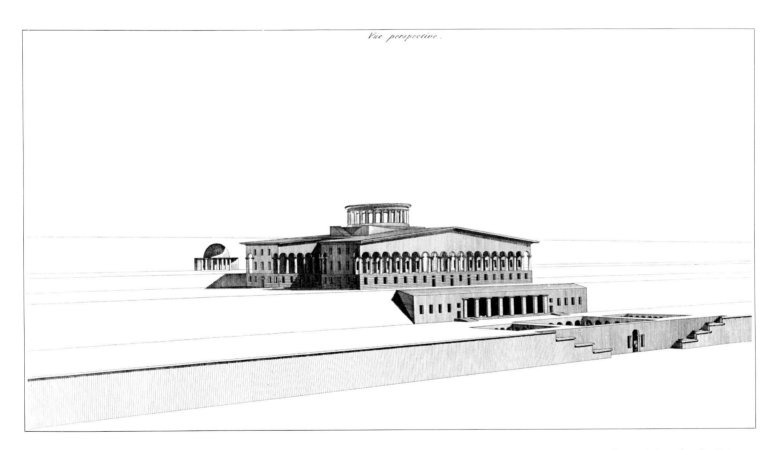

Vue perspective.

Ledoux, Palace for the Princesse de Conti, Louveciennes, project, c. 1787, perspective view. Engraving from Ramée, *Ledoux,* pl. 277.

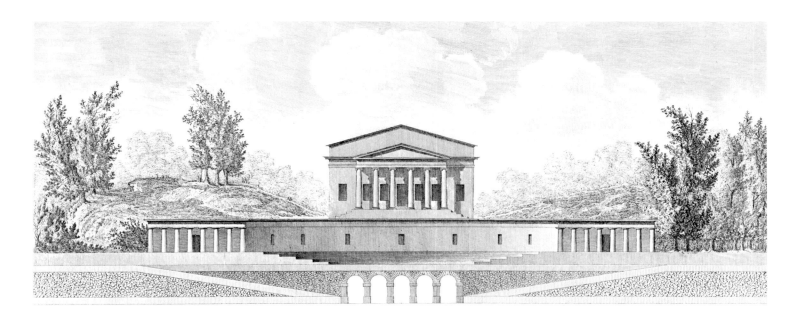

Ledoux, House on the rue
Neuve de Berry, c. 1787.
Above, elevation; *opposite,* plan
of second floor showing ter-
race theater. Engravings from
Ramée, *Ledoux,* pls. 213, 212.

younger brother was a vice-admiral and seigneur of Cézy.
The prince was further one of the largest holders of coal-
mining concessions in Franche-Comté. A Deputy to the Provincial Estates of Franche-Comté in Besançon, December
1788, and then a Deputy of the Nobility to the Etats Généraux, 19 July 1789, Charles-Roger was subsequently imprisoned during the terror—hence Ledoux's insistence on his
"qualities." Released, he retired to his estate at Cézy (Yonne)
and died in October 1795.

Ledoux, perhaps acting in his official capacity of Commissaire des Salines, had visited the prince's estate at Scey-
sur-Saône—Ledoux typically preferred the Roman appella-
tion "Sesusone"—traditionally a center of salt production.
During his visit, in 1778, as recorded by the date inscribed on
the (much later) engraving of his design, he was a guest at a
yearly gathering of local nobility, a celebration, as the architect recalled (211), in honor of Saint Hubert, the patron saint
of hunters.[74] Despite Ledoux's personal distaste for the
hunt—"What more miserable triumph could there be than
that won over a timid animal!" (212)—his description of the
chase, the kill, and the ensuing fête, followed by a banquet
attended not only by the warriors of the hunt but also by
poets, scholars, and artists, self-consciously evoked the antique aura of Caesar's *Commentaries*. The perspective view of
Ledoux's project for the Hunting Lodge no doubt depicts this
fête, with the participants dressed in Roman armor and driv-
ing chariots.

In his engraved design for Bauffremont's *retour de chasse,*
Ledoux conceived of a prototype for a classical lodge that
nevertheless evoked its medieval antecedent in its massing: a
cubic pavilion with, on the first floor, a central hall surrounded by banquet rooms; above, a grand salon encircled by
galleries overlooking the countryside and four principal bedrooms in turrets at each corner; surmounted by an attic containing dormitories for the hunters. This, flanked by
subsidiary pavilions, stood at the summit of a series of geometrically sculpted terraces: "What movement and variety
can be observed on these terraces disposed amphitheatrically
to multiply the charm of sensations! Everyone spoke favorably of the artist who had prepared the fête. The menacing

Ledoux, Hunting Lodge for the Prince de Bauffremont, c. 1778, perspective view. Engraving by Van Maëlle, dated 1778 but probably executed after 1789, from Ramée, *Ledoux,* pl. 287.

Ledoux, Hunting Lodge for the Prince de Bauffremont, detail of perspective view showing the return from the hunt with the hunters in antique dress. Engraving from Ramée, *Ledoux,* pl. 287.

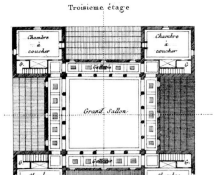

Troisieme étage

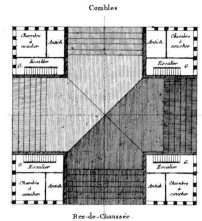

Combles

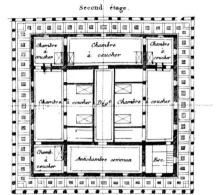

Second étage.

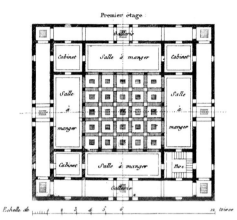

Premier étage

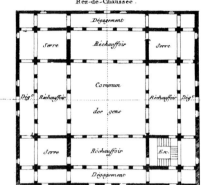

Rez-de-Chaussée.

Echelle de

Ledoux, Hunting Lodge for
the Prince de Bauffremont.
*Above, clockwise from lower
right,* plans of first, second,
third, fourth, and attic floors;
below, section and plan of ter-
racing. Engraving by Van
Maëlle and Simon from Ra-
mée, *Ledoux,* pl. 286.

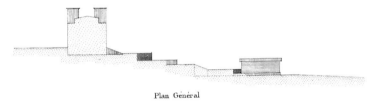

Plan Général

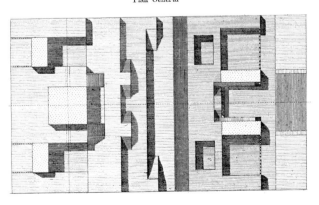

bastions, which evoked the terror of a siege, were replaced by pyramidal forms." (214) Ledoux was here referring to the character of the original château, which, belonging to the Bauffremonts from the second half of the thirteenth century, had been rebuilt during the 1570s and 1580s by Charles-Roger de Bauffremont, Bishop of Troyes, in the form of a fortified château defended by seven towers; in the sixteenth century it was already more a *maison de plaisance* than a castle. This structure was razed by Charles-Emmanuel de Bauffremont in 1697 and replaced by a house in the modern taste between 1700 and 1710. It consisted of a main building of three stories, with a domed central hall, flanked by symmetrical wings each with subsidiary domes at their centers. To the west the façade was fronted by a semicircular two-story arcade.[75]

In keeping with the character of the fête, Ledoux invested his "antique" restoration of this already restored house with overtones of medieval chivalric ceremonies, such as those described in La Curne de Sainte-Palaye's *Mémoires sur l'ancienne chevalerie,* where the entire countryside would be "covered with tents and superb pavilions" and the lists themselves surrounded by an amphitheater "often constructed in the form of towers . . . divided into lodges and steps, decorated with every possible magnificence, with rich tapestries, pavilions, and banners."[76]

Thus Ledoux's pavilions were decorated with panels of armorial bearings, which seemed painted on a temporary surface—the scenic covering erected to hide the façades of the old château—or embroidered on elaborate tapestries:

The hero, triumphant on the fields of Arlier, hastens his step, arrives and lays down his arms around the building that you see. Immediately, art, which knows how to embellish everything, groups them together and attaches them to the walls, beside the resplendent armor. There one sees the spears of Germanicus, of Dommaria and Divitiacus; the blunted swords of the Romans, the loyalty of the Scythian, traced on a shield inlaid with gold; the breastplates of the sires of Salins, of the Bauffremonts, joined to the sashes of the victors and of so many other warriors who have made these celebrated lands illustrious. (213)

Ledoux, Hunting Lodge for the Prince de Bauffremont, detail of perspective view, showing decoration in bas-relief on flanking pavilion. Engraving from Ramée, *Ledoux,* pl. 287.

Ledoux conceived this decorative program, like all of his heraldic conceits, in accordance with the status of his client. The Prince de Bauffremont claimed descent from an original nobility, established in Gallo-Roman times by the Caesars, and from their descendents through Clovis; his was a title "of quality," stressed Ledoux, unlike the spate of "new" titles that had been bestowed following the "burning of the titles [by Louis XI] in 1479." Ledoux lamented this expedient commerce in offices that had too often favored the "candidate of the day" over that "universal, social, and antique contract, obeyed by all and that none has the right to defame" (213). In consequence, armorial bearings and the display that represented noble descent had become, in his eyes, cheapened, with all the apparatus of late medieval art—crenellated towers and coats of arms "shaped at the whim of caprice" (212)— that were still evident in the Château de Scey.

But Ledoux's scheme, mingling antique imagery and medieval nostalgia, was also closely linked to the ceremony and sociability popular among Freemasonic societies in the provinces, where a local seigneur would act as the patron for a semiprivate lodge, bringing together the nobility and military officers of a region. Ledoux's project seems in this respect to be inspired by the special characteristics of the "chivalric" societies predominant in Franche-Comté and described by J.-M. Léquinio de Kerblay,

Before the Revolution they had associations of arquebusiers, known under the title of chivalry, and which were, in truth, only associations of pleasure. They had buildings, which still exist, under the name of chivalry. To draw, once a year, the arquebuse; to play, drink, and eat together much more often; to be formed into companies and bear uniforms, such were the duties of the chevaliers: it was the Freemasonry of the region. It seems that man cannot exist in any country without making for himself a separate society within society in general; this equally flatters his pride and his weakness.[77]

Ledoux's *éloge* to the decorative powers of the architect concluded with a reminder that, like Homer conserving the memory of Achilles, the artist, with his "allegorical marbles," has the role of preserving the memory of Gods and men. Here symbolic attributes were conceived as the mnemonic devices of civilization, the language through which the architect communicates to society. Ledoux's idea of character, first hazarded in the antique setting of the Café Militaire, was, in the hunting lodge, thereby confirmed as a force for social reform. After 1790, meditating on the destruction of his own monuments, Ledoux would reaffirm this ideal in the context of his memories of Bauffremont's hunting party:

These walls, these surfaces that you see, are imprinted with the life-giving flame that subordinates the world to primary ideas. . . . See what the architect can do when he purifies a principle and regularizes it. Predestined children of the god of persuasion, you have been chosen to raise the courage of humanity; you have been launched on the earth to eternalize the virtues, independent of their vacillations. (214)

It was such an architectural "writing," a rhetoric of characterization formulated in almost hieroglyphic terms, that Ledoux was to develop in the context of his public, institutional projects beginning with the Saline de Chaux in 1774. Here, however, the emblematics of representation were supported by and unified within an overriding concern with the form of distribution, a form that was to be both symbolic and functional. In this attempt Ledoux was to carry the art of characterization further than envisaged by Blondel, to create a genre of building that, as Ledoux was forced to argue, had yet to be invented: an architecture that would at once dignify and instrumentalize public, utilitarian programs once considered too mundane for aesthetic attention.

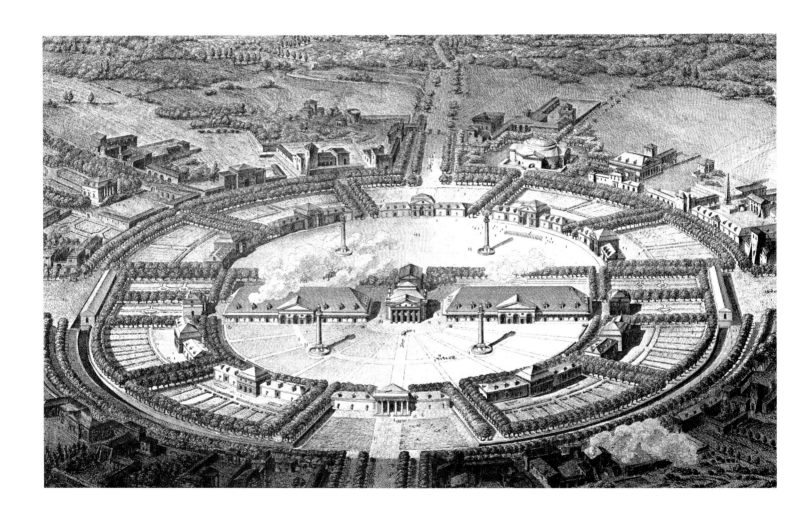

3 THE ARCHITECTURE OF PRODUCTION

The Saline de Chaux
1773–1778

███████████████████████

It is up to the architect to oversee the principle; he can activate the resources of industry, husband

its products and avoid costly maintenance; he can augment the treasury by means of the prodigal

compositions of his art. (122)

INSPECTING THE *SALINES*

Ledoux's two careers, private and public, came together on 20 September 1771, eighteen days after the inaugural fête at Louveciennes, when he was appointed by royal Arrêt du Conseil (Order in Council) Commissaire des Salines for Franche-Comté, Lorraine, and the Trois-Évêchés or bishop-rics of Verdun, Metz, and Toul in Lorraine, as an adjunct to the engineer Jean-Rodolphe Perronet.[1] His functions, like those of all engineer-inspectors of the Ponts et Chausseés, paralleled the work of the expanding corps of industrial inspectors that oversaw the quality and processes of manufacture in the royal factories. In the event of Perronet's absence, Ledoux was "to oversee the conservation and maintenance of the springs and salt-water wells of the said *salines* . . . as well as the buildings constructed or about to be constructed for the service of the said *salines*."[2] Evidently a direct reward for services rendered to Madame du Barry, the position might have remained a simple sinecure, paying some six thousand livres annually from the treasury of the Ferme Générale, which held the contract for the production as well as the tax-ation of salt. Ledoux, however, saw the chance to develop at least one commission and took the job seriously. In the event, he converted it within three years into his most celebrated completed work, the Saline de Chaux. "Could it be be-lieved?" he later remembered with awe. "The dream of a dis-turbed night set in motion the powerful lever of industry. . . . An episodic scene of thousands of actors employed on the great theater of events [the pavilion of Louveciennes] helped the artist with the means to join the interests of art with those of government." (57–58)

This appointment brought Ledoux into contact with a new group of patrons, official in the Intendance du Com-merce and quasi-official but just as powerful in the Ferme Générale.[3] The primary responsibility for the administration of the *salines royales* rested with the Contrôleur Général, the Abbé Jacques Terray, and under him with the designated Intendant du Commerce, Jean-Charles-Philibert Trudaine de Montigny. Trudaine, the son of the former Intendant, Daniel Trudaine, was in every way the model Enlightenment administrator.[4] Trained by his father—who, with Perronet, had continued the development of the highway and canal networks started by Colbert—Trudaine de Montigny was both scientist and *philosophe*. As a chemist, he had a direct knowledge of the processes of salt production and held commissions of enquiry and public experiments to determine the sources of contamination in Franche-Comté. As an agrarian reformer, he collaborated with the naturalist Georges-Louis de Buffon in raising new breeds of Merino sheep. As a *philosophe,* he was a friend of the Marquis de Condorcet and Denis Diderot, a passionate amateur of the theater, and a translator of Gotthold Ephraim Lessing. A friend of Jacques Turgot from 1758, he had traveled with the new finance minister and the poet Delille to meet Voltaire in 1776. While Ledoux found in Terray a somewhat reluctant supporter, in Trudaine he gained a faithful patron who, until his resignation after the demise of Turgot in 1776, consistently upheld the part of the architect over the objections of entrepreneurs, even recommending him for other commissions in Besançon and Aix. In an *éloge* Ledoux recognized his liberal talents:

A virtuous philosopher, he devoted himself from an early age to the study of the exact sciences, political economy, commerce, and to all the domains of knowledge necessary for those who are called on to hold high office; he struggled for a long time against the financial power that failed to recognize the important resources developed by a love for the arts. His extreme sensibility snatched him prematurely from his friends, and his passing was regretted by all those who knew how to appreciate him. (42)

The secondary responsibility for the oversight of the *salines* was in the hands of the Ferme, and Ledoux made long-lasting friendships with those officials immediately concerned with salt manufacture in Franche-Comté: the Fermiers Généraux André Haudry de Soucy and Alexandre-Parseval Deschênes.[5]

With their patronage, reinforced by his recent favor at the court, Ledoux was by 1773, as he remembered wistfully after the Revolution, "en évidence, . . . à l'apogée des faveurs"(39).

In retrospect, the nature of this double patronage was sufficient to brand him in the popular press as the most notorious and extravagant architect of his generation. Certainly his well-deserved image as architect to du Barry, hardly an epithet of praise after 1774 and enough to lead to the scaffold in 1793, was more than equaled by his public reputation as the favorite architect of the hated Ferme Générale, indistinguishably joined in general sentiment to the spectacle of corruption and opulence exhibited by the financiers and *fermiers* and the hardship imposed by the Ferme's agents in their ruthless collection of the *gabelle,* or salt tax.[6] Such support might explain Ledoux's preeminence as a practicing architect in the last twenty years of the *ancien régime,* but it would seem to sit less comfortably with his evident desire to be understood as a social and architectural reformer in the liberal philosophic tradition. Indeed, a superficial reading of his idealistic text has often led to the separation of the pre-Revolutionary and the post-Revolutionary Ledoux, the one spendthrift on behalf of his clients and prolific in grand and ruinous schemes, the other reflective in his prison cell and utopian in his aspirations. In fact, however, with the exception of specific and understandable disagreements over architectural style and building costs, there was little to distinguish Ledoux from his more enlightened clients in the 1770s and 1780s and, indeed, little in the ideological content of his later reveries with which they would have quarreled.

Both the liberal reforms envisaged by a section of the nobility and the economic restructuring proposed by second-generation Physiocrats like Trudaine de Montigny and Turgot shared with the *philosophes* an *esprit de réforme;* but this made them neither republican nor revolutionary. Despite its support of economic liberalism, its opposition to the traditional feudal protectionism and taxation structures of the state in a time of expanding commerce, Physiocracy was conceived strictly within the boundaries of an enlightened and despotic monarchy. Likewise, as François Furet has emphasized, no real contradiction existed between the institutional and agrarian reform envisaged by many aristocrats and their desire to retain the fundamental structures of the *ancien régime:*

The liberal movement, which called for the control of royal power by intermediary bodies, had nothing shocking in its principles, rather the opposite: the aristocracy launched the anglomania of the century, the admiration of English institutions. But it only advanced this political reformism in order to better eternalize the social state.[7]

Similarly, the incessant struggles between the king and the Parlements to define the limits and prerogatives of lawmaking were not in the first instance directed toward any vision of revolution or republican equality but simply toward the rebalancing of powers in the state as it was. In Montesquiou and Hocquart, Ledoux found liberal aristocrats and parliamentarians, even as in Trudaine and later in Charles-Alexandre de Calonne he found economic and social reformers, who recognized an affinity between their own brand of "radical" reformism and his belief in the power of architecture to reinforce such institutional change.

If his alliance with the Ferme Générale contained an element of opportunism, Ledoux also discovered many enlightened *fermiers* who envisaged, at least theoretically, a redistribution of taxation, less in its collection than in the redissemination of benefits. Besides Haudry, Ledoux met other *fermiers* who were themselves at the center of the philosophic circles, including, if not the philosopher Claude-Adrien Helvétius, certainly the naturalist Buffon and the chemist Lavoisier. Ledoux later gave to *fermiers,* bankers, and tax collectors an equal place in his utopia beside writers, artists, and artisans.

In the specific context of the design and building of the Saline de Chaux, Ledoux found it easy to ignore the immediate interests of the Ferme and its contractors in favor of a generalized appeal to the Physiocratic ideals of Trudaine's circle: The founder of the doctrine, François du Quesnay, had, after all, defined the manufacture of salt, like the mining of other raw materials, as a *productive* as opposed to a sterile, or commercial, activity. Turgot himself considered salt as a

kind of *bien-fonds,* provided by nature for the needs of mankind.[8] A dietary essential, crucially important for the preservation of food and the manufacture of cheese, its increased production was desirable even to those *philosophes* opposed to the Ferme and the *gabelle.* From the point of view of an economic and social reformer there was an overall need, inspired by the *Encyclopédie,* for the improvement of manufacturing methods made more pressing by the evident problems, identified by local officials and government administrators since the 1730s, experienced by the salt industry of Franche-Comté.

Ledoux, supported by the engineers of the Ponts et Chaussées, was further persuaded of the need for a comprehensive opening up of the border provinces to trade and industry. With such heterogeneous intellectual supports, commonplace enough in the 1770s, he designed a far-from-commonplace factory, one that from the outset he conceived as taking its place as a productive center, a rapidly expanding "natural city" in the fertile but barely exploited territory of the Jura and Franche-Comté.

THE SALTWORKS OF FRANCHE-COMTÉ

The *salines* of Lorraine and Franche-Comté, confided to Ledoux's care in 1771, were for the most part ancient foundations, often tracing the history of their production to Roman and medieval beginnings.[9] The techniques of manufacture were simple and had changed little over the centuries.[10] In vast, barnlike structures, or *bernes,* brigades of workers set up wide, flat boiling pans called *poëles,* constructed of hundreds of thin iron plates riveted together, hanging them from thick wooden beams over wood-burning furnaces by means of rods supporting the bottom of the pans. Other workers were responsible for evaporating the salt water, which was drawn from underground springs running through the salt beds in the Jura and lower Alps; they stoked the fires, maintaining a constant heat, gradually let in the brine, and skimmed the surface periodically to remove mineral impurities that formed during boiling. At the end of this continuous forty-eight-hour evaporation process, other workers raked off the wet salt crystals onto drying racks. Finally, in *salles des bosses,* or packing rooms, the salt was packed into panniers or compressed into flat cakes, to be sold—generally by agents of the Ferme—subject to a *gabelle.*[11]

Administering the *salines* from the outside were the different offices of the state and the Ferme Générale: first the office of the Contrôleur Général, within which was housed the Bureau du Commerce; then the office of the Inspecteur des Salines and his adjunct. In the regions of Lorraine and Franche-Comté, the state was represented by inspectors of architecture and engineering, inspectors of works and maintenance, inspectors of the waters (controlling the quality of the brine and conserving the wells), inspectors of the wood (controlling, in conjunction with the numerous officers of the royal forests, the supply of fuel), and inspectors of the salt (measuring and allocating production). The Ferme duplicated many of these positions. Periodically, the various officers visited the *salines* to oversee production and management. Within their walls, these *manufactures royales* were administered by officers of the crown or its sublessees, organized in a strictly hierarchical order: the director, supported by his receivers and treasurers; the clerks in charge of the office and records; the agent of the interior service of the *saline;* the clerks in charge of the delivery of salt, the weighing of salt, the supervision of wells, the process of graduation, and the supply of charcoal and other services. Supporting the work of these clerk-overseers were the gatekeeper and his underporters, the tax collectors, and numerous guards.[12]

The principal workers of the *salines* were divided among the salt workers, the *salineurs* and *socqueurs,* who formed the brigades operating the *bernes;* the carpenters and coopers, who maintained the pipes, reservoirs, and graduation buildings and fabricated the *bosses,* or casks, for the salt; and the blacksmiths, who repaired the boiling pans and fabricated the iron work. Each of these groups associated in a type of *compagnonnage,* or artisan guild; each practiced its trade according to rules of the craft learned through apprenticeship; each operated in a quasi-autonomous fashion in the *salines.*

Providing accommodation for at least some of the manufacturing work force was common practice in most of the *grandes industries* and in many of the privately controlled factories of the *ancien régime.* Necessary in isolated areas, an inducement to regularity in others, a supplement to meager pay rates in all, workers' barracks with minimal facilities were to be found in the royal glassworks, near the iron forges, and within the walls of most *salines* in Lorraine and Franche-Comté (though the decision of who lived in and who lived out remained unsystematic, with no common policy formulated as to the relative advantages of either).[13] As a result, the largest *salines*—such as those of Dieuze, Rosières, and Château-Salins in Lorraine and Salins in Franche-Comté—formed self-enclosed villages in their own right, with their pumps, wells, reservoirs, boiling pans, furnaces, storehouses, smithies, carpenters' workshops, cooperies, bakeries, winepresses, administrative offices, apartments for directors, overseers, and workers, chapels, prisons, and gatehouses, all surrounded by walls and ditches to defend their product against theft and fraud. As the historian Max Prinet noted,

Around the wells were a group of constructions forming a veritable village. Often the collection of these small buildings was surrounded by a wall intended to make fraud more difficult. From the eighteenth century, we know that the grand Saline de Salins was enclosed by a circle of walls. . . . These could become a true defense in time of war; they were flanked by towers and furnished with a small parapet.[14]

Altogether, as Léquinio de Kerblay remarked, "the operation of *salines* requires a great number of workers and overseers, and the dwellings necessary for the administrators and production form a kind of small city."[15] Built out of stone, with tiled roofs and overhanging eaves, their factory sheds and accommodations were indistinguishable from the rural barns of the region; their plans resembled any large cluster of farm buildings, grouped according to need and topography.

Beyond the ever-present difficulties of maintenance and growth, two problems of increasing magnitude preoccupied the administrators of the *salines* from midcentury. The first,

Saline de Château-Salins, Lorraine, plan as surveyed in 1787. From Etienne-A. Ancelon, "Recherches historiques et archéologiques sur les salines d'Amelécourt et de Château-Saline," *Mémoires de la Société d'archéologie Lorraine* (Nancy, 1880).

Legend:
1. Main gate
2. Second gate
3. Pumps and wells
4. Reservoirs
5–9. Buildings for the boiling pans
10. Ash pit
11–13. Storage for salt
14. Director's building
15. Cashier's house
16. Porters' lodge
17. New building
18. Old apartment for the controller
19. Apartments for the clerks, offices
20–21. Stables and yard
22. Old fortification
23. Stables
24. Old winepresses
25. Apartment for the contractor
26. Workshops for the blacksmiths
27. Storage for the smithy
28. Apartment for the second porter
29. Guardhouse
30–31. Aqueducts
32. Director's greenhouse
33. Drinking fountain
34. Icehouse
35. Director's garden.

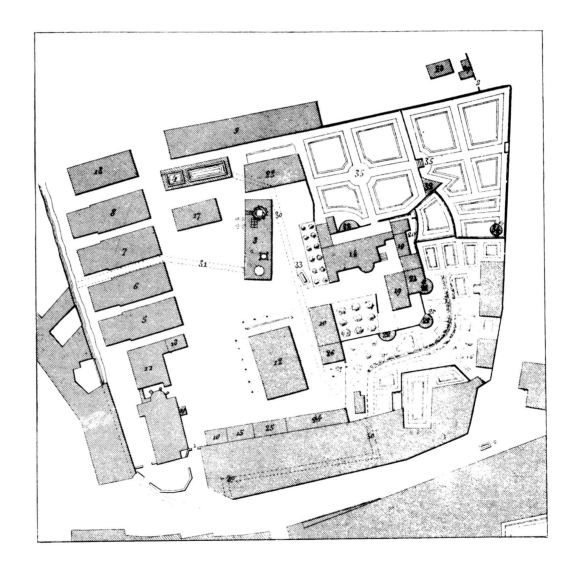

that of the quality of salt produced, engendered deep social resentment. Poor-quality salt, as the inhabitants of Franche-Comté had been quick to point out in 1756, when forced to use contaminated batches from Montmorot near Lons-le-Saunier, often resulted in sickness and death for animals fed during the winter on cured meat and in the decline of revenues from the sale of cheese made bitter and rotten by impure salt. Trudaine de Montigny, appointed by his father to enquire into possible remedies, reported being favorably received by the mountain populations following his public experiments into different techniques of evaporation.[16] But if the quality of the product was gradually subjected to scientific analysis and technical improvement in the 1760s, the second and most urgent problem proved more intractable: the *salines* enormous consumption of wood fuel, in short supply around factories that had been in existence for centuries.[17] The problem was twofold: practical, as it affected the costs of haulage; and political and social, as deforestation sparked grievances in localities where the royal *salines* consumed wood also needed by artisans, builders, and householders. Certain *salines*, beginning with Dieuze and Rosières, followed by Montmorot, adopted the partial solution of preevaporating the salt water by passing it over tightly packed bundles of thorn twigs, in narrow, open wooden structures called graduation buildings; the process exposed the water to the action of the air and thus concentrated its salinity before it reached the *poëles*.[18] Other *salines* that lacked the space for this fifteen-hundred-foot-long machine were simply forced to reduce production. This was true of the Saline de Salins: burning over twenty-two thousand cords of wood each year, from forests that had receded some twelve miles from the factory, the *saline* was prevented by the high costs of transport from fully using its saltwater springs.

The Saline de Montmorot had been a partial attempt to remedy the problem of fuel shortage by building a *saline* closer to a fresh source of wood. It was also, as completed in 1744, the first factory of its kind to be designed as a completely new and rationalized foundation.[19] Constructed by a student of Perronet, Jean Querret, later to be chief engineer

of Ponts et Chaussées for the province, its factory sheds, apartments, dormitories, workshops, storerooms, chapel, and gatehouse were grouped around a regular, square courtyard used for stacking cordwood. Montmorot also possessed the most elaborate system of graduation in the region, including—as the article "Salines" in the *Encyclopédie* noted—three separate buildings grouped in a semicircle to take advantage of winds from different quarters.[20] Ledoux seems to have retained both the square geometry of the *saline* and the semicircular arrangement of the graduation buildings in his first and second projects for Chaux. But Montmorot, which suffered a rapid deterioration in the quality of its salt after the 1740s, did not address the problems of expansion posed by the Saline de Salins.

THE NEW SALTWORKS OF CHAUX

Ledoux, who must have conducted his first tour of inspection sometime before 1773, was unimpressed by the haphazard layout of all the *salines* and struck by the general air of disrepair and neglect:

The Salines of Moyenvic, Château-Salins, Lons-le-Saunier display discordant surfaces, a mass of unsound materials abandoned to caprice. That of Dieuze, as important for its size as profitable for the abundance of its wells, exhibits sumptuous buildings at first glance. Alas, if only its expansion had been foreseen, a town of considerable size would have been able to be built. (30)

As a result of such lack of foresight, the Saline de Salins, built on a narrow site along the course of the river Furieuse, could not expand or profit from all its available water sources; its buildings "were marked by decay," its site, "constricted between two mountains (Mont Poupet and Fort St. André), had circumscribed its layout: in effect, where might one build?" (37).

As early as the 1720s the administration had proposed to build a new *saline* to which the overspill waters of Salins might be piped overland. Ledoux, implying that this scheme was revived at his instigation after 1771, recalled

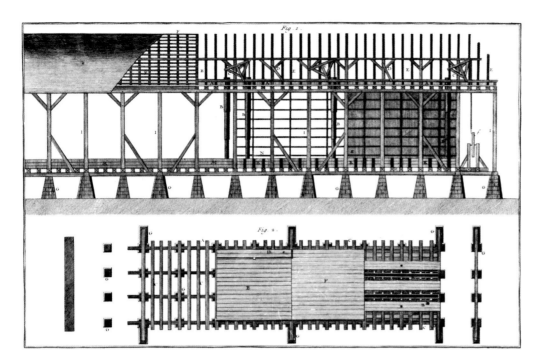

Salines de Dieuze et Rozières, partial plan and elevation of graduation buildings. Engraving by Bernard from Denis Diderot and Jean le Rond d'Alembert, *Encyclopédie, Planches* (Paris, 1751–65), "Minéralogie, salines," pl. 7.

Jean Querret, Saline de Montmorot, Lons-le-Saunier, Jura, plan of original project, 1744. Plan redrawn from the Archives Départementales du Jura, C.375.

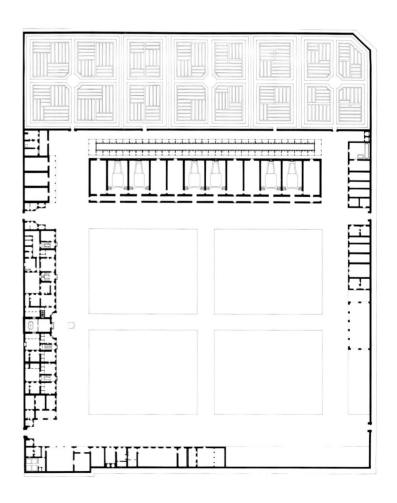

For a long time the administration had viewed the wastage of its sources with regret; it conceived the project of using the smaller springs—those of two or three degrees of salinity. Already the reports of interested parties filled the files and impotent echoes reverberated in the ministerial vaults. . . . A new motor was needed to guide the inevitably slow pace of decisions. (37)

Following the persuasive argument that, in Ledoux's words, "it was easier to make the water travel than to transport a forest in pieces" (38), late in 1773 a commission studied the question of building a new *saline:* "The undertaking was not without difficulty; an economic aqueduct had to be bored, using fir trunks, drilled and fretted, for a length of 48,000 feet; rocks had to be cut through, rapid rivers crossed, etc., etc."(38) The project was assessed economically, weighed against the increasing costs of transport at Salins— some sixty thousand livres annually: "The Supreme Council was assembled, the plan discussed; an exact accounting was rendered of the expenses, the expected production; the advantages were calculated and written up" (38). An Arrêt du Conseil, signed by Louis XV on 29 April 1773, finally directed the Ferme, represented by its Adjudicateur Général, Julien Alaterre, to call for construction bids on a *saline* to be built near the Forest of Chaux and the villages of Arc and Senans; thousands of acres of woodland were immediately appropriated for the future use of the factory, "His Majesty having been assured of the possibility of executing this project by the verification sent to him from the site, which sufficiently demonstrates a fall of more than three hundred feet between the Saline de Salins and the position of the new *saline.*" [21]

Over the following year little progress was made in these plans: the Contrôleur Général Terray was preoccupied with negotiating the next lease with the Ferme; Ledoux, perhaps, with the preparation of a preliminary scheme.[22] The dating of this first project, published in 1804 as the "Premier plan de la Saline de Chaux non exécuté," has been the subject of much debate among historians anxious either to prove or disprove a Ledoux "in advance of his time." The hypothesis that coincides with both Ledoux's own account and the political events of 1774–75 is that his first project was prepared in

concert with the new lease for the Ferme, presented to the king, in the presence of Madame du Barry and the Abbé Terray, and accepted together with an estimate prepared by a Parisian entrepreneur, Jean Roux Monclar.[23] This estimate was then the basis of a separate contract, drawn up between the Ferme Générale and Monclar and signed on 12 March 1774, just a month before Louis XV's death.[24] This sublease, to take effect in October, outlined a new managerial strategy for the *salines,* whereby the Ferme, in return for a fixed supply of salt, ceded the administration of the factories, their upkeep, and extension to Monclar for a period of twenty years. A large portion of the document addressed the construction brief for the new Saline de Chaux.

In his description of the first project Ledoux recounted its suspension on the death of Louis XV; the disgrace and exile of du Barry had no doubt placed Ledoux's own patronage in question. Lightly veiling the circumstances in allegory, he wrote, "The political clouds condensed and covered the atmosphere with their uncertain colors. Everything is subject to change, even in the heavens; new stars are discovered even as others disappear. . . . An order arrives; decisions are suspended, the question is discussed." (66) The political uncertainty lasted until August, despite the continuance of the Abbé Terray as Contrôleur Général; but on 24 August Terray and Augustin de Maupeau, Louis XV's Chancellor, were dismissed by the young Louis XVI, and the *philosophe,* economist, and former Intendant of the Limousin, Jacques Turgot was named in Terray's place.[25] His appointment strengthened, for two years at least, the Physiocratic and reform party in the administration—Trudaine and Malesherbes were friends and supporters of Turgot—and following Physiocratic doctrine, a number of traditional practices and economic institutions were called into question. The first of these, requiring an immediate decision in view of the impending lease in October, was the Ferme Générale itself. Turgot's instinct was to suppress the corporation and dismantle its powers, redistributing taxation and opening up the monopoly to freer trade; but the institution and its interests were too deeply entrenched to change. In the event, Turgot simply ratified the lease negotiated by Terray.[26] It was, no doubt, at this point that Ledoux's first project was seriously questioned: "New debates, new concerns," he wrote, "and why? What one minister does, his successor generally undoes" (41).

Ledoux's second scheme for the Saline de Chaux—the semicircular plan that was, with modifications, realized between 1775 and 1778—was, the architect related, a result of changes demanded by the administration. While the general project of the *saline,* with Monclar's lease, was ratified by Turgot, Ledoux's first plan was criticized from the point of view of safety and function, while its architecture already seemed inadequate to Ledoux himself: it had been, he noted, "conceived before seeing the map of the region (65)."

On 14 September 1774, the Directeur des Fermes for Franche-Comté Alexandre-Parseval Deschênes, one of Monclar's guarantors, was authorized to "visit the sites, order the works, settle the procedures, and keep the Ferme Générale informed."[27] Over a month later, Ledoux finally sent the first schematic diagram of his new plan to the site engineer, Claude Le Pin. This plan, simply showing the semicircular boundary wall of the future *saline,* as marked on the geometrical survey, was described as a *plan en masse:* "The *plan en masse* of this *saline* was ordered by M. Turgot, after having been agreed by M. Trudaine, with the sole concurrence of M. Haudry, invested with the powers of the Ferme Générale. This plan was sent by M. Turgot, joined to his letter dated 28 October 1774."[28]

An engineer for the aqueduct, pumps, and graduation building was selected and sent from Paris on 26 December; "le sieur Lebrun" was instructed to oversee "the plans and geometrical calculations" for the pipeline.[29] Nevertheless, not until January 1775 was the actual site for the *saline* finally identified. François-Marie, Maréchal de Longeville, councillor to the Parlement of Besançon and Commissaire Général des Salines for Franche-Comté, visited the area, "accompanied by architects, engineers, and others appointed by the court, in order to establish the most suitable site for the new *saline,* and, having walked over the entire extent of the plain [of the river Loüe] and supervised the digging of several

ditches to determine the depth of the firm ground and the height of the waters," a site was chosen beside the road leading from the village of Arc to that of Senans.[30] This, the highest ground between the river and the forest, was immediately staked out and reserved for the *saline* by royal *arrêt,* its proprietors to be indemnified appropriately; on 14 February the start of construction was itself authorized.[31]

The foundation stone of the *saline* was laid on 15 April 1775, very probably in the presence of Ledoux himself, who was certainly in Besançon visiting the Intendant, Charles-André de Lacoré, prior to August of that year.[32] During April and May of 1775, Ledoux slowly developed the plans for the individual buildings of the *saline,* sending "a *plan de détail,* only representing the *rez de chaussée,* to M. Le Pin, engineer of *salines* in Franche-Comté, charged with overseeing this construction. This plan, signed by M. Haudry and M. Le Doux, in amplification of the original was ordered by Mr. Trudaine, 2 June 1775."[33] Over the next month, work was begun on the foundations; Ledoux had yet to supply drawings for the elevations of the different buildings.[34] Trudaine, in a letter of 10 June, confirmed his wish that Le Pin—despite the fears of Monclar's association regarding the rising costs of construction—should "conform to the detailed plans both of the elevations and other [aspects] that would be sent to him by M. Le Doux." These elevations arrived on site at the end of June, and, as the entrepreneur had predicted, they were "loaded with decorations." A year later Monclar was forced to revise his estimates, and in a letter of 24 July 1776 he warned that the designs would greatly exceed the 600,000 livres estimated. The single most expensive item was Ledoux's projected Director's Building: "too sumptuous," it alone would cost 150,000 livres to complete. But Trudaine had, in the meantime, already "adopted for the construction of this building another plan, a little less sumptuous, but that still represented a cost of more than 40,000 livres." This second proposal for the Director's Building, sent by Ledoux on 22 July 1776, was "reluctantly" accepted by Monclar's guarantors, bound as they were by the orders of Trudaine and Haudry; but, as completed, it was "without so much deco-

Aqueduct from Salins to Arc-
et-Senans, 1775–78, plan
showing pipeline and basins.
Drawing by A. Vidler.

Legend:
1. Saline de Salins
2. Aqueduct
3. Port-Lesney
4. *Canal de graduation*
5. Graduation building
6. Saline de Chaux
7. Arc
8. Senans
9. Furieuse River
10. Loüe River.

ration." By the autumn of 1778 construction on the aqueduct and the *saline* was far enough advanced to prepare the factory for production: the first salt was drawn from the pans on 5 October.[35]

This chronology clearly distinguishes three stages in Ledoux's work on the design for the Saline de Chaux: a first project, developed between March 1773 and April 1774; a second, definitive plan for the *saline* as a whole, sketched in outline by October 1774 and in detail, at least to first-floor level, by June 1775; and, finally, the elaboration of elevations and details for the individual buildings, culminating in the two designs for the Director's Building between the end of June 1775 and July 1776.

ENGINEERING IN WOOD

From the outset, the construction of the Saline de Chaux had been envisaged as a regional undertaking, part of a general reform of the *salines,* roads, rivers, and forests of Franche-Comté. Monclar's contract gave him the responsibility not only of managing and repairing the *salines* of the east and building new *salines,* but also of coordinating the upkeep of forests and rivers and constructing new canals and roads in conjunction with the administration of the Ponts et Chaussées. The unification of all these duties in a single company would, it was thought, "prevent all competition and rivalry between different entrepreneurs in the same province," as well as ensure a uniform production and quality of salt, which, though "formed in the different *salines . . . ,* would be formed according to the same principles."[36]

First in line for building the new *saline* was the machinery and piping needed to transport the salt water from Salins to Chaux. The contract specified that Monclar should build

a saline, composed of evaporation sheds, or bernes, *drying rooms, reservoirs of water, storerooms,* étuailles, *accommodation for employees and workers, a graduation building, with pipes, sluices and locks, wheels, pumps, and other hydraulic machines necessary for the operation of said buildings; to fabricate and place the pipes and conduits necessary for the transport of saline waters from the Saline de Salins to the new* saline *and their distribution into the graduation building and boiling pans.*[37]

The engineering works were, in this context, at least as important as the buildings of the *saline* themselves; their route was surveyed and their construction begun before that of Ledoux's plans, taking approximately four years to complete.[38] The aqueduct, made of two rows of wooden pipes, bored from fir trunks at least a foot in diameter and joined end to end, followed a route along the valley of the Furieuse to its junction with the Loüe River, and thence along the Loüe until it reached the graduation building of the new *saline.*[39] At intervals, from the small Saline de Salins to Arc, the pipes entered catchment basins that regulated the flow of water in its three-hundred-fifty-foot fall over the length of the pipeline; to protect the salt water from theft and rain these basins were covered by sturdy, square sentry boxes built of stone. Where the aqueduct ran above ground, it was carried on stone

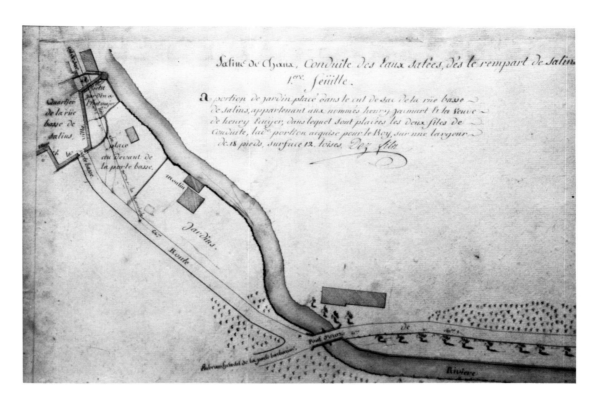

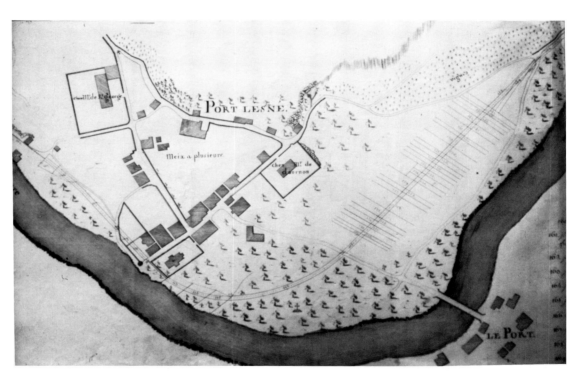

Aqueduct, surveyor's plan, showing pipeline and basin, Saline de Salins (*above*) and pipeline along the Louë River, Port-Lesney (*below*), 1775. Drawing by Denis-François Dez from the Archives Départementales du Jura, 8J 581-9.

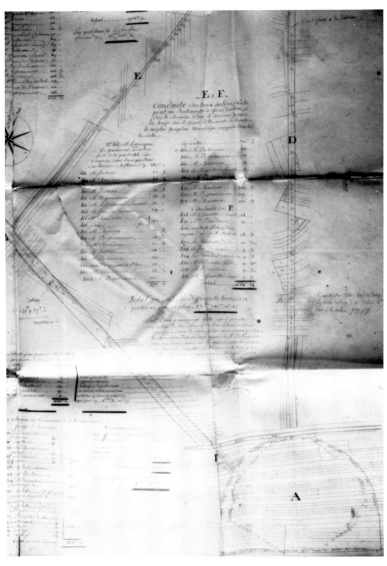

Aqueduct and graduation building, Saline de Chaux, 1775. *Above,* surveyor's plan showing site of *saline; below,* detail showing boundary wall. Drawing by Denis-François Dez from the Archives Départementales du Jura, 8J 581-9.

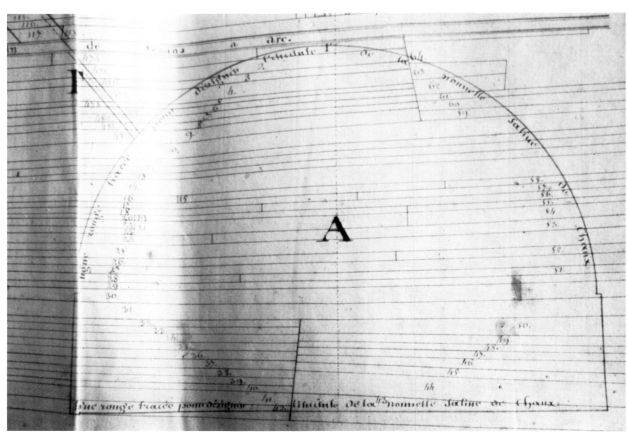

walls or, crossing the Furieuse River, on a stone bridge. Some fifteen thousand trees were felled and bored by mechanical drills turned by waterwheels established for the purpose;[40] Ledoux, on his first visit to the site, recalled

mountains of fir trunks piled up on each other; they were bored along their six-foot length, joined and bound with iron bands at each end; thousands of men leveled the ground, directed the canals, recovered the earth, constructed the reservoirs, raised the vents; I followed all the details of these economic aqueducts that passed over the mountains, the arid rocks, the rivers. (44)

When it reached the environs of the *saline,* on the opposite bank of the Loüe River, the aqueduct tunneled beneath the river to join the basin under the graduation building. There, six pumps, powered by waterwheels turned by the *canal de graduation,* raised the salt water to the top of this fifteen-hundred-foot-long wooden structure, whence it trickled down over the bundled fir twigs to be preevaporated by the air before two more pumps delivered it finally to the reservoirs inside the *saline.*

The graduation building itself, modeled after those at Montmorot, was covered along its length by a double pitched shingle roof; set diagonally to the main axis of the *saline* and standing isolated in the floodplain of the Loüe, it was a dramatic enough sight. The construction drawings support Ledoux's detailed description:

Here, the resinous fir, its bark dried up by the north wind, its center pierced by the drill, pours forth torrents of salt; there the rounded oaks shelter a light construction, platforms, hewn and braced, which counter the thrust and carry the shingle-covered roofs. The center is filled with masses of thorns covered with clay to purify the salt water and to preserve them from the rain that could pollute them. The water that has passed over the thorns at the first level is carried up by multiple pistons to the second, and so on, until it attains twelve degrees of salinity. (57)

Thence the water, partially evaporated, "fell drop by drop into a vast reservoir framed in fir" (57). The maintenance and operation of this *machine à évaporer* demanded the fulltime ser-

vices of an engineer, whose cottage, designed by Ledoux and later subjected to the inevitable idealization, still stands by the site of the wheels and pumps of the now-destroyed graduation building.[41]

For Ledoux, these wooden engineering works responded to his mechanical and Physiocratic interests; they were, as the Chevalier d'Éon put it, techniques wherein "art has searched to imitate nature."[42] In this sense, they corresponded to what Ledoux, together with Trudaine and Turgot, understood as productive forces, supplements to the "truth" Ledoux found embedded in natural resources. But they were not, for all that, works of architecture properly speaking. Indeed Ledoux questioned the form of the graduation building in a passage that interestingly anticipated later debates on the relation of engineering "aesthetics" to architecture: Why, he wondered, were the supports of so gigantic a construction so thin; why was the roof truncated, instead of following that "pure line demanded by nature and by art?" Its section was "vicious," the result of the traditional "prejudices" of carpentry rather than of the "purity of style" (57–58). He would no doubt have preferred to see this long arcade supported on primitive Doric columns, in the manner of the Greek porticoes eulogized by his putative *maître d'histoire,* David Le Roy.

INVENTING THE TYPE

This project was conceived before seeing the map of the region. A prospectus dictated by minor officials, who prepared obscure decisions, circumscribed the work. (65)

Introducing, in retrospect, his unbuilt first project for the Saline de Chaux, Ledoux was decidedly ambivalent toward its qualities. Certainly, as he emphasized, it was, as a "first thought," a "false germ conceived in nature," not at all "in accord with the main principles." Neither its response to the program nor its character in relation to the site was ultimately satisfactory. Yet it was, after all, the scheme ordered by Louis XV. Its plan was a first attempt to bring together the different functions of the *saline* within a unifying geometry; its conception was guided by a sense of management and community

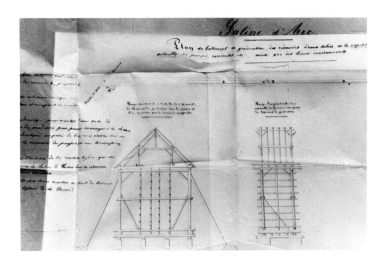

Graduation building, Saline de Chaux, sections, 1776. Construction drawing from the Archives Départementales du Jura, 8J 587.

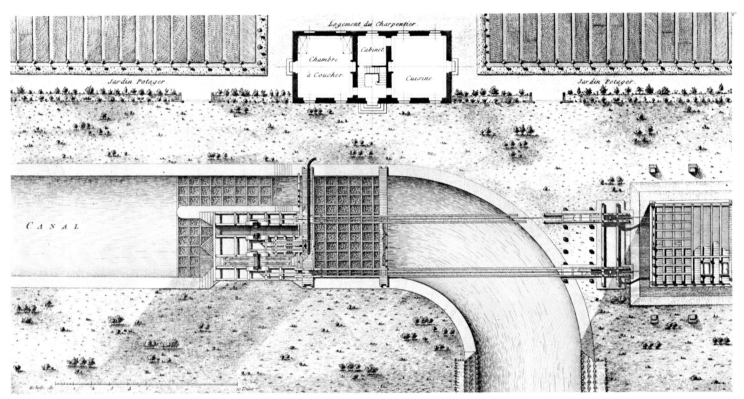

Graduation building, plan of canal, pumps, and carpenter's house. Engraving by Sellier from Rameé, *Ledoux,* pl. 111.

Graduation building, perspec-
tive view. Engraving by
Pierre-Gabriel Berthault from
Ramée, *Ledoux,* pl. 112.

that anticipated the geometries of the built project; and, finally, its architecture initiated Ledoux's search for an industrial style and introduced many of the motifs that later, in more developed forms, would become the hallmarks of his "public sublime."

On one level, the plan of Ledoux's first project was conventional enough: a simple transformation of the enclosed courtyard *parti* common to many late-seventeenth- and early-eighteenth-century institutions, such as the Hôpital Saint-Louis, it distributed the functions of living and working in a continuous structure around a square courtyard approximately four hundred seventy feet wide. At the corners and at the center of each side, square, two-story pavilions articulated the major functions of the *saline*. This main block of building was itself surrounded by a twenty-foot-wide band of gardens and courtyards, enclosed in turn by the wall of the *saline* that separated internal and external peripheral roads. The gatehouse occupied the central pavilion of the front façade and was approached through a front court from a road that prolonged the central axis of the plan south to the Loüe River. To the right and left of the gatehouse were the apartment of the director and those of the clerk-overseers of the Ferme. The southwestern and southeastern pavilions to the front were intended for the chapel and the bakery, respectively; each was circular in interior plan, the chapel with a colonnaded tribune—similar to that previously envisioned for the chapel of Bénouville—and the bakehouse with a round oven. The central pavilions to west and east housed the carpenters, coopers and blacksmiths, their workshops on the ground floor and their apartments above. The salt workers were housed in two separate, virtually self-contained quarters one between the chapel and coopery on the west and the other between the bakery and smithy on the east. The plan of these apartments, which Ledoux retained in the isolated pavilions of the second scheme, distributed the workers' rooms symmetrically on either side of a central, square communal space.

Ledoux planned the factory proper in the rear half of the building block. The three pavilions to the north each contained a reservoir and drying rooms as well as a storage room for salt that opened onto a covered porch for loading. The boiling pans, two to each reservoir, together with the *salles des bosses,* filled the remainder of the plan. In the *cour de bois,* the main courtyard used as a storage area for the cordwood, four covered galleries joined the entrances of each of the central pavilions diagonally, forming a sheltered passage that shortened the distance between factory, coopery, smithy, and gatehouse. At the center of this court stood a drinking fountain for the dray horses.

As an exercise in basic geometry, this plan might be interpreted as a simple regularization of the distribution that Querret had adopted at Montmorot, which similarly joined pavilions of different heights and size around a rectangular court.[43] Certainly its very regularity seemed to propose the image of a rational order, reminiscent of a barracks or military hospital, where previously, as Ledoux had noted, "it seemed that buildings had only been constructed haphazardly. Insofar as needs arose, they were built cheaply according to costly dimensions; heterogeneous materials were piled up on each other." (35) Ledoux's first project seemed to counter such anti-Physiocratic disorder with a geometry invested with a certain economic power. "I had wanted," he remembered, "to conform to the needs and conveniences of a productive factory where the utilization of time offers a first economy"; here the centralization of the plan in conjunction with the diagonal route of the circulation passages was calculated: "The diagonal line inscribed in a square seemed to unite every advantage: it would accelerate all the services" (66). Ledoux thought to supplement this economic order with a managerial control, the more perfect as facilitated by the lines of sight opened by the geometry: "The clerk-overseer, placed at the center of the axes, can embrace in a single glance the details confided to his care. Nothing escapes the dominant position of the director" (67). The section of the factory that showed the covered porticoes was, Ledoux affirmed, "in accord with the major principles. One can oversee the work; one sees everything at once" (68). This geometry of surveillance would be raised to a symbolic level in the second scheme. In all, Ledoux concluded, little had been neglected to make this factory a prototype of efficient manufacture, a blend of the monastic, quasi-fortified establishments favored by Colbert

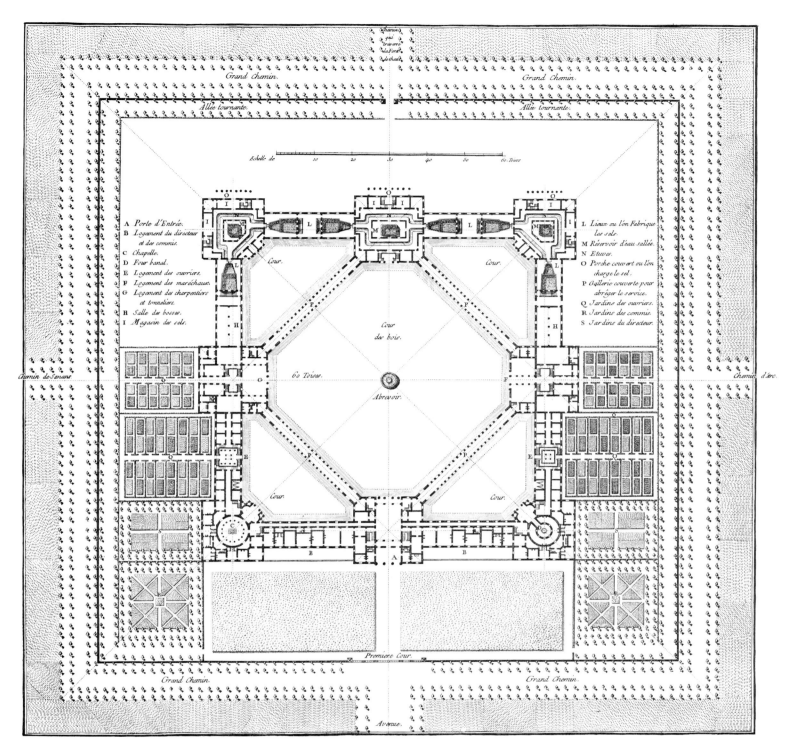

Ledoux, First project for the
Saline de Chaux, 1773–74,
unbuilt, plan. Engraving by
Sellier from Ramée, *Ledoux,*
pl. 113.

Legend:

A. Gatehouse
B. Apartments for the director
and clerk-overseers
C. Chapel
D. Bakery
E. Apartments for the salt
workers
F. Apartments for the
blacksmiths
G. Apartments for the carpen-
ters and coopers
H. Packing shed
I. Salt storage
L. Sheds for the manufacture
of salt
M. Reservoir for salt water
N. Stoves
O. Covered porch for loading
the salt
P. Covered galleries to hasten
the service
Q. Gardens for the workers
R. Gardens for the clerk-
overseers
S. Gardens for the director.

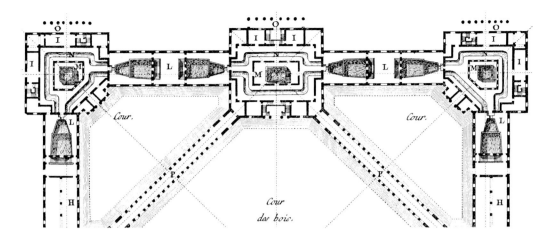

Ledoux, First project for the
Saline de Chaux. *Above,* plan,
detail showing layout of factory at rear; *right,* elevation
and section. Engravings by
Sellier from Ramée, *Ledoux,*
pls. 113, 114.

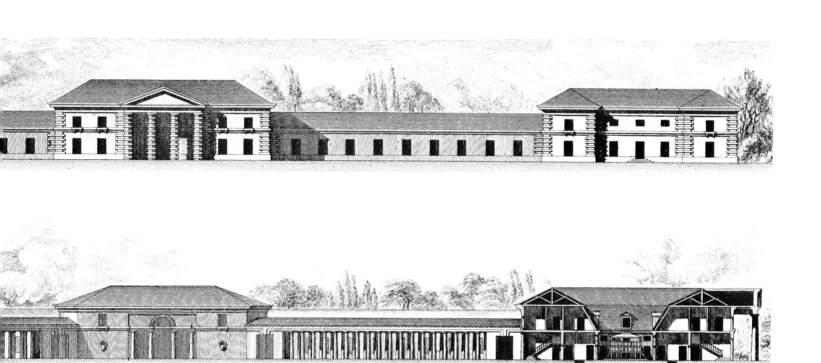

Ledoux, First project for the Saline de Chaux, detail of section showing covered colonnade and factory building with reservoir. Engraving by Sellier from Ramée, *Ledoux*, pl. 114.

and his inspectors and the rational spaces of production imaged in Diderot's *Encyclopédie:* "Man, under the cover of these preserving galleries, can export his materials without fear of the bad weather that dilutes them; nothing can stop, nothing can diminish his activity" (67). In Ledoux's opinion, later to be revised under criticism, the furnaces were distant enough from the living quarters to avoid the ever-present danger of fire; the linking together of the different pavilions in a single structure would give longer life to the building. Finally, the daily needs of the workers were accommodated, as a step away from the traditional reliance on discipline through policing toward a more subtle moralization on the social and communal level: "The workers are lodged healthily, the employees comfortably: all possess vegetable gardens that attach them to the soil; all can occupy their leisure time in that cultivation which ensures each day the first needs of life. Each one," affirmed Ledoux, "could be thankful for his individual comforts." (67)

The architectural expression of this clear plan was, however, less traditional. While many *manufactures royales* built in the previous fifty years had added a certain measure of architectural embellishment to an otherwise sturdy and almost military genre of construction, especially in the application of carved motifs and pilasters to gatehouses and administrative buildings, the *saline* had remained a thoroughly rural and empirical type.[44] Only rarely, as in the gatehouse of Montmorot, with its carved coat of arms, was the *saline* invested with any level of representation. Thus when Ledoux unveiled his first project, the results, as he reported verbatim, were predictable. His project used the orders in profusion, and in at least three different permutations of scale and rustication. Four giant, rusticated Doric columns crowned with a pediment announced the entry to the *saline;* twenty-four giant Doric columns supported the three covered porches to the rear of the factory; four Doric columns marked the Serlian entries to the coopery and smith—reminiscent of the Hôtel Tabary built two years before—off of which led colonnaded passages; moreover one hundred forty baseless Doric columns supported the covered galleries. Other columns encircled the chapel and decorated the entries to chapel and bakery. Certainly all were simple, "primitive," and even rustic, but their presence in such numbers in an economic building astonished the entrepreneurs. "The Fermiers Généraux, their appetites whetted by undigestible rhapsodies, cackled discordantly, tiring the ears with their impotent sounds. . . . Each of them said, laughing: 'Columns for a factory . . . !'" Even Louis XV, generally supportive of Ledoux, "said, caressing the idol of the day [Madame du Barry]: one cannot disagree that 'these views are grand'; but why 'so many columns, they are only suitable for temples and royal palaces.'" (40)

Architectural *convenance,* which according to classical doctrine was a virtual mirror of the orders of the state, had been offended by Ledoux's desire to ennoble the factory.[45] The architect's arguments in favor of the particular orders he had employed—"found neither in churches nor in palaces, nor in private habitations"—foundered in the face of orthodox prejudice. As built, the factory deployed only twelve columns in the gatehouse and the Director's Building, but perhaps with even more dramatic effect than the hundreds first envisaged.

THE THEATER OF PRODUCTION

One of the great moving forces linking governments to the profitable outcome of every instant is the general disposition of a plan that gathers to a common center all the parts of which it is composed. (77)

The change in Ledoux's plans for the Saline de Chaux, which occurred sometime between March and August of 1774, was far more than a simple shift in overall geometries from the square to the semicircle: it represented a complete reconceptualization of the functional and formal idea of the factory. First, Ledoux responded to a criticism of his initial project that the proximity of the boiling sheds to the living quarters would be not only a fire hazard but also injurious to the health of the workers:

The artist felt that he should isolate everything, that the communal and individual dwellings and the furnaces should be prevented from touching, always to be feared when a large number of people is enclosed. He felt that he should compose with the winds that ensure health. (67)

Ledoux, who in 1773 had been directly involved in the debate over the rebuilding of the Hôtel-Dieu in Paris after the disastrous fire of the previous year, thus showed himself susceptible to the arguments of doctors who projected plans for new hospitals according to criteria of ventilation and fire prevention.[46] For example, the plan for a hospital drawn up by the physician Antoine Petit in 1774 distributed isolated ward blocks radially, like the spokes of a wheel, about a common center that comprised a chapel and refectory: Petit himself had argued strongly against *la forme quarrée* adopted by Antoine Desgodets (1727) and Pierre Panseron (1773) as conducive to stagnant air and uneconomic for service.[47]

In this context, the semicircular plan that acted as a unifying device for the functions of the *saline,* now divided among separate pavilions standing around its perimeter and along its diameter, should be interpreted as a gesture toward this hygienic discourse. What before had been a single factory building Ledoux now broke up into the elements of a small town, planned—like Vitruvius's city of the winds—to take advantage of breezes from different directions, which would at once disperse the smoke and noxious fumes from the evaporation process and render the inhabitants healthier.[48] Ledoux, echoing the doctors, justified his quasi-radial plan:

The first laws are those of nature, those that ensure the health of inhabitants who establish their well-being on a preferred site. These first laws command the winds, and provide the means to preserve against their ill effects; their execution is confided to all the overseers of public administration. Here is what experience and researches tell us: the winds that blow directly are the most harmful that can be imagined. The cold hurts the delicate organs, humidity distends them, heat rots them. . . . The south winds engender fever; those from the west stimulate coughs; the north wind is insupportable. . . . Winds that strike obliquely are to be preferred. (70)

With the factory sheds housed in two separate buildings to the rear of the *saline* and the workers' houses distributed in four pavilions around the semicircle, "one had no longer to fear those contagious adherences that submitted a total fire to a partial mistake"; nor would the open plan "constrict the

Pierre Panseron, Project for an Hôtel-Dieu, 1773, plan. Engraving from Pierre Panseron, *Mémoire relatif à un plan d'Hôtel-Dieu pour Paris* (Paris, 1773).

Antoine Desgodetz, Project for an Hôtel-Dieu, 1727, plan. Engraving from the Bibliothèque Nationale, Cabinet des Estampes.

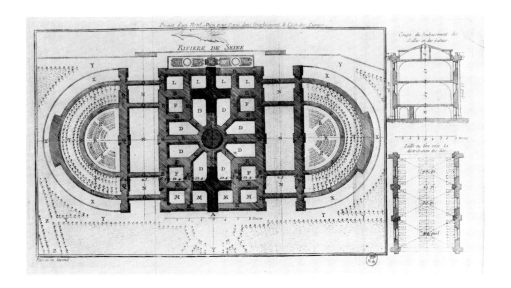

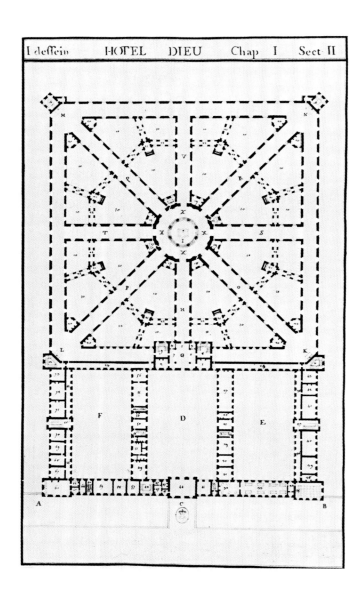

Antoine Petit, Project for an Hôtel-Dieu, 1774, plan. Engraving by Claude-Mathieu de Lagardette from Antoine Petit, *Mémoire sur la meilleure manière de construire un hôpital de malades* (Paris, 1774), pl. 1.

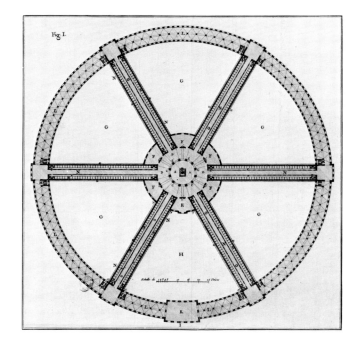

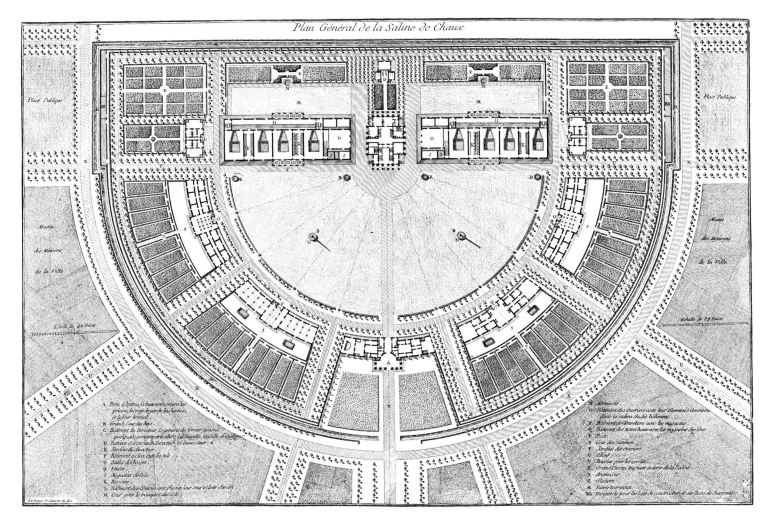

Ledoux, Second project for the Saline de Chaux, general plan, 1774–78. Engraving by Sellier from Ramée, *Ledoux*, pl. 117.

Legend:

A. Gatehouse (containing the prisons, the guardhouse, the courtroom, and the bakery)

B. Great court for the storage of wood

C. Director's Building, apartment for the Fermier Général, some individual apartments, the chapel, the audience chamber

D. Director's stables and coachhouse and rear court

E. Director's gardens

F. Buildings for the evaporation of the salt

G. Packing sheds

H. Stoves

J. Salt storage

K. Reservoirs

L. Clerk-overseers' houses each with their courtyard and garden

M. Courtyard for the transportation of the salt

N. Drinking pond

O. Workers' buildings with communal fireplaces in the center of each building

P. Coopers' building with storerooms

Q. Blacksmiths' building with storeroom for iron

R. Wells

S. Workers' courtyard

T. Workers' gardens

U. Avenues

V. Basins for soaking the hoops

X. Main road around the *saline*

Y. Front court

Z. Ice house

AA. Surrounding ditch

BB. Sheds for construction timber and carpenters' workshops.

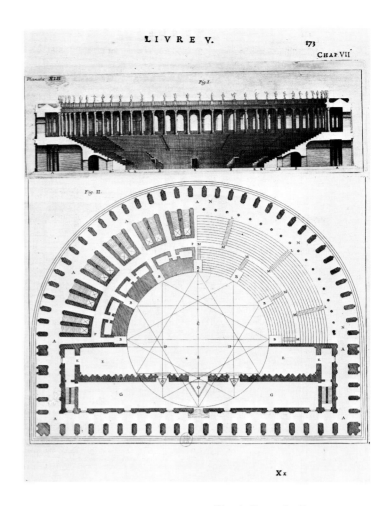

Claude Perrault, Reconstruction of Roman theater as described by Vitruvius. Engraving from Perrault, *Les dix livres d'architecture de Vitruve* (Paris, 1684), pl. 42.

lungs, restrain the faculties, and reflect the contagious breezes" (70).

But, as Ledoux also made clear, his reasons for revising the plan were as much aesthetic as functional. "Knowledge of the site changed the first dispositions": the open, picturesque landscape of the Loüe Valley to which he referred resembled a kind of natural *jardin anglais* and thus called for a variety better supplied by a group of *fabriques* than a single unified structure. An understanding of Ledoux's interest in words as "origins," derived from his classical education, points to the simple but suggestive effect that the name Arc might have had in the generation of the geometrical arc; while Ledoux himself was eloquent in describing his symbolic intentions in a plan that, in microcosm, referred to the arc "described by the sun in its course" (77). Such symbolism, referring to the royal patronage of the *saline,* reinforces Ledoux's evident reference to the classical form of earlier *places royales* in the semicircular radial plan—to Henry IV's projected Place de France as engraved by Claude Chastillon (1610)—but also, and closer to Chaux, to Jules Hardouin Mansart's semicircular arcade of 1688–89 in front of the Palais des Etats in Dijon, a *place royale* that directly expressed the power of Sun King in the provincial capital. But perhaps the most persuasive of sources Ledoux drew from the tradition of architecture itself, joining, in his imagination, all functional and aesthetic requirements in a single, powerful symbol of the kind of community he envisaged for the *saline:* that of the antique theater, described by Vitruvius, commented on by Perrault, and newly proposed as a type by Soufflot, De Wailly, and, in 1775, by Ledoux himself at Besançon.[49] A comparison of the general and detailed geometries of Perrault's reconstruction of Vitruvius's theaters with those of the plan of the *saline* shows this to be an unambiguous analogy. Long obscured by the notion that Ledoux's semicircle was from the beginning an "incomplete" form, merely the first half of an unfinished oval town, this obvious precedent is confirmed by recent demonstrations that Ledoux, at least at first, conceived the semicircular plan of the *saline* as a complete and finite entity. Only the theater, with its semicircular auditorium facing a proscenium across the diagonal, shares this typology. As type and as metaphor, it controlled and gave substance to Ledoux's complex political and social idealism, balanced between a prepanoptical symbolism of surveillance and a model of community; it also unified his decorative devices and supplied an appropriate allegory for the "production" of salt. In the event, the near simultaneity of Ledoux's projects for the Saline de Chaux and the Theater of Besançon was thus a coincidence of great formal significance.[50]

As designed, as built, and, in its heavily restored state, as it still exists today, the Saline de Chaux has resisted any monothematic interpretation: monumental and visually powerful, it certainly shared with Jeremy Bentham's Panopticon, as Michel Foucault pointed out, a desire to symbolize the "all-seeing eye" of surveillance and, in the French context, of royal authority; dramatic and picturesque, its pyramidal and cumulative compositions placed it within the tradition of the English landscape garden; its aesthetic of movement and contrast joined it to the painterly concerns of Horace Vernet, Hubert Robert, and, in theory, of Denis Diderot; constructed geometrically around an "enlightened center," with communal spaces for its workforce and with radial axes spreading into the countryside, it was in every aspect the type of an Enlightenment city, following the social idealism of Jean-Jacques Rousseau and the mathematical rationalism of Etienne de Condillac; as a *saline,* it succeeded in improving on traditional techniques of production and management to the extent that it was hailed as a model of its kind even after the incarceration of its designer under the Terror. For Ledoux, despite other commissions of apparently superior importance, it remained a central preoccupation for the rest of his life, becoming the fictional nucleus of an industrial and social redevelopment of Franche-Comté.

As built, the Saline de Chaux comprised ten major buildings, together with outhouses and stables, arranged along the perimeter of a semicircle seven hundred sixty-eight feet in diameter. The five pavilions that curved around the hemicycle were roughly similar in form, each with a central, double-height space flanked by single-story wings. To the front, a gatehouse, reached through a portico of eight baseless Doric columns and a doorway set within an imitation grotto,

with *urnes renversées* spouting "torrents of water, congealed," acted as a theatrical entrance to the works.[51] The central pavilion of the gatehouse accommodated the guards and porters. In the wing to the right, surrounding an open court, were apartments for the porter and underporter and, at the far end, a prison with two cells, or *cachots,* and its own courtyard; the left wing was occupied by apartments for the second underporter, the guards of the *saline* (with their bedrooms in the mansard of the central pavilion), and a common bakery with a fresh-water reservoir within a courtyard.[52] This "propylaeum" evidently referred to that of the Acropolis depicted by David Le Roy some sixteen years before, and published in a more complete and revised edition in 1774.[53]

The remaining pavilions housed the principal workers of the *saline.* The carpenters and coopers occupied the pavilion immediately to the west of the gatehouse. Each wing of this building was given over entirely to the carpenters' workshops; the ground floor of the central space served as the *atelier des bossiers,* or coopery. Ramped stairs led to the mansard, where three apartments for the coopers surrounded a large, circular room. The central hearth and chimney of this rotunda was common to all the workers of the building. The blacksmiths occupied the pavilion immediately to the east. Each wing contained four apartments and a larger end room for storing charcoal and iron. The forge proper filled the ground floor of the central space: a workshop and three forges with bellows. A stairway again led to the mansard, with five rooms for the blacksmiths. Completing the amphitheater on either side were the two pavilions that housed the *salineurs* and *socqueurs,* each building serving its adjacent *berne.* Each wing of the salt workers' buildings comprised six four-bed apartments along a corridor; in the main space of each pavilion was a communal kitchen, with stoves and a central hearth. Around this center, on the second story, ran a gallery supported on twelve wooden pillars, which gave access to the granary and storage loft in the mansard.

To the rear, across the straight diameter of the plan, were the administrative and manufacturing buildings. At the center, opposite the main gatehouse—literally and symbolically dominating the scene of production—stood the Direc-

Ledoux, Gatehouse, Saline de
Chaux, view from front court
(*above*) and view from inside
court (*below*). Photographs by
A. Vidler.

Ledoux, Gatehouse, perspective view and plan of ground floor. Engravings from Ramée, *Ledoux,* pls. 120 and 118 (pl. 120 by Joseph Varin).

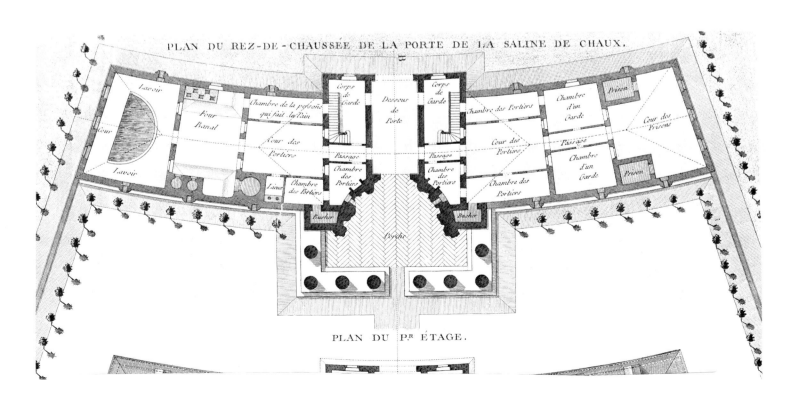

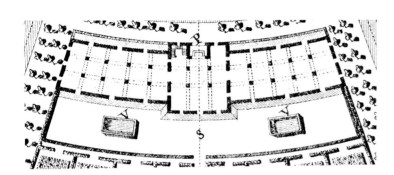

Ledoux, Coopers' building, Saline de Chaux, plan of first floor. Detail from Sellier's engraving of the general plan of the Saline de Chaux from Ramée, *Ledoux,* pl. 117.

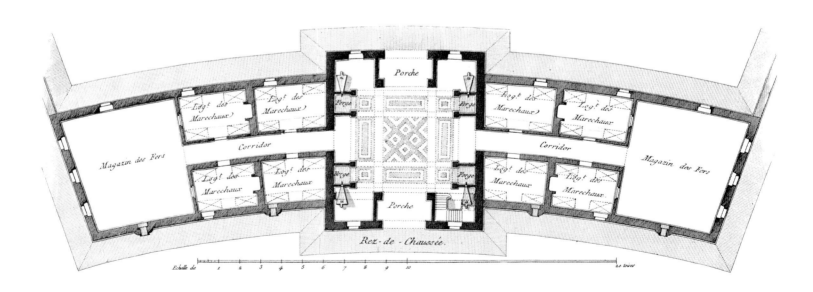

Ledoux, Blacksmiths' building, Saline de Chaux, plan of first floor, showing forges, bedrooms, and storerooms. Engraving from Ramée, *Ledoux,* pl. 131.

Ledoux, Salt workers' building, Saline de Chaux.
Photographs by A. Vidler.

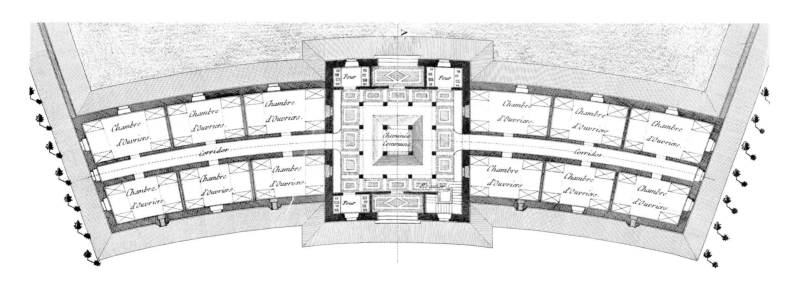

Ledoux, Salt workers' building, plan of first floor. Engraving from Ramée, *Ledoux,*
pl. 136.

tor's Building, fronted by a portico of six giant rusticated columns surmounted by a pediment, with a steep pyramidal roof behind. The functions of the building were ordered according to rank, hierarchically in section. The basement accommodated the individual needs of *employés subalternes*, wine cellars, stores for wood, coal and all other provisions that demanded cool temperatures for preservation. On the ground floor was a bank for agents and employees, an accounting office, a council chamber for meetings of the Fermiers, and a courtroom for the use of the chief visiting judge, who in consultation with the director would levy fines and pass sentences on those who had committed infractions of the salt laws or had broken the internal statutes of the *saline;* in Ledoux's words, "the rooms where Themis renders justice" (131). Also on this floor were kitchens, a doctor's office with storage for medicinal herbs, and a laboratory for the resident chemist, analyst of the salt waters and their impurities. On the floor above were a series of private apartments for the director and high officials of the *saline,* including a dining room, salon, two bedrooms, and offices, as well as tribunes and apartments for the Inspecteur Général of the Ferme. These rooms surrounded a central chapel, with its long flight of stairs designed for the assembled work force.

Flanking the Director's Building and connected by a covered passage running beneath the main stairs of the chapel were the two long *bernes*. Fronted by neo-Palladian porches in rusticated stone, each factory shed contained four *pöeles,* reservoirs, and drying racks. The layout of the *poëles* followed a more or less traditional arrangement in pairs on either side of the drying racks and in front of a continuous stove for the final baking of the salt cakes. But the distribution of the heat from the furnaces to these stoves had been considerably improved:[54] to retain as much heat as possible, the individual furnaces were separated by insulating walls built out of special bricks; a continuous system distributed the heat throughout both levels of the *bernes* in the form of a *modérateur,* or chimney, that connected the furnaces and stoves below to the drying rooms above.[55] Continuous upper-level galleries looked down on the *poëles;* and as if to reinforce the presence

Ledoux, Director's Building, Saline de Chaux. Photographs by A. Vidler.

Ledoux, Director's Building, second project, as built, plans of basement, second, third, and first floors (*clockwise from lower left*). Engraving by Sellier from Ledoux, *L'architecture,* pl. 70.

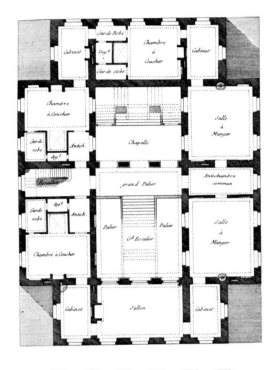

Plan du Premier étage.

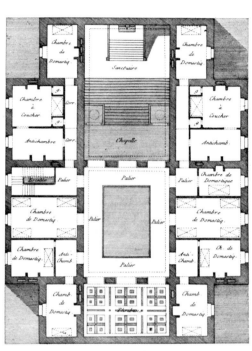

Plan du Second étage de la Direction.

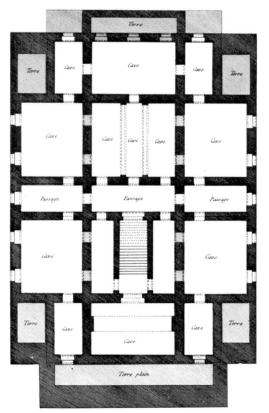

Plan des Caves de la direction.

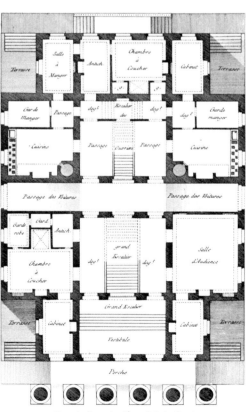

Plan du Rez-de-Chaussé de la direction.

Echelle de   10 Toises

Ledoux, Factory shed,
Saline de Chaux. Photograph
by A. Vidler.

Ledoux, Factory shed, plans of
first floor (*below*) and second
floor (*above*). Engraving from
Ramée, *Ledoux,* pl. 131.

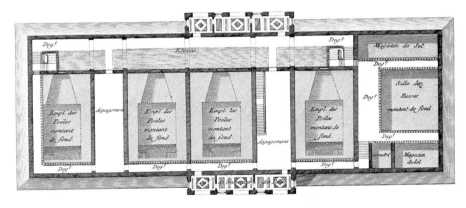

Plan detaillé du Bâtiment destiné à la fabrication des Sels

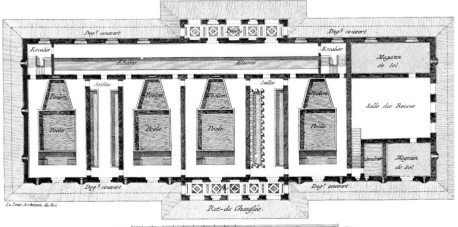

Rez-de-Chaussée.

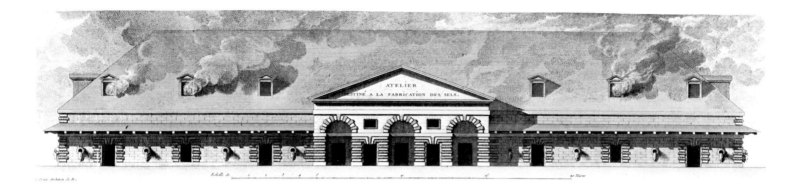

ATELIER
STINÉ A LA FABRICATION DES SELS.

Ledoux, Factory shed, front
elevation. Engraving from Ramée, *Ledoux,* pl. 132.

of constant supervision, an *inspecteur des poëles* was housed in
a small, no doubt extremely incommodious apartment in the
space over the central porch, in the pediment of the entrance
to the *bernes.*

To the west and east, at each rear corner of the factory
sheds, were semidetached houses for the clerk-overseers—
kinds of Parisian *hôtels* in miniature. Behind the Director's
Building was a coachhouse and stables, and behind each
workers' building a small stone shed for garden tools. To
service the semicircular forecourt were two fountains for
drinking water, with attendant horse troughs: standing symmetrically on either side of the central axis to the Director's
Building, two giant, unfluted Doric columns were planned
for the center of each fountain, acting as watchtowers, bea-
cons, and belfries, the instruments of worker surveillance and
time keeping. Placed in front of the gate, outside the walls of
the *saline* proper, was a small sentry box to shelter the controller of the wood, who administered the taxes on incoming
wood for the factory.[56] A high wall encircled the entire *saline,*
enclosing the gardens set aside individually for the workers,
the overseers, and the director. A dry ditch and perimeter
road completed the *enceinte.*

The architecture of this ensemble was unabashedly theatrical, a dramatic combination of three-dimensional geometries, described by the cubic and pyramidal forms of the
separate pavilions, each built simply using smooth-cut stone
and boldly pitched tiled roofs; the effect was reinforced by the
addition to this otherwise plain rural genre of architectural set
pieces, from porticoes to attributes. In Ledoux's terms, this
play of geometry and attributes symbolized, on the one hand,
the ever-present power of the director and his agents, themselves symbols of royal authority, in their surveillance ensuring a constant level of production, and, on the other hand, a
carefully structured community of worker sociability and
moralization, in its interdependent relations and daily routines ensuring good and productive conduct on and off
the job.

Ledoux, Clerk-overseers'
house, Saline de Chaux.
Photograph by A. Vidler.

Ledoux, Clerk-overseers'
house, plan of first floor. Engraving from Ramée, *Ledoux*,
pl. 134.

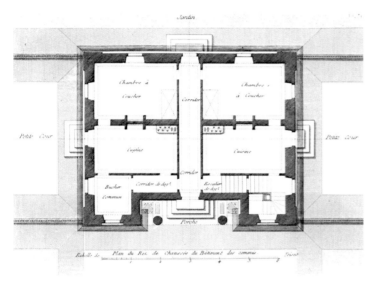

Ledoux, Director's stables
and carriage house, Saline de
Chaux. Photograph by
A. Vidler.

Ledoux, Director's stables and
carriage house, elevation. Engraving from Ramée, *Ledoux*,
pl. 128.

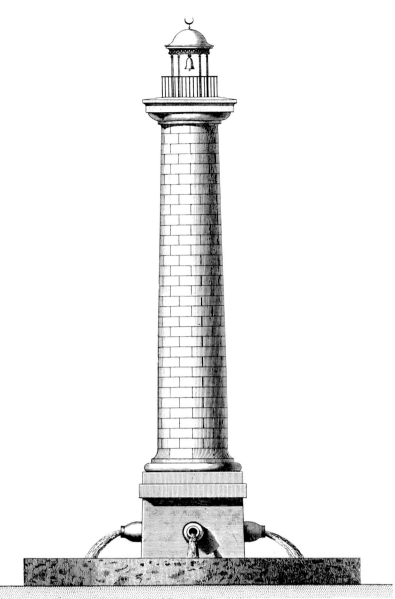

Ledoux, Fountain and beacon
in the central courtyard, Saline
de Chaux, elevation and plan.
Engraving by Sellier from Ramée, *Ledoux,* pl. 129.

Fontaine de la grande cour.

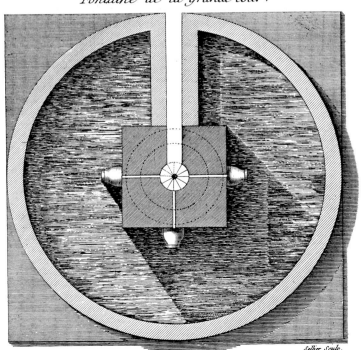

Sellier Sculp.

Plan de la Fontaine.

Echelle de   1   2   3   4   5   6 toises

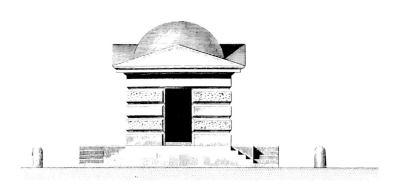

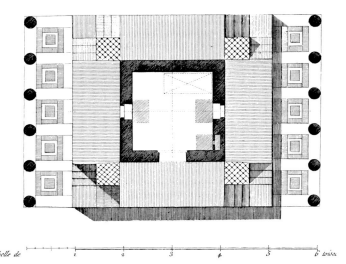

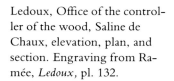

Ledoux, Office of the controller of the wood, Saline de Chaux, elevation, plan, and section. Engraving from Ramée, *Ledoux,* pl. 132.

SUPERVISING WORK AND MORALS

The twelve-foot-high wall, topped with thorn branches and reinforced by a dry moat, that encircled the Saline de Chaux enclosed a factory community that was for all intents and purposes self-sustaining. Some two hundred workers, living together with their families, were managed by a complex hierarchy of officials. Strict regulations ordered the day of every inhabitant, from morning prayers to curfew; the work procedures were rigidly controlled, divided according to traditional *métiers,* timed according to the calculation of the new industrial scientists; the use of fuel and other materials carefully watched to conserve wood, charcoal, and iron; incoming supplies and outgoing products were rigorously weighed, measured, and accounted for. A virtual fortress from the outside—even the agents of the Ferme required a written pass from the director to enter—it was a miniature kingdom inside, over which the director and his officials ruled, as the historian Pierre Boyé put it, "like a small band of tyrants," exercising constant surveillance over the workers and their production, celebrating feast days like the medieval lords of the manor they emulated.[57]

The activities of the *saline* were organized on a weekly basis. All records and the great register of the manufacture were calculated according to the reports submitted by the council of officers that met every Saturday, in which the *clercs des rôles,* secretaries, accountants, and archivists prepared a tally of receipts, salt production, and outgoing expenses.[58] The salt manufacture was calculated by *bernes* and the number of *cuites,* or bakings, completed in each, with the respective amounts of salt. These figures were recorded by the *chef de cuite.* The gatekeeper supervised all other expenses: the payment for wood and charcoal, tools, supplies, the salaries of laborers and workers. Each week the register recorded all these payments and amounts; they were then checked against other measurers—for example, the number of *cuites* against the amount of water drawn from the reservoirs and against the amount graduated, these against the number of casks of salt produced by each *berne,* and the amounts in stock against

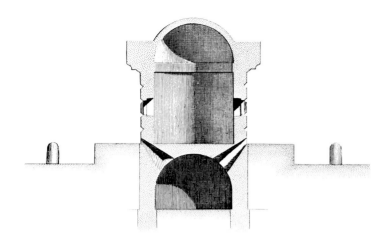

those exported—and drawn up in double columns. Also noted each week were the number and state of the *poêles* in use, the state of graduation, and details of the workforce.[59]

This ramified organization began at the gatehouse, which housed the offices for controlling movement in and out of the factory, the enforcement of the workers' timetable, and the registering of goods and services. "It is in this center of knowledge," wrote Ledoux, "that an indefatigable and vigilant eye follows the respective tasks of each hour and those that undertake them" (109). The regulations for the Saline de Montmorot, drawn up by Haudry in 1775, detailed the duties of the gatekeepers:

The porters and underporters will always be dressed when at work, either in the royal livery or in the agreed livery of their choice. They will carefully search all the male and female workers and other suspect persons on leaving and will carefully inspect everything that is taken out of the saline, whether it be vehicles, baskets, buckets, etc. They will not allow passage for any goods, wood, fire, ashes, raw materials, lye, etc., without the written permission of the Director, or, in his absence, of his representative; the same for any tree, fruit tree or not. They will conform in every way to the Order of the Commissioner of Council that forbids entrance to the saline *for all strangers, vagabonds, and beggars . . . and if any persons of distinction ask to see the* saline *they will ask them to wait while they inform the Director.*[60]

The porters were further to ensure that no pies, grain, or other foods were brought into the *saline* except by the workers; they were to supervise the use of the communal fountain, preventing its use to wash clothes, meats, or herbs. They were enjoined from striking the wagoners in the course of their duties; rather they should lodge a formal complaint with the director. Finally they were to open and close the gates at prescribed hours—dawn and nightfall—admitting none save the supervisors after closing.

The first concern of the administration was the supervision of the large and heterogeneous workforce of the *saline* to ensure smooth production, to guard against the wasting of fuel through ill-managed furnaces, to maintain a consistent quality in the salt, and to prevent theft, fraud, and bad conduct among the workers.

Surveillance began at the *poêle* itself, and within the brigade:

There is always one of the fourteen workers of the brigade who oversees the poêle *taking turns through the night; his functions consist in looking out for unforeseen accidents and in ensuring that the relief workers arrive on time at their posts for the work assigned to them.*[61]

Shift by shift, as *salineurs* replaced *socqueurs* in the long process of evaporation this *inspecteur des poêles* acted as alarm clock and watchdog, ready to report to the overseers any infraction of discipline, to remedy any hiatus in the transitions from one operation to the next. Directly supervising the work in the *bernes* and *salles des bosses* were the *moutiers*, overseers whose functions, as described in the *Encyclopédie méthodique*, were "to oversee all the service areas for the formation of the salt; to follow the operation of the evaporation, the making up of the cakes; to see to the maintenance of the irons, finally everything that relates to the quality of the equipment."[62] At Salins, the eight *moutiers* worked in shifts, three by three, throughout the evaporation period. Supplementing their surveillance were special controllers for the different operations outside the *bernes*: *contrôleurs des bancs*, who oversaw the distribution and transportation of the salt within the *saline;* and *contrôleurs des bois*, also called *veintres*, who regulated the use of wood and the supply of fuel to the furnaces.

The rules governing the conduct of the workers were strict: save for the skilled trades—the blacksmiths and coopers—and a minority of the *salineurs* who had become *maîtres*, the bulk of the workforce was not "self-regulated" by any tight guild structure. The brigades were operated by workers who gained their livelihood from other rural occupations in slack production periods; the transportation and laboring were supplied by day laborers who worked by the hour, also piecing together a living from the fields and forests.[63] Little used to the discipline of continuous production schedules, often unruly and unreliable in attendance, generally antagonistic to the *Fermiers Généraux* and their hated taxes, ever ready to engage in illegal salt production or to revolt against

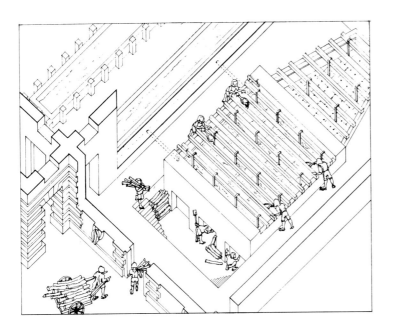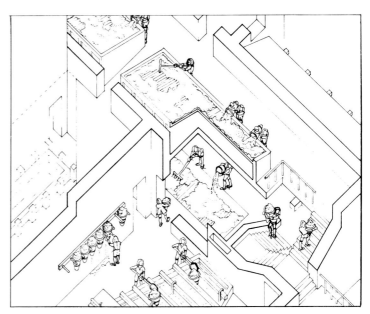

Producing the salt at the
Saline de Chaux. *Left to right:*
firing the evaporating stoves,
removing and drying the salt,
packing the salt in barrels.
Drawings by Deborah Oliver.

the officers of the *salines* and forests, this work force exhibited, from the point of view of management, all the intracta-
bility more generally associated with the early industrial
revolution in England.

Over the preceding century, the managers of the *grandes
manufactures* had gradually tried to establish norms for conduct and work, which by the 1770s had become generally
accepted throughout most forms of manufacturing: attendance, conduct in the factory and out, work routines, all became subject to minute regulation. In this respect, the *salines*
were no different from the wool, linen, glass, or paper factories: Bertrand Gille and Warren Scoville have demonstrated
the similarity of the great ironworks and the plate-glass factories to the *salines* in their close attention to worker regulation.[64] Attendance was enforced by the gatekeeper's recording
of times of entrance and the levying of fines for lateness;
drunkenness and theft were severely punished; married workers were made responsible for the conduct of their families;
often, talking was prohibited in the shops.[65] In all the regulations, administrative orders were as concerned with the details of production—work routines, economy in materials—
as with the moral order of the workers.

Thus work and conduct were controlled at one and the
same time in the royal *salines*. Salt workers were not allowed
to introduce their wives or children into the *bernes* under pain
of dismissal; late arrival was penalized by the loss of a whole
day's pay or, if repeated, by dismissal; the orders of all *sur-
veillants* had to be obeyed without question, again under
threat of dismissal. The craftsmen were charged to look after
their tools and other means of production provided by the
entrepreneur; they were prohibited from in any way trading
among themselves on the premises; they were enjoined from
quarreling, blaspheming, striking each other, or any other action that offended *bons moeurs*; they were never to be found
"intoxicated silly" or selling wine inside the *saline*. At the
same time, the workers were directed to watch over the order
of the *saline:* they should be attentive for signs of fire—negligence in this regard was punishable by imprisonment—and
guard against the wastage of wood or salt waters; inattentive
stoking, failure to detect leaks in the pans, and sleeping on the

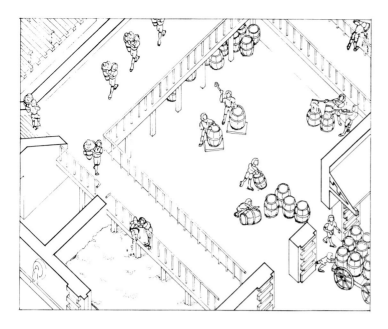

job were equally forbidden. None of the craftsmen might offer individual services to clients outside the *saline,* nor divert the materials owned by the management—iron or wood—to this purpose.[66]

But evidence exists as well of paternalistic concern by management: the registers of Montmorot, under the administration of Monclar, show a careful assessment of each worker's capabilities, with prospects for advancement; as the rules of the *salines* of Savoy noted, workers were to be evaluated "according to the evidence they give of the greatest skill, honesty, and attention to their work," before being advanced as *chefs du métier.*[67] At Montmorot, in 1776, five out of nine *cuiseurs* were listed as able to read and write and thus judged fit to become *chefs;* others, honest enough, could not read; others again were "not robust enough" or even "a little broken." The turnover in the work force was extremely small. In the third year of Monclar's contract no workers had changed their occupation; in the fourth year one had died and one had entered; in the fifth year one had left, in the seventh year two more. The average age of the work brigade was forty-one, with the oldest worker seventy-eight and the youngest twenty-seven.[68]

SYMBOLS OF SURVEILLANCE

Placed at the center of the radii, nothing escapes surveillance. (77)

Describing his second plan for the Saline de Chaux, Ledoux insisted upon what he considered the principal virtue of the semicircle: its ability to facilitate "surveillance." The concerns of oversight and economy present in the first project had become directly legible in the privileged central position of the director and in the lines of sight that radiated from his position to that of the workers, clustered in groups around the periphery. Such supervision was, in Ledoux's terms, a function of unobstructed vision: "The eye easily surveys the shortest line; the work traverses it with a rapid step; the burden is lightened by the hope of a prompt return. Everything obeys this combination that perfects the law of movement." (77) Such an obvious correlation between geometry and vi-

sual control has seemed to many commentators a confirmation of Ledoux's *esprit de panoptisme,* his anticipation of a form of surveillance perfected in Bentham's Panopticon schemes of the 1790s. Michael Foucault saw in Ledoux's plan the possibility for a "single gaze to see everything constantly," an intimation of panopticism, formed by the desire to construct a "perfect disciplinary apparatus": "A central point would be at the same time a source of light illuminating all things, and a place of convergence for everything that should be known: a perfect eye from which nothing escapes and a center toward which all regards are turned. This is what Ledoux had thought to build at Arc-et-Senans."[69] Ledoux's own discourse supports this interpretation: in the *Prospectus* to *L'architecture* he called the Director's Building a *temple de surveillance* and, speaking of the different functions of the *saline,* from the gatehouse to the factory sheds, he repeatedly stressed the need for continual oversight, day and night, on every level, from the lowest clerk to the director himself. Certainly the "lines of sight" marked on the general plan reinforced such a dictatorship of the eye.

But despite the overt similarity of many circular and semicircular plans for institutions—hospitals and prisons as well as factories—projected after the 1770s, the precise nature of "surveillance" varied widely in each particular case. In their plans for hospitals, Antoine Petit and Bernard Poyet selected the radial form as a way of providing visual access to the religious center; the radial shipyards planned by Pierre Touffaire for Brest and Rochefort were functional arrangements that allowed for the storage of many warships at once with access to a single basin; and in the case of Ledoux's factory, the semicircle was less a *machine à surveiller* than a *symbol* of such surveillance.[70] However unruly and undisciplined the rural workers of Franche-Comté might have been, the registers of the *salines* demonstrate none of the continuous preoccupation with police, control, and physical discipline manifested at the time by English management.[71] The presence of overseers, the existence of rules enforced by internal jurisdiction, and the craft nature of the work seem to have sufficed to keep order in the factory. Ledoux's "surveillance" appears to have

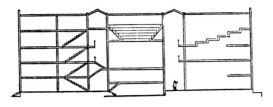

FIG. II.—SECTION

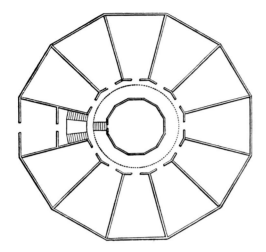

Jeremy Bentham, Panopticon Building, 1797, section and plan. Engraving from Jeremy Bentham, *Outline of a Work Entitled "Pauper Management Improved"* (London, 1797).

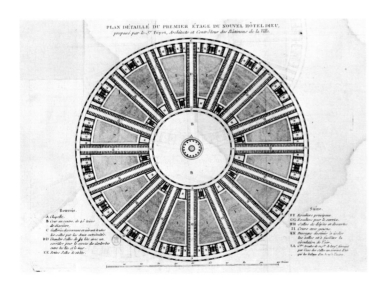

Bernard Poyet, Project for a new Hôtel-Dieu, 1785, plan of first floor. Engraving from Bernard Poyet and Claude Philibert Coquéau, *Mémoire sur la nécessité de transférer et reconstruire l'Hôtel-Dieu de Paris* (Paris, 1785).

been the aesthetic registration of a ramified system of oversight, already functioning and in place, rather than the invention of a new system of worker controls.

In fact, the actual plan of the *saline* did not facilitate direct visual access between director and workers—something in any event not demanded by the managerial process. Once the symbolic presence of power had been clearly marked, Ledoux seemed more concerned to disseminate discipline into smaller, self-contained, self-policing units. Hedges sheltered the workers' buildings from immediate scrutiny, at least in the later, idealized plan; and there was none of the relentless individualization enforced by Bentham's politics of control. Nor was the Director's Building the all-seeing cage invented for Bentham's overseer; at once a temple and a palace, it represented rather than instrumentalized power.[72] In this sense, Ledoux's insistence on the primacy of vision worked toward an aesthetic of expression rather than toward a machine of repression.

On this level, the architectural language was didactically clear. Cumulatively, building up along the main axis of the *saline,* from the bridge over the Loüe through the columns and mock grotto of the gatehouse, beneath the portico of the Director's Building, with its giant *colonnes à bossages,* to the last steps of the long stairway ascending to the alter of the chapel inside, Ledoux developed an allegory of natural, industrial and spiritual power marked at each step by architectural motifs. All these staged moments along the route established a narrative that moved from nature to worship. Starting at the banks of the Loüe River and entering the outer ramparts of the *saline* by way of an acropolitan propylea, this axis passed into the grotto, a "cavern issuing from the earth," which emulated the "sources" of the salt waters that Ledoux had visited in the underground caves of Salins. Carved so as to reveal its artificial, theatrical character, the rustication of the archway disappearing behind the thin stone appliqué of the rocks, this grotto also referred to the sources of the Loüe itself, waters springing forth from a famous and often painted cave. In a later design for a house intended for the overseers of the Loüe, Ledoux would pay homage to these "torrents of

Ledoux, Gatehouse, Saline de Chaux; section, entrance grotto, and detail of grotto. Engraving from Ramée, *Ledoux,* pl. 119; photographs by A. Vidler.

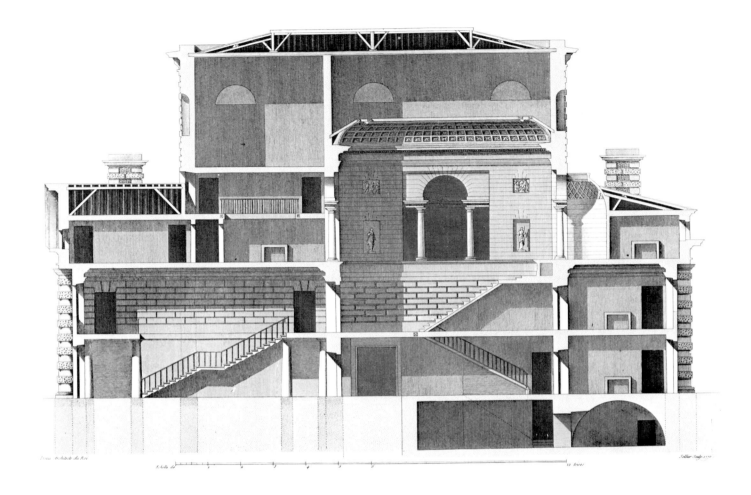

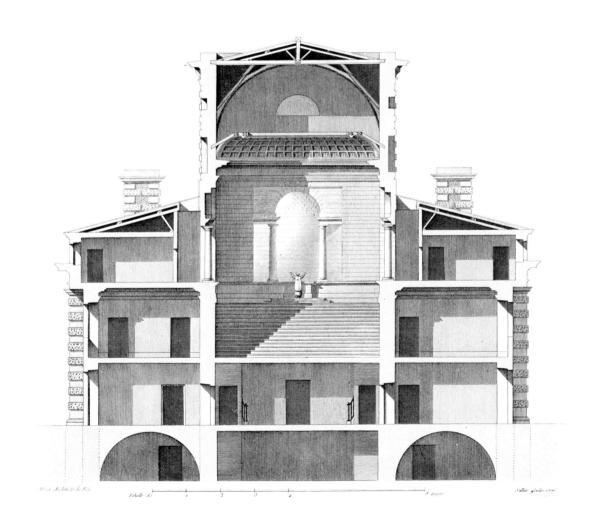

well-being" that, issuing from "deep cavities," fertilized the "arid deserts" of the plain.[73]

From the symbol of the source of natural power, the path moved across the semicircle to the portico of the Director's Building and, beyond this, ascended the stairs of the Chapel toward a single source of light, emblem of the Supreme Being. Perhaps, given Ledoux's later involvement with Masonic cults, a certain initiatory character to this route might be detected; clearly it bears comparison with a then-celebrated theatrical performance: the first Parisian staging of Christoph Willibald Gluck's *Orphée at Eurydice* on 2 August 1774.[74] Ledoux, who was surely in attendance, would have been struck by the mise-en-scène designed especially for the occasion. Moving in six acts from the laurel and cyprus groves where Eurydice was buried, past the Furies, into the abyss of Lethe, through "a cave of terrifying aspect across the river Cocytus," finally emerging in a "delightful region with verdant groves" to end at a "magnificent temple dedicated to Love," this quasi-Masonic scenography—entirely absent from his first project for the *saline*—evidently appealed to Ledoux. Over thirty years before, the tradition of such "descents" had been established by another of Ledoux's aesthetic mentors, Giovanni Niccolò Servandoni, in an elaborate performance of *The Descent of Aeneas into Hades* in the theater of the Tuileries.[75] Ledoux himself, recalling his visit to Salins in the early 1770s, spoke of his journey through Lethe, guided by a boatman "Cocytus."

But Ledoux, as we have noted, was also close to the burgeoning and increasingly fashionable Masonic movement of the early 1770s; the Grand Orient, established to legitimize and consolidate the already numerous lodges of English and Scottish inspiration, had been founded in 1773 under the protection of the Duc de Chartres with the active participation of the Montmorency. Among Ledoux's clients, de Montesquiou and Haudry were prominent Masons, as were many of his friends, including the Abbé Delille and Hubert Robert, and architectural colleagues, notably Brongniart and De Wailly. Ledoux's name does not appear in the scanty records of inscription between 1773 and the Revolution, though he was certainly a member of a non-Masonic lodge by 1784; but his

liberal use of motifs and allegorical references before then attests his more than fashionable interest. Beneath the iconology of nature, power, and sociability in the Saline de Chaux, especially embodied in the successive projects for the Director's Building, lay obvious Masonic influences: not only in the establishment of an initiatory route, whose stages directly imitated those of the Masonic ceremonies, but also in the form itself of the Director's Building.

Indeed, Ledoux's first project for this "temple" as completed in 1775 resembled some primitive "restoration" of Solomon's Temple, its giant rusticated pilasters and its central volume raised above the surrounding apartments reminiscent of Perrault's or Fischer von Erlach's drawings of Solomonic architecture.[76] This impression was reinforced by the geometry of the plan, where the chapel, enclosed within the main body of the building, echoed an ideal version of the Masonic lodge in proportion and decoration. Ledoux had perhaps seen the lodge built by Pierre Poncet for the Grant Orient in 1772–73.[77] A precise double square in plan, with the first third taken up by the tribune, entered between two isolated columns, ended by a plain semicircular niche, the chapel followed the Masonic rules exactly; the triple windows along its sides and front and the triple lucarnes in the pediment of the temple façade would have cemented the allusion for any contemporary observer. Ledoux made it equally clear that the "religion" for which he was designing was Deistic and "original" in form. Ledoux clarified the Masonic reference even further with the two colossal Doric columns he planned for the *Cour de bois,* flanking the façade of this industrial "temple" like those double columns of Jachim and Boaz, memorials of Solomon's originals, always to be found at the entrance of the lodge.

Guided by the religious history of Antoine Court de Gébelin or perhaps that of Charles-François Dupuis—"the great book that retraces the centuries and the cults"—Ledoux abstracted from all "those religions that vary to infinity" their common foundations in primitive worship.[78] Against the "temples of the Goths, filled with coarse images," and more modern churches like St. Peter's, repositories of "the products of superstition," he posed the natural religions of the Persians,

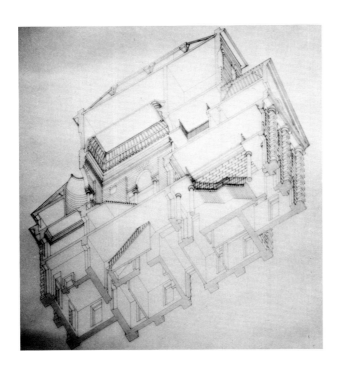

Ledoux, Director's Building, first project, cutaway axonometric. Drawing by Maurizio Deponte.

Ledoux, Director's Building, first project, plans of first, second, and third floors. Engravings from Ramée, *Ledoux,* pls. 121 and 122.

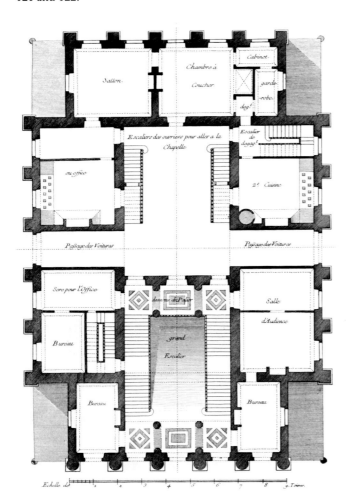

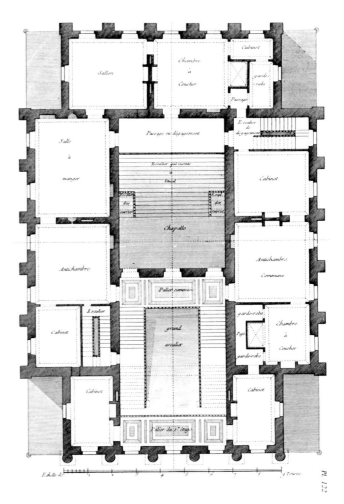

who built neither temples nor images; the saints of the Old Testament, who worshipped in the high mountains; the Chinese, who "never represent the *Tien*"; the Muhammadans, who substituted "moral and pious sentences" for images; and the Druids, who simply worshiped in the forests, setting up their altars "in the thick woods" where "a dark foliage and mysterious shadows covered the priests." All these Ledoux considered suitable models of origins. The temple he envisaged for the *saline* approached the natural Druidic space of worship, where the light itself provided the only divine symbolism: "The altar is at the center, the setting sun is radiant; only the priest is seen, only he is illuminated; one believes that the Divinity itself, descended from the heavens, occupies his place in all his majesty, in all his glory" (142).

This religion of light is perfectly illustrated by a cross section of the first project for the Director's Building, which shows the steps of the chapel and the altar lit from the rear through a hidden source that illuminates the priest, standing, hands raised in solitary worship, like Moses on the mount. By transforming the chapel into a primitive mountain, with its flight of forty steps, terraced for the assembly of the different ranks of workers, employees, and overseers, Ledoux returned what he hoped would become a natural society of production back to the origins of worship, in a generalized version of Freemasonic brotherhood. The pyramidal effect was even more pronounced in the built scheme for the Director's Building, where, in abandoning the basilica plan for the chapel, Ledoux reinforced the stair, pushing it back to the rear wall at a higher level: "It is there that the faithful, prostrate [call on] the Supreme Being . . . invoking the benefits of the morning; it is there where the end of the day receives the tender expressions of the most living thanks."

In order to display these combinations, the results provoked by the resources of art, it was necessary to establish the sixty steps that led to the altar, to darken the surfaces of the walls, to subdue light from divergent sources. . . . Everything had to contribute to valorize the principal object; the light that struck the sacrificer had to be the image of grandeur and supreme majesty, the mysterious shades that enveloped him had to represent the nothingness of nations. . . . It was necessary to raise up stairs that recalled the high heavens, the high mountains, and put between man and divinity that incommensurable distance crossed but never attained by the imagination. (143)

The cumulative effects of this gradual "ascension" from the gatehouse of the *saline* were, on a more precise architectural level, calculated in scale and position. Ledoux—following Le Roy—designed the columns of the gatehouse to stand out visually against the flat plain, giving them a "firm proportion": short and massive, closely spaced, with a deep entablature. "At the center of an immense plain that devours everything" and viewed from a great distance, tall, thin columns wold have been subject to visual, if not material, erosion. Similarly, Ledoux designed the columns of the Director's Building to be viewed from a fixed point at the gate: "One knows that all three-dimensional bodies diminish and become more slender to the eyes with distance; they lose

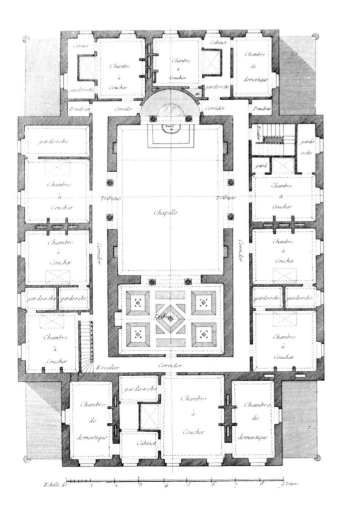

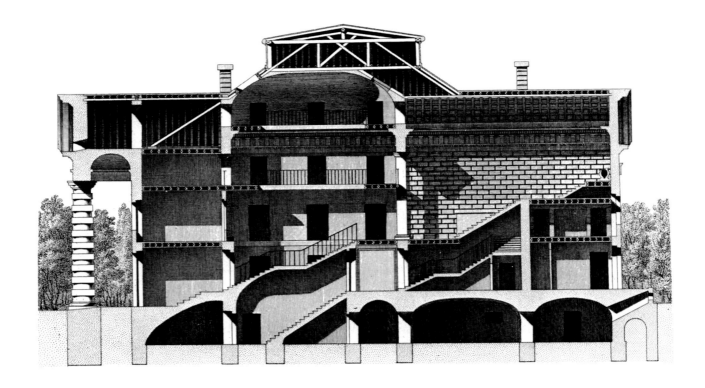

Echelle de 1 2 3 4 5 6 7 8 9 Toises

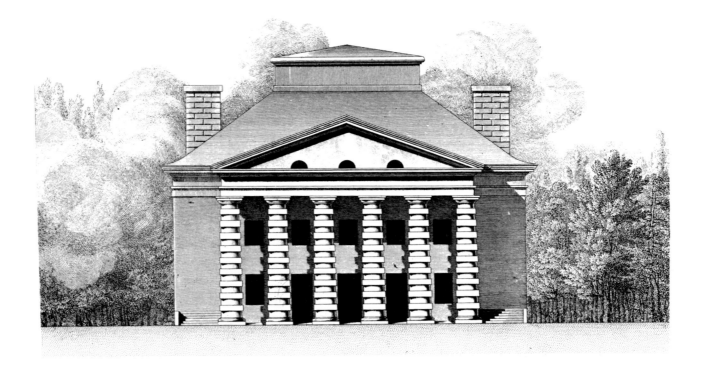

their proportion. The shortest orders are not protected from this decomposition; the most elegant are absorbed."(135) Recognizing that superimposed orders would only seem weak after the sight of the gatehouse, Ledoux invented a version of the rusticated column used by Palladio and Serlio, but pushed to giant proportions: "In a factory, round and square pillars, columns built of combined courses, seem to be more suitable than any of the known orders. The projections produce sharp shadows; this is a means of substituting strength for the weakness produced by distance." (135)

In a final, idealized version of the Director's Building, Ledoux increased this effect by creating freestanding rusticated porticoes to front and rear. The play of porticoes was completed to the right and left of the Director's Building by the pedimented porches of the factory sheds, supported by flat, rusticated arches, derived from Palladio via Fischer von Erlach, who used exactly similar arches as the imaginary entrances to his Egyptian pyramids.[79] This source for the entrance to the furnaces of the *saline* was a deliberate transposition by Ledoux of the iconography of the pyramids—the etymology of which, he pointed out, came from "the idea of the tapering flame" burning on the funeral pyres of the first Egyptian kings—to that of the boiling sheds of the traditional factory. Ledoux emphasized this resemblance to the pyramids in the cross section and rear elevation of the factory buildings, which, taking the precise geometry of the Great Pyramid, are shown belching smoke and fire;[80] later Ledoux, no doubt wishing to distance these buildings from the pyramidal crematoria designed by Pierre Giraud to receive the overflow of corpses from the Terror, asked the observer to "distinguish between the *saline* vapors that envelop the roofs of the *saline* and that putrid smoke exhaled from the altars where the victims are burned."[81] The pyramidal geometry present in the section of these buildings was reflected and centralized in that of the Director's Building, whose roof, if prolonged to the ground, would form a grand truncated pyramid, forcing "with its proud countenance" everyone who approached "to lower their head."

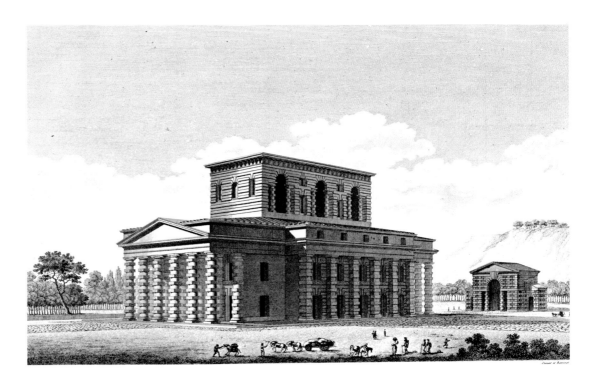

Ledoux, Director's Building, third, "ideal" project, plan of first floor. Detail from Sellier's engraving of the general plan of the Saline de Chaux from Ramée, *Ledoux,* pl. 117.

Ledoux, Director's Building, third, "ideal" project, perspective view. Engraving by Coquet and Edme Bovinet from Ramée, *Ledoux,* pl. 127.

Fischer von Erlach. "Magnificent Egyptian Pyramid, Thebes." Engraving from Fischer von Erlach, *Entwurf einer historischen architektur* (Vienna, 1721), pl. 43.

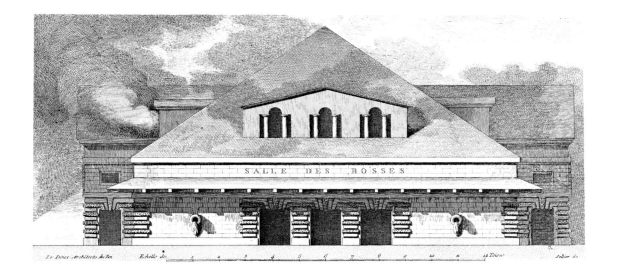

Ledoux, Factory shed, Saline de Chaux, side elevation showing idealized "Palladian" windows added to the engraving in the 1780s. Engraving by Sellier from Ramée, *Ledoux,* pl. 133.

Ledoux, Factory shed, cross section through evaporating pans. Engraving by Pierre-Nicolas Ransonnette from Ramée, *Ledoux,* pl. 133.

Saline de Dieuze, Lorraine, plan and section of the new building, c. 1750. Engraving from the *Encyclopédie,* "Minéralogie, salines," pl. 10.

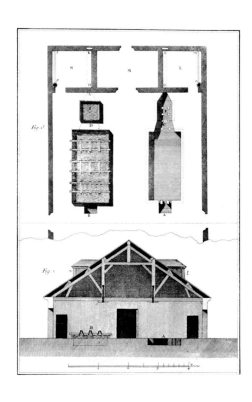

Five elevations, each thirty toises long, with the spaces in between planted with useful trees, describe a vast circle. (112)

Countering the forbidding iconography of the central axis of the *saline* and deliberately mediating its apparently absolutist implications, Ledoux used the properties of his geometry to establish the semblance of a community, one at least equal in its relationship to the scene of production that it faced. Here the imagery was provided less by the grand attributes of architecture than by a spatial confirmation of an idealized pattern of life. The plans of the four, nearly identical workers' buildings indicate clearly Ledoux's intentions: six apartments ranged along a corridor to each side of what he termed an *hôtel de réunion,* with a common hearth and chimney at its center and stairs leading to a loft with storerooms and extra apartments on an upper level.

Each room is occupied by a family; a gallery leads to a communal fireplace. This hearth offers all the means of preparing and tending the food; the clay oven in which it boils covers a hundred chafing dishes sustained by a continual flame. (111)

The hôtel de réunion *contains a fire that never grows cold, warmed by the gratitude of those brought together by beneficence. The galleries on the first floor, the benches, multiply the favors of well-being: it is an economic movement that knows no respite. (110)*

Ledoux evidently imagined a version of Rousseauesque happiness engendered by these centralized spaces, surrounded by square and circular galleries, and confirmed by their sections, which, though in fact roofed by mansards, the architect idealized with semicircular domes that projected their plans into three dimensions: "The section," he wrote of a workers' building, "gives a general idea of the reconciliation by common interest that recalls man to the social order." Here, as a first generation of modernists understood, were announced the principles of architecture as a social "condenser." Rousseau had first posited the formative effects of the home on familial society:

The first developments of the heart were the effect of a new situation that brought together in a common dwelling husbands and wives, fathers and children; the habit of living together gave rise to the sweetest sentiments known to men, conjugal and paternal love. Each family became a small society.[82]

Ledoux, too, was hopeful of the civilizing effects of his spaces. Of the communal rooms, he wrote: "It is in these charming places that everything is enjoyment; it is there where love has deposited its faithfulness, where man is still surrounded by his innocence." (110) These dwellings would, Ledoux believed, rapidly become "places of predilection" for their inhabitants; life would be lived "according to its natural laws." And if the worker, ill paid and overworked, had little in the way of property, at least he would be "surrounded by the sweetest illusions . . . with his wife and children during the hours set aside for rest." More important for the moral order of the factory and the smooth running of its produc-

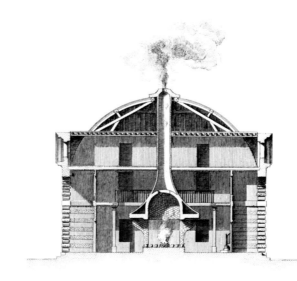

Ledoux, Salt workers' building, section through central community space and fireplace. Engraving from Ramée, *Ledoux,* pl. 119.

Ledoux, Blacksmiths' building, courtyard elevation with idealized "dome" replacing the mansard roof over the central pavilion. Engraving by Sellier from Ramée, *Ledoux,* pl. 137.

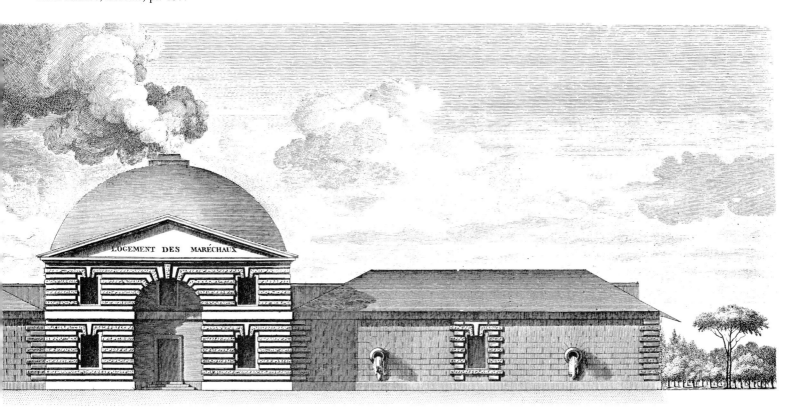

LOGEMENT DES MARÉCHAUX

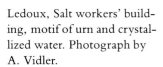

Ledoux, Salt workers' building, motif of urn and crystallized water. Photograph by A. Vidler.

tion, within his communal spaces the worker would be "sheltered from all those costly distractions and bacchic deliria that could disturb the marriage bond, tempting or surprising laziness." Inside, around the fire, "he finds, in this reunion with his dearest customs, his pleasures, the consolation for his afflictions, the gathering together of his needs; nothing forces him to expose his days to the unregulated time that harvests only imprudence and indiscretion." (111)

And the worker would be healthy. Supposedly warmed in winter by the heat traveling the passages from the common rooms to his apartments, he would also be better fed because provided with his own vegetable gardens to cultivate: "If he leaves these dear retreats it is to cultivate a productive field, which fills the intervals of labor, amuses his leisure time, and assures him of distractions that protect him from the errors and desires that shorten the days of those who live in the midst of temptations." (111–12) The workers, rural in origin, would thereby remain "attached to the soil," but within the confines of the factory. Thus leisure time would be functionalized on behalf of production, while the "first needs of life" would not be provided at the expense of the employer. In this model of a happy worker community Ledoux was perhaps following the argument of the anonymous author of the article "Manufacture" in the *Encyclopédie,* who criticized the overcentralized *manufactures réunies* where "the workers were more constrained and treated roughly," in favor of more dispersed factories where, in the nostalgic dream of Diderot's collaborator, "the companion is the friend of the master, lives with him as with his equal, has a place by the fire and a candle, has more liberty." [83] Whether the workers of the Saline de Chaux were affected beneficially by their accommodation or attached the more closely to their work by the sight of their kitchen gardens through the overturned water spouts that served them as windows—and as reminders of their labor— was never recorded.

A report of 1782, summarizing the state of completion of each of the buildings four years after the start of production, did, however, note a series of deficiencies in Ledoux's plans for a happy community. In the coopery, for example, "it was noted that because of the smoke given off by the common chimney and the coldness of this big room, it seemed indispensable to build four individual chimneys for the coopers, that is one to each worker." [84] Yet this might increase the danger of fire, and so—the report concluded—perhaps the coopers should be moved into one of the salt workers' buildings, where they would be "housed, and therefore less exposed to harm." But the salt workers' building had its own problems stemming from "the dampness that reigns throughout this building; it was observed that all the rooms . . . were extremely damp and that the communal kitchen was uncomfortable as much because it was regularly full of smoke as from other inconveniences; it seemed necessary and indispensable to abandon this chimney and to construct eight individual fireplaces in the salt workers' rooms." [85] Thus was Ledoux's felicitous dream of a working community gathered around its hearth for the long *veillées* of winter dispersed by a smoking chimney.

THE REGIONAL ECONOMY

Sustaining the order and continuity of production in the Saline de Chaux was a wide-flung external economy of fuel, transport, materials, and labor. The single most important external resource for the *saline* was the Forest of Chaux; it was as a direct appendage of the forest that the saline could operate at all, burning in its furnaces some four thousand cords of wood fuel each year. [86] Of the twenty thousand hectares estimated to comprise the forest, twenty-two thousand acres had been set aside for the use of the *saline* in 1773. [87] But this royal appropriation of wood on behalf of the *salines* did not take place without opposition, such were the powerfully competitive interests all converging on the right to utilize the forest wood. The regulation of the various rights to wood in Franche-Comté had been undertaken in stages, each hotly disputed by proprietors, communities, artisans, entrepreneurs, or the Parlement de Besançon according to their different interests. Traditionally, communities had enjoyed rights to the forest for their firewood and construction timber, as well as for their stoves to cure cheese—the primary domestic industry of the region. Beyond this, the forest was used as a pasturage for beasts, and as a source of fuel for the furnaces of innumerable small artisan industries, iron forges, and the like. These rights had all come under regulation with the conquest of Franche-Comté in 1674 and with the subsequent application to the region in 1694 of Colbert's reformation of the forest laws of 1669. The administration of Eaux et Forêts, thus established, continued in effect until the Revolution: the cost of administration fell most heavily on the same communities whose rights were severely restricted by successive edicts of the forestry department. Pasturage rights and rights of *affouage,* by which firewood could be gathered, were consistently withdrawn from these communities in favor of the privileges of large landowners, who enjoyed the support of the Parlement of Besançon. Meanwhile, numerous communities saw their wood subject to the particular exploitation of local industries under royal decree—*salines,* saltpeter factories, forges—or even to the overriding demands of large neighboring towns, such as Besançon itself with its ever-expanding requirements for fire and construction wood. The resulting disputes were settled by two Commissions de Reformation, established in 1717 and 1726, which held inquiries and fixed rights of use for the different communities, confirming many rights of pasturage and rights to glean deadwood, but often suppressing any rights for building wood or firewood.[88]

Surrounded by numerous villages that had all traditionally enjoyed certain rights, the Forest of Chaux, the largest in Franche-Comté, was especially subject to these conflicts of interest. The Commission de Reformation of 1717 had entirely suppressed all rights for firewood and construction; this led to immediate complaints from the communities, who could not afford the high prices demanded by the different forges and richer merchants of Dôle. Even the reduced right to collect deadwood from November to February, allowed in 1730, was finally suspended in 1765.[89] The response was again immediate: the entire forest went into revolt. Peasants, charcoal burners, and artisans, disguised as women, entered the forest armed, chased away the royal forest guards, and appropriated good trees for themselves, establishing saw mills and regulating their own cuttings.[90] While this *revolte des desmo-iselles* was eventually suppressed by force, the Parlement of Besançon took the side of the peasants and petitioned the Contrôleur Général accordingly. The reinstatement of deadwood gleaning rights (in August 1766) did not end these conflicts however. For the Forest of Chaux was the most intensely exploited of the region: the best wood went automatically to the shipyards of Marseilles and to the royal artillery, floated down the Loüe and Doubs Rivers to the Saône, thence to Lyons and the Rhône, thence to the Mediterranean. Furthermore, the saltpeter factories used wood to fire the saltpeter and to manufacture gunpowder; their privileges of cutting and gleaning were strong and much abused. The innumerable iron forges, paper factories, glassworks and tile factories also used immense quantities of wood; as did the wood industry itself, which supplied building material to cities like Lyons, as well as many small *métiers du bois* scattered throughout the forest. But the consumption of wood by the *salines* made them perhaps the most hated of all the forest industries, and the most often named as the principal culprits in the continual exhaustion of supplies.[91]

After wood, the *saline* had most need of iron: for the fabrication of the *poëles* and their accoutrements, for binding the hollow fir water pipes, for encircling the casks of salt, for making tools, and so on. A number of forges—one, marked on the "Carte des environs de la Saline de Chaux" drawn up by Ledoux—the forge of Roche, existed in the area, all suitable candidates for supplier to the *saline.* But precisely where the Saline de Chaux bought its iron remains unknown. One source notes that Charles Fenouillet de Falbaire was the proprietor of a forge at nearby Quingey on the Loüe River that made cast iron for export to Switzerland; the same source also mentions the forge and furnace of Roche.[92] And where the Loüe River first emerged, a much larger forge, owned by the king and operated by a Fermier Général, Cabod, had been newly established in 1771 for the fabrication of high-quality iron bars, again exporting to Switzerland.[93] According to an Enquête of 1772: "The factory will be susceptible to expansion, its position is the most advantageous, both for wood and for its abundant supply of water, which allows twelve mills to turn all the time."[94] Holding the exploitation of the factory for twenty-nine years, the owner Cabod proposed to open a new road to the factory and to "construct a shed for coal and a dwelling for the blacksmiths" in exchange for the right to take wood for repairs from the neighboring forest. Perhaps the most elaborate establishment in the region, however, was the forge at Baigne, whose buildings for a long time were ascribed by local tradition to Ledoux. This forge had been set up by one Rochet; and it is known that in 1756 an Edme Rochet had been engaged for six years to furnish to the brothers Bouchet all the iron necessary for the Salines de Salins and Montmorot.[95]

Such forges, while they did not themselves employ many internal workers (five workers for an *haut-furneaux,* or blast-furnace, and ten to twenty for a forge), were as dependent as the *salines* on external labor: in the area of Dôle alone a thousand carters a day were employed in the forges; while the forge of Perreciot employed some forty-five families (in all, approximately four hundred persons, including women and children, were needed to cut the wood, maintain the factory, care for the horses, and transport the materials).[96]

For the *salines* in particular, the management of this "veritable civilization of the woods" was critical to efficient production: inevitably, to ensure a continuous supply of wood for the furnaces, of charcoal for the blacksmiths' forges, of building materials and supplies, entrepreneurs were forced to control not only the forest, but the society of the woods itself: woodcutters, charcoal burners, sawyers, carpenters, carters, and the like. To cut the vast amount of wood demanded by the *salines* required a great number of woodcutters—approximately five hundred were estimated to work in the Forest of Chaux alone. To cart the wood to the *salines* and to distribute the salt produced there to the regional warehouses demanded an equally large number of carters. At Salins some one hundred fifty carts arrived and departed each day. It was not unusual for a *saline* to employ well over a thousand laborers in these external tasks.[97] Side by side with the woodcutters in the forest worked the charcoal burners—preparing a fuel increasingly used for its economy and slow rate of burning. The charcoal burners were either independent,

selling their charcoal in small quantities to the entrepreneur's middlemen, or contracted to furnish a fixed amount and paid by the batch.

Together, the woodcutters and charcoal burners represented an uncertain, often dangerous and unmanageable society, subject to no law but their own, to the continual irritation of entrepreneurs who needed to ensure a constant supply of fuel. The charcoal burners were well known for their wild and independent life in the woods.[98] They gained a reputation for what one ironmaster termed an "intolerable independence": "At the least appearance of authority they gather together with the woodcutters and leave the woods if not given [the price] they ask for."[99] Banded in confederations for many centuries, the independence of the charcoal burners was "intolerable" only for those who wished to control their product at a fixed price.

The directors of the *salines* were ultimately responsible for supervising the rights to wood in the forests under their control. A system of inspectors, surveyors, and guards almost as complex as that which oversaw the production of salt within the *saline* was accordingly developed to provide for the smooth and well-ordered supply of goods and services, the export of salt, and the cutting of wood. Thus in the area of Salins, immediately under the royal Commissáire Général charged with administering and policing forests, roads, and rivers (a post instituted in 1724) there were a subdelegate, a lieutenant, a procurer for the king, his substitute, two *gardes-marteaux,* an engineer and director of works, a receiver of spices and fines, two land surveyors, a collector of fines, two general guards, and thirty-eight other individual forest guards.[100] Besides the two *veintres* housed in the *saline,* two more lived outside its walls to oversee the *ventres,* or wood cuttings.[101]

Networks of *allées* were established throughout the forest and elaborate precautions taken to forestall any unlicensed taking of wood, forest guards patrolling on foot and horseback day and night, tax officials recording the transport of all wood in the area. Between 1778 and 1780 the first physical division of this territory was carried out; *triages,* or enclosures in the forest for the wood, marked for cuttings, were established along new routes made through the forest. This *quadrillage* of the forest continued until the early nineteenth century: "The network of different roads, tracks, and paths, gradually improving the existing highways, with each side of an artery marked by Doric columns (from 1826), evokes the rational organization of an intense exploitation.[102]

THE PRODUCTION OF SALT

Two years after the first salt was drawn from the pans of the Saline de Chaux in October 1778, production had risen to approximately 35,000 to 40,000 hundredweights per year. It was never to rise above this figure in more than a century of production.[103] The hoped-for 60,000 hundredweights specified in the original contract with Monclar was never attained, a result of a combination of problems—of supply, equipment, and administration.

Problems in the supply of salt water emerged almost as soon as the buildings had been completed. François-Marie, Maréchal de Longeville, inspecting the pipeline, found that it was losing some 31,000 out of 162,000 litres each day of pumping. He outlined the probable causes of this enormous loss in a report submitted on 19 July 1780 to Claude-Antoine Valdée de Lessart, assistant to Jacques Necker, the new Contrôleur Général des Finances.[104] Having inspected the entire length of the aqueduct, de Longeville blamed not only the uneven movement of the pumps at Salins, but also the state of the pipes themselves, which were badly bored, made from inferior wood, unseasoned and ill jointed, and laid in uneven slope. The chief offender was the engineer Lebrun:

The building of the pipeline had been entrusted to M. Lebrun, whom the contractors had brought from Paris with them, and who was entirely unknown to me: I had reason to think they had chosen him for his distinct talents. Nevertheless the pipes were so badly positioned and caulked over the greater length of the pipeline that they had to be torn up in order to begin the work again.[105]

An iron pipe, he concluded, would in the end have been as, if not more, economical. In November Necker responded, appointing the architect and engineer Claude Bertrand—a prac-

Doric column marking the crossing of routes in the Forest of Chaux, 1827. Photograph by A. Vidler.

titioner in Besançon and former collaborator with Ledoux—
to undertake a full enquiry into the engineering works and to
recommend improvements.[106] In December Bertrand received a letter from Perronet, outlining his view of the matter: "They claim that M. Lebrun, who was charged with the
supervision of the pipeline, had acquitted himself very badly,
having preferred hunting and other dissipations."[107] Perronet
exonerated Ledoux entirely, and probably correctly, from any
responsibility in the faulty works:

*M. Ledoux claims to have had no part in the building of the pipe-
line, for which reason you should not at all be displeased with him
because of the faults in construction that you find there. He places
the whole blame, as I have already said, on the negligence of M.
Lebrun.*[108]

Repairs began almost immediately; but the canalization continued to preoccupy successive administrations over the next
century—not only the state of the pipes but for the equally
difficult problem of theft. Leaks made it easy for local residents to tap the pipeline; inadequate policing enabled the reservoir of the graduation building itself to become a source of
contraband salt. In 1812 a report mentioned "persons from
surrounding communes" stealing from the reservoir, and in
1815 two gendarmes were posted on night duty to prevent
bands of some three to four hundred locals, well equipped
with evaporation instruments and tools, from raiding the
graduation building.[109]

The Rendue of 1782—drawn up by the director of the
Saline de Chaux on the occasion of Monclar's forced resignation from the administration of the *saline* and its return to
the direct control of the Ferme Générale—described the
buildings as partially or totally completed.[110] From this report
and from the weekly and monthly Register of the Saline an
image can be constructed of the Saline de Chaux in operation,
working like other *salines,* confronting shortages of fuel, labor problems, changes in weather, equipment breakdowns.[111]
The grand statements from Ledoux relating architecture, its
rhetoric and plan, to society were here "dried out" and placed
in their appropriate perspective. Architecture, and the entire
apparatus of expression developed by Ledoux, took their
place as the natural backdrop to a rough and difficult
production.

When de Falbaire de Quingey, in his new position as
Inspecteur Général des Salines (confirmed in May 1782), visited the Saline de Chaux in 1787, he found it working well, if
only at a reduced level of production. He was especially im-
pressed by the magnificent buildings. Their aesthetic appeared correct to a former playwright and poet:

*The eye easily comprehends its symmetry and different decorations,
which would have been still more complete if reasons of economy had
not prevented the building of the two domes with which the entry
gate and the Director's Building should have been crowned.*[112]

He was evidently referring to Ledoux's project for a domed
rather than a mansarded pavilion, presented in the idealized
engravings of the later 1780s. De Falbaire's aesthetic judgment was echoed after the Revolution by another visitor, Léquinio de Kerblay, who, in his two-volume *Voyage pittoresque
et physico-économique dans le Jura,* defended the "very modern"
architecture of the *saline* from its critics. While it had been
reproached with excessive massiveness, such *solidité* was, he
felt, entirely appropriate: "One cannot have too much massiveness in public buildings."[113] He immediately recognized
the affinity of the style to that of the *barrières* of Paris, and in
this respect considered the buildings overdecorated, "an imitation of the savage, a depiction of the natural rock in the
entry gate, like the entirely new antiquities they build in
Paris, or the small gardens in the English manner." The gate
was "bizarre," a ridiculous imitation of real nature, a "miniature" of the actual mountains surrounding Arc and Senans.
The columns of the Director's Building, like the *barrières* of
Enfer and Chaillot, were primitive also: "The first column,"
observed Léquinio, "was no doubt the tree against which a
savage leaned the first shelter."[114] But despite this unwonted
primitivism, the factory was to be considered a "superb establishment" that brought honor to France as well as to its
designer.

But the debate over the Saline de Chaux in the Revolutionary period was influenced by more than the personal ar-

chitectural taste of its visitors: the related questions of salt, of the *gabelle,* and of the *salines* themselves were, as was to be expected, hotly discussed from the very beginning of the Revolution.[115] Proposals ranged from the complete suppression of the factories, together with the taxes and the entire apparatus of the Fermiers Généraux, to the reform of individual manufactures, to the reuse of the plants for different purposes. An anonymous pamphlet that appeared in 1790, defending the Ferme, was immediately attacked by (Simon Vuillier, Deputy for the Jura).[116] He urged the immediate closing of the *salines* of Franche-Comté and Lorraine: "What can be done with the buildings of the *salines*? One will install superb factories in them, where the workers will be more usefully employed than in consuming precious wood as pure loss; and the salt waters could be put to other uses."[117] The idea of turning over the *salines* to other functions was followed through in the specific context of the Saline de Chaux by the prefect, Jean Debry, in an article on the commerce and industry of the Département du Doubs published in 1805.[118] He admitted the remarkable nature of the buildings, but pointed out that the return on the manufacture of salt was far from paying for the costs of construction, much less the daily upkeep of the factory. Accordingly, he proposed a new use for the double factory sheds, whose site, in the fertile plain "ouverte à toutes les communications," was perfect for manufacturing of all kinds: "One could usefully set up there a factory for printed fabrics; that portion of the Department called 'the mountain' offers many resources for such an undertaking."[119]

A more serious assessment of the productivity of the *salines* was provided by the special envoy of the Comité de Salut Public, Pierre-François Nicolas, in his meticulous report published in 1795.[120] Nicolas, who as a professor of chemistry in Nancy had written on the proper dietary habits for the newlyborn and, more professionally, on the chemistry of minerals in Lorraine in the 1770s, was fully qualified to review all aspects of the manufacture of salt—social, political, and technical. By 1794 he was already a professor of chemistry and natural history at the Ecole Centrale of the Département du Meurthe and a nonresident associate of the Institute

National. A response to the near cessation of production in 1794, when the war with European powers and the corresponding requisitions had slowed the transport of wood fuel to a standstill, his *Mémoire sur les salines de la République* carefully discussed the nature, sources, and processes of salt production, factory by factory, testing the order and duration of boilings, recommending purification procedures, and analyzing the chemical constitution of the product and by-products. His depiction of the Saline de Chaux, at which he carried out many of his experiments, included a breakdown of the operation of the three pumps supplying the *saline* with the overspill from Salins and an estimate of their average efficiency, as well as a chemical analysis of the three types of salt manufactured. The *saline* was, he remarked, "the most beautiful, without contradiction, in the Republic, as much for its agreeable site as for the magnificence of its buildings." And while the workings of the factory were, for the most part, similar to those of the other *salines* of the region, Nicolas observed that they were better ordered:

I observed that everything was carried out there with more cohesion and order, that the operations are more carefully conducted, and that the furnaces hardly lose any of their heat from the attention constantly paid to their maintenance in good working order. . . . The smithy is also much better organized, the boiling pans better maintained.[121]

But of the techniques of graduation at Arc, he offered no such praise: the operators had no knowledge of the principles of this valuable process, thinking only that they had to run water over the thorns, without regard to the direction of the winds or the efficient working of the taps. He similarly criticized the form of the furnaces and *poëles* and rejected the beating of the pans after evaporation as too harmful to the iron. Like Trudaine de Montigny, Nicolas was suspicious of the salt dried into cakes for storage and export: compressed with the partially evaporated water, it contained many of the same impurities:

Truly against the health of the citizens, it is equally against the interests of the Republic; it costs, for the salines of Salins and of

Arc, more than fifty thousand francs per year, in fuel and labor; and why? I ask the question: to maintain a prejudice as dangerous for men as it is expensive for the nation. I thus supported the suppression of salt in cakes.[122]

Of the two other forms of salt manufactured at Chaux, he found the slowly boiled large-grain salt the purest, and the quickly evaporated small-grain salt less free of foreign materials. As in the other *salines* of the Republic, that of Chaux used the by-products of evaporation—the so-called *schelot*—for the manufacture of glauber salts.

Nicolas's report was filled with practical measures by which to resume a more efficient production. A serious proposal was tendered to the German expert the Comte de Beust and a group of outside financiers to take over the operation of the *salines;* but their demand for a thirty-year lease was turned down in favor of a group of French investors headed by Catoire and Duquesnoy. The battle for control of the *salines* was opposed violently in the Assembly, however; and not until 1806—the year of Ledoux's death—was a new company, the Compagnie des Salines de l'Est, established and given the right to exploitation.[123]

Proposals for the further development of the factory continued throughout the nineteenth century. When, in 1843, the retired administrative director of the old Salines de l'Est, Jean-Marie Grimaldi, bought the Saline de Chaux for 321,270 francs on behalf of the Court of Spain, he immediately hired an architect to draw up plans for expanding production through the addition of twenty-three new *poëles* in the workers' buildings. Grimaldi, who seems to have run the *salines* of Montmorot, Salins, and Arc with a benevolence worthy of a Jean-Baptiste Godin, failed to raise production in this way, but nevertheless made his fortune out of salt, founding the thermal baths of Salins in 1853 and becoming the town's mayor in 1868.[124]

The history of the manufacturing life of the Saline de Chaux ended appropriately enough with a final legal complaint brought in 1894 by the inhabitants of Arc against the *saline,* opposing the pollution of their wells by the seepage of salt waters. The actual closure of the *saline* took place over a period of years, between 1895 and 1908, by which time the buildings were simply used as storerooms. The registers of the 1890s, recording the inevitable competition of the railroad (which still runs beside the factory today), state: "fabrication réduite." [125]

Ledoux, Director's Building (*top*) and salt workers' building (*center*), state before 1918. Photographs from the Archives Départementales du Jura.

Carved waterspouts, Saline de Salins, emblems from destroyed eighteenth-century factory shed, mounted back-to-back in imitation of Ledoux's project for the House of the Surveyors of the Loüe River.

Institutions of Public Order
1780–1789

The character of monuments, like their nature, sustains the propagation and purification of morals. There, theaters are built, following the progressive form that equalizes mankind; here are triumphal arches to deify it; further away are cemeteries that swallow it up. Laws come to the aid of morals: the enlightened temple of justice forms a salutary contrast to the dark lairs of crime. (3)

THE EMBELLISHED CITY

Between 1775 and 1789, from the laying of the foundation stone of the Saline de Chaux to the outbreak of the Revolution, Ledoux, despite numerous setbacks, real or imagined, developed one of the more brilliant and successful practices of the last years of the *ancien régime*.[1] While continuing to expand his patronage for *hôtels* and housing in Paris and the provinces, he devoted equal attention to public commissions. Supported until the end by the Ferme Générale, in the late 1770s he built a new salt warehouse for the administration at Compiègne and in 1783 began the construction of a large office building for its headquarters in Paris, the Hôtel des Fermes. Turning the friendship of Trudaine to good account, he obtained introductions to provincial intendants who recommended him for commissions: in 1775 the Intendant of Franche-Comté, Charles-André de Lacoré, called him to Besançon to design the new theater, finally completed in 1784; in 1776 the Governor of Provence asked him to prepare a report on the condition of the old Palais Comtale of Aix-en-Provence, a request that led to a series of designs for the new Palais de Justice and prisons for Aix between 1778 and 1784, the final versions of which were in construction by the Revolution. His work at Aix also enabled Ledoux to negotiate with competing land speculators for the commission to build the new theater at Marseilles. In 1776, Frederick II, Landgrave of Hesse-Cassel, invited him to Cassel, where he designed a triumphal arch, redesigned the royal library and museum, and projected grand plans for a royal palace.[2] Also outside France, some seven years later, he was asked to provide designs for the Hôtel de Ville of Neuchâtel.[3] Following opportunities presented by the institutional politics of Paris, Ledoux submitted two designs for a Discount Bank to successive Contrôleurs Generaux, Jacques Necker and Charles-Alexandre Calonne; he also proposed plans for a Market in the rue Saint Denis and a new cemetery for the city. Finally, from 1784 to 1787, Calonne and the Ferme engaged Ledoux to build a new tax wall around Paris, together with its attendant boulevards and *barrières*. The *barrières*, conceived as monumental entries to the city, were almost all completed before the Revolution, amid heated controversy and despite Ledoux's own dismissal from the work.

During these years Ledoux found his place in Parisian society. Recovering easily from a temporary loss of patronage following the disgrace of Madame du Barry and the fall of the Tugot-Trudaine administration two years later, he used his position as a favored architect of the Ferme and a member of Mlle Guimard's salon and of the Marquis de Montesquiou's circle to extend his friendships in the arts and to reinforce his practice. Connections to the musical and theatrical societies of the court, Paris, and the provinces not only sustained his reputation as an architect of theaters, but furthermore brought him into touch with the latest debates over the nature of theatricality and the shape of auditoria. Hubert Robert, painter of ruins and picturesque landscapes, and the Abbé Delille, poet of gardens and translator of Virgil, introduced him to the aesthetics of landscape and the poetics of agrarian improvement. Antiquarians like David Le Roy, lecturing at the Académie from 1774, expanded the repertory of classical precedents from the French bias of his predecessor Blondel to include a wider range of Roman, Greek, and Gallo-Roman models.

Sharing in the sociability of this milieu, Ledoux found support for an architecture with pretensions to social as well as aesthetic reform. What, in the late 1750s, had been the isolated demands of a few *philosophes* and critics for the "embellishment" of Paris had become, twenty years later, a commonplace of administrative and intellectual concern: the demand for the city—its streets, squares, and public monuments—to be renewed according to the latest principles of hygiene, circulation, and institutional planning.[4] To Pierre Patte, whose *Mémoires sur les objets les plus importants de l'architecture* was published in 1769, this implied not simply the

planting of trees, the decoration of public façades, and the cutting of new avenues, but also a more or less systematic reordering of the urban fabric: the development of a network of new routes for road and water traffic; scientific proposals for water supply, street lighting, and fire protection; the ventilation of the city for hygiene and the resiting of cemeteries, slaughter houses, hospitals, and prisons; the building of new markets; and, finally, the examination of all the institutions of education, justice, and poor relief to determine their proper programs and forms.[5]

Contributing to this movement were numerous scientists, doctors, lawyers, and administrators, as well as architects and engineers, often pressed into service by royal commissions or academic enquiries. The long-debated question of the renovation or replacement of the Paris Hôtel-Dieu after the fire of 1772; the enquiries into the state of the prisons, emulating those launched by John Howard in England and Europe; the designs and plans for new cemeteries were all products of this increasing concern for public health and social order. Images of reform found their way into journalists' accounts of present conditions and philosophers' visions of future utopias; Sébastien Mercier's popular novel *L'an 2240* of 1775 brought both of these levels together. Here, as in Laugier's *Observations sur l'architecture* of 1765 and in the Abbé Lubersac's *Discours sur les monuments publics* of 1775, a picture emerged of the *philosophe*'s ideal new city. It would, borrowing Laugier's imagery, take on the aspect of a hunting park, with the boulevards taking on the aspect of forest *allées*, the public squares of *rond-points*. As redesigned it would become a "natural" artifact, serviced by fountains and ventilated by fresh breezes. In this quasi-Physiocratic image, the important monuments of display, representation, pleasure, social welfare, and public order would be scattered throughout the "forest-city," set in clearings of their own as if in a landscape garden; tree-lined *cordons sanitaires* would surround the hospitals, cemeteries, and prisons to protect the population from infection, biological or social. This *ville verte,* policed, lit, serviced, and cleaned, would by implication shelter a society itself newly moralized by the combined effects of environment and instruction, health and institutional coercion.

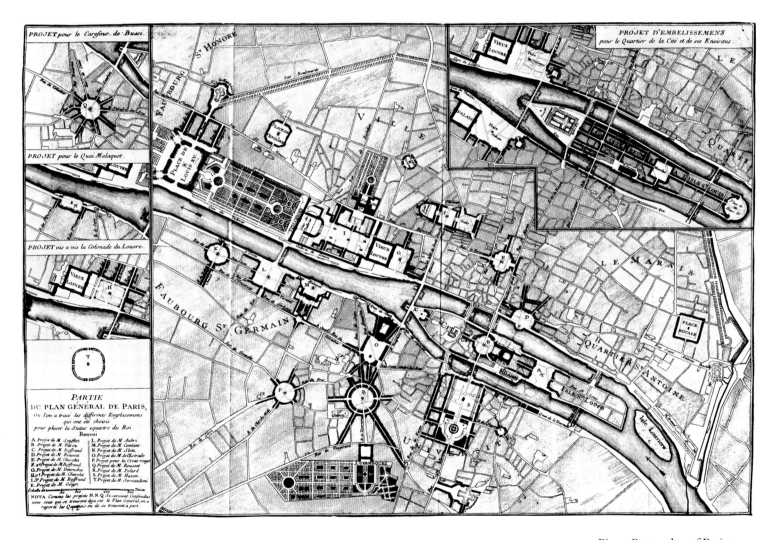

Pierre Patte, plan of Paris showing proposals for the siting of a monument to Louis XV, 1765. Engraving from Pierre Patte, *Monuments érigés en France à la gloire de Louis XV* (Paris, 1765).

From 1783, Ledoux gained support for his own contributions to this urbanistic reform movement from the new Contrôleur Général, Charles-Alexandre Calonne, his almost exact contemporary and also a former student of the Collège de Beauvais.[6] Appointed in October 1783 from the Intendence of Lille, Calonne had promised a fiscal regime dedicated to expansion in investment, industry, and trade and had, as well, shown an apparently unbounded optimism for social and political reform. His enthusiasm for public projects of every kind was infectious: from the development of agriculture to the opening up of roads, waterways, and ports, to the undertaking of larger urban reconstructions, Calonne demonstrated his commitment to an enlightened program of technocratic advance. Urban improvements were initiated at Bordeaux, Lyons, and Marseilles; the port of Cherbourg was opened by the king in 1786; the Canal du Centre and the Canal de Bourgogne were completed; trading companies like the Compagnie des Indes Orientales were revived. Physiocrats were employed in the Bureau de Commerce under the leadership of the economist Pierre-Samuel Du Pont de Nemours; another Physiocratic economist, Gérard de Rayneval, concluded a trade treaty with England, lowering the customs duties on industrial and agricultural products. Calonne, in emulation of English precedent, supported large-scale industrial developments in the eastern provinces, notably at Le Creusot. In Paris, he drew up legislation for removing houses and shops from the bridges across the Seine and for regulating the height of new development in relation to the width of the streets. Ledoux, who owed Calonne the commissions at Aix, the contract for the tax wall and *barrières* of the Ferme Générale, and the program for the design of a Cannon Foundry (perhaps conceived in relation to the new factories at Indret and Le Creusot) listed his mentor's achievements in an *éloge* that equaled those he accorded to Trudaine and the Abbé Delille:

The suppression of the guinguettes, *the construction of eight monuments for the recreation of the people.*
The enlargement of the market, its new exits and entrances, under the ministry of M. the Baron de Breteuil, who loved the arts

The new boulevards.
The discovery of the amphitheater of Nîmes.
The Propylaea of Paris.
He caused grain to be distributed to the farmers.
He established pension funds.
He helped the hospitals.
He had the courage to attack the financial regulations in order to impose equal taxation and to provide greater relief for the industrious class. How many ministers does one know who work for the public good with the certainty of losing their position? (177).

Three of these projects—the suppression of the *guinguettes,* or taverns, and the construction of eight state-run cabarets; the building of the new boulevards; and the erection of the "Propylaea," or *barrières,* of Paris—would be confided to Ledoux and represented Calonne's attempt, from 1784 on, to redefine the edges of the city, socially, commercially, and economically. The social question of the *banlieue,* with its shifting but growing population of indigent, criminal, and out-of-work poor, would thereby be addressed by a paternalistic control of their centers of recreation; the problem of transportation through an already obstructed Paris would be solved by wide, peripheral ring roads; the finances of the *ancien régime* would be shored up by the increased tax revenues of the Ferme. For Ledoux, these commissions represented the culmination of his urban architecture: the opportunity virtually to redesign the capital from the outside.

ACADEMIC PROGRAMS

Of all the circles to which Ledoux belonged, that which gave him the most theoretical and practical support in the development of his public architecture was undoubtedly the Académie Royale d'Architecture. Ledoux had aspired to membership since the late 1760s, applying unsuccessfully in 1767 with a summary of his first commissions that hardly convinced the director, the Marquis de Marigny.[7] But, with the ascendancy of Madame du Barry and the unseating of Marigny, who as Madame de Pompadour's younger brother represented the political opposition, Ledoux was more favored.[8] The Abbé Terray, a pliable ally of du Barry who for a brief interregnum succeeded Marigny as Directeur Générale des Bâtiments, was willing to press Ledoux's case. A critic of Terray described the ensuing, transparent maneuver:

He [Terray] has recently acted with zeal in favor of M. Ledoux, architect [of Madame du Barry]. This young man was known for different works of taste, nobility, and imagination, which, however, sometimes lack wisdom and good sense. Consequently he was unable to gain a vacant place in the Académie de l'Architecture in his own right, since there were many older architects [eligible] no less distinguished. M. le Directeur des Bâtiments wrote to the company that Madame du Barry wanted Ledoux to be elected, and he was. [9]

In August 1773, Ledoux's name had been submitted, together with those of Jacques Gondouin and four others; on 6 September he had been accepted for nomination, and on 15 November he was finally received by Terray himself at the minister's own installation ceremony. [10] Ledoux was to be joined at the Académie by Gondouin in 1774, Pierre-Adrien Pâris in 1780, and Alexandre-Théodore Brongniart in 1781.

At the time of Ledoux's admission as Architecte du Roi and second-class member of the Académie, the members, under their director, the elderly Jacques-Ange Gabriel, included, from the older generation, Jacques-Germain Soufflot and Jean-Rodolphe Perronet; among the teachers and theoreticians, Etienne-Louis Boullée and David Le Roy; and, among Ledoux's immediate peers, Jean-François Chalgrin, Marie-Joseph Peyre, and Charles De Wailly. They met regularly each month to discuss—according to the original statutes of 1671—matters of theory and judgments of taste and practicality in projects submitted for their approval and to set the programs for the prize competitions, the monthly *prix d'émulation* and the annual Grand Prix. Ledoux attended meetings initially and, after an interlude in the late 1770s that reflected his growing practice, from 1782, as assiduously as did any of his colleagues, sustaining an average of seven meetings a year until the Revolution.

While a reading of the *procès-verbaux* reveals a lessening of attention toward theoretical debates and historical issues and an increased concern with the business of running the Académie compared with the last decades of the previous century, it is clear that many of Ledoux's theoretical positions were derived from discussions among the academicians, notably with Le Roy and Boullée. Ledoux, whose aesthetic predilections were never static, found in the debates over the sensationalist theories of Nicolas Le Camus de Mézières and, no doubt, in the text of Boullée's own unpublished *Architecture*, reportedly known to a wide circle of friends before his death, a means of criticizing the received wisdom of Blondel and a basis for his own, idiosyncratic formulation of character. [11]

Equally important for Ledoux's definition of a public style were the programs set for the *prix d'émulation* and the Grand Prix competitions. Though still reflecting traditional academic concerns in their choice of subject matter, these competitions gradually responded to more public issues in the late 1770s and 1780s, replying to, and often implicitly correcting, current debates over the form of new institutions. A recent study by Pérouse de Montclos has underlined this pattern, hitherto obscured by the lack of a comprehensive list of prize program subjects. [12] Thus, the program for an Halle au Blé, set in 1764, was suggested by Le Camus's building campaign of the previous year; likewise, the program for an Hôtel de Ville of 1765 took note of the purchase by the city of Paris of a site previously occupied by the Hôtel de Conti. The program for the Salle de Comédie of 1768 was inspired by the designs of Peyre and De Wailly for the Théâtre-Français, that of the Hospice of 1773 by the fire at the Hôtel-Dieu a year before, that of the Ecoles de Médecine of 1775 by Gondouin's building of 1769, and that of the Palais de Justice of 1782 by the renovation of the Palais de Justice of Paris after 1776. Ledoux himself seems to have taken many of these subjects as excuses for designs, much in the same way as Boullée, who not only dominated their framing and choice in the Académie, but also prepared ideal "solutions" beforehand as a way of guiding his favorite students to correct entries. [13]

Two of Ledoux's commissions showed the influence of these programs: the Theater of Besançon, influenced by the Salle de Spectacle set in 1775 (when Pierre Fournerat, Ledoux's student, won the prize with a design that in many respects followed that of Ledoux), and the prisons at Aix by the program for Prisons Publics in 1778. Many of his so-called ideal projects were similarly conceived: the Public Baths of Chaux by the program of 1774 on the same subject; the Cemetery of Chaux by the Grand Prix subject of 1785 for a Monument Sépulchral; the Public Market of Chaux by the *prix d'émulation* for an Halle in 1784; the Church of Chaux by the Grand Prix subject of 1781 for a Cathedral for a Capital City (an implicit criticism of Soufflot's Sainte-Geneviève, for which Louis Combes and Boullée also prepared designs); the project for the Stock Exchange by the competition for a Stock Exchange for a Maritime City of 1782 and 1786.[14]

ANTIQUE TYPOLOGIES

Ledoux's designs for public institutions before the Revolution can be seen to stand apart from the solutions accepted by his contemporaries on at least two levels. On the one hand, while incorporating criteria of hygiene and functionality into his discourse, he showed himself unwilling to follow the reductive geometries of those doctors, lawyers, and some architects who in the 1770s and 1780s proposed diagrammatic schemes for hospitals and prisons. Architecture, for Ledoux, as for another institutional architect, Bernard Poyet, still resided more in the classical tradition than in pure formal determinism. But equally, Ledoux sought to avoid a literal historicism, an overt revival of an archaeologically verified style; while there may have been echoes of Le Roy's Greece, of Wood's Balbec, and later of Pâris's Pompeii in Ledoux's work, these remained at the level of general allusions rather than precise quotations. Ledoux sought instead to define a genre of public building that was entirely modern in its form and reference. To this end he founded his conception of character on the double play of form and representation already noted in the Saline de Chaux: a three-dimensional distribution controlled by a geometry that referred to its role and historical source by abstraction, in a style that might be termed "generic classicism." Precise enough in identifying its influences for a particular meaning to be communicated, it partook of an overall discourse of geometry that welded together the often heterogeneous sources of Ledoux's inspiration. Thus, for Ledoux, the

unifying force of three-dimensional geometry allowed a form such as the cube subdivided into nine squares in each dimension to be at once a referential figure, a trace of Palladio, and a new geometrical type-form (the modern villa), without perceptible strain. A similar mechanism had permitted the alternating cubes and cylinders of the rusticated columns of the Director's Building to stand both for "Serlio" and for a microcosm of the geometries of the building as a whole.

Within the parameters of such abstraction, Ledoux was, as the Saline de Chaux had also demonstrated, entirely open to the use of historical precedent. From Blondel's lectures and more especially from Le Roy's publications of Greek monuments, Ledoux invented a "history" wholly available for contemporary use. In this respect Le Roy's presentation of Athens as both ruined and "restored," a site of picturesque fragments and a field for the ideal restitution of Greek types, gave Ledoux a model that was both semantic and structural. Ruins, as Diderot had noted in his appreciation of Hubert Robert's paintings, showed the past, as it were, analytically, broken down into its component parts, the signs of ancient culture just as skeletons were the signs of once-living beings; complete building types, on the other hand, were the crystallization of social institutions in architectural form, models of social structure in spatial distribution. Ruins and fragments might act like hieroglyphs or pictograms to identify and signify an already lived culture; building types brought together and "constructed" different functions in typical patterns. The play between the fragmented ruin and the restored type was evident in Le Roy's engravings; the two were united in his composite plates that showed building types arranged in historical and comparative order, demonstrating, so to speak, the "descent" of types from their origins to the present. In these plates, as in Ledoux's public monuments, figurative devices and formal structures were joined by geometries to create buildings at once historically allusive and generically typical.

Ledoux's antique allusions were not, however, solely derived from Greek and Roman sources; his widening travels in France had introduced him to the scattered remains of Gallo-Roman culture, ruins that were gaining increasing at-

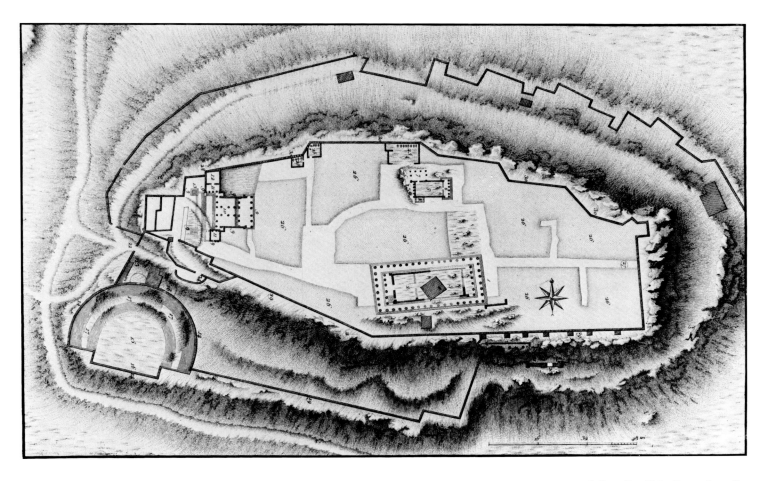

Julien-David Le Roy, plan of
the citadel of Athens, 1758.
Engraving from Julien-David
Le Roy, *Les ruines des plus
beaux monuments de la Grèce*
(Paris, 1758; 2d ed., 1770),
vol. 1, pl. 3.

tention from scholars, from the Président de Brosses to Charles-Louis Clérisseau, concerned to build a history of original classicism for France itself. For Ledoux, these signs of Roman grandeur on French soil gave an immediacy to the notion of antiquity that, without the experience of the obligatory grand tour, seemed remote when communicated by academic treatises. In Franche-Comté he had found the remains of a prefeudal France and had taken them to authenticate his own antique allusions in the Saline de Chaux: the Porte Noire of Besançon, with its profusion of allegorical bas-reliefs, and the *saline* of Salins itself dating back to Roman times. In the Midi, following his visit to Aix in 1776, he had discovered a complete repertory of Roman types, almost miraculously preserved, in the amphitheaters, triumphal arches, and mauseolea of Nîmes, Arles, Orange, Saint-Rémy, Marseilles, and Aix itself. The "Ruins" at Sant-Rémy, in particular, seem to have provided elements of his future designs for Aix and the *barrières* of Paris. From these he developed a sense that his own, new monuments were taking their place within defined "regional" monumentality, one invested with the authority of a living history:

My imagination wanders, it is transported to those sumptuous monuments that transmit to posterity the power of the emperors, the grandeur of Charlemagne. Nothing can contain the torrent that carries it; it penetrates those vaults that distribute abundance . . . those caverns that conceal the treasures of the Caesars [the grottoes of Auxelles]. It is expanded by the trace of their conquests, by those arches that recall their victories [the arch of Besançon]. (73)

The landscape, urban and rural, thus became a literal field for monumental display, ancient and modern, local archaeology providing the sources of a modern monumentality.

The design for a triumphal arch presented to Frederick of Hesse-Cassel in 1776 demonstrated Ledoux's interest in the development of a modern heraldry out of this eclectic mix. While derived in part from the stern classical prototype of François Blondel's Porte Saint-German, and borrowing some of its decorative motifs from Fischer von Erlach's Karlskirche in Vienna, it also clearly referred to the Porte Noire of Besançon. Above all it was composed to be *legible*. Writing to the landgrave on his return to Paris in January 1776, Ledoux explained his decorative program:

It would be better to place bas-reliefs on the columns, either in a spiral as in Trajan's column, or in alternate lines of rustication, separating them by smooth panels that contrast with those that are decorated; by this means one could present the different characteristics of the life of the prince who is to be celebrated. One depicts his civil or heroic virtues, his alliances, his taste for the fine arts and the sciences, etc.[15]

The arch itself seemed to be cut from a smooth cube of stone, inset into which a highly decorated Serliana formed the passage, while, applied to the upper part, a classical frieze echoed tradition. In front, as in the Karlskirche, two freestanding "Trajan" columns represented the scenes in the life of the prince. All the decorative motifs were clearly framed, contrasting with the plain surfaces for better effect, according to

The Porte Noire, Besançon. Photograph by Editions A. and J. Picard.

Les ruines, Saint-Rémy, Provence. Engraving after C. Lamy, late eighteenth century, from the Bibliothèque Méjanes, Aix-en-Provence, Est. A26; photographs from Arch. Phot. Paris/SPADEM.

Fischer von Erlach, Church of Saint Charles Borromeo (Karlskirche), Vienna, front elevation. Engraving from Fischer von Erlach, *Entwurf einer historischen architektur,* pl. 113.

Ledoux, Triumphal arch, Cassel, 1776, section, elevation, and plan. Engraving by Sellier from the Bibliothèque d'Art et d'Archéologie, Université de Paris, Fol. Rés. 169, vol. 2.

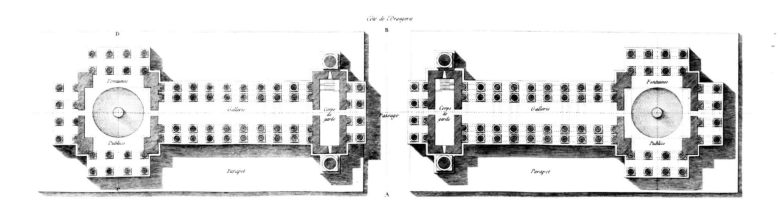

Ledoux's overriding maxim, previously stated for the Saline de Chaux: "Well-conceived decorations should be isolated, and cannot be dominated by any body that could be detrimental to them or constrain them" (12). In a design for a palace for the landgrave, probably engraved after the Revolution, Ledoux carried this principle further by reserving entire panels, such as the pediment formed by the gable roof, for a continuous bas-relief of a heroic triumph; this style of all-over decoration was to become a hallmark of Ledoux's later work, reappearing in the hunting lodge for the Prince de Bauffremont and in the Hosten Houses.

Ledoux's attempt to construct not only a decorative language but also a method of generating types was guided, however, less by the literal fragments depicted in the ruin fantasies of Piranesians like Hubert Robert—although the geometrical collages of Piranesi's Campo Marzio provided plan references for many individual buildings—than it was by the strict discipline of the nine-square Palladian grid. Ledoux's debt to Palladio, marked in his domestic work, was equally apparent in his public institutions. Palladio's "method" of controlling a limited repertory of classical motifs within a repeated geometrical schema, itself refined by proportional nuance, was abstracted and exploited by Ledoux in almost every design, from the first project of the Director's Building at Chaux to the final scheme of the Palais de Justice at Aix. Basilica and rotunda, the two dominant types adopted by Palladio, were alternated and combined in Ledoux's designs, while the centralized Villa Rotonda plan was transformed in every possible way.

THE RHETORIC OF CHARACTER

The word monument, *the idea that it expresses and the luxury or magnificence attached to it, is suited above all to those great establishments that enter first in line for the needs of peoples and which a strong instinct for decorum has called for art to impress with an external character to mark their importance and advertise their purpose to the spectator.*

Quatremère de Quincy, *Encyclopédie méthodique: Architecture,* vol. 2, 1 8 0 1.

In the development of his public style after the experience of the Saline de Chaux, Ledoux increasingly found the idea of character, as inherited from Boffrand and Blondel, entirely inadequate as a guide to the expression of and suitable form for the range of building types that he was called on to design. If the new institutions of public order and economic development were to be invested with the qualities of high architecture, then the traditional conventions and hierarchies of genre would have to be abandoned in favor of a language able to mark each of them, distinctively and unambiguously: "The character of the building should in no way be equivocal; the least knowledgeable spectator should be able to judge it" (119). Already in the *saline,* Ledoux had broken with the traditional ranking of *convenances,* insisting on elevating its architectural subject to that position previously occupied almost exclusively by palaces and churches. He had, as his later explanation revealed, also given the idea of characterization a determining role in the formation of his aesthetic, less in Blondel's terms as a proper framing for the decorative program, than as a totalizing force that controlled the internal form and the external expression of a building. For Ledoux, as for many of his contemporaries, characterization was synonymous with communication, a requirement on the part of the architect to search for an appropriate way of "speaking to the eyes." Boullée, indeed, defined character precisely in this way: "Let us cast our eyes on an object," he wrote in his *Architecture,* "the first sentiment we feel evidently stems from the way in which the object affects us. And I call 'character' the effects that results from this object and causes in us any impression whatever." [16] This shift from characterization by convention to characterization by sensation, from academic to empirical standards, was evidently based on the perception of nature as a source of powerful sensations and thereby as the origin of ideas, a notion derived from Locke through Condillac. Boullée stressed:

To embody character in a work is to use with efficacy all the means appropriate so as not to make us feel any other sensations than those than should result from the subject. To understand what I mean by character or the effect caused by different objects, let us consider the grand tableaux of nature and see how we are forced to express our-selves according to their action on our senses.[17]

Ledoux, as a reading of *L'architecture* suggests, subscribed to this ascription of character and its derivation from natural models. Here he agreed with Le Camus de Mézières as well as with Boullée, who both found in the imitation of natural scenes, from the darkest woods to the brightest meadows, a key to the generation of moods and passions in architecture; for them architecture was a kind of painterly art, joined to the idea of the sublime as developed in the late 1750s by Edmund Burke. For Ledoux character certainly encompassed such effects, as witnessed by his visions of the play of light and shade at the Saline de Chaux. But character in his understanding contributed further to a more cultural level of communication, where a building not only evoked fundamental sensations, but also was in some way a sign of its purpose. Natural character might reinforce conventional symbolism in Ledoux's architecture, but it would never remove the art from the social domain. Buildings, like natural beings, possessed their individual natures, and thence their own specific characters. As expressive of these, they became so many visual emblems, each signifying their purpose and role in society.

Indeed, such a criterion for expression held profound moral implications: "The character of monuments," wrote Ledoux, "like their nature, supports the propagation and purification of morals" (3). In this sense, Ledoux was echoing Rousseau's nostalgia for an original moral language, where social signs were presumably transparent to the things they signified, before, as Rousseau wrote, "art had fashioned our manners and taught our passions to speak an affected language." In such a time, "our morals were rustic but natural, and the difference between actions announced at first sight the difference among characters."[18] Such a utopia of characters, transparent to their appearance, where representation simply announced what it stood for without artifice, was joined in Ledoux with the idea that in this first Golden Age, language was in the first instance gestural, figural, and an immediate visual expression of the passions; "one speaks," Rousseau had put it, "better to the eyes than to the ears."[19] For Ledoux, as

for Rousseau, this sign language was perhaps the most energetic and forceful of all. Condillac, together with many of the Encyclopedists, was fascinated by the potentialities such a language would have for universal communication. It was an easy step to translate the burden of their arguments to other visual discourses, in particular those of painting and architecture. If a similar transparency could be attained between architecture and society as once operated between signs and society, buildings might regain the didactic role now restricted to written and spoken rhetoric. In Ledoux's conception, this would make of architecture a kind of moralizing stage set for guiding emotions and conduct. "Give us models that speak to the eyes; they will be more striking than precepts or those long-winded writings that weigh down and encumber the mind." (52)

This theoretical context helps to explain what Ledoux himself referred to as his "dramatic enthusiasm" (15), the "exalted" manner of speech that he argued was the proper style for the architect, and the equation of the forms of his art to the techniques of rhetoric:

Nothing is indifferent for the artist. When he conceives a grand project, everything that he brings together helps to elevate his thoughts and facilitate its execution; the detail that least strikes the ordinary man impresses on his soul a feeling that characterizes it. He sees in a plan that is apparently the least susceptible to development, everything that a stimulated imagination can create; he sees it aggrandized with traits that he draws from all the influences that surround it, in order to cover the needs of common life with a golden web; and if he deploys his powerful resources it is to animate a people of giants that he has drawn amidst the Lilliputians. (128)

Such a technique, known in rhetoric as amplification, operated not only to embellish a fact, but to transform it into a figure of speech or a trope. Ledoux spoke of this "figurative style" that he employed "relentlessly," and his urban and rural designs are infused with this belief in a form of architectural inspiration that confounded the building with its allegorical counterpart: "The house of a dancer presents itself as the temple of Terpsichore; the warehouse of a merchant develops the idea of the gardens of Zephyr and Flora" (16). In this light, all buildings should "speak" with a heightened emphasis of their nature, raising programs hitherto ignored by the architect to the level of art.

This emphasis on "elevation," both of the subject and of the style of the object, was, in rhetorical terms, naturally allied to the theory of the sublime—a term that, as inherited from the classical tradition, itself signified "elevated expression"—a theory that Ledoux, together with many of his generation, embraced and reformulated to dramatic effect.

THE PUBLIC SUBLIME

You will see that the only means allowed by the economy of art will lead you to the sublime. Establish fine masses, prepare happy contrasts, abandon the overrated affectations of timorous habit—those multiplied moldings, children born of blind fathers who have never savored the pleasure of light. (204)

Joining the idea of character to that of amplification was, as we have intimated, the notion of the sublime, a theme that became increasingly dominant in Ledoux's work in theory and in practice, from the building of the Saline de Chaux to his death. Announced at Chaux in the uniform geometry of the pyramidal composition and the funereal obscurity of the smoking factory sheds, in the symbolization of the Supreme Being in the diagonal ascent of the religious "mountain" and the hidden source of light in the chapel of the Director's Building, this aesthetic was elaborated at a number of levels in almost every one of his public designs thereafter. In this Ledoux went beyond the traditional idea of sublimity as a simple rhetorical category for high-flown speech, to register the increasing influence of theories based on Locke's empirical claims for the power of the sensations to generate ideas. Breaking with the concept of the sublime as propounded in the French classical tradition from Nicolas Boileau-Déspreaux to Jacques-François Blondel, Ledoux seems from early in his career to have been profoundly influenced by the writing of Edmund Burke: indeed, in the relatively small compass of the *saline* Ledoux had replicated, consciously or not, the roster of sublime effects described by Burke in his *Philosophical Enquiry into the Origin of Our Ideas of the Sublime*

and Beautiful, published in 1757 and 1759 and translated into French some six years later.[20]

Inherited from classical antiquity by way of the fragment attributed to Longinus, the term "sublime" as understood by seventeenth-century commentators was primarily a literary category applied, with rare exceptions, to writing, painting, and sculpture. Boileau, in the preface to his translation of Longinus, summarized and extended the idea in a way that was in the next century to be repeated as a commonplace:

It must be noted that by the sublime, Longinus does not only mean what orators call the sublime style, but rather whatever is extraordinary and marvelous that strikes one in a discourse, that causes a work to uplift, ravish, and transport. . . . One must therefore understand by the sublime in Longinus, the extraordinary, the surprising, and, as I have translated it, the marvelous in discourse.[21]

This somewhat idiosyncratic version of Longinus, while it seemed to many to privilege the "extraordinary" over the "high" style, nevertheless had the effect of expanding the range of the term's applicability; for it gradually came to take on the connotations, not only of a literary manner, but also of a form of experience, attributable both to the writer and to the objects that inspired such feelings in the first place. It was in this guise that the sublime was introduced to architectural theory. Most notably, Blondel recommended an "architecture of sublimity" as suitable for temples, basilicas, public buildings, and the tombs of great men—all monuments that acted to confirm their grand purposes by means of "grand lines." Paraphrasing Boileau almost to the letter, he defined the style as one that would "raise the mind of the observer, seize it, and astonish it."[22]

But the decisive intervention was that of Burke, popularized in France by Diderot, who after 1767 used many of Burke's concepts in his art criticism. Burke's understanding of the sublime radically extended that of Longinus and his classical interpreters, to make of it a fundamental principle of aesthetic perception founded on the psychology of sensation. Detaching the idea from any reference to tricks of style or rhetorical conceits, so much abhorred by the *philosophes,* Burke reduced it to a "single principle"—the effects of terror:

Whatever is fitted in any sort to excite the ideas of pain and danger, whatever is in any sort terrible, or is conversant about terrible objects, or operates in a manner analogous to terror, is a source of the sublime; that is, it is productive of the strongest emotion which the mind is capable of feeling.[23]

From the idea of the highest or grandest style, Burke moved to the absolute idea of the most powerful emotion, based on pain and its related sensations; such an emotion, far more powerful than mere pleasure, was founded on the horror that fear of pain evoked. Only in this way might the astonishment felt by man before the works of nature be explained. For a continuous chain of association worked from actual pain to anticipated or imagined pain; and horror and fear, in some way "apprehension of pain and death," worked on the mind analogously to real physical hurt. From these premises Burke developed a theory of cause and effect, listing all the possible objects in nature that might stimulate the mind to fear.

In this list of the causes of the sublime, architecture played a major and exemplary role. A building was, after all, experienced much in the same way as nature itself; the only difference between a cliff and a wall, a rock and a monument, was that of intention and self-conscious design. Thus Burke found his illustration for the general effect of obscurity and darkness in stimulating apprehension before the unknown in the primitive practice of darkening the temples to simulate the night:

Almost all the heathen temples were dark. Even in the barbarous temples of the Americans at this day, they keep their idol in a dark part of the hut, which is consecrated to his worship. For this purpose too the Druids performed all their ceremonies in the bosom of the darkest woods, and in the shade of the oldest and most spreading oaks.[24]

Darkness, confusion, uncertainty, all added to the sense of the sublime as necessarily connected to the practice of religious domination. Similarly, the imaginative experience of infinity, eternity, of supreme and unlimited power, such as might be ascribed to a deity, led inevitably to a feeling of the sublime. Thus impressions or experiences of vacuity, darkness, solitude, and silence, connected with a general feeling of deprivation; vastness in every dimension, height, breadth, length, and depth; magnificence and splendor; all these were sources of the sublime and might be stimulated equally by nature or architecture.

Burke specified in detail the techniques of stimulating the sublime, in a way that was for Ledoux, Boullée, and later generations of architects a prescription of the ready-made elements of an "institutional sublime" deployed in every building type worthy of the architect's attention. First was the effect of the "artificial infinite" to be produced by a combination of the succession and uniformity of the parts of the building. Whether exhibited in a rotunda, where no boundary interfered with the continuous turning of the eye and thence the imagination, or in a row of columns in a temple, basilica, or cathedral, where the "grand appearance" was created by the "range of uniform pillars on every side," Burke insisted on the need for absolute uniformity, in geometry or in the parts.[25] The similarity of each column to the next would, he argued, establish a cumulative effect, as opposed to the broken rhythm of alternating square and round columns or the rhythmless monotony of an entirely blank wall.[26] Beyond this were other effects to be sought: a grandeur of dimension, more a question of clever deceit than of real magnitude (Burke warned prophetically against the diminishing effect of overly large compositions); a sense of the difficulty encountered in attaining the effect, the great strength or labor required, exemplified for Burke by Stonehenge, with "its huge rude masses of stone, set on end and piled each on the other"; a feeling of magnificence, equivalent to that experienced at the sight of the starry heaven; a dramatic play of light and shade, with the emphasis on striking contrast; a color range that in buildings "where the highest degree of the sublime is intended" ought to tend toward "sad and fuscous colors, as black, or brown, or deep purple"; and, finally, an experience of absolutes, as in absolute darkness or absolute light, the *fiat lux* of Biblical creation.[27]

In the first years of his practice, Ledoux, while relishing the opportuniy provided by the factory to exploit all these devices, was more circumspect in his public monuments. Joining in some way Burke to Blondel, he developed a style that was both grand and simple. Emphasizing the simplicity afforded by the play of primary geometric solids and bare walls, relieved only by the contrast of severe but deeply carved bas-reliefs or rustication, Ledoux seemed to anticipate Kant's more nuanced relfections on the sublime in the 1790s, with his insistence on encompassing the simple and the reduced within the term. Gradually, in the 1780s, Ledoux began to explore other dimensions of the genre: in his generation of theatrical illusion, his contrast of the moods of enlightened justice and terrible punishment, the combinatorial gigantism of the *barrières* seemingly assembled by some cyclopean hand or ruined by a natural cataclysm. In the mid-eighties, beginning with the Cannon Foundry, designed as if it were some realm of the underworld, and culminating in the Cemetery, which intimated the absolute negation of life, Ledoux completed his repertory of sublime effects.

AN INSTITUTIONAL GENRE

What is suitable for the decoration of a factory, for the entry columns of a city (the Propylaea) does not aways accord with the severity that accompanies high architecture.(134)

Joining, in this way, a general sense of the sublime to an even more generalized historicism, Ledoux gradually developed an idiosyncratic genre, a specific style appropriate to that intermediate class of buildings, hitherto ambiguously defined in theory, public monuments. This "public genre," somewhere between the classical "high" and "low" manners, forged out of a combination of antique allusion and geometrical simplification, allowed Ledoux to retain the classical hierarchy of genres, from the palace to the private house, while expanding it to include subjects previously excluded from decorative treatment.

The hallmark of this style was, as we have suggested, simplicity: the reduction of the plan and massing of the building, expressed in combinations of geometrically defined volumes and surfaces, and the assimilation of the traditional forms of the orders and their decorative attributes within this abstracted geometry. Writing of the need to invent a new, geometric order for the Director's Building at Chaux, Ledoux stated the case for a genre that encompassed those tasks not generally accepted into the ranks of high architecture. As if extending Laugier's prescriptions for "buildings wherein one uses no architectural order," where the Jesuit theoretician had advised the exploration of "all the regular geometrical figures"[28] to supply the variety generally furnished by the orders, Ledoux proposed that the orders themselves be "reduced" to similar geometries:

All the forms that one describes with a single stroke of the compass are allowed by taste. The circle, the square, these are the alphabetic letters that authors employ in the texture of their best works. Out of them one creates epic poems, elegies; one hymns the gods and celebrates the shepherds; one builds temples to Valor, Strength, Voluptuousnes; one constructs houses and the most ignored buildings of the social order.(135)

Ledoux's public monumental style, a version of the primitive Roman or Tuscan vernacular favored during the same years by the painter Jacques-Louis David, here emerges as a decorous answer to programs that demanded architectural treatment without a proliferation of ornament or orders, and, at least in the context of these designs, seems to contradict the legend of a Ledoux scornful of the conventions of genre and hierarchies of *convenance*. Thus, writing of his design for the Public Baths, Ledoux pointed to his conscious avoidance of exterior decoration: "No apparent openings; no development; no trace of the interior distribution" (169), he noted, following Blondel and Laugier (who had demanded, criticizing Boffrand's portico to the Hôpital des Enfants Trouvés next to Nôtre Dame, that "the poor be housed as poor").[29]

The decoration of a building intended for the cure of contagious illnesses should be constrained by the humility of a use already de-

graded in public opinion and efface itself before the eyes from the fear of being seen; . . . this is no colossus whose proud head demands magnificence, but a pigmy who hides his poverty beneath the sheltering masses of the high trees, allowing only a glimpse of the entry that receives its sick. (169)

Elaborating on Laugier's suggestion that geometry alone might provide the effects lost by the suppression of the high orders, Ledoux outlined his theory of characterization for types serving public utility:

The decoration of a building should derive from the inspiration provided by its subject; its effect depends on the choice of pyramidal masses, the plane surfaces, contrasts that produce shadows. . . . Costly and useless openings should be avoided as well as cornices without a purpose, those accessories of fashion. Everything that is not indispensable tires the eyes, nullifies thought, and adds nothing to the whole. (169)

Such an economy of form, mustered in three-dimensional combinations that endowed his monuments with an interplay of dramatic spatial effects and powerful exterior massing, marked all Ledoux's public projects from the early 1780s. In the salt warehouse at Compiègne, designed sometime after 1775, the style that Ledoux had developed for the Fermiers Généraux, first advanced in the Saline de Chaux and gradually to be refined and extended as a generalized form of public representation, was codified and reduced to its component parts. Combining the functions of storage and judicial tribunal for the hearing of cases involving infractions against the Ferme, this structure was fronted by a giant semicircular arch on a rusticated base—an urban version of the proscenium of Besançon—with a pediment containing the royal arms above. This opened into a semicircular niche with a covered ceiling, like that in the façade of the Hôtel Guimard, from which the warehouse was entered on the first floor. Curved stairs led up to the registry and court room. This play of semicircles cleverly compensated for the angled site and accommodated the necessary shift in axis. The whole structure, which still exists, anticipated Ledoux's public style of the early 1780s—the Market, Baths, and Church of Chaux and

the Hôtel de Ville of Neuchâtel—with its banded rustication, simple geometries, and grand arched and pedimented orders.

The commission for the Hôtel de Ville of Neuchâtel, a canton under Prussian domination, was the result of a legacy left to the town by a wealthy merchant in April 1783.[30] A site was chosen the following month, and Ledoux, who apparently enjoyed some local notoriety—Geneviève Levallet-Haug has surmised as the reason the town's proximity to Besançon and Chaux, joined with the former patronage of the Swiss d'Hallwyl and Thélusson—was almost immediately asked to submit designs. His project, completed before the end of 1783, was, however, rejected in favor of one prepared by Pierre-Adrien Parîs in January 1784, the construction of which was completed by October 1787.[31]

Ledoux's design, engraved by Varin, took the form of a simple rectangular block freestanding in the town square. A base of horizontally banded rustication ran around the first floor, cut by simple arched openings. The walls above were plain, the windows clearly framed. The building was entered through an Ionic peristyle of six columns with a pediment and strongly carved mutules. This led, on the first floor, into the grand public gallery, a hall stretching almost the entire length of the building and given the aspect of some primitive basilica by two rows of squat, baseless Doric columns. This gallery opened at each end into circular vestibules and at the center to the formal stairs leading to the council chambers on the second floor. Above this, on the third floor, was the city arsenal, a large, atticlike hall set across the block on the central short axis and flanked by low arches on pilasters to either side. This double play of axes, major volumes on the first and third floors compensating each other by exploiting major and minor axes in turn, was to become typical of Ledoux's spatial treatment of public monuments.

This "public style," now fully formed, was returned to its origins, so to speak, in the same year, 1783, when Ledoux was asked to prepare designs for the central offices of the Ferme Général in Paris. The new Hôtel des Fermes was to replace the old Hôtel Ségnier on the rue de Grenelle, following the huge expansion and rationalization of the bureaucracy

Ledoux, Salt warehouse,
Compiègne, 1775, partial section and front elevation. Engraving from Ramée, *Ledoux,*
pl. 107.

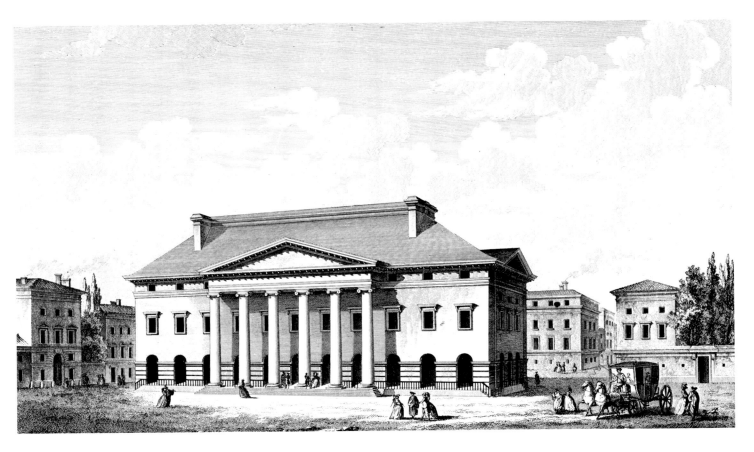

Ledoux, Hôtel de Ville, Neuchâtel, 1784, perspective view
and plan of first floor. Engravings by Varin from Ramée,
Ledoux, pls. 40, 37.

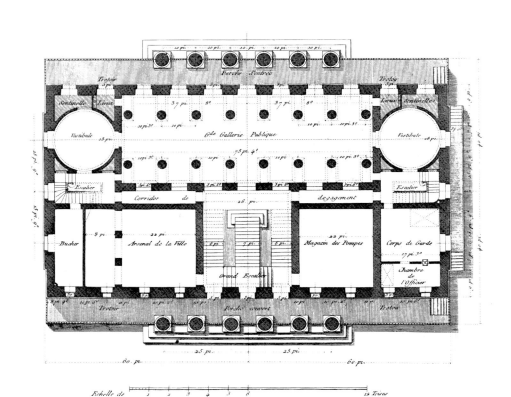

of the Ferme in the preceding decade. From the 1760s the Ferme had moved from a system whereby each *fermier* maintained his own administrative offices in his *hôtel* to a central administration in the rue de Grenelle in the Hôtels de Longueville and Bretonvilliers. The number of employees paid by the Ferme increased rapidly, until in the 1780s some 824 chief clerks, controllers, and inspectors, divided into four classes of offices, worked in the central building.[32] Bruno Fortier has pointed out the uniqueness of this "first great system of offices ever imagined and created in Paris," a system to which Ledoux responded by developing what must be one of the first type forms for the urban office building.[33] Ledoux took over the large site between the rue de Grenelle and the rue de Bouloir, deploying the offices around four square courtyards in blocks six stories high, the offices themselves systematically planned on single-loaded corridors to each side and double-loaded corridors in the central block. Ledoux gave over the western half of the building to the Ferme Générale and the eastern half to the customs officials. On the ground floor to the west, reached through an antechamber, were the offices of the receiver general and the offices of payment, banking, control, and dispatch; to the rear stood the chapel of the Ferme, aisled with a tribune at the mezzanine level. To the east, the customhouse included an office for the public receiver, offices of royal weights and measures, a library, sheds and warehouses for unclaimed, prohibited, and seized goods, and rooms for the firemen and guards. The courtyard of the customhouse was to be used for inspecting all the bales, packing cases, and chests intended for export. On the first floor, above the offices and apartments of the mezzanine, were the main salons and assembly rooms and the offices for the major officials—the chief clerks and underclerks. These, together with the four floors of offices above, were reached by a grand square stair at the center of the plan. Subsidiary stairs placed at the ends of each office block completed the circulation. The entire building was detailed in the same manner as the Hôtel de Ville of Neuchâtel, with rustication along the ground floor and mezzanine and with continuous arcades surrounding the courtyards; the only decorative relief was the frieze with triglyphs and the pyramidal stepping of the rusti-

cation over the entrances, as if to form a pediment composed of cyclopean blocks. This portion of the offices, already completed in 1787, was remarked on by Luc-Vincent Thiéry and Sebastien Mercier for its massivity and threatening character, entirely appropriate for its unpopular clients. Ledoux's evident attempt to express the power and security of the Ferme, while avoiding the sumptuary codes of church or state, was also noted by architects critical of the new emphasis on characterization. Viel de Saint Maux, ironical in his perplexity over the ambiguous style of this building, described this pediment as topped by a statue of Mercury.[34]

Other projects for public monuments of this period included a Market, the Maison de Commerce, between the rue Saint Denis and the rue Saint Lazare, a grand development taking up an entire block. Covered arcades and passages joined by stores cut through its center, forming a Greek cross; the corners of the block were taken up with pavilions containing four shops each. At the center, on the first floor, was a huge sale room. Greek cross in plan, double height, and lit from the sides, it was entered through Doric porticoes and surmounted by pedimented gables that led out to antechambers and terraces on the upper level. The perspective view of this development shows its abstract and strong geometries deployed as if in a Roman setting, with a temple, stoa, and fortifications in the background. While this project does not seem to have been built, J.-C. Krafft published a detail of the roof timbers, as projected by Ledoux, in his *Traité théorique et pratique sur l'art de la charpente* of 1819, entitled "Sections and elevations of a roof truss in the form of a vault, executed in planks with a gallery on each side formed by columns, built in the Maison de Commerce, rue Saint Lazare, Paris."[35]

Perhaps the most telling example of Ledoux's stylistic development in these years would be the comparison of the two projects for the Caisse d'Escompte, or national Discount Bank. The idea of such a bank had been launched in January 1767, under the finance ministry of Clément de l'Averdy, who established the bank with credit for ten years; the bank was to provide short-term credit for commercial operations by buying stock with its own capital on behalf of the company in question. But it was Turgot who authorized the es-

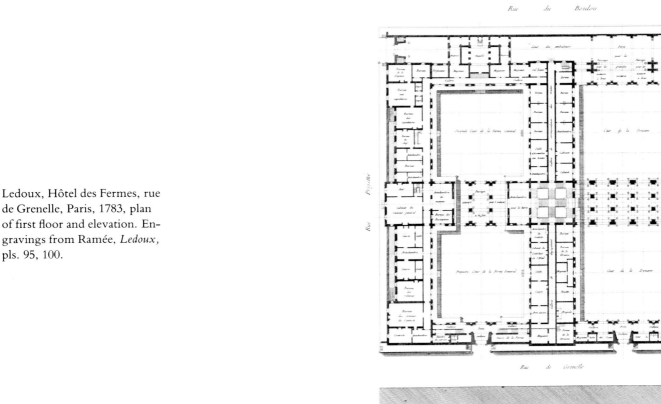

Ledoux, Hôtel des Fermes, rue de Grenelle, Paris, 1783, plan of first floor and elevation. Engravings from Ramée, *Ledoux*, pls. 95, 100.

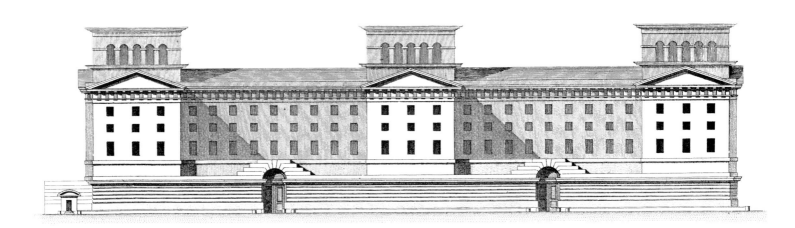

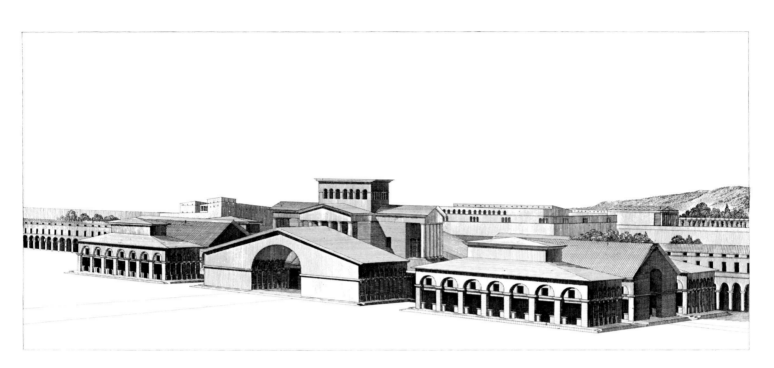

Ledoux, Project for a market
development on the rue Saint-
Denis, Paris, perspective
view. Engraving from Ramée,
Ledoux, pl. 225.

tablishment of the permanent institution on 24 March 1776,
just before his enforced resignation, and provisional quarters
were found in the Hôtel de Talaru, rue Vivienne. In 1777 the
bank began to issue its own notes and by 1783 had built up a
circulation of up to forty million livres; in the same year its
independence from the state was compromised by the Contrôleur Général, Fabre d'Ormesson, who ordered it to make
an advance to the treasury, and gradually under Calonne, who
extended credit for the bank, it was brought under state control. In 1785 Calonne opened a limited competition for its
design; Antoine, Brongniart, and Jalliers de Savault presented
projects. Ledoux—whose relations with successive ministers
of finance, from Turgot to Necker to Calonne, were established by his patronage by the Ferme—proposed two
schemes for a new building on a site, belonging to the banker
J.-J. de la Borde, between the rue d'Artois and the Chaussée
d'Antin. Stylistically they seem to belong to the period 1776–
82. Perhaps the first scheme corresponds to Turgot's initiative
of March 1776, the second to Calonne's.

In what seems to be his first scheme,[36] Ledoux proposed
to house the institution in a form of semipublic *hôtel,* according to the tradition of the time. The main *corps de logis* was
rectangular and two stories high. The bank was entered from
portes cochères at each side leading into a cavernous vestibule
vaulted with a coffered arch, like the proscenium of Besançon. The grand stair, lit from above by a skylight, turned the
visitor back toward the front of the building and thence,
through a sequence of anterooms, around to the rear and the
main assembly room. In this way Ledoux emphasized the security of the banking hall, a theme dramatically displayed on
the front elevation. There the giant Doric order and pedimented portico, which stood out two bays deep and continued the line of the cornice, were reached by steps that simply
stopped at the porch level, halfway between the first and second floors, allowing of no entry into the building and reinforcing the effect of closure presented by the blank two-story

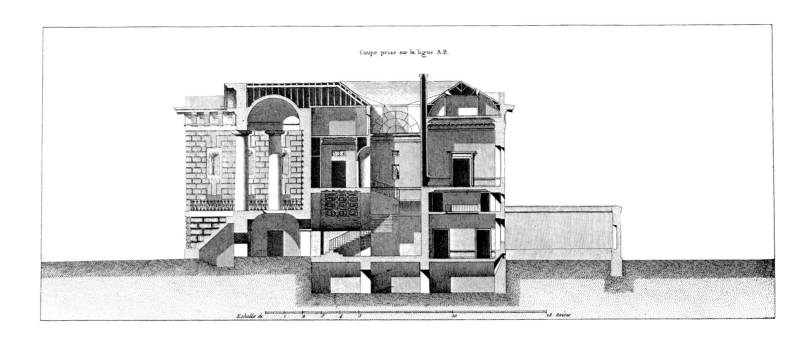

Coupe prise sur la ligne A.B.

Echelle de 1 2 3 4 5 10 15 toises

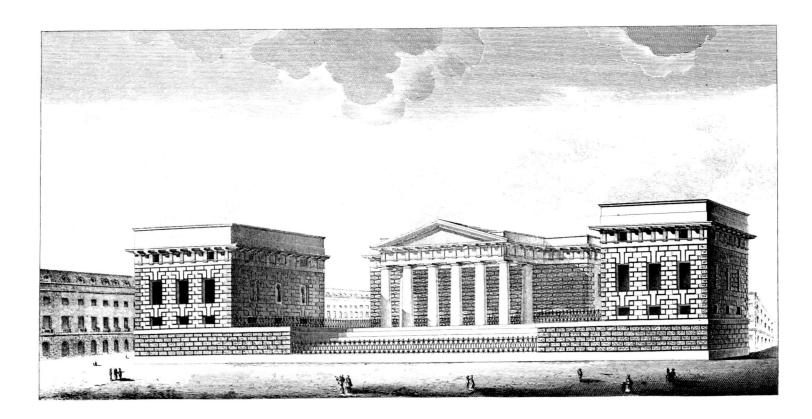

front wall. Entirely covered with diamond rustication, this façade represented the security afforded by the bank, a characterization supplemented by the heavily rusticated corner pavilions housing offices and marking the vehicular entries—entries that in the interests of a graphic display of closure are suppressed in Sellier's perspective engraving.

In the second scheme, perhaps Ledoux's entry to the competition proposed by Calonne, the bank became a building type in its own right, along the lines proposed by Brongniart and Antoine in the same years. A square, free standing "temple," the bank was surrounded by a continuous peristyle of unfluted, baseless Doric columns, as if emulating the Grecian stoas described by Le Roy. The body of the building was rusticated on the first floor, and the difference in height between the one-story banking halls and the central rotunda was masked by a blind fascia standing above the architrave, which created the impression of a two-story rectangular block. The center of the plan was taken up by a circular banking hall, covered with a Pantheonlike coffered dome, lit from above. A glazed gallery isolated this rotunda from the surrounding banking rooms, octagonal at the rear corners, oval to the front, and reached by diagonal passages from the main hall. Each of these, like Sir John Soane's individual rooms at the Bank of England in London, built some years later, was lit by individually shaped skylights. The whole building was represented standing isolated in a square surrounded by continuous arcades, as depicted in the project for the market on the rue Saint Denis. In this scheme Ledoux brought together all the elements of a new type, the bank, in a prescient formulation. Brongniart's scheme of 1785, with a similar rotunda and top-lit banking rooms, was at once more decorative and more of a hybrid between the great *hôtel* and the bank: the façade, rusticated on the first floor and at the corners, finished by a continuous frieze of consoles and embellished with a bas-relief, awkwardly attempted a characterization falling between a prison and a bank, while the section showed the dome of the entry hall standing half-above and half-below the attic.[37]

These two projects for the Discount Bank anticipated Ledoux's designs for the Stock Exchange, or Bourse, of Chaux. The first version, shown in the aerial perspective view of the town of Chaux standing next to the Public Baths, is templelike; its peristyle of columns and arched dormer remarkably anticipate the Saint Petersburg Bourse, built by one of Ledoux's students, Thomas de Thomon, in 1805. The second scheme, in the form of a square Ionic temple with pediment, raised on a stepped podium, idealizes the functions of an exchange. Brongniart proposed a similar temple for a combined exchange, Bank of France, Commercial Tribunal, and Sinking Fund Bank on the site of the Madeleine, using the Ionic peristyle of his first proposals for the Bourse of Paris in 1808.[38] Ledoux's temple, with its porticoes three columns deep surrounding a central, square banking hall rising from the first floor and open beneath the roof of the colonnade, merges the idea of the temple with that of a treasury, endowing the operations of commerce with an aura of antique morality.

Ledoux, Discount Bank, rue d'Artois, Paris, first project, section and perspective view. Engraving by Sellier from Ramée, *Ledoux,* pl. 102.

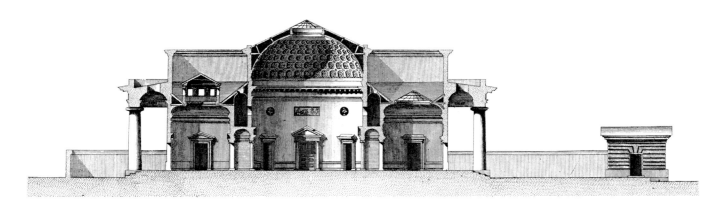

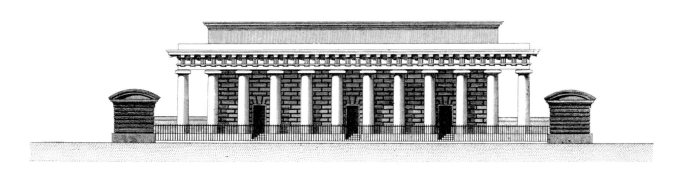

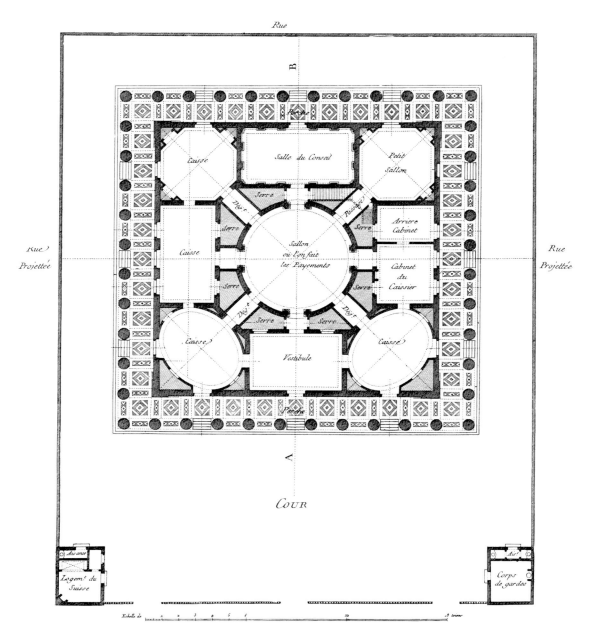

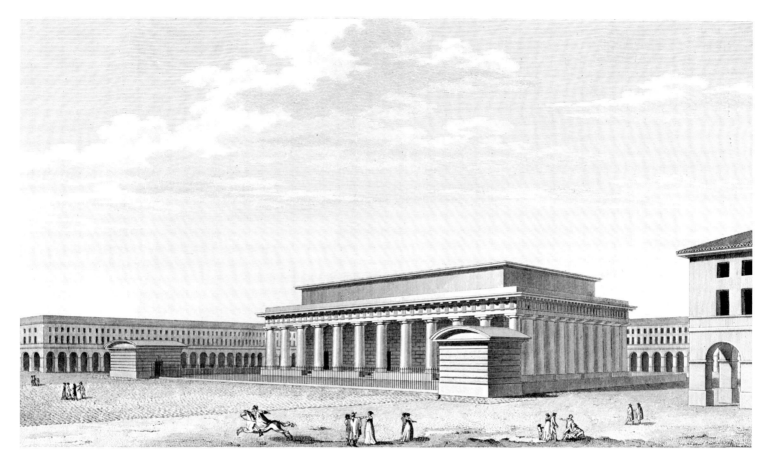

Ledoux, Discount Bank, second project. *Above,* perspective view; *opposite,* section, elevation, and plan of first floor. Engravings from Ramée, *Ledoux,* pls. 105 (by Coquet) and 103 (by Sellier).

These projects share stylistic characteristics with a number of others, later to be included in the gamut of types assembled in the fictional city of Chaux: the Church, Public Baths, and Market, all designed between 1780 and 1786. With their rusticated bases, plain walls, central, domed rotundas, Greek-cross and square plans, pedimented porticoes, and plain Doric orders, these take their place in Ledoux's catalogue of public institutonal forms developed according to the programs of the Académie. The first two, in particular, derived from the model of the Pantheon, with its porches repeated on four sides following Palladian precedent, weld antique allusion to contemporary needs in a simple, direct way, parading neither antiquarian accuracy nor overscaled dimensions. Their aesthetic of nudity and elemental relationships was thus combined with a selection of typical forms taken from Roman antiquity, Palladian practice, and eighteenth-century historiography. The Baths, for example, were composed from the rotunda of the Pantheon, Palladio's Villa Rotonda, and the oriental baths illustrated by Fischer von Erlach, united by the severe and planimetric geometry of the whole, and given Ledoux's unique stamp by the majestic Doric or the circular peristyle around the pool.

These individual projects—none of which, save for a portion of the Hôtel des Fermes, was built—were, during the decade from 1780 to the Revolution, overshadowed by the three major commissions of the theater of Besançon, the Palais de Justice and prisons of Aix-en-Provence, and the *barrières* associated with the wall of the Ferme Générale. Here the

Ledoux, Stock Exchange of Chaux, first project, perspective view. Detail of the "Perspective View of the Town of Chaux" from Ramée, *Ledoux,* pl. 116.

Ledoux, Stock Exchange of Chaux, second project, perspective view, elevation, section, and plans. Engraving by Van Maëlle from Ramée, *Ledoux,* pl. 71.

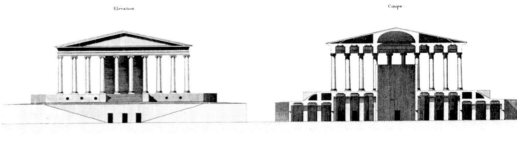

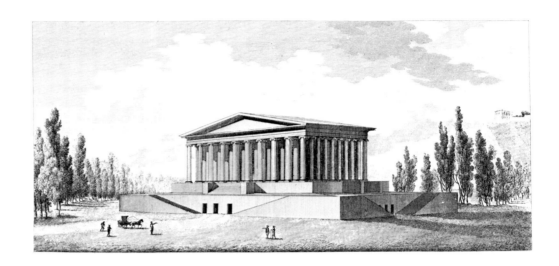

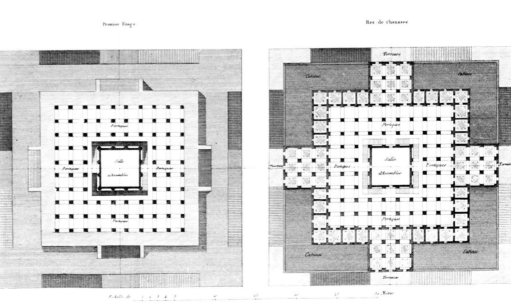

Ledoux, perspective views of
Church, Public Baths, and
Market of Chaux (*top to bottom*). Details of the "Perspective View of the Town of
Chaux" from Ramée, *Ledoux,*
pl. 116.

different building types were, at least in Ledoux's eyes, virtually without contemporary precedent, and he was forced at once to improvise and to search antiquity for their assumed "origins." Such beginnings, while giving to his inventions a form of authority, could only appear to be invented themselves, representing both a deracinated antiquity and a yet-to-be-defined modernity.

THE THEATRICAL VISION:
BESANÇON AND MARSEILLES

Our theaters . . . are still in the infancy of the art and leave much to be desired in relation to the purity of morals, solidity, salubrity, commodity, and the general effect. This last concern is seriously neglected, even though everyone knows that one of the greatest advantages of a performance is to see everything and be, in turn, well seen. (222)

THE THEATER IN THE CITY

The new Theater of Besançon, while not opened to the public until 1784, and then with its decorations incomplete, was in fact designed in tandem with the Saline de Chaux. Commissioned sometime before August 1775, its preliminary drawings were finished by then, and a final model built by the end of the next year.[39] The concurrence of the two projects, the one for a theater, the other for a small factory town, was of the greatest thematic and formal importance for both. Indeed, Ledoux made it clear that he regarded the one as the microcosm of the other. The plans of Besançon were the only built designs included in the first volume of *L'architecture* that did not concern the *saline* directly, thus emphasizing the intimate link, not only regional but also theoretical and architectural, between the two. This relationship was established on the most immediate level by the similar geometries employed; the semicircles of the *saline* and the auditorium of Besançon referred in both cases to the model of the antique theater. But the parallel was intended on a social level as well: as a commonplace analogy between theater and society, on the one hand, and as a more complex allegory of Ledoux's ideas of

social and political reform and their representation, on the other.

Writing to the Intendant of Franche-Comté, Charles-André de Lacoré in August 1775, sometime after a visit to Besançon no doubt undertaken in conjunction with his responsibilities at Arc-et-Senans, Ledoux outlined his first project for the theater, drawings of which he enclosed.[40] The letter, excerpts from which he inserted almost unchanged in *L'architecture* some twenty-five years later, indicated the extent to which Ledoux was already deeply committed to a social and architectural "reform" of the theater. He spoke quite seriously of his design in terms of "establishing a new religion," and of the costs entailed. More realistically, he spoke cautiously of the "prejudices to overcome" in a "provincial town that models itself on the capital." He anticipated that "at first sight I will pass for a fool," but hoped that ultimately his voice would emerge as one of reason.[41]

In the event, however, while Ledoux's anticipation of opposition seemed justified in the light of the difficulties that Charles De Wailly experienced with his similarly radical desgn for the Comédie-Française, the ten-year delay in the completion of the Besançon theater was in no way the result of his admitted innovations. De Lacoré immediately accepted his design; and the municipality, which had earlier resisted the establishment of a permanent *salle de spectacle*, agreed with Ledoux's monumental aims: to provide a building "that on the one hand would be fitting for the century . . . and on the other in line with the modest budget available."[42] Even this last concern, normally so frustrating to Ledoux's hyperbolic imagination, was in the case of Besançon entirely in concert with his search for the simplest architectural expression of his principled scheme. The theater, in fact, would ultimately count among his more successful financial ventures, its cost of construction comparing favorably with other contemporary provincial auditoria of equal size.

The delays were, instead, the product of a long-drawn-out dispute between de Lacoré and the magistrature of the town over the proper site for the new theater. Both parties agreed on the utility of the project; both held similar aesthetic and functional criteria; both wanted this object of municipal

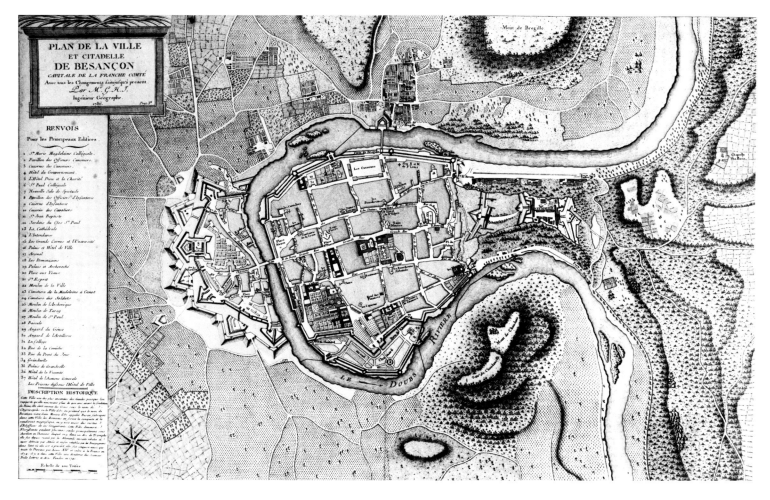

and regional pride to be sited at the center of the town. But
they differed profoundly on their respective definitions of this
central position.[43] De Lacoré, in the process of finishing construction of the new Intendancy, preferred a site close by, at
the geometrical center of that portion of the town enclosed
by the loop of the Doubs River; he therefore suggested a piece
of land then occupied by a series of houses and shops called
locally the Transmarchement and by the university-owned
botanical gardens. The magistrature, representative of the
town as a whole, including the garrison and the more popular
quarters on the right bank of the river, argued for a site at the
center of the town's commercial life, on the Place Neuve next
to the bridge that connected the two sides of Besançon.

The arguments of the magistrature were convincing
enough, and even de Lacoré professed initially to be swayed
by them. Set forth in a long memorandum in July 1776, they
constituted ten points that embraced the latest principles of
urbanism in the service of the "will of the public" of Besançon.[44] Their proposed site lay at the true center of town, at
equal distances from its extremities and from the barracks.
The traditional site of the town theater, which had once occupied the tennis court, the quarter of the Place Neuve was in
any case more populated (that is, more popular) than that of
the Transmarchement. As the land already belonged to the
town, its purchase would entail no expenses for the municipality. Moreover, the Place Neuve offered a space entirely appropriate for the freestanding monument conceived for the
theater. "The building, isolated on each side, will form an
island that will give it entries on each of its façades," they

wrote; the square itself would be replanned to form a suitable context: "It will give to an irregular square, the regularity to which it is susceptible." [45] Standing beside the public granary, the theater would act as the cultural symbol of a prosperous economy. Visible from all directions, decorated on four sides, the new building would be "one of the most considerable embellishments that the town could procure." Beyond this, the functional conditions of the Place Neuve were far superior to those of the Transmarchement: wide avenues from each quarter would ensure free access for carriages; a large space was available for parking and circulation; the proximity of the river afforded security in case of fire, "an accident always to be feared for a *salle de spectacle*." Finally, the position would be appreciated by the actors themselves, presumably lodged on the right bank. On such a site the magistrature agreed it would be possible to construct a theater "with all the advantages that even Paris could envy, and of the proportions that were capable of occupying the time of the most talented artists in France and, if possible, of recalling the memory of antiquity to our sight." [46] Following the example of over twenty-five other provincial centers after 1750, Besançon would at last possess its own permanent theater.

In his reply to this memorandum, de Lacoré seemed to agree with the council, promising to submit their suggestions to Ledoux and to await the architect's response. [47] A week later, he communicated Ledoux's reactions to the magistrature: "I have emphasized to M. Ledoux the necessity of adopting your views on the siting of the theater. He is in agreement with me that it would be very well placed on the Place Neuve, and he will make use of a portion of the land that you propose for this purpose." [48] According to de Lacoré, in order not to alter the already completed project, the model of which was almost finished, Ledoux had set his theater in the place, projecting into the square beyond the siteline established by the city and thereby emphasizing its monumental proportions. The architect had also added "some ideas about the context that would make the place more regular and agreeable." And he proposed, concluded de Lacoré, "to set a pedestrian statue in the middle, to build, on the side of the fountain, kinds of

open sheds or arcades." [49] Ledoux certainly would not have opposed the choice of so open and malleable a site, one perfectly suited to his aesthetic of "isolation" and characterization. But by the end of the following year, de Lacoré had reelaborated his arguments for a more central location, accessible to "those people who frequent the theater most often," that is, the upper bourgeoisie and the intendant's own circle. Although the quarter of the Transmarchement was evidently less populated and more dilapidated than the Place Neuve, he saw the building of the theater and its surrounding shops in a new square as a means of renewal and embellishment. [50] In January 1778, de Lacoré changed his mind once more, ordering that plans be drawn up and work started on the theater in yet a third position—the gardens of the Hôtel Grandvelle, which had housed the town's temporary theater for over fifty years. [51] Almost immediately, de Lacoré, having received the consent of the municipality for this revised plan, reverted to his original preference. The Magistrature impatiently petitioned the Duc de Duras, outlining their previous objections and resubmitting the arguments for the Place Neuve in two memoranda. [52] The governor's reply, received in Besançon on 2 February, was flatly negative; supporting Ledoux and the intendant, he ordered the theater to be built on the site of the botanical gardens. [53] Some days later de Lacoré thanked the magistrature for their acceptance of this request and asked them to begin acquisition of the surrounding houses. A local architect, Claude-Joseph-Alexandre Bertand, who was to act as Ledoux's site manager throughout construction, started the surveys; ground was broken in March 1778.

The subtext of this apparently aimless dispute, where the superficially supple politics of the intendant succeeded in wearing down the obstinancy of the city, was not simply one that pitted local against royal and centralized power. It concerned the fundamental division between an economic and popular view of urban development and an aesthetic and aristocratic vision of embellishment. The two "centers" of Besançon identified by the disputants exactly symbolized these oppositions: the Place Neuve, an architecturally formless but socially vital commercial center, against a new square in an unfrequented quarter that would, however, provide a suitable backdrop for a theater to represent the beneficent and civilizing administration of an enlightened royalty. An inscription written in 1771 for the foundation ceremony of the new Hôtel de l'Intendance demonstrated the extent to which de Lacoré saw himself as an "awakener of the arts," a rival of Jean-Baptiste Colbert in his "just and wise" administration of public works.[54] But the debate also marked a distinct shift in the nature of the public theater itself. Theater was no longer a popular spectacle to be situated in the marketplace or a tennis court, nor a private aristocratic luxury to be housed in an *hôtel;* its formalization as a public monument confirmed the place of performance in the pattern of provincial middle-class entertainment. Patronized by the royal administration and open to the well-behaved working population, the theater had become a specialized and professionalized realm where an orderly audience appreciated the particular aesthetic values ascribed to the performance and the play.[55] The crystallization of this relatively new understanding of theatricality into the building type "theater" was, as Ledoux recognized, to be accomplished at the expense of both popular and aristocratic tradition.

THE REFORM OF THE THEATER

Ledoux drew up his designs for Besançon in the context of the lively debate over the reform of the public theater that had engaged *philosophes,* writers, critics, and architects since the late 1740s. This discussion explored the proper nature of the genres—as in Voltaire's appeal to antiquity on behalf of a purified tragedy or in Diderot's definition of a new genre of bourgeois comedy. But it also focused on the aesthetics of theatricality in general in view of the social and moral effects of performances on the audience.[56] For Diderot, whose criticisms and proposals were perhaps the most systematic and far-reaching, these concerns were intimately linked to the morality of the actors and to the attentiveness of the audience. A play that depicted human conditions faithfully, or rather created the illusion of verisimilitude by a correct use of gestures and voice, acted by performers whose interior morality

ideally corresponded to their affected performance, would operate on a properly disposed audience like a veritable school of ethics. In his "Entretiens sur Le fils naturel" of 1757 and, more systematically, in his "De la poésie dramatique" of the following year, Diderot outlined a plan of reform and a theatrical aesthetic that confonted the traditional commonplaces of a drama imprisoned in the attenuated formulae of classical rhetoric performed for a self-interested public.[57] His new model was, like that of Voltaire, founded on a return to antiquity joined to a complex aesthetic of the senses. As Jean-Claude Bonnet has remarked, "It was a question of renewing with Antiquity, by reestablishing the theater in its pedagogic and social functions. This implied a national cultural politics, with acting schools and a new architecture of theaters."[58]

A similar return to antique prototypes had also been advanced by architects, at least in principle or in image. Jacques-Germain Soufflot's trip to Italy in the company of Charles-Nicolas Cochin and Gabrielle Dumont between 1749 and 1751, followed by the construction of his theater at Lyons, had stimulated a series of projects that adapted the Roman amphitheater or its Palladian derivation to French uses.[59] Soufflot was struck with the "natural" form of the theater at Herculaneum, which seemed to mimic the spontaneous grouping of an audience seated in a semicircle on a hillside; thus for his theater at Lyons he adopted an elliptical plan, seeking to overcome what Cochin pointed out as the gravest fault of traditional auditoria: "that they are all too deep."[60] Cochin himself proposed to cut the ellipse on its long axis, bringing audience and stage even closer and widening the aperture of the proscenium, while Gabriel Dumont proposed an entirely circular form.[61] Both tried to preserve the image of the Roman amphitheater by stepping back the private boxes that traditionally had been stacked vertically, one row above the next. Charles De Wailly and Marie-Joseph Peyre, in their successive projects for the new Comédie-Française between 1769 and 1778, returned to the geometry of the semicircle as described by Vitruvius and uncovered at Herculaneum; they similarly preferred open boxes ramped back amphitheatrically.[62] In 1776 the architect Jean Damun published a "Prospectus for a New Theater Designed According to the Principles of the Greeks and the Romans," noting that the semicircle followed the most instinctive patterns of a crowd watching a traveling player.[63] The following year, the theatrical machinist and carpenter André-Jacques Roubo proposed an almost unchanged Roman type for the Comédie-Française.[64]

Each of these projects attempted to reconcile the fixed type of antiquity with the mixture of social and aesthetic needs of the eighteenth century by means of complex geometrical formulae. The social demand for private boxes, or *loges,* for highly decorated *salles,* for the evident distinction of ranks and classes, traditionally satisfied by deep, oval or horseshoe-shaped auditoria with vertical rows of *loges,* had to be satisfied by a combination of side partitions and hierarchically arranged galleries. The equally difficult problems of acoustics and visual contact with the stage, while entirely ignored in existing theaters, were not solved by the pure semicircle; and architects vigorously debated the merits of different combinative geometries. By 1782 the confusion was such as to be described by Pierre Patte, who tried to resolve the debate in favor of the truncated ellipse utilized by Soufflot, in terms that seem to indicate an unending battle of geometries:

Some pretend that the circular or semicircular shape is the most favorable; others want it to be oval or half oval; others, and they form the greatest number, believe that they are free to adopt all curved forms indifferently—that of a bell, a racket, a horseshoe, an octagon, an oblong, a parallelogram, etc.[66]

All solutions were, however, supported by the belief that some reform of theatrical practices was essential and, moreover, could be aided, if not effected, by the precise form of the *salle* and its geometrical relationship to the stage.

As Patte was later to point out with elaborate calculations, the assumed correspondence of a theater planned according to the Vitruvian type to that conceived by the modernizing antiquarianism of Voltaire and Diderot was by no means evident. The relation, for those of De Wailly's generation excited by the archaeological discoveries in southern Italy and Greece, was as much aesthetic as practical. For De Wailly, Ledoux, and Gondouin, and later for Boullée, the image of republican Rome afforded by the amphitheater, combined with the acoustical and visual properties claimed for the circle, was enough to join their preferred plans to the theater of natural gesture and unaffected mores, of powerful passions and unambiguous signs envisaged by Diderot and his followers. But in practice, as De Wailly's experience demonstrated, resistance to such reform was strong, at the court as well as among the corps of actors and dancers themselves. Ledoux, some thirty years later, recounted the opposition of the Abbé Terray's mistress to the first project of Peyre and De Wailly: the "progressive system" of stepped-back *loges,* "the equality that causes ranks to disappear and gives preeminence to the mass of a numerous assembly," offended her pride. Ledoux, protected by Diderot's admirer and friend Trudaine de Mon-

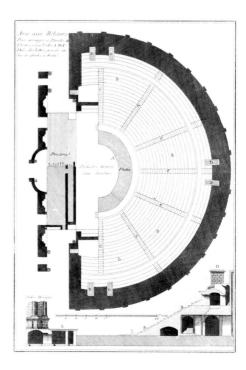

Theater, Herculaneum, plan and section. Engraving from the *Encyclopédie,* "Théâtres."

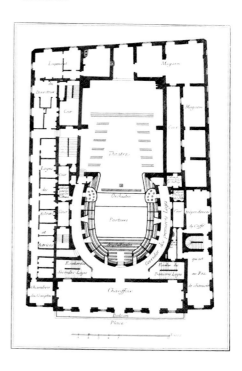

Jacques-Germain Soufflot, Theater at Lyons, 1753–56, plan of first tier of boxes. Engraving from the *Encyclopédie,* "Théâtres."

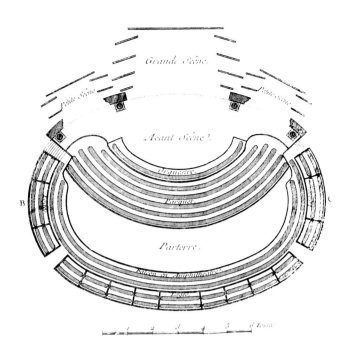

Charles-Nicolas Cochin, Project for a theater, 1765, plan. Engraving from Charles-Nicolas Cochin, *Projet d'une salle de spectacle pour un théâtre de comédie* (Paris, 1765), pl. 1.

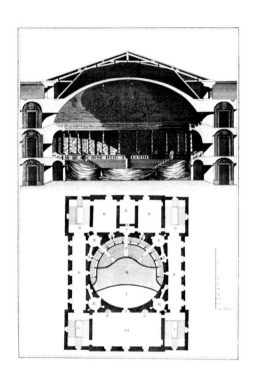

Gabriel Dumont, Project for a circular theater, section and plan. Engraving from the *Encyclopédie,* "Théâtres."

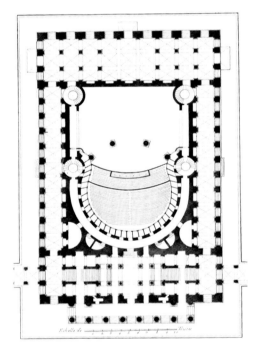

Joseph-Marie Peyre and Charles De Wailly, Second project for the Comédie-Française, 1771, plan of first level of boxes. Engraving from the *Encyclopédie, Supplément,* "Architecture, Théâtre," pl. 2.

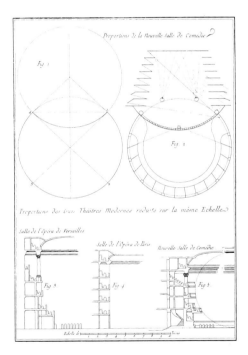

Charles De Wailly, Diagram comparing the proportions of three modern theaters—the Opera of Versailles, the Opera of Paris, and the new Comédie-Française—showing the regulating geometry of the circle in the latter. Engraving from the *Encyclopédie, Supplément,* "Architecture, Théâtre," pl. 5.

tigny and by the Maréchal de Duras, Governor of Franche-Comté and First Gentleman of the Bedchamber to Louis XVI, was more fortunate in his patronage. De Lacoré, whose ambition was to rival Turgot in the administration of his province, proved an equally consistent supporter.

Carrying all the traces of its aristocratic and private origins, the eighteenth-century theater provided for an audience more generally interested in being seen than in seeing. Seated in order of rank and fortune, the majority of the audience lived at the theater much as in its salons. The boxes were treated like small society reception rooms, scenes of intrigue, debates, lovers' rendezvous, and infidelity as dramatic as those presented on stage.[66] Ledoux was scornful of these "hutches," or "wooden cages" "like vast aviaries, where the powers of the earth cling to their high luxurious perches, colored like the birds of the air." Not only did their curtains hide the stage from sight and impede hearing, their very secrecy "troubled modesty and offended morals." Those who could not afford boxes stood in the flat pit, or *parterre*, between the *loges* and the stage. The noise was continuous: "Our theaters were places of tumult. . . . One hears from one side, 'Make way for the women'; from the other, 'Raise your arms, M. Abbé'; from somewhere else, 'Take off your hat'; and from all sides, 'Quiet there, silence the chatter.' It was an incredible din," remembered Diderot.[67] And while he was to lament somewhat the calming of the crowd in later years, to a serious playwright or theatergoer such tumult was intolerable. The heat and the smells were equally repulsive: "It is there," wrote Ledoux, "that our fellow men, those least favored by fortune, are so pushed and pressed that they sweat blood; a murderous vapor hangs round them" (219).[68] Even when seating was provided, the pit remained a place of "tumult and convulsive movement."

Part of the audience is forced to stand on tiptoe to compensate for lack of height; another part, half a head taller, hides the scene entirely. Those who occupy the sides of the auditorium in the first tiers can only see the actors by craning their necks; those in the second, third, and fourth tiers, stimulated by the theatrical action that continuously escapes their sight, stand up in vain, turn around, lose their

balance, shrug their shoulders impatiently, disheveling their dress in their preoccupation, so as to gain by stretching forward what is refused them by the proportions of the seats or the inconvenience of the lines of sight. (219)

The loud noise, foul smells, lack of ventilation, difficulty of seeing and hearing turned what should have been a place of moral instruction into a "trench, where passions of every kind stir in their own detritus."

Ledoux's solution was outlined in his letter to de Lacoré that accompanied his preliminary design for the new theater. No doubt influenced by his friendship with De Wailly, he appealed to what he understood as the natural principle of theatricality:

Let us return to principle, let us trample underfoot the centuries of ignorance where the form of our theaters was that of a tennis court. Let us take for our model the simplest actions of humanity that occur every day in front of our eyes. How, for example, do people gather around a charlatan in a public square when they want to hear better? Everyone clusters together and surrounds him in a circle; the strongest approach the closest, the weak are the furthest away, but, as the radius of the circle is short, the barker is equally distant from all of his assistants.[69]

When applied to a theater audience, this model, as Ledoux recognized, would in effect reverse the traditional order of seating. For, as he pointed out, "the strongest, that is to say, he who pays the most, should be the closest; he who pays the least should be the furthest away." Because of this reversal Ledoux feared he would be resisted by those who frequented the theater more to be seen than to see, or by the traditional *amour-propre* of the society of Besançon, more ramified than in other provincial towns by the presence of the garrison. His proposal was radical enough: to seat the audience as much by its ability to pay as by rank, assuming that its predominant interest lay in viewing the performance.

Of his first project only an elevation survives. For a second project, represented by a section and a partial sketch plan,[70] Ledoux designed an auditorium ramped in four or five stages: an amphitheater that replaced the old *parterre*, to be

ÉCHÉLLE DE DOUZE TOISES DE ROI LINÉAIRE dont une divisé en 6ᵖⁱᵉᵈˢ

Ledoux, Theater of Besançon,
first project, c. 1766, elevation. Drawing from the
Archives Municipales de
Besançon, Yc B2.

Ledoux, Theater of Besançon,
second project, section. Drawing from the Bibliothèque de
Besançon, Fonds Pierre-
Adrien Pâris, *Etudes d'architecture,* vol. 5, pl. 304.

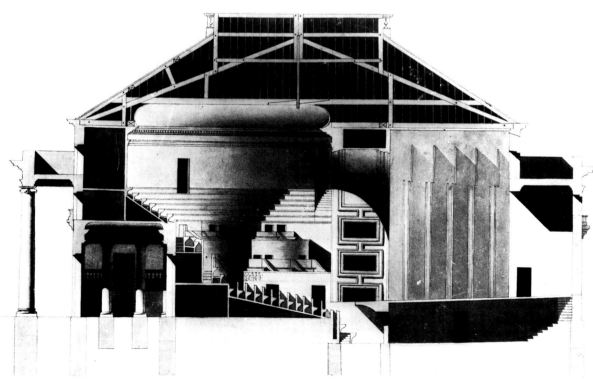

"filled by those who pay the most"; a balcony for the staff officers of the barracks; the first boxes for rich women; the second boxes for the second estate; and the resited *parterre* in the "gods" for "those who pay the least, but who will be better treated and placed than they have been till now."[71] Despite Ledoux's claims for the semicircle and his evident desire to evoke the image of Rome, the equally graded steps and pure geometry of the latter were thus distorted in section and plan to conform, at least minimally, to social degrees. In plan, the amphitheater and first and second boxes formed an open bell shape, similar to that which Charles De Wailly provided for the Comédie-Française; only the six rows of the new *parterre* achieved the pure semicircle, which was prolonged on either side to join the proscenium. In section, the stepping was similarly unequal, with the slopes of the amphitheater, the boxes, and the *parterre* at differing angles and vertical separations.

In the third and fourth projects, perhaps those elaborated for the model completed in 1776, Ledoux refined this breakdown of Besançon society in the light of a more comprehensive program.[72] The plans and section conserved in the collection of Pierre-Adrien Pâris reveal a multiplication of distinctions enforcd by the social codes of the town, while showing the influence of the model of Palladio's Teatro Olimpico at Vicenza. The amphitheater was renamed the *parquet,* a memory of the once common practice of seating dignitaries on the stage itself and a way of dignifying what was formerly the pit. The gallery, mentioned in Ledoux's letter but not shown in the section of the early project, now separated the amphitheater from the rows of first and second boxes, while the *parterre* itself was divided into two by a colonnade similar to that completing the auditorium of Palladio's theater at Vicenza. This division separated the occupants of the *parterre* proper from four rows reserved for the soldiers of the garrison at the very rear of the theater. The *parterre* itself contained places reserved to either side for domestic servants.

As in the early project, the highest nobles and officers of the province were provided with private, enclosed boxes. The most important were planned in the thickness of the proscenium arch in four levels on either side. The royal boxes, for the king and queen respectively, heated with their own fireplaces, were on the level of the gallery. Four other boxes for lesser officials were planned beneath the gallery at the upper level of the *parquet,* two to either side.[73]

As built, the theater went even further in specifying place according to social status and economic power.[74] Closed boxes in the proscenium, barred boxes below the gallery, each accommodating four to eight spectators, were reserved for those who could afford to rent them by the year or by the season. The *parquet* remained the favored seating for the rich bourgeoisie. The gallery, on the same level as the royal boxes, also used from time to time by the intendant and his circle, was reserved for the commanders and chiefs of the army, officers of the military, and civil police. At either side and separated by a moveable bar from these central positions, seating was open to others who could pay. The first row of boxes was specifically reserved for nobles, or "those living nobly," and proscribed for the bourgeoisie by order of de Lacoré.[75] The second row of boxes, for the "honest bourgeoisie," were placed to either side of open seating for workers and shopgirls. The third row of boxes was divided into three sections—with seating for men only centered between seating for men and women individually—and comprised the level of the *parterre* in the earlier projects. Behind these sections, defined by a row of Doric columns, a fourth tier of seats was divided among bourgeois, sergeants and soldiers, and domestic servants, with specific places set to each side for soldiers and for domestics.[76]

These dispositions, enforced by law and marked by architectural form, served the social order of the theater on a number of different levels, practical and ideological. First, they no doubt went a long way toward fulfilling Ledoux's initial intention, "to satisfy all estates." Second, the very real threat of disorder posed by the traditional *parterre* was literally removed. Ledoux's aim in this case was both social and aesthetic: "The general order will gain from this; the pedestrians, who in our theaters give off a smell like that of people pressed into a carriage, will no longer be able to complain of the jolts, the press of the crowd, the din that people make when standing up. The *cabale* will cease."[77] Thus, with the attention of the

Andrea Palladio, Teatro Olimpico, Vicenza, 1580–85, section through auditorium and
stage. Drawing by Pâris from
the Fonds P.-A. Pâris, *Architecture,* vol. 5, pl. 58.

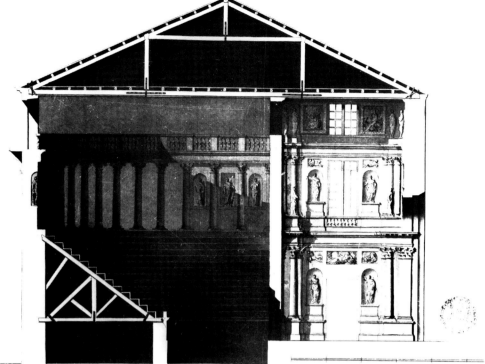

Ledoux, Theater of Besançon,
third project, elevation and
section. Drawings from the
Fonds P.-A. Pâris, *Architecture,*
vol. 5, pls. 305, 303.

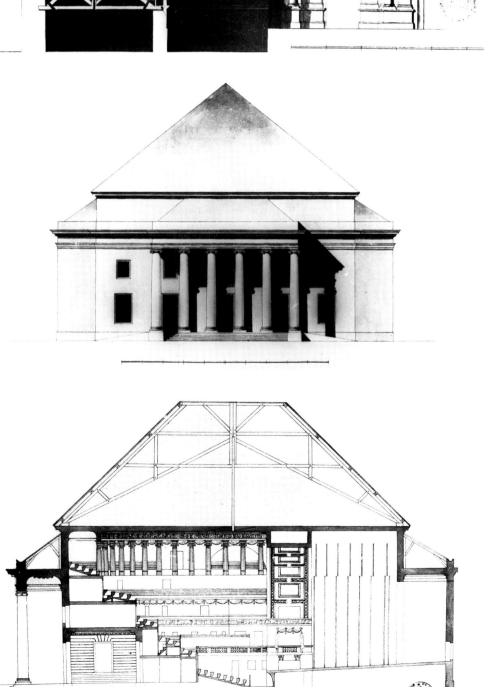

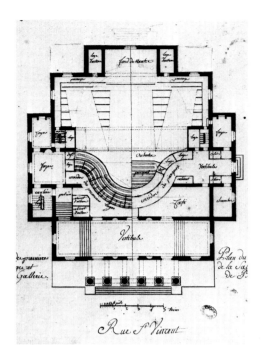

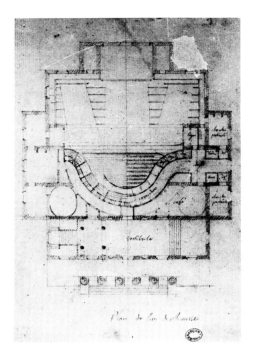

Ledoux, Theater of Besançon, third project. *Left,* plan of first floor and first level of boxes; *right,* sketch of first-floor plan, showing alternative layout for vestibule. Drawings from the Archives Municipales de Besançon, Yc B2.

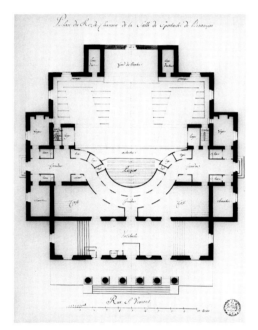

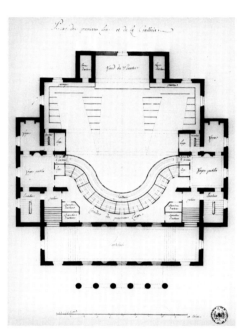

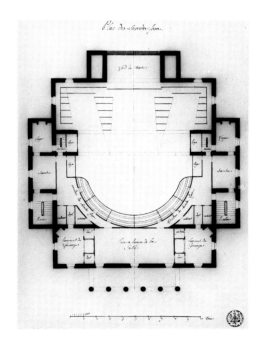

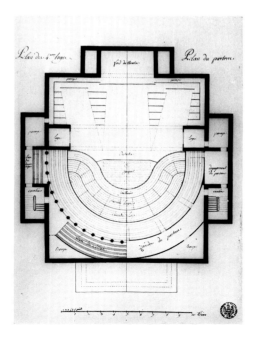

Ledoux, Theater of Besançon, third project, plans. *Above left,* first floor; *above right,* first level of boxes and gallery; *below left,* second level of boxes; *below right,* fourth level of boxes (left half) and *parterre* (right half). Drawings from the Fonds P.-A. Pâris, *Architecture,* vol. 5, pls. 299–302.

Ledoux, Theater of Besançon, plan of properties to be purchased to form a square around the theater. Drawing from the Archives Municipales de Besançon, DD35.

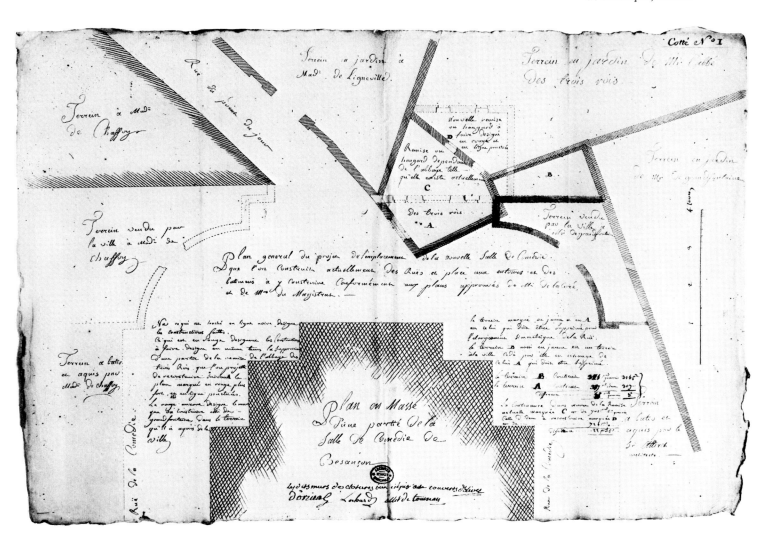

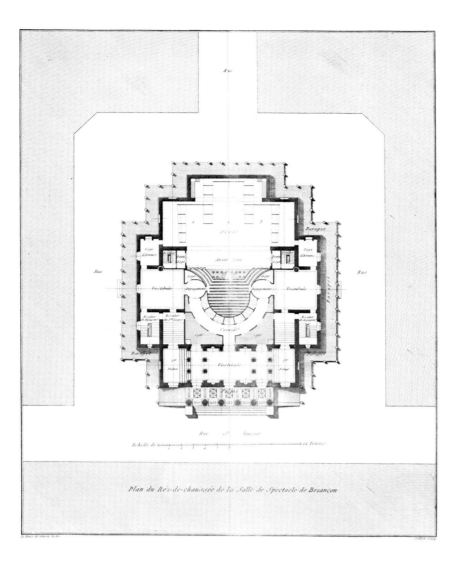

Plan du Rèz-de-chaussée de la Salle de Spectacle de Besançon.

Ledoux, Theater of Besançon, final project, 1778–84. *Left,* plan of first floor; *below,* plans of first, second, third, and fourth levels of boxes; *opposite,* section through auditorium and stage. Engravings from Ramée, *Ledoux,* pls. 73, 74, 75, 77 (pls. 73 and 77 by Sellier).

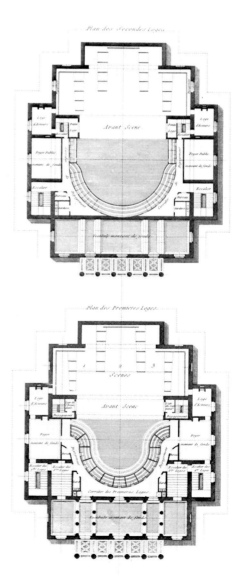

Plan des Secondes Loges.

Plan des Premieres Loges.

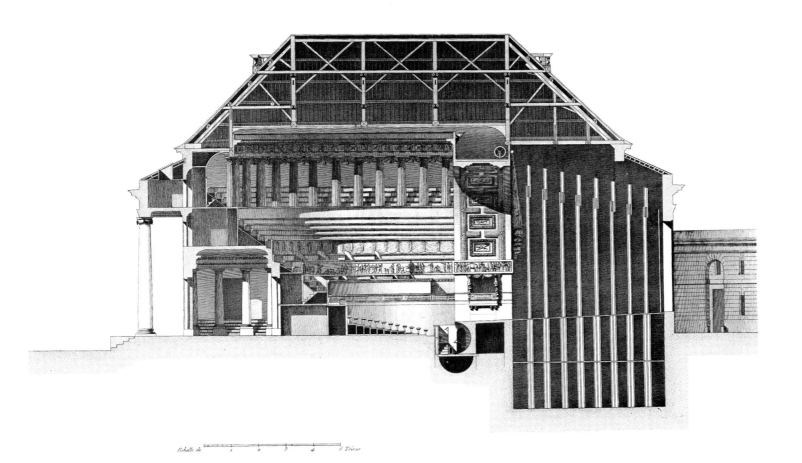

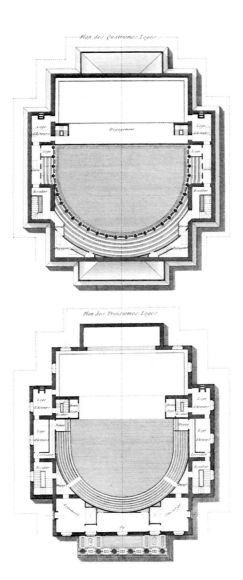

Plan des Quatriemes Loges.

Plan des Troisiemes Loges.

entire audience focused on the stage, now visually and acoustically accessible to all, the performance itself—the actors, the play, and the mise-en-scène—would become the central preoccupation: "By destroying what is falsely called the enthusiasm of the *parterre,* the authors will be judged more sanely." [78]

Finally, Ledoux's social reformism extended beyond the *cabale* to counter what he considered one of the outstanding faults of contemporary theaters: their encouragement of social immorality and licentiousness at every social level. Echoing Rousseau—whose strictures against the libertinage sustained by urban theaters had been stated in his *Lettre à M. d'Alembert* and popularized in Saint-Preux's reactions to the Parisian theater in *La Nouvelle Héloïse* [79]—Ledoux castigated the system of closed private boxes as favoring illicit liaisons. Hidden in their wooden cages, behind double-net curtains and gauze veils, the occupants of these boxes were assured anonymity:

They made it a crime in Greece to build monuments to lubricity . . . whereas here one sees altars on which the priestesses of corruption burn the insipid incense of impurity under the cover of a piece of gauze; their sacrifices are performed in these mysterious places, and the doors of licentiousness are only opened at the voices of initiates. (220)

Opening the majority of boxes to the auditorium as a whole allowed the audience not only to see better, but also to be constantly seen. In Ledoux's terms, such visibility would serve the double requirement of social display and the social surveillance of morals. While this argument seems slightly forced expounded by an artist who assiduously attended the far from moral gatherings of Mlle Guimard, it was without doubt a reasoning calculated to appeal to the bourgeois morality of a garrison town that for precisely these reasons was likely to be suspicious of a permanent theater. But Ledoux, as his later, more utopian projects demonstrated, was less opposed to licentiousness in itself than to its generalized dissemination. The institutions he would dedicate to libertinage were exactly calculated to confine and control its practices and effects on behalf of morality. In a theater, dedicated exclusively to the presentation of a performance both pleasurable and didactic, any activity that distracted the attention of the audience was to be rigidly excluded: "One sees well everywhere, one is well seen, which contributes to the pleasure of the spectacle and maintains decency" (232).

The advantages of the amphitheatrical plan, where "the levels increase tier by tier, until they acquire the strength of the semicircle, the only form that allows the possibility of seeing all the scenes of the theater" (223), extended equally to the acoustics of the auditorium. Ledoux, countering Patte's arguments on behalf of the truncated ellipse, blended contemporary science and Renaissance Neoplatonism in his espousal of the properties of the sphere in the reflection of sound: "It must not be forgotten that rays of sound, like those of light, are propagated in inverse proportion to the square of their distance from the center of origin, and that this follows from the properties of the sphere." (229) But the theater was a more complex form, differing in its effects on sound from the "simple and perfect action of the sphere": "If the universal harmony of the world is principally composed of a certain proportion and relationship between spherical and rectilinear actions, one must strive to imitate this proportion and these relations, as much for the effects of light and colors as for sounds, in theaters." (229)

It followed from this that an auditorium approaching a perfect circle in plan might avoid the "opposition and confusion" produced by a composite mixture of curved, straight, and angular lines; it would not "distort, break, decompose, and confuse the effects of the sound" (229). [80] Such a confusion was most pronounced in the competition between the voices of the actors and the sound of the orchestra. Whether placed on stage or in the auditorium itself, the musicians inevitably triumphed over the actors, deafening those closest to the stage, "effacing the voice," and "depriving the audience of the faithful expresson of thought" (229). To correct this disproportion, Ledoux relocated the orchestra in a sunken pit between the *parquet* and the stage. There the visual presence of the musicians would no longer detract from the performance, and their sound, reflected by a curved, acoustically constructed sounding board at the rear of the orchestra, would be disseminated equally throughout the *salle*. Concentrated and reflected like the sound of a single instrument or voice, "masked in the exercise of its functions," the sound of the orchestra would no longer be "confounded with the general action of the theater" (229). Ledoux speculated further on how orchestral acoustics might be enhanced throughout the auditorium to give rise to the most sublime effects: "Experiments have not yet been conducted to determine to what degree the orchestra, treated as a whole as an instrument, would give by the form and grandeur of its dimensions a deeper sound than that of the deepest note of a doublebass. This new kind of experiment, subjected to calculation, could become a fertile source of effects in music and acoustics." (229) He even dreamed of recuperating Vitruvius's suggestions of filling the theater with vases of clay, bronze, or brass, which, containing various levels of water, would form a harmonic scale among themselves that would echo and reinforce that of the singers and players. Art would supply the effects that nature provided in the echoes of mountains and forests.

With the orchestra buried in front of the stage, the audience would be presented with the scene entirely disembarrassed of superfluous or intervening distractions. For this reason, Ledoux paid particular attention to the form of the proscenium opening. It was, as he noted, the embrasure of the performance, equivalent to the frame of a picture or the opening of a window onto a landscape. It was, moreover, the very point of transition between the real and the fictive, the living society of the audience and the illusory society on stage.[81] As a place of transition it should, in Ledoux's terms, be both seamless—a "smooth surface"—and a space in its own right—an "intermediary thickness that separates the action from the outside . . . a place of rest where the eye prepares itself" (221). Ledoux's proscenium was thus virtually undecorated, painted as if constructed out of massive, smooth blocks of masonry. The spandrels alone were occupied by representations—of victory chariots seemingly carved in bas-relief, a memory of the antique Porte Noire. The contour of the arch, compared unfavorably by the English traveler Arthur Young to the entrance of a dark cave, perhaps also recalled the profile of a bridge, a favorite framing device for

artists from Piranesi to Hubert Robert—and emulated by Ledoux in his framing of the Hotel Thélusson by a giant, semiburied arch as well as in his view of the Rural School of Meillant seen from beneath a bridge. But in the context of the theater, the complex geometries of the arch derived from another source, which Ledoux clearly indicated in his engraving of the "Coup d'oeil du Théâtre de Besançon," depicting the amphitheater of the *salle* as reflected in the pupil of an enormous eye. The "frame" of vision, formed by the eyelid as it cuts the pupil across the top, follows a contour exactly that of the proscenium, rounded at the sides, flattened at the top. Seen in this way, the engraving suggests a view through a transparent pupil to the empty auditorium as well as its reflection. The eye, as Ledoux pointed out, was indeed the "first frame" through which the world was seen, and remains the frame of vision for each individual member of the audience. The proscenium, focusing the collective vision of the *salle* at a single point, thus echoed in its form the natural boundaries of sight. It was thereby, the image of a view transparent to the scene itself.

The auditorium of Besançon reinforced Ledoux's initial intentions through a carefully elaborated decorative program supervised by the architect at each stage. From the first project Ledoux had envisaged a plain architecture, whose surfaces would reveal the geometry of the auditorium, in a primitive classical style that both harked back to the abstract forms of Perrault's illustrations for Vitruvius and anticipated the sober *hemicycles* of the Revolutionary chambers. The sole decoration on the exterior of the theater was a portico of six Ionic columns derived from Palladio, the effect of which relied on sharply defined cubic masses and a steep pyramidal roof—clear echoes of the Director's Building at Chaux. This simple but monumental scheme was continued on the interior. The vestibule, at first planned as a single space walled in stone, was in the final design decorated with a plain Doric order, attached and freestanding, which marked the entries into the *salle* on either side and the stairs to the first level. The auditorium itself, entirely painted to simulate white marble, was relieved only by the blue of the seats, the gold applied to some of the painted friezes, and the row of twenty-eight fluted

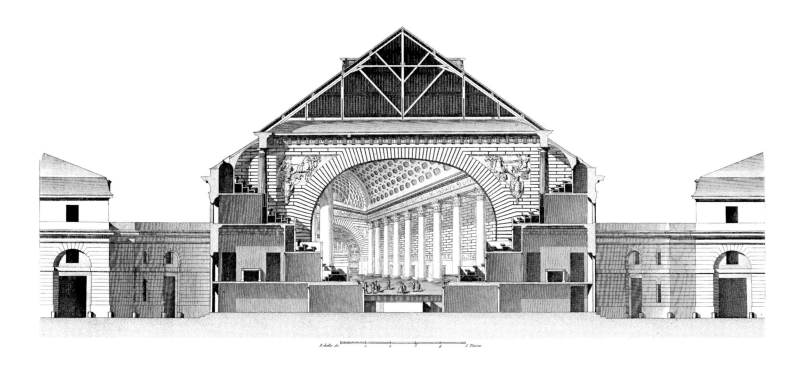

Echelle de .... 5 Toises

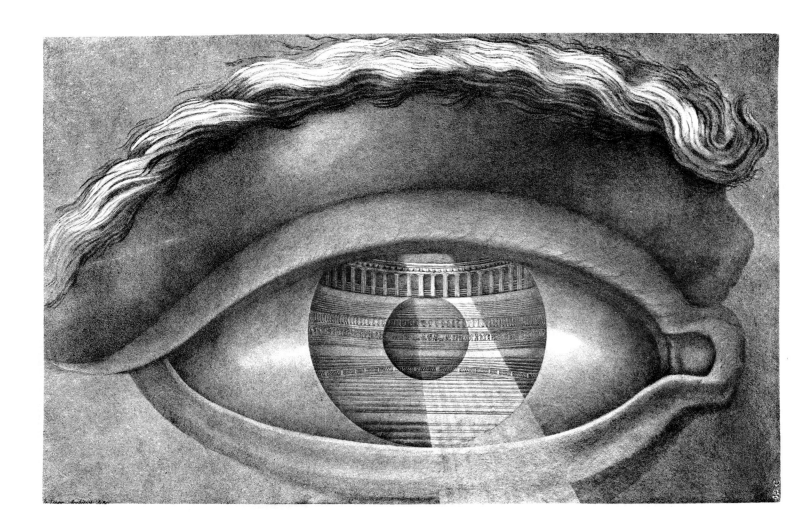

Doric columns, *à la* Paestum, that surrounded the upper *parterre.* On the vertical surface separating the gallery from the first *loges,* a frieze displayed allegorical subjects connected to tragedy, comedy, and dance; the balustrade between the first and second boxes revealed painted draperies. However simple, the effect of the white, blue, and gold was, in the accounts of contemporaries, magnificent: "un coup d'oeil magnifique," noted the journalist of the *Mercure de France.*[82] Over the auditorium, an azure blue ceiling—painted in imitation of an awning hung from the colonnade, heightening the open-air effect of the amphitheater—depicted the ascent of Apollo and his attendants, with a gilded sun at the center of a circle that echoed the circle of the theater.[83]

Ledoux thus tried to avoid the overdecorated appearance of conventional theaters—"with garlands on the first level, garlands on the next, garlands on the last"—while emphasizing by contrast "the interest of the main lines that cannot be interrupted." This asceticism was on one level economic, but at root it supported the moral overtones of the entire theater. Of the lack of decorations on the upper levels, Ledoux wrote: "Wishing to associate public instruction to those whose means do not allow them to obtain seats, desiring to form mores by the purified choice of representations, I thought that it was unsuitable to encircle the crowd by that dangerous custom of depraved scenes that degrade and debase good taste." (226) In the event, the spectators themselves would provide the major decoration of the *salle:* "thirty-six rows of spectators, placed one behind the other. The dress of the first bench is in graduated opposition with the last. What varieties, what richness of tones!" (233). Such "natural" decoration would replace the affected masks and dresses of the vertical *loges* with an entirely representative vision of the social order, each estate dressed according to its means. This Rousseauesque version of moral representation took its authority from the example, advanced by Ledoux, of popular festivals. In such "a spectacle given freely to the people," a vast crowd would gather on the steps of a temporary wooden stadium according to a natural order of precedence, covering the rough benches with its own spectacle of picturesque mixtures of dress and physiognomy.

This image of a crowd assembled in the open air, on the semicircular levels of an auditorium constructed according to tradition and type, provided Ledoux with the moral justification for his own theater: "On this vast theater, balanced in the clouds, circles on circles," society would find its "primitive estate . . . the equality that it should never have lost" (223). Writing at the same time, after the Revolutionary festivals had given to this crowd a specifically political dimension, Boullée similarly imagined a coliseum filled with three hundred thousand spectators, "brought together in amphitheatrical order," where the only necessary decoration was the audience itself.[84] But whereas Boullée conceived of this vision in terms of a grandiose, sublime restoration of republican Rome, Ledoux preferred the scale of the public square. Boullée's utopia aspired to the compass of an antique tragedy; Ledoux's remained within that of a domestic comedy. Ledoux's "realism," close in this respect to Diderot's, refused the nos-

Ledoux, Theater of Besançon,
detail of ceiling painting
showing Apollo. Engraving
from Ramée, *Ledoux,* pl. 81.

talgic communitarianism of Rousseau on the one hand, even as it rejected the pomp of David and Boullée on the other. In a sharp exchange of letters accusing the architect Bernard Poyet of plagiarizing his designs for Besançon, Ledoux underscored this insistence on the refashioning of existing estates and mores: "What is suitable for a republican state is not so for a monarchy; our mores, our customs, our spectacles are different. The steps that are applicable to our public schools do not fulfill the needs of our theaters. . . . There must be boxes, comfortable boxes, where the ranks and fortunes are distinguished."[85] What Ledoux called "the solution to the riddle" lay in the combination of boxes and amphitheater built at Besançon.

MORAL TABLEAUX

One must not lose sight of the fact that among the ancients their spectacles formed a part of their religion. . . . If our theaters are not places of worship, it is at least desirable that their arrangement ensures the purity of morals; it is easier to correct men by the attraction of pleasure than by religious ceremonies or customs accredited by superstition. (232)

The theatrical reform envisaged by Diderot had as its first aim the renewal of enthusiasm on the part of the audience, the provocation of the most powerful emotions, the complete involvement of the spectator in the drama.[86] For this, he argued, the stiff, rhetorical poses, the recitation by rote, the static scenes of traditional classicism had to be rejected in favor of a new *verisimilitude,* a new realism, which comprised not only the techniques of acting, but also the genres of drama and their aesthetic unity. A new genre of tragedy—the domestic and bourgeois—would engage the sentiments of a new bourgeois audience. Its depiction of the states and conditions of society rather than the conventions of characters would lead to identification on the part of this audience. The lessons of pantomime and dance would transform the gestural art of the actor, stimulating the movement of the entire body and increasing the effect of the passions and emotions simulated. A concern with the three unities of time, action, and place would, if interpreted seriously, produce a performance closer

to nature. The theatrical "event," subject to stricter criteria of temporality and joined together with other events in a sequence that appeared reasonable, now took on the role of an aesthetic "unit" in its own right. Like the words of a discourse, the ideas of a logical argument, or images linked together in a chain of associations, events were in themselves discrete entities; and their effect would be heightened if treated as so many *tableaux* composed and sharply differentiated among each other. Here the visual analogue was not simply to a painting, but to those sequences of paintings and popular engravings that, like the moralizing prints of William Hogarth, themselves modeled on the scenes of the theater, told a story in pictorial language, framed image after framed image. The actors, uniting the arts of dance, pantomime, and rhetoric, might self-consciously group and regroup in *tableaux vivants,* each one composed, like a didactic painting by Jean-Baptiste Greuze, for intensity of emotional effect. Diderot's ideas, novel in the 1760s, were by the 1770s generally approved. Adopted by Gotthold Ephraim Lessing, they had gained favor in France with the general fashion for German culture and had returned by way of his translated works, some introduced by Trudaine.[87] Ledoux, whose *anglomanie* had already predisposed him to the empiricist, sensationalist aesthetic of Hogarth and Henry Fielding, was fully in accord with a theory of drama that privileged the power of sight over that of the emotions.

The comparison between the composition of a painting and the scenes of a theater that dominated Diderot's theatrical aesthetics necessarily pointed to the importance of the frame. In either case, the frame marked the outer limit of the scene and formalized its contents according to the visual laws of balance and harmony, variety and contrast. Ledoux, perhaps remembering Alberti's description of a painting in terms of an image seen through a window, similarly defined the requirements of theatrical framing: "The auditorium being to the scene what an inhabited room is to the empty space discovered outside, the stage should be wider and deeper than the space that contains the spectators. It is the veritable site of the magic illusions of the scene." (231) Even as the perspective offered through a window enlarged or diminished objects ac-

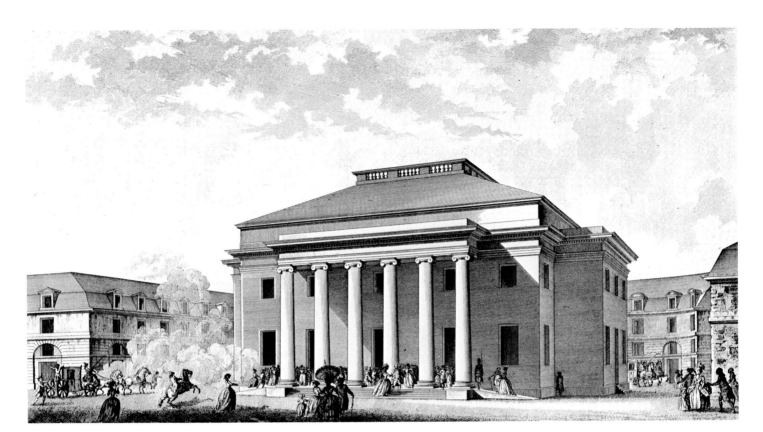

Ledoux, Theater of Besançon,
perspective view. Engraving
by Varin from Ramée, *Ledoux*,
pl. 76.

Ledoux, Theater of Besançon,
view of auditorium before the
fire of 1958. Photograph by
Marcel Bovis.

cording to the width or narrowness of the aperture, so the wider the proscenium opening, the more varied the scenes presented to the spectator. Therein lay one of the main advantages of the amphitheatral plan over the oval or elliptical.

For the stage itself, following De Wailly's first project for the Comédie-Française, and like Cochin in 1765 undoubtedly referring to Palladian precedent, Ledoux adopted a triple scene. This technique involved placing two smaller "perspectives" on either side of the central *tableau* in order to present simultaneously a variety of settings. De Wailly himself had argued the case in his memorandum of 1770, taking as his example Voltaire's *Semiramis,* which required a temple, a palace, and a tomb, more conveniently represented as three different sets.[88] De Wailly, however, insisted on framing each scene separately within a triple division of the proscenium. Ledoux, by contrast, unified the three parts of his scene beneath a single arch, avoiding the columns that hid the scenes from the view of much of the audience. More important, Ledoux's formulation of the triple scene implied the essential relations of the *tableaux* to each other and confirmed the continuous play of variety within a pyramidal hierarchy. He thus tried to reconcile the technical requirements for multiple scenes within an aesthetic that satisfied the demands for a "truth" in temporal and spatial representation.

The technical difficulties of the triple scene were, however, less easy to overcome than the theoretical. The stage engineer appointed to oversee the construction of the machines and equipment of Besançon showed little enthusiasm for Ledoux's innovations. A student and successor to Servandoni at the Tuileries, Guillaume Dard de Bosco did admit the novelty of Ledoux's invention: "If it is established that the stage of the theater has an entirely different form to that of other theaters, it is equally true that the decorations proposed by M. Ledoux are of an absolutely new genre since they represent three scenes."[89] But his frustration with the shallow depth, the lack of vertical space either above or below the stage, the poor resources afforded by a provincial town for the building and maintenance of machines and the employment of skilled operators caused him to conclude that "the mad idea of a triple scene on the part of the architect" had complicated his task unnecessarily.[90]

Ledoux himself contributed designs for some of the sets, notably those for a "salon and gallery together" and part of the decoration for a "public square," and also delineated the painting of the curtain. These, unlike others painted by local artists, were attested by a member of the Académie d'Architecture and a professor of the Académie de Sculpture et Peinture of Besançon to be in an "architecture of the very best taste," with "nothing neglected in the perspective in order to render the illusion perfect."[91] Yet perhaps the most striking of his designs for the scenery of the new theater was that depicted in his engraving of the cross section, looking toward the stage. Framed by the rusticated proscenium, a stage set representing a huge basilican hall, with a colonnade of the giant Corinthian order and a coffered barrelvault, was deployed in diagonal perspective. But at the rear, instead of the traditional apse, Ledoux painted a clear representation of

Ledoux, Theater of Besançon, view of entrance portico, 1947. Photograph from Arch. Phot. Paris/SPADEM.

the proscenium of the theater, through which, at the far left of the stage, was visible the amphitheater of the auditorium, as if seen in reflection from the stage itself. The audience in the real auditorium was thus presented with a vision of itself, a mirror image of the *salle* in the scene. This ingenious illusion can be explained by Ledoux's adherence to a tradition of representation in which the published engraving of a theatrical design generally showed the stage as set for the formal opening of the theater, its royal inauguration.

The Theater of Besançon was rushed to opening during 1784, to coincide with the proposed visit of the Prince de Condé, Governor of Burgundy, and his son, the Duc de Bourbon.[92] The ceremony on 9 August 1784 included a reception by the magistrature and de Lacoré and the performance of two plays. In addition, a preliminary piece was presented, in the words of the record of the Hôtel de Ville, "a spectacle *analogous to that of the presence of their royal highnesses,*" that is, a theatrical representation of the opening of the theater.[93] Ledoux's backdrop no doubt depicted this ceremony. From the royal box, to the right of the proscenium, the fictive royal box of the scene would have appeared in a direct line, explaining the set's forced angle perspective. In the event, the princes, taking their cue from the amphitheatrical architecture, as Ledoux would have wanted, "after having examined their boxes, had preferred to sit in the middle of the gallery, directly in front of the stage."[94]

Ledoux's theatrical allegory, as Daniel Rabreau has pointed out, did not simply refer to the specific conditions of Besançon.[95] His understanding of the theater as a microcosm of the city, and of the social world as a whole, was perfectly expressed in this image of a theater audience at once extended, so to speak, into the city by way of the scene, and yet closed on itself by a city that represented a theater. Over thirty years later, Schinkel would confirm this idea of the city as theater, the theater as city in his own painted backdrop for the inauguration of the new opera house in Berlin. His perspective, now calculated from the central position of the king in the auditorium, showed the opera house itself, exactly as it would appear, were the intervening buildings cleared away, from the private apartments of the royal palace. Kurt Forster

has demonstrated the complex manner in which Schinkel thus integrated his own perspectival vision of the urban landscape with this privileging of the royal view.[96] Such a doubled reflection of the power of sight was intimated by Ledoux's engraving of the *coup d'oeil,* which summarized the political aesthetics not only of his theater but also of his town within the Saline de Chaux. In this extraordinary "envisioning" of the theater, Ledoux, as noted, showed the auditorium as if reflected in the pupil of an eye, the tiered seats rising to the upper colonnade. From a hidden source above the entablature a beam of light expands, as if to flood the stage itself. But instead of containing the beam within the reflection proper, Ledoux extended it beyond the eye to the borders of the engraving. The light, originating at the rear of the auditorium like any stage light, consequently seems to come from inside the eye, as though emulating the commonplace "all-seeing eye" of Freemasonic iconography. Thus the eye, which realistically must belong to an actor or director standing on stage, both gains light from the auditorium and, in turn, floods the audience, or the viewer of the image, with light: the light of vision, of reason, but also of power. In the context of the theater, this image clearly represented the reciprocal relations between audience and play, informed by the multiple powers of sight. In the theatrical plan of the Saline de Chaux, such a visual contract seemed to be sustained by the central position of the director, flanked by his theater of production, overseeing an audience that, in the curved amphitheater of its social housing, played a double role of spectator and actor.

This merging of the aesthetic of the scene with the aestheticized perception of the world was, of course, common in the last half of the eighteenth century. The dramatist and writer L. Carrogis, known as Carmontelle, who created what he referred to as a *pays d'illusions* in the landscapes and fabriques of the Jardin Monceau for the Duc d'Orléans,[97] the architect Nicolas Le Camus de Mézières, who staged plays in the private *salle de spectacle* on his family estate at Charonne and dreamed of a naturally expressive architecture;[98] Louis-Sébastien Mercier, whose dramatic vision informed his *tableaux* of Parisian life;[99] even utopian reformers like Nicolas-Edme Rétif de la Bretonne, whose *Mimographe* elided the engraved versions of Ledoux's designs, published by Ramée, show that he had taken the opportunity to enlarge and perfect the amphitheatrical model to accommodate three thousand spectators, while suggesting a far more elaborate and monumental exterior treatment, suitable for a town of the first order. It was his private response to De Wailly and Poyet.

For his initial submission, of which only one rendering survives, a three-quarters perspective of the theater, Ledoux designed a portico with a giant order of eight Corinthian columns leading to an entry into the high, rusticated base on which the theater was raised.[115] At the first level this base in turn served as a terrace overlooking the square, with a series of Corinthian Serlianas that opened to the outside from the first row of boxes. The "base" of the theater acted as an interface between the city and its *salle de spectacle* not only formally but functionally: along each side stood a row of ten shops, reflecting those that encircled the square, while the main entrance led into a huge vestibule with sixteen freestanding columns and thence into a "grand café" of the same size beneath the auditorium. Together, Ledoux noted, the vestibule and café could accommodate two thousand people for fêtes and balls.[116] The auditorium itself was more perfectly amphitheatrical than that of Besançon, rising in six semicircular tiers from the *parquet* and *parterre*. Sensitive to the different social composition of the Marseilles audience, Ledoux retained a standing *parterre,* in front of which a seated *parquet* reflected the more traditional disposition; above this he placed a first row of boxes for rich merchants and nobles, rows for the bourgeoisie, and finally the *paradis* for servants and soldiers. Ledoux also marked the specific requirements of a theater in a seaport town by providing separate seating for "artisans and prostitutes."[117] No doubt, following his attempt to instate a kind of social order by means of architectural form at Besançon, Ledoux felt that the separation of the prostitutes, inevitably a large part of the audience, would contribute to their better policing. His opinion was not shared by de Beauvau, who found this disposition the weakest part of Ledoux's scheme:

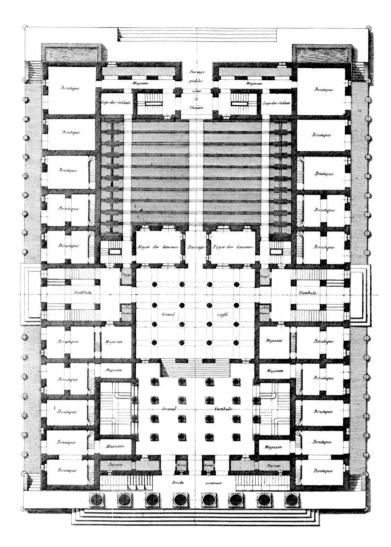

Ledoux, Project for the Theater of Marseilles, 1785, plan of first floor showing vestibule, shops, and large central café. Engraving from Ramée, *Ledoux,* pl. 82.

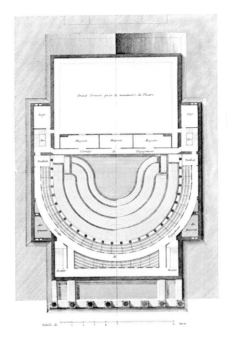

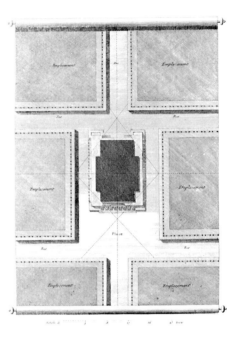

Ledoux, Project for the Theater of Marseilles. *Above left,*
plan of sixth level of boxes;
above right, site plan; *below,*
section through auditorium
and stage. Engravings from
Ramée, *Ledoux,* pls. 86, 87.

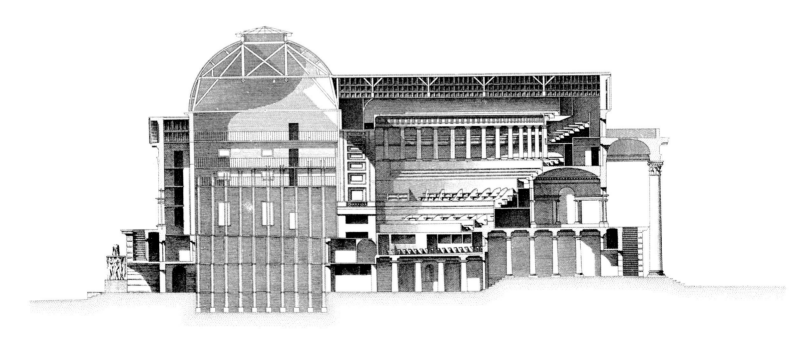

These very impractical arrangements everywhere will be of the greatest consequence in Marseilles because of the number and type of people who go to the theater and the difficulty presented by the project of Ledoux of maintaining good order, since the sailors and workers, etc., would occupy the amphitheaters of the fourth boxes and the prostitutes would be on the third level. How to contain twelve hundred people of all nations and estates, piled up on levels multiplied to excess and easy to pass between in every direction. What disorders, what accidents would result from such a layout.[118]

For Ledoux, however, the conception of his grand theater, *à l'antique,* symbolized the return of Marseilles to its ancient dignity, its Greek foundation rivaling in age the Roman origins of the capital of Provence, Aix-en-Provence, and its new monumentality equaling the ancient remains of Orange, Arles, and Nîmes.[119] In the engraved revision of the perspective view, later published by Ramée, Ledoux set his theater in a scene that might have been drawn from Serlio, with fortified towers, walls, and an amphitheater in the background, as if Marseilles had regained its *Romanità.* The chariot of Apollo drawn by a quadriga, which surmounted the Corinthian portico, was now seen against a dome, replacing the original pyramidal roof over the stage, in an echo of an imaginary Pantheon. Such an evocation of Rome in the old center of the Gallo-Roman empire was entirely consistent with the emerging sensibility of antiquarians, historians, and legislators toward the visible signs of a local and Gallic Rome, more intimate and accessible than those of Italy. Increasingly, from Charles-Louis Clérisseau and Jacques-Guillaume Legrand's monograph of 1778 on the amphitheater at Nîmes, to Calonne's efforts to encourage excavations there and elsewhere, in emulation of those begun further south in Pompeii and Herculaneum, this sensibility took on all the aspects of a primitive movement for the conservation, if not restoration, of monuments that were for the first time seen as essential memorials of the national patrimony.[120]

PHYSIOGNOMIES OF JUSTICE: AIX-EN-PROVENCE

CITY AND PARLEMENT

If in the Theaters of Besançon and Marseilles Ledoux had successfully framed a return to antiquity within a suitable contemporary guise, in the commission for the new Palais de Justice at Aix-en-Provence he was confronted with a difficult and unavoidable choice between the protection of a major historic landmark and its destruction in favor of a new development.[121] The old Palais de Justice, in a dangerous state of disrepair since 1775, had served as the home of the Parlement of Provence since its foundation in 1501.[122] Earlier, the palace had been the fortified residence of the Counts of Provence. Moreover, enclosed within its walls stood two of the round towers that marked the entrance to the Roman foundation of Aquae Sextiae and outside its ancient ramparts a square tower later verified to be a Roman mausoleum.[123] The fabric of the palace thus literally exhibited every stage of the growth and history of Aix. Arranged around the Palais de Justice were the town hall, the Cathedral of Saint Sauveur, the archbishop's palace, and the university. It thus stood as the center of a group of buildings in the old Bourg and Ville Comtale that together represented the position of Aix as site of the provincial government and first town of Provence.[124]

The Parlement of Provence, one of the twelve sovereign parlements in the nation administering a mixture of local and royal justice, had been founded at the beginning of the sixteenth century. It was comprised of a president (who since the end of the seventeenth century was regularly the Intendant), nine vice-presidents, and, by 1783, some eighty-four counselors, together with numerous prosecutors, lawyers, and clerks. Its powers were wide, embracing the judgment of cases brought on behalf of the king, the church, colleges, privileged communities and corporations, and individuals; the administration of local and provincial police; the oversight of the guilds and communes; the political functions of registering royal acts and annexing the papal bulls, as well as the right of remonstrance against what it considered a too great

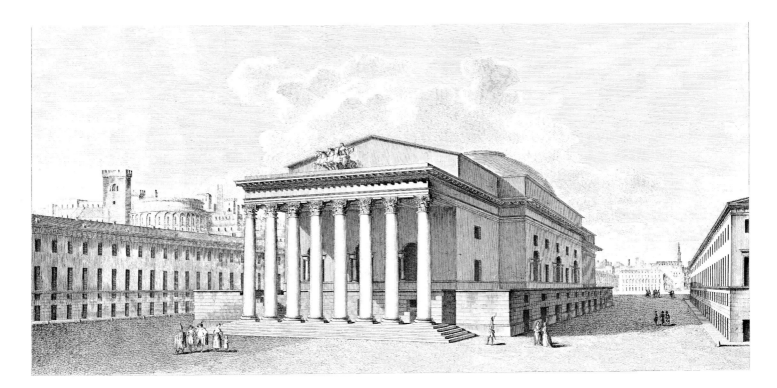

Ledoux, Project for the Theater of Marseilles, perspective
view. Engraving from Ramée,
Ledoux, pl. 88.

Plan of the Palais de Justice,
Aix-en-Provence, in the late
eighteenth century before its
demolition in 1786. Drawing
by A. Vidler.

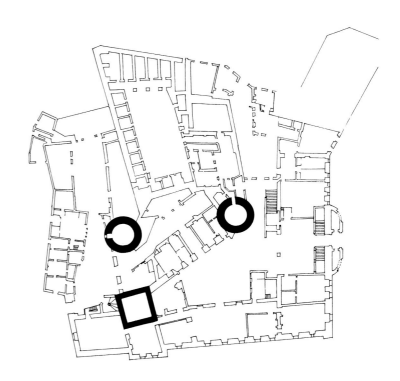

extension of royal authority. Since the sixteenth century the Parlement had been divided into three main houses: the Grande Chambre, which registered legislation, royal and papal, regulated the lower courts, and administered civil judgments over the nobility, royal officials, and higher clergy; the Chambre de la Tournelle, or criminal house, which heard appeals in criminal cases, administering corporal punishment, and shared some jurisdiction with the Grande Chambre over the privileged; and the Chambre des Enquêtes, the lowest court, which heard the appeals of the nonprivileged. Side by side with the Parlement sat three other bodies: the Cours des Comptes, Aides et Finances, the second sovereign court of Provence, which administered all cases of civil and criminal infractions involving taxation; the office of the Trésoriers Généraux de France, or provincial tax collection bureau; and the chief seneschal court of Provence, the highest of twelve, concerned with civil and criminal cases smaller than those appealed to the upper houses of parliament.[125] Not accidentally, the parlements were centers of opposition to royal centralization; subject only to the Royal Council, the *nobles de robe* built their power on local grievances and would often withhold their right to register royal edicts.

Proud of its independence, tracing its legislative tradition to Roman times, its magistrates were powerful nobles in their own right, often descended from family dynasties as eminent as those of many nobles of the sword.[126] Thus the Intendant and Premier Président from 1748, Charles-Jean-Baptiste des Gallois de la Tour, was the son of the former Intendant and Premier Président; the Président Jules-François-Paul de Fauris de Saint-Vincens was similarly descended from a family that had been ennobled for services to the Parlement at the beginning of the century. Many, presidents and counselors alike, were erudites and historians, collectors of local antiquities, legal scholars, and political theorists. Fauris de Saint-Vincens, who wrote several essays on the history of Provence and of the Parlement, was a member of the Académie de Marseilles and a correspondent of the Académie Royale des Inscriptions et Belles Lettres, amassing a huge library that he left to the city of Aix. Lawyers to Parlement, such as C. F. Bouche, G. Grégoire, and J. B. Boyer de

Fonscolombe, wrote histories of Provence from partisan points of view, emphasizing traditional rights and customs in their struggle against royal privileges. In the close-knit Aixois society many were also joined by ties to the Masonic lodges of the town—Etoile Persévérance, Les Amis Réunis, Saint-Jean d-Ecosse, Saint-Jean de Jérusalem, and l'Amitié, which last was founded in 1781 by nine magistrates of the sovereign courts.[127]

Aix, as a parliamentary town with some twenty percent of its population in the 1780s employed in administrative positions, relied on the prosperity of the parliamentarians for its own; the Palais de Justice was the veritable center of city life, and its rituals and festivals rivaled, and often combined with, those of the archbishopric. During the eighteenth century, despite a chorus of nostalgic voices lamenting the loss of power, splendor, and economic force of the Parlement and city, the entire town south of the old Palais Comtale was replanned and extended according to the precepts and forms of Enlightenment planning. The Cours, the long avenue running across the city from east to west, was embellished by fountains, new *hôtel* façades, and *allées* of trees. The public baths, to the northwest, was rebuilt in quasi-antique form; large-scale speculations in property development gave rise to new residential quarters.

On 29 September 1771, together with the other parliaments of the realm, the Parlement of Aix had been "exiled" by the royal chancellor, Augustin de Maupeou, to be superseded by a counterparliament whose members, drawn from the Cours des Comptes, were eager to gain their own personal power. Reestablished in the winter of 1775 under the ministry of Turgot, the old Parlement reinstalled itself with great pomp and celebration; it was to remain in session until the end of 1788 and the recall of the Estates to Paris.[128] Many contemporaries and later historians were convinced that it was resentment against the temporary parliament of Maupeou that fired the initiative to tear down, rather than restore, the old Palais Comtale—a kind of political revenge against the monument that sheltered the unlawful parliament. For, its prestige notwithstanding, the building was uninhabitable according to the parliamentarians, returning in January 1775 after their three years of exile. The ceilings of the Grande Chambre were falling in, and a passerby had been injured by a fragment of masonry detached from a balcony.[129] Pending repairs the palace was evacuated. Surveys were conducted by a local architect, Brun, as well as by Ledoux, who was called to Aix in October 1776.[130] Ledoux's report cited water damage and unstable foundations, and concluded that no useful restoration could be undertaken.[131] By the beginning of 1778 he had drawn up a project for a new parliament building, resited on open land outside the old walls, well to the southwest of the Bourg at the end of the Cours.[132] To connect the palace to the center he envisaged extending the Cours to the east, which would form a wide avenue cutting across the town, framed at one end by the parliament and at the other by a triumphal arch. Ledoux thus applied to Aix the precepts of urban embellishment common among post-Enlightenment thinkers from Patte to De Wailly. This proposal—together with two others prepared between 1779 and 1783 that also avoided the site of the old palace—was rejected out of hand by the Assemblée de Provence, which resented the intrusion of "foreigners" into its affairs and refused the expense of what it considered grandiose schemes.[133]

But behind this refusal, as Ledoux reluctantly realized, was a strong allegiance to the site of the old building. A move to the periphery would relinquish a privileged position in the city. As one of the two traditional foci of religious and secular festivals, the processions and rituals of which took place between the palace and the cathedral, the parliament building was locked, not only physically but also socially, into a more or less fixed location. As late as 1787 Claude-François Achard, listing the endless fêtes and ceremonies in his *Description historique . . . de la Provence,* and, a decade earlier the Abbé Grégoire, meticulously analyzing the weeklong festivities for Corpus Christi, situated the Palais de Justice at the heart of a closed network of streets and monuments that served as the theatrical backdrops for public processions and *bazoches,* or carnivals.[134]

While almost everyone agreed on the need to maintain the site of the palace, opinion was divided on the different strategies for refurbishing the old building. Evidently, by

1784, a majority had been persuaded on the course of demolition and complete rebuilding. Rumors spread that the proud parliamentarians were pleased to raze a structure that had, even if only for four years, housed a rival judicial body. Other factions accused the lawmakers of wanting to profit from the financial speculation in an area of the town where many owned property.[135] But for most enlightened justices, the destruction of an ill-maintained, ill-ventilated, and inconvenient building without evident architectural merit, one that had stood empty, half-ruined and useless for nearly ten years, was a matter of progressive logic and simple common sense. The financial contribution of the crown was undoubtedly a deciding factor. Such was the basis for the final support of Ledoux's new projects of 1784–85, which, as ratified by the crown in 1786, proposed to install the new palace directly on the site of the old and to demolish a block of houses to accommodate the new prisons.[136] Demolition, tentatively begun in 1776, was hastened, and in 1787 work commenced on the foundations of Ledoux's Palais de Justice and prisons. In the event construction of both buildings, advanced to first-floor level by 1789, was suspended in 1790, and never recommenced. The Palais de Justice and Prisons would be completed, but according to the designs of Michel Pench and between 1822 and 1832.

But in the face of the imminent disappearance of the old palace, a current of opposition emerged led by local antiquarians and historians, a number of them distinguished members of the Parlement: the Président Fauris de Saint-Vincens, the painter Esprit Gibelin, and the lawyer Charles-François Bouche were among those who voiced their anger at the destruction of the three Roman towers within the palace.[137] Saint-Vincens, in a report of 1786 submitted to the Abbé Barthélemy in Paris, summarized their position: "In demolishing the old Palais de Justice of Aix, they have destroyed to its very foundations an ancient monument enclosed within its walls."[138] Gibelin followed the course of the demolition with the help of Ledoux's contractor, Brunet: "It is with sadness, I tell you," he wrote, "that I learned of the destruction of the towers of the Palais of Aix."[139] Both Saint-Vincens and Gibelin prepared detailed archaeological reports, establishing

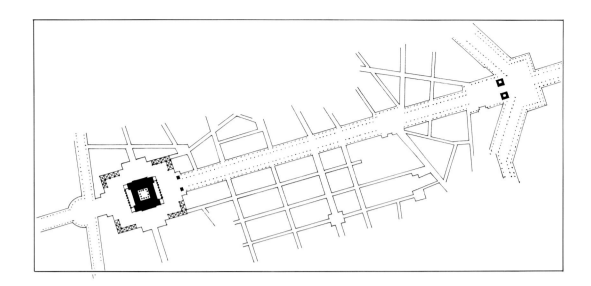

Ledoux, First project for a new Palais de Justice, Aix-en-Provence, sited at the end of the Cours, outside the walls, c. 1777–78. Redrawn from the plan in the Bibliothèque Méjanes, Aix-en-Provence, 1059, 10.

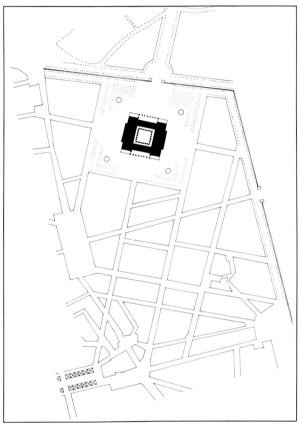

Ledoux, Second project for the new Palais de Justice, Aix-en-Provence, behind the district known as Le Prêcheurs, c. 1779. Redrawn from the plan in the Bibliothèque Méjanes, 1059, 9.

Plan of Aix-en-Provence in the late eighteenth century, showing the sites of Ledoux's second and third projects for the Palais de Justice. Drawing by A. Vidler.

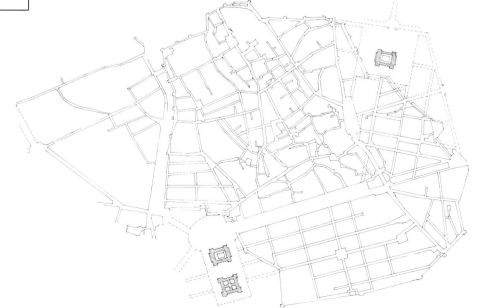

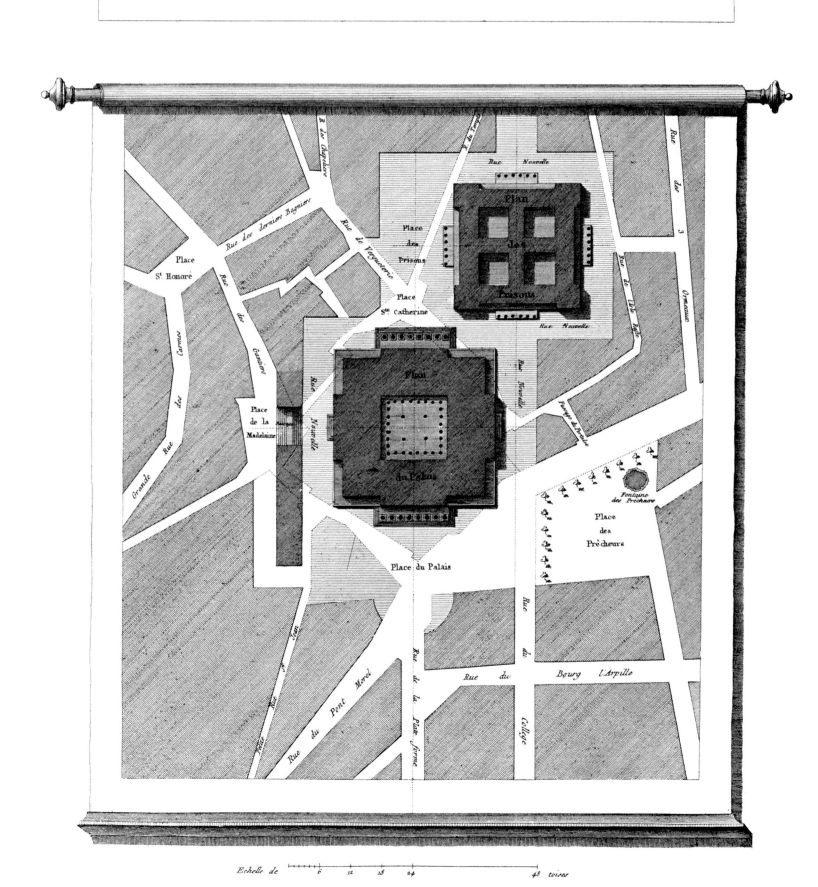

Echelle de | | | | | | | | | | 6   12   18   24   48   toises

Ledoux, Definitive project for the Palais de Justice and prisons, Aix-en-Provence, on the site of the old Palais, 1787. Engraving from Ramée, *Ledoux,* pl. 44.

The Treasury Tower and Clock Tower, Palais de Justice, Aix-en-Provence. From Esprit-Antoine Gibelin, *Lettre sur les tours antiques qu'on a démolies à Aix-en-Provence* (Aix-en-Provence, 1787).

LA TOUR DU TRÉSOR, d'après GIBELIN

3. - GIBELIN

the date and function of the square tower and analyzing the objects found in its base—medals, annulets, and two urns. Gibelin supervised the recording of the towers before their final demolition. The most outspoken opponent, however, was Bouche. As early as 1785, in his history of Provence, he lamented the disappearance of the towers, developing a long polemic on behalf of the restoration of historic monuments and suggesting that it would have been more in the spirit of the eighteenth century either to have resited the towers, according to ancient Greek practice, or to have planned the reconstruction around them.[140] Two years later, in his contributions to Achard's *Description historique,* he repeated his *éloge* of the towers and detailed his earlier plan of partial restoration. In a passionate attack on "modern architecture" and its ephemeral virtues, he called for the memorialization of the lost monuments by bronze columns placed on blocks of marble—a recognition of the first masons of Aix by a prominent eighteenth-century Freemason.[141]

Ledoux, aware of the belated movement for preservation, seemed unconcerned. Writing to his friend and fellow developer Joseph Saveur Mignard in November 1786, he observed dryly that "with regard to the urn and the portrait, I think that the urn is good to see, but its form is of little interest and can only be pleasing to those who gather in the *cabinets des antiquités*."[142] Certainly, while he had avoided building over the old palace for as long as possible, he did not envision the towers as works of art; their interest, solely archaeological and antiquarian, did not compete with the values of his own building. In the event, his design for both the palace and the prisons incorporated enough overt references to the antique past of Aix to satisfy the majority of Parlement. They were, moreover, embodied in a composition that responded at once to the complex programmatic needs of the daily and monthly rituals of justice and to their symbolic representation.

THE PALAIS DE JUSTICE

The old palace had accommodated its diverse functions in an agglomeration of buildings built at different periods, loosely grouped around three irregularly shaped courtyards.[143] To the front, opening onto the Place des Prêcheurs, were the courts of finance and justice; to the north, the prisons; to the rear, the governor's apartments, with stables and carriage houses. Sometime during 1783, following the appointment of a new governor, the Prince de Beauvau, the prisons and governor's quarters were distinguished from the function of the Parlement proper: Ledoux was asked to draw up plans for a new governor's mansion—a project that he still hoped to finance in 1785 by virtue of the savings he predicted on his proposal for the Theater of Marseilles—and separate designs for the prisons appear on all projects after 1783.[144] This gradual "specialization" of the program allowed Ledoux to consider the form and character of the Palais de Justice as a single coherent type, distinct from those of the prison or the private *hôtel*. At the same time, it enabled him to exploit the dialectical relations between justice and punishment, literally enclosed in the same building in the old palace, juxtaposed functionally and rhetorically in Ledoux's design.

In his treatment of both parliament and prisons, Ledoux clearly attempted to preserve the traces of a spatial and even an architectural order that had served the traditional courts for so many centuries. These arrangements, originally the result of haphazard growth and the necessary compromises of an existing building, had nevertheless gradually become embodied in the habits and many of the formal ceremonies of the Parlement. The hierarchy of the courts had dictated a distribution that placed the Cour des Comptes with its chapel and public waiting room, or *salle des pas perdus,* on the ground floor, and reached by a grand stair from the east entrance, the Parlement with its three courts, their *salles des pas perdus, salles d'audience,* and chapel on the second floor. Ledoux adopted this vertical division, articulating it in plan and section to reinforce what had become ingrained tradition. Similarly, the lower offices of the Seneschal of Aix and the Tresoriers Généraux, squeezed between parliament and prisons in the old palace, were in Ledoux's plans accommodated in the mezzanine. Finally, the prisons themselves, originally built behind the Roman wall connecting the two round towers, seem in Ledoux's treatment to have literally been detached from their former site and reinstated, with four corner towers, as an isolated building.

On the level of architectural expression, also, Ledoux overtly referred to the demolished palace and to the historical monuments of Aix in general. The efforts of Serge Conard to demonstrate that Ledoux assimilated "traces" of the old towers into the geometries of his palace are unconvincing, given the complete lack of two- or three-dimensional correspondence between the site or the massing of the Roman remains and Ledoux's scheme. In the four-cornered prison building, however, Ledoux certainly remembered them.[145] The resemblance, pointed out by Conard, to the hypothetical "restoration" of the Roman structure drawn in the fifteenth century by Giuliano Sangallo, during his journey through the Midi, is striking.[146] Sangallo not only duplicated the two towers into four, but positioned a second courtyard behind, as if to imply,

as Conard also suggests, the celebrated transition, well known to Ledoux, between the Temples of Virtue and Honor built by Marcellus in Rome. But even if Ledoux did not have immediate access to this image, conserved in the archaeological tradition of Aixois scholars from Jean-Scholastique Pitton and Nicolas-Claude Fabri de Peiresc in the seventeenth century to Gibelin in the eighteenth, his "quotation" of the towers in the prison was unmistakable. Perhaps a more likely iconographical source would have been a collection of engravings published in Aix in 1760, one plate of which showed the two round towers at the corners of an apparently complete rectangular building of solid Roman masonry.[147] The same plate also depicted the mausoleum as a freestanding structure, rising from its square base to its two cylindrical upper stories, each surrounded by columns. The tempietto-like form of the upper portion of this monument might well have provided the inspiration for Ledoux's own "tempietto" crowning the pyramidal central roof of the Palais de Justice. This latter motif would also have been seen, especially in view of its function as a lantern to the *grande salle* of the Parlement, as a restoration of the so-called Temple du Soleil, a circle of antique Corinthian columns integrated into the baptistery of the Cathedral of Saint Sauveur and represented in the engravings of 1760 as an open-air temple precinct.[148]

Nonetheless, the two buildings designed by Ledoux between 1783 and 1787 were conceived as self-enclosed, monumental exemplars of their types, more concerned with the representation of their late-eighteenth-century needs and roles than with any eclectic citations from the past. Unwilling to forge a compromise that incorporated ancient and modern fragments, unable to accept a literal historicism, Ledoux remained consistent to the architectural aims of the *saline* and the theaters: to achieve by geometrical and formal synthesis the constitution of fundamentally modern monuments.

Indeed, the outlines of the Palais de Justice changed only slightly from their first depiction on the plan of 1778 to their final form.[149] A square block with an interior courtyard and colonnaded porticoes to front and rear, echoed on either side by equal projections, comprised the basic *parti*—a play of the square and the Greek cross. In the definitive project, Ledoux utilized the axial and volumetric properties of this combination, already exploited in the Director's Building of the Saline de Chaux and in the Theater of Besançon, to reinforce the different hierarchies of the judicial bodies as well as to unite them around a common center. Thus he enclosed the open central courtyard to provide *salles des pas perdus* for the Comptes on the ground floor and for the Parlement on the *piano nobile*. The ribbed, lantern-topped dome lit the Parlement from above, while the Greek-cross plan of the parliamentary *salle* provided four square light wells at the corners for the Comptes below. This centralization was further emphasized by the hypostyle hall of the Comptes; a square room, four steps lower than the outer offices, it was surrounded by baseless Doric columns, four columns freestanding in the center. The *grande salle* of Parlement was similarly surrounded by a colonnade, a giant Corinthian order a story and a half high. Above, the uniform gallery of the archives, carried on Ionic columns, encircled the *salles*. As in the Director's Building at Chaux, this centrality was in turn inflected by the great central stair, which, divided at the ground level to provide access to the Comptes, joined at the mezzanine in monumental preparation for the *grande salle,* beyond which it continued in steps leading to the chapel of the Parlement, and again further in a final series of steps up to its altar. In longitudinal section, this emulated the ascent to the chapel of the *saline*. The continuous upward movement from the front to the rear of the building was punctuated by secondary movements into different *salles d'audience* along the way, marked from above by three sources of daylight—over the stairs, the *grande salle,* and the chapel itself—and resolved to the rear of the building by the double *salles d'audience* flanking the chapels of the Comptes and Parlement on each level.

On the exterior, Ledoux marked the intersection of axiality and centrality by the differentiation of entrances and façades on the one hand and by the overall pyramidal composition of the building on the other. The most important entrance, that to the Parlement, facing southeast toward the Place des Prêcheurs and the rue de la Plateforme, was fronted

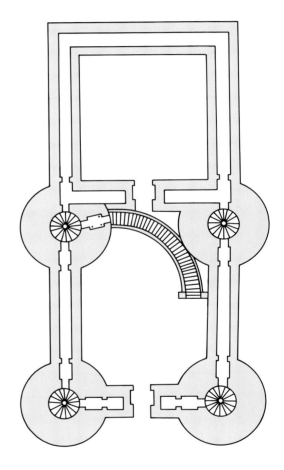

Plan of the old Palais de Justice or Palais Comtale, by Giovanni da Sangallo, 1494–96. Redrawn from Michel Clerc, *Aquae Sextiae: Histoire d'Aix-en-Provence dans l'Antiquité* (Aix-en-Provence, 1916), 430.

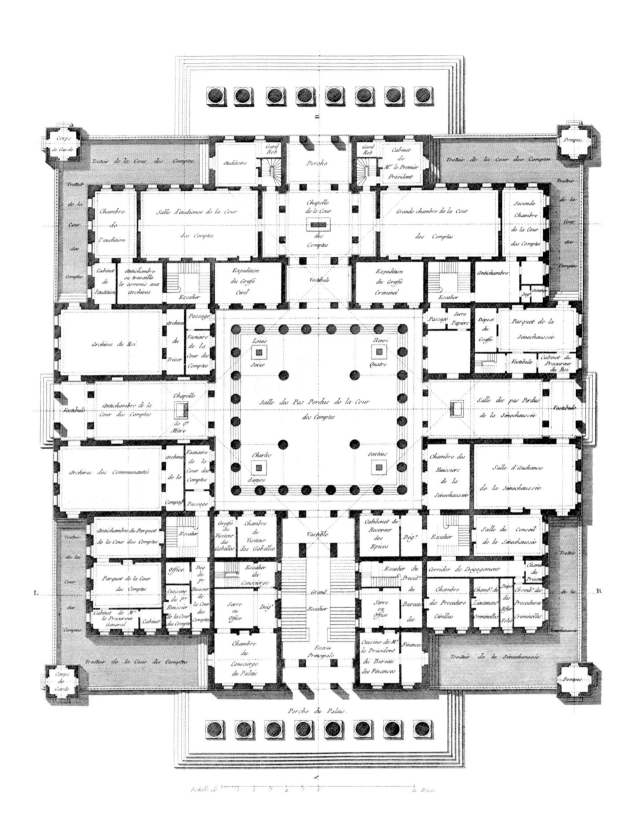

Ledoux, Palais de Justice, plan
of first floor. Engraving from
Ramée, *Ledoux,* pl. 46.

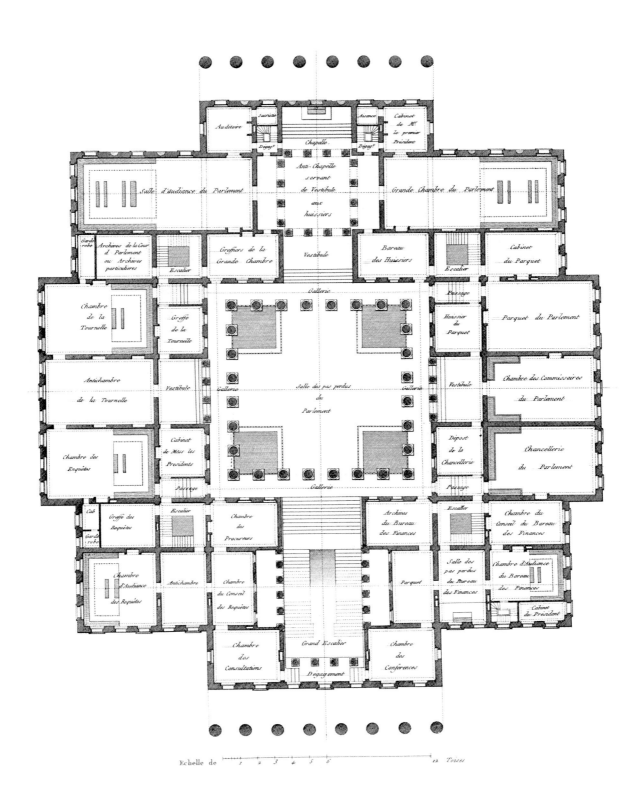

Auditoire Sacristie Aisance Cabinet de M.^r le premier Président

Chapelle

Anti-Chapelle servant de Vestibule aux huissiers

Salle d'audience du Parlement   Grande Chambre du Parlement

Garde robe   Archives de la Cour d. Parlement ou Archives particulières   Greffiers de la Grande Chambre   Vestibule   Bureau des Huissiers   Cabinet du Parquet

Escalier   Escalier

Chambre de la Tournelle   Greffe de la Tournelle   Gallerie   Passage   Huissier du Parquet   Parquet du Parlement

Antichambre de la Tournelle   Vestibule   Gallerie   Salle des pas perdus du Parlement   Gallerie   Vestibule   Chambre des Commissaires du Parlement

Chambre des Enquêtes   Cabinet de M^{ss} les Présidents   Dépost de la Chancellerie   Chancellerie du Parlement

Passage   Gallerie   Passage

Cab   Greffe des Requêtes   Escalier   Chambre des Procureurs   Archives du Bureau des Finances   Escalier   Chambre du Conseil du Bureau des Finances

Garde robe   Chambre d'Audience des Requêtes   Antichambre   Chambre du Conseil des Requêtes   Parquet   Salle des pas perdus du Bureau des Finances   Chambre d'Audience du Bureau des Finances

Cabinet du Président

Chambre des Consultations   Grand Escalier   Chambre des Conférences

Dégagement

Echelle de   1 2 3 4 5 6   12 Toises

Ledoux, Palais de Justice, plan
of second floor. Engraving
from Ramée, *Ledoux,* pl. 48.

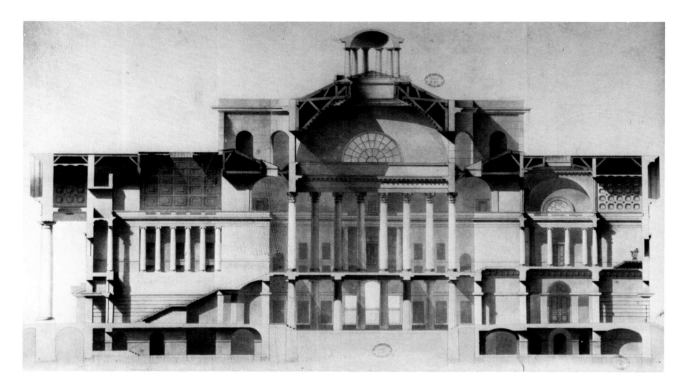

Ledoux, Palais de Justice, longitudinal section, east-west. Drawing from Ledoux's office, Bibliothèque Méjanes, 1059, 35.

Ledoux, Palais de Justice, cross section looking toward the west. *Opposite above,* cross section through the chapels and audience chamber; *opposite below,* front elevation. Engravings from Ramée, *Ledoux,* pls. 59, 57, 53.

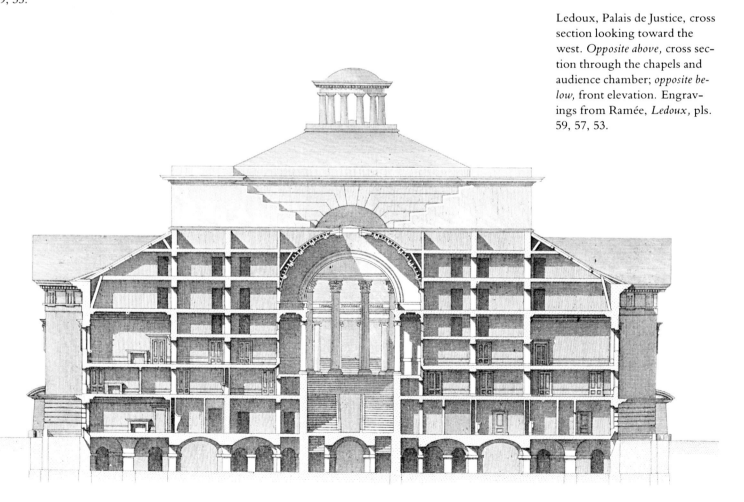

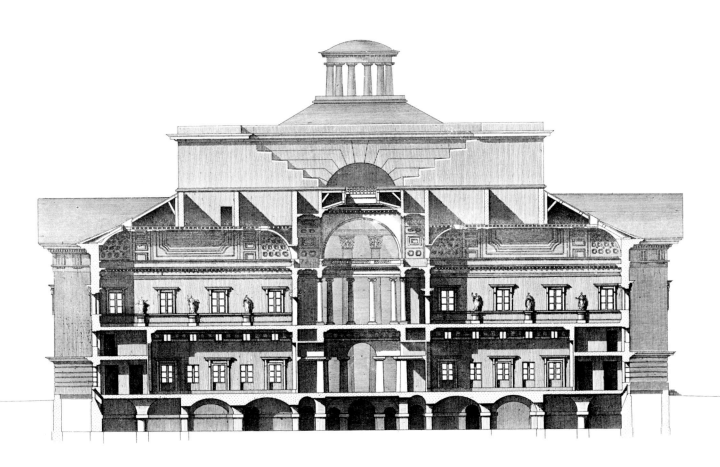

Echelle de 1 2 3 4 5 6 12 toises

Echelle de 1 2 3 4 5 6 12 toises

by a giant portico of the Tuscan order—reinforcing the public seriousness of the type—surmounted by a pediment with triumphal bas-reliefs. The side elevations lacked orders. Instead, square panels of bas-reliefs depicting figures of Victory with trumpets framed the Serlian doorways, above which pediments carried the royal arms. The rear elevation, giving onto the chapel of the Cour des Comptes, received slightly more decoration, as statues in round-headed niches alternated with the plain rectangular windows that encircled the building. The walls were plain, rising from a simply rusticated base to a continuous frieze of carved metopes and triglyphs. On all sides, the roof ascended in a pyramid to the lantern, broken only by the vertical walls of the four stairs leading to the archives, stepped down to the center to reveal the lucarnes of the *grande salle*.

What Ledoux was later to call an "enlightened temple of justice," or a "praetorium," in memory of its Roman origins, thus emerged as a self-conscious synthesis of antique types and motifs, Palladian compositional geometries, and his own, already formed institutional language. Juridical tradition was installed in a combination of basilica, ancient seat of the law, and a temple, which, in the colonnade and architrave surrounding the *grande salle*, recalled at once the original collective temples of the Druids—who legend maintained had installed their own temple in Aix—and Bramante's Tempietto, itself a memory of an antique model. But Ledoux was also recalling his own repertory of types: the Church of Chaux, with its similar Tuscan front, frieze, and section; the Market of Chaux, with its rusticated base and simple fenestration; the Public Baths of Chaux, with its rusticated base, Doric colonnade, and plain walls. All three shared with Aix a Greek-cross and square plan as well as centrally lit, domed rotundas; and like the Palais de Justice, all three seemed the product of a set of antique precedents, as if fabricated from a restricted but rich kit of parts.

THE PRISONS

In the Palais de Justice, Ledoux had been presented with a well-developed program that remained to be, so to speak, given appropriate form and iconography; in the prisons, almost exactly the reverse was true. A host of iconographical experiments and exercises in proper characterization for prisons had followed Piranesi's between 1745 and 1775; from *capricci* to stage sets, the prison had become a favorite subject for the exploration of the "terrible sublime," as defined by Burke in 1765 and applied in theory to the various categories of prison by Blondel in 1771.[150] In the early 1780s Ledoux could draw on a well-established expressive code, which included not only the traditional emblems of heavy rustication, chains, and figures of Justice that had been exploited with mannerist skill by George Dance, Jr., at Newgate, but also a range of stylistic quotations, from the crenellated "Gothic" of J. A. Houssin to the funereal Roman of Jean-Charles Delafosse.[151] The same could not be said, however, of the programmatic or typological form of the prison, which in the 1780s had yet to receive the concentrated attention devoted

Stage designs for the tragedy *Numitor*, 15 July 1783, showing the temple and temple crypt. Drawings from the Fonds P.-A. Pâris, *Architecture*, vol. 5, pl. 68.

Jean-Charles Delafosse,
project for a prison, c. 1780.
Watercolor from the Cooper-
Hewitt Museum.

since 1773 to that of the hospital. The commission of enquiry appointed by Necker and led by Jacques Tenon in 1780 had opened the debate on conditions in the worst Parisian prisons; Pierre-Louis Moreau, city architect of Paris, and then Boullée had proposed ameliorations and additions to the Hôtel de la Force; the Académie had included the subject in its competition program for 1778: but these tentative approaches to the problem displayed a little consistency.[152] No architect set out a model with the same comprehensive views as those of Antoine Petit, Jean-Baptiste Leroy, or Bernard Poyet; and the influential catalogue of types assembled by John Howard had not yet been distributed widely in France.

Ledoux's plan for the prison, drawing on all these sources, nevertheless pushed the formulation of an iconographical and typological program further than any of his contemporaries, attempting to join questions of representation and distribution in a unified type-form. His plan was square, divided into four parts by intersecting galleries on two levels. Each quarter of the prison, following the wisdom of ward separation in hospitals, was segregated by age, sex, and type of crime: quarters for men, women, and children criminals and for civil prisoners. Each quarter was furnished with its own infirmary at the corners of the building. Separate exercise courtyards were formed by the lower level of the galleries, which intersected in the center. On the second floor, this intersection, marked by a circular colonnade of heavy Doric columns, formed the chapel of the prison. On the ground level beneath the infirmaries were workshops, again segregated according to the types of prisoner. Interior corridors overlooking the courtyards serviced the three levels of cells, which were furnished, lit, ventilated, and secure.

In adopting this distribution, seemingly in advance of its time, Ledoux reflected the recommendations of the polemicist, Grub Street critic, and later Revolutionary Jacques-Pierre Brissot de Warville. His *Théorie des lois criminelles,* a prize essay demanding the reorganization of institutions of justice, had been published in 1781.[153] In it Brissot called for a quasi-Physiocratic dissolution of state-controlled institutions, claimed that mendacity would disappear with its causes, and railed against conditions in prisons and hospitals.

Ledoux, Prisons, Aix-en-Provence, 1787, plans of first, second, fourth, and third floors (*clockwise from lower left*). Engravings from Ramée, *Ledoux,* pls. 61, 62.

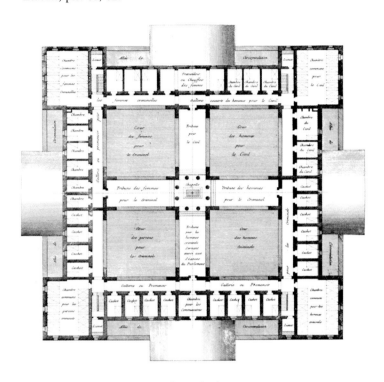

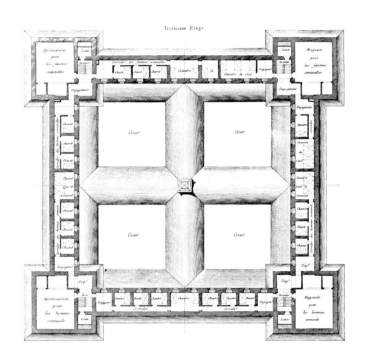

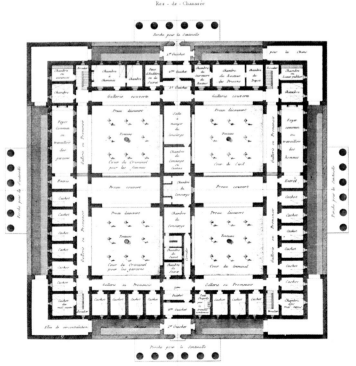

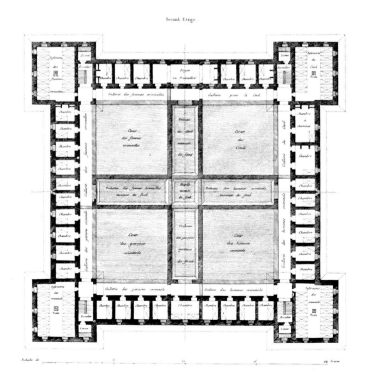

Ledoux, Prisons, section
through east-west axis. Drawing from Ledoux's office, Bibliothèque Méjanes, 1059, 26.

Influenced by Jeremy Bentham's *Remarks on the Hard
Labour Bill* of 1778, to which his essay was in part a response,
Brissot sketched a prison, or "House of Correction," that relied for its effect equally on its plan and its appearance.[154]
Placed on a large open site, his prison, like Ledoux's, was to
be four stories high. He conceived it as a perfect square, divided into four.[155] Each "quarter" was to be set aside for a
different kind of criminal—women and children; debtors; libertines; and murderers or convicted felons awaiting death or
deportation—and each was to be provided with its own services and a separate, open courtyard for exercise. Classification, as in the hospital plans of the 1770s, was thus reinforced
by spatial layout. Separate workshops, each properly heated
and ventilated, were assigned to each quarter, and each would
administer a type of labor carefully proportioned to the severity and type of the crime. Tasks would be calculated by
analogy to impress social and moral virtues on each kind of
criminal: "Thus the vagabonds, the libertines, and convicts
will be occupied in cutting stones, polishing marble, grinding
colors, and in chemical undertakings wherein the life of honest citizens is normally in danger."[156] Brissot, as Michel
Foucault has remarked, seemed to be implying that the continuous activities of cutting, polishing, blending would ultimately be interiorized as a civilizing, rationalizing force that
acted on the prisoner's moral state.[157] Ledoux was to envisage
similar punishments, analogically "fitting the crime," in the
quarries of Chaux; no doubt echoing Brissot, he generalized
this belief in the power of the environment over the personality: "One can be made virtuous or vicious, as the rough or
polished stone, by the friction of our surroundings" (3).

At the center of Brissot's prison would stand the chapel.
Mass would be celebrated daily, the prisoners opening the
windows of their cells to hear the sacred music and religious
instruction. But Brissot also designed his prison as a spectacle
of terror. He prescribed an *épigraphe terrible* over the main
door, heightened by an emblem composed of crossed chains;
he specified that the walls of the prison itself be painted black,
as a fitting background to the "silent sentinels" standing

guard at the main gate. Twice each year the entire institution was to become a kind of living, social sign of its contents, a theater of criminality, opened to the public in order to give to the citizens "the spectacle of the expiations of crime."[158] Balanced between a Piranesian idea of the sublime and a Benthamite machine for punishment, Brissot's scheme was imagined to satisfy the aspirations of artists and administrators alike.

In adopting a similar distribution, Ledoux, perhaps with the agreement of Calonne, was associating himself with a juridical reform movement that implied a comprehensive reformulation of public institutions, ultimately envisaging the disappearance of the prison altogether—a utopia that he was later to adopt in his fictional account of Chaux. Certainly Ledoux was concerned to show himself as connected to the reform movement of the hygienists; having been excluded from the hospital program, he evidently wanted to establish Aix as the center of a new theory and practice of imprisonment. Writing in 1785 to the Intendant de la Tour, he described the urgent need for work on the palace and prisons to start immediately: "I think I have left nothing out. The continual epidemic that rages in the prisons, the humid and unhealthy air that one breathes in the palace placed in the [Place de] Prêcheurs are overriding reasons to accelerate the entire operation of this affair."[159] In this instance, however, despite his allegiance to a rational distribution of needs, Ledoux was less impressive as "hygienist" than as rhetorician of architecture.

PHYSIOGNOMY AND CHARACTER

In the Saline de Caux, Ledoux had employed a mixture of "theatrical" attributes and three-dimensional compositions as a means of investing his buildings with appropriate character, developing an elaborate allegory of power and production. In the prisons of Aix, he attempted to endow the building with a "physiognomy," a personality, that would not depend on the addition of emblematic attributes but would turn the whole edifice into a sign of its character. Like Buffon's animal's or Linnaeus's plants, the building expressed its nature

through its *organization,* its total form. The individual elements—short and massive baseless Doric columns, corner towers capped with funereal roofs, "Gothic" corbeling—recalled previous exercises in characterization; they were, however, integrated into an abstract and purely geometrical mass, plainly expressive of its internal order, but assembled in such a way as to suggest the aspect of a lowering, sombre face. Ledoux was no longer simply drawing on the classical theory of physiognomical characterization of Jean de La Bruyère and Charles Le Brun, but taking his inspiration from more recent, quasi-scientific investigations into the psychological and behavioral interpretation of physiognomy. This "science," elaborated by the Swiss pastor Johann Caspar Lavater between 1775 and 1778, was based on the premise, stated in his *Essays in Physiognomy,* that "the exterior, the visible, the surface of objects indicate their interior, their properties; every external sign is an expression of internal qualities"; and that by careful analysis of the "characteristic lines," the contours and surfaces of a face, the nature of the soul within might be discovered.[160] The Abbé Pernetti in 1750 had already rewritten traditional commonplaces of character reading with psychological emphasis, and anatomists and doctors for the rest of the century—until the critical attacks the phrenologist François-Joseph Gall—were preoccupied with this seemingly fertile line of enquiry.[161]

In architecture, the analogy had been worked by Le Camus de Mézières, who had developed a theory of characterization drawn from a "physiognomical" reading of nature.[162] Noting that in nature "each object possesses a character that is suitable for it, and that often a single line, a simple contour suffices to express it," Le Camus derived for architecture what Le Brun had provided for painting: a proof that emotions and ideas might be evoked by single and therefore easily classifiable lines. Even as "the face of the lion, those of the tiger and the leopard are composed of an assemblage of lines that render them terrible," or "the head of a cat [gives it] the character of betrayal," so, Le Camus claimed, in "inanimate objects," "their form" provoked similar feelings: "Their form makes some pleasing to us, some disagreeable. . . . A building fixes our gaze by means of its mass; its totality attracts or repulses us. In examining a monument we experience different sensations that are opposed to each other: there is gaiety, here melancholy." [163] On this foundation he argued for a synthesis of architecture, painting, and sculpture, "this triple magic," that would repeat the almost magical stage effects of the legendary Servandoni—but with permanent effect.

Ledoux, who was, as Daniel Ramée later noted, a keen student of Servandoni, and whose theory of characterization was, like that of Le Camus, derived from Blondel, likewise compared the character of buildings to "the dominant passions of man: one sees on the face the calm of good conscience, the charitable virtues, generosity, merit, exhaltation, anger, the abuse of pleasures" (119). Like the characters of man, those of architecture might be ranged in order of propriety and morality; they were, or should be, equally unmistakable to the sight. The walls of buildings were in the sense so many depictions of states of mind and morality, each one corresponding to the activity it housed: "When the soul is tranquil, all the parts that constitute the man are in a state of repose; it is the same with the expression of each building. Do you want to represent the tranquility of the interior? Then the exterior should announce the calm and sweet harmony that sustains unity." (204)

Ledoux, long accustomed, as he recalled, to "the habit of analyzing and judging everything in men from their external forms," made the direct connection between these ideas of architectural physiognomy and his designs for the prisons of Aix. In a footnote to his comparisons between human and architectural character, appended to his description of the idea of "anger" in architecture, he recounted his visit, sometime in the 1780s, to the laboratory of a "distinguished anatomist" in Aix, a doctor "Tornatory. [164] An amateur criminologist, this scientist had collected "the bodies of many of those condemned by the criminal code and dissected them" (119). Despite the doctor's reputation—Ledoux remembered that "they reproached him for favoring the systems he held dearly; they regarded him as mad"—his visit was unexpectedly interesting.

I was introduced to him; the presentiment that he had of my impartiality disposed him in my favor. He sat me down in the middle of a select collection of heads, ranged in order. "You who are an artist, who have studied the conformation of the human body and its relations to the brain and stomach," he said, "judge the characters, vices, and crimes of these humiliating remains of the dignity of man." After having reflected, I assembled my thoughts: "The first and the second," I said, "were assassins; the third died of anger." This was enough. He ran to his records, leafed through them: "Ah," he cried, "I am not indeed mad." (119)

Ledoux's visit to the anatomist Pierre-Claude-Jean Tournatoris, whose museum of pathology and osteology had become celebrated in Provence but whose enthusiasm for dissection was regarded locally with suspicion, gave him a direct model for the expression of the prison. Between face and façade Ledoux proposed an analogy; for the *têtes parlantes* of the executed criminals, he substituted *murs parlants*.

Avoiding the more literal transcriptions of facial character to buildings fashionable in the early nineteenth century, notably in the physiognomic experiments of Lequeu, and at the same time resisting the more purely metaphorical analogies of Boullée, Ledoux welded a veritable "expression" of criminality—heavy, lowering walls, slitlike "eyes," and a forbidding "mouth"—to a set of antique references, primarily funereal architecture, by means of an abstract three-dimensional geometry. The result was, in the light of his later ideal designs for Chaux, an intimation of a style of public monumentality entirely new in his work. Properly deployed in the prisons to contribute to the "terrible sublime," it would become the overriding manner for every kind of ideal institution he was to design in the 1790s. Quotation and historical reference would be incorporated as a way of endowing hitherto unknown types with legitimacy and a shadow of meaning, but within an almost all-subsuming vocabulary of abstract form. In the prisons of Aix the ambiguity between pure form and iconographical citation was virtually complete, the one emerging from the other indistinguishably. Thus the specific sources of the tomblike cellular interior, the *pierres-tombales* of the entrance and corner towers—signaled

Ledoux, Prisons, front elevation. Drawing from Ledoux's
office, Bibliothèque Méjanes,
1059, 21.

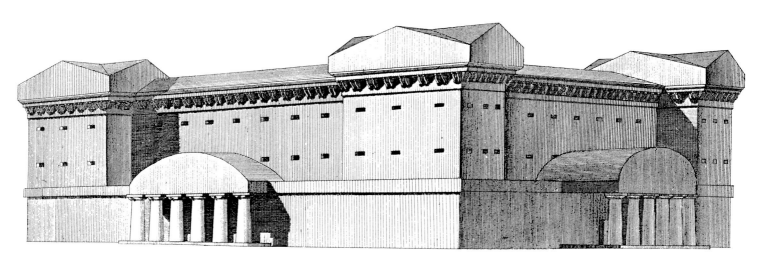

Ledoux, Prisons, perspective
view. Engraving from Ramée,
Ledoux, pl. 64.

accurately enough by Serge Conard as references to the columbaria at Pozzuoli and the fantasies of Delafosse—are less important than the generalized funereal aspect of the place: carved as if from a single block of stone, a primitive sepulchre for the condemned. Inscribed on the "pediment" over the entry was the clear message, reinforced by the architecture: *Securitas publica*.

COMBINATORIAL MODELS: THE *BARRIÈRES* OF PARIS

None of Ledoux's designs, projected or built, were so immediately and consistently the objects of outrage, criticism, and condemnation as were the *barrières* of Paris.[166] The Saline de Chaux had shocked the conventions of court and contractors, but might be dismissed as an aberration in a distant region, in any case no more than a lowly function overaggrandized. The magnificences of the private *hôtels,* from the Pavillon du Barry to the Hôtel Thélusson, were remarked on with curiosity and amazement but were considered no more than expressions of the luxurious follies of their clients. The ideal projects for the city of Chaux would be dismissed after Ledoux's death as characteristic of his madness, or at least megalomania, but in the end they belonged to the relatively harmless realm of utopia. The *barrières,* however, were inextricably joined, in conception and realization, with the fate of the *ancien régime.* Erected in its last years, in secrecy and haste, they were inevitably seen as the visible emblems of fiscal tyranny, the overblown signs of the despised Ferme Générale; their monumentality and strange forms, exaggerating traditional architectural motifs in scale and placement to the point of caricature, seemed apt demonstrations of economic profligacy. They were attacked on every level: to latter-day Physiocrats the *barrières* epitomized a useless investment in urban embellishment and the evils of a monopoly system of centralized taxation. Reform ministers claimed that they denied by their very cost the benefits they were erected to accrue. Journalists seized on their "bizarre" nature and ubiquity as

objects around which to rally criticism of the government and its agents. A wide-ranging coalition of special interests, from the tavern keepers outside the old circuit, whose wine was now taxed, to legal and illegal wine traders, saw their profits undermined by the *barrières.* Property owners resented the expropriation of their lands. Architects and critics railed against the outrageous flouting of all classical canons. What for Ledoux, and a small circle of loyal friends, represented the height of his aspirations as an architect, bringing together the general amelioration of urban circulation at the scale of the entire city, with the monumental embellishment of every quarter—a truly "Roman" project—became in a short time the cause of his downfall and subsequent reputation as an *architecte maudit.*

THE BOUNDARIES OF THE CITY

After the demolition of the old fortifications in 1670, the limits of the city of Paris were no longer determined by defensive needs but instead defined fiscally, as the boundaries of an area of taxation.[167] The enclosure of milestones erected in 1672, supplemented throughout the eighteenth century by wooden palisades, marked the points of collection of the Parisian *droits d'octroi,* duties on provisions brought into the city: the *droits d'entrée,* levied on wine and other liquids; the *pied fourché,* levied on livestock; the various *droits* imposed on straw, wood, coal, cooked fruits, spiced meats, game, and poultry. The collection of these dues was in the hands of the Ferme, which complained continually about the difficulties of administering and policing an often nonexistent "wall" that no longer represented the true limits of a rapidly growing city, that was subject to multiple local laws, that physically was easily breached by tunnels or openings, and that, in the event, was rendered ineffective by the numerous *guinguettes* that traded in untaxed wine outside the *barrières.* In the early 1780s, the pressure for funds not requiring the assent of the Parlement led the Ferme to commission a report on the wall from one of their company, Antoine Lavoisier. In a plan submitted in 1782, the scientist estimated that some six million livres were lost each year through fraud and lack of surveillance and proposed the building of a new, permanent wall, commencing with the left bank quarters that stretched from the Quai d'Austerlitz to the Invalides. Lavoisier's projected route extended the southern boundary of the city to enclose the hitherto external properties of the Hôpital Générale, the Salpêtrière, the districts of Vaugirard, Gros-Caillou, the Ecole Militaire, and the Invalides themselves. His plan clearly associated the demands of fiscal order with those of social policing: the quarters around the Salpêtrière were notorious centers of criminal life, their *guinguettes* bringing together the unemployed, the destitute, and the petty thief, those "dangerous and laboring classes." [168]

Tabled under Necker, Lavoisier's scheme was resurrected in the first year of Calonne's administration as part of a grand plan of amelioration throughout the faubourgs. The Baron de Breteuil sent copies of the proposal to Calonne and to the city of Paris, which asked for a report from the city architect Moreau. Accepted in principle by Moreau, the plan was finally adopted by the Prévôt des Marchands of Paris in early May 1784. The city committed itself to share the expense of construction with the Ferme, clearly anticipating benefits beyond those of efficient tax collection: "We estimate that the project presented by the Fermiers Généraux can only be useful for the collection of the royal dues and that it will have great advantages for the circulation of vehicles and all the operations of commerce." [169] In his *Mémoires,* published long after the Revolution, the Comte de Mollien, in 1784 a young assistant to Calonne, recollected these arguments:

It was not enough to oppose the fraud by a high wall; this fiscal fortification had to have its peripheral road, it had to be isolated inside and especially outside from private habitations. We conceived the conversion of this external space into a boulevard that could encircle the whole city; this would facilitate communications and improve the surveillance by the clerks of the Ferme. At the same time it would provide the inhabitants of Paris with a new promenade, on an open site, with a circuit of some thousands of toises. [170]

Such a peripheral boulevard would not only serve as a kind of *cordon policière* for the better oversight of the tax collectors, it would also provide a route around Paris for heavy traffic

that otherwise would destroy the internal streets. Ledoux, similarly, found justification for the extensive nature of the works in their attendant contributions to every level of urban embellishment, symbolic and practical.

In January 1785 Calonne and Louis XVI, anxious to begin construction of the southern tax wall without too much publicity, arranged for what a later critic would characterize as "only a simple Arrêt du Conseil" [171] to ratify a project already several months under way. In May 1784 Ledoux, as the favored architect of both the Ferme and Calonne, had been asked to prepare preliminary designs; by September the contractors had been selected; and a month later Ledoux had appropriated some ten thousand livres to buy the first materials. By the beginning of June 1785 ground had been broken around the Salpêtrière under the administration of M. de Colonia, Premier Commis des Fermes. By midyear the project was extended to encompass the whole of Paris.

Conscious of the political and financial pressures, Ledoux was indefatigable in pushing ahead the work as fast as possible, preparing designs and estimates, visiting sites, and even intervening directly in disputes over expropriation costs. A proprietor in the Vaugirard district, who demanded some sixty-three thousand livres for a piece of marshy ground that the Ferme valued at twelve thousand livres, was honored by several visits from Ledoux "to make him see the ridiculousness of his request." [172] Couching his vision of the new building program in biblical terms, he assumed personal responsibility for the total urban reconstruction of the city boundaries:

I will transplant mountains; I will drain the marshes, level the precipices whose vapors, raised up by the sun, fall again on human heads when the clouds of the sky condense; I will increase the slopes of the plain to allow sluggish water to run off; I will present projects for roads to deobstruct the interior of the city—these magnificent boulevards, without precedent in their length; I will protect them from excessive loads that crush their paving, a danger for the fearful or preoccupied inhabitant. (18)

The wall and its tollgates should, in this context, be understood as part of a comprehensive plan for the calculation, control, and statistical knowledge of the Parisian population; Lavoisier's inquiry undertaken on behalf of the Ferme was only a part of the Ferme's attempt to transform itself into a modern bureaucracy. The offices on the rue de Grenelle also played a part, as did Ledoux himself, bringing to bear the wisdom of the previous decades: the research into hospital and cemetery planning; the recommendations of Patte and others; the reports of the Académie des Sciences. Fortier has characterized Ledoux's contribution as operating on three levels: "Ledoux imagined a triple functional network: unhealthy activities and industrial establishments (sited far from habitations as recommended by the Académie des Sciences); immense inns whose luxury ought, in theory, to make the population forget the wine and *guinguettes* outside the tax boundary; but, above all, the *barrières,* sumptuous and paradoxical."[173] Here, as Fortier points out, the work of Ledoux should be seen not so much as an impossible contrast between utopia and reality, but rather as the paradox caused by a monumentality displaced beyond its usual programs.

THE WALL OF THE FERME GÉNÉRALE

The general plan called for the construction of a continuous wall, almost eleven feet high and over fourteen miles long, along a route that enclosed a wide strip of largely undeveloped land, increasing the area of Paris itself from approximately 2,720 to 8,320 acres. A peripheral road would follow the wall inside the city; surrounding the city outside the wall, a thirty-nine-foot-wide boulevard would form part of a zone, some 328 feet across, within which, as a security measure, building would be prohibited. At the intersections of entering roads would stand the *barrières* themselves. The Ferme Général estimated the need for a staff of some eight hundred employees to operate the wall: six hundred guards, or *chasseurs,* to police the boundary and two hundred receivers and clerks to assess, collect, and maintain records of the taxes and dues. This force was to be distributed among forty-five points of entry around the wall, according to the relative importance of the individual gates. A typical *barrière* would provide living and sleeping quarters for a brigade of seven to eight guards, and an *avant-garde* of four or five, plus their *brigadier,* rooms for a clerk or receiver, as well as a kitchen, an office, and a cellar for wine and wood storage. Separate *guérites,* or sentry boxes, would shelter the officers on duty. Supplementing these accommodations at the larger entries would be warehouses and *dépôts* for confiscated goods, customs sheds, stables, and carriage houses; at strategic intervals along the wall there would be observation posts. Ledoux provided designs for forty-five entrances, proposing altogether sixty-five buildings (including the double pavilions of some sites) and their accompanying *guérites.* Despite public outcry, official enquiries, a change of architects, and repeated assaults on the *barrières,* by 1790 forty-two of the gates were sufficiently advanced in construction to be finished according to reduced versions of his plans.[174] Before his death in 1806, Ledoux could see, more or less complete and in full operation, the entire circuit as he had imagined it in 1785, with sixty-two of the projected buildings standing in a great circle around Paris.

The first complaints were voiced toward the end of 1784. The bookseller Hardy noted in October that "everyone protested the building of the strange project of the Fermiers Généraux" when they saw the walls, then already three feet high, appearing round the Salpêtrière; he lamented the loss to the city dweller of "the sweet pleasure of being able to contemplate the green fields, as well as that of being able to breathe, on feast days and Sundays, a pure air, having worked all week in dwellings as sad as they were unhealthy."[175] This often-invoked theme of a Paris made unhealthy by a kind of forced incarceration, its citizens deprived of light and air by a "prison" wall, turned the aspirations of the urban embellisher into an attempt to institutionalize the city population. The epigrams current in 1785 reinforced this metaphor: "The wall, walling Paris, rendered Paris discontent," more effective in the original: "Le mur, murant Paris, rend Paris murmurant."[176] A popular rhyme, repeated in opposition pamphlets, extended the analogy:

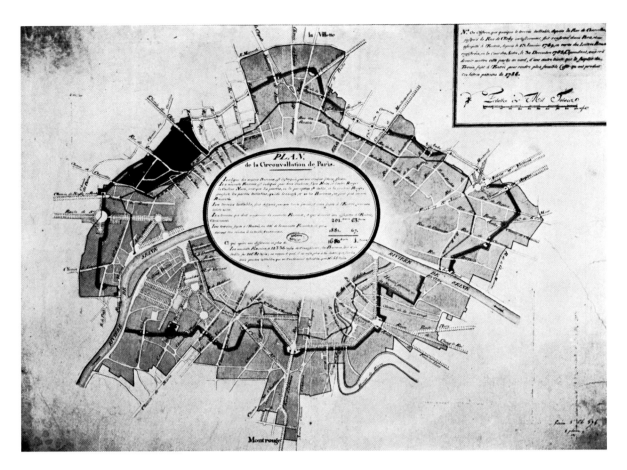

Plan of the new wall of the
Fermiers Généraux, Paris,
1789. From the Archives
Nationales, Cartes et Plans,
AN NIII Seine 874.

To increase its cash,
And diminish our horizon,
The Ferme has thought it necessary
To put Paris in prison.[177]

By 1787 the author of the *Mémoires secrets* had solved the riddle and justified Ledoux: "In vain have they mocked the extravagance of the immense wall with which you incarcerate us in Paris, by lampoons and writings. As for me I approve of your reasons and judge your plan wise enough; Ledoux, according to the old saying, must embellish his prison."[178]

By the beginning of 1786 the Première Chambre des Enquêtes was hearing complaints from the landowners of the faubourgs whose property had been or was about to be expropriated; a delegation from Montmartre representing one hundred twenty inhabitants, led by the abbess of the convent of Montmartre, registered its discontent with the path of the wall between Clichy and Rochouant.[179] All such manifestations produced no effect, however, with Calonne secure in his post and supporting the decisions of the Ferme and Ledoux.

From 1785 the works advanced rapidly, and by the spring of 1787 they were sufficiently finished to invite detailed criticism of their obviously unorthodox architecture. The most complete indictment was published under the title *Réclamation d'un citoyen, contre la nouvelle enceinte de Paris* by Jacques-Antoine Dulaure, a sympathizer with Physiocratic tenets. Dulaure based his attack on the argument that such a wall prevented the free circulation of air throughout the city: It "destroys the health of the air," he asserted, concluding that this *enceinte* would deprive the city, already in a basin surrounded by hills, of some 45,000 cubic toises of air each second, amounting to 1,620,000 cubic feet each minute.[180] And restricting the circulation of air, he argued, went entirely against the best medical advice, then agitating for the removal of the cemeteries, the *fosses d'aisance,* and the hospitals from the center of the city precisely to prevent epidemics. The Ferme was therefore guilty, for the sake of its revenues, of sacrificing the health and lives of hundreds of thousands of citizens. In addition, and again according to Physiocratic doctrine, Dulaure objected to extending the city limits by enclosing a wider, yet unbuilt area, as this would simply encourage a growth in the population. Already the stream of vagrants and job seekers from the countryside had created a city where "crimes and their needs are greatly increased," where "the example or degradation and of crime recompensed, of virtue humiliated, of opulence alone respected, and of a blind emulation established by luxury, leads every day to brigandage, to dissolution, to atrocious crimes."[181] Thus expanded, the city would invade the countryside, which would in turn be deserted and demoralized: the entire youth of the nation would be corrupted.

But the fall of Calonne in April 1787 deprived Ledoux of the total support he had enjoyed from the royal administration, and the renewed attacks on the by then conspicuous wall and its megalomaniacal gates forced Louis XVI to accede to an enquiry. Ledoux was called to render an account of the expenses incurred from May 1786 to February 1787; as a result, in July, the Intendant de Finances, Douet de La Boullaye, ordered him to economize by some 700,000 livres. Another, more serious enquiry was launched at the beginning of September: Ledoux was ordered to submit all plans, estimates, and documentation to a commission of architects, formed of François-Victor Pérard de Montreuil, architect and *censeur royale,* together with Jacques-Denis Antoine and Jean-Arnaud Raymond, both members of the Académie. Raymond was also the personal architect of Calonne's successor, the archbishop Etienne-Charles de Lomménie de Brienne. Lomménie's Contrôleur Général, Antoine-Louis Lambert, ordered the commission to verify and inspect the work accomplished to date; but its investigation was hindered by Ledoux, who chose to ignore its activities. On 4 October Lambert personally instructed Ledoux to provide all the relevant papers

"within the day." The architect's further resistance was followed by visits to his atelier, first from the officials of the Contrôleur Général's office, then from Lomménie de Brienne himself: Ledoux either refused to appear or went into hiding for the day. Finally, on 25 November, the king was induced to suspend all work on the *barrières* pending the outcome of the enquiry. The commission, hitherto ineffective, was augmented by two more members of the Académie, Michel-Barthélémy Hazon, Intendant Général des Bâtiments du Roi, and Maximilien Brébion, Contrôleur Général des Bâtiments du Roi. Site visits were arranged, and Ledoux was once again ordered to turn over all records to the investigators, as well as to meet with them and abide by any economies they suggested. Nevertheless, Ledoux was still strongly protected within the administration, no doubt with the backing of the Ferme, which resented this royal interference in what it regarded as a purely internal matter. In February 1788 he was reinstated in his full functions as architect.

Three months later, the Contrôleur Général's office tried to reconstruct the commission of enquiry by replacing Pérard, an avowed supporter of Ledoux, with a functionary, Roche; the acquisition of land was given over to another royal administrator. But not until the fall of Lomménie, and the reappointment of Necker in late 1788, did Ledoux's position again become untenable. The reports submitted to Necker indicated massive increases in building costs on every *barrière*. The Bureau de l'Etoile, for example, estimated by Ledoux at 96,000 livres, had cost some 500,000, while the Bureau de Monceau had risen from 26,000 to 70,000 livres, bringing the entire costs to date to over seventeen million livres. Necker removed Antoine from the commission on the charge of having helped Ledoux increase his expenses and, in May 1789, definitively dismissed Ledoux from the works. Ledoux immediately asked to be judged by his equals in the Académie, which, however, refused to become involved. Throughout June and July, he sent Necker a series of letters declaring innocence of wrongdoing and injury from injustice—a claim largely denied by his early activism—appealing first to Necker's sense of professional probity, then to his compassion.[182]

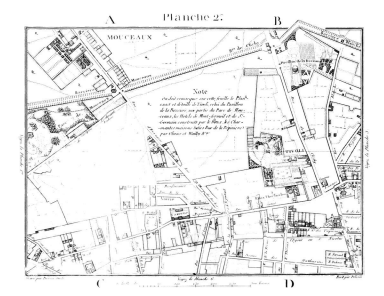

Plan of the wall of the Fermiers Généraux, 1784–1789, detail of northeastern portion, from the Barrière Blanche to the Barrière de la Chopinette. From the Plan Maire, 1808.

But Ledoux, and eventually Necker himself, no longer worked in a state that recognized such appeals from an academician and royalist of the *ancien régime*. A week after Ledoux's final petition to Necker, on 10 July 1789, and continuing for five days, the *barrières* were systematically looted and burned by groups recruited from the unemployed and destitute of the *banlieue*. While these events intersected with the storming of the Bastille on the fourteenth, they were probably orchestrated by those with direct grievances against the Ferme and the *octroi*: tavern owners, dispossessed landowners, wine smugglers, and the like.[183] In all, out of fifty-five nearly completed structures, forty-six suffered considerable damage and the destruction of their contents.

Antoine, who had been recalled on the final dismissal of Ledoux, was given the task of repairing the damage and finishing the construction work. By the spring of 1790, the wall and its tollgates were ready for operation. The Ferme organized its force of six hundred *chasseurs* to protect its new offices, pushed through a decree in the Constituent Assembly that reaffirmed its rights to collect dues within the newly enclosed territories, and began to install its agents in June. Over the next year, the *barrières* and the officers of the Ferme were subjected to increasing attacks from a population estimated by the Marquis de Lafayette to include approximately twenty-two thousand workers living outside the gates, joined by "smugglers also in great numbers," and aided by the general populace in certain areas. An anxious government voted to suspend the entry taxes beginning 1 May 1791: on that day, while a procession of the Garde Nationale, with musicians at the head, patrolled the wall in an effort to reduce looting and further destruction of the gates, the population, supplied by a stream of wine carts, celebrated around each *barrière* before marching to the Place Louis XV. Eight years later, the city of Paris reinstated the *octroi* in a form that survived until the end of 1859.

Ledoux's attitude to such a new city wall was inevitably ambiguous. Earlier he had found authority for the establishment of the Saline de Chaux in the foundation rites of the Romans: "I ploughed the boundaries of a laboring commu-

nity [*une peuplade laborieuse*] in the most beautiful place in the world" (42), he wrote, speaking of "ploughing the bounds of an innocent town" (196). These boundaries were, of course, firmly established by an actual wall in the *saline*, only to be eroded, at least visually, by the emerging vision of a town expanding into the landscape. In the case of Paris, a city of evidently continuous expansion, Ledoux seems to have adopted the view of the Physiocrats, that the city should be finite in size and physically bounded; Ledoux's "wall" was designed to clarify this edge, to sharpen the contrast between city and country and prevent further unplanned spread. His aim was, as he stated, "to *de-villagerize* a community of eight hundred thousand people in order to give it the independence that a city gains from its isolation" (18). Closing the city, however, did not mean that its connections to the countryside were to be explicitly invisible: thus the *barrières* were designed so as to maintain clear lines of sight between inside and outside, pavilions placed at the sides of the entry roads, rather than gates centrally sited that would create "closed exits that obstruct the lines of sight" (18). The wall, both for the Saline de Chaux and for Paris, was a formal, architectural means of establishing order out of formless, natural chaos: "It was in this way that the founders of Rome brought this celebrated

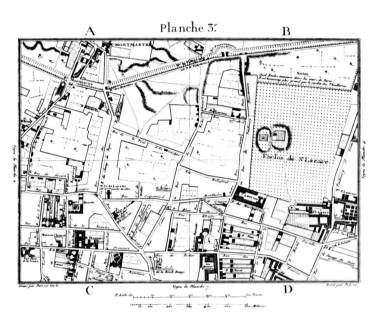

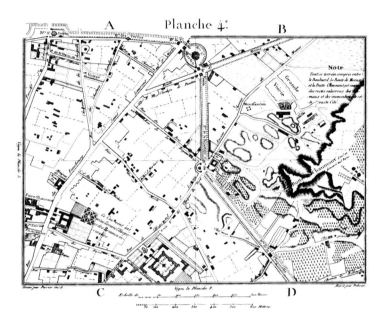

town that dictated the laws of the universe out of chaos. Themistocles built the walls of Athens; those of Thebes were built to the sound of Amphion's lyre; Semiramis constructed the thick walls of Babylon." (42) After his dismissal from the work, Ledoux recounted how Theodoric, king of the Ostrogoths, had repaired the walls of Rome, calling on the architects to march with him "golden staffs in hand." Implying that such respect for architecture from one generally classed among the great "barbarians" placed the barbarism of the Revolutionaries at an even lower level, Ledoux ironically concluded that the blind architects of today "only carry the white stick!" (42).

TRIUMPHAL TOLLGATES

The old fiscal *barrières* installed after the demolition of the ramparts had been no more than wooden palisades erected at the principal entrances to the city and serviced by small wooden sheds on wheels, called *roulettes,* that sheltered the tax collectors. Both their appearance and their functions overtly contradicted the image—fostered by Colbert and cherished somewhat nostalgically by a number of *philosophes,* from Voltaire to Grimm—of a Paris surrounded by monu-

mental arches. The Abbé Laugier voiced the general complaint in 1753:

There is nothing more wretched and poverty-stricken than these barrières *that, today, form the true gates of Paris. From whatever side the capital is approached, the first things one sees are some miserable palisades roughly set up on wooden rails, swinging on two old hinges and flanked by two or three piles of manure. This is what is dignified with the pompous title of the gates of Paris. Nothing as mean can be seen in the smallest towns of the realm. Foreigners who pass through these* barrières *are thunderstruck when told that they are now in the capital of France. One has to argue with them to convince them, they can hardly believe their eyes, imagining that they are still in some nearby village.*[184]

In place of these "indecent" entries that marked an "irregular" and "deformed" boundary around the city, Laugier called for "grand triumphal arches" on the Roman model, set in the middle of vast squares around a regular polygonal *enceinte.* He took for his model Blondel's Porte Saint-Denis, which, with its simple semicircular arch and bold bas-reliefs, equaled, if not surpassed, any antique precedent; indeed, both its geometry and its simplicity were closer than the Roman type to Laugier's own aesthetic preferences. The Roman model, moreover, transgressed Laugier's first principle of separating columns and arcades: columns were, he argued, out of place in a triumphal arch, as "always carrying with them the idea of houses intended for habitation: a triumphal arch can only be a place of passage." [185]

Ledoux agreed with Laugier on the "wretched" aspect of the existing gates. His grandiose aim to replace them with "trophies of victory" was apparent in his presentation of his designs for the *barrières* as propylaea, evocations of the Athenian citadel. But Ledoux was confronted with a program that precisely mingled "habitation" with a "place of passage." This fusion of traditional monumentality and modern requirements necessitated, in his mind at lease, that he invent a genre that would merge the high symbolic role of the triumphal arch with that of the new functions he was to shelter— guardhouses, offices, and tollbooths. Whether modest two-room pavilions of a single story or extensive complexes of several stories, all his entries were invested with a similar architectural character: fabricated, as it were, from a versatile kit of parts created out of antique and Renaissance prototypes, one with seemingly infinite properties for combination and recombination. [186]

The plan types that Ledoux selected were simple and few in number: temples, amphiprostyle and peripteral; the Greek cross in a square, stressing either the cross or the cube, playing all the variations on Palladio's Villa Rotonda, with central lanterns, cylindrical, cubic, or domed; cubic pavilions with pediments on two or four faces; pavilions with rusticated porticoes attached; pure circular rotundas; and combinations of two or more of these plans. Ledoux also reduced the set of architectural elements to a minimum: Venetian openings for windows and doors, sometimes joined in series with single or double columns; a primitive Doric order, generally unfluted and baseless, with an exaggerated entasis derived from Paestum; rustication, liberally used for podia, ground floors, and bases, on columns applied as reticulated, alternate courses (as in the Director's Building at Chaux) or rounded (as in the director's stables of the *saline*); and occasionally linking two columns on each side of a Venetian opening; and pediments, broken by Serliana, faintly marked by

low-pitched gables, formed segmentally or invaded by projecting keystone motifs. Ledoux mustered these basic elements to generate a series of single or paired pavilions that at once responded individually to the compositional and symbolic requirements of their specific sites and formed a family of structures unmistakably identified with the same institution.

The more important entries were marked by major building complexes, significant architectural commissions in their own right. To the north, the Barrières de La Villette and de Pantin shared a large customhouse: the Barrière Saint-Martin with its high central rotunda, enclosing an open courtyard and surrounded by Venetian arcades, set on a square base and entered through four equal porticoes formed on a pediment and eight square Tuscan columns. The Barrière d'Enfer, similarly, had as its customhouse and observation post a rotunda topped by a cylindrical, flat-domed lantern and entered through three porches with pedimented gables and rusticated Serliana. To the east and west, the river entries were controlled by *pataches,* or customs boats, operating out of the Barrière de La Cunette and the customhouse of the Quai de la Rapée. At La Cunette, the *barrière,* formed of a wide gable pediment over three Venetian arches, with double columns *à bossages,* was entered through a heavily rusticated, grotto like archway above a basin sheltering the *pataches* on the Seine. The Barrière de la Rapée was a circular building around an open central courtyard with an external peristyle of baseless Doric columns, entered through four porches whose gable pediments were decorated with projecting keystones; it, too, was serviced by rusticated stairs leading up from the river. For this gate Ledoux also prepared an elaborate design for the *patache*.

These functionally important *barrières* were balanced in scale and magnificence by the symbolically important "royal" entries. By custom and right, Ledoux was constrained to submit the designs for Louis XVI's approbation. On the west, the entry from Versailles along the Quai des Bonshommes was marked by a free standing pedimented pavilion, with a screen of Doric columns and a semicircular porch with a coved and coffered arch, reminiscent of the Hôtel Guimard.

Ledoux, the *barrières* of Paris,
1784–89, perspective views of
the *barrières* of Fontainebleau,
l'Oursine, Saint-Jacques, Orléans, Montparnasse, Maine,
Vanves, and Plumet. Engraving from Gaitte, *Recueil des
plus belles maisons et des plus
beaux édifices de Paris* (Paris,
n.d. [1792]), pl. 7.

Ledoux, the *barrières* of Paris,
perspective views of the *bar-
rières* of the Ecole Militaire,
Grenelle, Seve (La Cunette),
Versailles, Chaillot (Sainte-
Marie), and Chaillot (Longch-
amp). Engraving from Gaitte,
Recueil, pl. 8.

Ledoux, the *barrières* of Paris,
perspective views of the *barrières* of Reservoirs, Etoile,
Courcelles, Monceau
(Rotonde de Chartres), Roule,
and Monceau. Engraving
from Gaitte, *Recueil,* pl. 9.

Ledoux, the *barrières* of Paris, perspective views of the *barrières* of Clichy, Blanche, Rue Royale, Martyrs, Saint-Denis, and Vertus. Engraving from Gaitte, *Recueil*, pl. 10.

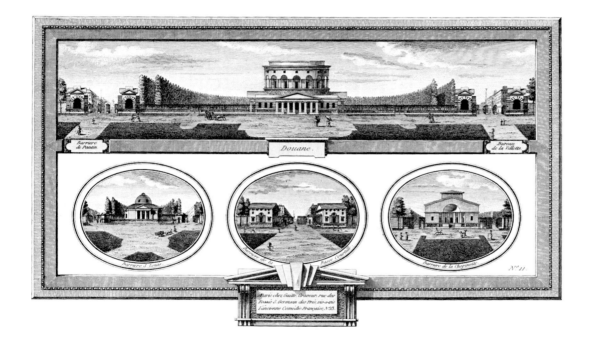

Ledoux, the *barrières* of Paris, perspective views of the *barrières* of La Villette (including Pantin and the Rotunda), Saint-Louis (Combat), Basse Courtille (Chemin de Belleville), and Chopinette. Engraving from Gaitte, *Recueil*, pl. 11.

Ledoux, the *barrières* of Paris, perspective views of the *barrières* of Deux Couronnes (Trois-Couronnes), Ménilmontant (Belleville), Fontarabie (Rue de Charonne), Poissonière, Folie Regnault and Rats, and Amandiers. Engraving from Gaitte, *Recueil*, pl. 12.

Ledoux, the *barrières* of Paris, perspective views of the *barrières* of Montreuil, Charenton, Bercy, Rapée, the customs rotunda, Barrière d'Orléans (Enfer), and Vaugirard. Engraving from Gaitte, *Recueil,* pl. 13.

Ledoux, the *barrières* of Paris, perspective views of the *barrières* of Vincennes, Saint-Mandé, Picpus, and Reuilly. Engraving from Gaitte, *Recueil,* pl. 14.

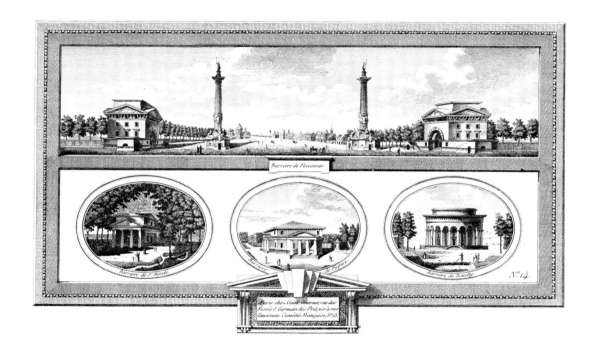

Ledoux, the *barrières* of Paris, perspective views of the Barrière d'Ivry and the customs sheds of the Barrière d'Orléans (Enfer). Engraving from Gaitte, *Recueil,* pl. 15.

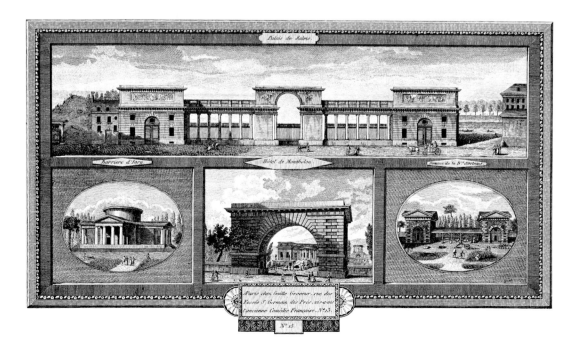

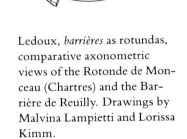

Ledoux, *barrières* as temples, comparative axonometric views of the *barrières* of Gentilly, Saint-Jacques, Courcelles, and Rats. Drawings by Malvina Lampietti and Lorissa Kimm.

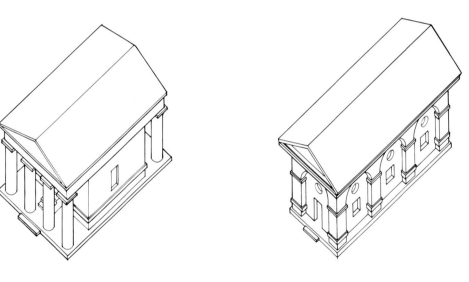

Ledoux, *barrières* as rotundas, comparative axonometric views of the Rotonde de Monceau (Chartres) and the Barrière de Reuilly. Drawings by Malvina Lampietti and Lorissa Kimm.

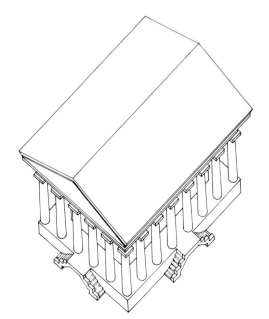

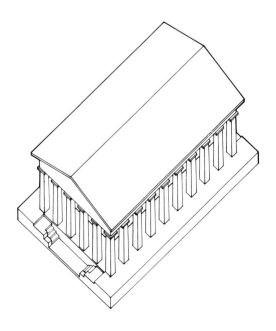

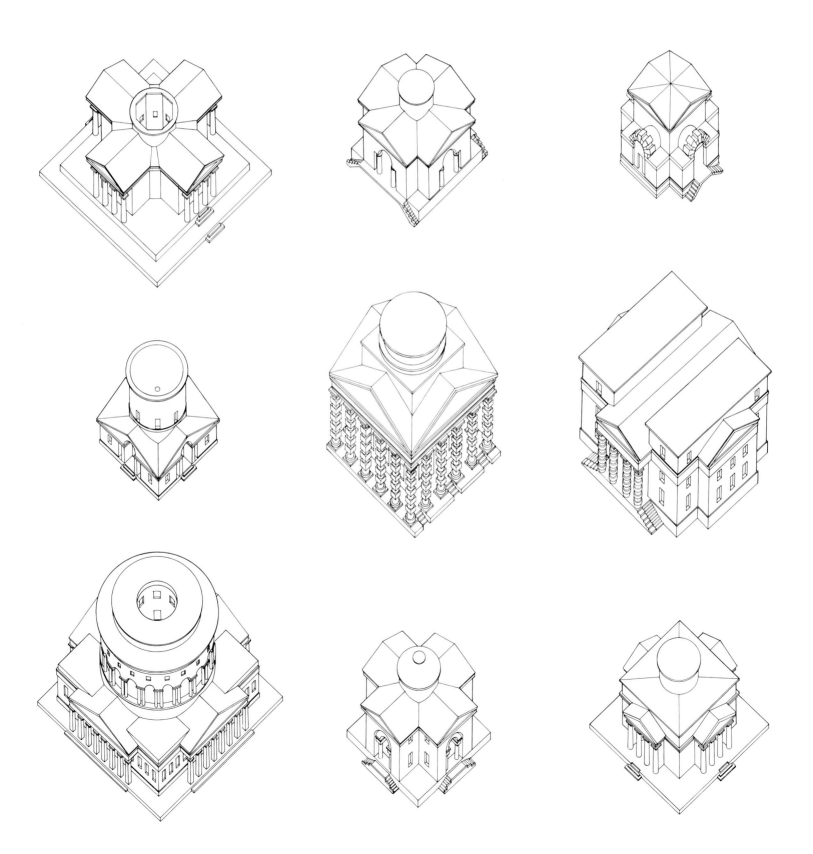

Ledoux, *barrières* as centralized pavilions, comparative axonometric views of the *barrières* of Ivry, Vaugirard, Ecole Militaire, Chaillot, Etoile, Saint-Denis, La Villette, Trois Couronnes, and Picpus (*top to bottom, left to right*). Drawings by Malvina Lampietti and Lorissa Kimm.

Ledoux, Barrière d'Enfer.
Photograph by Gouviot from
the Bibliothèque Historique de
la Ville de Paris.

Ledoux, Barrière des Bon-
shommes. Photograph by
Gouviot from the Bibliot-
hèque Historique de la Ville de
Paris.

Ledoux, Barrière de Saint-
Martin (La Villette).
Photograph by Giraudon.

Ledoux, Barrière de l'Etoile.
Photograph, 1860, from the
Bibliothèque Nationale,
Cabinet des Estampes, va 279
Fol. T.IV.

J.-J. Delaporte, View of the
Bureau de l'Etoile in winter.
From the Bibliothèque Histo-
rique de la Ville de Paris;
photograph from Arch. Phot.
Paris/SPADEM.

Intimating the great east-west axis yet to be realized, the double pavilions of the Barrière de l'Etoile and of the Barrière de Vincennes or du Trône—the former with their façades directly borrowed from the portico of the Director's Building at Chaux, the latter flanking two monumental columns on cruciform bases—completed Ledoux's not entirely altruistic homage to the monarchy. In justificatory memoranda of 1785 and 1786, Ledoux recorded the roles of Calonne and the Comte d'Angiviller, Directeur des Bâtiments Royales, in the design of these gates. For the Champs Elysées, then the avenue de Neuilly, "the King wished that the *barrières*, . . . interesting because of their position, should announce the Place de Louis XV and the entry to the Louvre."[187] For the avenue de Vincennes, "he desired that the *barrières,* placed . . . in an immense space, should perpetuate the idea of the project of Perrault [the Place du Trône]." The designs were submitted to d'Angiviller, who professed satisfaction and offered advice as to how to give the buildings "the importance required by the site."[189] Ledoux attributed to him the idea of the porticoes of the Etoile, "isolating the columns without changing the general disposition."[190] It was also in conversation with d'Angiviller that Ledoux suggested surmounting the two pavilions of the Etoile with appropriate sculptures: Cybele carrying the products of the earth, Thetis carrying those of the sea.[191]

Ledoux's comments on the style of these royal *barrières* summarized his general approach toward the creation of a new "public" genre: "We have been content," he noted in relation to the Barrière de l'Etoile, "to present the needs of the Ferme with an exterior order that is regular, manly [*mâle*], and not too refined [*peu élevée*]."[192] Writing three months later on the same subject, he continued: "The artist has been content to give to these offices a public character, and so that their architecture not be decomposed and destroyed by the spaces, which are immense, he has thought it best to use the most severe and determined style."[193] These marks of a style specifically calculated to represent both a public *enceinte* for the city and the offices of the quasi-public Ferme Générale were consistently deployed throughout the other *barrières;* Ledoux's

Ledoux, Barrière du Trône.
Photograph by Eugène Atget
from the Bibliothèque Historique de la Ville de Paris; from
Arch. Phot. Paris/SPADEM.

Ledoux, Barrière du Trône,
axonometric view. Drawing
by Malvina Lampietti and
Lorissa Kimm.

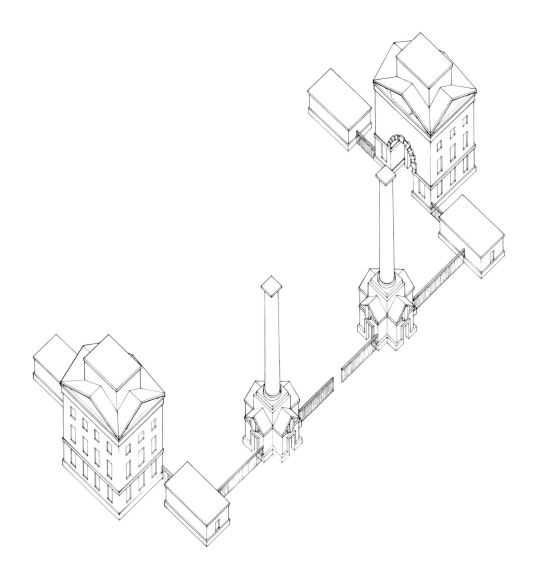

adoption of classical types gave the wall a monumental, Roman aspect, while his requotation of motifs used for the Ferme's earlier buildings, at Chaux and in the Hôtel des Fermes, endowed the whole with a proprietorial stamp—unfortunately, in the event, unmistakable. But Ledoux was also, as with all his other public commissions, exploring the limits of a new form of classicism, creating new entities out of the dismembered fragments of the old. What gave all these experiments a unity—one not entirely appreciated by his contemporaries, who preferred to see the gates as emblems of political and aesthetic ruination—was Ledoux's commitment to a form of primitivism exemplified in the Barrière de Courcelles. Derived as much from the examples of early Greek and Etruscan monuments illustrated by Le Roy and Piranesi as from the conflation of the idea of origins with geometrical reductivism, this primitivism was more pronounced in the *barrières* than in many of Ledoux's earlier commissions.

Indeed, in the context of the equally primitive, "Etruscan" backdrops sketched by De Wailly for the heroic paintings of the younger David between 1785 and 1789, perhaps themselves derived from the observation of Ledoux's new works, it might be possible to speak of a primitivism of the mid-1780s entirely distinct in style from both its more elegant predecessors (theorized by Laugier and practiced by Soufflot and Gondouin) and its more historicized successors (as exemplified by the designs of Durand and reified in the theory of Quatremère de Quincy.[194] This primitivism, marked in the mannerism of the Barrièrre des Fourneaux, also espoused by Brongniart and De Wailly and later to become the primary source of John Soane's idiosyncratic style, was, as the historian and architect Jacques-Guillaume Legrand realized, the personal invention of Ledoux.

Thus the various "temples" surrounding the city were conceived as transformations of an "original" type at once less "purist" and more architectonic than that suggested by Laugier. Best represented by the project for the Barrière des Rats, it consisted of a peripteral plan formed by square "Etruscan" columns of stocky proportions, baseless and with rudimentary capitals. These carried a gabled roof without architrave or frieze, echoing restorations from Inigo Jones to Perrault of Vitruvius's description of an Etruscan temple, but in a highly simplified form. Ledoux, at the same time, designed a variation of this type for the center of the village of Maupertuis; as depicted in the bird's-eye-view perspective, the temple was invaded by an even more primitive type, the stepped pyramid, conceived as a prolongation of the stylobate, rising through the peristyle and cella to form a high central "alter".[195] Ledoux designed another "stage" of temple development for the Barrière de Courcelles, a peripteral, hexastyle temple in a Doric order, baseless, unfluted, and without a frieze—an order repeated in the tetrastyle porticoes of the small amphiprostyle temple of the Barrière de la Glacière, or de l'Oursine. Perhaps, in Ledoux's transformational imagination, the development from square to round columns was itself signified by the rusticated columns of the two temples actually built for the Barrière des Rats, whose porticoes re-

Ledoux, Barrière de Courcelles. Photograph by Gouviot, 1859, from the Bibliothèque Historique de la Ville de Paris.

Ledoux, Barrière des Fourneaux. Photograph by Gouviot from the Bibliothèque Historique de la Ville de Paris.

Elevation Laterale

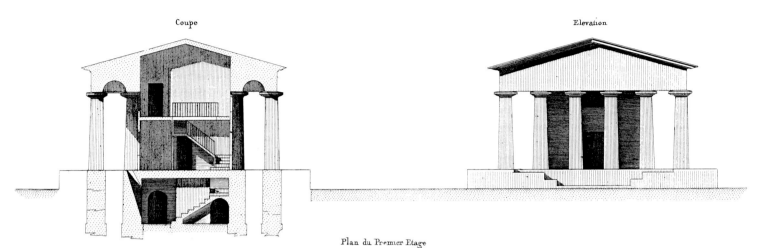

Coupe

Elevation

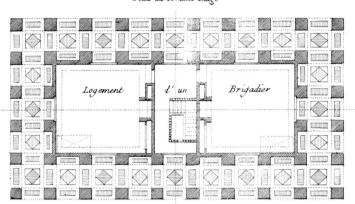

Plan du Premier Etage

Logement   d'un   Brigadier

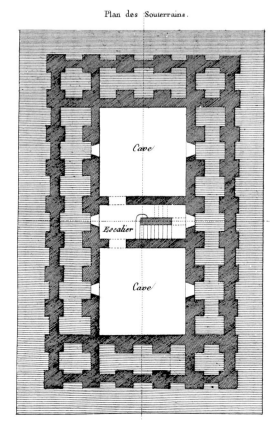

Plan des Souterrains.

Cave

Escalier

Cave

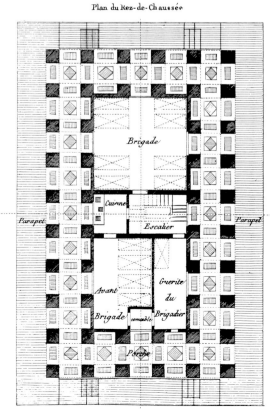

Plan du Rez-de-Chaussée

Brigade

Parapel

Cuisine

Escalier

Parapel

Avant

Brigade

Guerite
du
Brigadier

comble

Porche

sembled those of the Director's Building at Chaux. Other versions of primitive temples were built at the Barrière de Bercy (carrying crude pedimented gables without attics) and at the Barrières de Saint-Mandé, de Montreuil, and de Charenton (with attics raised over the main block).

If these virtually "unformed" types offended a nascent neoclassicism, Ledoux's contamination of the temple model with "Palladian" interpolations, directly opposed to Laugier's austere principles in the combination of arch and column, presented a species of "monster" to critical opinion. Linking Venetian arches on single columns to form porticoes to amphiprostyle temples, as at the Barrière de Clichy, or employing them on double columns, as at the Barrière de Belleville, Ledoux created a type somewhere between the temple and the basilica. In its perfect peripteral form this type was realized in the double pavilions of the Barrière de Ménilmontant, with three arches on double unfluted Doric columns to a side; in the project for the *patache* at the Barrière de la Rapée, this "Venetian Temple" was returned to its true home, so to speak, on a form of neoclassical gondola.

Even more Palladian in inspiration, and clearly based on the model of the Villa Rotonda, were a series of *barrières* for which Ledoux employed variations on the plan of the Greek cross within a square, with central lanterns or rotundas. In addition to the large Barrières Saint-Martin and de la Rapée, Ledoux projected cruciform gatehouses for the Barrières d'Ivry and de la Santé, neither of which were built. The former, as engraved in Ramée and in Gaitte, had four porticoes of unfluted Doric orders carrying a plain frieze and pediment as well as a central, cylindrical lantern over an octagonal courtyard. In the latter, almost medieval in aspect and perhaps, as engraved, dating from a later epoch of Ledoux's design, barrel-vaulted solids were substituted for pediments and the high, rectangular attic was embellished with keyhole-shaped windows resembling arrow slits, heavy consoles, and a round, domed lantern. Ledoux repeated the type around the *enceinte*: in the large Barrière du Roule, with a central dome; in the Barrières de Vaugirard, des Trois-Couronnes, and de Royale-Montmartre, with variations on Venetian-arched porches; and in the Barrière de Picpus, with pedimented por-

ticoes of unfluted Doric columns each opening into semicircular porches.

In these office-villas, Ledoux conflated a domestic and a bureaucratic type. But in many of the *barrières* the model was more simply that of a private *hôtel,* entered through monumental porticoes as a sign of its public role: thus, the *barrières* of the Place d'Italie, their continuous Venetian arcades introduced to shelter the customs agents at work; the two pavilions of the Barrière d'Enfer, their triple Venetian arches on double columns heavily banded by rustication; the Barrière de Monceau, with an attached portico of rusticated columns; the Barrière Saint-Denis, originally designed as a pedimented peristyle joining two detached pavilions, but built as a pavilion with an attached portico; the Barrière de Fontarabie, similar to those of the Place d'Italie; and the Barrière du Maine, whose two pavilions, recessed at the center, were entered through arched Serlianas surmounted by a "pediment" formed out of stepped blocks of rustication (a motif borrowed directly from the Hôtel des Fermes, then in construction).

Other *barrières* were less reducible to types, or rather, formed types of their own, invented specifically by Ledoux. Among these, the most common were cubic pavilions, pedimented on four or two sides, according to their exposition on the site, and generally entered through grand arches enclosing setback Venetian doorways, as at the Barrières de L'Ecole Militaire and de Vincennes. Several *barrières* played variations on nested pediments; at the Barrières des Paillassons, des Vertus, and de Sainte Marie, or Chaillot, deeply projecting broken segmental pediments over Venetian arches formed entries that were contrasted to triangular pediments crowning the cross axis of the pavilion. Some *barrières* specifically used by Ledoux in parklike settings, were pure rotundas; the observation post of the Barrière d'Enfer; the Barrière des Amandiers in the quarter of market gardens, its high Venetian-arched entries framed by reticulated rustication; the Barrière de Reuilly, with its pure peristyle of eighteen arches on columns. Completing this group was the Rotonde de Chartres, the "tempietto" of the Parc Monceau, built on land belonging to the Duc d'Orléans. Designed with his approbation, it contained his private apartment on the top floor. As built, the

Opposite: Ledoux, Rotonde de
Monceau, site plan and
plans. Engraving from Ramée,
Ledoux, pl. 3.

Ledoux, Barrière de Reuilly.
Watercolor by Palaisseau for
Les barrières de Paris (Paris,
1819).

Ledoux, Rotonde de Mon-
ceau, elevation. Engraving
from Ramée, *Ledoux,* pl. 4.

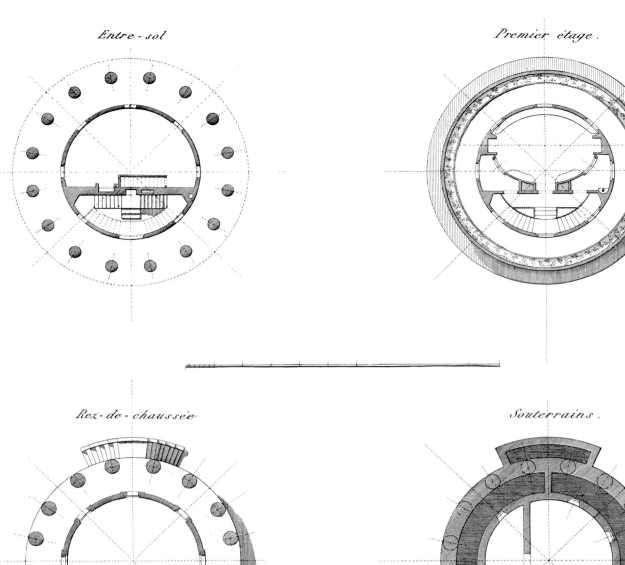

Entre-sol

Premier étage.

Rez-de-chaussée

Souterrains.

Plan général.

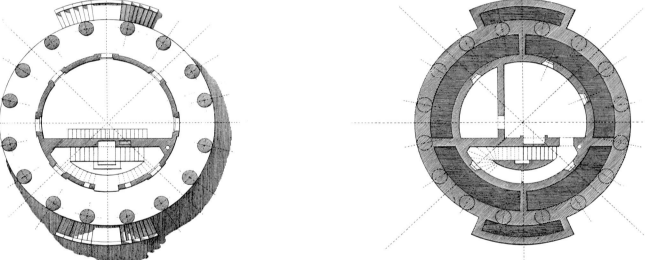

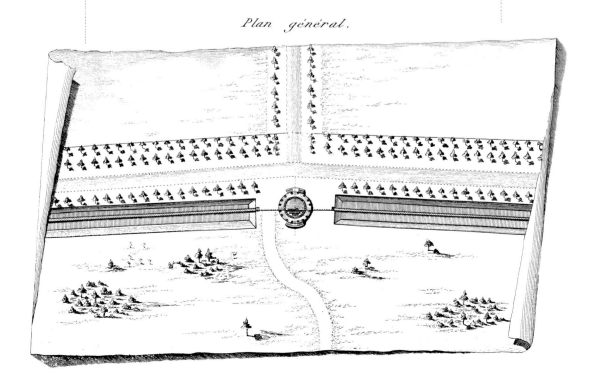

Doric columns were unfluted and the dome shallower than in the restoration that survives. Another, smaller group of *barrières* took as their model the wayside tombs or chapels of Italy: the Barrières Saint-Jacques, de Montparnasse, des Ministres, and des Martyrs, with different rustication, entries, and pediments, were all of this type. Finally, Ledoux planned three gates in the form of triumphal arches, albeit of a kind unknown in antiquity: the Barrière Poissonnière, illustrated by Gaitte, and those presented in Ramée as plates 28, 29 and 33 show a gabled building cut by a wide arch through its short axis. At Poissonnière and in the project depicted on plates 28 and 29, the passage, lined on either side by Doric colonnades, was lit by lanterns, respectively cylindrical or cut into a huge barrel-vaulted attic. In the project shown in plate 33, a covered passage moved through the center of the *barrière,* with open, segmentally planned courtyards to either side. This project used the motifs of Ledoux's *style de la Ferme* in profusion: deep consoles carrying the pitched roof; rusticated columns framing the windows, echoing Palladio's Villa Thiene; angular rustication around the base and a rusticated stepped arch, like those of the Barrière du Maine and the Hôtel des Fermes, over the side entrances. Ledoux reemployed the same vocabulary in another of his unbuilt projects, illustrated on plate 35 of Ramée: a tall rotunda lit by a cylindrical lantern, served by a central spiral stairway, and set on a rusticated square base. These unbuilt projects evoke Ledoux's picturesque vision even more strongly perhaps than Gaitte's engravings of the built *barrières.* The centralized pavilion with four pedimented gables depicted on plate 32 of Ramée stood on a square base serving as a terrace and marked at the corners by four round *guérites;* the pavilion was, in turn, topped by a hollow monumental column, embellished with the prows of ships, that functioned as a lookout from its tempietto-like lantern. The smaller *guérite* with a Pantheon plan shown in plate 36 was entered through a square-columned portico and lit by keyhole apertures and a cylindrical, domed lantern. Finally, Ledoux projected a floating temple for the idealized *patache* at the Barrière de la Rapée.

In these last projects, the style approached that of the ideal designs for Chaux, drawn up after 1790, and indeed Van Maëlle was used as an engraver for both. The resemblance was clearly not fortuitous. Whether at the time or in retrospect, Ledoux obviously used the commission for the *barrières* as a kind of experimental laboratory of type forms and their combinations. Dissociated from their previous functions, these types were open and accessible to new ones: Ledoux seemed almost to recognize that the Ferme's occupation of the *barrières* was only temporary, and that they awaited their adoption by a different social institution. Perhaps it was as a form of opportunistic hindsight that Ledoux repeated, or redrew the themes of the gates in many of his projects for Chaux: the triumphal arches of the Barrière de la Poissonnière and of the *barrières* on plates 29 and 33 of Ramée became the Double Houses for Milliners. The barrel vaults of the arch depicted on plate 29 and of that for the Barrière de la Santé anticipated the barrel-vaulted House of the Surveyors of the

Ledoux, Project for a *barrière* as a triumphal arch, perspective view, section, and elevation. Engraving from Ramée, *Ledoux,* pl. 29.

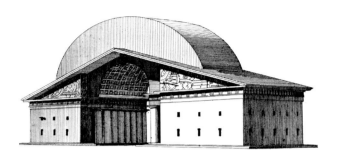

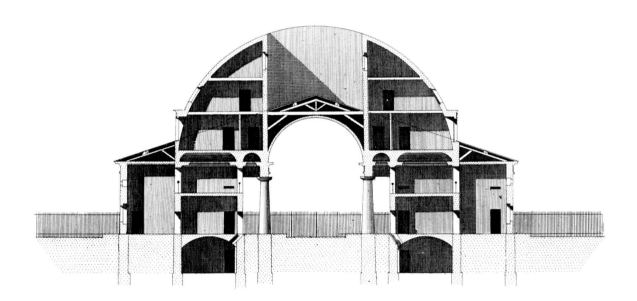

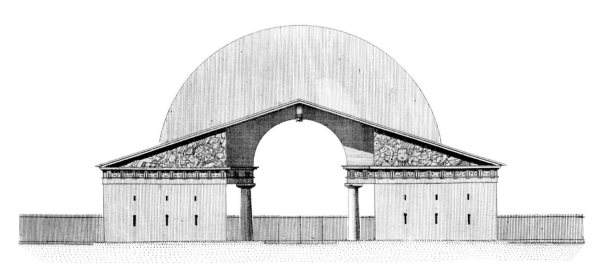

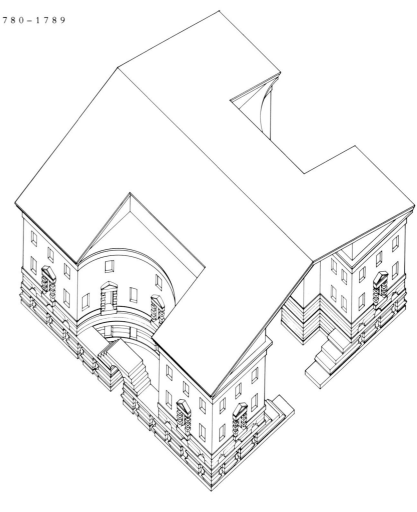

Ledoux, Project for a *barrière,* axonometric view. Redrawn from Ramée, *Ledoux,* pl. 33, by Malvina Lampietti and Lorissa Kimm.

Ledoux, Project for a *barrière,* elevation and section. Engraving from Ramée, *Ledoux,* pl. 35.

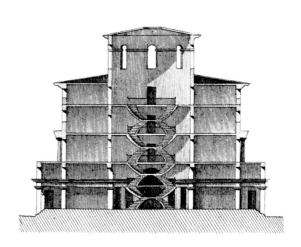

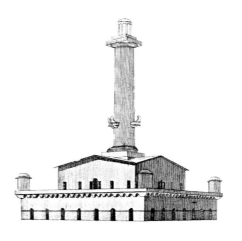

Ledoux, Project for a *barrière,* perspective view. Engraving from Ramée, *Ledoux,* pl. 32.

Ledoux, Project for a *barrière,*
elevation, section, and plan.
Engraving from Ramée,
Ledoux, pl. 36.

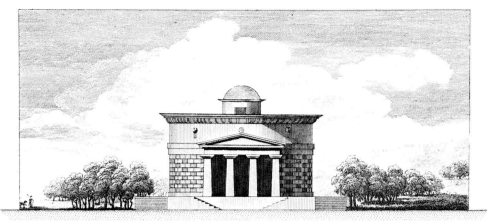

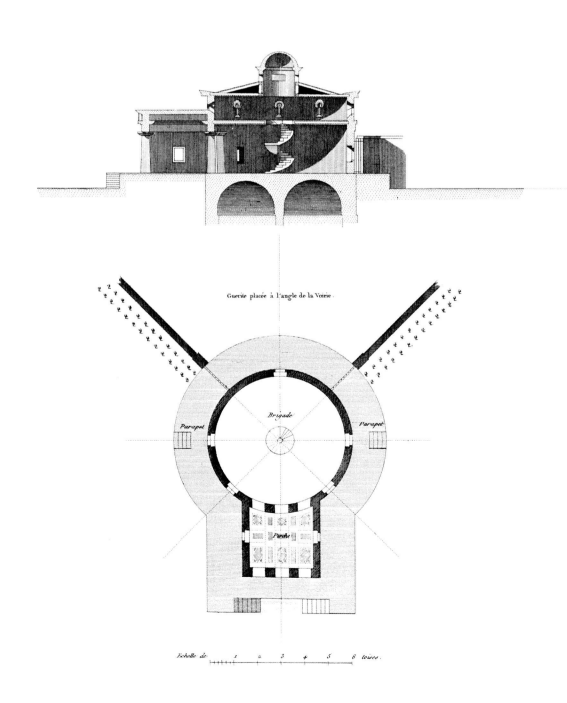

Guerite placée à l'angle de la Voirie.

Brigade

Parapet

Parapet

Parvis

Echelle de   1   2   3   4   5   6   toises.

Ledoux, Project for *patache* at the Barrière de la Rapée, perspective view, elevations, section, and plan. Engraving from Ramée, *Ledoux,* pl. 14.

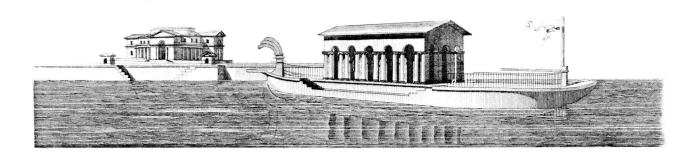

Elevation

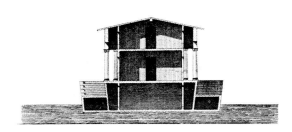

Coupe

Elevation Laterale

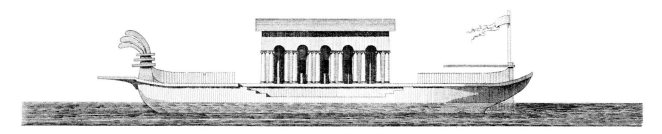

Plan

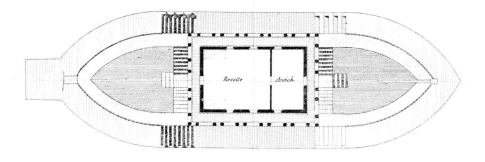

Echelle de   1   2   3   4   5   10 toises

Loüe River. The Barrières de La Villette and de Pantin prefigured the typical Worker's House on plate 17 of *L'architecture,* as the Barrière Saint-Martin and the project on plate 35 of Ramée did the cylindrical Country House for a Stockbroker. The rustication of the Barrière Sainte-Marie imitated the "logs" later used for various rustic *ateliers.* And the amphiprostyle temple of the Barrière de la Glacière reappeared intact in the Country House for a former Councillor to the Parlement of Besançon.

More immediately, this "museum" of types held a particularly didactic role in Ledoux's mind. Full-scale models of antique precedents adapted to modern uses, the *barrières* were conceived as object lessons for the architect and the citizen:[196] the architectural student could study a series of "compositions as varied as they were numerous," models of characterization and combination; the inhabitants of Paris, for their part, could easily recognize the emblematic values embodied in each pavilion, "external virtues assembled in a circle in order to level public feeling" (18). Ledoux's urban aesthetic extended to the scale of the city as a whole the circular landscape of the panorama. The contrast and variety exhibited from *barrière* to *barrière* would, he noted, produce "pictures that are joined to the most piquant sites and whose effects are close to the illusory magic of our theaters" (18). In this sense, the "transformational grammar" of the gates was calculated to produce the effect of a chain of association, stimulated in the perception of an observer moving along the new boulevards that bounded the city by the decomposition of one *barrière* and its recomposition in the next: "constructions whose diversity quences the thirst of desire" (18).

TAVERNS FOR THE PEOPLE

Ledoux's double aim of aesthetic and moral "embellishment" was most strongly exemplified in his designs for eight huge taverns, prepared, at the behest of Calonne, as an integral part of the urbanistic program of the *barrières.* These *guinguettes* were intended to replace the popular resorts of the *banlieue* that had grown up outside the walls to escape the tax on wine. Despite their obvious recreational role, the inns had become meeting places for a crowd that, in the years before the Revolution, was increasingly perceived as a threat to social and political order.[197] New taverns, state-run and properly policed, would not only neutralize the danger of riot, revolt, or simple brigandage, but also recuperate on behalf of the Crown revenues hitherto uncollectable. As described by Luc-Vincent Thiéry in 1783, the traditional *guinguette* was frequented by artisans and *gens du peuple* on Sundays and feast days: "All the cabarets in these places have vast courtyards planted with trees and furnished with tables where food and drink are served. There violins play, and most of the people dance in the great courtyard, finding in this pleasure relaxation from the fatigue of the week." Ledoux adopted this program, but transformed it into that of an institution of moralizing intent:

Oh People! So respectable an entity by reason of the importance of each part that it comprises, you will not be forgotten amidst the constructions of art: at proper distances from the towns monuments will be built for you that rival the palaces of the governors of the world; houses for your meetings and your pleasures. There you will be able to efface the memory of your hardships in the games prepared for you; to drink your fatigue to oblivion, and, in a restorative relaxation, you will derive new strengths and the courage necessary for your labors. (6)

To this end Ledoux invented a new type—the ancestor of the nineteenth-century *café concert*—composed of centralized salons, long eating and drinking galleries, private rooms, and spacious courtyards surrounded by arcades and peristyles. The largest measured some three hundred fifty feet across, the smallest, two hundred. He planned each *guinguette* in combinations of the square and Greek cross, save for one, which he enclosed within a circular *enceinte.* At the center of many were two-story buildings, cruciform or rotunda in plan, resembling the larger *barrières.* Ledoux conceived each with a quarter in mind, every one already a place of popular resort: the Faubourgs Poissonnière, du Temple, Saint-Antoine, Saint-Marceau, Vaugirard, Chaillot, the rue Ménilmontant, and the Quai de la Rapée. This last he designed as a

Ledoux, Project for a *guin-guette,* Faubourg Poissonnière, plan, elevation, and section. Engraving from Ramée, *Ledoux,* pl. 226.

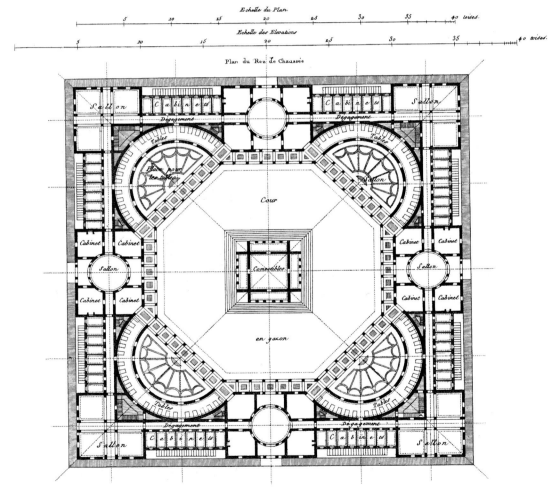

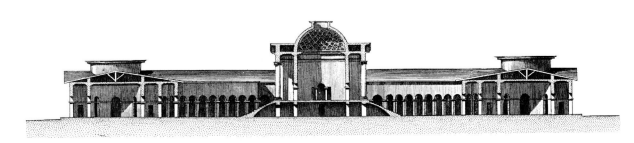

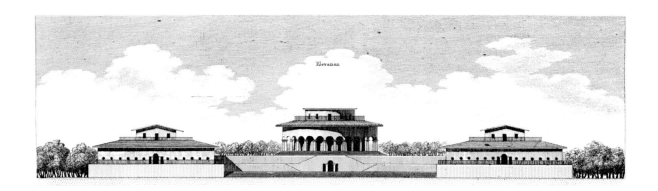

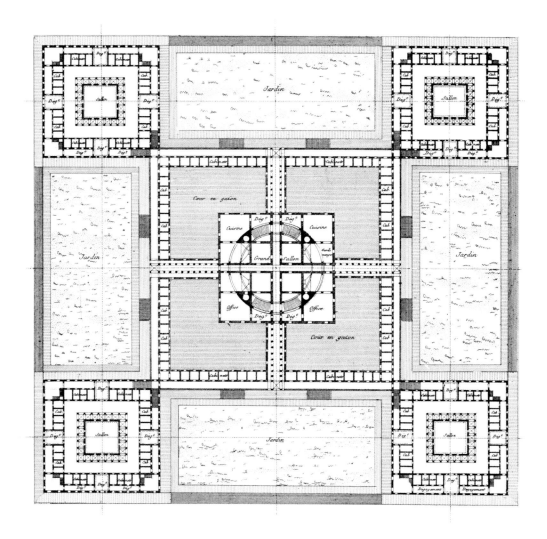

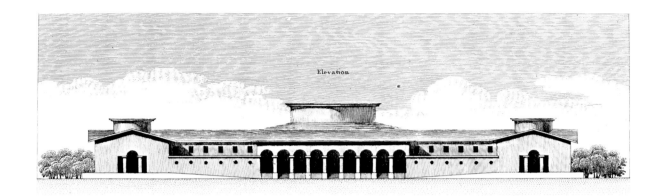

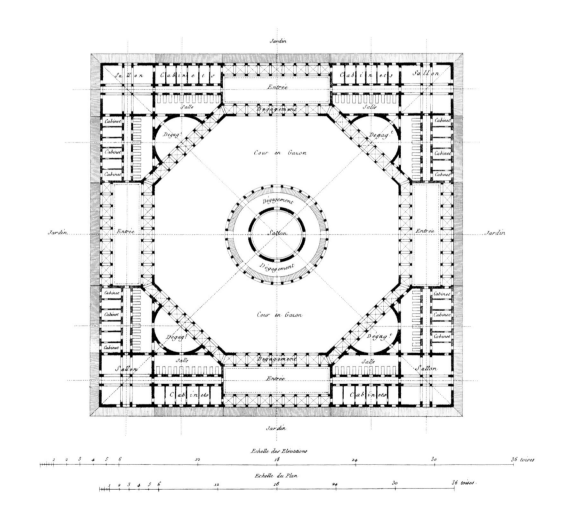

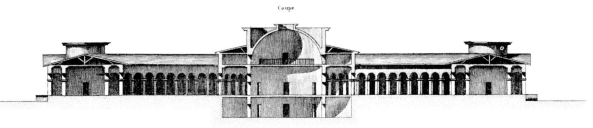

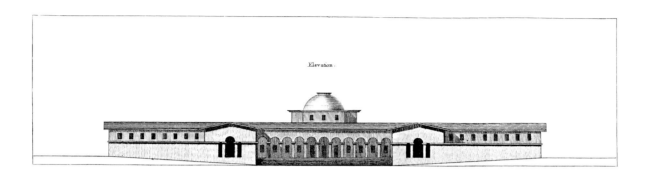

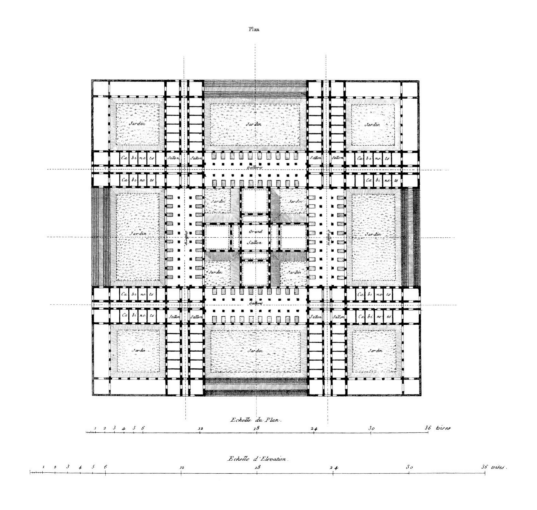

Ledoux, Project for a *guinguette,* Quai de la Rapée, plan, elevation, and section. Engraving from Ramée, *Ledoux,* pl. 230.

Plan

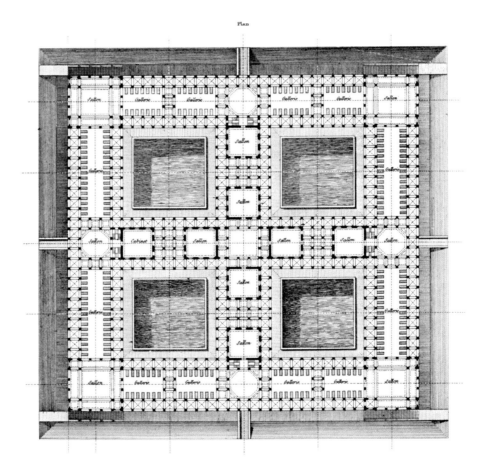

Coupe

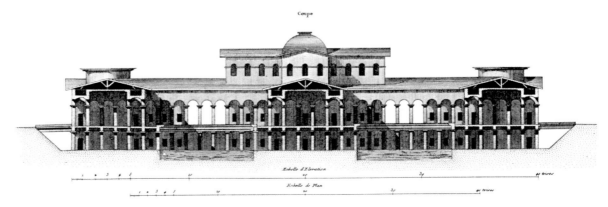

Ledoux, Project for a *guinguette,* Faubourg Saint-Marceau, plan, elevation, and section. Engraving from Ramée, *Ledoux,* pl. 231.

Plan

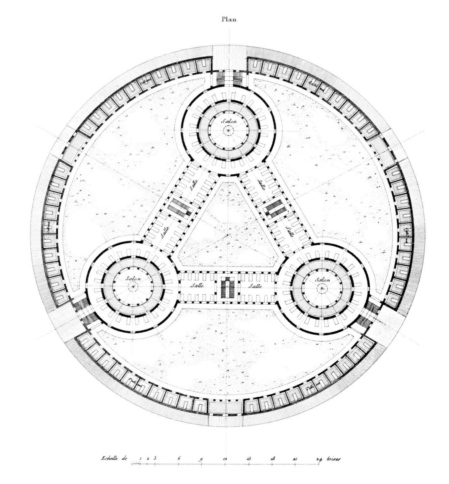

Echelle de 1 2 3   6   9   12   15   18   21   24 toises

Coupe

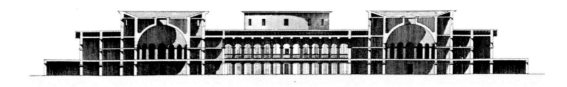

Echelle de 1 2 3 4 5   10   20 toises

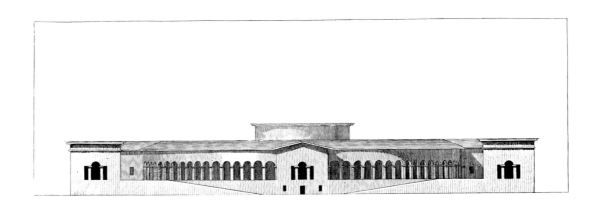

Plan

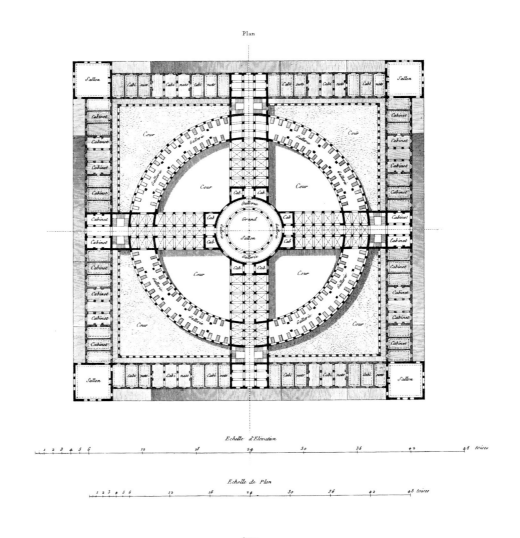

Echelle d'Elevation

Echelle de Plan

Coupe

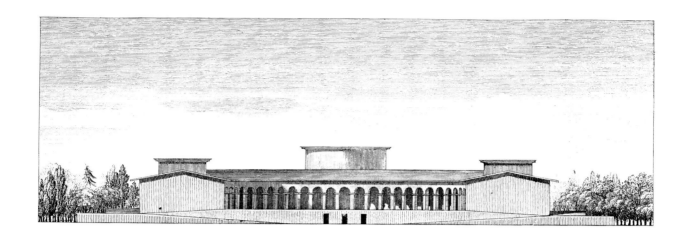

Plan

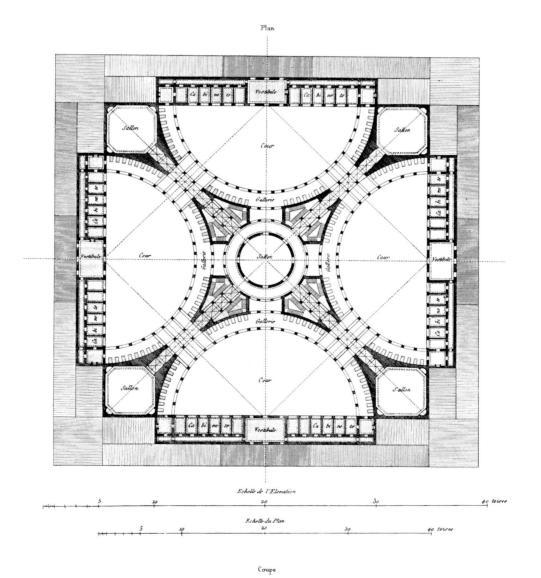

Echelle de l'Elevation

5   10   20   30   40 toises

Echelle du Plan

5   10   20   30   40 toises

Coupe

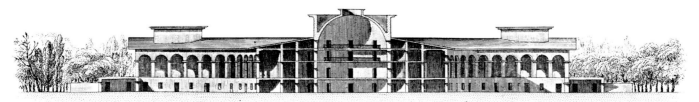

riverside tavern, replacing its courtyards with swimming and boating pools. For Montmartre, recognizing the singular character of the quarter, Ledoux conceived an even more specialized place of recreation, a House of Pleasure, whose function was revealed wittily in the intrusion of a phallic-shaped "temple" into its vast, circular *enceinte*. In section, this licensed house of prostitution seems to occupy the entire hill of Montmartre, with long stairs and ramps leading up to the monument itself, envisaged as a high cylinder standing within a square. "For the first time," claimed Ledoux, "one will see the magnificence of the tavern and the palace on the same scale" (18). Completing this series of "People's Houses" was a design for what Ledoux termed a Monument of Popularity, the social program of which was similar to that of the *guinguettes*: an enclosed institution with controlled access, it seems to propose a new type of government-sponsored facility. At the center of an ideally square terrain, the square main pavilion contained a domed circular dining salon of two stories, placed above its kitchens and lit from a skylight. This room was furnished with curved tables around the central space and radially set tables beneath a surrounding gallery. On the ground floor, a continuous gallery sheltered tables placed around the perimeter of the circular kitchen. Around the edge of the site, a series of small private booths for drinking and dining formed a wall to the outside, while, at each corner, pavilions housed dance rooms, a gaming room, and a billiard room. Most remarkable, however, was not this panoptical play area, but the architectural style envisaged as appropriate for a "popular" house. Uniquely in his work, Ledoux conceived the pavilion as a variation on a theme of popular architecture: the gable roof was covered in pantiles and its eaves extended over the second-floor terrace; the posts supporting this terrace were obviously wooden, of no architectural order; and the inner cylindrical volume was of brick, plain on the first floor and decorated with inset timber, as in a half-timbered cottage, on the upper floors. The entire composition resembled a kind of institutional "Swiss chalet," or perhaps a farmhouse of the Jura, raised to the public scale and furnished with mass-produced cast-iron railings and balustrades.

Ledoux's overall plan for the boulevards and *barrières* of Paris should thus be seen in the context of a number of initiatives that, between the late 1750s and the Revolution, attempted to map and to plan its useful and representational embellishments at more than the local scale. Moreau's plans for the quais, Patte's imaginary map of the city scattered with projected places for the statue of Louis XV; Verniquet's systematic mapping between 1774 and 1791,[199] all led to a sense of the city as a totality, out of which Ledoux's own project was developed. The first comprehensive plan for the city to emerge from this current was that prepared by Charles De Wailly and exhibited at the Salon of 1789, and entitled

Project of utility and embellishment for the city of Paris, which conforms with the projects already ordered by the government, in which have been brought together new monuments, public squares, roads opened to provide accessibility and to supplement the currents of air, and in which have been proposed the unification of the three islands in a single island; means of directing the current from the northern arm of the river to make it more navigable and from the southern branch to create a port at the center of the capital.[200]

In his plan De Wailly included a number of already proposed projects: the completion of a square in front of Saint Sulpice, the creation of a new square for the fair of Saint-Germain, the project for the large new Hôtel-Dieu designed by Poyet for the Ile des Cygnes, and the joining of the Ile de la Cité and Ile Saint-Louis. In addition he proposed new projects: avenues from the Barrière du Trône to the Etoile, from the Panthéon to the rue Vieille-du-Temple, and around the Champ de Mars; an opera in the Carrousel of the Louvre; a palace for Monsieur by the Luxembourg gardens; a public promenade running to the river beside the Hôtel de Ville; and a new Hall aux Blés and public baths matching Poyet's Hôtel-Dieu:

The Halle aux Blés being recognized as inadequate for the provisioning of Paris, it has been thought necessary to supplement it by establishing, beside the river beyond the Ile des Cygnes, a circus, symmetrical to the projected Hôtel-Dieu where the boats could enter to remain loaded throughout the winter if the storehouses were al-

Ledoux, Project for a *guin-guette,* Chaillot, perspective view. Engraving from Ramée, *Ledoux,* pl. 278.

Ledoux, House of Pleasure, Montmartre, plan. Engraving from Ramée, *Ledoux,* pl. 238.

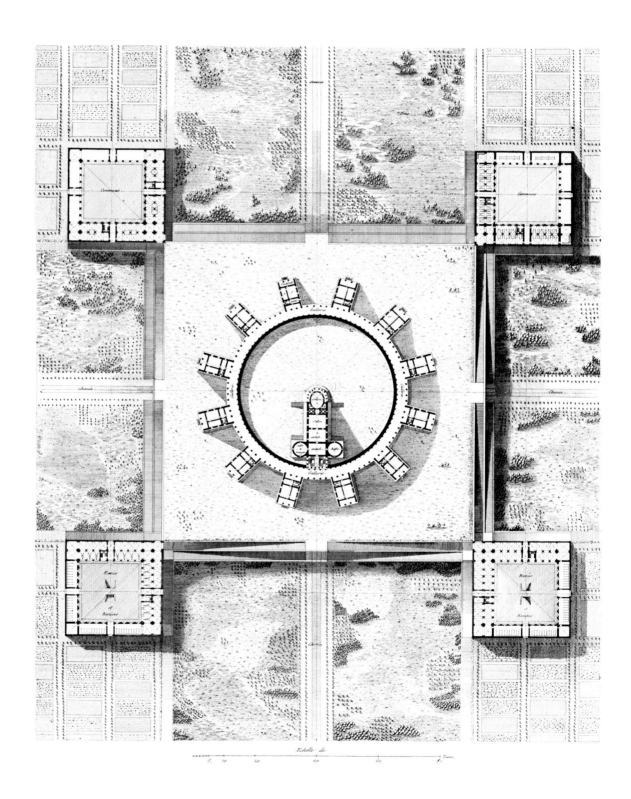

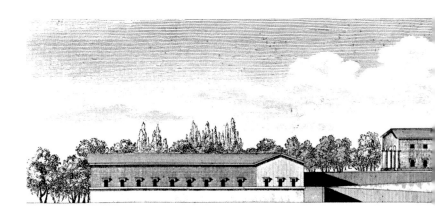

Coupe
fur la ligne C.D

Echell

Ledoux, House of Pleasure,
elevation and sections. Engraving from Ramée, *Ledoux,*
pl. 239.

Elévation.

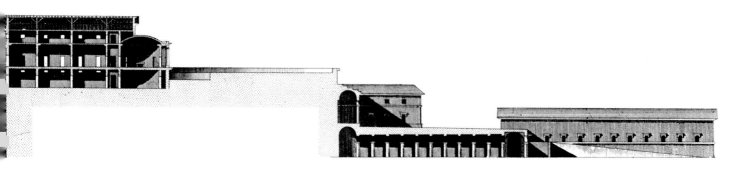

Coupe
fur la ligne A.B.

Coupe
fur la ligne E.F.

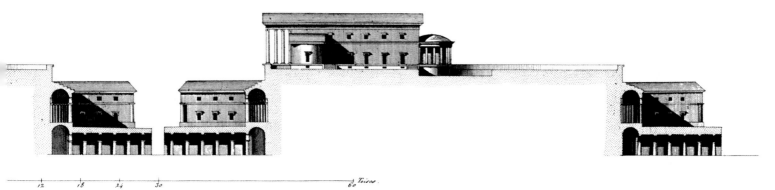

12   18   24   30   3 Toises.   60

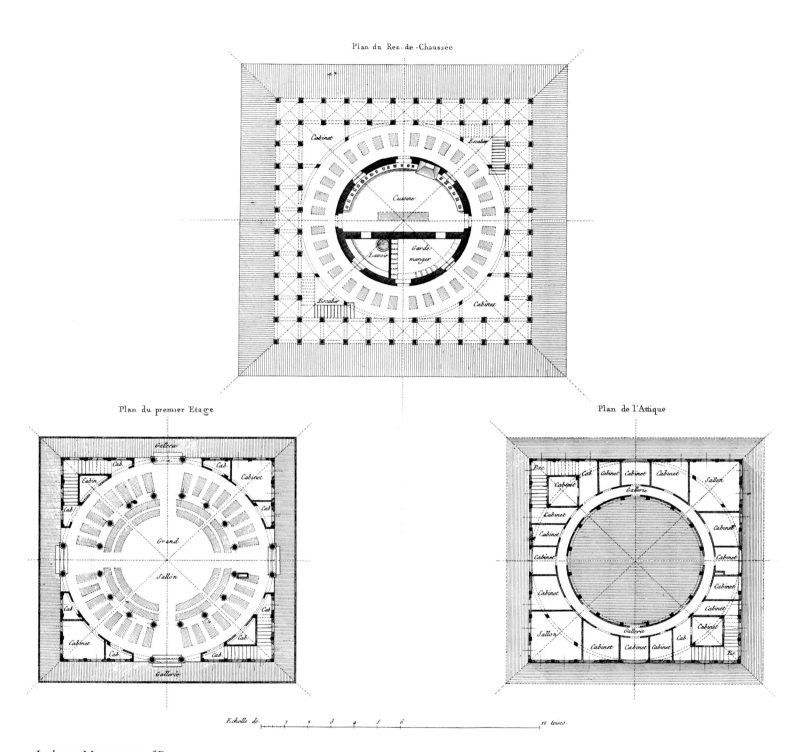

Plan du Rez-de-Chaussée

Plan du premier Etage

Plan de l'Attique

Echelle de

Ledoux, Monument of Popularity, plans, section, elevation, and site plan. Engravings from Ramée, *Ledoux,* pls. 234 and 235.

Coupe

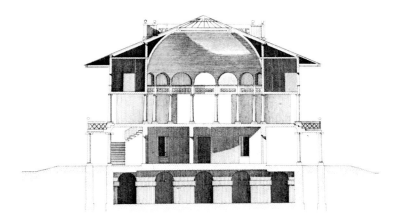

Plan des Souterrains.

Garde manger | Serre | Deg.t | Serre
Serre | | Serre
Serre | Cuisine | Serre
Deg.gt | | Deg.gt
Serre | Office | Serre
Deg.gt | | Serre
Serre | Deg.t | Serre

Elevation

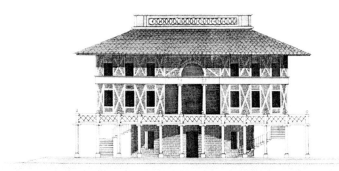

Echelle de 1 2 3 4 5 6 12 toises

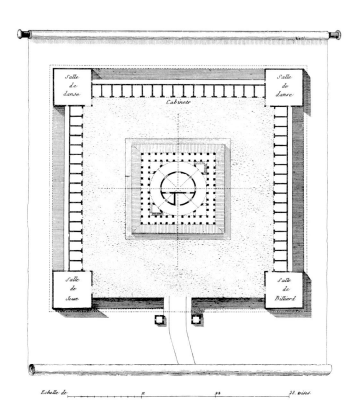

Salle de danse | Cabinet | Salle de danse
Salle de Jeux | | Salle de Billard

Echelle de a 22 33 toises

ready full. In the summer this basin could be used for jousts and swimming. The foundation of the circus at the level of the river will serve as public baths.[201]

ARCHITECTURE DENATURED

From the beginning, architectural criticism of the *barrières* had to wrestle with what was, for all intents and purposes, a fundamental breach in the doctrine of decorum: in the attempt to develop a new genre of public architecture, Ledoux had invested a minor, utilitarian function with all the monumental dignity of high architecture. What in his rhetorical transposition had dignified clerks' offices as the heirs of classical propylaea, thus elevating them to the realm of public art, had in effect made an object of use monumental, or worse, made a monument useful. Ledoux, moreover, had not been content simply to apply the rules of traditional classicism to this task. He intentionally broke every one of them in the search for a new genre, and on every level, from the typological references selected for the pavilions as a whole to the individual elements and ornamental motifs. Not only did he refuse them the characteristics of triumphal arches—the only classical precedents suitable for monumental gates—he also endowed each of them with a specific and different character ranging from temples to prisons. Dulaure noted that "these offices, intended for the collection of the entry dues, should be only simple, convenient, and entirely without a luxury, which would be very out of place and even insulting; they can differ among themselves in their size and interior plan, but they should all have the same character, since they all have the same function."[202] For such modest constructions Dulaure recommended an "architecture that should be simple and conforming to the hardly brilliant and little esteemed estate of the inhabitants." He considered bizarre those built by Ledoux, signifying temples, caves, or prisons—this last suitable, he noted ironically, for the imprisoning wall of the Ferme. Each one contravened the laws of suitability, even of morality: "We should protest against this abuse that publicly injures good taste, that prostitutes the riches of architecture to the clerks of the *barrières,* that insults the poverty of the people by flaunt-ing the objects that aggravate the burden of its existence with a triumphant and magnificent display, and by forcing it, so to speak, to admire the instruments of its unhappiness."[203] Sebastien Mercier, who agreed more mildly with this assessment, simply concluded his catalogue of Ledoux's architectural sins with "Monsieur Ledoux, you are a terrible architect."[204]

The strongest and most perceptive critic of the *barrières* was Quatremère de Quincy, who immediately seized on their totally subversive nature, their propensity to explode all the controls of a classical aesthetic. In the first volume of his *Encyclopédie méthodique: Architecture,* he repeatedly returned to the subject, in the articles "Abus," "Bizarrerie," "Bossages," and "Barrières." In the second volume, he finished his attack under the heading of "Dorique."[205] In each article he presented the *barrières* as negative examples of an architecture that oversteps the limits, that demonstrates the abuse of license, the over-use of rustication, the wrongheaded "invention" of new species of the Doric order.

Quatremère's argument was pitched on three levels: that of the social and political implications of the designs; that of their "typological" form; and that, most important of all, of their assault on every rule of order, proportion, and syntax. Politically, the new *bureaux des fermes* represented for Quatremère a direct example of the extent to which works of art reflect intimately the manners, customs, and morals of a people: following the maxim "The arts are the most faithful mirror of the ideas of a people." he reasoned that the exaggerated and overluxurious forms were only explicable in a country where the word *barrière* had for so long been connected to the existing, half-ruined wooden palisades surrounding Paris.[206] Compared to the gates of Greece and Rome, triumphal arches precisely suited to their dominant position in the city, or even to the gates of Louis XIV, Saint-Antoine and Saint-Denis, these new constructions violated all precedent and were thus to be seen as a reflection of the degraded taste of contemporary France. Quatremère cited Laugier's call for magnificent entries to Paris; fewer and larger entries were needed, not the proliferation of sixty or so monuments, the smallest of which was more costly to build than the Porte Saint-Denis. Second, on the level of typology, he also agreed with Laugier in calling for triumphal arches: for Quatremère, the "type" of the triumphal arch was the simple gate; between gate and arch there existed the same link as between cottage and palace, hut and temple, and, on a larger scale, building and architecture. Tombs, temples, prisons not only contravened the typical origin but also offended the propriety of tombs and temples themselves. A gate, after all, straddled a route, like the door to the city, "announcing an entry"; Ledoux's *barrières,* like "two houses placed on either side of a road, indicate nothing, and the railings needed to defend them and bar the exits will have been only a banal addition to this fault."[207] These new *monuments bâtards"* would turn away a stranger who should be welcomed.

But Quatremère's most analytical comments were reserved for Ledoux's architecture. He admitted the validity of the public's astonishment at the novelty of the *barrières,* their "strange and unusual decorative taste"; he admired their imposing "pyramidal" effect, their "broad and grandiose style;" their character of strength and contrast. He even complimented Ledoux on his use of the "proud austerity of the most male and ancient of Greek orders." But beyond this he saw only "modern puerility." The hitherto unknown combinations, "columns applied with species of torture unheard of till now, frightening rustication, shock in some way all the senses." Quatremère seems to have seen Ledoux as the Marquis de Sade of architecture, dismembering classicism with the delight of a torturer. In every gate Quatremère found "licences": arches inscribed within pediments, pediments without friezes, abaci spanning two columns, freedom of rustication, couplings of columns, distortions of capitals and moldings, false doors of all kinds, "discordant plans, fantastic elevations."

To such works Quatremère applied the qualification *bizarre:* "Almost all these monuments seem to be amalgams of every bizarreness found or not yet found to the present, a new residue of combinations until now impossible." This ascription held a special place in Quatremère's negative criteria. It

was to be distinguished from the mere *caprice,* which implied the deliberate forgetting of rules, and from the simple *folly,* which resulted from a madness, an unknowing fault. The bizarre, by contrast, was the determined product of reflection; "it announces a definite project to commit mistakes or create novelties." A caprice would lead to an abuse and a folly to more follies, but bizarreness gave rise to *vices:*

By an unknown mixture of strength and weakness, richness and poverty, grandeur and puerility, severity and bizarreness, of the colossal and the mean, by the barbarous union of the most discordant and antipathetic principles, these buildings, for the most part, have become monstrous productions, as foreign to the architecture that disavows them as injurious to the good taste that should hasten to proscribe them.

Quatremère had accurately detected in Ledoux the beginnings of that "sleep of reason" that would engender the genre of the monstrous and the romantic grotesque. It was as if he understood Ledoux literally to be dismembering the organic, classical body of architecture—itself founded on the proportional principles of the human form—and, having dispensed with all anthropomorphic relations, to be playing a fantastic game of "heads, bodies, and legs" to give birth to some proto-Frankensteinian monster. As a sculptor and idealist neoclassicist, Quatremère was dedicated to the opposite course: the restoration of the broken body of classicism, in architecture and in statuary, theoretically through the idea of type and practically by the piecing together of fragments.

Yet Quatremère, consistent to his intellectual appreciation of typological invention of all kinds, hesitated to condemn Ledoux's efforts entirely, whether because he thought invention in itself should be encouraged or because he was bound to the view that new conditions of social life give rise to new forms of art. "A new type of monument has seemingly required from architecture a new genre of building," he concluded. The fault, in this sense, resided less in Ledoux's initial premise—to invent a new type—than in the generic nature of the type that he adopted as a basis for his invention. For, "when the type or the primary idea offers nothing grand to the idea of the artist, he finds himself led toward bizarreness in order to hide or dissimulate the vices of his subject." [208] The mean models of the former *barrièrres*, hovels built roughly out of planks, could not have been expected to stimulate the architect to produce great works. From base originals only base new products could be created.

Quatremère's judgment was shared by classicists and romantics alike throughout the nineteenth century. Hugo, decrying the banalization of classical taste, would ask in 1832, "Are we fallen to such a degree of misery that we should be forced to admire the *barrières* of Paris?" [209] Little regret was expressed at their gradual demolition and at their near total eradication after 1859. Almost alone of Ledoux's contemporaries, the historian and architect Jacques-Guillaume Legrand presented a favorable review of the *barrièrres*, intelligently recognizing their novel qualities as essential to the life of a modern architecture.

One sees by the choice of these forms, consecrated by antiquity, that modern architecture has known how to give to each of these buildings the monumental character that they should carry, since they form part of the public buildings of a great town; and because a public building, it cannot be repeated too often, in the type of its construction and the character of its form, must differ essentially from the hut of a gardener or the house of an artisan, with which buildings it should not in any way be confounded. [210]

Here Legrand, followed by the engraver Gaitte, understood the need for a public genre that was neither high nor low, a rhetoric easily comprehended by a wider public than that comprised by the court or church.

THE CITY AS THEATER

In evoking a theatrical metaphor to describe the visual effect of the sequence of *barrières*, Ledoux confirmed what in the Saline de Chaux and the Theater of Besançon had been intimated on the scale of a single building type: that the city itself was to be regarded as a vast social theater, with the didactic effects of its monuments and "landscapes" calculated like so many scenes in a modern bourgeois play of morals. In this constructed series of *tableaux*, the model of the theater was taken directly: "The picture must be confined within the frame that suits it in order to avoid its dispersal" (134). But in the projects and buildings for the *barrières*, Ledoux made it clear that the social theater of the city was to be framed visually and programmatically by the architect. Here, invoking the multiplied effect of a large number of different and strongly contrasted monuments, each recalling a different building type or types from antiquity or the Renaissance and thereby giving to the whole city an antique air, as if Paris were suddenly Rome reborn, Ledoux was appealing to another tradition of theatricality that was, in essence, urban: the design of public festivals for royal, civic, or corporative celebration. These fêtes, with their temporary architecture of allegorical monuments, triumphal entrances, *feux d'artifices*, and ceremonial altars, occasioned the display of imaginative and playful virtuosity in every art. In the words of Alain-Charles Gruber, "The festival brings together architecture, sculpture, painting, fireworks, music, choreography, opera, and theater, not to speak of the minor arts." [211] The fusion of the arts within the theater was, in the fête, demonstrated on an urban scale. The "scenes" of the festival, marked by the ephemeral architecture of temples, rotundas, pavilions, and statuary, merged naturally with the permanent setting of the street: ideal and real intersected in staged illusion. And if, for Ledoux's contemporaries, trained in the climate of archaeological and antiquarian reconstruction and citation that permeated the French school in Rome, the fêtes represented an opportunity to explore, experimentally, the dimensions of a restored antiquity, unobtainable with real commissions—to realize, so to speak, the promises of a Piranesian fantasy—for Ledoux, the fêtes provided a model to be permanently rendered in monumental architecture. What during the festival turned daily life into a mock utopian romance was to be, through architecture, universally instituted. This is why the pavilions for the *barrières* have, despite their evident solidity, such a festive and almost hallucinatory quality: they are neither more nor less than the settings for a permanent urban fête. The festivals of the Revolutionary period even transformed the Barrières de Chaillot into *feux d'artifices*, the stage sets for an allegory of Fame, standing on a sphere set on a huge rock grotto, trumpeting the memory of Revolution.[212]

Ledoux, while not participating in the design of these festivals, spent these last years imagining the allegorical monuments for a utopian city dedicated to social life envisaged as a continual festival. His designs for the ideal institutions of Chaux similarly bear the marks of their ephemeral origins; and, drawn between 1790 and 1802, they form an exact counterpart to a similar sequence of "ideal" designs by Brongniart for the fêtes of year IV.[213] In a sense, whether politically acceptable or not, Ledoux's utopia took its place within the tradition of Revolutionary festivals, much as the equally utopian manifestoes of François-Noël Babeuf formed part of the revolutionary discourse as a whole.[214] Babeuf imagined the egalitarian aims of the Revolution generalized to the entire countryside, in a Rousseauesque dream of a "natural" equality. So Ledoux extended the moralizing *fabriques* of the urban festival to the surroundings of Chaux, endowing the ideal city with a social theater, equally Rousseauesque, that encompassed every space and each building, in the same way as its nucleus, the Saline de Chaux, embodied the theater as productive mechanism.

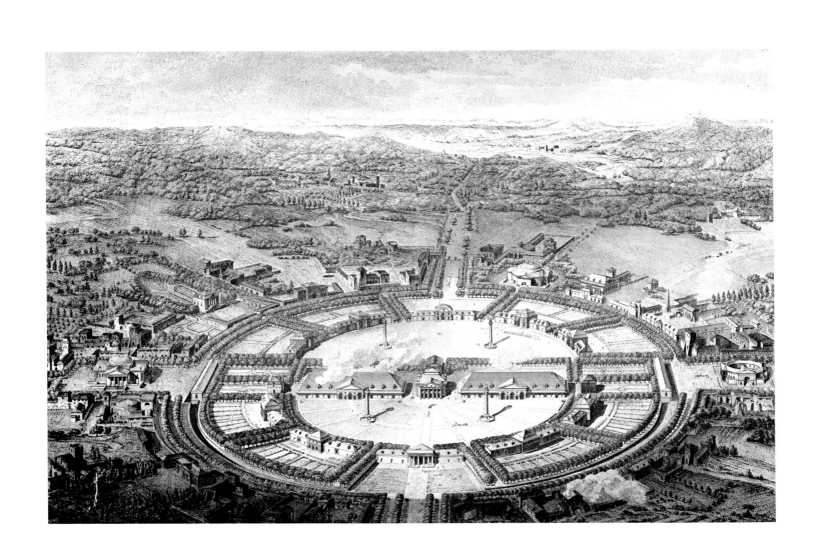

*The Ideal City of Chaux
1780–1804*

███████████████████████████████

I had been traveling for two years to educate myself, when I learned, in Lyons, that the government had opened up extensive works in a part of Franche-Comté. This province offers a vast quarry for natural history, commerce, and industry. (43)

PHYSIOCRATIC REGIONALISM

THE DEVELOPMENT OF FRANCHE-COMTÉ

Though planned in response to a specific program, the Saline de Chaux took its place in the 1770s, as the contract with the entrepreneur Monclar had clearly intimated, within a general policy of opening up the province of Franche-Comté to expanded industry and trade. Annexed to France only a century earlier, with an independent population, customs, and parliament, the region was nevertheless both economically and strategically important: its forests supplied a growing iron industry, while its proximity to the Swiss cantons gave it military significance.[1] The breaking down of linguistic barriers, the connection of its roads and rivers to the French network, the encouragement of new production would, the government believed, strengthen the borders as well as stimulate competition with Geneva. Accordingly, the administration of Trudaine and Turgot and later that of Calonne actively supported the development of the eastern provinces: the highway system was improved and extended, canals for shipping and the transport of timber were projected and begun, and state financing was advanced for new industries.

From as early as 1744, in conjunction with the survey of France begun by the astronomer and cartographer César-François Cassini of the Paris Observatory, and with the encouragement of the elder Trudaine, the old Comté de Bourgogne was surveyed and mapped by the Ponts et Chaussées; the chief engineer of the province, Jean Querret, presented the results to Cassini and the Académie Royale des Sciences in 1748. In a later memorandum Querret noted that roads were necessary for communication and commerce; they should be "beautiful, secure, easy, and practical."[2] Problems of safety, upkeep, and ease of travel were interlinked:

It is not enough for the roads to be short, straight, linked together, convenient, and well maintained, they must also be safe, pleasant for travelers, and disengaged from the woods on either side, which could serve as a place of ambush and retreat for the thieves that the present circumstances make it all the more necessary to fear. Even more than in peacetime the number of those uprooted from the cultivation of the land and accustomed to dissipation could lead to trouble. . . . This is why it is important to cut back the woods that border the roads to a certain distance.[3]

At the height of the Seven Years' War, fears of brigandage were plausible enough; the *corvée,* or mandatory service on the roads, had virtually ceased to function (Turgot even attempted briefly to suspend it in Franche-Comté); many roads were impassable in the winter and the majority of the watercourses were blocked. Indeed, only the roads directly dependent on the *salines* were in good repair; a report of 1776 found them to be "the finest and best maintained of the roads despite the continual passage of vehicles carrying wood and salt."[4] Under Querret's leadership, the Ponts et Chaussées tried to improve conditions, training a corps of young engineers for service in the region. Ten years later in 1774, in his capacity as Contrôleur Générale and Directeur des Bâtiments du Roi, the Abbé Terray commissioned a painting from Claude-Joseph Vernet, *The Construction of a Great Road,* to celebrate their success: a chief engineer, perhaps Perronet, is seen inspecting the completion of a road through the mountainous Jura, in a picturesque landscape that Ledoux would later evoke as the site of his ideal city.[5]

Equally important for commerce were the rivers and canals, the *canaux de flottage* for the delivery of timber from the high forests to the sawmills. In a long report, submitted a year after the completion of the Saline de Chaux, the engineer Philippe Bertrand proposed a systematization of the waterways of Franche-Comté.[6] He found the need for navigable routes acute. Only the Saône could handle boats of any size, and these had to be hauled by men or horses; iron and stone, together with fragile goods such as wine and glass, had to be carried overland, where they were subject to excessive tolls. The other rivers—the Doubs, the Orgnon, the Loüe,

and the Dain—could only accommodate floating timber and, rarely, barges. The Doubs, obstructed with sawmills and at its junction with the Saône completely blocked by silt and flotsam, conveyed no boats at all. Bertrand suggested the construction of a new canal, three and a half leagues long, joining the Doubs to the Saône. The results would, he claimed, be felt immediately:

Not only will this new stretch of canal carry the navigation of the Rhône and Saône to Dôle and thence to Besançon; but the region strongly urges that navigation be possible through to Alsace, and that there a canal should be built to join with the Rhine, which would unite Holland to the Mediterranean and which would, by means of the Canal de Bourgogne already undertaken to join with the Seine, render Franche-Comté the center of commerce for the three seas and make it the most magnificent establishment possible to glorify among any of the most flourishing nations.[7]

Supporting these projects to open up the eastern provinces were the strong economic doctrines of Jacques Turgot and his circle, derived from the programs for agricultural reform and free trade advanced by the Physiocrats in the 1750s.[8] As originally formulated by François du Quesnay and elaborated by Honoré-Gabriel de Mirabeau, Physiocracy envisaged a return to an entirely natural economy, based on farming and the use of raw materials. As opposed to the nonproductive activities of commerce and financial speculation, which were *sterile* and without natural foundation, these products of a *fertile* earth were, the doctrine ran, the only bases of real wealth.

Quesnay, personal physician to Madame de Pompadour, was interested in agricultural practice as well as medicine and wrote a number of articles for Diderot's *Encyclopédie,* including the influential essays "Farmers," "Corn," "Men," and "Taxation." Extending his knowledge of physiology to the social world, he drew up an economic "table" that described the flow of wealth and exchange in terms of circulation: against monopolies and protective tariffs, he supported free trade, internally to France and externally. His followers included Pierre-Samuel Dupont de Nemours, who published Quesnay's major writings in 1767,[9] and the Abbé Nicolas Baudeau, as well as Turgot and Trudaine de Montigny. Their philosophy was premised on the belief that "nature," and specifically economic nature, was an all-pervasive and all-beneficent force: their hope was, in the words of Dupont de Nemours, "to join the natural right of men, the natural order of society, and the natural laws most advantageous for men brought together in society." [10] In methodological terms, this meant using all the tools of analytical reason to construct a model of natural economy, a "model" of natural flows, the circulation of wealth and goods, along the lines of the circulation of blood in the human body. The free circulation of goods necessitated a well-functioning communication network: Quesnay and his followers supported transportation of every kind, and urged the development of canal and road works, especially in isolated rural areas, in order to bring agricultural produce to the markets. Quesnay, in his article "Men," supported the canal between the Sâone and the Loire as well as a project for piping water to every house in Paris—both projects that had been resisted by the water carriers. Physiocratic opposition to monopoly interests fought all forms of *dirigisme* by the state and closed guilds; in the words of the Abbé Baudeau, "liberty, total liberty, perfect immunity, this is the fundamental law." [11]

Opposed to the concentration of wealth and luxury in the towns and arguing for a "return to the countryside," the Physiocrats extended their criticism to the aesthetic realm, against "frivolous ornamentation" as wasteful of resources better used to further agriculture. Quoting Cicero on the happiness of the farmer, Quesnay lauded the "worthy inhabitants of the countryside" and espoused rural festivals that celebrated productive virtues in place of the artificial amusements of the towns. In his article on farmers he concluded,

It is the riches of farmers that fertilize the earth, multiply livestock, that attract and fix the inhabitants of the countryside and that are the strength and prosperity of the nation. Manufactures and commerce, supported by the disorders of luxury, accumulate men and riches in the big towns, oppose themselves to the amelioration of goods, devastate the countryside, inspire disgust for agriculture, augment the expenses of individuals excessively, destroy the sustenance of families, oppose the propagation of men, and enfeeble the state. [12]

Commercial profit was thus criticized, as contributing to the movement of money rather than to the enrichment of primary resources; free trade and a natural level of prices was preferable to the monopoly of a dirigist state. Certain machines were admitted into Quesnay's system, notably those which, like the taffeta looms in Lyons, acted to reduce the cost of labor; but the emphasis was predominantly rural and entirely pre–Industrial Revolution in outlook. [13]

Turgot, while adopting the substance of this doctrine, had extended it in significant ways. First, what had been for Quesnay a rigid, geometrical diagram of a system—the productive "circle" that began and ended in nature—was historicized and given a flexible, progressive dynamic. In his initial discourses, read at the Sorbonne while still a student, Turgot insisted on the inevitability of progress, which in his terms included a measure of commercial development. [14] Second, like Diderot, Turgot was as favorable to the artisan and his *métier* as he was to the farmer. Third, Turgot held that industries, if founded on the transformation of natural raw materials, might be admitted into the system if their profits were, so to speak, returned to the soil. [15] While Intendant de Limousin, Turgot had tried to put his theories into practice, notably in his support for the development of roads and waterways; and his appointment as Contrôleur Général in 1774 had seemed to many liberal economists the opportunity, finally, to put Physiocracy to the test. In the event, Turgot's abortive attempts to free the price of grain, suspend the *corvée*, and attack the entrenched monopolies of the corporations and the State proved the ruin of his career. But in the brief interval between 1774 and 1776, the considerable support that Turgot found from Trudaine and Malesherbes inspired the hope for a regeneration of agriculture and trade on the English model. [16]

Joined to Turgot's circle by his friendship with the Abbé Delille, Ledoux adopted its reformist optimism with enthusiasm and made out of it his own heterogeneous program for rural development. From Trudaine and Perronet and the younger members of the Ponts et Chaussées in Franche-Comté, he derived his understanding of the necessary infrastructure of roads and waterways. From the "late" Physiocracy of Turgot and Dupont de Nemours and its vulgarization by the Abbé Baudeau and Jacques-Pierre Brissot de Warville, he conceived the agricultural foundations of his imaginary town as well as its peculiar institutional supports. Finally, Ledoux found in the Abbé Delille a theoretical and aesthetic mentor who combined a commitment to agrarian reform with its idealization in pastoral poetics.

FROM SALINE TO NEW TOWN

In this context, Ledoux's claim that, from the outset, he had envisaged the Saline de Chaux as the industrial nucleus of a new town that would form the center of such regional development is entirely credible. "I presented the projects for a town together with the growth to which it was susceptible," he stated in describing the incredulous reception of his first plans for the *saline* by the contractors and tax agents; he recorded the words of his clients on seeing his "grand views": "Temples, public baths, markets, houses of commerce, of games, etc., etc. . . . What a mass of incoherent ideas!" But clearly Ledoux had not designed these institutions in 1774, nor, as the chronology of the building campaign demonstrates, did he necessarily conceive the *saline* with any future extension in mind—the theatrical *parti* was, after all, complete in itself. Nevertheless, as Jacques Cellérier recorded, Ledoux very possibly presented the idea of such a new town to the Trudaine-Turgot administration, which might well, in turn, have accepted in principle the notion of government-sponsored housing.[17] Ledoux himself implied that he had been inspired by the failure of the government's plans for the new town of Versoix on the shores of Lake Geneva, projected in the 1760s by the Secretary of State for Foreign Affairs, the Duc de Choiseul. Writing in 1802, Ledoux was clear as to his own intentions: "Here the town is built," and to avoid any ambiguity he added, "The Town of Chaux. The project for building Versois had been abandoned, M. the Duc de Choiseul having left the Ministry" (*Prospectus,* 9).

The plan for Versoix, or La Nouvelle Choiseul as it was originally called, had first been conceived in 1762 as a military and economic challenge to a Geneva weakened by revolution.

Sponsored by Choiseul himself, together with the Chevalier de Jaucourt and Fabry, the work of building the port was started five years later, on the completion of the post road between Lyons and the site of the new town; an engineer was then appointed and construction began on the town proper. On the disgrace of Choiseul in 1770, however, plans for the town were suspended. Nevertheless, despite the opposition of Trudaine and the obstructionism of Terray, the town was backed by an important group of *philosophes,* led by Voltaire and Malesherbes, who argued for the establishment at Versois of religious tolerance.[18] In 1775 the engineer Jean Querret proposed completing the work based on a new plan; and the Comte de Vergennes, the new Foreign Secretary, envisaged that the town, while not large, might become "the center of export for all our merchandise coming from the south for Switzerland, Germany, and even a part of Italy."[19] The town was only finally abandoned at the end of 1782.

Querret's plan, drawn up and engraved, significantly enough, by François-Noël Sellier in 1774, transformed the older version, which had been envisaged as a traditional Renaissance "ideal city" within fortifications that might have been planned by Sébastien le Prestre Vauban, into a more modern settlement whose walls were replaced by encircling boulevards and *rond-points.* Querret retained the square, camplike plan of the first scheme, but rendered circular its one central square and supplemented it with four rectangular, neighborhood squares each corresponding to one of four entrances to the town, three from the land, one from the lake. The surrounding boulevard took the form of an octagon, truncated by the port, its points marked by semicircular *places,* in the manner advised by Laugier or Patte; the town was served from the hinterland by a canal that entered from the northwest into a circular basin and ran axially along the middle of the main boulevard to the port. This centralized new town, planned both as a reinforcement of the frontiers and as a philosophic experiment in liberty of religion and trade, at precisely the same time as Ledoux's commission for Chaux, engraved by his own engraver, and competing with it for Trudaine's support, cannot but have influenced his own design.

Jean Querret, Plan of the new
town of Versoix, 1774. Engraving by Sellier from the
Bibliothèque Nationale,
Cartes et Plans, GeD 10139.

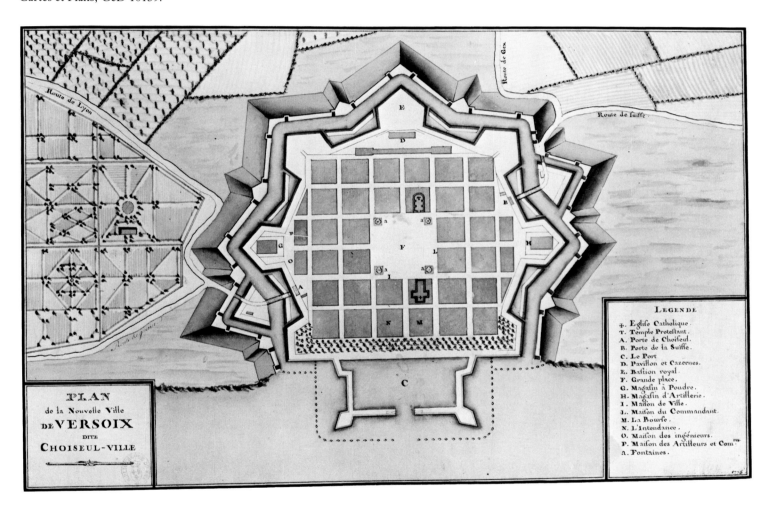

LEGENDE

✝. Eglise Catholique.
T. Temple Proteftant.
A. Porte de Choifeul.
B. Porte de la Suiffe.
C. Le Port.
D. Pavillon et Cazernes.
E. Baftion royal
F. Grande place.
G. Magafin à Poudre.
H. Magafin d'Artillerie.
I. Maifon de Ville.
L. Maifon du Commandant.
M. La Bourfe.
N. L'Intendance.
O. Maifon des ingénieurs.
P. Maifon des Artilleurs et Comⁿˢ
a. Fontaines.

PLAN
de la Nouvelle Ville
DE VERSOIX
DITE
CHOISEUL-VILLE

Ledoux's ambitions were also no doubt supported by the work of his fellow academician, Charles De Wailly, at Port-Vendres on the southwest coast. This port, strategically and commercially useful for access to the Mediterranean and the Atlantic, had been enlarged between 1773 and 1775; throughout the War of American Independence work continued on the building of a church and public monuments. De Wailly, commissioned in 1779 to design an obelisk in honor of the king, took the opportunity to draw up a more comprehensive plan for an entire new town planned radially around two semicircular basins. It was presented, like the plan for Chaux, in an elaborate bird's-eye view: The great obelisk stands in front of a chapel in the form of an antique temple; to either side of the central *hôtel de ville* and stock exchange stand a convent and the parish church, this latter modeled on the Pantheon.[20] In the event, only the obelisk and its surroundings were built, on a reduced plan that replaced the temple/chapel with a maritime warehouse, between 1782 and 1783.

The influence of both these projects on Ledoux's ambitious extension of the *saline* into a new town is suggested by a map in the Bibliothèque Nationale of the *saline,* the Forest of Chaux, and the planned new access roads.[21] Undated and unsigned, this drawing was thought by Herrmann as of too small a scale to have served as a basis for the engraved "Map of the Surroundings of the Saline de Chaux," and it has escaped the notice of subsequent commentators. Entitled "Plan of the Forest of Chaux, of the site of the *saline,* the graduation building, the canal, and the roads projected in this forest for the service of the *saline,*" it shows the Loüe River, the villages of Arc and Senans between the village of Chissey to the west and the Château de Roche to the east, and the entire Forest of Chaux to the north, ringed by the communities of Dôle, Orchampt, Fraisans, and Saint Vir. The routes through this forest are drawn according to the old grid of *allées* as shown, for example, on Querret's map of 1748. In these respects, the map shows the "surroundings" of the *saline* precisely as drawn in Ledoux's published engraving, and, despite Herrmann's claim, in equal detail, but simply extending to a larger area. More interesting, however, is that the *saline* is shown as

built, but with the complete oval of the town of Chaux drawn in red and surrounded by a ring boulevard, thus denoting the land to be reserved for what would be taken up by the barracks and *hôtel de ville* of the new town, yet prior to the planning of the individual buildings. Further, also in red, superimposed on the existing routes, an axial road leads to the Loüe to the south and to the forest to the north, as in the engraving. Beyond the confines of the engraving, and in the center of the forest, this north-south route ends in a *rond-point* with a pyramidal obelisk at its center. From this point three roads, marked in red across the old grid, radiate out to Dôle, to Orchampt, and to Saint Vir, thus connecting the new town to the outside world in a radial pattern that extends its internal planning principles to the territory.

All the internal evidence points to this plan being drawn up sometime between the plans for the *saline* as built and the final engraving published in *L'architecture,* and the plan seems, stylistically, to date from before the Revolution. It was no doubt prepared according to Ledoux's design and suggests that the doubling of the semicircle of the *saline* to form the oval containing the barracks and *hôtel de ville* might have occurred earlier than generally thought, perhaps even between 1776 and the early 1780s. One is tempted to see in this schematic plan the project Cellérier tells us was presented to Turgot before 1776. This first, almost pragmatic map of the proposed new town became the basis of the idealized version finally published in *L'architecture,* first in the "Perspective View of the Town of Chaux" and then in the engraved "Map of the Surroundings of the Saline de Chaux," a rendering that, as Herrmann correctly observes, has itself undergone two stages of development.

The map in the Bibliothèque Nationale seems then to represent an intermediate version of Ledoux's projects for the new town, one corresponding to the "Perspective View of the Town of Chaux." This would be expanded with the addition of a second band of housing in the second state of the plate showing the surroundings of the *saline.* It was no doubt this expansion, added sometime between 1795 and 1802, to which Ledoux refers when, optimistically, he stated in the *Prospectus* that he was then in the process of developing the plans for a

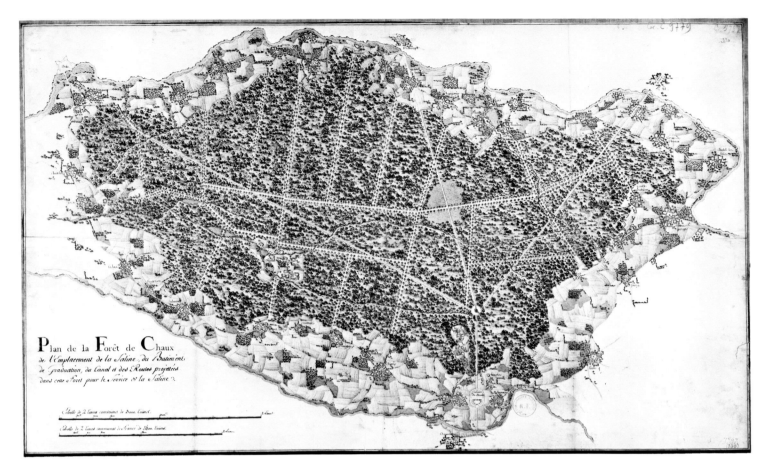

Plan of the Forest of Chaux, showing the siting of the *saline,* the graduation building, canal, and the routes projected in the forest for the service of the *saline.* Undated, but probably around 1780. Drawing from the Bibliothèque Nationale, Cartes et Plans, GeC 9779.

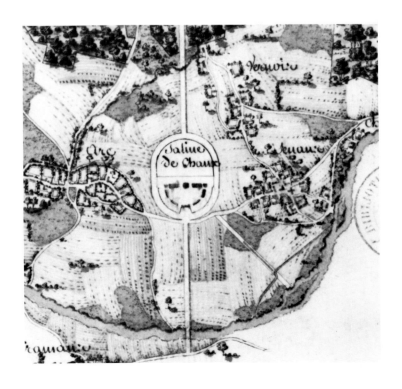

second town: "I will execute in a second town what I have conceived in the first: there one will see the luxury of ideas reproduce themselves on the antique volume of nature" (*Prospectus,* 25). Such a hypothesis would at once bear out Ledoux's claims that the project for the town was conceived and presented to the administration while the *saline* was still being built and, at the same time, confirm Helen Rosenau's sense that the formalization of the terrace housing in the "Map of the Surroundings" dates from a later period.[22]

If this is so, then the parallel between Ledoux at Chaux and De Wailly at Port-Vendres becomes telling; it places Ledoux within a general current of new-town speculation, tied to the reinforcement of the frontiers, the encouragement of trade, and the more generic project of "mapping" the space of the realm. This mapping, as Bruno Fortier has shown, held within its own techniques the project of interpreting and utilizing the territory through the establishment of roads, canals, ports, agricultural colonies, and of course, new towns.[23]

Ledoux's first signed proposal for the town of Chaux, envisaged as an extension of the *saline,* was recorded on the first state of the "Map of the Surroundings of the Saline de Chaux." The plan is compact and enclosed within the oval formed by the doubling of the Saline de Chaux; the *saline* is shown as built and still enclosed by its wall and surrounding ditch. This detail reinforces the assumption of an early date for this scheme; for in his insistence on continually revising his idealized designs, Ledoux would have, at a later stage, added rear porches to the factory buildings. The semicircle of buildings to the north that exactly mirrors that of the *saline* is

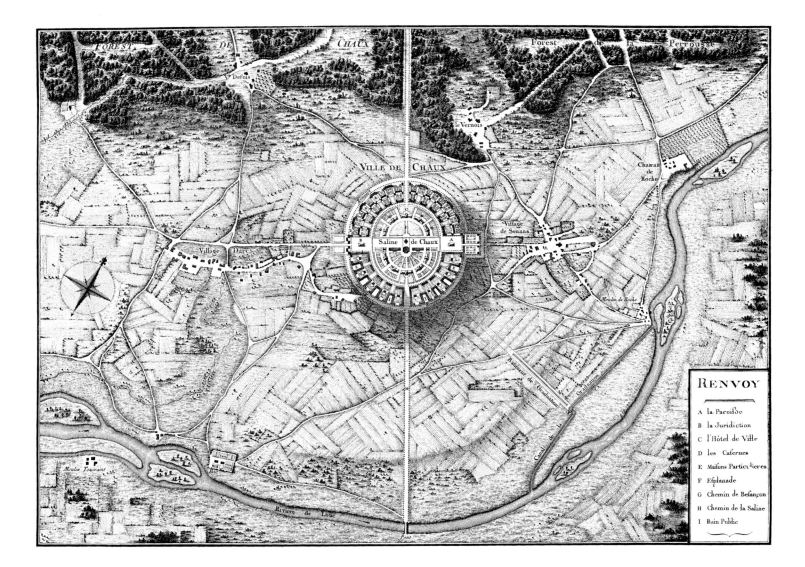

Ledoux, "Map of the Surroundings of the Saline de
Chaux." Engraving by Dupuis
from Ramée, *Ledoux,* pl. 115.

Legend:
A. Parish church
B. Law courts
C. Town hall
D. Barracks
E. Private houses
F. Esplanade
G. Road to Besançon
H. Road to the *saline*
 I. Public baths.

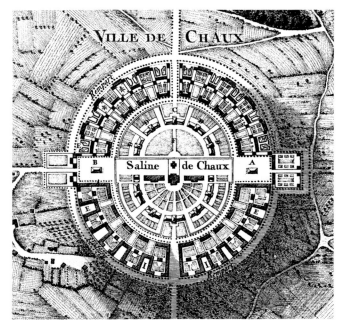

Detail of the map showing the
Town of Chaux.

similarly enclosed by a wall, with barracks corresponding to the workers' pavilions of the *saline* and an *hôtel de ville* taking the place of the gatehouse. To the east and west on the cross axis of the oval are public squares with simple buildings, entered through peristyles, labeled the Parish Church and the Law Courts, respectively. Other institutions, such as the Public Baths, are indicated only by letter. Around the oval formed by the barracks and *saline* runs a tree-lined boulevard that provides circulation for a town whose center, so to speak, is inaccessible. This ring road services the private houses of the town, which are planned in reticulated patterns around courtyards and gardens, the layout differing, no doubt for reasons of orientation, from south to north. These terraces, with their geometries reminiscent of the crescents and terraces of George Dance, Jr., and John Wood in England, are themselves enclosed by a peripheral boulevard, designated, in reference to the "fortified" nature of this military border town, "The Rampart." The only roads leading to the town from the surrounding countryside are the two main axial routes: one running south-north, from the Loüe River to the Forest of Chaux and Besançon beyond; the other, west-east, less pronounced and simply a regularization of the road between Arc and Senans. Ledoux left unchanged the land of the region, its houses, the Château de Roche and its water mill, the ferry downstream, the parish church of Senans, the foresters' clearings, as well as the graduation building and its accompanying, later idealized, cottage. The impression is of a plan conceived, probably sometime between 1779 and 1785, to rival that of Versoix, with similar graphic conventions and institutional program to those of Querret.

A second version of the new town, however, depicted in the "Perspective View of the Town of Chaux," reveals a very different conception: the closed, geometric character appropriate to a garrison was replaced by a more open, almost picturesque aspect that doubtless reflected the influence of the new fashion for landscapes and gardens composed according to English precedents. The central oval of *saline* and barracks remains in place, but enlivened by clouds of smoke from the factory and by troops assembled in their parade ground. The developed design for the Church to the east and the first

scheme for a Market replacing the Law Courts to the west occupy the public squares; visible to the rear are the Public Baths and what seems to be a first project for the Stock Exchange. The regular terraces of housing, however, are gone; and in their stead, old and new buildings are mingled as in a picture by Hubert Robert. Neo-Palladian villas similar to the one Ledoux designed for the Chevalier de Mannery of Salins stand next to rambling farmsteads, monasteries, and warehouses. A building with a domed, semicircular addition seems to indicate a school, in the manner of Gondouin's auditorium for the Ecole de Chirurgie. Villages, marked by chapels, parish churches, and farms, are scattered through the Forest of Chaux, which recedes to the distant horizon. The aesthetic is that of the Abbé Delille's popular evocation of the landscape garden, *Les jardins* of 1782, significantly subtitled "the art of embellishing landscapes." [24]

This view, certainly one of the most striking and beautifully executed plates of *L'architecture,* was engraved by Pierre-Gabriel Berthault. He was also responsible for the perspective views of the Public Baths and the graduation building of the *saline,* which confirm in their style the early date of the aerial perspective. The view of the graduation building also depicts the cottage of the carpenter in charge of the pumps as built (and indeed as it still exists), prior to Ledoux's post-Revolutionary redesign. A second aerial view of the town, taken from the southwest and showing the definitive project for the Market, drawn after 1784, obviously used Berthault's first view as a basis; it too shows the Public Baths and the first scheme for the Stock Exchange, but it handles the perspective less confidently and was evidently given to a less competent engraver whose knowledge of the plans for the *saline* and baths was confined to Berthault's version.

A third version of the town plan, which Ledoux described in his text as a town with "sixteen streets that converge toward a common center," that is, a radial town with *allées* expanding into the countryside in the manner of Karlsruhe, was perhaps the latest to be conceived. Its form is indicated by a late state of the engraving of the "General Plan of the Saline as Built," a state that appears in none of the pre-Revolutionary collections of Ledoux's engravings. As Jo-

Ledoux, "Perspective View of
the Town of Chaux." Engraving by Berthault from Ramée,
Ledoux, pl. 116.

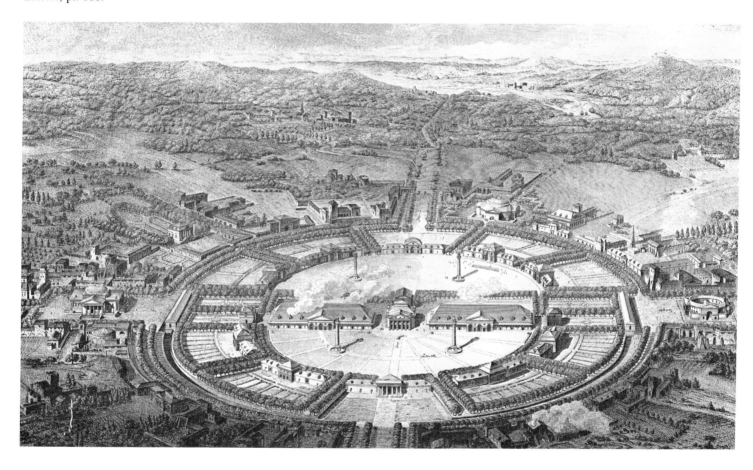

Ledoux, Market of Chaux,
perspective view. Engraving
from Ramée, *Ledoux,* pl. 145.

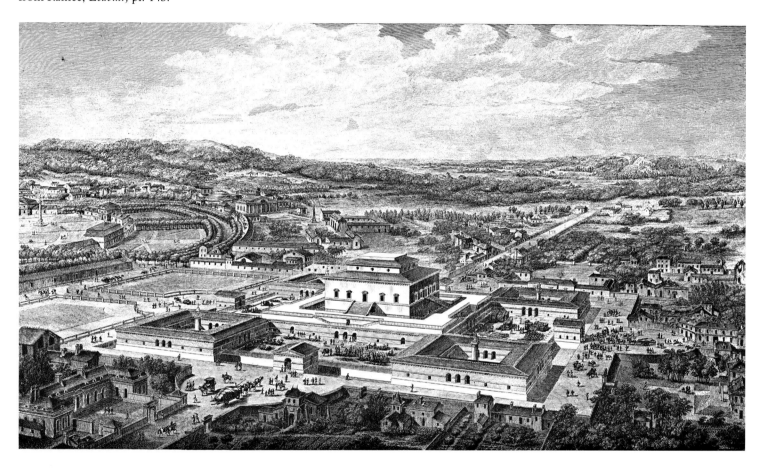

hannes Langner has shown, this version, printed for the first time in *L'architecture,* was superimposed on an original plan of the *saline,* engraved by Sellier around 1776, that bears no trace of the later ideal town nor of the doubling of the semi-circle into an oval. On this plan—proof of the original theatrical concept of the *saline*—Ledoux marked the lines of nine of the sixteen radial roads, tree-lined boulevards that seem to extend the lines of the paths between the workers' buildings, themselves now formalized into miniature avenues. Between these radials Ledoux simply noted the sites for the "mass of the houses of the town." To the original state, drawn before the rejection of the first scheme of the Director's Building and showing the ground-floor plan also as engraved by Sellier in 1776, Ledoux added porticoes to the rear of the factory buildings and to the front and rear of the Director's Building, as it would be drawn in the idealized version of Coquet and Bovinet's perspective view. Finally, no doubt sometime around 1800, Ledoux added the reticulated housing and encircling boulevard to the "Map of the Surroundings of the Saline de Chaux."

In the text of *L'architecture* all these versions were elided to form a single all-embracing vision of the ideal city. Its nucleus was still the *saline* and the barracks; actually oval, but assimilated by Ledoux to the "elliptical" course of the sun, its generic form was circular, thus mimicking the Physiocrats' economic metaphor of the circle of production. Even as Quesnay, preoccupied throughout his life by the circle and circulation, was convinced, as Ronald Meek has put it, that "in nature everything is intertwined, everything moves through circular courses which are interlaced with one another," [25] so Ledoux took the imagery of the circle to represent the genesis and expanding influence of his city: "Everything is circular in nature; the stone that falls into the water propagates infinite circles; centripetal force is incessantly countered by a rotary motion; the air and the seas move in perpetual circles"(223). Ledoux transferred this image, used to justify the form of his theater, to the town of Chaux, which he spoke of as "an immense circle," with a form "as pure as that described by the sun." And he compared the foundation of Chaux to the mythical formation of the Milky Way by a drop

of milk falling from Juno's breast, replacing, in the case of Chaux, milk with salt water: "Here a drop of water suspended in the air acquires a progressive value in falling, and founds the city"(69). [26]

Sustaining this economic foundation, Ledoux imagined a complete repertory of industrial and agricultural institutions generating a new commercial center, linked to the rest of France and to the world by the completed network of roads and canals envisaged by the Ponts et Chaussées.

The line intersecting the diameter [of the saline] crosses the Loüe, immense plains, the town, the forest, the Doubs, the Geneva canal, the Swiss pastures; to the left lie the Meuse, the Moselle, the Rhine, the port of Antwerp, and the North seas carry the first and much desired fruits of our commerce and arts to the very deserts of Siberia.(72)

Echoing the memoranda of the Ponts et Chaussées to the letter, Ledoux depicted the completion of the canal network begun by Daniel Trudaine:

Here the Dôle canal is married to the Yonne; . . . its children roll their waters to the south seas. . . . There, the Doubs petitions the Meuse in order to join with the Rhine. The port of Antwerp is open and divides with hardworking Batavia the precious fruits of commerce. . . . You see the Rhône canal, that of Iverdun, which carry to Lake Bienne the marine timber taken from Switzerland and Savoy; . . . you see the Arve, cut over a short distance, ease transportation from the Pays du Gex, from Bugey, Chatagne, Chablais.(74)

In the last years of the eighteenth century, with the completion of the Canal du Centre by Emiliand Gauthey in 1793 opening the route from the Loire to the Saône, the completion of the Doubs-Saône canal in the same year, and the extension of the Canal du Languedoc opening the route from the Mediterranean to the Bay of Biscay, such a dream was less than utopian. [27]

INSTITUTIONS OF SOCIAL REFORM

This expanding vision was accompanied, from the very early 1780s, by Ledoux's designs for an equally expansionist institutional infrastructure for his city. Following his grand statements to Trudaine and Turgot, Ledoux gradually assembled detailed plans for, as he was to claim on the title page of *L'architecture,* a "collection that brings together all the kinds of building used in the social order." After the group of institutions designed between 1780 and 1785, and depicted in the engravings discussed above—the Church, the Public Baths, the two projects for the Market, and the first scheme for the Stock Exchange—came a second group of institutional designs for Chaux, which can be dated with some confidence between 1785 and 1789. These carry the marks of a more abstract style, associated with that of the *barrières,* and may be related to Boullée's "visionary" designs from the same years; they respond equally to programs either set by the Académie or proposed by Calonne before his dismissal in 1787. For the most part, they were engraved by Coquet, Edme Bovinet, and Pierre-Nicolas Ransonnette. This later group included the Cemetery of Chaux, whose sphere clearly echoed Boullée's Cenotaph to Newton of 1784, and which corresponded in style exactly to Ledoux's spherical House of the Agricultural Guards for Maupertuis. According to the evidence of the other houses for the new village of Maupertuis on the estate of the Marquis de Montesquiou—the plans for which were drawn on the same sheet as those for a number of *barrières*—this engraving must be dated between 1785 and 1787. Coquet and Bovinet also drew the bird's-eye view of the Cannon Foundry, designed, according to Ledoux's account, following a prospectus envisaged by Calonne between 1785 and 1787; Bovinet drew the view of the Bridge over the Loüe River, apparently stimulated by Calonne's request in 1787 for variations on Perronet's design for the bridge leading from the Place Louis XV, then in construction. These last two perspectives include other designs that seem to have been drawn up in the mid-1780s: the Grange Parée, the small *hôtellerie,* the commercial buildings, the double houses under triple arcades, the barrel-vaulted Worker's House (seen both in the

aerial perspective of Maupertuis and in the left background of the view of the bridge of boats). From this intermediate period, identified as much by their style as by Ledoux's preoccupation with the design of *fabriques* for Maupertuis and Bourneville, may be dated the "rustic" workshops and houses for the woodcutters, coopers, sawyers, forest guards, and charcoal burners. Two more communal institutions, the Cénobie and the phallic-planned Oikéma, linked to the House of Pleasure for Montmartre, should also be added to those designs conceived, if not actually engraved, before the Revolution.

A third and final group of ideal projects, easily joined by their abstract style and repeated motifs as well as by their more purely "utopian" programs—the product of Ledoux's post-Revolutionary reveries—must be dated between 1793 and 1802, that is, between Ledoux's release from prison and the publication of the *Prospectus* for *L'architecture.* These include at least twelve of the country houses, mostly engraved by Van Maëlle and his collaborators Simon and Maillet; the rural buildings, the *portiques,* or warehouses, and the Cour de Service; the Hospice, the House of the Surveyors of the Loüe River, the House of Education, the Hunting Lodge, and the Stock Exchange; the two recreational buildings, the Monument to Recreation and the House of Games; and the suite of moralizing monuments, from the Pacifère, the House of Union, and the Temple of Memory, to the Panarèthéon.

The stylistic differences among these three groups of designs parallel, despite the unifying intent of his text in *L'architecture,* Ledoux's changing social and political interests over this long period of time and, equally, reflect the particular nature of his private and public commissions year by year. Ledoux's initial interest, following that of his patrons in the Intendance du Commerce, was economic and regionalist. Thus the debates over freedom of worship for Versoix together with the discussions over the proper form for the Cathedral of Sainte-Geneviève, left incomplete by the death of Soufflot, inspired the Deist and multi-altared Church of Chaux. Ledoux's involvement in the planning of new hospitals in Paris from 1773 and his arguments against the centralization of health care on the side of the conservative Physiocrats, led to an extension of his medical interests, represented by the Public Baths of Chaux—equally inspired by his visit to the baths of Aix and his discovery of the healing properties of the waters of Salins. The Market of Chaux, a response to an Académie program, was also directly a result of Calonne's renewed interest in the development of regional centers for the distribution of produce; likewise, the Cannon Foundry was an expression of Calonne's support of industry based on the exploitation of natural raw materials, conflated with a more strategic and defensive aim. In the mid-1780s, with Ledoux's reengagement in the planning of the estate of Maupertuis, his commission for the *fabriques* in the park of Bourneville, and his involvement with circles of *agronomes,* his focus shifted slightly to practical proposals for the reform of agriculture and the housing of the rural poor. After the Revolution, when Ledoux was preoccupied with salvaging a destroyed reputation, his projects became more concerned with the moral, if not the moralizing, role of institutions, joining the idea of a social world united by brotherhood and communal values—a mingling of Freemasonic and Rousseauesque ideals—to an architectural, symbolic program that would serve to institutionalize the new order.

Whether designed specifically for the town of Chaux or following an actual program and only later assimilated into the all-embracing ideal city, these projects formed in Ledoux's mind an exemplary gamut of types, set, in his ever-expanding vision, in the fertile and picturesque landscapes of Franche-Comté. They were to be the instruments of reform and happiness for the region's rough but natural population of peasants, workers, and farmers—restored to their true nature by a combination of Rousseauesque educational principles, paternalist coercion, and architectural representation and enriched by the wise application of Physiocratic and agronomic doctrines. In this sense, the "ideal" town of Chaux never lost its grip on reality. The complex dialogue between existing social conditions and their architectural reformulation was, in Ledoux's ultimately realist vision, never far removed from the way of life he observed in the countryside; the architect interrogated this intractable and stubbornly rooted tradition to re-

veal its "essential" forms, which he then endowed with new meaning through their architectural display.

RELIGIOUS FESTIVITIES

Ledoux's project for the Church of Chaux was perhaps the first institution not connected to the *saline* itself to be joined to the enlarging plans for the town of Chaux. Designed after 1781 and probably engraved between 1783 and 1784, the church took its place beside other contributions to large-scale religious architecture following Soufflot's death in 1780 and developed in the context of the Académie program for a "Cathedral" of 1781. Inevitably, given the fierce debate over the successive plans for the still incomplete Sainte-Geneviève and the theoretical contributions of historians and critics from Laugier to Le Roy, these were all in some way designed as implicit criticisms of Soufflot's monumental precedent, while at the same time recognizing it as a point of departure, the prototype, so to speak, of the Enlightenment church-temple.[28] Thus both the prize-winning design by Louis Combes and the idealized project for a "Metropole" by Boullée, which have often been compared with Ledoux's scheme for the Church of Chaux, followed the Greek-cross plan of Soufflot's first project for Sainte-Geneviève in 1757; but where Soufflot added an almost freestanding temple front, with its giant Corinthian order, as an entry portico, Combes and Boullée stressed the equality of the cross with four pedimented porticoes. Combes joined these to continuous colonnades surrounding the building, thus preserving the purity of the geometric cross; Boullée emphasized the plain surface of the enclosing wall, setting his colonnades into the geometric solid. Reinforcing the absolute symmetry, both designs placed the altar in a central position beneath the dome, in Boullée's scheme raised on a kind of circular, stepped pyramid and reached by long flights of stairs around the crossing. Both adopted a dome on a high colonnaded drum, according to the precedents of Michelangelo's Saint Peter's or Wren's Saint Paul's; both used the lantern above the dome as the single strongest source of light for the interior, reversing Soufflot's "Gothic" taste for colonnades flooded with light

Ledoux, Church of Chaux,
perspective view. Engraving
by the Varin brothers from
Ramée, *Ledoux,* pl. 140.

from the surrounding walls, to provide a somber, enclosed
volume dramatically lit from above.

Ledoux's church design followed many of these shifts
from the original model, but with significant differences. His
plan was a pure Greek cross, with pedimented porticoes (Tuscan in the perspective view, Corinthian in the cross section);
the altar stood in the center, raised on a square pyramid of
steps and lit from above; the surrounding walls were blank.
There, however, the resemblances ceased. In its three-
dimensional development, in its scale, and in its references to
classical precedent, Ledoux's project departed radically from
the model set by Soufflot and "corrected" by Combes and
Boullée. Elaborating the sectional characteristics of the chapel
in the Director's Building at Chaux, Ledoux transformed the
naves along the axis of entry into continuous stairs, forming
a pyramidal approach to the main altar. The naves were
roofed by barrel vaults, coffered, and lit from above, supported on a straight entablature and high Ionic columns. The
eight side "aisles," or chapels, each with its own altar, were
set in giant niches, enclosed by huge semicircular arches,
reminiscent of the proscenium of the Besançon theater. To
either side, beneath the two sides naves that remained horizontal at the level of the crossing, Ledoux introduced entries
to the crypt below. Here, a central altar was surrounded by
squat, baseless Tuscan columns and covered by a low vault.
On this level, the side chapels led out to the four corners of
the cross, which were taken up by walled cemeteries.

From the outside, the church, while imposing in scale
for a parish the size of Chaux, was entirely lacking in the
grand inflation of Boullée's project. Without the high, colonnaded drum supporting the dome, Ledoux's design seems to

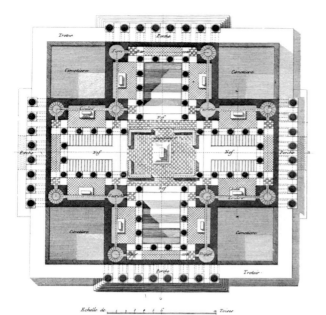

Ledoux, Church of Chaux,
plans of first floor and crypt.
Engraving by Delaitre from
Ramée, *Ledoux,* pl. 138.

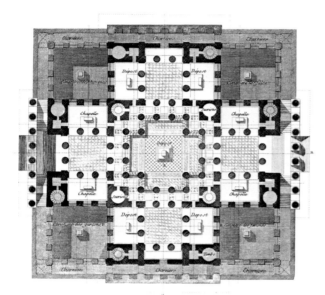

Ledoux, Church of Chaux,
section. Engraving by Sellier
from Ramée, *Ledoux,* pl. 139.

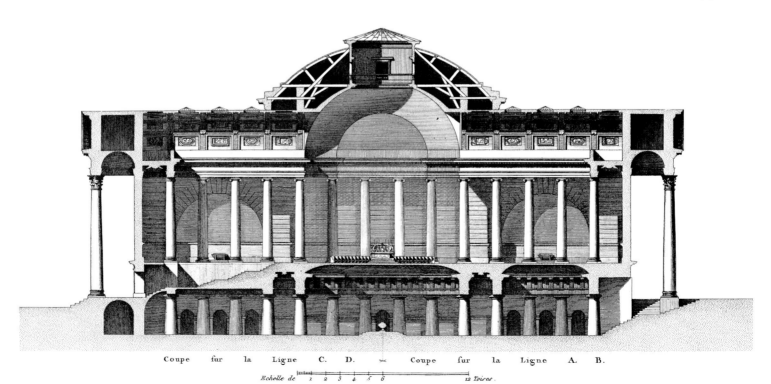

refer less to Christian precedents, whether in Rome or London, and more directly to the Roman Pantheon, a general allusion to the antique that was reinforced by the continuous bas-reliefs surrounding the whole church on the level of the cemetery wall.

Such formal differences between the projects of Ledoux and those of Boullée and Combes point to deeper divisions, both on the level of aesthetic intention and liturgical program. For Boullée, the church, or "basilica," was the occasion to explore a work that would exhibit the character of the highest sublime in keeping with its dedication to the worship of the Supreme Being. His design was matched against the grand images of immensity provided by Saint Peter's, spaces that suggested the sense of infinity suited to the subject, while implying the terror and awe associated with the "contemplation of the Creator." Paraphrasing Longinus, with overtones of Edmund Burke, Boullée defined the idea of the sublime and its architectural representation in terms of a grandeur that is both beautiful and horrifying: "A volcano vomiting flames and death is a horribly beautiful image." [29] Again following Burke, Boullée suggested that the sense of immensity most suitable to the grandeur of a temple dedicated to the infinite might be rendered by the use of successive colonnades subjected to the dramatic play of light and shade. The architect, model of the Creator in his ability to "say *fiat lux*," might plunge the cathedral in shadow to inspire religious fear or flood it with light to inspire joy, according to the nature of the celebration. Two perspectives show, in turn, the interior of the temple "au temps de la Fête-Dieu" and the same "au temps des Ténèbres." [30]

Ledoux certainly shared in Boullée's celebration of the grand sublime and the effects of light and shade, writing of the shadows cast by the torches and the severity of the orders as appropriate to a funeral procession. But for him the monument as a whole was dedicated less to absolute grandeur than to the celebration of the rhythms of daily and yearly life, to the consecration of the social order of Chaux. His project firmly established the realm of the sacred in plan and section, but without removing it from the experience of the citizen. Against Boullée's endless colonnades, high, cloud-painted

domes, incommensurable distances, apparently infinite surfaces, and innumerable masses of worshipers, Ledoux proposed a stable center for civic ritual.

Standing at the center of the active, festive life he envisaged for the population of Chaux, the church, for Ledoux, was also a didactic instrument for conveying the principles of a rational, Deistic religion that would inform the individual and social morality of the city. Its walls were covered with bas-reliefs that traced the history of religions and the great actions of society: "There the spectator is perfected by his own sensations; he sees from nearby a bas-relief that surrounds the building; he is directly enlightened. . . . It retraces for his eyes the history of the most distinguished men."(152)

These lessons were to be supplemented by a continuous celebration of the stages of life, in Ledoux's imagination at once a formalization of the traditional fêtes of birth, marriage, and saints' days in the villages of the *ancien régime* and a remodeling of the grand aristocratic and monarchical festivals of Paris and the towns. On the one hand, the village celebrations lacked a clearly defined program, a universally agreed timetable; on the other, the *feux d'artifice* and *pompes funèbres* were showy and ultimately "useless." Civilized luxury and self-interest had denatured the original, natural festivals dreamed by Rousseau, of which rustic games were the distorted echo. "The egoism of governments has disfigured the origins . . . only to sustain at great cost a pyrotechnics, that frivolous art whose brilliance strikes the ear, dazzles the eyes, disappears, and says nothing to the heart"(156). In place of this individual and isolated display, Ledoux proposed a new system of the fête. Admitting that "public customs require illusory fêtes" and that popular credulity could be made to work toward moral order, that "passions of every kind" could be agents of perfectibility if associated in the mind with the practice of virtue, Ledoux called for a natural sequence of "celebrations of the calendar," a kind of festive almanac tied to everyday life.

Why not adapt public fêtes to all the interesting aspects of life? Births, marriages, even burials present so many united interests that it is difficult to conceive how they are confined in the tacit custom of

*a civil act. Insofar as the public expression of all the interests awak-
ened by these moments can be of general utility, who could be es-
tranged from so many advantages felt by the virtuous masses?(156)*

The very number of births and marriages occurring each day
would suffice to make such festivals continuous: "How many
ways there are of obtaining that pure gaiety that constitutes
the virtuous man and how many ways of effacing his miseries!"(156). Like architecture itself, the festival would act on
the sensations, provoking the strongest feelings of pleasure,
gratitude, and sorrow, purifying and developing the social
and moral instincts of the population.

   As we have seen, Ledoux planned the Church of Chaux
to receive these ceremonials, setting aside separate and specific altars for each kind of service—baptism, marriage, and
death. In this way he replaced the single altar, which mingled
all types of worship indifferently, with appropriately decorated and positioned monuments, each contributing to the effect of the ceremony. In the perspective view, Ledoux showed
a public procession emerging from the main door of the
church while funeral cortèges disappear into the crypt at the
sides. He arranged the section in a slightly different manner,
to balance the processional to the central altar from the front
of the church with a similar descent to the crypt from the rear.
On the main floor, eight side altars supplemented the freestanding table in the sanctuary beneath the dome; in the crypt
a similar number of chapels offered services for the dead.
Such specialization followed the populace to the grave: in the
corners of the plan separate burying grounds were identified
for men, women, boys, and girls.

   Complementing the Church, and completing the ritual
equipment of the new town was, of course, the Cemetery
itself, designed like the Church according to a program developed, in the Académie and outside, during the mid-1780s.
The program for the Cemetery of Chaux, probably drawn
up in 1785, was suggested by a number of proposals in the
early 1780s for closing the Parisian cemeteries and replacing
the human remains in the disused quarries of Montrouge,
closed since 1778. The Cemetery of the Innocents, the largest
and most problematic of the urban burial grounds, was closed

Ledoux, Church of Chaux, religious fête (*above*) and funeral
procession (*below*). Details of
engraving by the Varin brothers from Ramée, *Ledoux*, pl.
140.

in September 1780. In 1782 an anonymous author (one Vil-
ledieu) proposed a *Project for catacombs for the city of Paris,
adopting for this purpose the quarries that are found both in the
outskirts and surroundings;* this proposal was put into effect in
December 1785, when the bones from the Innocents cemetery were exhumed and transferred to the quarries to the
south of the city.[31] The resulting ossuary was popularly
named "The Catacombs." The idea of using the quarries especially appealed to the contemporary interest in antique
forms of burial and fascination with the catacombs of Rome
and Naples.[32] Quatremère de Quincy, writing in 1788, while
arguing against the principle of the common cemetery that
"confounded and annihilated without distinction all men in
the same abyss of oblivion," nevertheless found catacombs
useful enough to serve as cemeteries: "It is very true that almost all the great towns have in their proximities cavities resulting from the working of the quarries, which seem still to
wait such a function to become useful"—he insisted that here
he was speaking above all as an economist and not as an
artist.[33]

   Ledoux himself was well aware of the hygienist arguments, noting that "the selection of site for a cemetery is not
unimportant; its evil influences must be relegated to the highest solitudes of the air; . . . the inhabitants must be preserved
from the desolating effect of the north wind, which carries
corruption and the illnesses that follow with it"(193). Later,
in the text for *L'architecture,* Ledoux transferred the notion of
the Parisian quarries to Chaux, imagining that the quarries
used for building stone for the new city would be filled in
with the new cemetery: three levels of catacombs below
ground level, arranged along radial tunnels that led into a vast
central sphere, half-below and half-above ground. Ledoux
gave first a functional explanation, speaking of how he had
"covered the extent of the land excavated by the extraction of
stones with an immense vault . . . to obtain at the top the
evaporation of the mephitic odors of a cemetery"(195). This
raison d'être was, however, subsumed within a larger symbolic meaning enclosed by the sphere.[34] Ledoux clearly linked
his form to other necropolitan symbols such as the pyramid:
"Everyone knows that the kings of Egypt, in order to occupy

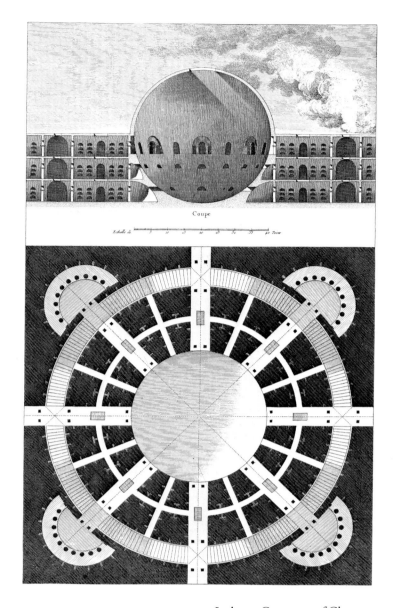

Ledoux, Cemetery of Chaux,
c. 1785, section and plan. Engraving by Ransonnette from
Ramée, *Ledoux,* pl. 141.

the leisure of their slaves, . . . built the pyramids at great cost. . . . The idea of the flame that tapered (Σπιζα) under the pressure of the air determined their form. Do you think that the earth cedes to them in grandeur?"(194) Ledoux selected the sphere over the pyramid not only for its more universal connotations but also for its more egalitarian implications. He spoke of the "opulence" that "had as its aim only a sepulcher disdainful of humanity"(194) in the pyramid, an evidently hierarchical form, destined for the burial of a single prince; the spherical Cemetery of Chaux, by contrast, would display the remains of all the citizens, brought back to equality by death on a "common bier"(193).

The religious ceremonies of burial and memorial, Ledoux wrote, would take up the center of the building, lit from above by the heavens; the spectacle of the burning braziers, the smoke from the cremations, endowed the cemetery with the aspect of a mysterious netherworld. Indeed the symbolism of earth and nature, embodied in the half-sunken sphere, was evidently also an evocation of Hades and Heaven. Ledoux spoke of the "two stairs, cut into this imperishable mass of rock," that "descend into the antipodes of the world," and saw the eternal cycle of life, death, and burial as informed by the activities of cremation: "The dead are purified to excite the living to virtue"(193).

Ledoux's project for the Cemetery of Chaux has often been compared to another essay in spherical geometry, that of Boullée's Cenotaph to Newton of 1784.[35] A symbolic monument of the earth itself, Boullée's sphere was also designed, at least in its second version, as a giant planetarium, where, at night, an artificial sun would illuminate a three-dimensional diagram of Newton's principle and, by day, light would percolate through holes in the dome to produce the effect of the stars. A number of sources have been adduced by historians for this dramatic design. As summarized by Pérouse de Montclos, they have proposed Boullée's concept of the sphere as a primary geometrical form, the essence of architecture; an "autobiographical" play on the similarity between the name Boullée and the word boule, or ball, which would make the cenotaph a direct substitution of Boullée for Newton; different projects for spherical tomb monuments in the Middle

Ages and Renaissance; the spherical tomb of Archimedes described by Cicero; allegories of scientific representations of the moon seen through telescopes; a pictorial play on the Mongolfier balloon, first flown in 1784; and a reference to antique temples described as cosmological models, with domes covered in stars and circular architraves decorated with the signs of the zodiac.[36] Pérouse de Montclos himself convincingly argues the relationship of the earlier of the two drawings, that of 1784, to accounts of buried, spherical Druidical temples and suggests that, in fact, the "planetarium" scheme was first designed, like the spherical projects of Jean-Jacques Lequeu some years later, as a kind of universal Masonic lodge, only being joined to the Newton Monument program of the Académie from expediency a year later in 1785. A comparison of the drawings reveals two distinct schemes: The first shows a cubic altar and worshiping priest dedicated to the religion of the central sun; the altar, emanating light, as if from some Rosicrucian underground tomb, is surrounded by a cosmic diagram displaying not the Newtonian but the Copernican universe. The second scheme, however, replaces the altar with a sarcophagus, Newton's tomb. Pérouse de Montclos examines a series of accounts of spherical tombs and temples associated in the eighteenth century with the primitive religions or Zoroaster, Mithras, and the Druids, all connected with the symbolic and initiatory repertories of Freemasonry; most convincing is the spherical, underground "Druidic" temple depicted by the eighteenth-century architect and antiquarian Beaumesnil. In this respect Ledoux's design for the Cemetery of Chaux seems even more closely linked than Boullée's Newton monument to this half-buried Druidic temple. It posited even more extremely the idea of negativity, of the absence of light, of the absolute void as a sublime image of finality.

Ledoux's design seems calculated to follow the precepts of Boullée's own funerary architecture, exemplified in a series of "Temples of Death" imagined at the time of Napoleon's expedition to Egypt.[37] For these cemeteries, loci of the terrible sublime, Boullée created what he thought of as new genres of architecture: a "buried architecture" fashioned out of the principle that "the skeleton of architecture is the abso-

Etienne-Louis Boullée, Cenotaph for Newton: 1784 drawing, section showing daylight effect of artificial sun; 1785 drawing, section showing night effect of apertures in pattern of the stars. From the Bibliothèque Nationale, Cabinet des Estampes, Ha 57, pls. 9, 8.

lutely bare wall" and an architecture composed entirely of shadows, a negative architecture where all the positive elements of construction—columns, pediments, and the like—were traced on the façade in dark cutouts of their absence: "It seemed to me impossible to conceive of anything sadder than a monument composed of a plane surface, naked and stripped, made of a material that absorbs the light, absolutely deprived of details and whose decoration is formed by a painting of shadows delineated themselves by shadows still more somber."[38]

Like Boullée, and taking his cue from Burke, Ledoux found in the bare, undecorated sphere, inside and out, "an image of nothingness" that "presented to the eye neither woods nor meadows, valleys nor rivers, and even less the benefits of the sun that vivifies nature"(195).

Like Boullée's, Ledoux's sphere was also a direct evocation of the terrestrial sublime: "This round machine, is it not sublime?"(194) he asked. And the universal sublime into which the souls of the departed merged—"See this sublime harmony that composes the parts of this vast picture"—was illustrated in Ledoux's startling vision of the "Elevation" of this cemetery, depicting the earth and the planets lit by the rays of the sun. This "astronomical" image, evoking Ledoux's excitement over the recent discoveries of the astronomer William Herschel and the parallel temptation of the heavens represented by the balloon flights of 1783–84, was apparently of Ledoux's own invention, a pictorial fantasy that confirmed his claim to artistic skills as developed as those of Boullée. Its inclusion in an architectural treatise as one of only three such "allegorical" plates would seem to imply a theater of action for architecture as vast as the imagination might envisage.

THERAPEUTIC MONUMENTS

Ledoux's attitude toward the institutionalization of social problems was initially Physiocratic. The Abbé Baudeau and Dupont de Nemours had consistently argued against the increasing tendency for poverty, illness, criminality, and immortality to be "solved" by means of specific institutions—workhouses, hospitals, and prisons—that were supposed to render the poor and idle virtuous, healthy, and productive.[39]

In their view, the era of what Michel Foucault has called "the great confinement" in the *hospital-general* of the late seventeenth and eighteenth centuries had only succeeded in creating centers of poverty and sickness, the breeding places of what they were supposed to cure. Their sharpest polemic was reserved for the architects of projects to replace the old Hôtel-Dieu by giant, centralized facilities.[40] Bernard Poyet's five-thousand-bed hospital projected for the Ile des Cygnes was the most monumental symbol of this kind of solution, and was criticized both for its architectural display—its resemblance to the Colosseum—and for its anticommunitarian implications.[41] The Physiocrats argued instead for small, decentralized hospices, each run along the lines of religious centers of charity, and for a medicine that emphasized home care within the family and neighborhood. A myth of an "organic society" lost by the decline of religious morality, the increase of state interference, and the dissolution of stable, self-knowing communities pervaded their discourse. Ledoux, who as a practicing architect had no scruples in taking on commissions for prisons and who had, with Chalgrin, served on an initial commission following the fire at the Hôtel-Dieu in 1773, was, in his utopia, able to deny these institutions in favor of more "natural" environmental and social remedies. Thus in Chaux there would be no institutions that simply incarcerated and isolated the criminal, the sick, the poor: there would be no prison because "the newborn town . . . will perhaps be inhabited by less criminal men"; there would be no hospitals, not only because, as Ledoux wrote of the workhouse or hospice, "a specialized asylum for poverty is so humiliating for moral equality"(215), but also because the surroundings were so healthy. Crimes and indigence would be unknown in this city of egalitarian charity, where "each individual is known"(127).

"At first sight," he wrote, paraphrasing his report in favor of replacing the Hôtel-Dieu with four, smaller hospices, "hospitals offer a great good; England has increased their number, France has concentrated them too much. There are few men who cannot be employed in occupations useful

Ledoux, "Elevation of the
Cemetery of the Town of
Chaux." Engraving by Bovinet from Ramée, *Ledoux,*
pl. 142.

either to themselves or to the government. If one wishes to
follow this principle, one will see that there will be fewer
destitute"(215).

In place of a hospital, Ledoux proposed the institution
of the Public Baths, a favorite among his roster of social
building types. When imprisoned under the Terror, he would
repropose the design, suggesting its use by the French armies
and its patriotic nature. In *L'architecture* he lamented that such
"constructions sheltering miseries presented great difficulties
in execution"; sickness was hardly a political force, for "miseries have no other expression than silence and the pent-up
cry of sadness"(167). Nevertheless the establishment of a
number of watering places dedicated to curing the sick—
among them he cited that of Spa in Belgium, which despite
its "affluence and corruption" was a useful precedent—gave
him hope that the overspill salt waters of Chaux might be put
to good use: those of Salins had been used for centuries. Salt
water had long been known for its healing properties for the
skin; those living far from the sea, however, "suffer without
hope," unable to afford the voyage. Economically, as well as
medically, his scheme would "unite all the respective interests
with those of the government." Drawing from the text of his
letter to the Revolutionary authorities in 1794, he avowed that

*the use of these baths can be considered one of the surest means to
counter the deterioration of health; it is a gift provided by the gods of
the earth. Experience proves that they hasten the cure of wounds
more effectively than the common surgical remedies. No one is ignorant of the fact that saline baths are suitable for all ages, for ardent, bilious, melancholic, and nervous temperaments; for women
subject to convulsions, to those who experience suppurations; they
are useful for nervous illnesses, rheumatisms, sciaticas, venereal and
cutaneous illnesses; for scurvy, impurities of the blood, and for dis-*

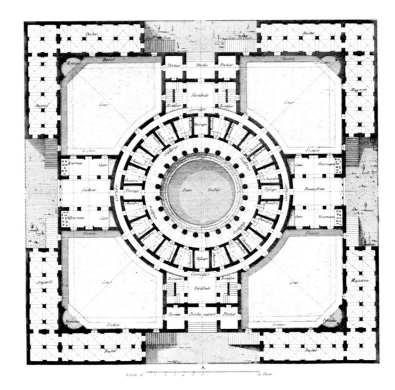

Ledoux, Public Baths of Chaux, plan of first floor, section, and perspective view. Engravings from Ramée, *Ledoux,* pls. 146, 147, 148 (pl. 148 by Berthault, pl. 147 by Sellier).

eases spread by contact devastating our armies; the substances found in salt water provide an aperient action to the tissue of the skin. (168)

To this end, the Public Baths should be built "at the center" of the town, "for those whose misfortune does not allow them to pay for special care"(168). Set at the edge of the forest, and beside a canal that would supply the water, drawn from the aqueduct between Salins and Chaux, the establishment contained a circular central bathing hall for the public, with a plain, top-lit dome, open to "dissipate harmful vapors," and a surrounding gallery of baseless Doric columns. Individual rooms reached from an external corridor opened into this gallery, while laundries, drying rooms, wood stores, and apartments for the concierge were deployed in the arms of the Greek cross that, enclosed by a square podium, framed the interior and exterior promenades. The entire establishment was heated by furnaces distributing hot air through a system of vents. This was, in every respect, Ledoux's final answer to the hospital debate that took place between 1772 and 1789.[42] He concluded wryly, no doubt aware of his proscription as hospital architect for the Duc de Praslin's charitable campaign of 1787, "The architect who proposes a useful monument is not always crowned by success"(167).[43]

But Ledoux's preoccupation with the institution of the baths was not, by the 1780s, novel in itself. An antiquarian interest in the grand plans of the Roman baths, evoked in the measured drawings of the Baths of Diocletian by Peyre, De Wailly, and Moreau-Desproux prepared in 1757 and exhibited at the Salon of 1771, was supported by an increasing awareness of the benefits to health of contemporary baths. A long tradition of "taking the waters" was thus allied to a fascination with the compositional grandeur of the antique examples. In England, James Wood had literally joined the two concerns, remodeling the Roman baths at Bath in 1724; while in France, the bathing places at Vichy, Plombières, Aix-en-Provence, Mont-Dore, Evaux-les-Bains, and Digne had been enlarged or reconstructed between the end of the seventeenth century and the late 1760s.[44] In Franche-Comté, the engineer

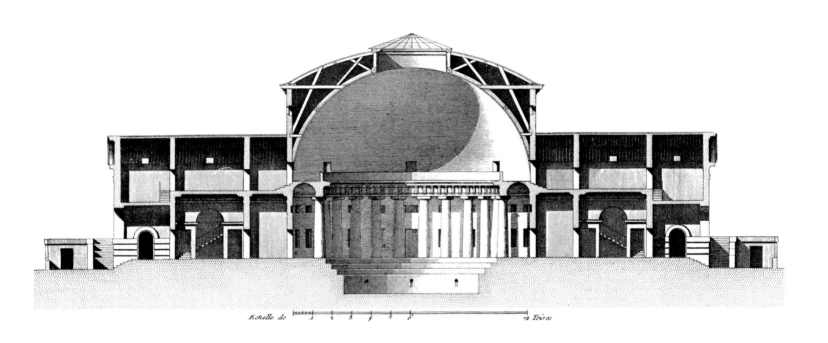

Echelle de [scale markings] Toises

BAINS PUBLICS

Querret had, on the orders of de Lacoré, reconstructed the baths of Luxeuil-les-Bains between 1762 and 1768. Thus the Académie program of 1774 for "Public Mineral Water Baths" confirmed a developing trend. It specifications were monumental, designed to encourage projects as splendid as those of Rome:

These baths will consist of buildings decorated with porticoes that will establish covered communications between the various parts and serve as promenades for those who take the waters. There will be a chapel, decorated and sufficiently large, two large rooms for the baths (the one for men, the other for women of the people), smaller rooms and private chambers in which men and women of substance and of the Third Estate will take baths. All these rooms will be vaulted and rise the entire height of the building. On the rest of the site will be disposed the dwellings, for those who come to take the baths as well as for the governors, concierge, and those serving its police and administration; these buildings, as well as a theater and tennis court will only be indicated in their massing on the general plan, which will also show the promenades and pools suitable for fêtes.[45]

Daniel Rabreau has analyzed the winning design, by Mathurin Crucy, in terms of the "stylistic exercise" posed by the subject, fulfilled in Crucy's design by the planning of the large rectangular monument divided into multiple rooms and crowned by a low central dome. But while the plan displayed an attempt to rival that of a Roman baths, the elevation, with its blank walls decorated by clearly marked bas-reliefs, and the bare surface of the dome showed a consciousness of social appropriateness already registered in the program, with its baths for the people and its provision of a complete roster of community services for worship and recreation: "The citizen who takes the cure finds in this vast enclosure all the necessities for bodily hygiene and spiritual life."[46]

Ledoux, who was no doubt stimulated by this competition subject as by many others, took this social aspect even more seriously, trimming the stylistic extravagance of the Grand Prix designs to create a suitable expression for "silence and the concentrated cry of sadness." The lack of openings, the restricted planning, reflected, in his terms, "the decoration of a building intended for the cure of contagious diseases [that] should be submitted to the humiliation of a custom degraded in public opinion and efface itself before the eyes in the fear of being seen"(169).

Architecturally, Ledoux was perhaps less influenced by the restorations of De Wailly and Peyre or the monumental designs of Crucy than by actual projects for regional baths. Those at Aix-en-Provence, for example, must have had a special significance for Ledoux, whose mission to study the state of the old Palais de Justice in 1776 had been conducted in the guise of a journey undertaken for reasons of health, that is, to take the celebrated waters of the town. The baths at Aix, built on the ruins of the old Roman baths, were begun under Louis XIV in 1705 by the architect Laurent Vallon. Vallon projected, in the description of the historian Jean-Jacques Gloton, "a public pump room in the form of a rotunda, built entirely in carefully cut stone, with its Doric order alternating with blind bays and surmounted by a large semihemispherical cupola, lit from the top by a fine oculus, like the Roman Pantheon."[47] At the time of Ledoux's visit, this structure was still unfinished and open to the sky, an eighteenth-century ruin some already thought dated from Roman times. In September 1780 the sculptor Gilles Cauvet, in conjunction with the plan for a Place de la Rotonde suggested by Jean de Boisgelin in 1776, drew up a plan for rebuilding the baths on a freestanding site outside the town. His design followed the tradition of Vallon, with a large, circular pool at the center, eighteen smaller baths for the sick, apartments for the director, a hostelry, and gaming rooms.[48] It would not be unlikely that Ledoux's project for Chaux, was, in the first instance, prepared as a "restoration" of Vallon's classical "restoration," as a counterproject to the more monumental and impractical scheme of Cauvet. Whether or not this was so, his design certainly seems to echo the pseudo-Roman foundation of Aix, thus reinforcing Serge Conard's assertion that the projects for Aix and those for Chaux were intimately linked, programmatically and even geographically tied by an axis that formed one side of a great triangulation between Chaux, Aix, and Paris.[49]

ECONOMIC PROGRAMS

For the more traditional forms of socially coercive institutions, Ledoux substituted forms of economic support. The Market, returned to its primary function as the center of agricultural wealth, also became a center for the instruction and charitable sustenance of the poor. The Stock Exchange, besides functioning as a commercial and industrial financial center, also acted as a distributor of benefits to the needy. Both were reconceived, in Ledoux's terms, to preserve the dignity of those they helped; both, it was hoped, would transform the normal system of supply and exchange into instruments of equalization and general enrichment.

The Market, first conceived as a variation of Le Camus de Mézière's Halle au Blé for Paris of 1763 and utilizing a similar combination of cylindrical drums and porticoes to that of the Barrière Saint-Martin, was dramatically expanded after 1784 to equal the Saline de Chaux in size and complexity. Surrounded by a wide moat, some six hundred feet square, with separate courtyards for each kind of produce, it stood as a kind of market city in its own right. At the center of the plan, rising above the surrounding buildings, was a large, roofed store for wheat, rye, barley, oats, lentils, and acorns. Covered passages led out on each side to the four large open markets for wine; fruit and vegetables; wood, coal and iron; and livestock. At the corners of the plan were four smaller courts for fish, meat, poultry and game, and cloth and linen, each court surrounded by covered porticoes and storerooms. The market was entered through four gates across the moat on the main axes, each containing a small inn or hostel.[50] Ledoux described the measures taken to ensure ventilation and sanitary conditions, especially for the slaughterhouses:

They are made salubrious by the north winds and by the moving water that runs unceasingly in the ditches. Precautions against fire, which fertilize the resources of art, offer abundant water supplies, deep drinking troughs, open aqueducts, preserved against concentrated putrefaction. The steepness of the slopes is so far developed that it rapidly washes away those heterogeneous materials and the putrid disorder that follows stagnation.(165)

The aim of this establishment was both economic and moral. Its economic functions were to be overseen by an independent company, set up at the behest of a wise government that wished to centralize the distribution of agricultural products in the frontier region of the northeast. A solution to the incessant and politically disastrous scarcities of the second half of the eighteenth century and a containment of the corruption and speculation over prices that attended the bad harvests, the Market departed from strict Physiocratic principles and extended the logic of "natural riches" to their rational exploitation and repartition.[51] Completely free trade was abandoned in favor of a just distribution of profits:

The centralization of all the functions offers great advantages: the administration is less costly, the oversight more active; products of every kind flow from all sides, exportation becomes easier; the way to restrain the activities of greed, of containing them in the rigorous principles of political economy, is to permit exchange only insofar as the warehouses are full and exceed demand. . . . One can ensure inexpensive food for the poor as well as support the sale of the rich traders' produce.(162)

Based on his belief that "agriculture, commerce, and the arts are primary riches," Ledoux privileged the honest capitalist, backer of necessary credit: "Without credit," he admitted, "there is no trade." Such a merchant was to be compared to the earth, inexhaustible source of wealth, as he supported agriculture with loans and profits from its harvests. In contrast, the financial speculator who invested only outside the country or the stockbroker dealing in the inflated price of paper reaped a mere "illusory asset" (162)—a perfect paraphrase of the Physiocratic position.

But the Market also served a moral function in Ledoux's imagination. He drew the picture of "Roman charity," symbolized by the erection of *colonnes lactaires* in ancient herb markets, asylums for abandoned children; an equally charitable government overseeing the Market of Chaux would emulate antiquity by erecting four monuments "that would appeal to the national interest and awaken fraternal charity." Each would be inscribed with an appropriate maxim reminding the public of their duties to the young and old: "To aban-

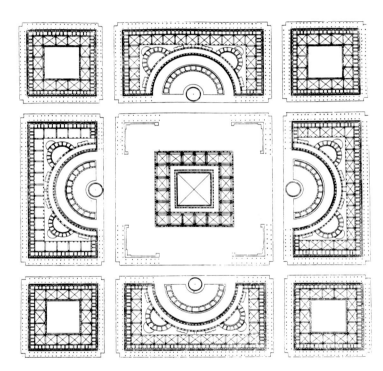

Le Clotte, Project for a Market, *prix d'emulation,* 1784. Engraving from Pierre-Athanase
Détournelle, Antoine-
Laurent-Thomas Vaudoyer,
and G.-E. Allais, *Projets d'architecture* (Paris, 1806).

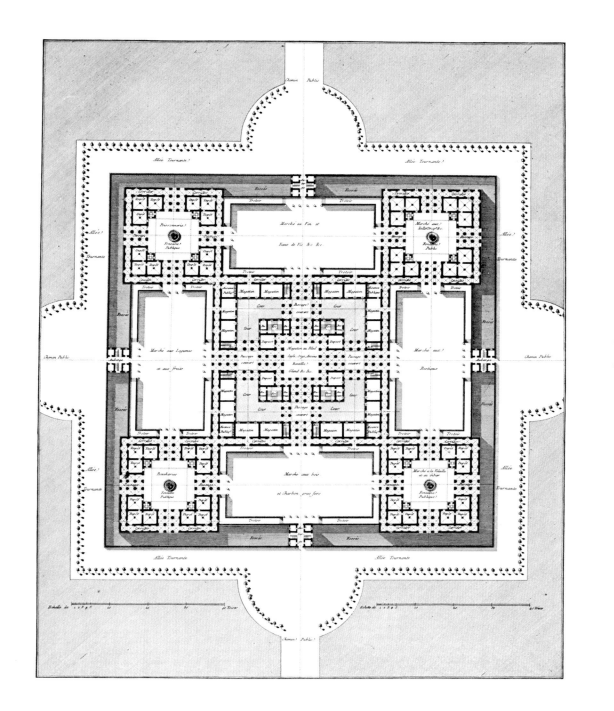

Ledoux, Market of Chaux, plan and section. Engravings by Sellier from Ramée, *Ledoux,* pls. 143, 144.

doned children"; "For the education of orphans"; "For periods of enforced unemployment and for unforeseen accidents that prevent work"; "To ensure the security of old age, the tranquility of retirement" (165). Ledoux put forward his project, derived from his reading of an article in *La bibliothèque britannique,* as an experiment that would abolish begging, "the shame of the government," thus linking his architecture to the entire reform of the poor laws, as ineffective in France as in England. And indeed, he claimed, the planning of the Market itself would have beneficent results for public charity, as, beneath its multiple arcades, merchants and farmers would gather to discuss the principles of social morality.

This economization of morality would be in Ledoux's scheme continued by the activities of the Stock Exchange of Chaux. First depicted in the "Perspective View of the Town of Chaux" in the mid-1780s, it was redesigned after the Revolution as a square "temple" consisting almost entirely of open porticoes on the main floor and covered arcades in the plinth, surrounding the central *salle d'assemblée,* itself open, as a kind of cella, at the roof.[52] Ledoux defined the nature of this institution as against the conventions of the day: "What does one understand by a Stock Exchange? In large cities it is a monument that ought to attest to the purity of morals; in a town founded by philosophy, it is a gathering of chosen men who deal in good faith, either in real materials or in exchanges." (126) An improvement on the companies founded, and often collapsed, to encourage trade in Europe and the East—the corporations of Hamburg, Russia, Greenland, the East Indies, and Turkey—this association would be bound to standards of absolute virtue and honesty. None of its financial undertakings would be at the expense of national or public interest—"gold is not exchanged for poverty"—none would be dictated by any one government or interest. It would act as the economic heart of the new city and thereby form its chief political and social strength. Its principal business would be the regulation and encouragement of foreign trade: "This assembly covers the seas with numerous vessels, levies taxes, establishes prices, regulates the interests that will be tempted to speculate on vile monopolies"(127). No secret deals, no

monopolistic policies could restrict its actions as it operated as a great clearing house and export company for French products: "Already you send to Monopotapa . . . our pictures, sculptures, cloths from Lyons, our artistic masterpieces."

The architecture of the Stock Exchange would reflect and support this probity. Built out of *pierres durables,* with stone courses as level and regular as the morals they would shelter, as equal as the invariable procedures of the institution, it would be decorated by inscriptions and bas-reliefs illustrating its principles.

There one does not read those placards produced in such numbers by a self-interested corruption to charm the leisure of the idle; one reads on these incorruptible walls everything that can elevate the public mind—a merchant who builds a charitable monument with the unexpected returns on his investment or the symbol of the arts placed on a scale with commerce, carried by the figure of abandoned agriculture.(127)

In this set of correspondences, both symbolic and iconographic, emerge the first principles of an *architecture parlante* that endows the architect with the status of an acknowledged legislator, one who "knows that he must awaken feelings in order to generate productive seeds . . . awaken desire with models that strike the eyes."

Supporting this economic expansion Ledoux imagined a vast industrial development growing up in the environs of the more traditional *salines.*[53] Constructed according to the model of the ironworks, foundries, and blast furnaces being installed to the southeast at Le Creusot, the Cannon Foundry had like Chaux itself a double function of defense and production. This foundry would take its place beside other factories—glassworks, porcelain factories, textile *manufactures*—that would compete with the clockmaking industry of Switzerland and even the ironworks of Birmingham: "The cross axis of the Saline joins the routes to Arc and Senans, the forges of Roche, the paper mills, the polishing mills; what activity! Some polish the steel, chase the brass, blow the crystal, others cast the molten metal that sustains the rights of nations" (72). Raw materials would be mined from the mountains: "The earth is opened up on all sides and its fertile flanks produce coal, iron, brass, pyrites" (74). The initial incentive for Ledoux's designs for the Cannon Foundry was the renewed interest of the Minister de la Marine, Sartines, in establishing a cannon forge first at Indret, near Nantes, between 1777 and 1780, then at Le Creusot in Burgundy in 1782. At Le Creusot, a society under the leadership of the artillery officer Ignace-François de Wendel employed the English ironmaster William Wilkinson and the French engineer-architect Pierre Touffaire. The works comprised two blast furnaces and four reverberating furnaces, together with extensive buildings for other trades and housing for the workers.[54] The first large-scale iron foundry constructed on modern principles in France, it was, by 1785, an object of interest for the government. Calonne, reversing the policy of Jacques Necker, advanced funds for the operation of Wilkinson's first factory at Indret, and, in 1786, succeeded in transferring the royal glassworks from Sèvres to Le Creusot, thus enlarging the industrial complex considerably. Louis Daubenton described the works as one of the wonders of the world: "Formerly impassable mountains are leveled daily to make sites for establishments as interesting as they are useful, and while their bowels are excavated for that inexhaustible mine of high quality that activates machines of all kinds, one sees this mountain covered with furnaces, pumps, and steam engines."[55] Ledoux, who cited a "prospectus" conceived and dictated by "a minister of probity," a characteristic he applied elsewhere to Calonne, drew up a plan for a large cannon foundry dedicated to the manufacture of arms for the eastern armies. "Cannons are necessary to impose reason," noted Ledoux, trying to justify the warlike nature of such a factory in the utopian realm of Chaux: "The inhabitants of Chaux, by the confluence of rivers that transport abundant supplies, will provide the armies of the east with the means to join their interests with those of the government" (240).

Four giant, pyramidal blast furnaces marked the corners of the square plan of the factory; workshops for carpentry, joinery, chasing, casting, locksmithing, cartwright's work, and the production of hand weapons were ranged along the sides. Four two-story workshops housing the forges intersected at the center of the factory in the building of the ironmaster, director of the foundry. A canal and subsidiary basins provided water throughout the works, which was finally surrounded by a defensive ditch.

Bovinet's engraving of the Cannon Foundry shows a veritable *cité industrielle,* with the foundry at the center, its blast furnaces in full operation, a collection of houses for merchants, artists, cabinetmakers, wholesalers, and artisans of all kinds, warehouses, porticoes, and workshops all set on a level plain presumably at some distance from the center of Chaux. The small canal opened up between the watermill of Roche and the graduation building of the *saline* is aggrandized as the center of commercial development for the ideal city: "a hundred porticoes are built on the banks of the Roche."

RURAL ARCHITECTURE

If you return to the cultivation of the precious earth those ungrateful souls who belittle it, even though it has showered them with its prodigality, how many powerful levels would thereby be created to overcome inactivity and move industry forward; how many outlets would be opened for the economy! (74)

THE REFORM OF THE FARM

The theoretical models of the Physiocrats provided a formal basis for understanding economic processes and, by their moral commitment to agrarian cultivation and the extraction of raw materials, supported an ideology of rural reform; but it is in the practical experiments and exemplary farming of the enlightened landowners and scientists of the second half of the century that we find the programmatic roots of the rural architecture that so preoccupied Ledoux from the 1770s on.[56] While the economists confined their speculation to the pure realms of political economy, concerning themselves with the reform of taxes, the redistribution of land, and the methodological techniques for economic analysis, the *agronomes,* largely under the influence of their English counterparts, concentrated on the businesses and methods of farming. Their emphasis was practical, utilizing findings from botany, chem-

Barthélémy Jeanson, Queen's
Glassworks at Le Creusot,
1785, perspective view.
Engraving from Ecomusée,
Le Creusot.

Ledoux, Cannon Foundry,
section, plan, and elevation.
Engraving by Heluis from
Ramée, *Ledoux*, pl. 149.

Ledoux, Cannon Foundry,
perspective view. Engraving
by Coquet and Bovinet from
Ramée, *Ledoux*, pl. 150.

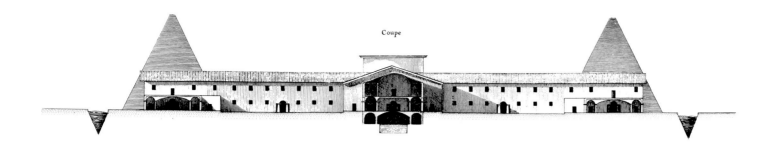

Coupe

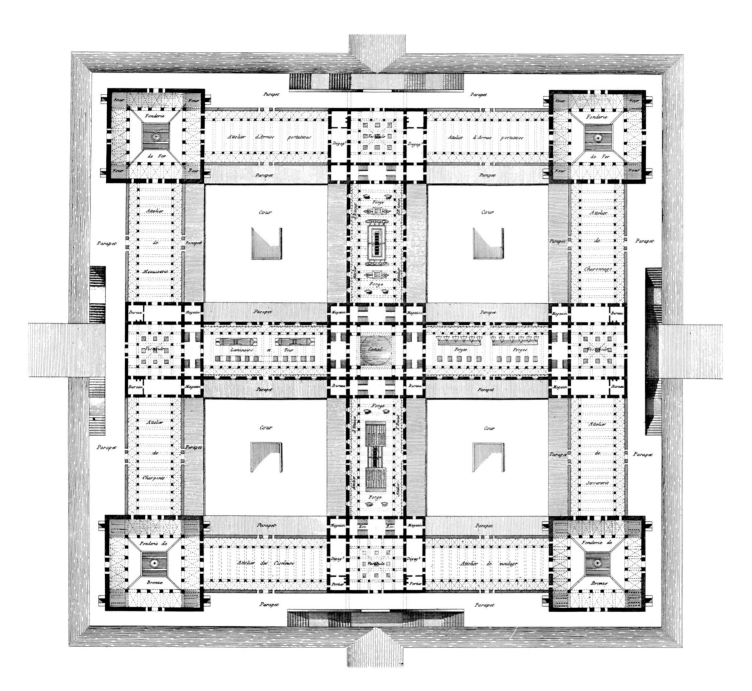

Elevation

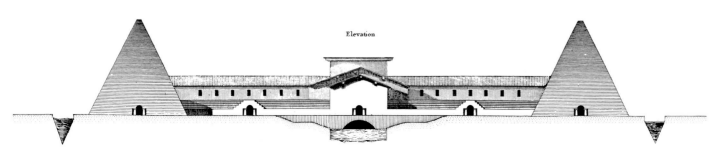

Echelle de   5   10   20   30   40 toises

istry, and physics, searching for technical means by which to reform agricultural routines and practices; where the Physiocrat was abstract and systematic, a *philosophe* of principle, the *agronome* was empirical and didactic. In 1779 the agronomist Butet-Dumont wrote, "The word *agronome* has been introduced in the last few years in the French language to signify he who teaches agriculture, or who treats of its rules, or even simply someone who has studied them well."[57]

Besides reporting on the latest systems of cultivation in England, (the *noveau système* studied by Henri-Louis Duhamel du Monceau, with its methods of crop rotation, breeding, new tools, drainage, and enclosure techniques), the texts of the agrarian reformers also engaged in the campaign against rural ignorance and peasant routine, that is, in the *social* implications of agriculture.[58] Between the elaborate experiments of Buffon at the Jardin du Roi as well as on his own estate at Montbard and the daily life of the peasant or tenant farmer was a link that most theorists of the new agriculture understood to be vital to success: without education and social improvement, the traditional practices, governed by mixtures of astrological and mythical beliefs, what was called *la routine,* could not be broken down. The entire social condition of the countryside thereafter became a domain for speculation and even some practical attempts at reform: Trudaine at Courtagny and, with Buffon, at Montbard established model sheep farms; Turgot experimented with raising livestock in Berry; Malesherbes, an enthusiast for botany, studied in his model tree plantations the science of arboriculture and proposed a research program for agriculture.[59] But side by side with these scientific activities, the *agronomes* projected model villages, schools, and agricultural institutes, participating in the general, sentimental current of moralisms on the theme of *bonheur dans les campagnes,* which after the 1770s took on an increasingly sharp moralistic tone.[60] The Société de Médecine of Paris studied the health of rural artisans. The Marquis de Perusse de Escars envisioned the foundation of *colonies agricoles* and in 1765 drew up a plan for a model community consisting of eight hygienically and economically built houses, planned in relation to a central street. The Abbé Louis Desbiey in 1776 responded to a question of the Acadé-

mie des Sciences of Bordeaux, on land distribution and cultivation, by planning an *unité d'exploitation* based on drainage canals and road grids. At Lyons in 1763 a school for rural instruction was proposed, and one was established at Tours two years later; the *enfants trouvés* of La Rochette were set to study tree culture in a school founded in 1765.[61] And though these initiatives were isolated and for the most part ineffective, especially when compared to the overwhelming success of English agronomists, they did succeed in establishing a climate of reform that, programmatically at least, explains Ledoux's intense interest in, and projects for, rural dwellings and farm establishments after the completion of the Saline de Chaux. For him, the activities of Trudaine, Malesherbes, and later the Duc de Charost were exemplary, demanding an architecture of corresponding vision, one that would, from the base up, reform French society. He shared with the *agronomes* the ability to accept their privileged place in the social order, even while attempting to ameliorate the lot of the rural poor. As André Bourde notes, "The *agronomes* more open to the problems and the mentality of the humblest classes, without at all rejecting the distinctions accorded to those who occupied the summit of the social scale in the countryside, also made a place for the peasants in their projects."[62]

Ledoux's experience with the techniques and resources of rural construction while in the service of the Département des Eaux et Forêts has already been noted. If Gallet's hypothesis is correct and Ledoux visited England sometime before 1773, this interest in rural reform would have been confirmed. Certainly he was struck by the bridge architecture and, especially, by the careful treatment of horses in England. In contrast, in France "dwellings are built for the animal species with as much negligence as in the plantation of our parks"(145). Ledoux's concern with the hygiene, ventilation, and fireproofing of the buildings of the *saline* was exemplified for him in the small pavilion for the director's stables. Classical texts that "descend into the minutest details of instruction" did exist for such humble buildings—those, for example, of Columella and Pliny—and Ledoux cited them as "high" writers who did not disdain low subjects; but his own detailed recommendations reflect more closely eighteenth-

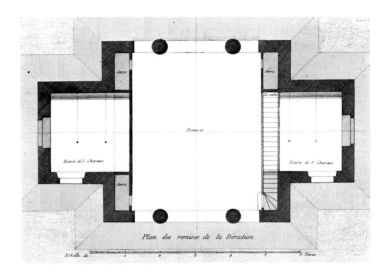

Ledoux, Director's stables and carriage house, Saline de Chaux, plan. Engraving from Ramée, *Ledoux,* pl. 128.

century discussions of the proper ventilation of rural buildings and of fireproof construction in the countryside. Writing on the stables, Ledoux noted the commonly used works, such as *Le parfait maréchal* of 1706 and the *Hippiatrique,* and gave precise instructions on tethering horses in stalls.[63] He argued against the use of sandstone and in favor of wooden flooring, as more elastic and less jarring to the horses; he supported the use of ventilators with judicious placement and sizing; he opposed the stacking of hay and rotting straw on upper floors. In each case, he contradicted, in the manner of a true *agronome,* "current custom":

In effect, you can see the results of a bad plan; granaries are placed above stables; straw, hay, and grains are piled up leading to every kind of fermentation; the horses occupy a damp ground floor; the air is confined and its poisons affect the weakest parts of the animal, who deserves more care from us in return for the services he renders.(145)

Following the recommendations of Stephen Hales and his French followers, Ledoux insisted on the proper ventilation of the stalls:[64] the horses, tethered by their individual hay racks, "so that the passing air does not immediately cause the animal to cough," deserved as much consideration as patients in hospitals and certainly prisoners in cells. Correctly proportioned *trappes d'évaporation,* together with pigeonholes spaced under the rafters, would ensure the circulation and renewal of air. Above all, the rural architect should construct in fireproof materials; the risk of fire, so present in the traditional buildings of wood, thatch, and daub, could be avoided by stone construction and by the provision of storage facilities for hay and fodder. Running through the text of *L'architecture* like a refrain borrowed from Jacques Vannière's *Praedium Rusticum* or the Abbé Rozier's *Cours complet d'agriculture* are admonitions, recipes, and homilies on good building practice in the countryside.[65] These prescriptions were not based entirely on theory: before his work on the *saline,* Ledoux had been involved in the construction of several large-scale outbuildings for the Château de Maupertuis, the large *communs,* the pavilions for the estate guards and concierge, as well as the orangery and pheasant preserve; he had also designed the grand *hôtel des équipages* for Madame du Barry at Versailles, with individual stalls for thirty-two horses, drinking fountains, and the enormous, but unrealized, "petite ménagerie."

Later, just before the Revolution, Ledoux drew up plans for a *ferme parée,* or model farm, and a *bergerie,* or sheepfold, for the estate of La Roche Bernard, owned by Louis-Bruno de Boisgelin, brother of the Archbishop of Aix. In this, the largest of his ideal rural projects, Ledoux reconciled contemporary debates over the merits of the *parc* as against the *bergerie* by extending the long covered arcades of the sheepfold to enclose a large central *parc* and four peripheral areas.[66] He designed the *bergerie* itself as a linear system of troughs set on either side of a drainage pit covered by a grating. A Doric arcade on either side of the troughs provided protection from the weather for the sheep, which would be subjected—like any productive element of an economic order—to constant surveillance. Ledoux noted that within the railings of the central passage over the drainage pit "the sheep dog circulates to gather together instantly the entire flock." At the center of the entire plan—recalling the placement of the building of the master of the iron foundry or the director of the saline— stood the building of the farmers, or shepherds, who would sustain the well-run husbandry of the *bergerie.* The enormous *ferme parée* similarly enclosed all its functions within a square plan that contained some nineteen open courtyards surrounded by every conceivable amenity. At the extreme corners yards for the hay ricks were enclosed by a series of barns for storing oats, hay, barley, alfalfa, and straw. Stores for flour, iron, wood, tools, and leather served workshops for wheelwrights, locksmiths, shoemakers, and saddlers. Bakeries, washrooms, winepresses, and laundries surrounded courtyards given over to the shepherds and their small sheepfolds, cowherds and their cowsheds, grooms and their stables. Accommodation was provided for the laborers, day workers, wine growers, wine pressers, and threshers. Next to offices and storehouses for goods received as feudal dues, two large dwellings faced each other across the central courtyard of the complex, the house of the farmer and the house of the lord of the domain, the *bâtiment seigneurial.*

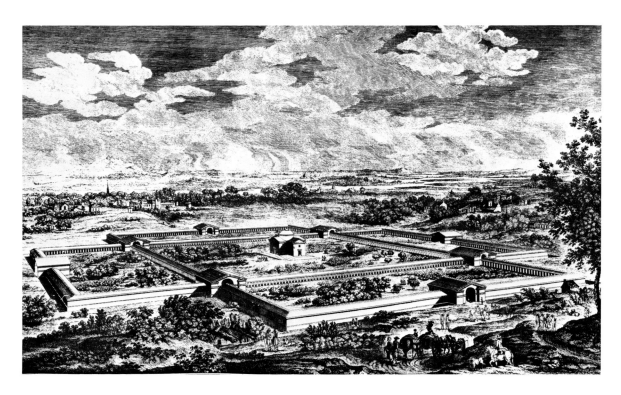

Ledoux, *Bergerie,* La Roche Bernard, Brittany, perspective view. Engraving from De No-belle, *L'architecture de Ledoux.*

Ledoux, *Bergerie,* La Roche Bernard, plan. Engraving from Ramée, *Ledoux,* pl. 297.

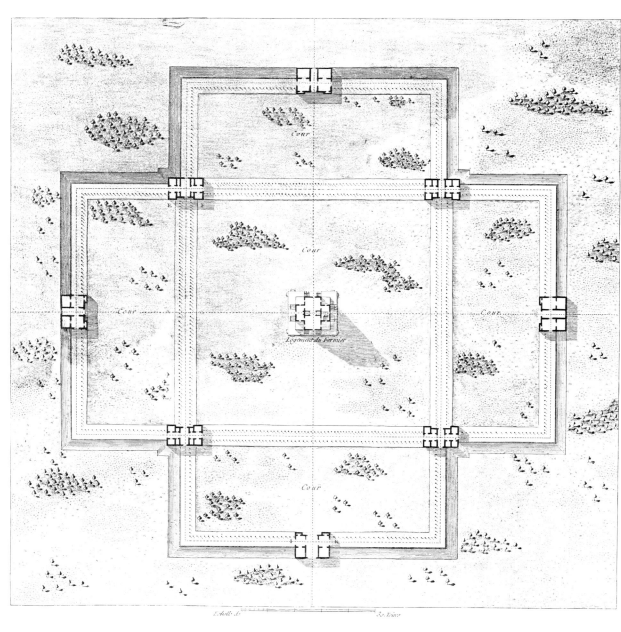

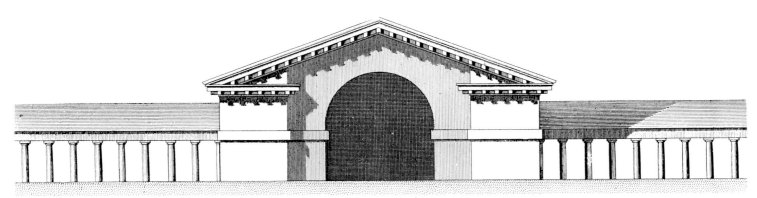

PORTE D'ENTRÉE

Elevation sur la Ligne GH

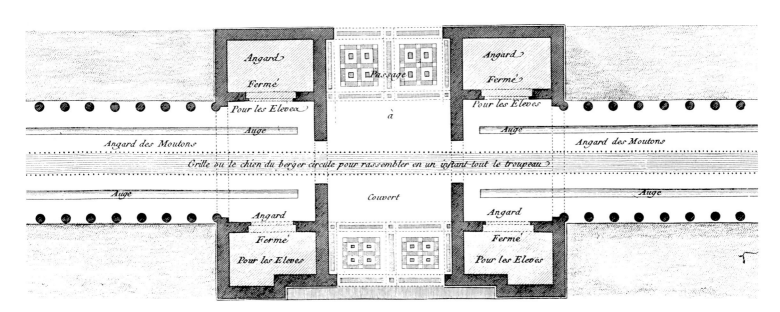

Angard

Fermé

Pour les Eleves

Angard des Moutons

Auge

Passage

à

Couvert

Angard

Fermé

Pour les Eleves

Angard des Moutons

Auge

Grille ou le chien du berger circule pour rassembler en un instant tout le troupeau

Auge

Angard

Fermé

Pour les Eleves

Auge

Angard

Fermé

Pour les Eleves

Ledoux, *Bergerie,* La Roche
Bernard, partial elevation and
detailed plan of sheepfolds.
Engraving by Sellier from Ramée, *Ledoux,* pl. 298.

Plan général de la Ferme parée de la Roche Bernard.

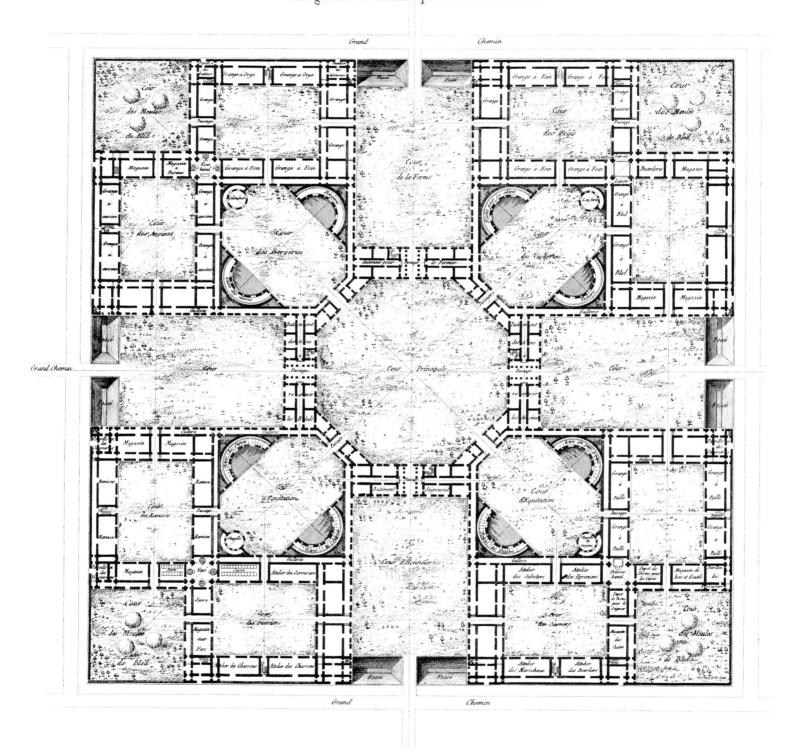

Élévation de l'une des Façades

Another of Ledoux's ideal designs, the Rural School of Meillant, was engraved in year III (1795). It was equipped with every facility necessary to disseminate the new learning in agriculture to the local population.[67] On the ground floor, open on two sides with colonnades fronting the park, were a large hall for public festivals and a storage room for full-scale demonstration models of new agricultural implements. On the mezzanine, an agricultural library, a *salle des plantes,* and a free dispensary for medical supplies were disposed together with a room for small-scale replicas of tools. Ledoux devoted the upper floor to the activities of the local agricultural societies established in many areas as the regional committees for the encouragement of improved methods of farming, providing rooms for their elected assemblies and secretariat and their agricultural shows. The dramatic perspective of the agricultural school, evoking the "sublime" position of the building, dedicated to natural principles and subjected to the elements, depicts the school in an active, productive landscape. Framed by the massive Piranesian arch of a rural stone bridge—the idealization of those proposed by Ledoux for many small communities in the 1760s and early 1770s—supported on two rows of massive Doric columns, the school stands in a *jardin anglais* of artificial rock grottoes and hillocks.[68] On the lawns that slope down to the river, gardeners, visitors, and scholars occupy themselves in front of the building; on the river, fishermen dredge their catches; at the edge of the washhouse, washerwomen ply their trade; a groom leads his horses to drink from the watering trough; a large hay cart drawn by four splendid horses of English breed crosses the road above. The entire scene is subjected to the sudden blast of a summer storm, which tosses a carter's hat over the bridge and bends the trees by its force, while a rainbow, reinforcing the connection between the forms of nature and those of art, appears through the clouds. The picture deliberately animates the more didactic scenes of rural *métiers* in the *Encyclopédie* and Rozier's *Cours complet,* captured at the moment of interaction between demonstrated Physiocratic principle and agronomic activity.

Ledoux advanced these concerns for rural architecture, theoretically at least, in the agricultural buildings conceived as a part of his ideal city. Ledoux saw these simple structures, set in the picturesque landscape of Franche-Comté, as illustrations to some Virgilian eclogue; through the rhetorical conventions of the pastoral he endowed his designs with a direct pedigree from antiquity:

In the countryside, Agriculture and all the rustic gods have their temples. Their names inscribed on the altars testify to their rights to our love. To this entirely natural religion are associated the parks, however proud they might be of the neighboring châteaux. On all sides are inexpensive buildings, barns, farms, productive sheepfolds, monuments that are too often scorned.(4)

In this vision, Ledoux was less concerned with the grandiose establishments of noble lords, the Boisgelins or the Montesquious, than with the holdings of the small farmer, emblem of economic virtue and moral humility before nature. Thus he designed the Grange Parée as a small farmhouse for an estate not affluent enough to build separate barns, stables, or stores for each use, to, as he stated, "isolate all the particulars of a farm." Instead, Ledoux brought together all the functions in a single building. In the basement he set the wine cellars, kitchen, laundry, and dairy side by side with the wood store and the smithy; on the ground floor, following traditional rural practice, he planned stables and stalls for horses, pigs, cows, and sheep and a run for chickens. Above these he placed the bedrooms for the farmer and family and the grain stores, and on the upper floor the quarters of the domestic servants. In the attic he planned reservoirs of rain water as a precaution against fire, that most threatening of rural domestic disasters. The farmer described by Ledoux was a true *agronome,* railing against the ruinous and ill-directed practices of the neighboring estate:

"Do you see," he asked me, "that magnificent château that harbors the anxieties that stem from the weight of large holdings? Those high walls that surround the numerous flocks, the young shoots withered by murderous teeth, the precious trees lost to the present generation. . . . Their ruin is near, it is inevitable."(49)

Against this emblem of thoughtless exploitation, forest neglect, and traditional methods, the farm of the *petit économe*

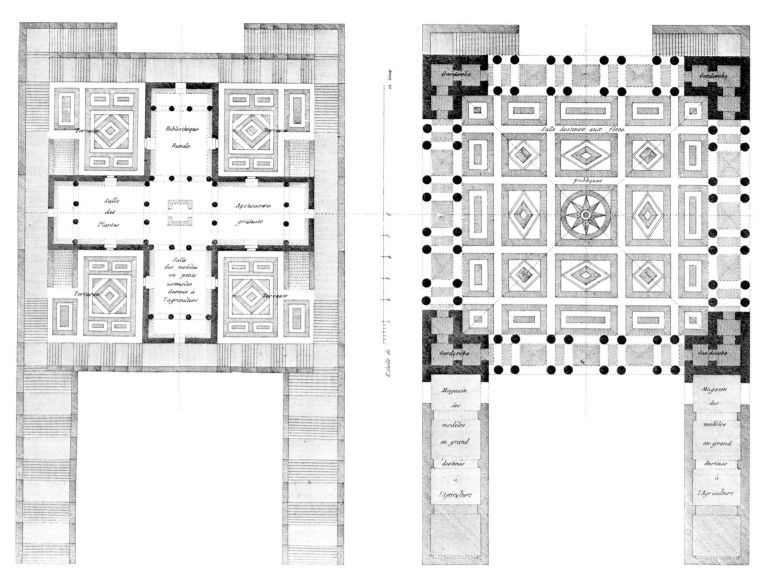

Ledoux, Rural School of Meillant, 1795, plans of mezzanine,
first, and second floors and
section. Engraving by Beutrois from Ramée, *Ledoux,* pls.
289 and 290.

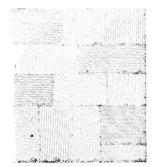
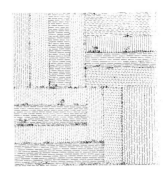
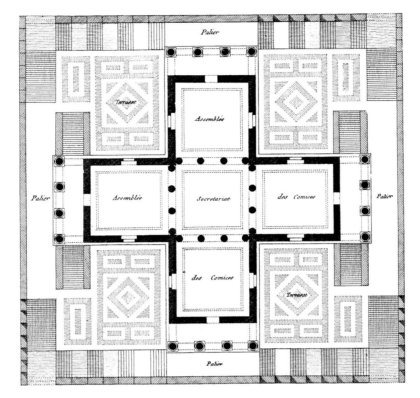
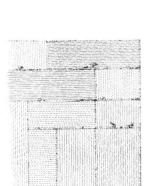
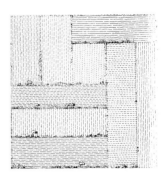

Palier

Terrasse

Assemblée

Assemblée

Secretariat

des Comices

Palier

Palier

des Comices

Terrasse

Palier

Echelle de   1   2   3   4   5   6   12   toises

Ledoux, Rural School of Meil-
lant, perspective view.
Engraving by Piquenot and
Ransonnette from Ramée,
Ledoux, pl. 288.

Ledoux, Washing place and
bridge, Meillant, elevation
and section. Engraving from
Ramée, *Ledoux,* pl. 289.

Plan du Rez-de-Chaussée.

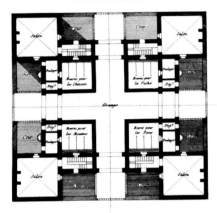

Plan des Souterrains.

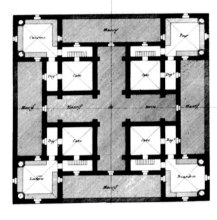

Grange parée.

Elevation Latterale

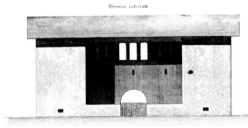

Coupe.

Elevation

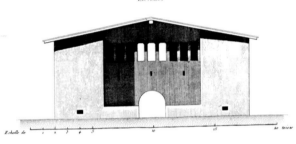

Echelle de

Plan du Second étage

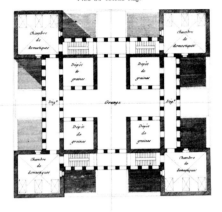

Plan du Premier étage

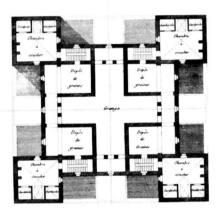

Ledoux, Grange Parée,
Chaux, plans of basement,
first, second, and third floors,
elevations, and section. Engraving by Varin from
Ledoux, *L'architecture,* pl. 5.

was a model of contemporary English practice: nothing was unnecessary or against reason; the estate was small enough to be administered, without the help of "greedy agents," entirely by a single farmer, whose revenues would exceed his expenditures. Even the view was reminiscent of Gainsborough or Kent: "Unconfined by any stone wall, I am linked to the neighboring lands by a ditch and a hedge; I enjoy at once the products of my cultivation and all the land open to my view" (49).

Ledoux designed an even more modest farm, the Cour de Service, for a cultivator with no financial resources but a small property. Surrounding a centralized covered courtyard, accessible from four sides, were stables, cowsheds, sheepfolds, a dairy, and chicken run on the ground floor, and bedrooms and living quarters for servants and the farmer on the upper floors. In this little farm, ventilated by galleries and arcades and built in fireproof materials, Ledoux took traditional distributions and converted them into architecture, with the use of motifs abstracted from Palladio and Tuscan vernacular. Such a farm was no doubt to be serviced by the *portiques* that in Ledoux's idealized design mimicked the traditional form of the medieval covered market raised on columns, now isolated in the countryside as a building type in its own right. Ledoux dreamed of the philosophical farmers walking and talking beneath these arcades in a transposition of Alberti's classical vision of the role of antique porticoes. Finally, Ledoux contributed to the rural utopia of Chaux a freestanding, rusticated shelter for a drinking pond and washing place. The structure was entered through Serlian pilasters; its central pool, covered by a flat vault, was fed by rain-water reservoirs under the eaves. Ledoux compared this useful structure to the antique *lavoirs* of Nîmes, but the program exactly recalled a number of washing places built in the 1770s by hygienically conscious municipalities: the circular plans and covered arcades of those at Tonnerre and Brienon-sur-Armançon in Burgundy were notable examples. But taken together, these ideal rural projects constituted a body of work that in the late eighteenth century, in the realm of architecture at least, was original enough. As Ledoux noted, "What I have said about the general precautions to be taken by the architect can be considered a warning rather than as an instruction. If developed, the material would fill many volumes"(146).

THE HOUSE OF THE POOR

The destruction of the thatched cottages is an act that restores man to his dignity, his security; it preserves large cities from destructive fires. . . . To destroy the thatched cottages is to level the appearance of poverty with the comfort by which industriousness should be honored.(103)

Ledoux's designs for agricultural buildings, in accordance with economic premises, deliberately eschewed the picturesque embellishments of the more fashionable *fermes ornées* built in the 1780s, of which Marie Antoinette's hamlet and dairy at Versailles, partly the work of Hubert Robert, were the most celebrated examples. This refusal of the decorative in matters of rural reform extended as well to the general

Ledoux, Cours de Service, Chaux, perspective view, elevation, section, and plans of basement, mezzanine, first, and second floors. Engraving from Ledoux, *L'architecture,* pl. 65.

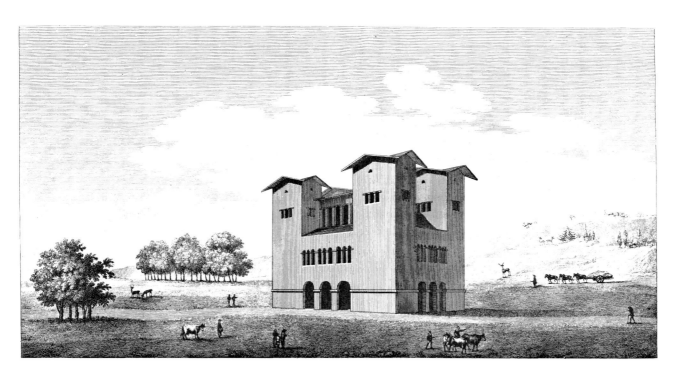

Elévation

Coupe

Entresol

Premier Etage.

Souterrain

Rez-de-Chaussée

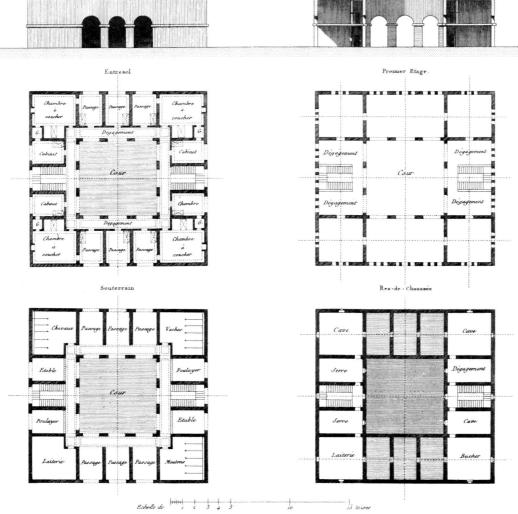

Echelle de 1 2 3 4 5 10 15 toises

Elevation.   Coupe

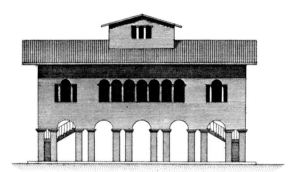   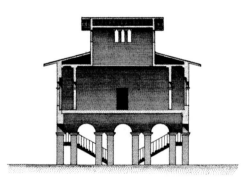

Rez -de Chaussée   Premier étage .

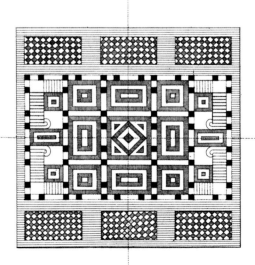   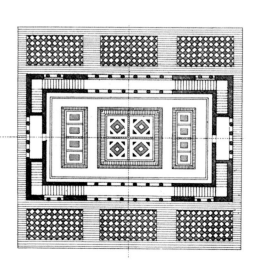

Echelle de ┣┼┼┼┼┤ 1   2   3   4   5   10 toises

Ledoux, Portiques, Chaux, perspective view, elevation, section, and plans of first and second floors. Engraving by Van Maëlle and Simon from Ledoux, *L'architecture,* pl. 31.

Ledoux, Drinking pond and washing place, elevation, plan, and section. Engraving from Ramée, *Ledoux,* pl. 130.

Elevation

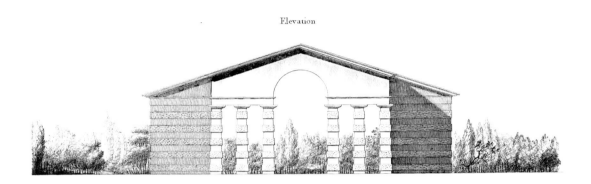

Plan

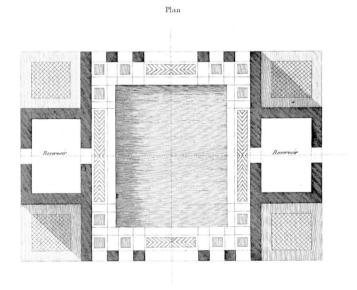

Coupe

problem of housing the poor, whose unhygienic, fire-prone, damp cottages were seen by many *agronomes* as the most evident signs of a derelict and backward cultivation.[69] In the last twenty years of the century many proposals were advanced in England and France for economic, durable, and healthy alternatives to these squalid huts and cottages that visibly interfered with the concept of a countryside at once fertile and benign. (The most prolific campaigner for fireproof dwellings was François Cointeraux, whose patent method of construction in *pisé,* a kind of cement formed out of compressed earth, was propounded in numerous reports between 1784 and 1810.)[70] Practical, cheap, and simple in form, these designs had little, if any, architectural qualities, dealing only with the basic needs of the poorest families, day laborers, and peasants.

Ledoux, however, in a series of designs prepared after 1780, not only followed the more advanced reformers in calling for the eradication of the thatched cottages, but also advanced political and aesthetic criteria for his comprehensive program of rural reconstruction. It was in the interests of government, he claimed, to destroy "these insubstantial constructions," to efface them from the map of France, and to build in their stead model homes, encouraging the dissemination of knowledge in building techniques, health, and hygiene. Beyond this, it was an affront to the proclaimed enlightenment of the century to ignore the vast majority of the population, that reservoir of honest labor and productive forces: "Everywhere *la classe nombreuse* is disdained; the tyrant fears the people, the people fear the tyrant"(102).

The poor man in the eighteenth century has nothing with which to shelter his head. He runs in the fields and when he is tired he rests on a bed of stone in the shelter of a sycamore or weeping willow, and the fields, so fertile for others, are arid for him alone.(104)

In an ironic reversal of the mid-eighteenth-century myth of architectural origins that, in the optimistic narrative of Laugier, presented a vision of a self-sufficient "natural" man building his own shelter out of the materials of the forest, constructing a model for all subsequent architecture, Ledoux in *L'architecture* depicted this "poor man's shelter" as a lone stunted tree growing out of a stony islet set in an infinite sea. Beneath it a naked, shivering pauper holds out his hands in supplication to the skies, where, atop a bank of clouds that disperses the rays of the sun toward the earth—the first rays of Enlightenment—the gods of Olympus and the muses of the arts and sciences are assembled, apparently ready to dispense their munificence. "The Architect is there," wrote Ledoux, "surrounded by clouds"(195). Clearly, if specialization of *métiers* has removed from the poor the path of self-help, the modern architect should be prepared to serve. Ledoux was contemptuous of the rustic primitivism that treated the "hut" as a decorative conceit, a sentimentalized stage prop for gardens *à l'anglais:*

Since the hut of Romulus, huts are still built; luxury perpetuates them, placing them in sumptuous gardens. . . . How is it that in a century that gathers the knowledge of those that have preceded it, so much favor is given to huts? Why not efface the traces of poverty to present it under the sign of happiness, even of the marvelous?(102)

For Ledoux "origins" were rather to be found in the strict dictates of need, *le besoin,* described materialistically, the natural foundation of life; architecture, returning to origins, should be based on these needs, perfecting them according to the laws of nature and art.

Taking the basic needs of solid construction, ventilation, drainage, and economy as his program, Ledoux formulated a typical "model home," a prototype that he envisaged would be built in a number of examples in the surroundings of the Saline de Chaux and that he claimed had, in principle, been accepted as a part of the building campaign of the original factory. This Worker's House was drawn up in its simplest form on plate 17 of *L'architecture* and presented in some four variations in following plates: "The government, wishing to give models to the less fortunate of men, had constructed many houses that united every quality of utility and solidity and had not even neglected to give them a relative measure of architectural order"(78). This simple two-story house, with living spaces on the ground floor and bedrooms on the first floor, was abutted by lean-to stables and storerooms incorporated into a service podium that accommo-

dated wine cellars and wood stores. A barrel-vaulted roof enclosed an attic ventilated from above. The architecture was plain, with only the arched façade and its abstracted Palladian motif serving to remind the viewer of the conventions: it was in the composition of the masses, their juxtaposition and linking with stairs and roofs that Ledoux developed the aesthetic. The whole design was a didactic exercise in the "form of need," an origin for architecture that socially as well as formally operated as a moral beginning for the building of the social order.

Each of the four *maisons de commis* or *maisons de l'employés* clerks' or workers' houses, illustrated in *L'architecture* was a variation on this plan. Low pitched tile roofs replaced the vaulted roof and detached dependencies replaced the consolidated cellars and livestock courts, and the patterns of porches, arcades, and covered passageways differed; but the same general pattern of living and bed spaces remained as well as a similar stripped aesthetic. The principle of the type for Ledoux lay in this very susceptibility to endless variation; where the orders and decorative emblematics were proscribed, the variety of distribution and composition and the contrast of the simple, cubic volumes with the surrounding colors and profusion of nature provided the *ordonnance relatif* required by humble *besoins*.

While, in the utopia of Chaux, he conceived these dwellings as standing free within clearings in the forest or amid small cultivated holdings, returning in this way a clerk or factory overseer to the soil, Ledoux also made it clear that he had designed a house type that would equally find its place, aggregated, in a village or small town.[71] If all settlements were composed of detached houses, each set on a small plot

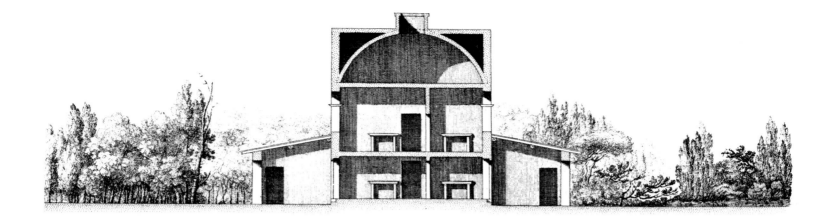

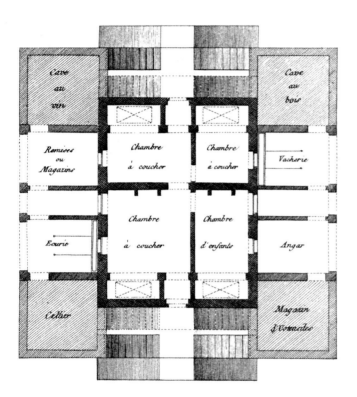

Cave au vin

Cave au bois

Remises ou Magazins

Chambre à coucher

Chambre à coucher

Vacherie

Chambre à coucher

Chambre à coucher

Chambre à coucher

Chambre d'enfants

Ecurie

Chambre à coucher

Chambre d'enfants

Angar

Cellier

Magazin d'Ustenciles

Chambre d'enfants

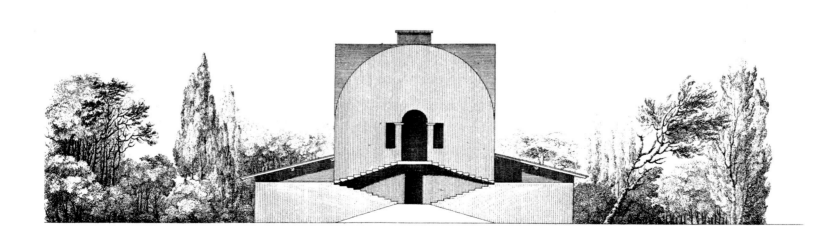

of land, then the dangers of fire present in contemporary towns would be avoided; at the same time, the peasant, day laborer, or functionary could supplement his income by growing food. Sometime after 1784 Ledoux planned such a village for the domain of Maupertuis, presumably to be built by de Montesquiou himself to replace those dwellings destroyed in the redevelopment of his landscape gardens.[72] The perspective view shows a collection of variations on the Worker's House ranged along two streets that intersect at right angles at the village square. Each house has a different roof formation and massing; each sits on a fenced plot containing orchards, arbors, and kitchen gardens, fronting onto the main street and backing onto the village *communs*. This settlement seems to recall the happy vision of Rousseau in describing the villages around Neuchâtel, where the mountain was "entirely covered with dwellings, each one of which constitutes the center of the lands that it controls, so that these houses, separated by distances as equal as the fortunes of the proprietors, offer to the numerous inhabitants of this mountain both the tranquility of a retreat and the sweetness of society."[73] But Ledoux's political utopia was more paternalistic than Rousseau's, and in the village of Maupertuis the "equality" was rigorously enforced by the plan. The moralization of its inhabitants was also a matter of seigneurial concern: In the perspective view of Maupertuis, Ledoux depicted a procession of villagers wending its way to a huge "temple" that occupies the center of the village square, a peristyle of primitive Tuscan columns standing on, and vertically invaded by, a pyramid of stairs ascending to the altar, a center of public celebration and religious order.

THE MÉTIERS OF THE FOREST

At the heart of forests of an immense extent may be seen the sacred roof of their conservator who, new Sylvan, surveys them and protects them; the pyramidal retreat of the woodcutter who, among the giants that people the forest, strikes at his master's signal . . . ; the domestic cupola of the charcoal burner who prepares the fuel needed by the furnaces of the chemists . . . ; finally the subdivided galleries where, next to his dwelling, the carpenter fashions, trims, and levels his wood.(4)

If in the workers' houses for Maupertuis Ledoux responded to the enlightened paternalism of the reforming landowner class, in a series of ideal designs for rural dwellings invented between 1784 and 1789, he took his program from the already defined needs of the external economy of the Saline de Chaux. The omnivorous demand for cordwood, construction timber, charcoal, iron, casks, and barrels to sustain the production of salt was, for Ledoux, the occasion to imagine housing and workshops for those *métiers* of the forest—charcoal burners, woodcutters, sawyers, coopers, and forest guards—immediately concerned with the control and exploitation of the forest itself.[74] Set in clearings, isolated from one another but joined by a network of *allées,* these small pavilions or *fabriques* were envisioned as architectural "figures" of production, dramatizing by their primitive rhetoric the rural occupations dignified by Diderot and his collaborators.[75] In Ledoux's mind, they would at once confirm the domination of the factory over the region and act to reform the social life and morals of their rough inhabitants, who lived, according to one observer, much "like wolves" in their dens, surrounded by half-naked children, hardly sheltered by branches and leaves.[76]

The architecture of these new houses, however, was directly inspired by their original type-form and by their social program. The type-form that Ledoux seemed to have had in mind was the workshop for the fabrication of pegs and vine stakes from the *Encyclopédie,* illustrated as a hexagonal structure with a pyramidal roof open at the apex for a chimney and with benches around the walls for sleep and work.[77] Throughout the eighteenth century, similar pyramidal huts, less idyllic than this, were routinely described by visitors to country districts. "All their huts," noted Emile Souvestre of the coopers in Brittany, "were round, built of branches, which they filled in with grass or moss."[78] Desiré Monnier, a collector of folklore and an amateur anthropologist of the customs of Franche-Comté, described the charcoal burner's hut in the Jura as a pyramidal roof that reached the ground on all sides.[79] And indeed, this type was well embedded in the tradition of classical architecture: Claude Perrault had depicted primitive rural huts in his translation of Vitruvius,

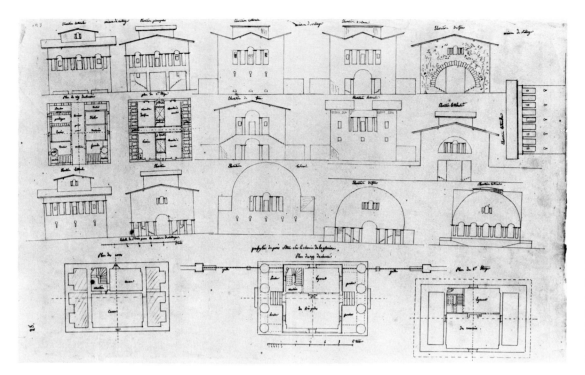

Ledoux, Houses for Maupertuis, elevations and plans,
drawn on same sheet as plans
for the Barrière de la Glacière.
Drawing from Ledoux's of-
fice, Musèe des Arts Décoratifs, Paris, CL 12917.

Ledoux, Village of Maupertuis, perspective view.
Engraving from the Archives
de Seine-et-Marne, Melun.

Workshop for the fabrication
of clogs and vine stakes. Engraving from the *Encyclopédie,*
"Economie rurale" pl. 55.

thereby "verifying" the antique myth of origins.[80] Taking this natural form as his model, Ledoux developed architectural variations, with a particular character suited to each *métier,* according to the geometrical permutations of simple, centralized plans, themselves derived from the reduced Palladian tradition assayed in the *barrières.*

Built of unfashioned timber—the original hut of Laugier now turned to social use—these *fabriques* were all planned around a common fireplace, like Ledoux's earlier designs for the workers' buildings of the Saline de Chaux, with bedrooms and workshops deployed around a central, double-height room. These houses might be read as primitive versions of that bourgeois and aristocratic space of sociability, the "lodge," the brotherly circle idealized in the Masonic societies of the late eighteenth century. But Ledoux was also aware of the deep-rooted associational life of the rural artisans, whose own lodges were, after all, the original types, as it were, of the bourgeois circles. Woodcutters, charcoal burners, carpenters all had their own forms of *compagnonnage,* derived from their isolated life in the woods and the collective nature of their work. Living in temporary, roughly built huts, sharing hearths and food, eating and working in common, the forest workers had highly developed associations. The woodcutters, whose *coupes,* or cuttings, took place in the fall and winter months, would unite in a band of four or five fellows to buy a certain number of acres over which they would have the right of cutting; the *fendeurs,* who split and cut the wood after felling, likewise had their brotherhoods. Carpenters too had their fraternities, naming the members of their corporations after animals such as rabbits or foxes. The societies of the charcoal burners were especially close.[81] The initiation rituals of these societies dated back well into the Middle Ages; and churchmen in rural districts were continually complaining of the "ceremonies that profane all that is most sacred," celebrated by iron workers and charcoal burners.[82] Late-eighteenth-century bourgeois foundations such as the Bons Cousins, Charbonniers, or Fendeurs were often outgrowths or direct imitations of these earlier, operative guilds.[83] Monnier recorded his attendance at a *vente,* or felling of timber, held in a clearing in the forest on the feast day of Saint Thiebaud, where he was received as a member of the Bons Cousins in a ritual celebrated in a "house of logs."[84] Ledoux, as social designer, was concerned to reform these primitive associations, reconstructing them according to the civilized laws of architecture and production. By investing the huts of the forest workers with architectural attributes and by designing each of them as a small community in its own right, Ledoux evidently hoped to bring their inhabitants into a natural state of harmony in a "communal center." Of the House and Workshop of the Charcoal Burners he wrote,

Here man learns to support himself; sad amidst his fellows, he inhabits the forests; he passes, in obscurity, days that are inaccessible to the malaise of ambition. Charcoal burner draws near to charcoal burner; he develops his activity beneath this compliant arch, which [the architect] has curved within the forest to preserve his asylum from the bad weather and the incursions of wild beasts.(209)

And of the House of the Woodcutters he wrote, "It is here that exercise regularizes the passions, that it develops the faculties of the body; it is here that love, that imperious sentiment, submits nature to the consoling calculations of happiness"(197). Ledoux was lyrical in his description of the Rousseauesque life of these reformed men of the forest. The daily round of burning coals, cutting trees, and sawing logs, freshened by the sweet charms of life in their well-ventilated communal dwellings, would again institute, this time in a truly productive setting, natural man in arcadia. This was Physiocratic man, healthy, rugged, enjoying the fruits of labor, and moral, endowed with a high sense of his task in the natural order. The working out of such a "felicific calculus" in all its pedantic mathematical detail was to be the self-imposed task of Jeremy Bentham; Ledoux, similarly drawing on the Helvetian notion that the environment could produce calculable changes in the balance of pain and pleasure, insisted on the role of a properly constituted architecture. The space of this new order of sociability was crucial. It was not incidental that the common hearth stood at the center of all these *fabriques:*

One sees the bustle imparted by active morality as a means of facing the troubles of life; one sees the clay pots multiplied around the wide circle; the nourishing juices of the day bubble and boil without respite; the common flame rises and warms from afar the period given over to rest; the meats are seasoned by appetite, the inseparable companion of the god of health.(197)

The circle of clay pots, each holding the simmering soup for the evening repast, not only symbolized the communal feast, but—recalling in idealized terms those traditional *veillées* around the hearth, common in every rural community—also instrumentalized the circle of brotherhood.[85]

But the radial and axial plans of these constructions did not simply refer inward to the communal hearth; they directed the attention of the inhabitants outward, making of them the natural agents of the very surveillance that ordered their lives. Ledoux extended the limits of surveillance through openings, visual and formal, incorporated into the plans of the buildings. Moreover, he sited each structure at the intersection of a number of forest routes, as station points of an all-controlling perspectival vision. Thus he placed the House and Workshop of the Sawyers "at the center of six *allées* of the forest"(103); the House and Workshop of the Woodcutters, whom Ledoux gave the supplementary title of forest guards, put "work and surveillance" at "the center of many routes whose shadowed vaults extend to the horizon" (197); the House and Workshop of the Charcoal Burners stood "at the center of four routes," its porches constructed to "ensure their surveillance"(209). The principle of surveillance, logically enough, found its consummate expression in the House of the Forest Guards, whose form was entirely determined by the employment of its occupants. Bringing together work and habitation, Ledoux abandoned the wall altogether—a move of which Laugier, for other reasons, would have wholeheartedly approved—in favor of a grid of square pillars supporting a pyramidal, overhanging roof. From inside, nothing should interfere with the act of visual oversight: "Everything must be seen, nothing must stop the eye . . . every obstacle should be contrary to the principle"(191). This "principle" of visual surveillance, a kind of

panopticism before the fact, of a more instrumental kind than informed the radial plan of the *saline*, would be ensured in its effectiveness by this "kind of cage, open on every side"(191). From the communal fire, through openings in the vaults, the inhabitants could view the surrounding countryside, alert to any infraction or illegal incursion into the forest.

SIGNS OF PRODUCTION

Ledoux's merging of architectural and social reform found expression in dwellings and workshops that took the idea of character to its extreme, no longer in the service of a monumental circuit around the city of Paris, but as an educational device by which to instill a sense of order and place among the rural proletariat. Ledoux devised plans and three-dimensional geometries that mirrored their social content; invented new, rustic orders, expressive of the differences between each *métier;* and, in some cases, gave emblematic form to the entire building as a sign of the occupation of its inhabitants.

The plan of the House and Workshop of the Charcoal Burners was a square divided equally into nine squares and entered on four sides through open porches. Each corner was taken up with two beds and the center with a fireplace, the chimney of which rose up to the apex of a cross-vaulted dome. Beneath this dome, on an upper level, were four more bedrooms and stores, reached by means of a gallery that surrounded the chimney. The House and Workshop of the Sawyers was a semicovered, single-story space. The fireplace formed the core of a circular communal room that rose as a two-story drum to a shallow, conical roof; from this room three bedroom wings extended radially, dividing the workshop areas, which were outside but covered with a lean-to roof. The entire building was slightly raised on a circular platform. The square plan of the House of the Woodcutters, with four bedrooms at the corners, was divided by the upper and lower entrances on axis and surrounded on all sides by a covered portico, surmounted by a pediment with each doorway marked by a rounded arch. A full basement accommodated stables, cowshed, chicken run, and meat store. A cylinder,

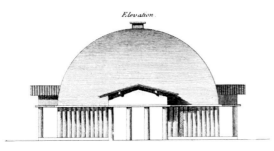

Elevation.

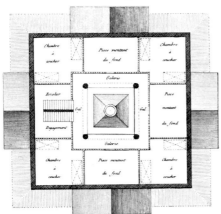

Premier Etage.

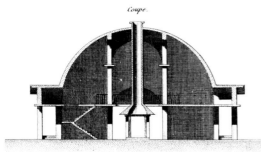

Coupe.

Plan du Rez-de-Chaussée

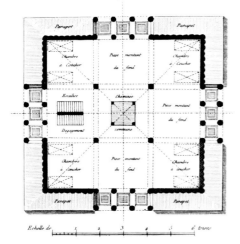

Echelle de

Ledoux, House and Workshop
of the Charcoal Burners,
elevation, section, and plans
of first and second floors. Engraving from Ledoux, *L'architecture,* pl. 109.

Ledoux, House and Workshop
of the Sawyers, elevation,
plan, and section. Engraving
by Ransonnette from Ledoux,
L'architecture, pl. 32.

Elevation.

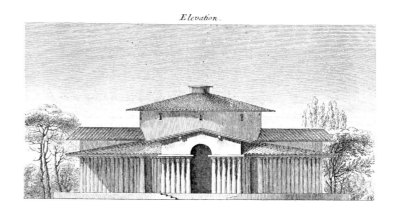

Plan du Premier.

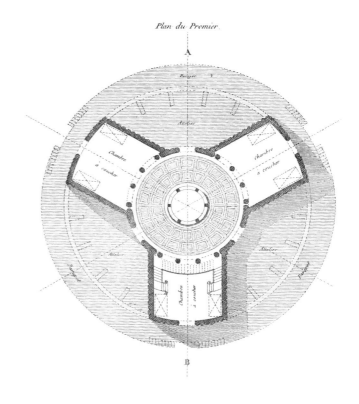

Coupe sur la ligne A B du Plan

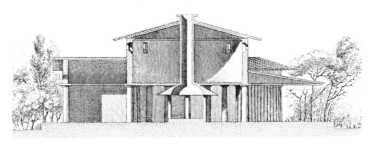

Echelle de

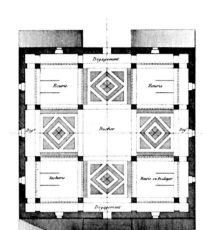

Ledoux, House and Workshop
of the Woodcutters, perspective view, section, and plans of
basement and first floor. Engravings from Ledoux,
L'architecture, pls. 102, 101.

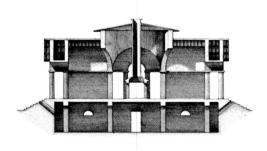

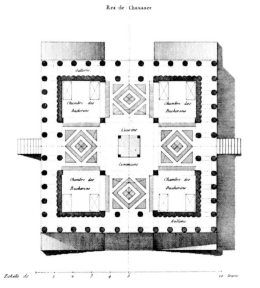

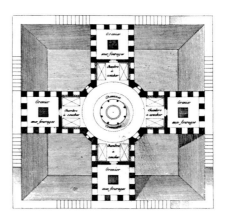

Coupe

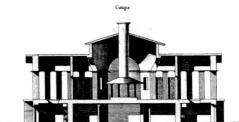

Elevation

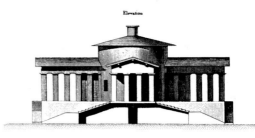

Plan du Rez-de-Chaussée

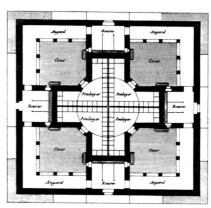

Echelle de

rising from the four central posts, encircled the hearth and chimney.

Deriving his architectural expression from the role of the *métier* and its place in the hierarchy of *métiers,* Ledoux invented for the House and Workshop of the Charcoal Burners first the "dome," reflecting the traditional huts of bent branches, now formalized; then a "pediment" over the porches, formed simply out of a shallow-pitched roof over the entry; finally, a new order, a "tree-trunk" or "log" order, posts placed vertically side by side to form the walls. Ledoux designed the House and Workshop of the Sawyers and the House of the Woodcutters with similar wooden orders. These log cabins demonstrated, as it were, the active results of labor, but they also referred to the ideas of origins developed by the *philosophes* of the mid-century. Ledoux, however, was not content to replicate the structural "grammar" of Laugier's primitive hut; he required a powerful expression of the economic and productive forces that in a real sense motivated these signs of Physiocratic activity. Thus the primitive wooden order was most appropriate for the House of the Woodcutters: "The woodcutter's workshop returns us to first ideas. The oaks of the forest are felled, bound closely together, and attached to boards placed edge to edge; they are reinforced by subsidiary supports to sustain the roofs."(198) The resulting effect was, for Ledoux, "unequivocal." The play of light and shade; the contrast between rough, unfinished timber and simple architectural attributes; the rustic tile roofs with their steep overhangs, all this would endow these buildings with suitable character. In any case, historical precedent existed for the tree-trunk orders, from the first hut on the Capitoline Hill to the principle emblem of Laugier: "This is not the first time that architecture has been represented in logs"(198). Ledoux's use of the word "figuré" for "represent" implied the use of these supports as rhetorical motifs. For the House of the Forest Guards, Ledoux likewise employed a primitive, but more finished order, appropriate to the higher status of the inhabitants, fabricated out of square pilasters. While rarely used in antiquity (Ledoux cited the Temple of Trevi) and then only at the corners of buildings, the square

Ledoux, Workshop of the
Charcoal Burners, perspective
view. Engraving from
Ledoux, *L'architecture*, pl. 102.

pilaster was suggestive of a primitive strength: "Square pillars
are erected, the spaces between filled with jointed plants; the
lines of stone courses are marked on them. . . . Such was man
in his simplicity, before ceding to the power of encroaching
luxury."(191)

Ledoux's method is clearest in a design—illustrated
only in perspective—for a workshop, labeled a woodcutters'
house but possibly intended as a workshop for the charcoal
burners.[86] Pyramidal in shape, it was made of horizontal logs
rising from a square base, with ramped roofs forming a kind
of pediment over the porches. Here Ledoux gave to the charcoal burners' pyre—perhaps extant beneath its new roof—
the character of a truncated pyramid, entered, like those illustrated by Fischer von Erlach, through a "Palladian" doorway.
Again, the object was more than a complex of high and low
references; it literally returned the supposed origin of the
Egyptian pyramids in the shape of the eternal flame to its
source. Pyramid once more became pyre, this time produc-
tively. The form of the *métier* was thus made into architecture;
a constructed place was fabricated out of a temporary position; the errant charcoal burner was "dignified" and fixed in
place by the architect-manager.

The House and Workshop of the Coopers took this idea
of proper characterization to another level and, with the
House of the Agricultural Guards of Maupertuis, stood as the
logical conclusion of Ledoux's rhetorical exercises. In each of
these designs, Ledoux attempted to make "hieroglyphic"
signs out of the material of the program, turning architecture,
so to speak, into pictographic writing. He suppressed or ban-
ished altogether the rustic orders and architectural motifs, let-
ting the three-dimensional form of the structures "speak"
clearly to the eyes. In plan and section these buildings were
laid out rationally enough. The House and Workshop of the
Coopers was square in plan, possessing all the functional
characteristics of collective life and work observed in the
other rural *fabriques:* living quarters around a central fireplace
took up the ground floor and bedrooms at the corners divided
the workshops on the upper floor. In elevation, however, it
presented itself as a giant series of inscribed circles, with a
circular hole in the center. In three dimensions the intersection of the four circular sides and their attendant roofs generated the form of two intersecting cylinders, the circular
bands inscribed on their ends. The symbolism was readily
apparent: The entire house formed a double barrel, its façades

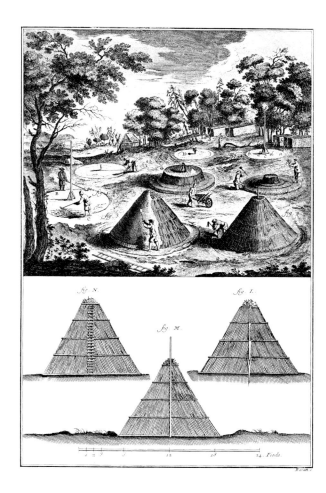

Ledoux, House and Workshop of the Coopers, elevation, plan, and section. Engraving from Ledoux, *L'architecture*, pl. 88.

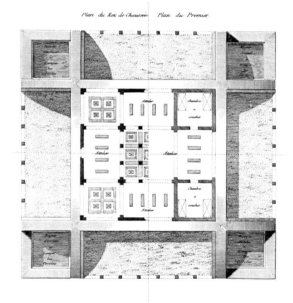

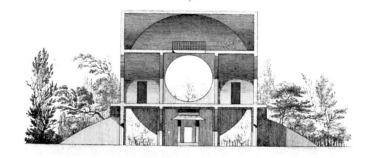

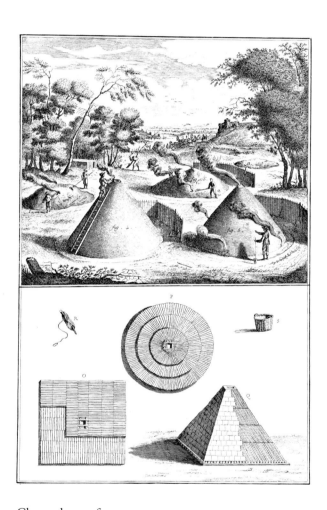

Charcoal manufacture, perspective views of charcoal burners' pyramids in the forest and construction details. Engraving from the *Encyclopédie,* "Economie rurale," pls. 56 and 57.

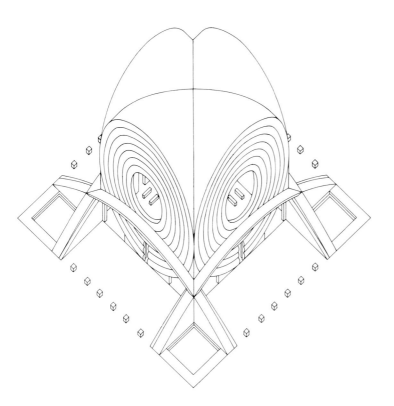

Ledoux, House and Workshop
of the Coopers, axonometric
reconstruction.

Coopers' Workshop. Engraving from the *Encyclopédie,*
"Tonnelier," pl. 1.

grooved in a pattern of *cercles,* the hoops that bound the barrels. Similarly, the curves of the hoops were echoed by the segmental ramps leading from the first-floor workshops to the soaking basins that occupied each of the lower corners and down which the barrels were rolled. The house thus became a literal confirmation of the work, the coopers surrounded by the shape of their product. The shape of the craft was also brought into play to relate to a higher symbolic order. The apertures through the center of the house served, in Ledoux's words, to "overlook the great routes of the forest," allowing a view of "the pines, whose masses correct the winter, the oaks, the sycamores, the acacias, which renew themselves every spring and produce contrasts that soften the aspect of stone"; likewise, the incised circles of the façades "extend the indefinite lines of the hoops and link them with the azure vault whose form and marvels they espouse"(179).

The House of the Agricultural Guards had a plan similar to that of the House of the Forest Guards, with bed alcoves grouped around a central fireplace and with stables and stores on the basement level below. The origins of its shape, a complete sphere, might have been more obscure to the agricultural laborer or to the shepherds who lived in it. Ledoux, however, made its meaning clear in his perspective view: The sphere, which rests lightly on the ground, supported by flying buttresses that serve as bridges to the main entrances, is triangulated between, on the left, a rude shed of branches and leaves—the traditional shelter of shepherds—and, on the far horizon, the rising sun, whose rays bathe the scene in bucolic splendor. The original "type" of the rural hut is here mediated through the "type" or origin of nature into a symbolic form of universal guardianship. In addition to linking the shepherds' house to the heavenly bodies, Ledoux emulated in its form many late-eighteenth-century idealized designs for Masonic lodges and private houses, from Antoine Vaudoyer to Jean-Jacques Lequeu.[87]

Ledoux did not write about the spherical house, which remained among the engravings that were intended for the other volumes of his unfinished work. But he clearly understood the "experimental" nature of these designs. He called the House and Workshop of the Coopers "an experiment, to

Ledoux, House of the Agricultural Guards of Maupertuis, elevation, section, plans of basement, first, and second floors, and perspective view. Engraving from Ramée, *Ledoux,* pl. 254.

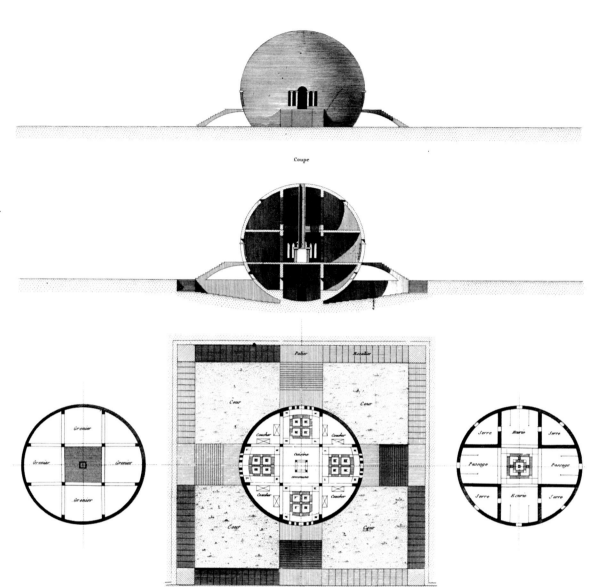

Freemasonic vignette, c. 1775,
showing rising sun and foundations of Masonic temple.

awaken with boldness of thought and execution" the "apa-
thetic sleep" of architects and reformers. He pointed out the
ease and economy of its construction, its rational and healthy
plans, and argued strongly for its aesthetic qualities.

*Even though it might seem unimportant that a workshop of some
forty to fifty feet square, situated in a little-frequented forest, should
produce more or less effect, nevertheless you should follow the principle, Is there anything that should not be capable of offering to the
eyes the attraction of useful progress? Is there anything that the ini-
tiating breeze of art cannot galvanize?(179)*

Even those who found the idea strange enough in itself
would, he concluded, perhaps be led to reflect on its subject,
the rural dwelling: "Often an idea that is unimportant by itself, however bizarre, contains an excellent concept that a
suitable manipulation, addition, or subtraction could turn
into a model"(179). This, in the end, was Ledoux's double
purpose: to overlay the geometry of work with that of architecture, generating a sign that by its dramatic character would
draw attention to both use and user; and, at the same time, in
this way to develop a series of models—economic, functional, and replicable—that might become standard solutions. The conventions of the architect might then become
social conventions as the disseminated rhetoric of production.

SYMBOLS OF NATURAL POWER

Taking their place beside these characteristic forms for the *arts
et métiers* in the productive landscapes of Chaux were others
dedicated by Ledoux to the idealization and reification of the
technical control of natural forces, among which the rivers
were of the highest importance. Channels of irrigation for
agriculture, routes for the economic transportation of goods
and the flotation of timber, sources of power for the pumps
and wheels of the salt and iron industries, the rivers and canals
of Franche-Comté had played a prominent role in Ledoux's
projects for regional development. The Bridge over the Loüe
River and the House of the Surveyors of the Loüe River, both
in different ways, celebrated the triumph of civil engineering
represented by the Corps des Ponts et Chaussées, both graphically and technically. In their design, Ledoux solved the aesthetic problem he had confronted with the engineering works
of the *saline,* the pumps, wheels, and graduation building.
Faced with this entirely functional structure, Ledoux had expressed reservations: "The ancient and modern colossi had
left some traces in my mind. This [monument] presented dis-
similarities, contradictions: if the parts were in accord with
the spirit of utility that had dictated them, my scruples, while
applauding the principle, called for more analogy in the
whole."(57) Ledoux, as previously noted, criticized the "attenuated members," seemingly too thin to support the gigantic structure, the "truncated form" of the roof, and concluded
that the "common practice of carpentry," a tradition that prevented innovation, had given rise to "this vicious section," "of
Gothic proportion," against the "purity of style" he would
have preferred. The key to his criticism is to be found less in
his complaints against "les préjugés de charpente"—a commonplace of encyclopedic rationalism that would subject all
traditions to logical and thereby geometrical scrutiny—than
in his call for "more analogy."

For the sight of the graduation building had, despite its
aesthetic drawbacks, inspired Ledoux to a reverie of surprising force on the powers it harnessed. The structure, "like a
huge ship launched on the liquid plain," evoked "the conserving ark of mankind prey to the universal deluge"(57). Before

its incessant activity, the pumps, wheels, and pipes forcing water from the aqueduct through its hundreds of channels and dripping them down over the bundled twigs, Ledoux felt "surrounded by water." "I was preoccupied with the industrious work of the pumps; an overflowing river with full canals agitated my thoughts; a hundred reveries amused my isolation."(54) Giving rise to a graphic daydream of the corruption and fall of Babylon, this scene was, for Ledoux, emblematic of the necessity of water to civilization. Babylon, in Ledoux's fantasy, imagined through the fiction of "one of the worlds of Fontenelle," was destroyed by fire, its canals and rivers dried up and thereby useless to save the city. A new city rose in its place, founded on a newly dredged river, linked to the sea by engineering works. Fountains were built to refresh the public squares, to provide water for the horses, and to protect the citizen against fire. "Canals and open aqueducts were substituted for temporary and more perishable measures"(56).

If such were the intimations of the graduation building, then its design demanded more than simple engineering; by "analogy" Ledoux meant a form that would represent as well as serve such life-giving functions. Thus the bridge over the Loüe River—"a true bridge," Ledoux called it—was conceived according to an analogy parallel to that which had seen the graduation building as some primitive Noah's Ark: "The sight of many vessels unmasted, sails unfurled, with rails raised to protect a road over the trembling brilliance of a turbulent river, recalled to my memory those first thoughts on which one can establish the succession of ideas and the progress of science."(45) The temporary bridge of boats—a traditional means of military and civil crossing illustrated in the *Encyclopédie*—constructed by the entrepreneur for the *saline,* supplied Ledoux with an equally common analogy for his bridge: that of Xerxes over the Hellespont.[88] Transforming a principle of analogical origin in this way, Ledoux shaped the four piers of his three-arched span into sturdy Roman galleys complete with the shields and oars of their rowers, the cabin and rudder of their navigator, their crossed masts delineating the arches. The form of the piles was thus entirely derived from analogy; but it also served the purpose of guarding against erosion, a constant preoccupation of Perronet and his engineers. Indeed, Emiliand Gauthey had already constructed a similar "analogical bridge" in Franche-Comté, that of Navilly over the Doubs River, finished after 1780: its piers, shaped like the hulls of boats, oval in plan to resist erosion, supported rusticated obelisks; its "Roman" arches were coffered.[89] The structure was located only thirty-seven miles from the site of Ledoux's own projected bridge of boats. No doubt Ledoux was also influenced by Boullée, who, in 1787, on the orders of Calonne, proposed a similar scheme for the redecoration of the Pont de la Concorde, then in construction by Perronet; in another example of the aesthetic "correction" of engineering, Boullée stated that, like Ledoux, he had "conceived the decoration of this bridge by returning to first ideas, which consisted in establishing, by means of boats, a passage over the water."[90]

A second bridge by Gauthey provides a clue to the interpretation of Ledoux's most dramatic exploitation of "analogy" in the celebration of water, the House of the Surveyors of the Loüe River. In this bridge, at Echavannes over a tributary of the Saône, Gauthey, to present less resistance to floods, opened up the piers with large, elliptical openings that would act as overflow channels at high water. It would seem directly to have inspired the oval section of the House of the Surveyors. Sited in Ledoux's imagination at the source of the Loüe, several miles to the northeast of Chaux, where a grotto and waterfall celebrated in travel literature and later in art gave rise to the river that irrigated the surroundings of Chaux and provided power for its pumps, this "house" took the form of a combined bridge and watercourse. It spanned the river at the foot of the falls, so that the water flowed through its lower half, enclosed by the giant oval section. The top half connected the two sides of the house by an arch across which ran a central salon, or billiard room, that overlooked the water beneath. Above, on the third level were servants' bedrooms; below, to either side, were salons, dining rooms, and bedrooms. These pedestrian accommodations were subordinated in Ledoux's account to a literary description of the falls that took on almost pictorial dimensions, as the architect sought to rival, in his words, Guaspre, Poussin, Salvator Rosa, and

Ledoux, Bridge over the Loüe
River, perspective view. Engraving from Ramée, *Ledoux,*
pl. 109.

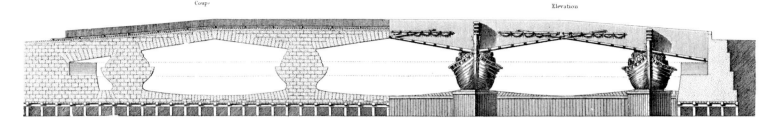

Coupe   Elevation

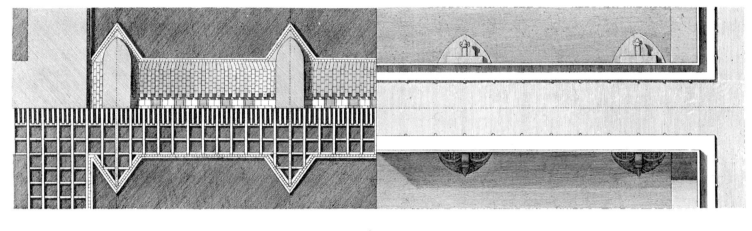

Plan des fondations   Plan des Parapets

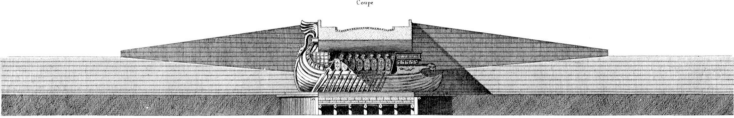

Coupe

Echelle de

Ledoux, Bridge over the Loüe
River, sections, elevation, and
plans. Engraving from Ramée,
Ledoux, pl. 108.

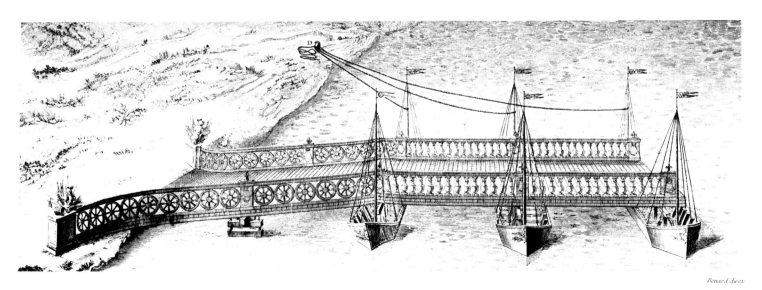

Benard direx

Military bridge of boats, perspective view. Engraving from
the *Encyclopédie,* "Charpente,"
pls. 198 and 199.

Emiliand Gauthey, Bridge,
Echavannes, detail of supports
with oval overflow channels.
Photograph from F. de Dartein,
Etudes sur les ponts, vol. 4
(Paris, 1909).

Ledoux, House of the Surveyors of the Loüe River,
perspective view. Engraving
from Ramée, *Ledoux,* pl. 110.

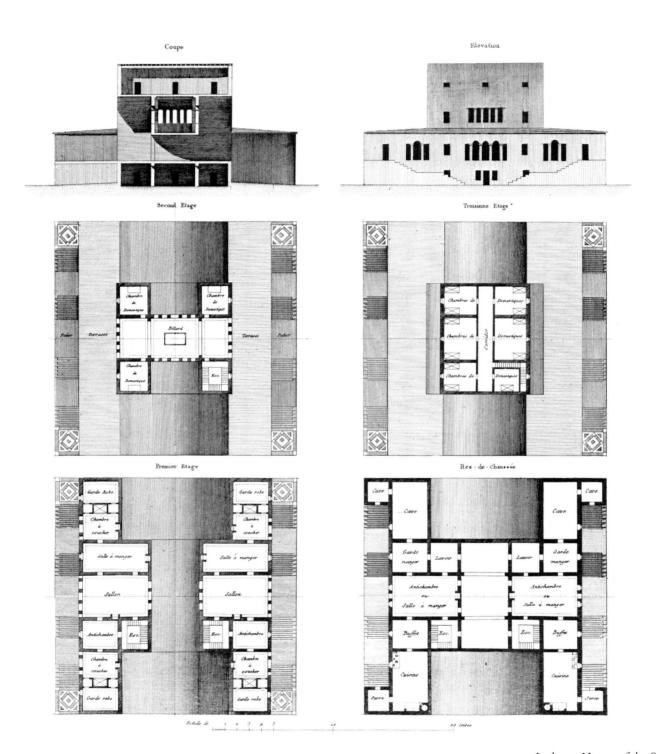

Coupe

Elevation

Second Etage

Troisieme Etage

Premier Etage

Rez-de-Chaussée

Echelle de 1 2 3 4 5 10 20 toises

Ledoux, House of the Surveyors of the Loüe River, section,
elevation, and plans of first,
second, third, and fourth
floors. Engraving from Ramée, *Ledoux,* pl. 110.

Bourdon. The torrents falling from the rocky cavern seemed to emulate those of Cocyx, their noise emulating the Fates themselves; tamed, the waters irrigated the countryside, "fertilizing the arid deserts."

Neptune grows old, and already he builds for his children, on these humid rocks, drained by art, a palace of surveillance. The fields could thus dispense with the accidental dews of the morning; the uncultivated soil will produce constantly, watered by the imperious filters that provoke industry. . . . The Architect commands; this delegate of nature searches for its mobile elements in order to trace for your eyes the effects of this coalesced strength.(51)

These apocalyptic visions of the forces of nature are strongly reminiscent of the catastrophic visions of an earlier engineer-architect, Nicolas-Antoine Boulanger, whose religious and antiquarian meditations on the nature of the gods, *L'antiquité dévoilée par ses usages,* had been published in 1766 with an introduction by Diderot himself. A former student of rhetoric at the Collège de Beauvais, a member of the Ponts et Chaussées working in Champagne, Lorraine, and Burgundy, Boulanger had also contributed eloquent articles to the *Encyclopédie* on society, the *corvée,* and, more significant, the flood, before his early death.[91] His thesis of a universal flood as the true "source" of all religious ceremonies, the origin of all myths, was, as befitted an engineer and amateur geologist, proved by reference to the nature of the earth's crust. Boulanger depicted in graphic terms the image of the earth rent by fissures, eroded by subterranean streams that broke through its surface, and devastated by volcanic activity; he was similarly lyrical in describing the postdiluvian reestablishment of arcadia and the gradual recovery of society. Following Boulanger's pleas for the acceptance of the laws of reason and nature that alone would impel the progress of the arts and sciences, Ledoux clearly joined the idea of the fertilizing torrents to the metaphor of artistic creation itself, imagining the architect as the natural force delegated by nature to harness its benefits, an almost Physiocratic circle formed between nature and art.

FROM THE VILLA TO THE COMMUNE

These palaces reflected in the limpid waters of the Brenta; these palaces respected by the corroding seasons; these masses corrected by the impassive scruple of knowledge; these details escaped from the barbarous flood, resuscitated for the instruction of fortunate ages; what have they produced for the popular classes? Nothing. (Prospectus, 16)

In the background of Ledoux's engraving of the Village of Maupertuis, overlooking the productive landscapes, the cottages and workshops of the estate, stand a number of villas, evidently Palladian in inspiration, geometrically purified and combined out of the repertory of elements already refined by Ledoux in the 1770s. One, in the far distance, seems to repeat the forms of the Villa Rotonda, with a dome and four porticoes; another, closer to the village, has a wide gabled roof intersected by an attic story with Serlianas. Both imply the presence of the landowner as a reforming and paternal force; both resituate Palladian precedents in a context of agricultural regeneration, thereby returning, so to speak, Palladianism to its own origins. What, in Ledoux's earlier work, had been the product of a general fashion for English neo-Palladianism, resulting in the pavilionate style of the Parisian *hôtels* and the occasional garden *fabrique* (such as the little "temple" house for the poet Charles-François Saint-Lambert at Ermenonville, built in the mid-1770s for Joseph-Florent Lenormand de Mézières), ten years later took on more serious, social connotations.

In this shift from style to substance, Ledoux was following the lead of his friend the Abbé Delille, whose preface to *Les jardins* of 1782 departed from the purely aesthetic delights of Saint-Lambert's *Les saisons* of 1769. Delille pointed to the positive benefits of the new fashion for "English" landscape design, arguing that landowners would be encouraged to take greater interest in the management of their estates: "The money that would have supported the artisans of luxury," he proposed with Physiocratic emphasis, "goes to sustain the cultivators, and wealth returns to the source."[92] Delille was himself following the tendency of treatises on landscape gardening, after the mid-1770s, to stress the economic and social advantages of estate management linked to aesthetic pleasure. Perhaps the most celebrated of these, and one that could not have failed to influence Ledoux, was written by the Marquis René de Girardin, friend and last patron of Rousseau, who had laid out his park at Ermenonville according to the visual codes of the *jardin anglais* and the literary sensibility of the gardens described in Rousseau's own *Nouvelle Héloïse*.

In his work *De la composition des paysages,* written in 1775 and published almost three years later, Girardin stressed the need to "embellish nature around dwellings by joining the useful to the agreeable," a commonplace requirement in the eighteenth century, but one given economic and social implications by the author's insistence on the design, not of gardens, but of "the countryside, its embellishment, cultivation, and subsistence." [93] Criticizing the enclosed aspect of the formal garden stemming from André Le Nôtre, Girardin espoused the English aesthetic of a view unencumbered by "intermediary obstacles" between garden and surrounding countryside. [94] But this visual extension would, for Girardin, simply reinforce social and agrarian reform. Having visited England, he noted with approval the structure of the typical village, still, despite the disruptive incursions of the enclosure movement, surrounded by common lands that "contributed much to the health of the community by allowing the free flow of purifying air. Surrounded by trees and fences, these common pastures were at the same time a place of amenity for walking and for the games of the village." [95] Inspired by the health of the countryside, the landowner would return to the management of his estates and there be inspired to raise the condition of his peasants: "The good man returns to purer air and, reunited with the joys of nature in the countryside, immediately senses that the suffering of his fellow men is the most unhappy spectacle for humanity." [96] Drawn from Rousseau's recollections of the villages around Neuchâtel, Girardin's vision of agrarian happiness linked the aesthetics of variety to the regeneration of agrarian society:

The habitations of happy and tranquil Cultivators will be built right in the midst of all their united and adjoining cultivated lands. By *this means their* fields *will become as easy to cultivate as their gardens; flocks of every kind, peaceful and without guardians, will spread out and graze in the fields beneath the wise eyes of their Master. And, in fact, could a more agreeable abode exist, and one more suited to the wise man, than that of a house of a simple and rural kind in the middle of a sweet and tranquil landscape?* [97]

Such a description might well apply to Ledoux's conception of Maupertuis and its adjoining village; informed by a typology of dwellings, from the cottage to the villa, generated from Palladian precedent reduced to simple geometrical formulae, it became the basis for a number of designs in the 1780s dedicated to the reform of the peasantry and the celebration of a reforming aristocracy.

In this context, Ledoux's projects for the Maison de Witt of 1781 and for the Château d'Eyguières probably of the same year may be seen as seigneurial villas, standing at the center of their territories as emblems of a Palladianism in the service of reform. Both were conceived as raised upon rusticated ground stories above irrigation canals and surrounded by landscapes drawn in the style of Dutch landscapists, populated with fishermen, shepherds, and cattle as if illustrating agricultural subjects in the *Encyclopédie*. In the more strictly Palladian Château d'Eyguières, with its centralized plan and four porticoes, Ledoux redeployed the motif of the natural grotto for its half-rustic, half-geometric podium that served as the entrance to a tunnel, lined by columns with square rustication, that covered the canal running beneath the house. This might well have been a branch of the Canal de Boisgelin, planned by the Archbishop of Aix, Jean de Boisgelin, and engineered by Fabre between 1784 and 1786. [98] Designed to bring water from the river Durance to Aix, Marseilles, and Tarascon, this canal was completed as far as Eyguières and the river Crau in 1784; the *château* projected by Ledoux might have been for the family of de Benault de Lubières, marquis of Roquemartine, or possibly for a member of the de Sade family, *grand seigneurs* of the region. It should be noted here that, despite the dispute between the Archbishop of Aix and Ledoux over the plans for the Palais de Justice after 1784, de Boisgelin was a serious proponent of agricultural reform and

Ledoux, House for M. de
Witt, 1781, perspective view.
Engraving by Sellier from
Ramée, *Ledoux,* pl. 195.

Ledoux, Château d'Eyguières,
perspective view. Engraving
from Ramée, *Ledoux,* pl. 258.

Ledoux, Episcopal Palace
of Sisteron, perspective view.
Engraving from Ramée,
Ledoux, pl. 68.

Physiocratic economics, a disciple of Vincent de Gournay and
sometime associate of Turgot, Trudaine, and Malesherbes.[99]

The picturesque and savage landscapes in which these
two *châteaux* were set may be compared to that surrounding
another project for de Boisgelin's entourage, a palace for the
Bishop of Sisteron, Louis-Jérôme Suffren de Saint-Tropez. In
Ledoux's engraving, the Alps, scattered with the traces of Roman and medieval aqueducts, fortifications, and modern Palladian villas, form a background to the town of Sisteron,
imagined as a Roman settlement with temples and coliseum,
in front of whose walls stands the episcopal palace. This similarly takes its place among the villa projects of the early
1780s, with its four Doric porticoes projecting on the axes of
a Greek cross, and a temple like rotunda, modified by Serli-
ans, lighting the central volume. Ledoux drew all these landscapes, like those some years later illustrating projects for the
ideal city of Chaux, to evoke his favorite scenic artists: Salvator Rosa, Nicolas Poussin, and his contemporaries Joseph
Vernet, Philippe-Jacques Loutherbourg, and Hubert Robert.
In them, Ledoux joined intimations of a natural sublime, of
wild and mountainous terrains subjected to storms and the
changing seasons, to a more domesticated vision of cultivation and productivity.

It is in the context of this program of agrarian reform,
dedicated to the return of the landowner to the land, that the
numerous country houses, designed in the late 1780s and
1790s and published in the first volume of *L'architecture* as an
integral part of the imaginary town of Chaux, should be considered. Bringing together the socioaesthetic ideal of the
expression of individual character and the typology of the
villa, each of these projects allied a detailed program of familial and professional needs to the transformational logic of
the nine-square plan. The result was, in Ledoux's terms, a
celebration of contrast and variety: "Variety," he emphasized,

"is so useful, so necessary, that one can look on it politically, as a public duty, a social acquisition, since it contributes toward the propagation of business; it can be attained more easily in the countryside by being related to different sites that produce contrasts. . . . "The plans and elevations of houses in the town and the countryside should be as varied as there are shapes; none should look like another, even though they are all composed in the same way: their distributions should differ only slightly relative to the fortune that dictates them." (110, 130)

Each house thus took its particular character from the needs of its occupants; each related to every other house in Chaux by virtue of its typical, neo-Palladian plan. Thus the House of a Physicist, or Inventor of Machines, on plates 19 and 20 required libraries, rooms for collections of mathematical and physical instruments and models of machines, furnaces, forges, woodworking shops, and laboratories. At its center Ledoux placed a study, which, he stressed, perhaps autobiographically, was "withdrawn from the noise inseparable from domestic chores, sheltered from the amorous caprices that could delay, or even annihilate, the inspiration of the moment"(83). Its exterior was simple, "suited to the modesty of a man who finds all glory in service to his fellows"; its rooms were small, without salons or *chambres de parade*. The House for a Grand Master of Waters and Forests, on plate 18, on the other hand, surrounded by gardens and picturesque in its composition of masses in the landscape, was furnished for large gatherings. Galleries and dining rooms were disposed around a square public salon that took up the center of the first floor; above, a *salon d'été,* again at the center, was enlarged by hemicycles on each side, each giving onto a colonnaded terrace overlooking the countryside. More complicated programs were spawned by familial problems: for example, that on plate 21 of *L'architecture* for the Monsieur ★★★ who desired a large house for solitude, while his wife carried on her voracious sociability in pavilions set beneath covered arcades ("Madame ★★★ lives in one of the pavilions; she loves to converse with a minor provincial relative who has much wit"(86), noted Ledoux with pleasant gossip); or that on plate 29 for the miserly father of a family that included three children, each insufferable—a narcissist, a sower of discord, and a daughter who had known neither love nor friendship. For them Ledoux provided four separate houses, at the corners of a large central courtyard, joined by covered galleries. Other houses were conceived for bankers and stockbrokers. One House for a Stockbroker, on plate 37, while conserving the nine-square grid in the distribution of apartments, reflected in its cylindrical form not only the turning fortunes of the broker's trade, but also his ownership of a factory for painted cloths, a visual pun on the calendar, or polishing cylinder of the *manufacture.* The design on plate 69 for a House for a Man of Letters was a gift from Ledoux to the Abbé Delille, a "temple of glory"(147) set in a Virgilian landscape. Other country houses were evidently the result of lost or suspended commissions—that on plates 22 and 23 for a Former Councillor to the Parlement of Besançon, for ex-

Ledoux, Country House for a Grand Master of Waters and Forests, perspective view, elevation, section, and plans of basement, first, second, and third floors. Engraving by Van Maëlle from Ledoux, *L'architecture,* pl. 18.

Elévation Géometrale

Coupe

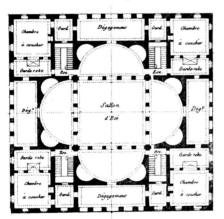

Premier Etage

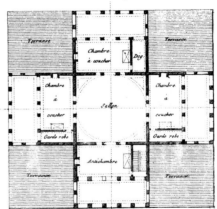

Second Etage

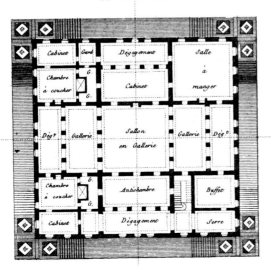

Rez - de - Chaussée

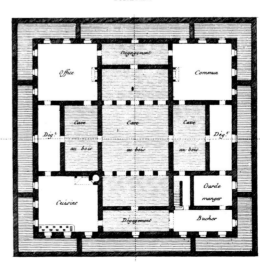

Souterrains

Echelle de 1 2 3 4 5 10 15 20 toises

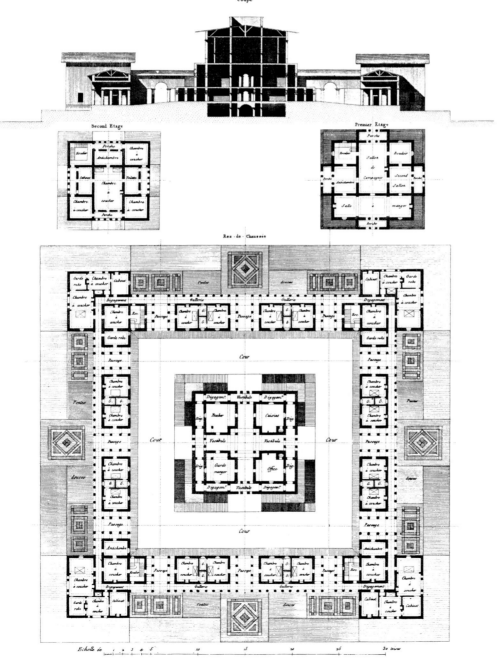

Ledoux, Country House for M.———, perspective view, section, and plans of first, second, and third floors. Engraving by Van Maëlle from Ledoux, *L'architecture,* pl. 21.

Ledoux, Country House for a Father with Three Children, perspective view, section, and plans of first, second, and third floors. Engraving by Van Maëlle from Ledoux, *L'architecture,* pl. 29.

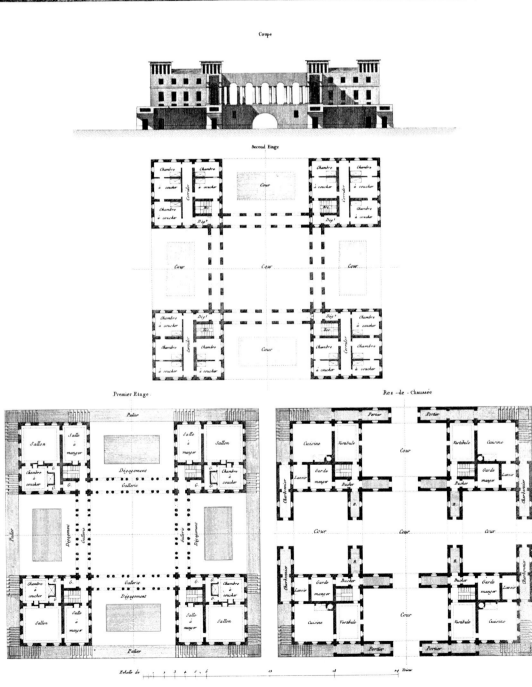

Elevation   Coupe.

Second étage   Troisième étage

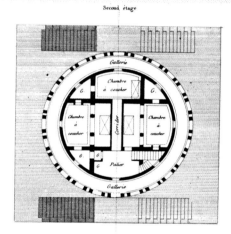

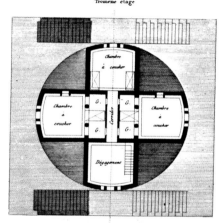

Premier étage   Rez-de-Chaussée

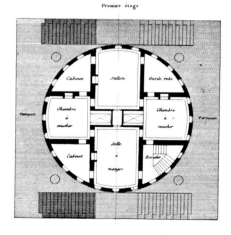

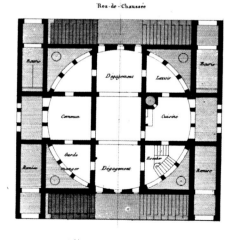

Echelle de

Ledoux, Country House for a
Stockbroker, perspective view,
elevation, section, and plans
of first, second, third, and
fourth floors. Engraving by
Van Maëlle and Simon from
Ledoux, *L'architecture,* pl. 37.

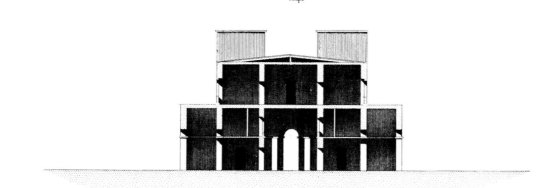

Coupe

Ledoux, Country House for
a Man of Letters (Abbé
Delille), perspective view,
section, and plans of first,
mezzanine, second, and attic
floors. Engraving from
Ledoux, *L'architecture,* pl. 69.

Premier Etage

Comble

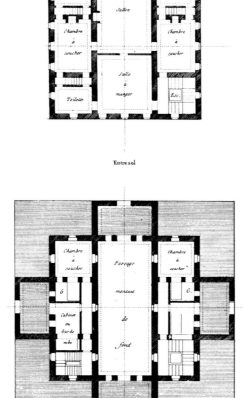

Entresol

Rez de Chaussée.

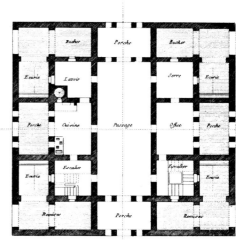

ample, or that on plate 46 for a Merchant of Besançon. Ledoux planned every one according to the possible variations on the Villa Rotonda scheme: some with central spaces, others (such as that illustrated on plate 55) with open, central stair halls; some with the central bay emphasized by rotundas or pedimented gables, others with the corners stressed by turrets or terraces. The simplest or most typical of all, on which the others seem to have been based, was that illustrated at the end of *L'architecture* on plate 123, in which Ledoux modified the Palladian villa form for bourgeois purposes: services took up the first floor and a ramp led to the second floor with its dining room, salon, and bedroom, while corner bedrooms for servants and a central billiard room, a newly fashionable game for the middle classes toward the end of the century, occupied the upper floor.

Finally, Ledoux invented another "type" for the houses of Chaux, one related to his stated need for a monumentality that would invest the territory with reminiscences of its former Gallo-Roman glory. These were a series of four double houses joined as pairs within larger architectural frames. On plates 26–28, Houses for Merchants, perhaps intimating the benefits of commercial competition, and Houses for Cabinet-makers were joined together by arcades, leaving a courtyard in the middle, as prototype row housing for the area of Chaux adjoining the Cannon Foundry. Similarly, and even more monumental, on plates 94 and 96 two Houses for Milliners, *marchandes des modes,* were combined beneath a single pedimented gable, arched in the middle and supported on a giant Doric order to form a double house in the shape of a triumphal arch. Ledoux dedicated a final exercise in this series to two of his architectural peers, Charles De Wailly and Marie-Joseph Peyre, whose difficulties with the first project for the Comédie-Française Ledoux chronicled. The Houses for Two Artists, illustrated on plates 95 and 96, consisting of two pavilions linked by arched arcades, graphically illustrated Ledoux's social and artistic ideal of individuality within community.

This ideal, which pervaded the quasi-Rousseauesque program of the imaginary city of Chaux, based on a version of the social contract—Ledoux called it the *pacte sociale*—was

embodied most completely in the project for a secular commune, the Cénobie. This community, named after the early cenobites (from the Greek meaning "common," "life in community," and used in Latin "coenobita," "coenobium," to refer to communal life), was imagined by Ledoux in the form of a unified dwelling with common facilities in a central pavilion joined by covered galleries to sixteen single-family apartments disposed four to each corner. The L-shaped layout of the apartments enclosed a service courtyard and terraces private to each group of four families, while the square central block housed communal kitchens on the first floor, a circular salon for recreation and billiards on the second floor, and, overlooking this high, domed space, a dining room with semicircular tables on a third, gallery, level. Designed in the late 1780s in the manner of the *barrières,* this "asylum of happiness" constructed in a forest clearing was an intimation of the ideal city of Chaux in microcosm. Ledoux described the idyllic life led by the cenobites, their natural piety and morality, reinforced by isolation in community and the support of nature:

Sixteen families lived together in the calm of the woods; they each had a complete apartment; all the needs of an isolated life—vegetable gardens, others for useful and medicinal plants, orchards, meadows, cultivated fields, others reserved for pastures, vineyards, winepresses, services, the communal salon, the dining room—all the accessories that ensure comfort and convenience were brought together. The heads of the family governed by trust; good example and feelings of piety propagated the lessons of wisdom more than any school of morality. Religion attached them to the laws of the country; they found in its consoling exercise a sweet and tranquil life, the hope for good and a fear of evil. Their religion was that which reason has bestowed on our own enlightened thinkers; they expressed their gratitude to the Creator and lived to accomplish the duties imposed by the Divinity: surrounded by all the virtues, they had no idea of evil.(181)

This mixture of primitive piety and eighteenth-century naturalism, the program of a self-supporting, agrarian commune organized under natural laws of production and consumption, informed by a belief in a rational Supreme Being, was,

Ledoux, Houses for Merchants (*above*) and Houses for Cabinetmakers (*below*), perspective views. Engraving by Van Maëlle and Simon from Ledoux, *L'architecture,* pl. 26.

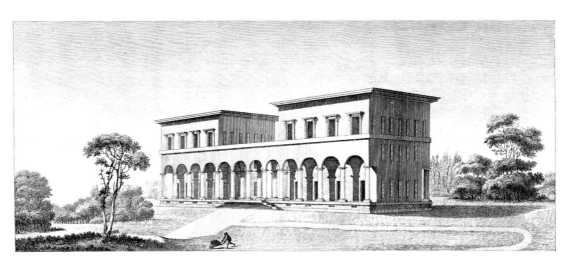

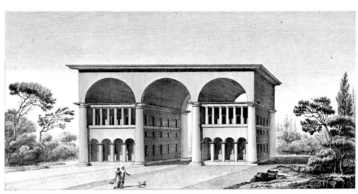

Ledoux, Houses for Milliners
(*above*) and Houses for Two
Artists (*below*), perspective
views. Engraving by Van
Maëlle from Ledoux, *L'architecture,* pl. 96.

Ledoux, Cénobie, perspective
view. Engraving from
Ledoux, *L'architecture,* pl. 89.

Ledoux, Cénobie, elevation,
plan of third floor, and section.
Engraving by Heluis from
Ledoux, *L'architecture,* pl. 91.

Elevation

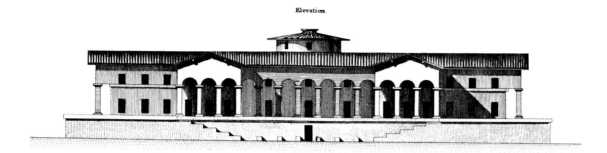

Plan du Second Etage.

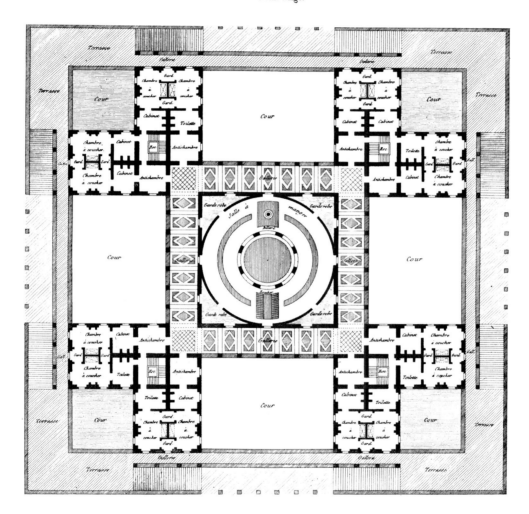

Coupe

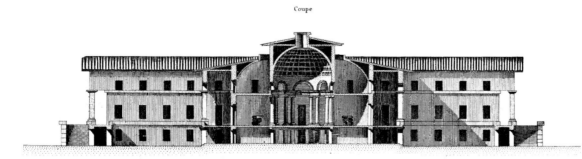

of course, common enough at the century's end—the Abbé Morelly and Rétif de la Bretonne elaborated versions of it— and it anticipated the full-fledged nostalgia of Charles Fourier and his contemporaries in the early nineteenth century.[100] But Ledoux, in describing his imaginary community, added a moral of his own that distanced him from progressive utopi- ans and economic theorists alike. This perfect example of so- ciability was, he noted, already a thing of the past, destroyed by the entry of a "modern philosopher, an economist" in its midst:

Happiness fled, unease commenced, everyone was anxious; the read- ing of a new social system occupied their minds; ideas crossed, mul- tiplying from different conceptions, and, as those who are not yet tainted by corruption are easy to lead astray when presented with something better under specious appearances, they took the art of reasoning for reason itself.(181)

Written after the Revolution, Ledoux's fable of lost in- nocence through the false application of rationalism in politics and society, his tale of *la jeunesse plus exaltée* breaking with the communal and "familial pact," was only a lightly veiled com- ment on the destruction of the natural order of the *ancien ré- gime*. A long disquisition on the political systems of the world, historical and contemporary, from the Athenian oli- garchy to the feudal regimes of the east, decrying corruption and despotism, ended "En France . . ."(182). Dispersed by a vain search for a better life, wandering like some modern An- acharses, the cenobites, in Ledoux's post-Revolutionary fan- tasy, finally returned to their ancestral home, "returned to principle":

Worn out by a voyage as arduous as it was without rewards, our cenobites searched in vain in the Forest of Chaux for the first habi- tation of their infancy; all had disappeared, there remained only vast ruins: they recognized then that the better life, after which they had run, is no more valuable than the good that we possess, in ourselves; that, independent of the vacillations of the globe, it is almost always the enemy of the happiness that is at our disposition.(183)

For Ledoux, abruptly withdrawn from political influence and forced into premature retirement after 1789, the imaginary reconstruction of such ruins became his only solace, con- vinced that this act of "restoration," at once historical and po- litical, would be recognized by future generations as it was scorned by his own.

SPACES OF SOCIABILITY

There I see true citizens, obliging and grateful, united and happy; there are pleasant recreations and noble amusements; there, merit is amiable and willing; there, the talents are civilized; there reigns that exquisite taste preferable to crude science; there the mind enjoys the rights of sovereignty and politeness tempers domination; there wis- dom shines—not an unsociable or savage wisdom, but wisdom em- bellished with enjoyment, the enemy of pompous appearance and artificial airs; there, finally, reason presides, not that phantom so often mistaken for it, but humanized reason.

Abbé Marquet, *Discours sur l'esprit de société*[101]

INITIATORY FORMS

The idea of a space that would, so to speak, construct and reform social mores by means of its particular shape and sym- bolic representation was in the eighteenth century deeply embedded in the ideology and practice of bourgeois and aris- tocratic sociability. The image of a civilized gathering, unit- ing the estates, the arts, and the professions, dominated popular texts on sociability and pervaded the debates of the mid-century *philosophes*. The salon, the club, the academy, the café, and the lodge all contributed to the general sense that a spirit of political, moral, and artistic improvement might be fostered by an extension of the "arts of sociability" through- out the upper and middle classes and, consequently, among *le peuple*. As Diderot wrote, "From the principle of sociability there flow, as from a spring, all the laws of society."[102] Such a principle, founded on natural laws, was understood to inform meetings of dining societies as well as rustic festivals; intimate in the private salon of a rich Fermier Général, public in the organized ritual of religious and secular fêtes, sociability would, it was hoped, lead to that triumph of *bonheur* dreamed of by utopian and political thinkers alike. "If man is sociable," concluded the Abbé Pluquet in his essay on sociability of 1767, "morality, legislation, and politics should have no other principles than those of sociability, which he receives from Nature." [103] And if man was by nature sociable, then the environment of sociability, the space that surrounded and protected the circle, would, if properly conceived, support and possibly bring about the bonds of friendship and fraternity. It was not for practical reasons alone that the definition of specialized places for meeting, their decoration and planning, became in the later part of the century a recognized part of the architect's practice. The café, the salon, the academy, the school, the Masonic lodge all took their place in the repertory of types emerging as necessary for a bourgeois and professional elite, imitative of the spaces of traditional aristocratic gatherings, but with the critical difference of specialization.

Of these spaces none became more paradigmatic nor more idealized than that of the Masonic lodge. In the last thirty years of the century, following the consolidation of Freemasonry under the aegis of the Grand Orient in 1773, the lodge, as built and as imagined, attained the status of a type dedicated to the formation of a happy society. It housed a community dedicated to brotherhood and mutual support; its layout was calculated to inform and structure rituals of initiation and festivity that themselves were thought to embody the principles of sociability and bring them to life. Its architectural references were drawn from the ideology of the community, itself derived from the old "operative" Masonic charges, and utilized the Temple of Solomon as metaphor and iconographical source in order, as it was said, to "return" to the original and natural forms of social life. The Masonic lodge was also the weekly and monthly gathering place for the most fashionable and extensive society in the *ancien régime:* in Paris alone some eighty lodges, with a recorded membership of over ten thousand, were active between 1773 and the Revolution. And this counted only those "orthodox" lodges directly affiliated with the Grand Orient; beyond these were thousands of members of the schismatic Grand Lodge together with hundreds of breakaway and occultist societies and their counterparts, the women's "Lodges of Adoption." The life of the lodges touched almost every level of society, lending its discourse and symbolism to the general utopianism of writers, philosophers, and architects and being imitated by artisans and workers in the countryside and forest. [104]

For architects, especially, membership in a lodge took on a particular significance, beyond the patronage opportunities and general conviviality common to all brothers. The very terms in which the Masons couched their rituals and social aims were "architectural," and the architecture of the lodge itself played a major role in the life of the group. The spaces of ritual initiation and fraternal celebration were seen not only as theatrical backdrops to club life, but as the instruments by which that life turned into a species of lived utopia, eventually to be extended into a more general concern for the reform of society as a whole.

As we have noted, Ledoux, while not inscribed on any of the surviving membership lists of the regular lodges, was intimate with many architect-Freemasons and associated with patrons who were themselves officers in the Grand Orient. Familiar with this ambiance from the early 1770s, he was also drawn in the 1780s to more unorthodox secret societies. According to the evidence of the English writer William Beckford, visiting Paris in the spring of 1784, Ledoux was an architect for, and participant in, the rituals of a strange sect that met outside Paris in the grounds of a *château* apparently redesigned by Ledoux for the purpose. [105] In this account, written in the form of a letter to his sister-in-law, the former Louise Pitt-Rivers, Beckford described an experience that he was later to elaborate in detail in a number of drafts that remained unpublished at his death. [106]

Beckford, who, as his biographer J. W. Oliver has noted, moved in circles that were close to those of Ledoux—Hubert Robert, the young Comte de Buffon, Jean-Joseph de La Borde, Madame Necker, and the Emperor Joseph II—had already been introduced to the architect on a previous visit. [107] In 1784, he visited Ledoux's *atelier,* recalled as "one of the strangest mock-palaces you ever saw," and spent some time leafing through the renderings of Ledoux's public and private commissions: *hôtels,* follies, projects for the ideal city of Chaux, and preliminary designs for the *barrières* ("which from their massive, sepulchral character look more like the entrances of a Necropolis, a city of the dead than of a city so damnably alive as this confounded capital"). Beckford remembered a number of these drawings:

Some of them are glorious—many ridiculously grotesque and not a few very like what Sir John Vanburgh would have invented had he lived at the present period—triumphal chimneys, and heroic smoke-ducts extending their long lines over arcaded walls more than substantial enough to bear them.

Among them, by accident, a particularly elaborate design fell from the pile, "a beautiful drawing of a ceiling in colors heightened with gold." To the author's surprise, Ledoux was reluctant to discuss this project:

He put on a look of mysterious gravity and . . . replied in an altered tone of voice, "This is the ceiling of the most sumptuous apartment I ever erected—it belongs to a revered friend of mine, whose thoughts, words and actions are not of the common world—his habits, his appearance, his garb are peculiar—very peculiar—so much so indeed that he never wishes to manifest himself—unless to persons born under peculiar influences."

Persuaded that Beckford possessed certain hermetic powers—he had reportedly "mesmerized" a lion in the Jardin des Plantes shortly before—Ledoux, however, agreed that they might visit the house in question, subject to a rule that the young Englishman would have to renounce all questions as to the locality and nature of the premises. The following day, just before dusk, the two were conducted in a closed carriage to a site outside the city; the journey, as Beckford could recall, lasted over an hour, with many turns, until they finally alighted in front of a long, greyish, moss-eaten stone wall, "like the wall of a burying ground." Entering through a gate, Beckford found himself "in a vast space entirely occupied by wood-piles, some of enormous dimensions and very lofty, others with thatched roofs acutely pointed resembling views

I have seen of Tartarian villages." These woodpiles, apparently pyramidal forebears of Ledoux's designs for woodcutter's shelters, were lined up in seemingly endless avenues; the landscape was uncannily silent, save for the incessant chirping of sparrows wheeling in clouds in the cold, clear sky. The two visitors passed down one of the longer alleys, in the shadow of the timber piles, and came to a halt in front of the largest pyramid. Its low door was covered by a few rough boards; Ledoux, whom Beckford begins to refer to in Masonic terminology as his "conductor," knocked twice on the door, which sprang open with a sharp whistling sound. They entered into a gloomy vestibule, "more like a barn than a hall" lit only from leaded casements in the roof. Groping their way through this hall they came to another small door, knocked again, and were admitted into a small, plain room, "like the chamber of a cottage with its deal table and straw-bottomed chairs overlooking a little garden surrounded by well-clipped hedges." The gate of this small, rustic cottage led into a better-furnished apartment. Thenceforth Ledoux no longer made easy conversation, "nor did he smile—all his courtly blandishments seemed to have forsaken him." Advancing into a high, square room, decorated with marble pilasters and lit from above, Beckford noted a large white cockatoo standing on a high, gilded perch in one corner. The two then passed through a tapestry curtain into the major apartment, the salon. Beckford immediately recognized "the coved ceiling, richly painted with mythological subjects," as that he had seen earlier in Ledoux's drawing. Under a highly decorated chimneypiece a fire blazed, giving off exotic scents. In front of this aromatic fire a formal-looking old man of small stature but imposing presence sat on a strangely shaped, elaborately worked chair: "He was habited in an antiquated court suit of changeable colored silk—his severe, forbidding countenance was overspread with the livid paleness of a dead body, but his eyes were as the eyes of the living—most vivid and most piercing." With no acknowledgment of their greeting, the old man bade his visitors examine the room and its decorations. Every recess was ornamented with elaborate armories of brass and tortoiseshell. Beckford focused his attention on an

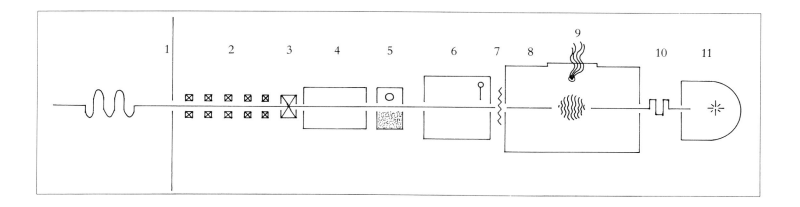

enormous bronze urn raised upon a green porphyry base, with large handles in the form of tritons and nereïds, filled to the brim with a transparent liquid. The red setting sun played on its surface. But as the old man approached, Beckford saw that "the water, becoming agitated, rode up in waves. Upon the gleaming surface of the undulating fluid, flitted by a succession of ghastly shadows somewhat resembling the human form in the last agonies of dissolution." As these horrible visions passed before Beckford's eyes, he had the presence of mind, not without a little English sangfroid in his terror, to exclaim, "This is most frightfully extraordinary!" The old man turned on him with a chilling voice, and Ledoux, shaking his head, refused to answer his questions. When he turned back to the giant laver, the water had subsided. At once the sound of deep voices chanting in harmony rose up from beyond the salon; the old man motioned for Beckford and Ledoux to pass through the doors, which again "opened sympathetically as it were." Ledoux encouraged the writer forward, speaking of the staircase of which he was proud. He led Beckford up the stairs, which reminded Beckford of the Scala Regia of the Vatican, and into a tribune that overlooked a chapel. "Day was closing in, and darkness beginning to prevail, when suddenly a stream of light, such as might be supposed to emanate from the tapers of an altar, shone forth through the perforations of a lofty screen of carved work." The sonorous voices chanted psalms, including passages that referred to the fall of the mighty and the exaltation of the meek, while Beckford knelt on the cushions of the gallery, lost in mournful revery. Remembering the visions in the urn, he was prompted to recite the Lord's Prayer; this broke the spell, and Ledoux appeared troubled. In response to Beckford's questions he admitted that "this truly sacred edifice is set apart for a high, tho' not entirely a religious purpose," but confessed his disappointment that Beckford had not followed the ceremony to the end: "You have lost an opportunity of gaining knowledge which may never return. Had you undergone a slight ceremony we were on the point of proposing, you might have asked any question, however abstruse, with the certainty of its being resolved. You would not only have

Diagram of the lodge described by William Beckford. Drawing by A. Vidler.

Legend:
1. Wall
2. Woodpiles
3. Pyramidal entrance
4. Barnish hall
5. Antechamber and cottage
6. Room with the white cockatoo
7. Curtain
8. Main salon
9. Aromatic fire and giant laver
10. Grant stair
11. Tribune and chapel.

Ledoux, Chapel of Bourneville, section. Engraving from Ramée, *Ledoux*, pl. 296.

heard—but seen things ineffable." Silently, they retraced their steps; the fire had dimmed, the bronze vase had disappeared and with it the old man's chair and the white bird. In the open air, they were met by a servant with a lantern, who led them through "the dreary labyrinth of wood-piles" to the gate and their carriage.

The ceremony described by Beckford, a mixture of Mesmerist and Freemasonic ritual, was in no way uncommon to the secret societies of the 1780s. The symbolism of the pyramid, reputed entrance to the underworld; the giant laver, replica of that which stood before Solomon's Temple; the stages of initiation conceived as so many "tests" to be undergone before the aspirant, led by his "conductor," was admitted to the inner circles, all formed part of the elaborate and eclectic apparatus of the lodges, as they drew their scenography from Egyptian, medieval, mystical, and biblical accounts of initiations. But, as Beckford described this particular lodge, it is evident that Ledoux, the architect-initiate, had added another level of symbolism to the ritual, confirmed by the sequence of spaces leading to the final sanctum. From the dead landscape of woodpiles to the chapel, Ledoux had mirrored the entire history of civilization in architecture. The woodpiles, like some primitive village, were evidently symbolic of origins, the abandoned huts of early man; the hut-pyramid marked an Egyptian stage; the "barnish hall" seemed to signify the Middle Ages, home of chivalry and magic; the cottage, of a Rousseauesque simplicity, no doubt referred to the eighteenth-century ideal of natural life and rustic morality; the cubic room with the white bird denoted the beginning of civilization, confirmed in the decorations of the eighteenth-century salon. But the end of the rite was, in some sense, beyond civilization, in a spiritual realm formed out of light in darkness, the sublime vision of a new society. In Ledoux's design, architecture formed the instrument for provoking appropriate states of mind along this ritual route, and its symbolic reification.

The design Beckford described, while it cannot be located with any certainty, even as its patron remains a mystery and its secret society unknown, seems entirely credible as a

work of Ledoux. The reference to the pyramidal woodpiles are consistent with the rural "lodges" for woodcutters already discussed; the stair seems to echo that of Bénouville, the salon and chapel those of Maupertuis. Perhaps the work that most approaches Beckford's description was the Château of Bourneville, redesigned before 1785 for the treasury official Praudeau de Chemilly, together with extensive landscaping and *fabriques,* including a chapel, a "Temple terminating the view of the garden of Zephyr and Flora," and a monumental entrance flanked by two Doric columns. The domed chapel, with its tribune and hidden crypt, and the double columns at the entry of the park, reminiscent of the two columns always standing at the commencement of the Freemasonic ritual (emblematic of the columns of Jachim and Boaz before the Temple of Solomon), would have perfectly corresponded to the ritual remembered by Beckford. The English connections of Praudeau would have made a visit to his newly refurbished territory entirely natural. Such identification, however, must remain tentative; what is important in Beckford's account does not depend on them.

For, from the mid-1780s, Ledoux drew on such Freemasonic imagery for his increasingly idealized designs for *fabriques* and monuments, and by the time of the Revolution he was incorporating the symbolic forms, ritual paths, and even the idealized "type" of the Masonic lodge into the utopian institutions of Chaux. Indeed, in one sense, this utopia, dedicated to the realization of a society of happiness, joined by bonds of brotherhood and confirmed by the architecture of its specialized places for association, may be read as the

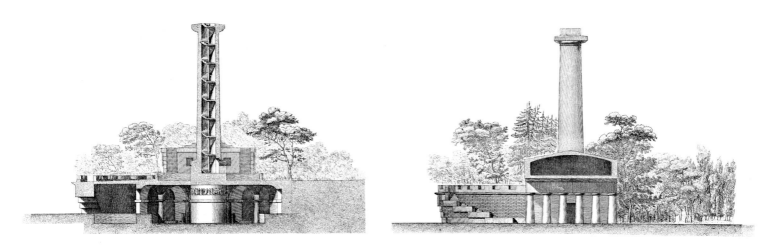

Ledoux, Gate to the park of
Bourneville, elevation and sec-
tions. Engraving from Ramée,
Ledoux, pls. 294 and 295.

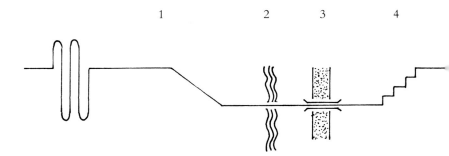

natural extension of Freemasonic ideals into the business of social reform. At the Revolution, while the lodges dissolved themselves in the general enthusiasm for a new social order in the process of becoming, and their iconography became a part of the festivals and processionals staged to commemorate the grand public acts of the regime, Ledoux, refused a practice and a living, turned to a more private vision of such generalized Masonry. In this he found sustenance in the architecture of the lodges, as prototypes for a social architecture not yet invented, as experiments in the welding of form and society on every level, ideological, instrumental, and symbolic.[108]

THE ROUTE TO UTOPIA

Punctuating the long and heterogeneous text of *L'architecture,* as if cut up and inserted at random, are the fragments of a utopian discourse, written in the manner of an eighteenth-century travel romance somewhere between Swift's *Gulliver's Travels* and Rousseau's *Rêveries du promeneur solitaire.* Ledoux's "traveler" describes a visit to Franche-Comté, to the *saline* and to its imaginary context, the ideal city of Chaux. In places the narrative is continuous, as in the preliminary sections of the book, where the traveler recounts the journey from Lyons to Chaux, by way of Salins and the aqueduct, and where his discussions with the "inspector," or "conductor of works," lead to aesthetic debates over the apparently strange architecture of the bridge, the graduation building, and the *saline* itself. Elsewhere the narrative is discontinuous, breaking off for more than twenty pages at a time to give way to programmatic descriptions, apostrophic eulogies, meditations, and even short stories; but it always returns, generally as an awakening at a fresh dawn that prefaces a new experience in the utopia of Chaux. In this way Ledoux, omnivorous reader of voyages, oriental tales, and utopian fantasies, self-consciously claimed for his own picaresque sequence of architectural images the status of a literary *récit,* as if matching, monument by monument, his own designs against those of ancient Greece discovered by the Abbé Barthélemy's fictional traveler in the *Voyage du jeune Anacharsis en Grèce.*

The narrative of the journey, so picaresquely elaborated as the "plot" of *Joseph Andrews* or of *Tom Jones,* took on in the later eighteenth century much of the apparatus of the "initiatory" routes staged with so much ceremony in the lodges. The carefully structured ramblings in the mountains of Rousseau's Saint Preux were more than allegories of interior, moral transformations: they were virtual instruments of that transformation achieved through the medium of the natural landscape itself. The journey through life of Goethe's Wilhelm Meister was an equally initiatory experience, a *bildung* that echoed the Freemasonic initiations of the Society of the Tower. Similarly, the characters of de Sade's novels, who, as Roland Barthes remarked, seemed always to be going on journeys, sought escape from their contemporary moral world into a defensible realm of natural immorality, a bounded space for the enactment of unbounded liberties. In each of these narratives the environment of the journey played an active role; each stage was marked by a place, of specific character, that stimulated or confirmed the mental or social state arrived at. For Saint Preux, the ascent of a mountain acted to reinforce an almost transparent communion with nature, where inner mental life and outer nature were in harmony; for Wilhelm Meister, each experience operated a decisive change in his own character; for the libertines of the *120 Jours,* the passage across the Rhine, through dark and wild forests, across infinitely deep ravines, into a realm surrounded by impassable peaks and defended by moats, doors, and tunnels, represented a withdrawal from civilization as total as if reversing the progress of culture itself, returning it to absolute, savage nature.[109]

For Ledoux the device of the journey, presented at the outset of his "rambling" text, served a slightly different but related purpose. On one level, it operated as a unifying narrative form, recounted by a single voice, not that of the author or architect but of a fictional *voyageur,* which could weld together reality—the landscape, factories, and built work of Ledoux in Franche Comté—and utopia—the realm of imagined institutions and activities of a city not yet built. The journey presented reality in a fictional guise and fiction as

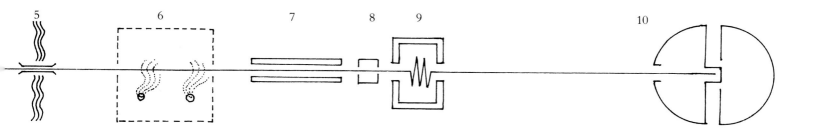

"discovered" reality. On another level, as in the Abbé Terrasson's *Séthos* or Beckford's *Vathek,* it provided a ritualized approach to the ideal city, a sequence of experiences and dreams that prepared the visitor, so to speak, for entry into this privileged realm.[110] Ledoux's ideal city of happiness, like the Freemasonic *société du bonheur,* was conceived as "a world isolated from the world," protected by environmental and institutional barriers whose overcoming rendered the newly received inhabitant worthy of his place.

The descent of Ledoux's narrator into the underground caves beneath the Saline de Salins was followed by a visit to the site of the new Saline de Chaux.[111] The first monument to be registered was the Bridge over the Loüe River, where the traveler met a young artist, overseer of the works (Ledoux in fictional disguise), from whom he drew out the rationale for so strange a series of architectural fantasies. He next encountered the symbolic form of the House of the Surveyors of the Loüe River, guarding and directing the waters that irrigated the valley; he then visited the graduation building and the carpenter's workshop close by. Struck by the immense length of the water-filled structure, the traveler fell into a dream, noted above, of a Babylonian city in its last period of decadent decline. The magnificence of its fine arts and the finery of its women stood in sharp contrast to is corrupt institutions, sightless sages, and scandalous houses of pleasure. Here philosophy had led not to the purification of morals but to their destruction; eloquence and rhetoric, as in the first Babel, had become meaningless. The city, in the traveler's dream, was suddenly destroyed by a flash of lightning; and from its ashes a new city was built, on the stable foundations of commercial abundance and morality, with an architecture that sustained both. This reverie, resembling the Masonic legend of the fall of Babylon and its reconstruction by the associated arts, was Ledoux's prelude to the entry into the ideal city proper, by way of an institution that acted not only as the "gate" but also as the guardian of moral values for the protected realm of Chaux: the Hospice.

Diagram of the "route" to Chaux as allegorically described by Ledoux. Drawing by A. Vidler.

Legend:
1. Descent into the "underworld" of the Saline de Salins
2. Crossing the "Styx"
3. Bridge over the infernal marsh
4. Ascent into the light
5. Bridge over the River of Life (the Loüe River)
6. Dream of the fall of Babel and the reconstruction of the world by means of architecture
7. "Noah's Ark," or the graduation building
8. Revelation of the architect
9. Hospice, or initiation into the ideal society
10. Gate to the city of Chaux, through the grotto, leading to the chapel in the center of the director's "temple."

Ledoux, Buildings by the
Loüe River, Chaux. Detail
from the perspective view of
the bridge over the Loüe
River. Engraving by Bovinet
from Ramée, *Ledoux,* pl. 109.

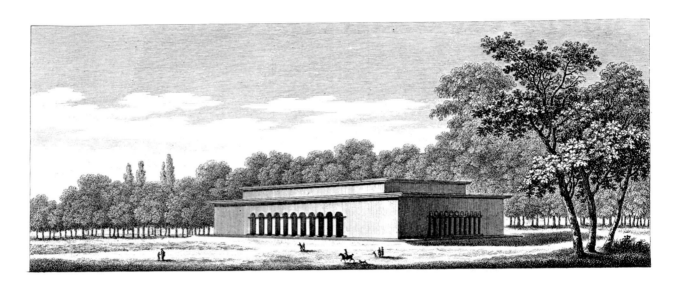

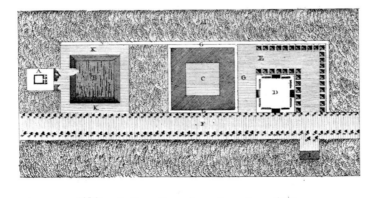

Ledoux, Hospice, Chaux, per-
spective view and site plan.
Engraving from Ramée,
Ledoux, pl. 94.

Legend:
A. Pagoda
B. Purifying pool
C. Hospice
D. Bazaar
E. Rue de Bazaar
F. Public road
G. Surrounding space
H. Fragrant woods
 I. Director's house
K. Covered walks
L. Covered road.

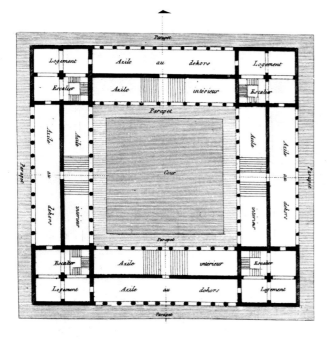

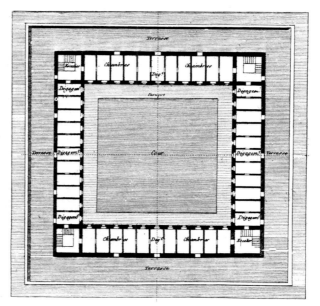

Ledoux, Hospice, elevation,
section, and plans of first and
second floors. Engraving from
Ramée, *Ledoux,* pl. 94.

Unlike the workhouses or hospices of contemporary
France, Ledoux's Hospice was envisaged as an oriental conceit, an anti-hospice, evoked in slightly mocking vein as a
playful criticism of contemporary poor-law administration,
specifically the *ateliers du charité* that had caused so much damage to the *barrières*. A dream fantasy, an Indian fable, perhaps
influenced by Beckford, this design served for Ledoux to contrast a wondrous ideal society against eighteenth-century reality. He raised the image of "le cortège du riche Nabab de
Golconde," traveling with a crowd of slaves, finding shelter
in a grove of palms, setting up camp among the trees like the
old retainers of the Café Militaire, hanging their trophies on
the trunks, enjoying the pleasures of the bazaar. Travelers to
the domain of Chaux, who might also have read the history
of the East, would enjoy equal rights to shelter. For them
Ledoux designed a complete oasis: pagoda, sacred pool, bazaar, fragrant woods, together with the hospice itself, directly
modeled on the description of a caravanserai in the *Encyclopédie.* A walled enclosure around a central, fortified courtyard
surrounded by arcades on the ground floor and apartments
on the upper stories, the Hospice was also reminiscent of
many workhouses of the epoch, with their square exercise
courts surrounded by cells. The imaginary function of this
structure thereby blended oriental fantasy with social
surveillance.

Here the good and the evil are equally received for the first night; but first thing in the morning, the good continue tranquilly on their journey; the others are questioned, found out, and condemned to assist in our public works. Their ill will is imprisoned and they render to society what they wanted to steal from it. The day of repentance will come (64)

Ledoux thus employed an Arabian Nights romance as a fictional cover for a social filter, an institution that would guarantee the ideal city against the intrusion of undesirable inhabitants, on the one hand, and act as a reformatory, on the other: "The hospice, always open to the traveler, will, by its useful purifications, only allow entry to the frontiers for the man worthy of penetrating therein" (3). As in any workhouse or prison, the "director" had the power to interview, judge, and finally pardon. Divested of his Oriental trappings, he would appear with similar powers at the center of Bentham's Panopticon. As in the Panopticon, the aim of the Hospice was to "purify the social order"; but unlike Bentham's ideal prison, it worked first by seduction—"by the example of charity"—and only secondly by coercion—"by changing vicious inclinations with the example of work and subjecting licentiousness to the laws of subordination"(64).

Ledoux couched his orientation in the terms of many eighteenth-century *contes arabes,* from Montesquieu to Diderot and thence to Beckford; indeed, the hospice itself bore a direct resemblance to that described in *Vathek,* which carried an inscription over its door at once romantic and hermetic: "This is the asylum of pilgrims, the refuge of travellers, and the repository of secrets from all over the world."[112] Its function, however, was entirely transformed. As a hospice and not a caravanserai, it served, on the boundaries of Ledoux's city of virtue, to protect and guard; in the heart of the forest, haunt of thieves and vagabonds, it stood as an emblem and instrument of morality: "Who can doubt that the views of humanity are admirably placed at the center of forests where crime has too often based its hopes of impunity?"(64). While Ledoux had insisted that *within* his ideal city the philosophical virtues and healthy morality of the citizens would render a prison or workhouse unnecessary, on its *boundaries* a workhouse would have the essential task of filtering and reforming aspiring inhabitants. After this, inside, the only task of institutions would be to sustain and extend the morality of an already moral populace.

MORALIZING INSTITUTIONS

The first of these institutions to be introduced in Ledoux's text was the Pacifère. An acknowledged neologism, it stood in Ledoux's city, for the law, for its beneficent administration, and for its calculated effects.[113] Conceived in opposition to the terrifying vision of ancient justice and barbaric criminality, where "in these sad and somber halls tribunals are set up or severe and pale judges are seated" (114), and out of a refusal to follow the fashion for building useless garden *fabriques* dedicated to an equally useless abstract idea like *bonheur,* the Pacifère represented a conciliatory justice fairly meted out among the reasonable citizens of Ledoux's philosophic city:

Ledoux, Pacifère, Chaux, section, plans of first and second floors, and perspective view. Engraving by Van Maëlle from Ledoux, *L'architecture,* pl. 40.

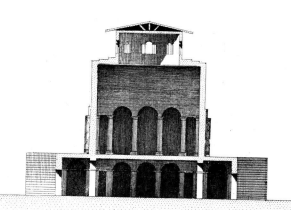

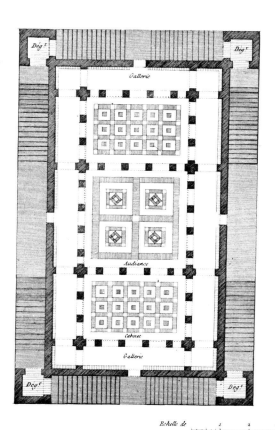

Galleric

Audiance

Cabinet

Galleric

Echelle de   1   2   3   4   5   10 toises

Salle

Publique

Audiance

Cabinet

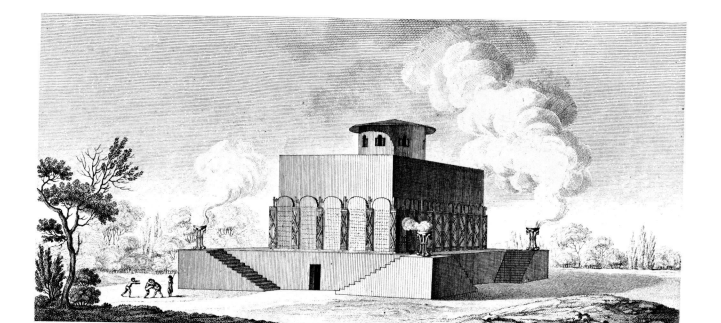

"The newborn town, each building of which I want to motivate, will perhaps be inhabited by less criminal men, over whom reason and their own interest will exercise some power" (114). Mediation was to take the place of imprisonment. Thus there would be no need for the sublime and terrifying images of power and retribution assayed in the prisons of Aix, that physiognomy of "the terrible lair where Themis, sword in hand, renders justice to men" (113). The counsels of "a wise and conciliatory arbiter" would be enough to restore the momentary lapses into jealousy and self-interest that were the only possible crimes in Chaux.

The Pacifère consisted of a rectangular, two-story building, its main tribunal raised upon a one-story podium. On the ground floor were the offices and waiting rooms; on the tribunal level a *salle publique* led into a square, central audience chamber, lit from above by a cylindrical lantern. Its form participated in what Ledoux described as an entire *système symbolique*," inherited from the iconography of antiquity and the Renaissance: "The form of a cube is the symbol of Justice; she is represented seated on a square stone prescribing punishments for vice and rewards for virtue" (115). Such a form, abstract and allegorical, was not, of course, of the same order of representation as the more pictogrammatic compositions for the rustic population. Rather, its function was unmistakably characterized by the addition to its bare surfaces of attributes that surrounded the outer walls of the main tribune: tablets, in the shape of mosaic stones, on which were literally inscribed the principles of the new justice, "the principal maxims of the moralists, ancient and modern," together with the names of philosophers and lawmakers such as Socrates, Plato, and Marcus Aurelius. Framing each tablet was a monumental order in the form of the Roman symbol of unity, the fasces. The central tablet at each end of the tribunal also acted as the entry door, giving the effect when closed of a hermetically sealed, secret chamber. On each corner of the podium tripods held up braziers, whose eternal flames recalled Roman precedents.

But the resulting effect was far from evocative of classical types, or of antique architecture of any kind: "silent" and as "simple as the laws that are pronounced therein," the forms referred more to some new and severe rationalist lodge than to any restored vision of an antique temple. In plan and in outside massing, the form of the lodge was unmistakable, at once an abstraction of Solomon's Temple and a symbol of the *asyle* to which any Deist lodge might aspire. Inside the Pacifère, the reticulated pavement, the three arches separating audience chamber from public waiting hall, the hidden source of light immediately above the judge's head, all reinforced the Masonic image.[114] Ledoux here gave didactic force to the tripartite system of Masonic virtues and an active, mediating role to the master/judge seated on the tribunal: "With a pleasing and sweet voice he will reconcile their reciprocal interests, force them to embrace each other in front of him, and enjoin them to the love of justice and peace"(114). In the perspective view, Ledoux depicted two citizens outside in the forest clearing in the act of deciding their argument, under the watchful eyes of their seconds, by the simple and direct means of unarmed combat—a sentence handed down by the "pacifier" within.

Ledoux's second institution of moralization, the House of Union, carried in its title a direct reference to the notion of brotherhood. "Union," claimed Ledoux, in a particularly Masonic passage, "is so necessary to maintain order and hasten the flights of virtue that nature itself, by offering us its marvels, has dictated its indefeasible laws"(117). Found throughout nature, union had its apotheosis in the human form, building all parts into a whole; stronger than simple "cohesion" or even than familial relations, it was the strength and glory of empires and societies. Its formal analogue was, for Ledoux, mirrored in the plan of Chaux with all radials tending toward the common center of a universal circle. Accordingly, the House of Union was entirely centralized, a symbol of totality. Its cubic form was raised on a base of pyramidally ascending stairs; open arcades surrounded the central *salle d'union* on the first floor; living rooms, studies, and bedrooms occupied the second floor; internal galleries and a central salon lit from above by a cylindrical lantern took up the top floor. Wrapped around the upper level of the outer walls, fasces "that sustain harmony" again called attention to the character of the monument.

In Ledoux's imagination, this institution would not simply symbolize union, for "principles are valuable only insofar as they are put into practice" (117). The building would provide a didactic example of union in action, its walls inscribed with maxims and commonplaces from every textbook of morals:

Union produces every good.

Probity determines the choice.

If happiness were bought with gold could one obtain it without union?

Reinforcing this quality of the primary school, the House of Union would offer all the facilities of a "popular university." To be supported by a grant of twenty thousand francs, matched by a contribution from the Ferme Générale accumulated by a tax of a sou on each cake of salt ("This charitable tax is imperceptible," Ledoux noted hopefully), the facilities included research laboratories, study rooms, meeting rooms, galleries, and libraries for agricultural subjects. Outside, Ledoux planned vast covered walks and experimental medicinal gardens. Union, thus conceived, would be—as Ledoux concluded, according to masonic doctrine—"the source of happiness," "an honorable institution," which could not be ignored by society; its dissemination and support would bring about that *nouveau pacte social* dreamed of by Rousseau.

Complementing the institutions of Peace and Union was a third, carrying the neologism of Panarèthéon, or "accomplished virtue," that Ledoux conceived of as the symbolic manifestation of the good mores of Chaux, a kind of architectural and iconographic school of virtue, "a school of morals where the duties of man are taught." Raised on two stories of ramps and arcades, a pure cube enclosed a cylindrical *salle d'assemblée*, lit from above by a circular light. Formed so as to emphasize its permanence by means of the exterior cube, here "the symbol of immutability," it surrounded and protected the circle of citizens gathered around their teacher-philosopher inside. The ramps that led up to the highest room emblematized so many "degrees of perfection," earned by the inhabitants, like the grades of Masonic rite. Along the outer walls of the cube Ledoux placed a series of allegorical sculptures that included the Graces, the Days, the Hours, Wisdom in the guise of the Minerva of Sosicles, Reason modeled on the canon of Polyclitus, and the social Virtues, with Justice flanked by Temperance and Moderation, followed by Continence, Generosity, Prodigality, Magnanimity, Prudence, Piety, and Love. Carved according to Ledoux's theory of contrast, character, and proportional relativity, these statues followed all the criteria for high Greek sculpture outlined by theorists since Winckelmann; like columns, each had its proper height, width, and spacing. They were of a "delightful proportion, avowed by exigent architecture, drawn from the laws of harmony; neither too large nor too small, too light nor too strong; the outline is pure and does not hide the figure; the pose is tranquil; the appreciative eye takes pleasure in running over this beauty in the details" (185). Ledoux seemed to echo Winckelmann directly in his call for noble simplicity and quiet grandeur. Between these figures of virtue were a series of inscriptions taken from a wide range of philosophic works, including "d'apologues indiens, orientaux."

The Panarèthéon thus served as a veritable museum of characteristics, a carved book of emblems and devices, maxims and mottoes, in a long tradition of similar monuments from the ancient Temple of the Sun, as evoked by Jean-Louis Viel de Saint-Maux, to Greek and Roman temples dedicated to particular gods.[115] It was also, of course, a kind of neoclassical memory theater established by a modern Phidias; historicist in inspiration but not in style or intent, it seemed to prefigure the more literal Pantheons of public and private museums from Canova to Schinkel.

Ledoux confirmed this association of the monuments to Peace, Union, and Virtue with a revived "art of memory" in a fourth symbolic institution, the Temple of Memory. Conceived as a "country house," with a nine-square plan that corresponded to the series of houses published in *L'architecture,* its function was displayed by four monumental columns engaged at each corner. A cross between Trajan "memory" columns and oriental minarets, they transformed their Palladian precedent into a temple seemingly taken from the pages of Fischer von Erlach; they reinforced the hallucinatory world

Ledoux, House of Union,
Chaux, perspective view, elevation, section, and plans of
first, second, third, and fourth
floors. Engraving by Van
Maëlle and Simon from
Ledoux, *L'architecture*, pl. 43.

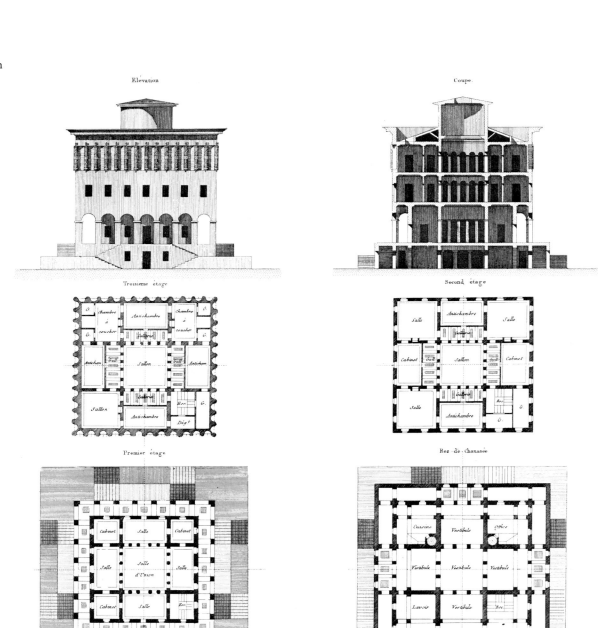

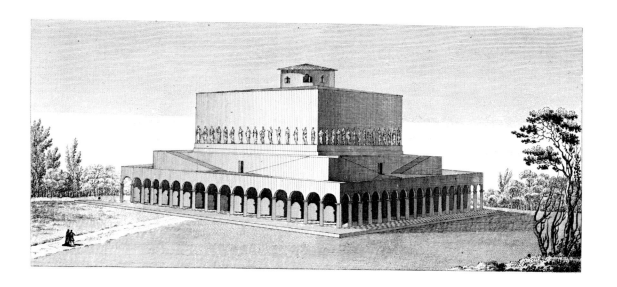

Ledoux, Panarèthéon, Chaux,
perspective view, plans of first
and second floors, and section.
Engraving by Van Maëlle and
Simon from Ramée, *Ledoux,*
pl. 242.

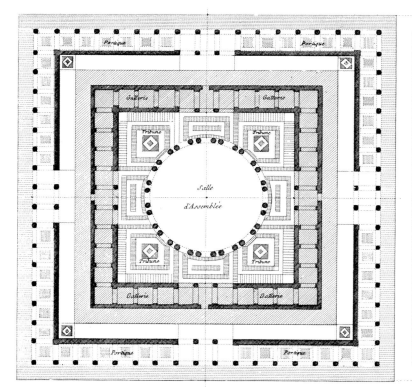

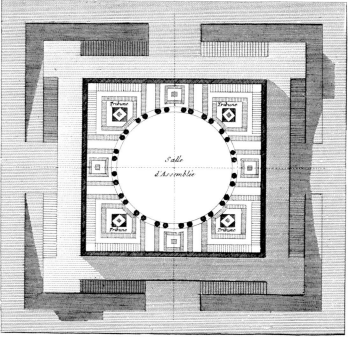

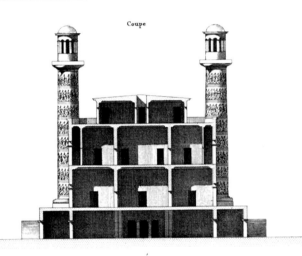

Coupe

Élévation

Second Étage

Troisieme Étage

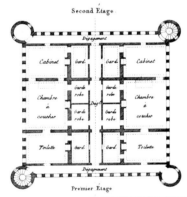

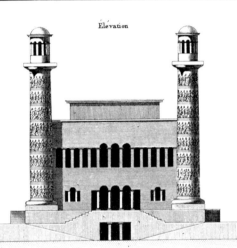

Premier Étage

Rez-de-Chaussée

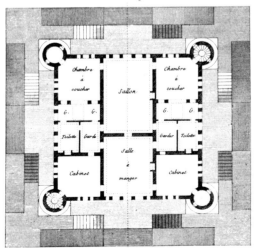

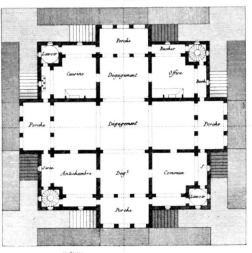

Echelle de

Ledoux, Temple of Memory, Chaux, perspective view, section, elevation, and plans of first, second, third, and fourth floors. Engraving by Coquet from Ledoux, *L'architecture*, pl. 75.

of Chaux, suspended halfway between East and West. Wrapping these columns were bas-reliefs recounting the exploits of women, public or private heroines, sustainers of mores, and inculcators of natural virtues. Ledoux's dedication of this "lodge" to women equalized the stern male qualities symbolized in the other three: while Peace, Union, and Virtue echoed the Masonic triad of Justice, Union, and Strength, the Temple of Memory served as the city's "Lodge of Adoption," enclosing and celebrating the female principle. Built, according to Ledoux, in the fairest place in the city, it also enclosed his memories of childhood and his anticipation of death: indeed, he dreamed of a final resting place among the "virtuous passions that guard the interior" (*Prospectus,* 26). Built at the "summit of the promontory that ends the vista of the park," this *fabrique* was at once exemplary for all sons, an object lesson in stone to which a father might point—"the virtues of your mother are traced on these high columns"—and Ledoux's own private memorial to his mother(160).

The moralizing effect of these quasi-Masonic temples, elevated in their high symbolism to the status of architectural maxims, was reinforced, at the base of the society, so to speak, by an institution dedicated to instilling the precepts of a natural education, the House of Education. An upbringing far from the vices of the city as well as ideas selected for their compatibility with reason and a generalized Deism, taught with enthusiasm and mingled with exemplary activities, had been an integral part of the *philosophes'* program.[116] In returning the subject of this education to his origins in *Emile,* Rousseau had popularized the assumption that, given the right environment and preceptors, man could be molded in any direction: Ledoux extended the principle, conceiving the ideal city itself as the framework of such education. Its Edenic surroundings, its didactic buildings covered with inscriptions and emblematic lessons, its moral population, and the incessant theatrical reinforcement of morality in the fêtes contributed to ensuring a youth adapted to perfection and prepared for happiness. "We can be made virtuous or vicious," claimed Ledoux, "by the friction of our surroundings"(3).

Nevertheless, the indefatigable logic of specialization by space and building type demanded a "school" where the values of education might be centered and rendered most effective. Significantly enough, Ledoux planned the House of Education in the form of a church, a Greek cross: a grand, open hall in the center contained the chapel and its pyramidal altar; the four wings accommodated the schoolrooms on the main floor and apartments for the masters and dormitories for the children on the upper two floors. Continuous galleries linked all the activities, and open courts provided sheltered spaces for recreation. The form of the building was simple, its pure geometric lines reinforcing the purity of its educational function:

The artist who conceives an educational monument will present you with simple forms, tranquil exteriors; he will place Religion at the center, that inestimable gift of the god of health, that necessary rein on the concentrated desires of newly aroused passions; he will, by means of uninterrupted lines, aid that surveillance that ensures

Ledoux, House of Education,
Chaux, perspective view. Engraving by Van Maëlle and
Maillet from Ramée, *Ledoux,*
pl. 220.

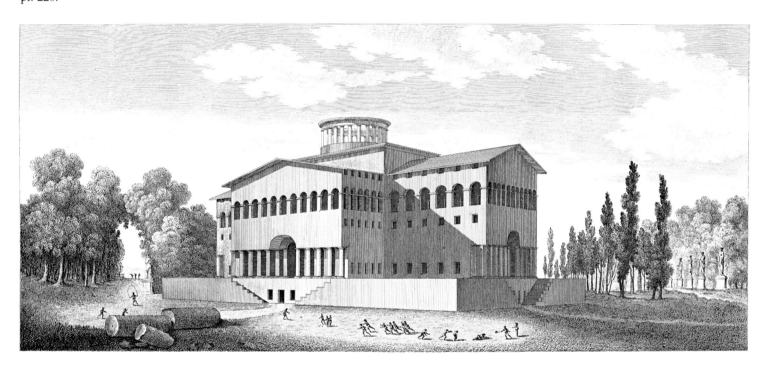

Ledoux, House of Education,
model. Photograph by A.
Vidler.

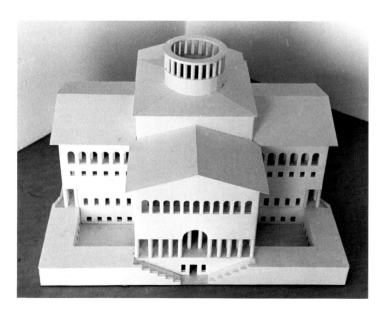

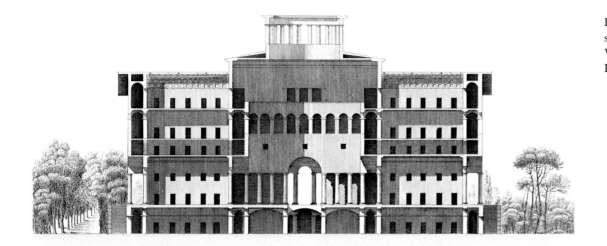

Ledoux, House of Education,
section. Engraving by
Van Maëlle and Simon from
Ramée, *Ledoux,* pl. 219.

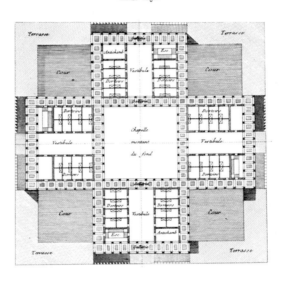

Ledoux, House of Education,
plans of first, mezzanine, second, and third floors. Engraving from Ramée, *Ledoux,*
pl. 218.

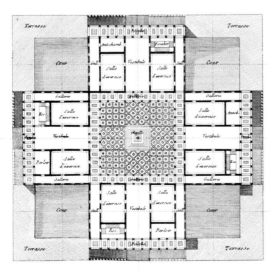

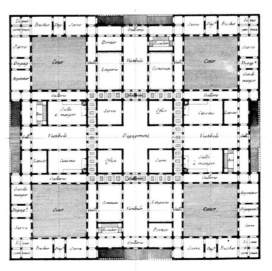

morality; he will bring together every kind of study and communication.(204)

Utopia did not diminish the need for continuous surveillance; the architecture of utopia, with its apertures and porticoes, open spaces and centralized plans, reinforced oversight in every way.

Ledoux planned the school according to all the criteria of the hospital: The isolation of the building guaranteed it against the danger of fire; its open, arcaded façades encouraged the circulation of air; its parklike grounds allowed the children free run in the open air. "The public schools will be isolated and independent of any attachments that could cause a fire. The children should never be too numerous: the air should be dry, healthy, incessantly renewed in order to refresh the lungs." (295) Ledoux registered Lavoisier's experiments on the composition of the air, depicted with graphic drama in Abraham Wright's portrait of the bird in the bell jar; he was concerned that a sudden change in the quality of the air, from city to utopia, would have a harmful effect: to change the climate was, for the late eighteenth century, to change health. In Ledoux's perspective view of the gardens of the school, statues of the arts and virtues provide reminders of the lessons inside; children play traditional games, with bat and ball or with stones, in a landscape marked with all the aura of Masonic lore: in the foreground lies a fallen column, broken but ready to be "reassembled" by education; in the left background, framed beneath an arbor of forest trees, three children, reminders of the triad of Masonic vows, stand side by side awaiting entry into the new world outside.

These calm and pristine monuments to *bonheur social* enclosed and confirmed a vision of Freemasonry, seemingly at once philosophic and Deist—of the kind propagated by Ledoux's contemporaries in Les Neuf Soeurs or the Grand Orient, with its three almost austere rites. There was no hint of occultism, of Egyptomania, or, for that matter, of the heterogeneous initiatory rituals espoused by adherents of *les rites écossais* and other hermetic cults. The spaces of Ledoux's "temples" were static, non-narrative; there were no axes of progression or ritual consummation; all was resolved, for, in

his conception, the inhabitants of Chaux were already initiates.

Only when Ledoux treated of the problems of adolescent sexuality, of the adjustment of youth to adulthood in his society, in the context of a temple dedicated to the celebration and exorcism of libertine pleasures, the Oikéma, did a hint of the ritual route of Beckford's description emerge. This formidable institution, invented to ensure the security of the marriage bond in Chaux, was conceived as a place of absolute dissipation, indeed overgratification, where, following a taste of its infinite delights, the exhausted and satiated youth would turn naturally to the calm and ordered pleasures of matrimony.[117]

Architecturally, this elaborate public brothel took the form of a pure Ionic temple from the front, covering its modernity by posing, in Ledoux's terms, as the "fragments of a Greek monument" restored by the architect-archaeologist, in the manner of David Le Roy. In plan and general composition, the building was based on an elaborate "negative fantasy," developed out of Ledoux's readings in the ancient cults of love and virility, and incorporating in its plan "fragments" of quotations from, among other "phallic" temples, Piranesi's imaginary temple dedicated to Augustus in the Campo Marzio. The Ionic portico led into a wide vestibule, with rooms for the porters, parlors, and galleries for dining; at the center of the chequered pavement of this entry stood "a tripod found in the ruins of the Temple of Venus, its flame rising up in the form of a pyramid" (202); the surrounding bas-reliefs represented "the lascivious companies of Perfica (a goddess revered among the Romans) and of Pertunda (the goddess of voluptuousness)" (202). This space led in turn to a long, two-story gallery on axis with the main entrance, arcaded on the first floor beneath a continuous balcony on the second. Under these arcades and giving onto the balcony at each level were a series of elegantly furnished bedrooms for the permanent inhabitants of the institution, turning this one-hundred-foot-long room into a veritable *passage d'amour*. At the end of this sequence, a large, oval salon opened onto the gardens beyond and the pools, baths, and terraces below. This evidently phallic plan, reaching its consummation in the final sanctuary of

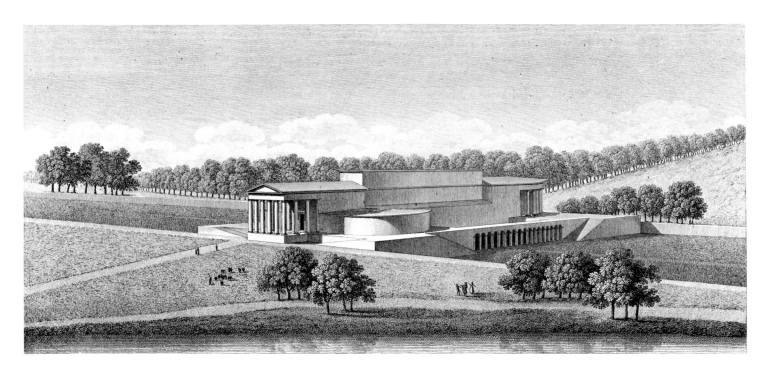

Ledoux, Oikéma, Chaux, perspective view, plans of first
and second floors, and section.
Engravings by Coquet from
Ramée, *Ledoux,* pls. 241, 240
(perspective view by Coquet
and Bovinet).

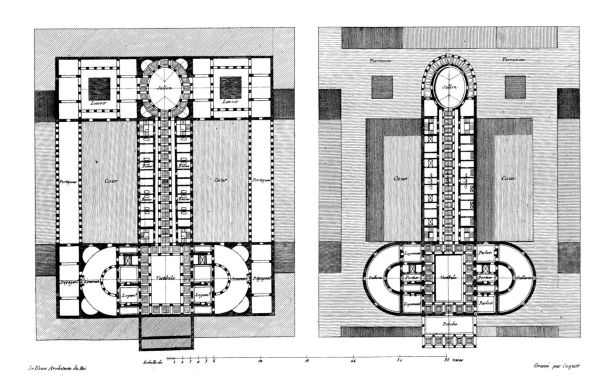

love—a device similar to that used by Ledoux in his House of Pleasure for Paris—transformed the route of initiation into a sign of its erotic purpose. From the front a temple, from the rear an oval pavilion, from the side a long, arcaded basilica, the Oikéma revealed its true message in plan alone—a secret known only to the initiate-architect or one who had traversed its sequence of spaces. As Ledoux wrote, its "tranquil walls hide the agitation inside" (202).

The cult, described by Ledoux in detail worthy of de Sade or Laclos, was dedicated to the use of combined sensual depravity and moral corruption as, paradoxically, and departing from de Sade, a purifying force:

Viewed from nearby, vice influences the soul no less strongly; by the horror it instills it causes the soul to react toward virtue. The Oikéma presents depravation in all its nakedness to the ardent and fickle youth it attracts. The sight of man's degradation reanimates slumbering virtue, leading man to the altar of virtuous Hymen, who embraces and crowns him.(2)

This "workshop of corruption," as Ledoux called it, assembled all the characteristics of the archaic Greek mysteries. Set in an arcadia, it was surrounded by the sights and scents of seduction, the erotic site of a mid-eighteenth-century romance; Ledoux was, of course, aware that the popular name for the valley of the river Loüe was the Val d'Amour. Delighting in contrast, social as well as aesthetic, Ledoux developed a mythic ritual somewhere between the dark myths of Eleusis as described by Virgil and the pleasurable metamorphoses of Ovid.

The idea of moral reform through the institutionalization of prostitution was not new in the late eighteenth century; a number of writers—as Détournelle, the reviewer of *L'architecture* in 1804, noted—had already proposed similar projects. The most celebrated example was that of Nicolas-Edme Rétif de la Bretonne, whose ideal moral code had been set out in *Le pornographe* as early as 1769. Here, the popular novelist, whose treatment of the vices of the cities and the virtues of the countryside were to captivate a large public in the mid-1770s, outlined a plan for an institution he called, again using a Greek neologism, a "Parthénion," taking the name of the sacred, initiatory temple near Eleusis.[118] This state brothel was conceived in the first place as a means of controlling the spread of venereal disease and envisaged as a tightly controlled, closed "convent," where the inhabitants might be subjected to a strict hygienic regime. A self-supporting and self-perpetuating institution, where the children were brought up within the walls to the trade of the house, the Parthénion possessed all the hierarchical structure of the traditional utopia; it resembled, and probably inspired, the antiutopian version described by de Sade in *Les cent vingt jours de sodome,* some twenty years later. Rétif even described its planning in terms that reflected the functional discussion of hospitals in the late 1760s and early 1770s. Built around closed courtyards and gardens, the institution was divided along bedroom corridors, according to six categories of prostitutes, aged from fourteen to thirty-six and carefully graded by beauty; each corridor was to open into a large communal salon, where the inmates, working eight-hour shifts, would gather to be selected by their visitors.[119] On the one hand entirely functional and propaedeutic, this proposal was on the other hand buttressed by a long history of the noble art of prostitution among the ancients, a sacred pleasure rather than a debauched and depraved occupation. This double face of antique nostalgia and modern reformism was taken up by Ledoux, who, in the long gallery lined by bedrooms and the oval salon, seems to have taken Rétif's Parthénion as his program.[120] In his description of the Oikéma's delights, however, Ledoux depicted a sensuality that had nothing of the dry, codified forms of Rétif or the mechanical systematic repetition of de Sade. It was equally distant from the systematic treatment of Fourier's *Nouveau monde amoureux* elaborated a quarter of a century later. Ledoux's fantasies were still those of Montesquieu's *Lettres persanes* or Diderot's *Bijoux indiscrets;* with their overtones of preromantic sensibility derived from Delille's nature poetry, they displayed the light eroticism of a Fragonard or a Boucher. The quasi-aristocratic *fête d'amour* Ledoux imagined was couched in the language of the courtly masque, or, more immediately, a picnic with Madame du Barry at Louveciennes.

HAPPINESS IN THE COUNTRYSIDE

All these monuments were finally dedicated to a combined program of recreation and moralization that would lead, according to Ledoux, toward the ultimate goal of happiness for the entire population of Chaux. The theme of a happiness that originated in natural pastimes ran through much of the popular literature and tracts on social reform in the late eighteenth century. Fundamentally conservative in outlook, these writings were overtly paternalistic, emphasizing a combination of religious uplift, practical reform, and enforced moralization. The polemics of the Marquis de Lezay-Marnésia were exemplary. Celebrating the picturesque nature of Franche-Comté in his *Essai sur la nature champêtre,* a sentimental verse description in the manner of the Abbé Delille, he also put forward schemes for rural reform. In his widely read *Le bonheur dans les campagnes* he wrote, "I have seen the ills of the countryside and I have searched for remedies." [121] Like the Physiocrats, he opposed the concentration of the "sterile glories" of wealth in the court and capital cities and argued for a return of absentee landlords to their domains. Supporting this "return to the *châteaux*" would be a hierarchically ordered set of institutions and preceptors for the moral guidance of the people; a live-in curé or vicar for each parish would assume the responsibilities for religious and agricultural instruction, the wise distribution of charity, and a careful program of rural amusements. As a reviewer in the *Mercure de France* noted, Lezay-Marnésia "preferred those sports that, while exercising the body, required skill, like running, archery, bathing, bat and ball, water tilting. . . . He reserved dancing for winter and for days when the weather prevents exercise in the open air." [122] A popular theater would also be organized, as well as a program of fêtes and spectacles, which, following Rousseau's strictures against the immorality of urban theaters, would be reserved for special and solemn occasions—veritable schools of virtue, adapted to the simple mores of the countryside. In these theatrical entertainments, again as suggested by Rousseau and by Rétif de la Bretonne, the actors would be the model citizen themselves. The scenes would emulate the moral pictures of Jean-Baptiste Greuze:

The good father of the family, impelled by his heart and directed by his prudence, divides his care and tenderness among an estimable wife, obedient children, and faithful servants; the charitable peasant . . . the good son, the good friend, the good mother, the good master, the zealous servant, the charitable lord, the generous curé, etc.,etc. [123]

Ledoux invested his program of rustic games for the ideal city of Chaux with a similar moralizing purpose. If the *guinguettes* of Paris could be reconstructed as "houses of meeting and pleasure" in which the people took part in fêtes and games prepared for them by a munificent government, then the population of the countryside should be no less fortunate. Living in a kind of arcadia, the inhabitants of Chaux would be in some sense "children of nature" and their recreations would be adjusted accordingly; untroubled by and therefore unenvious of *la classe agissante,* they would be satisfied with a modicum of pleasure to drown the sorrows of labor. [124] Ledoux assured the future people of Chaux that "rest comes after work, and joy, arriving at intervals, leads to the forgetting of the ills attached to humanity. Simple tastes discover happiness amidst uniform pleasures; far from exhausting the body, they augment one's skill and conserve one's strengths" (172).

To ensure that these pleasures would be taken in moderation, the recreational habits of the rural workers were to be strictly supervised: spatially, by assembling all amusements within a large, formal park, with separate pavilions for each activity, and institutionally, by combining education with instruction. "Public morals being the basis of good governments and the happiness of peoples, the government has thought it useful to establish a new school of rural amusements"(172). There, a literal "re-creation" of traditional country sports would engender popular loyalty, increase public order, and generate commercial wealth. For the Monument intended for Recreations, as he called this institution, Ledoux appropriated the entire roster of traditional games, which he listed with almost anthropological enthusiasm. [125] He noted spaces for skittles, archery, tennis, softball, boxing, discus, fencing, swimming, chariot and horse racing, and various games of chance as well as a running track that followed an elliptical route lined by fir trees. In his narration of

Plan Général.

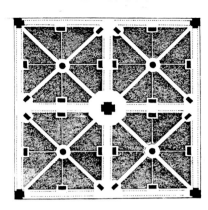

la Lutte
le Pugilat
le Disque
la Course
le Surte
la Lance
le Saut
la Paume
Salle d'Armes
Lutterhtique
le Javelot

le Billard
le Jeu d'arc
le Jeu de bague
combat de Coqs
Jeux de hazard
course de Chars
course de Chevaux
le jeu de Siam
le jeu de Boule
le jeu de Quilles
le Tami

Ledoux, Monument intended for Recreations, Chaux. *Left,* site plan; *opposite left,* plans of first and second floors, elevation, and section. Engraving by Varin from Ramée, *Ledoux,* pl. 236.

these games, recalling a scene from his visits to Franche-Comté, Ledoux described a wrestling match staged by two forest workers, "two black charcoal burners flashing ivory teeth," the victor awarded a long drink; in depicting the fight then taken up by two salt workers, he provided an incidental object lesson for painters or sculptors interested in verifying the positions of the Laocoön. The javelin thrown by a huge blacksmith, felling a goose, became a moral lesson against the arts of the war; the spherical balls in the game of bowls played beneath a long arbor by "peacable men" provided another universal allegory. A cockfight made a sanguine contrast to the card games played under long, open shed roofs.

At the center of the park, overlooking the gardens, a vast restaurant would serve cold and roast meats on the ground floor and wines in the first-floor recesses. In the adjoining ballroom, a square, double-height room with an elliptical area marked out for dancing, the assembled inhabitants could recover a sense of the rustic dances of primitive times: "Gaiety hovers in this enclosure, and the air, disturbed by its wings, fans with its caresses the robust beauties that decorate it. Here everyone knows everyone else; scruple guides the choice of partners: one no longer, as in populous cities, has to cajole with soft words the son of the assassin of one's father"(172). In contrast to the festivals and dances of contemporary Paris—those "cheerless and awkward" dances that Rousseau had witnessed in the *guinguettes*—Ledoux's dance was governed by the social morality of the small rural community.[126] As in Rousseau's favorite Swiss examples, "everything glows with contentment and gaiety . . . well-being, fraternity, and concord," subject to the benign supervision of the elders.[127] In Chaux everyone would go to bed early: "At last, at eight o'clock, everyone retires. . . . Everyone, a little tired, content with the day, promises themselves new pleasures for the next fête" (172).

If, in the Monument intended for Recreations, Ledoux scrutinized each traditional pastime for its positive qualities and transformed it into an instrument of moralization, in the second institution dedicated to the people's leisure, the House of Games, he carried this transformational logic to its conclusion. His subject was gambling and related activities, the at-

traction of which, corrupting in large cities, Ledoux proposed might, under proper surveillance, be utilized for good—the profits taxed for poor relief. In smaller towns, where a theater could not be afforded or its morality was considered corrupting, and where idleness led to crime, games provided a means both to occupy the otherwise criminal and to satisfy social beneficence. Where *un asyle special du malheur,* a hospice or workhouse, might be an affront to human dignity, gambling receipts would simply take from the rich to give to the poor. In the ideal city, however, even this modification of traditional corruption would be proscribed; instead, Ledoux designed the House of Games as a monument to sociability. On the ground floor, opening through arcades to the surrounding fields, he planned a *salle de dance,* or *salle de bal champêtre,* with a gallery above for observing this social theater. On the upper floor he designed a *salle de jeux,* surrounded by smaller rooms that would once have been used for gambling, but which Ledoux gave over to libraries, concerts, meetings of agricultural societies, clubs for the teaching and practice of rhetoric, the belles lettres, poetry, and art. Ledoux thus brought together the academic and salon life of the eighteenth-century bourgeois for the benefit of the rural population, creating in the House of Games a predecessor of all those reading rooms for worker improvement built in company towns in the next century.

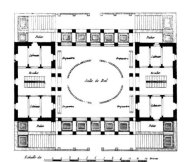

Elevation

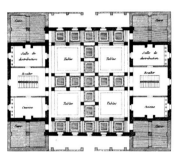

Plan du Premier Etage

Coupe

Ledoux, House of Games,
Chaux, elevation, section, and
plans of basement, first, mezzanine, and second floors.
Engraving by Van Maëlle
from Ramée, *Ledoux,* pl. 237.

Elevation

Coupe

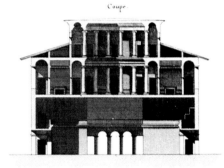

Premier Etage

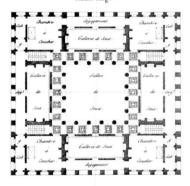

Entresol

Plan des Caves

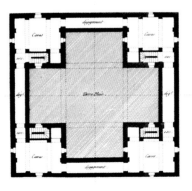

Rez de Chaussée

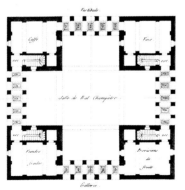

Echelle de

L'ARCHITECTURE

CONSIDÉRÉE

SOUS LE RAPPORT DE L'ART,

DES MŒURS

ET DE LA LÉGISLATION.

L'architecture
1789–1804

███████████████████████████

Events, overwhelming in their nature, cut the thread of my work before the autumn of my days.

Suddenly, positions attained by means of a long struggle passed into sacrilegious hands. I lost the

fruit of thirty years of honorable service. Amidst the clouds that enveloped my affairs it was inevi-

table that one part of myself would yearn for the other. (33)

ARCHITECTURE AND REVOLUTION

Throughout the Revolutionary years and the foundation of the Empire Ledoux was left virtually without work, friends, or money. His close affiliation with the courts of Louis XV and Louis XVI, and especially with the hated du Barry, his sustained connections with the aristocracy in exile, including Calonne, the foremost organizer of resistance from abroad, and, above all, his ubiquitous reputation as architect to the Ferme Générale rendered him unemployable and forced him into a kind of internal exile. His fall, however, despite his dismissal from the *barrières,* was not immediate; in the first months he clung to a guarded optimism. Against the judgment of Dufresne, Intendant of the Treasury, that "Ledoux is a turbulent and extremely dangerous man by reason of his extravagant and expensive projects," he pressed his claims for reimbursement for work completed on the wall and *barrières,* demanding 1,250,000 livres in 1790 and a more modest 616,728 livres the following year.[1] As a result of his former relations with the Ferme he was asked to act as arbitrator in a dispute between his friend the architect François-Joseph Bélanger and a client, the Fermier-Général Augéard.[2]

Ledoux, with many of his friends, had at first viewed the revolutionary events as a temporary interruption of the old order. Looking forward to a restoration of his work and honor, he drafted a memorandum to the king in 1789, requesting the long-promised bestowal of the Cordon Noir, the order of Saint Michel.

The King grants honorable distinctions to architects who have the honor to be attached to his person . . . for having constructed a public auditorium, fêtes, or a distinguished building. . . . Ledoux has built more than a hundred useful monuments; he has built in Russia, in

Germany, in Holland, in England, and in almost all the provinces of the realm; he has built theaters, palaces of justice, prisons, etc., etc.; he has engraved five hundred plates at great cost, in order to enlighten his century; there remain an equal number to complete his work, which will cost him more than a hundred thousand livres; a single example of a collection as varied and large cannot be cited. Louis XV saw fit to promise him the Cordon de St. Michel under the ministry of M. the Abbé Terray. M. Delongville, Commissaire des Salines, recalled this promise in his report of 28 June 1787. His request, justly founded, was granted for the end of the year 1787; only the particular and independent situation of Ledoux has suspended this decision.[3]

In this vein, feeling wronged but not at all cowed, Ledoux observed the daily events of the Revolution from the *entresol* of the Palais Royal, according to his own account playing billiards and reading the newspapers in the rooms of the Club de Valois, together with the painter Joseph Vernet and Michel Le Peletier de Saint-Fargeau, soon, with Marat, to become a martyr of the Revolution.[4] Writing to the developer Joseph Saveur Mignard on the opportunism of Isaac-René-Guy Le Chapelier in the Assembly, Ledoux noted ironically that "when places are vacant one will certainly see capable men who will fill them."[5] In the same letter he reported on the vigorous defense of church properties mounted by the liberal Archbishop of Aix, his former adversary, Jean de Boisgelin; with amusement he observed that the new controls on the church and the aristocracy ("the priesthood and the nobility had committed abuses," he agreed) would no doubt force the archbishop to spend more time at home: "It seems by this arrangement you will see the archbishop in his diocese often; the provincial assemblies make the provinces more important; the landowners will be obliged to inhabit their property, and this becomes necessary for their interests and for the new regime."[6]

In the circle of the Club de Valois, Ledoux, as always, preferred the company of liberal aristocrats and cautious reformers to that of radical republicans. The club, under the patronage of the Duc d'Orléans, numbered among its members Lally-Tollendal, Clermont-Tonnerre, Mounier, Malo-net, the Prince de Conti, Condorcet, La Rochefoucauld, the Abbé Sieyès, Lafayette, Mirabeau, and the Duc de Montmorency.[7] Politically the Orléanists were followers of Montesquieu, considering themselves constitutional monarchists, partisans of the English system with its House of Lords, and advocates of the check to monarchical power represented by a high chamber formed of the provincial estates. If the anonymous pamphlet entitled *Un bon-homme aux Etats-généraux,* published in "London" in 1788, is, as seems very likely from internal evidence, by Ledoux, his political liberalism was entirely favorable to this form of government, one that his mentor Calonne had believed it possible to manipulate to the advantage of the king.

And while the chances for such a liberal compromise receded as the Revolution developed, Ledoux, like many architects, continued to feel confident of "proving" his Revolutionary sympathies without too much compromise, simply by seeming eager to submit designs for public works. The police later reported that "he took part in political life during the first six months of the revolution in the district of the Filles-Dieu."[8] On 1 April 1790 he presented a project for moving the site of the opera to the Commune de Paris; but, no doubt in view of his previous reputation, the Assembly ordered that his report should not be read. As a further precaution, on 28 July 1790 Ledoux voluntarily enrolled in the Parisian National Guard.

Deprived of the commission for the *barrières,* his immediate concern was to ensure the continuation of work at Aix. There, in 1789, work was still proceeding on the foundations of the Palais de Justice and prisons. Ledoux wrote in September specifying the stone for the façades and advising the use of chain reinforcement for the thinner interior walls; he concluded by pointing out the value of public works in times of hardship. But his real vexation was reserved for Brunet, the contractor, whose political activities had interfered with his responsibilities in Aix:

He has donned the patriotic habit, the epaulette decorates his shoulder and he runs through the countryside to find subsistence for the capital. He has also taken on a civil office: he is commissioner, vice-

president or even president of his district. One can only applaud all these patriotic views; but while he searches for subsistence for others he neglects his own. . . . His character always leads him to cede to the circumstance of the day.[9]

Writing to the Procureurs du Pays de Provence in December, Ledoux was still hopeful of reengaging Brunet, but his letters and those of Mignard remained unanswered. He assured his clients that the worst of the work was over and restated his arguments for useful public works. In the light of the *ateliers publics* instituted by the Assembly, generally employed in minor and profitless labor, Ledoux felt able to press his philosophy, rooted in his Physiocratic beliefs, against charity and for productive undertakings, that is, for the building of the Palais and prisons:

In unfortunate times that demand public works to support the most indigent of the population, it would be extremely impolitic not to continue, during the winter, the cutting of stones of all kinds and the other work capable of employing the laborers. The government has built a road that leads to Montmartre: it is not useful to the public; it has made the poor work under the name of Charity Workshops. The single and disturbing Montmartre road has cost 1,900,000 livres, without counting the sums used since by the municipality for the repairing of a few roads. One could have built a magnificent palace with these expenses dictated by the needs of the moment and clothed in the humiliating word charity.[10]

In January 1790 the site engineer, Vallon, was even optimistic that the buildings might be completed by 1792.[11] Indeed, while the opposition of the Regional Assembly forced the suspension of construction in May 1790, Ledoux's project was not definitively abandoned until 1803, and he remained hopeful for over a decade that he might succeed, with the help of the entrepreneur Mignard, to open the *chantier* once more.[12]

His attendance at the Académie, now almost his only professional activity, continued as before to reflect the pace of his practice. In 1789 he signed the register in March, May, June, July, and August; at the meeting on 13 July, while the *barrières* burned and the municipal revolution was proclaimed at the Hôtel de Ville, the academicians listened, no doubt

without any immediate sense of paradox, to a reading of Vitruvius on the subject of the choice of healthy building sites. In 1790 he was almost entirely absent, signing only for July, but in 1791 he was present for nine of the eleven meetings, sensing the fragility both of the Académie and of his own position. By contrast, in 1792 he attended only two meetings, an indication of his briefly renewed professional activity with the commission for the Hosten houses. Proposed as a candidate for the First Class on 5 March 1792, he began again to attend the monthly meetings, signing in April and again in July.[13] But this was to be the final meeting of the Académie Royale d'Architecture: on 27 November 1792 the academies were suspended on the initiative of Jacques-Louis David, to be definitively suppressed nine months later.[14]

At the beginning of 1792, Ledoux had begun to reestablish his practice with a commission to build fifteen houses for a rich sugar planter from Santo Domingo, Jean-Baptiste Hosten, on a large site off the rue Saint-Georges.[15] This development, which included Hosten's own house, was planned, like the London terraces where many of Ledoux's former patrons had found refuge, around a landscaped garden, complete with miniature temples, *fabriques* designed as carriage houses, and even a serpentine pool crossed by an ornamental bridge, emulating that in Saint James's Park. Perhaps this evident reference to English urban housing reflected a journey Ledoux was rumored to have made in 1787, following Calonne's flight to London, to design a house for his former patron near Hyde Park Corner.[16] Ledoux had projected a similar development in the late 1780s, also reflecting English precedent, for the de Saisseval family, prominent Freemasons and investors in Left Bank property, where four houses, raised on a high rusticated ground floor, formed a linked series, separated by recessed courtyards.

The style of the Hosten project was Palladian, with motifs and decoration severely abstracted and framed in panels, in the same manner as the hunting lodge for the Prince de Bauffremont and the palace for the Landgrave of Hesse-Cassel. A rusticated base and a continuous arched colonnade at the level of the *piano nobile* unified the linked houses, which were distinguished by pedimented gables over the projecting

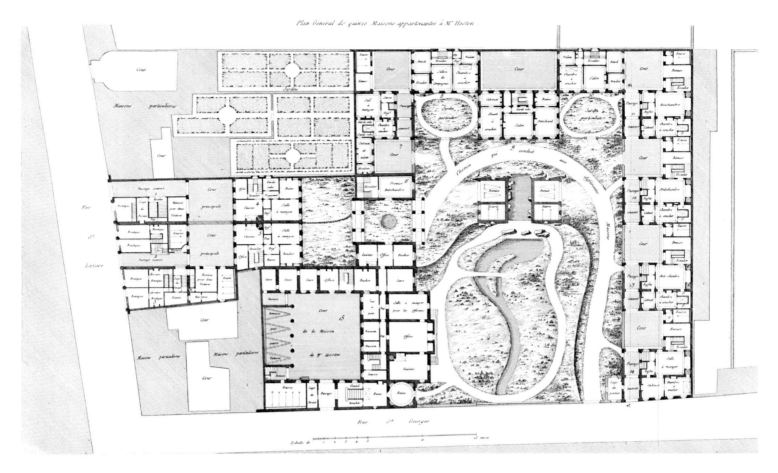

Ledoux, Houses for M. Hosten, Paris, 1792, site plan. Engraving by Ransonnette from Ramée, *Ledoux,* pl. 178.

Ledoux, Houses for M. Hosten, perspective view, c. 1792. Watercolor executed for M. de l'Arbre, the contractor for the houses, from the Musée Carnavalet.

Elévation sur la Cour.

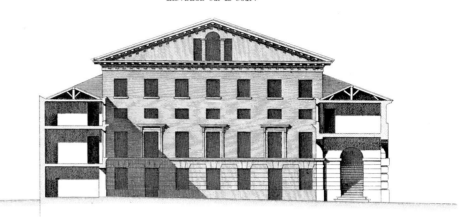

Ledoux, House for M. Hosten, no. 15, elevations. Engraving from Ramée, *Ledoux,* pl. 180.

Elévation sur la Rue .

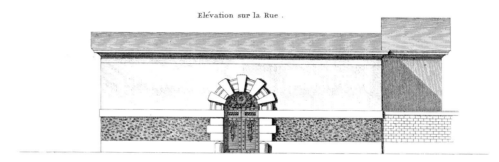

Elévation sur le Jardin .

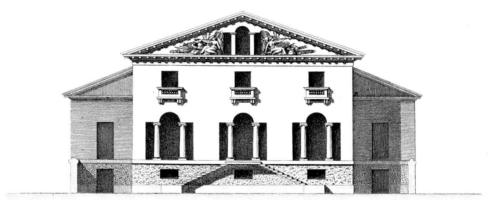

Echelle de   1   2   3   4   5   6   12 Toises .

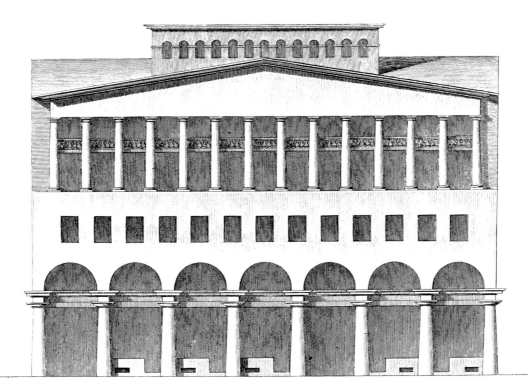

Echelle de   1   2   3   6 *Toises*

Ledoux, Houses for M. Hosten, nos. 1, 2, and 3, elevation on the rue Saint Lazare showing stores on the first floor. Engraving from Ramée, *Ledoux,* pl. 188.

Ledoux, Houses for M. Hosten, nos. 11, 12, 13, and 14, elevation on inner courtyard. Engraving from Ramée, *Ledoux,* pl. 183.

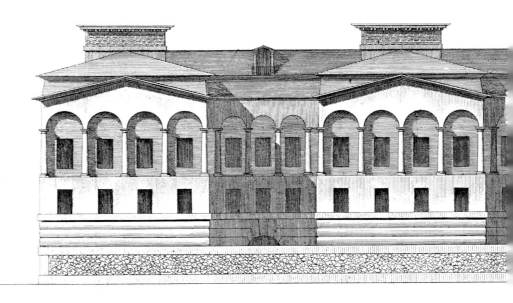

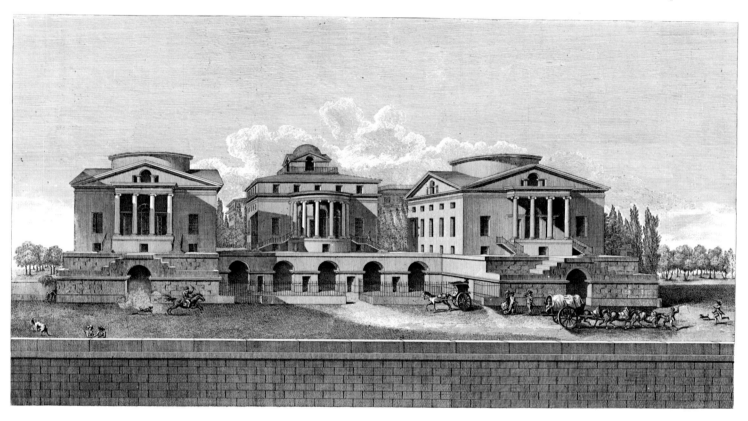

Ledoux, Houses for M. de Saisseval, Paris, c. 1787, perspective view. Engraving from Ramée, *Ledoux,* pl. 192.

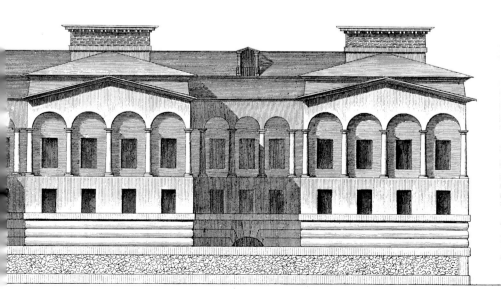

bays that faced the garden. Hosten's own house was fronted with a pediment carved with trophies in bas-relief interrupted by a central Serliana. Inside this main pavilion the decorations were derived from the recently published wall paintings of Herculaneum, a literal historical quotation rare in the work of Ledoux but reflecting his attempt to shift toward the taste of the younger generation of Jean-Nicolas-Louis Durand, Jean-Thomas Thibault, Charles Percier, and Pierre-François-Léonard Fontaine. These were complemented by landscape paintings executed by Ledoux's old friend Hubert Robert.[17] The square main salon was surrounded by mirrors framed by pilasters decorated with gilded arabesques; the ceiling was painted with mythological subjects; the chimneypiece was in marble with bronze inlays. The adjoining bedroom was more Pompeiian still, with a painted bas-relief in grisaille.[18]

At the end of July 1792, with the Hosten works proceeding speedily, Ledoux felt confident enough to buy new property. But at the end of August Ledoux's wife, apparently already separated from him, died in the house of the former contractor for the Saline de Chaux, Jean Roux Monclar.[19] By the beginning of the next year Ledoux was forced to take out loans from various friends, and his practice showed no signs of developing after the Hosten commission.

The events of year II (1793–94) abruptly ended any hopes for a liberal compromise between enlightened aristocrats like the Duc d'Orléans and the Third Estate. Seventeen ninety-three had started with the execution of Louis XVI on 21 January; it had continued with the declaration of war on Great Britain and Holland in February and on Spain in March. Mass conscription of the French population was rendered the more necessary by internal revolts, the most serious of which was that of the Vendée, in the northwest. To counter this double threat, external and internal, in April the Convention established the soon to be infamous Committee of Public Safety, which itself was soon divided by the campaign against the liberal, utopian wing of revolutionaries, the Girondins. The growing success of the Vendéan uprising throughout June, July, and August; the insistent pressure of the most unstable of revolutionary forces, the sans-culottes, who began serious demonstrations in September; and the divisions within the Convention itself led increasingly to a state of war, inside France and outside, and determined the economic and political responses of the Committee of Public Safety, evermore under the domination of Robespierre following the assassination of Marat on 13 July. By the beginning of year II (September 1793), the notion of "Revolutionary government" had entirely shifted from the first bourgeois, democratic aspirations of the National Assembly and early Convention after 1789. The adoption of the Law of Suspects of 17 September, which required evidence of *civisme* to his or her section from every citizen and the general incarceration of all who might be suspect of even lack of sympathy with the revolution, together with the execution of Marie-Antoinette on 16 October confirmed the new strong-arm policies of the Committee, the success of which was manifested in the defeats of the Vendéans on 10 November and 23 December.

The wide-ranging law against suspects enacted in September had been followed by an order directing the local revolutionary committees to examine suspects for certificates of civic zeal and to draw up expanded lists. The Faubourg du Nord, Ledoux's quarter, was as zealous as any. On 29 November 1793 Ledoux was arrested and incarcerated in La Force prison; his previous connections and well-known commissions seemed certain to lead to the guillotine.

THE PRISON NOTEBOOKS

According to the records of the Comité Révolutionnaire of the Faubourg du Nord, Ledoux had been apprehended at his house in the rue Neuve d'Orléans, in a sweep that included fourteen other inhabitants of the section, among them a stockbroker, a former noble, a grocer-distiller, a "so-called American," a gauze maker, a clerk, and a former commissioner of police. Despite his later dissimulation (noting in *L'architecture* that his arrest was a question of mistaken identity for a doctor of the Sorbonne with the same name), Ledoux was correctly identified by his interrogators:

An architect, before and after the Revolution, especially for the former nobles, notably du Barry. It was he who built for her the small pavilion of Louveciennes, for which he obtained from the father of the last tyrant, King of the French, 6,000 livres of rent from the salines. It was at that time he began his career as architect of the aforesaid [nobles]. From there he [became] architect for the Ferme [Générale, for the enclosure of Paris, and author of those celebrated barrières *at the entries of Paris.*[20]

Documents sealed at the time of his arrest, and collected from his house on 8 January 1794 in his presence, demonstrated to the committee that he was hardly a sympathizer with the Revolution. His very way of life made him suspect; although he claimed to have only five to six thousand livres a year in revenue, he "had not," it was pointed out in the charges brought against him, "diminished the style of his household, keeping his cook, coachman, and servant." He had not even admitted in the first round of questioning that he was in the process of claiming fees for the *barrières,* an omission that itself was "a proof of infidelity."[21] The discovery of the memorandum soliciting the Cordon Noir, together with the yearly almanac of the Club de Valois, betrayed his royalist sentiments. Although he had apparently changed his attitude abruptly following the execution of Louis XVI, the committee found that his subsequent absence from revolutionary meetings displayed his "false approbation":

A character decidedly for royalism before the death of the tyrant and wanting to persuade, since, of his patriotism by chatting with patriots. With regard to his political opinions, they cannot be known publicly because he has not appeared at all at the assemblies of the section since the revolution of 10 August, which in itself could prove that he disapproves of that happy day and that of 21 May, happier still for the support of the Republic.[22]

Not surprisingly, they could find little in his papers to indicate his support for their cause.

Ledoux, helped by his daughters, Alexandrine-Euphrasie and Adélaïde-Constance, prepared his defense. A letter from Alexandrine, dated 22 July 1794, listed his answers to the accusations. He had, she explained, already demonstrated the value of his architectural work, documenting the more than twenty years he had spent in search of the true principles of design, by presenting drafts of his text to the

committee; his age and health had been the reasons for his absence from political meetings; he had indeed spoken out in favor of the execution of the king, for, as Alexandrine noted, "born with the love of liberty," her father "had always applauded the destruction of tyranny"; social clubs like the Club de Valois were permitted in 1789, their members flattered to be in the company of famous artists—Ledoux claimed to have been inscribed at the instigation of Le Peletier de Saint-Fargeau, together with many other so-called patriots, and to have used the facilities for reading newspapers and playing billiards only two or three times in 1788; the letter requesting the Cordon Noir was, after all, only an unsigned draft with no proof that it had been sent; finally, he had "thought that a citizen who worked to enlighten his fellow citizens in the domain he knew best served his country better than by occupying positions he did not know how to fulfill."[23] Other letters from the two daughters cried piteously for aid and the return of a dearly beloved father (an emotion to be quickly forgotten by Alexandrine in the later struggle for her mother's legacy after the death of Adélaïde-Constance in October 1794).[24] Ledoux himself petitioned ceaselessly, writing to the Commission des Artistes, the officials of the Section du Nord, and to former patrons.[25]

In a letter written on 19 July (1 Thermidor), eight days before the fall of Robespierre, Ledoux requested permission to retrieve drawings, notes, and memoranda from his house in order to complete his projects.[26] He noted that "under the Despotism" he had built "Republican" theaters; that his designs would benefit young architects and the public in general as "infused with liberty and humanitarian views." In this vein, he went on to offer his designs for public monuments as gifts to the Revolution, responding formally to the competition for rural architecture announced on 2 May:

Following the invitation extended to artists to occupy themselves with useful and agricultural institutions, citizen Ledoux offers the plans, sections, and elevations of a model farm that contains services of every kind; a sheepfold [no doubt that for La Roche Bernard] on a large scale with demonstrable principles and utility—one can cite few as fine either in Spain or in England; a public market that brings together the principal means of subsistence at the frontiers; granaries for surpluses; public baths, using the overflow of the salt springs, for use against those destructive plagues that afflict the poor, for the cure of the intractable scabies, skin diseases, scorbutic infections, nervous illnesses, and the fungous complaints of the weary soldier.[27]

This latter project, "already approved," Ledoux noted, would, like the baths recently established at Boulogne-sur-Mer, have the effect of "eradicating disastrous diseases from the social order." These were plans for establishments that "satisfied needs and offered real economies," for farmers, merchants, and those who "gave new value to beneficent waters, revivifying the countryside with new products." Ledoux was aware, he wrote, that "Poverty, which solicits its needs, has not the same credit as Opulence, which builds luxurious monuments," but he affirmed his belief in a "Nature that sees everything with the same eye," that "did not vary in its principles when it disseminated its benefits to the opposite ends of the scale." Government would, Ledoux concluded, undertake nature's task, "occupying itself with the good of everyone, taking care to revenge past misery and the scorn of opulence."[28]

Ledoux sent another version of this letter two weeks later, on 5 August, to the Commission Temporaire des Arts, asking for support in gaining his release:

It is to artists that we address ourselves to request hastening the release of one of their colleagues; . . . Le Doux (architect) has undertaken a work that is very important for the public welfare, he requests his liberty only to demonstrate his love for the Revolution; and his entire devotion. . . . An artist who has divided all his time between paternal affections and the multiplied occupations of the most active work would be only too happy to contribute to the progress of knowledge that could interest the success of the Republic. Salut et fraternité, Le Doux.[29]

The commission's minutes recorded cursorily, "Ledoux, architect, solicits the benevolence of the Commission and especially the artist members of this Commission in order to obtain his liberty. The Commission passes to the business of the day."[30]

Ledoux's "prison notebooks" not only confirm the pre-Revolutionary dating of the *ferme parée*, the *bergerie* of La Roche Bernard, the Market of Chaux, and the Public Baths, but moreover they provide an image of Ledoux as unwavering as ever in his faith in architecture as social propaedeutic and as certain of his own genius. They sketch the themes later to be developed in *L'architecture* and indicate the tenor of much of the text written in these months of solitude. According to a fellow prisoner, the General Custines, "Ledoux, architect, dreamed and talked only of columns of five-twelfths."[31] Among his fellow prisoners, besides a number of his former clients' children—the sons of Thélusson, of Trudaine de Montigny, and of Béthune-Charost—were other authors whose works might well have influenced his own emerging text, including the Comte de Volney, whose reflections on the historical sublime in *Les ruines* of 1791 formed a model for Ledoux's meditation on the fragments of civilization left after the Revolution. Choderlos de Laclos, a member of the Orléanist circle in the Club de Valois, whose *Liaisons dangereuses* of 1782 seems to have anticipated the imaginary "programs" of Ledoux's country houses designed after 1794, was also briefly interned in La Force.

THE LAST DECADE

Unlike many of the former members of the Académie, Ledoux had resisted joining the Commune Générale des Arts, founded in August 1793 under the influence of David as the Revolutionary equivalent of the academies; nor, later, would he take part in the more radical Société Populaire et Républicaine des Arts or the Société Républicaine des Arts. No doubt Ledoux knew that he would be unwelcome, and his public involvement with the Ferme did not allow him to take the distanced position of Boullée, who, pleading illness in Meudon, acted like an elder statesman of architecture in retirement. But this did not prevent him, in extremis, from appealing to the new bodies and even hoping for their professional support.

The competition for rural architecture, for which Ledoux had evidently intended the designs outlined in his letter to the Commission Temporaire des Arts, had been announced on 2 May 1794 by the Société Populaire et Républicaine des Arts. It had the support of the Abbé Grégoire, whose *Rapport et projet de décret sur les moyens d'améliorer l'agriculture en France* had proposed the establishment of a "Maison d'Economie Rurale," or center for agricultural studies and teaching, in each department. The official closing date for entries was fixed for 31 July; the competition, however, had still not been judged by December, when a new jury of the arts was elected to replace that selected earlier under David's influence. This second jury, elected by an assembly of artists convened at the Louvre, was both more moderate and more academic than its predecessor: with Quatremére de Quincy as its president, it included the architects Boullée, Le Roy, Léon Dufourny, Jean-Augustin Renard, Antoine-François Peyre le Jeune, Jean-Baptiste Rondelet, and Jacques-Charles Bonnard. Such a group evidently leaned toward conciliation with former members of the Académie. Such a tendency was confirmed by the unprecedented election of the still-imprisoned Ledoux, anticipating and perhaps hastening his release. Jacques-Guillaume Legrand, a continuous supporter of Ledoux, and François Soufflot Le Romain, Soufflot's nephew and employer of Lequeu, were appointed as alternate members. A number of Ledoux's former collaborators and friends were also elected: Augustin Pajou, sculptor of Madame du Barry's pavilion at Louveciennes, and the painters Jean-Marie Vien, Honoré Fragonard, and Hubert Robert. The engraver Jean-Michel Moreau le Jeune, painter of the celebrated scene of the opening of Louveciennes, was an alternate. Ledoux, released on 13 January 1795, could therefore join the jury in the hopes of a full rehabilitation.

This regrouping of former members of the Académie and their students, in evident reaction to the political extremism of the earlier jury, did not go undenounced. Lequeu "copied" the text of a placard that he records as having been affixed to the door of the Louvre Museum and the headquarters of the Comité d'Instruction Publique. In language that recalls Lequeu's own indictments of pre-Revolutionary architects, the notice warned against this academic "conspiracy":

Artists who demand that justice be done, awaken. A party has been formed among the members of the jury of the arts named according to the decree of the National Convention; based apparently on some esteem in society this powerful party has dominated the whole assembly; a species of fool in architecture, the septuagenarian Boullée is at the heart of it; this man has organized everything to this end; importunate canvassing, seductive proposals, nothing is too much for him, and that is why the judging is still in the hands of the Academicians; also these friends carry off the honor and the fruit of your labors.

Architects, fellow competitors, your work is not yet given to the Comité d'Instruction Publique, as you know well; for myself, I hope to expose other details before the jury takes place.

Don't trust Dardel—however much he dissimulates, he hates artists—and watch out for the fawning Ledoux, and for the phlegmatic charlatan Le Roy, etc., etc.[32]

The author of this placard, who signed himself "The Just" (and who might well have been Lequeu himself, discontented at not having been awarded a prize), in this way connected *le patelin* Ledoux to a resurgent academicism: "The opinions of the Boullée party," Lequeu noted, "were said to be fully academic and royalist."[33] Lequeu, whose own projects for a "Gate for Paris that could be called a People's arch" was in some sense a vicious satire on Ledoux's *barrières,* a giant figure of Hercules seated on two rusticated sentry boxes that recall Ledoux's *guérites,* was equally scornful of the competition winners. He called Philibert Moitte's triumphal arch a "Coachmen's Arch" or "The Gate of a Butcher's Shop." But while two of Ledoux's students were among the competitors—Louis-Emmanuel-Aimé Damesme and Jean-Nicolas Sobre—there is no evidence that his views prevailed in the jury, and the prizes were in the end awarded to two of Boullée's protegés, Jean-Nicolas-Louis Durand and Jean-Thomas Thibault, themselves, like Boullée himself, enthusiastic supporters of the Revolution if not of its excesses. In the face of their high "Republican" style, Lequeu's caricatural efforts to win approval seemed exaggerated to Boullée, a judgment later confirmed by Lequeu's ironic comment written on the back of his project for the Parisian gate, "Drawing to save me from the guillotine. Everything for the Fatherland!", an inscription that belied any serious profession of revolutionary faith.[34]

The work of the jury finished on 9 October 1795; after this date there are few public references to Ledoux, who seems to have withdrawn into semiretirement, like Boullée, to complete the text and drawings for his long-announced masterwork. The Rural School of Meillant, his final appeal for recognition as a rural architect, was engraved in this year. The next three years seem to have been exclusively dedicated to the designing, engraving, and writing of projects for *L'architecture*. Occasional notes in the press indicate that he still participated somewhat in public life. In 1798, for example, at the request of Athanese Détournelle, he signed a letter to the Minister of the Interior, with Sobre, Moitte, Bonnard, Poyet, Percier, Fontaine, Pierre-Théodore Bienaimé, Pierre-Jules Delespine, and Félix-Emmanuel Callet, complaining of the length of time taken by the jurors in the competition for the Chateau-Trompette in Bordeaux.[35] In the same year he was recorded as being a member of the intellectual society the Athénée des Etrangers, meeting in the former Hôtel Thélusson. Still under surveillance, he was cited by the police, no doubt correctly, as corresponding with emigrés and royalists in 1799.[36]

The ascendancy of Napoleon after 1798 seemed to Ledoux to offer the conditions for at least a partial rehabilitation. Recommended to Lucien Bonaparte by his old friend Le Brun, now Commissioner of the Musée Centrale des Arts, who called him "a man of genius with an ardent imagination" (24 September 1800), he successfully petitioned for the acceptance of his project to complete the decoration of the triumphal columns at the Barrière du Trône with "trophies, bas-reliefs, inscriptions, and other ornaments."[37] The next year, he was appointed to the commission to judge the competition for a monument to General L. Desaix de Veygoux, together with old friends such as Moreau, Chalgrin, Bélanger, Baltard, and Le Roy as well as younger architects such as Durand, Thibault, Fontaine, Bienaimé, Dufourny, and Détournelle.[38] In the less politically charged atmosphere of the Consulate and Empire, this younger generation was more inclined to pay homage to its teachers.

Ledoux's mood, however, as recorded by Cellérier, was increasingly bitter and resentful, aggravated by the long-drawn-out dispute with his surviving daughter, Alexandrine, who, having left home to live with a musician, Jean Chol, began a suit against her father over her mother's legacy, a litigation that dragged on until 1805. More disappointing still was his exclusion from the new Institut de France, founded to replace the old academies in October 1795, an exclusion made harder to bear by the election of many of his former fellow academicians, including Boullée, Gondouin, De Wailly, Peyre le Jeune, Raymond, and Pâris, as the architect-representatives of the Third Class, Literature and Fine Arts. Ledoux was unable to mask his anger.[39] He argued privately against the restricted number of six architects and, according to Cellérier, "did not hide his ill humor in this regard, when he spoke of it. He could show particular feeling in these sallies, but this is excusable in an honored member of the old Académie who saw himself forgotten."[40] In 1800 he was subjected to another attack, albeit in veiled terms, from the hospital architect Charles-François Viel, whose *Décadence de l'architecture à la fin du dix-huitième siècle* spoke of "two all-too-famous architects," "one celebrated for the extent of his ruinous enterprises; the other for the multitude of his drawings, products of a wayward and disordered imagination," whose "capricious spirit" had diverted a number of architects from the proper study of antique architecture and had "brought about a veritable revolution in the ordonnance of buildings."[41] Ledoux, commonly criticized for his "ruinous enterprises," and Boullée, for his ideal designs, were here accused of setting the fashion for overpublication, the proliferation of new styles, and the general "exhaltation of overweening pride." Viel, like the anonymous pamphleteer cited by Lequeu, saw them at the center of a "kind of sect," the more responsible for the decadence of architecture as it dominated "the tribunal that awards the ordinary prizes of the students" as well as the jury for prize competitions.[42] Writing in 1800, Viel hoped that their success, encouraged by the recent "political convulsions," would last no longer than the century that had reached its end.

The publication of *L'architecture* occupied Ledoux from the late 1790s to 1804, and he evidently hoped that its impact would lead to renewed interest in his work. By the end of 1802, despite lack of external support, Ledoux could write in the *Prospectus* that was distributed in the following year, "The work is finished and engraved by the best artists. The typography, in Didot face, will be of the highest quality, and confided to the presses of C.-F. Patrix."[43] He wrote to his friend Mignard in March 1803, "It is written with energy and in a good style. It is printed and the work is of the greatest luxury: I think it will have much effect."[44] Such was his enthusiasm that he sent copies of the *Prospectus* throughout France—to Mignard, to the officials of Aix (including the son of Saint-Vincent and the lawyer de Gualifey), to the Prefect of Aix with a letter concerning the prisons, to the learned societies of Marseilles, and to others in different provinces.[45]

Opening the *Prospectus,* he optimistically compared himself to the newly awakened Epimenides of Cnossos, whose prophecies, delivered after a long retreat in a cavern, had led to the foundation of Orphism and had guided Solon in the development of a new code of laws for Athens, an obvious parallel to Ledoux's vision of his role in pre- and post-Revolutionary France. He imaged himself as rising from the tomb amidst the ruins of his works—the *barrières*—destroyed by "vandalism." Using a word only newly coined by the Abbé Grégoire in 1793 to characterize the excesses of the Revolution against historical monuments, Ledoux thus associated his own recent monuments, modern versions of antique triumphal entries, with the patrimony of France: "The first rays of the rising sun play upon this heap of stones soiled by vandalism; Nature weeps amidst this political debris" (*Prospectus,* 1).

Late in 1803 the initial sections of the first volume began to appear; the text, printed by Perronneau, accompanied the final installment of plates in 1804. Ledoux was triumphant. This was the work that would justify him to posterity and perhaps renew his favor with the state. Evidently encouraged that the work at Aix might recommence, he received the Mayor of Aix ("He seems a well-born man; I am ignorant of his real character but appearances are in his favor"), listened to the financial straits of the town, now forced to bear the whole expense of the Palais and prisons, and wrote immediately to Brunet.[46] Certainly the reviews, and especially the long, five-part appreciation by Détournelle in the *Journal des arts,* were favorable, even eulogistic; the proclamation of the Empire on 18 May 1804 and Napoleon's coronation seven months later seemed to indicate a new stability and an explicit demand for a public architecture on the scale Ledoux envisioned.

Ledoux lived in such hopes for more than two years, waiting for a recognition that never came. He found few supporters in the milieu of the *style Empire* for the pre-Revolutionary brand of what the anonymous reviewer in the *Journal des bâtiments* called his "architectural metaphysics," a mixture of the sublime and the caricatural.[47] He continued to see old friends: Delille had returned from exile in 1802 and a younger group of architects, including Cellérier, Détournelle, and Pierre Vignon, seems to have courted his favor in these last years. In 1806 Ledoux renewed his professional qualifications by taking out a patent and took part in a jury at the Ecole Impériale des Beaux-Arts with Cellérier, Antoine-Laurent-Thomas Vaudoyer, Mathurin Cherpitel, Antoine-Joseph Debourge, Charles-François Viel, and Charles-Alexandre Guillaumot. The same year Vaudoyer included him, together with Cellérier, in a list of architects to form a proposed new Société Académique d'Architecture, evidently an attempt to provide a professional association for those excluded from the Institut.[48] But in August he was already ill, declining a dinner invitation from Bélanger; on 15 September, preparing for the future, he sold the drawings, plates, proofs, and manuscripts for the completion of *L'architecture* to his young friend and protégé Vignon for 24,000 francs.[49] The subscription to the second volume was then announced in November.[50]

On 12 November Ledoux finally drew up his will, dividing his goods equally between the architect Vignon and his surviving daughter.[51] He had, according to Cellérier, "for a long time, for over three months, lost the gaiety that was at

L'ARCHITECTURE

DE C.N. LE DOUX.

PREMIER VOLUME,

CONTENANT DES PLANS, ELEVATIONS, COUPES,

VUES PERSPECTIVES

de Villes, Usines, Greniers à sel, Bâtiments
de graduation, Bains publics, Marchés, Eglises,
Cimetières, Théâtres, Ponts, Hôtelleries, Maisons
de Ville et de Campagne de tout genre, Maisons
de Commerce, de Négociants, d'Employés, d'Edifices
destinés aux récréations publiques, &c. &c.

Construits ou commencés depuis 1768 jusques en 1789.

*Collection qui rassemble tous les Genres de Bâtimens
Employés dans l'ordre social.*

Ledoux, First title page to
L'architecture, vol. 1. Engrav-
ing, 1789, from Ledoux,
L'architecture.

the basis of his character; he was weighed down with sorrows
and as many regrets that derived from the subjects of his affection."[52] Seven days later, following a protracted attack of
paralysis, he died. His funeral attracted, according to a witness, "almost all the architects, intellectuals, and artists of
Paris," who, despite the rain, followed the cortege of twenty
carriages on foot to the cemetery of Montmartre.[53] Ledoux's
friend the poet Luce de Lancival delivered a brief *éloge,* read a
verse by Delille, and placed a wreath on the tomb; Vignon
read what an observer called "a very moving discourse that
showed his attachment to his master and friend."[54] The ceremony concluded with the announcement of a design competition in memory of Ledoux, the second prize for which
would be a copy of *L'architecture.* Cellérier was to claim that
at least sixty students from the Ecole Spéciale d'Architecture
entered the first competition.

When, some days later, Pierre Vignon and Alexandrine
Chol, née Ledoux, together with their respective notaries, arrived at 16 rue Neuve d'Orléans to settle the estate, they
found an establishment much reduced in style from that of
twenty years before.[55] The furniture was worn, the paintings
few and of doubtful quality, the decorations meager. Fifty
bottles and a barrel of old Mâcon wine were left in the cellar;
a plaster figure of the dying Achilles decorated the dining
room; an ivory bust of Voltaire and an *écritoire* containing Ledoux's drawing instruments were in the bedroom.

Ledoux's library was small, in comparison, for example, to those of his contemporaries Boullée and De Wailly:
only some two hundred twenty volumes were listed in the
inventory. They included thirty large folio volumes on architecture shelved in Ledoux's study, "among which was Blondel's *Cours d'architecture,*" according to the notary, who had
perhaps mistaken the title of Blondel's folio work, the *Architecture françoise.* A small mahogany bookcase in the dining
room contained fifty-five volumes in quarto, including De-
leyre's *Histoire des voyages* in twenty-one volumes, the Abbé
Raynal's *Histoire philosophique et politique des établissements et du
commerce des Européens dans les deux Indes* of 1770 in six volumes, the *Oeuvres* of Alexis Piron in nine volumes, and the

Dictionnaire des grands hommes in six volumes, among other literary works. Delisle de Sale's *De la philosophie de la nature* of 1777 and the *Bibliothèque des Romans* were together with a hundred bound volumes in an armoire in the bedroom. A further thirty-five books were recorded in a small boudoir given onto the salon, including the works of Tasso in Italian. To these works must be added the even shorter list provided by Cellérier, who confirmed that Ledoux's library was modest: Vitruvius, Palladio, Serlio, Inigo Jones, and "two or three authors of this caliber."[56]

The drawings, engravings, and notes for *L'architecture* were not listed; no doubt Ledoux had already passed them on to Vignon in September, when he had named his student, together with Cellérier and Damesme, as responsible for completing the publication. Of these, only those plates retrieved under obscure circumstances by Daniel Ramée and published in 1846 survived.

A TEXT WITHOUT A GENRE

SENTIMENTAL ARCHITECTURE

The first volume of *L'architecture considérée sous le rapport de l'art, des moeurs et de la législation* had, as we have seen, been a long time in preparation; conceived as a collection of plates in the 1780s, it had been frequently announced from 1784 on. By 1787, Luc-Vincent Thiéry, author of a popular guide to Paris, was almost resigned to its indefinite postponement: "This artist [Ledoux]," he wrote, "is incessantly announcing to the public a considerable collection of engraved plates."[57] These delays were the result more of Ledoux's continuous reworking of the plates than of a lack of subscribers: Joseph II of Austria, Marie-Antoinette's brother, had met Ledoux at the house of Mlle Guimard in 1777, and later subscribed; Paul I of Russia, then Grand Duke, had accepted the dedication of the book on his visit to Paris in 1782. In the two collections Ledoux prepared for presentation to the Contrôleurs des Finances, Joly de Fleury (seventy-eight engravings in 1781) and Le Fèvre d'Ormesson (eighty-five engravings in 1783), none of the ideal projects for Chaux were evident; in a third, that

now in the collection of the Bibliothèque d'Art et Archéologie, only the Church, the Market, and the Public Baths of Chaux are included among one hundred sixty engravings of built and commissioned works. Paul I had finally received a set of two hundred seventy-three drawings in the spring of 1789; it is not known whether these were engravings or originals. The first title page in fact dated from this year. Simply called *L'architecture de C.-N. Ledoux,* it listed the general contents:

Towns, Factories, Warehouses for salt, Graduation Buildings, Public Baths, Markets, Churches, Cemeteries, Theaters, Bridges, Hostelries, Town and Country Houses of every kind, Commercial Buildings, Houses for Merchants and Employees, Buildings for Public Recreation, etc., etc.

In this list of building types, "constructed or begun from 1768 until 1789," the quasi-didactic, quasi-encyclopedic nature of the final work was already apparent, while the social idealism of the projects was announced in a qualifying note that characterized the book as a "Collection that brings together all the Kinds of Buildings Used in the Social Order."

Gradually the text, which had evidently been conceived originally as a traditional commentary on a collection of designs, took on a more elaborate theoretical and literary shape. Ledoux, between 1789 and 1800, brought together fragments of his writing—pieces of letters to friends and clients, descriptions, and official reports—and inserted them into a continuous "meditation" on his career and on architecture and society in general.

The first indications of this change appeared in a summary of the forthcoming book that Ledoux prepared as a part of a submission to the Institut, no doubt to solicit membership, on 10 September 1801. This fragment was, as Monique Mosser has correctly pointed out, a first draft of the *Prospectus* of 1802.[58] It announced a number of important themes. To begin with, the *recueil,* or collection, now had a title: *Architecture sentimentale, contenant tous les genres d'édifices connus dans l'ordre social.* With this conceptual framing, "sentimental architecture," the work was now associated with a philosophic, or more properly a psychological, principle of art: the effect of architecture on the sentiments, its moral and didactic power as experienced through the sensations, a theory based on the materialism of Locke, Condillac, and Helvétius, mediated through the literary sensibilities of Rousseau, Bernadin de Saint-Pierre, Saint-Lambert, the Abbé Delille, and, in art and architecture, Watelet, Le Camus de Mézières, and, of course, Boullée, whose manuscript was well known to members of his circle before his death. Ledoux was, in this initial extension of the theme of a "collection," reflecting a renewed interest in the nature of the feelings stimulated by the members of the circle around Destutt de Tracy and the Institut, the self-named *idéologues,* as they attempted to generalize a theory of knowledge and language based on a systematic application of Condillac's principles. The question of sentiment was equally raised by the preromantic heirs to Rousseau's meditations on feeling, and most notably by quasi-mystics such as Pierre Ballanche, first patron of the young Charles Fourier, whose book *Du sentiment considérée dans ses rapports avec la littérature et les arts* was published in Lyons and Paris in 1801. Ballanche's title, together with his plea for the free play of sentiment in the poetics of the arts, freed from the restrictions of the schools of logic and rhetoric, was to be echoed by Ledoux.

Furthermore, the work as Ledoux described it in this preliminary outline was greatly expanded from the original one-volume *recueil.* As now announced it was to appear in six volumes, one per year, and to contain a longer list of designs, including most of the rural and symbolic designs of 1789–1800. Ledoux himself characterized the work as somewhere between Diderot's *Encyclopédie* and the new Napoleonic museums: it was "an Encyclopedia or Architectural Museum." In this way, Ledoux joined his collected designs on the one hand to the rational definition of types displayed in encyclopedic completeness and on the other to the more literal collections of buildings assembled in engraved form by Durand and as scale models by Cassas, or even, as the fragmentary nature of the text intimated, the Musée des Monuments Française of Alexandre Lenoir.[59] The word "museum" was, besides, to be read in conjunction with the title, *Architecture*

Sentimentale, a work dedicated to and conceived under the guidance of the Muses.

For the first time, outside of his letters to clients, Ledoux's views on the relations of architecture to society would be directly presented; the précis stated, "Analysis of the social virtues, political economy, commerce, industry. The development of the great resources that extend the power of nations. Analysis of progresive ideas. . . ."[60] Among these progressive ideas, which, Ledoux claimed, "stimulate the products of the imagination," were listed practical reforms that included the proper siting of towns for reasons of health, together with the aesthetic concepts of formal variety; "analogy," by which Ledoux meant the association of a form with an idea, in the terms of a Lockean "chain of associations"; and the nature of the picturesque, as explored in the *fabriques pittoresques* designed for the parks of Bourneville and Belleville. These ideas, as befitted a treatise informed by philosophical rationalism, were each in turn founded on the concept of "origins": "Of the origins of all things, of the first cults adapted to morality, to architecture; of its progress and deviations. . . . The moral and philosophic aim of the work, supported in its entirety on the principles of nature and returned to the universal system that constitutes the happiness of the greatest number."[61] From the origins of architecture, to its progress, to the happiness it provides for the greatest number: these ideas ran through the gamut of Enlightenment themes, Encyclopedic and Benthamite. Their peculiar mixture of rationalism and sentimentality, expounded in Ledoux's discursive prose, was to make his text, for his contemporaries and later interpreters, so singularly difficult to read.

At sixty-four years old, weakened by imprisonment and privation, impoverished by his lack of work, Ledoux was well aware of the difficulties of the task he had set himself: "This elementary concatenation of ideas is until now unprecedented; to finish it demands much time, the willpower to command the best, an enormous expense: the possibility of writing."[62] In the face of the impossibility of building, the "possibility of writing" had become the architect's last hope.

Confirming and extending these announced themes, the published *Prospectus* of 1803 outlined the now five volumes projected for publication, under the rubric of what was to be the definitive titles, *Architecture considered in relation to Art, Mores and Legislation*. The first volume was to collect the designs for the Saline de Chaux, the town of Chaux, and the institutions and building types conceived for the region of Franche-Comté; the second, third, and fourth volumes would unite, in no very systematic order, Ledoux's private and public projects for Paris and the provinces; the fifth was to be dedicated entirely to the "Propylaea of Paris."[63]

FROM RECUEIL TO ENCYCLOPÉDIE

As published in 1804, the first and only volume of *L'architecture* to be completed by Ledoux comprised one hundred twenty-five engraved plates accompanied by two hundred forty pages of text. It contained the first title page of 1789, a second title page of 1804, a dedication page, and a frontispiece. This image, engraved by Charles-Nicolas Varin, showed a portrait bust of Ledoux set in a blind window framed by female caryatids in the style of Jean Goujon's portico at the Louvre. A frieze of shields taken from the *barrières* decorates the architrave, while the caryatids hold up a curtain in front of the opening, inscribed with the full title of the work. The quasi-initiatory character of this image, an invitation to enter the book as if through an architectural opening, derives further force from the emblems surrounding the bust of Ledoux. Beside the partially unrolled drawings showing the Palais de Justice and prisons of Aix and two of the *barrières* are a compass and square (commonplace signs of the architect), a telescope (signifying the architect's powerful gaze), and a branch of acacia. These motifs invoke the iconography of Freemasonry and, when placed within the two columns, leave little ambiguity as to their intended reading. Ledoux had appropriated the imagery of the seal of the Grand Orient and the signs of the Neuf Soeurs lodge to imply his role as architect-initiator, one that he had already displayed to Beckford twenty years before.

The dedication, originally promised to Paul I of Russia, was, after his death on 24 March 1801, now given to his successor, Alexander I, with a convenient rhetorical flourish that compared him to the first, Greek, Alexander:

The Scythians, attacked by Alexander of Macedonia in the midst of the deserts and rocks that they inhabited, said to that conqueror: you are thus not a god because you do ill to men!

All the peoples of the earth will say to Alexander of the North: you are a man! since you wish to subscribe to a social system that will contribute to the happiness of the human species.

The new title of the book, with its emphasis on the relations between architecture and society, its mutual dependency and influence on laws, mores, and the arts, alluded in an evidently self-conscious way to a range of similar investigations that had been published in other fields. Ledoux himself referred in the *Prospectus* to his desire to emulate Montesquieu's *Esprit des lois*—"Montesquieu created a code of laws for nations. For the first time, art brings together natural laws and composes a social system"—and undoubtedly he joined this to the "Morals and Legislation" of Bentham's treatise. But other, more recent titles seem to have been evoked; that of Ballanche has already been noted. The formula "considered in relation to," or "considered in its effects on," had indeed been introduced by the Institut, which in 1795 had set the prize question, "What has been and what could be still the influence of painting on the mores and government of peoples?" The mathematician George-Marie Raymond had gained third place with his *De la peinture considérée dans ses effets sur les hommes de toutes les classes et de son influence sur les moeurs et le gouvernement des peuples*, published in 1804 but widely reported in 1798. In this otherwise undistinguished treatise, Raymond stressed the relation, already developed by Quatremère de Quincy, between the character of nations, peoples, and their arts and argued for the preservation of the arts of every period.

The joining of "legislation" and "mores" in Ledoux's title was derived not only from Montesquieu and Bentham but also from Diderot, whose consideration of the effect of legislation on the mores of a people was formulated in the article "Moeurs" for the *Encyclopédie*. Here *moeurs* were defined as "the free actions of men, natural or acquired, good or bad, susceptible to rules and directions," a vision of man as a being that might be "modified" that was expanded in the

Ledoux, Frontispiece to *L'ar-chitecture*, 1804. Engraving by Varin from Ramée, *Ledoux*.

Ledoux, Dedication to *L'archi-tecture*. Engraving by Dien.

A SA MAJESTÉ

L'EMPEREUR

DE TOUTES LES RUSSIES.

Les Scytes attaqués par Alexandre de Macédoine, jusques au milieu des déserts et des rochers qu'ils habitaient, dirent à ce conquérant : Tu n'es donc pas un dieu, puisque tu fais du mal aux hommes !

Tous les peuples de la terre diront à l'Alexandre du Nord : Vous êtes un homme ! puisque vous voulez bien accueillir un système social, qui contribuera au bonheur du genre humain.

J'ai l'honneur d'être, avec la reconnaissance la plus respectueuse,

de Votre Majesté Impériale,

Le très-humble & très-obéissant Serviteur,

Le Doux.

Gravé par Dien.

article "Modification." [64] "It cannot be doubted," wrote Diderot in 1769, "that laws, in time, change the mores of a people." [65] But where Diderot felt that this was a slow and sometimes imperceptible process, resisted more often than not by the innate, natural "turn of mind of a people," Ledoux was more optimistic, claiming that the art of architecture would surpass that of the law in shaping social morality. Where legislation had failed architecture would succeed.

The text of the first volume was, however, an unabashed collage of fragments written throughout his life, assembled out of pieces of letters to clients (the earliest, the letter to de Lacoré of 1775 describing and justifying his first project for the Theater of Besançon), memoranda, from the report on the *salines* to his justification *mémoire* on the *barrières* drawn up while in prison, and paraphrases of contemporary works. It was divided, often quite arbitrarily, by the titles of engravings, at points that did not necessarily correspond to their "description." At moments Ledoux interrupted the text dramatically to register breaks in the writing. Thus, on his arrest in 1793, he inserted a space: ". . . . . ."—a typographical symbol of his imprisonment—only to resume, not without irony, "I was interrupted . . . The national axe was raised, they called for Ledoux, but it was not me, my happy star guided it: it was a Doctor of the Sorbonne with the same name. Unhappy victim! . . . I continue" (230).

The engravings themselves were brought together from all stages of his career, often "revised" to bring them into line with his later ideas of style. Early engravings by François-Noël Sellier for the Saline de Chaux and the Theater of Besançon took their place beside the late ideal projects engraved for the most part by Van Maëlle and his collaborators, Simon and Maillet. They were responsible for over twenty plates, including the Hospice, the Pacifère, the Stock Exchange, the House of Union, the House of Education, the Panarèthéon, the Hunting Lodge, and most of the Country Houses. The calligrapher-engraver Dien, who had inscribed the months on the most popular engraving of the Revolutionary calendar, prepared the dedication. Charles-Nicolas Varin, in addition to the new frontispiece, engraved some of the later agricultural projects, the Grange Parée and the House of the Forest Guards; his brother, Joseph Varin, depicted the Theater of Besançon and the Hôtel de Ville of Neuchâtel in perspective (this last project not included in Ledoux's first volume). Together the brothers Varin completed the meticulous perspective view of the Church of Chaux. Pierre-Nicolas Ransonnette, engraver by appointment to Monsieur, brother to the King, and contributor of plates to the *Encyclopédie,* drew up the Bridge over the Loüe River, the small *hôtellerie,* the Workshop of the Woodcutters, and the plan of the Cemetery. The beautiful perspectives, on which the reputation of the book rested for a long time, were the work of a number of experts in landscape effects. Pierre-Gabriel Berthault, a specialist in perspective drawing who had contributed to Saint-Non's *Voyage à Naples et en Sicile,* engraved the graduation building, the Public Baths, and the grand vision of the "Perspective View of the Town of Chaux," plates that must have been among the earliest completed. Edme Bovinet elaborated the view of the Bridge over the Loüe River and the dramatic "Elevation of the Cemetery of Chaux" and, with Coquet, those of the Director's House of the *saline,* the Oikéma, and the Cannon Foundry. Dupuis (perhaps François-Nicolas, who exhibited at the Salon between 1795 and 1802) recorded Ledoux's final scheme for the Town of Chaux on the "Map of the Surroundings of the Saline de Chaux." Other, single plates were farmed out to Heluis, Boutrois, Ciony, Delaitre, J.-J. De La Porte, Crépy, A. Moitte, and N.-F.-J. Masquelier le Jeune.

On one level, the ostensible form of the book followed the pattern, outlined by Blondel and Boullée and realized for the Académie by Prieur, of a collection of programs accompanied by model solutions. Boullée had described such a collection as a "museum," calling for its permanent exhibition for architects and their students. In his unpublished treatise he had expanded this format to incorporate long meditations on the appropriate characterization of specific types, on the aesthetic correspondences between nature and art, and on the high role of the architect, using the assemblage of particular exercises to compose a general treatise on architecture. Ledoux, who was no doubt familiar with Boullée's *Architecture,* which passed into the hands of his student Joachim Bénard after his death in 1799, took the form even further: he creatively recast the traditional "program" as a combined literary and architectural fantasy, the medium for the invention of new programs and their corresponding architectural equivalents. Each ideal and real design in *L'architecture* is joined to a gloss that purports to be both its genesis and explanation. Program and design work together, as in the *Encyclopédie,* to give authority to each other. The assemblage of these virtually self-contained texts, again as in the *Encyclopédie,* but without the apparent order provided by the alphabet, reads like a rambling, plotless, picaresque novel. Families are endowed with pedigrees to explain new house types; individuals from every class are described in their lives and productive activities as a means of endowing otherwise inexplicable designs with verisimilitude; communities are depicted in collective acts that range from the hermetic to the pornographic in buildings whose idiosyncratic plans "represent" and literally "institute" them. In this way Ledoux developed a commentary on, and a kind of revenge against, the programmatic obsessions of the previous thirty years that had, first in the domains of hospital and prison planning and then, in the hands of Durand, extended to all public functions, gradually reduced the role of representation.

The effect of Ledoux's "fictions of function" was, in fact, to transform the idea of the academic "program" on two distinct levels. First, by narrating the fiction of living occupants for his ideal designs, Ledoux at once cemented the assumed relations of social mores to architectural form and elided hypothesized behavior and projected object, in a way that ascribed a level of reality to the architecture itself. Such a relation between text and form would, indeed, become the rule for all nineteenth- and many twentieth-century urban and rural utopias, being fully elaborated in, for example, the relation between the utopian novel—Emile Zola's *Travail*—and the utopian city—Tony Garnier's Cité Industrielle. Second, in the elaboration of detailed descriptions, often of an exotic nature, the abstract forms of his architecture were, as he noted, given their own "speech," sometimes as an extension of the iconic form of the design and sometimes, as in the juxtaposition of design and fable in the project of the Hospice, as a way of rendering the architecture entirely dependent

on the text for its meaning—an intimation of the death of architecture at the hands of the book rhetorically claimed by Victor Hugo thirty years later.

Certainly, too, Ledoux wanted his book to rival not only the *Encyclopédie* but also the *Cours* of his master Blondel; from the outset, the *Prospectus* and the introduction to the first volume propose a consideration of architecture in terms of its theoretical categories and their definition. Thus, in an elaborate allegory that opens the *Prospectus,* Ledoux drew an image of the "Temple of Imagination," seat of the virtues, qualities, and attributes of the arts. On first inspection this "temple," an obvious homage to the Abbé Delille, who had included a eulogy to Ledoux's ideal city in his own poem "L'imagination," was a simple commonplace device for the rhetorical presentation of abstract concepts, a transposition of the pictorial into the poetic. Ledoux's image might, in this sense, recall Cochin's engraved frontispiece to the *Encyclopédie,* or, alternatively, the painterly allegories of André Chénier.[66] Thus Ledoux's artistic company, ranged dutifully beneath the auspices of Nature herself, is headed by Apollo and includes, in order of rank, such "divinities" as Beauty, Health, and Temperature—a hygienic extension of the traditional canon—as well as the classical qualities of *convenance, ordonnance, style, bienséance, symmetrie, variété, sévérité, unité, commodité, distribution, décoration, proportion, génie, jugement, raisonnement, méthode,* and, to conclude, the goddess Minerva, deity of the handicrafts. Ledoux's temple-dictionary composes, so to speak, the "theory" of the art of architecture according to the mid-century wisdom outlined by Blondel.

But, on another level, it is clear that Ledoux has not summoned up these spirits simply to demonstrate his scholarly erudition or his addiction to the doctrine of the schools. Rather he envisages himself, like Epimenides, as a *new* lawgiver, rising from the ashes of political turmoil, a herald of the future: the Temple of Imagination has not, in fact, resisted the new forces of change, and was indeed, in his account, profoundly modified by his own assimilation of progress into his practice:

This was the composition of the Council of majestic Nature, when Industry, born on the confidence of financial transactions, on that insensible tax that causes affluence to circulate by rendering to the solstice of winter the laborious sweat of the summer, was admitted to this august tribunal: there she deployed her vast wheels. (2)

By thus infiltrating "the vast wheels" of industry into the Temple of Imagination, Ledoux has imaged the transformation to be registered by all theoretical categories in his post-Physiocratic universe. This process of redefining Blondel's definitions was continued in the introduction to *L'architecture.*

Ledoux's last work was also, in this era of "Confessions," a personal *mémoire,* a long reverie on an incomplete career, a spirited vindication of its reversals, a testament to the best of intentions. Even as Rousseau proposed to reveal, in the model of the genre, "simply himself," so Ledoux the architect opened with a personal appeal to this court of last resort, the sympathetic reader:

Amidst the host of preoccupations, the size of which may be judged by the immensity of the work that I submit to the view of nations; in the midst of agitations with which they have exhausted my constancy; enmired in persecutions that are inseparable from the publicity attendant on great conceptions, and passions that have spent themselves against my energy; almost all the while subjected to reduced budgets, timidly deployed fortunes, and shifting policies that neutralize the flights of genius, I will not present to my readers the kind of projects that are lost in the vagueness of imaginary combinations, or whose frightening possibilities preclude their execution in advance. (1)

If Ledoux's book was the first architectural treatise to introduce in its title the subjects of art, legislation, and mores, in its text it was the first to introduce the author, the first-person self as its major protagonist. The tired but undefeated creator, emotionally spent and socially broken, still has as a last recourse the autobiographical text. From this text readers may well derive insights into the state of architecture, the conditions of architectural practice, and the utopian ideals of a designer, but as a whole it serves to present an apologia and a history of Ledoux's personal self. And it is this self, not any systematic or institutionalized society nor any honored tradition of architecture, that gives authority and legitimacy to the work of design. In this, despite all arguments over the specific qualities of "neoclassicism," "romantic-classicism," or "romanticism," Ledoux showed himself, like Rousseau, to be self-aware, self-preoccupied, self-generating, an autobiographical, and thereby fundamentally modern, architect.

Feeding this nostalgic self-preoccupation was Ledoux's sense of a change in the nature of history itself. For side by side with the ideal of the spatial sublime, atemporal and ahistorical, the instrument of neoclassical eternalization, there was emerging toward the end of the century another sensibility, also linked to the sublime, that might be termed "historicist." Epitomized by the celebrated frontispiece to the Comte de Volney's *Ruines,* which depicted a solitary and reflective traveler surveying the ruins of Palmyra, this was, in retrospect, a threat to the static versions of historical precedent espoused by Ledoux's generation. Volney, followed by Chateaubriand and the first generation of romantics, would regard the very transience of history as a sublime fact:

The view of an illustrious city deserted, the remembrance of past times, their comparison with the present state of things, all combined to raise my heart to a strain of sublime meditation. I sat down on the base of a column, and there, my elbow on my knee and my head resting on my hand, sometimes turning my eyes toward the desert, sometimes fixing them on the ruins, I fell into a profound reverie.[67]

Like Gibbon among the ruins of the Capitol or Séroux d'Agincourt in the catacombs, Volney was struck by the funereal aspect of a ruined past, the city reduced to a "mournful skeleton," the "silence of the tomb" replacing the noise of the living street. Against such a vision of eternal change and mutability, one certainly warranted in the context of the Revolutionary years, Ledoux marshaled his defences. Preferring his history to be entirely absorbed in a universal aesthetic of abstract allusions, he stated on the first page of *L'architecture* that "the annals of time" should be "abbreviated," summarized to engender eternal principles, models for general application and individual imitation. No hint of acceptance of stylistic eclecticism or historical relativism appears in the entire work. Read in this way, Ledoux's text and plates represent a last and protracted defense against the incursions of the ruinating effects of history and the revolutions, rise and fall of empires, it brought in its wake. Ledoux intended his "museum," finally, to be made out of living antihistorical types, not one of already formed quotations from an already dead past.

CRITICAL RECEPTION

The reviews of Ledoux's masterwork were largely favorable, and their number indicates that the author was far from forgotten, if not yet entirely rehabilitated in the public mind. In January 1803 the *Journal des bâtiments, des monuments et des arts* noted the publication of the book, trying to set a proper tone for its reception: "It is always a renewed pleasure for us to announce the productions of artists: above all those that disseminated among all the powers of Europe, have attained for their author a celebrity that none can attack or put in doubt."[68] Such an evaluation, however against general opinion, was at least an attempt to revindicate the old royalist architect. Conscious of the need to apologize for one so deeply implicated in a discredited regime, the announcement went to great pains to explain the circumstances of what Ledoux himself called his "rebirth":

To describe thus a man who, having turned grey amidst a host of buildings of every kind, has contributed to the glory of French architecture and who, withdrawn to the silence of his study, has created for himself, in some way, a new existence, is it not to indicate in advance that we are not afraid to propose Citizen Ledoux, this consummate architect, as a model for artists and amateurs of every country?[69]

The phrase "withdrawn to the silence of his study" intimated the condition of practice enforced by political revolution, the enforced and unhappy state of an architect without work, the condition of a suspended career that might at any moment be reconstituted.

The review articles that appeared in the *Journal des bâtiments* (or *Annales de l'architecture* as it became in 1806) were enthusiastic; in April 1806 the *Prospectus* was summarized and in November the book itself was reviewed, followed in the next month by a deeply sympathetic *nécrologie*. The work, stated the anonymous reviewer, was indeed a veritable "architectural encyclopedia." It was at once a treatise on architecture and its aesthetics ("the unity of thoughts, variety of forms, taste, suitability, fitness, analogy, method, the characters, proportion, beauty, distribution, decoration . . ."), a scientific handbook (on "the healthiness of towns and villages, of sites and temperature"), a manual for rural instruction (for "the inhabitants of the countryside far from the resources of large towns"), and a treatise on political economy, commerce, industry, and public welfare to be read by artists and administrators.[70] In 1806, with Revolution having been transformed into imperial stability, should not, the reviewer asked, Ledoux be accorded the honors of one who would contribute to the glory of the Empire? "In the same way as the former Académie Française, most of whose members were plunged into the most absolute oblivion, will not Ledoux, like Molière, survive for all ages to come?"[71]

The most substantial assessment was published by Athanase Détournelle, architect and journalist, for the *Journal des arts, des sciences et de littérature,* appearing in five installments in April 1804.[72] Détournelle, who had already reviewed Durand's *Précis des leçons*, Dubut's *Architecture civile,* Rondelet's *Traité théorique et pratique* and Quatremère de Quincy's *De l'architecture égyptienne,* had found Ledoux's *Prospectus* "more or less amphigoric" and "extremely curious" in its written style and had quoted extensively from its opening paragraphs.[73] He found the introduction to the first volume equally difficult, an "obstacle" to comprehending the work as a whole and full of "écarts en littérature."[74] Despite this, he selected a number of passages from this introduction to demonstrate that Ledoux, behind this overblown rhetoric, was full of "thoughts, grand ideas, and genius," worthy of a philosopher. He noted with approbation Ledoux's ideas on the high task of the architect, the need for liberty of conception and artistic style, and the chain of figurative allusions that led to the correct choice of motifs, and he sympathized with Ledoux's sense of persecution and his bitterness over his dismissal from the *barrières*. Détournelle, who had fully entered the debates over a proper "revolutionary" architecture, argued in favor of Ledoux against those who from jealousy or political intrigue had "deeply wounded" him.[75] These passages of moral and personal reflection caused Détournelle to modify his initial judgment of Ledoux's writing as "*amphigourique*" and to admit its real qualities.

Détournelle's long review was conceived as a way of introducing a work that was "costly and difficult to find" to the general public, while at the same time advertising a newly opened reading room sponsored by the publisher of the *Journal des arts*. This Salon des Arts on the Quai Conti, beside the Pont Neuf, had been established a few months before; in the notice that appeared in the journal in February, it had been described as a *cabinet littéraire* for artists and architects, a place for "tranquil conversation and discussions full of wisdom, on the arts of design, their theory and practice."[76] The works of Durand, Dubut, Krafft, Landon, Percier, Boutrois, and Delettre were already available, together with the physiognomical studies of Lavater and the new publication of the Grands Prix; "in a few days," the notice had concluded, "the architectural works of M. Ledoux will take their place among the riches of this cabinet."[77] Accordingly, Détournelle organized his review as a plate by plate commentary, a readily assimilable accompaniment to a visual inspection at the Salon des Arts. Starting with the frontispiece, he followed the order of Ledoux's text and engravings through this first volume, encompassing in these notes the two hundred thirty pages of text and the one hundred seventeen plates available to him. It appeared that Détournelle had been supplied with an imperfect edition: "The work of M. Ledoux is in very few hands. One can leaf through it in a literary reading room, at the Salon des Arts, Quai Conti. The example on show there is not made up of the best proofs; it seems that they are plates that have served as first proofs to be corrected; it also lacks some plates, and there are many still without the name of the engravers."[78]

But Détournelle's observations were not simply descriptive. At the outset he defended his right to criticize judiciously, in a passage that, in a period when the forms of artistic criticism were being worked out, stood as a manifesto for a yet nonexistent architectural criticism:

The architects do not say what they think of their works among themselves, and still less publicly. Would that artists employed by the government might speak out on the work, on which they would surely have many observations to make, and how useful this would be for the advancement of the art! But they do not wish to provoke quarrels and stick close to their pusillanimous considerations. We ourselves, who have proved in many circumstances how open we were on this subject, have in our moments of leisure promised ourselves to review the different works that appear publicly; and we will make every effort to torment their authors as little as possible, while never forgetting to praise and to analyze whatever is good in them."[79]

With regard to Ledoux, Détournelle set himself the task of explaining the work, as he put it, "like a father who explains to his son the mores and circumstances of a country where he is being sent for instruction."[80] In the process, he provided a detailed summary of contemporary responses to Ledoux's ideal designs.

His criticism was above all practical: the workshops of the House of the Sawyers are too close to the living quarters; the salons of many of the country houses, placed in the middle of the buildings, are too dark; bedrooms are too small, often the bed must be placed three feet from the fireplace, with no room for other furniture; surrounding galleries deprive rooms of light; the servants are often treated better than their masters; courtyards thirty feet square surrounded by buildings fifty feet high are unhealthy; the assembly room of the Stock Exchange has the "proportions of a well"; the circular stairs in the triumphal columns of the Temple of Memory are too narrow and long; windows in many of the country houses are too small and too high; the audience chamber of the Pacifère is too dark; the rooms of the House of Union are similarly badly lit—"we doubt that one could read a book in daylight"; the oval salon of the Oikéma would be disagreeable to decorate. Assessing the character of the various designs, Détournelle was generally favorable, save for his dislike of the *colonnes à bossages* of the Saline de Chaux and an occasional warning against the use of conceits such as the tree-trunk orders of the House of the Woodcutters. Of the ideal designs, he preferred the Bridge over the Loüe River ("a very ingenious idea"); the Hospice ("one of the most beautiful plans in the book: simplicity, unity, balance, health, severity in the elevation; nothing too much, nothing forgotten"); the commercial buildings ("Here the most severe critic should be silent: masterpiece of planning"); the porticoes ("One cannot praise too much the motive and intention of such a good idea"); the Market of Chaux ("The disposition is magnificent; the style and decoration suitable. This scheme attests to knowledge of economy and politics"); and, finally, the Oikéma ("One can only praise this project. Many buildings of this kind would be extremely necessary in a large town such as Paris; and many authors who have written on this subject have always thought that morals would be improved by this"). On Ledoux's architecture in general Détournelle was laudatory: "The architecture has a very individual style; it is extremely picturesque, original, and new." But, as the engravings of the Theater of Besançon show, Ledoux was, Détournelle concluded, better in his built than in his ideal projects:

All the monuments that M. Ledoux has built are much better than those that have only been confided to a portfolio. On the occasions when he has had to realize a project, the author has studied it more and shown more wisdom, more true taste than on other occasions. The Hôtel d'Uzès, the infinity of barrières, *and the Theater of Besançon are monuments whose reputation, justly gained, will last longer than that of his engraved works; and these authentic witnesses to talent will assign him a distinguished place among the most celebrated architects of our day. In terms of composition, he has contributed more than any other to throw off the yoke that architecture bore under Louis XV.*[81]

While Détournelle thus concluded in favor of Ledoux's buildings and expressed reservations about his ideal projects and "too poetic," "fiery" prose, an anonymous reviewer of the *Prospectus* in the *Journal des monuments et des arts* in 1804 was more favorable to his style of writing. He perfectly characterized Ledoux's problematic genre and the difficulties that a younger generation might have with Ledoux's stripped, almost ahistorical designs:

If in the lines and plans there are minute errors to be found, there are no fewer generating ideas and these alone will be enough response to small minds who, perceiving these errors and searching for them, find in them material for jealous criticisms. One must therefore identify with the author, and follow him still more in his text than in his designs, which are only its result. . . . In a word, the precepts of Ledoux are traced less in the arid lines of his architecture than in the figuration of his text; it is from this that they must be drawn. This architectural metaphysics, if it is possible to use the term, could be compared to the art of sculpture, which presents in its figures only what imagination has been able to create concerning the ideal of a god, but which is not the god himself and leaves many stages to be overcome before exhausting all possible ideas.[82]

Less taken with Ledoux's "figurative style," other reviewers were content to admire the plates for their quality but dismissed the text as unreadable. This reputation has followed the book well into the twentieth century. J.-M. Quérard, for example, in 1833, delivered a judgment that has served many commentators since: "As for the plates and the typography, this work is fit for the richest libraries; but its text has been written by Ledoux with an emphasis and flights of imagination that render it hardly intelligible."[83]

In retrospect, perhaps the mythical unreadability of Ledoux's book does not really stem from the amphibological style in which it was written (it might be compared to many minor preromantic works of similar tone and flourish from which Ledoux, indeed, freely drew), nor even from the way in which Ledoux treated the various subjects of his discourse. There were many so-called utopian texts in the late eighteenth century that pose more formidable tasks of interpretation. Rather the problem seems to arise from Ledoux's deliberate confusion of *genres,* in a mixture that would have perplexed a purely literary audience and that entirely baffled his architectural readers.

The book was evidently not a simple *recueil* of drawings, gathering together, as first proposed, the designs of an architect's career. Certainly the text could not be understood as "theory" in the traditional sense inherited from Alberti through Blondel. Nor, in its unsystematic arrangement, could it be construed as a dictionary or encyclopedia along the lines of Quatremère de Quincy's volumes for the *Encyclopédie méthodique;* although it pretended to didactic intent, it lacked any apparent order and resisted either interpretation or imitation. And while Ledoux spoke in general terms of "abbreviating the annals of time" and of following a "chronological" order, there was little if any history in his text.

Some critics have preferred to read the book as a utopia; but the conventional form, as developed from Thomas More to Fénelon, was tied to a more continuous narrative and sustained story line than that offered by Ledoux. Compared with the radical political utopias of the eighteenth century, such as the *Code de la nature* of Morelly or the rural economics of Gracchus Babeuf, Ledoux provided little in the way of explicit recipes for a new way of life. Despite his attempt to preserve a form of unity, however fragmentary, by introducing the "traveler" whose visit to Franche-Comté provided an excuse for the discussion of some of the designs for Chaux, the work was not a fully developed travelogue either, in the sense of Léquinio's description of the region. Literary genres were also confounded. Neither a picaresque novel along the lines of Richardson or Fielding nor a sentiment *récit, confession,* or *rêverie* in the manner of Rousseau, if it might be categorized according to any genre at all, Ledoux's text was decidedly a bastard form.

"REVOLUTIONARY ARCHITECTURE"

It was Emil Kaufmann, following his prewar thesis of Ledoux as protomodernist, who in the early 1950s invented a trio of so-called Revolutionary architects: Boullée, Ledoux, Lequeu.[84] Even though he made it clear that by this ascription he did not mean those architects who worked directly for the revolutionary authorities between 1789 and 1799, his attempt to link their work with the broader currents of ideas that led up to the Revolution, to attribute to them a "revolution" in architecture that paralleled in form the revolution in politics,

has given rise to much misunderstanding. The linking of three names, despite the difference in generation, style, and ideology between them, has created an artificial triumvirate that has distorted the historical consideration of more accurate affiliations and influences.

Indeed, Kaufmann's famous trilogy not only brought together three different generations—Boullée born in 1728, Ledoux in 1736, Lequeu in 1757—but also three entirely different political and aesthetic sympathies. Boullée, in retirement and ill health during the Revolution, continuing his stern, idealized visions of an architecture, was preoccupied as much with death as with revolutionary life, referring back to a pre-Revolutionary vision of Egypt out of Fischer von Erlach or Robert for his ominous cemeteries. He could not have been more opposed to the bizarre imagination of Lequeu, who lost his job and possibilities of upward mobility with 1789, and whose various poses—architect, aristocrat, sans-culotte, madman, bureaucrat, pouter, mystic, voyeur—bear the stamp of ironic disassociation and mad alienation more than of opportunism. His Temple of Sacred Equality and Temple of the Earth and his competition submission for the triumphal gage for Paris seems to be more projects of revenge against Boullée and Ledoux than genuine revolutionary products. None of the three may be invested with the aura of a "Revolutionary architect," properly speaking.

Yet the problem of identifying their influence on revolutionary architecture still remains. On an iconographical level, it is clear that they took from as much as contributed to the range of symbols that, after 1789, were invested with special significance. The Freemasonic repertoire of "Egyptian" motifs, the all-seeing eyes, fasces, tables of the law, double columns, deployed most tellingly by Ledoux both before and after Napoléon's expedition to Egypt, had been quickly assimilated into the Revolutionary vocabulary and resemanticized. Thus it is difficult to judge whether the mosaic tables that surrounded the Pacifère anticipated or were drawn from the same tables as they ubiquitously displayed the new constitution. Likewise, the all-seeing eye in which is reflected the auditorium of Besançon seems to be a late invention of Le-

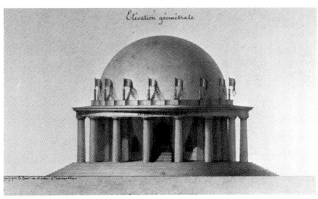

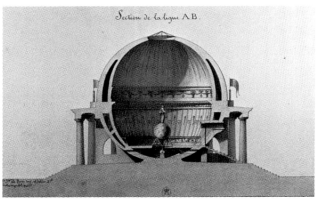

Jean-Jacques Lequeu, Temple of Sacred Equality, 1793 (*above*) and Temple of the Earth (*below*), elevations and sections. From the Bibliothèque Nationale, Cabinet des Estampes, Ha 80c, 80b.

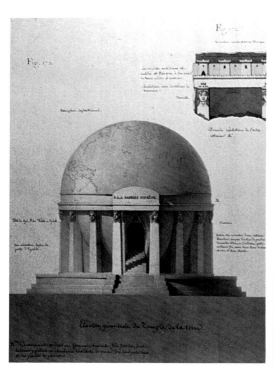

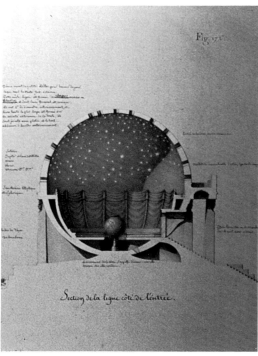

Pierre Giraud, Crematorium, 1801, perspective view. Engraving from Pierre Giraud, *Essai sur les sépultures* (Paris, 1801).

doux, possibly inspired by both Freemasonic and Revolutionary sources. This ambiguity may be illustrated by the fact that Ledoux's elaboration of the ideal city of Chaux after 1789 seems to owe as much to the scenic dispositions of the Revolutionary festivals as to pre-Revolutionary sources, while the architectural symbol of the Terror that so moved the historian Jules Michelet, the crematorium of Pierre Giraud, architect to the cemeteries of Paris (a project dating, in fact, from 1801), reveals itself to be little more than a replaying of Ledoux's favorite motifs of pyramid and circular porticoes, in a landscape as arcadian as that of the ideal city.[85]

It is equally clear, as Kaufmann and others have pointed out, that the so-called "Revolutionary style" characteristic at least of some architects after 1789 was hardly an invention of those years. Victor Hugo's characterization of the architecture of the Terror, the "style of Messidor" (June 1794, the height of the Terror), has to be modified in this respect. In his description of the auditorium of the Convention, he used adjectives such as "violent," "savage," "regular," "the correct in the cruel," "Massive and shrill," "prudish," a "style so sober that it became emaciated," "skeleton-like." But these characteristics, after all, had been present in the arts since the 1750s with Joseph-Marie Vien's celebrated painting *The Seller of Cupids*. Despite Hugo's conclusion, produced with a magnificent piece of art-historical rhetoric, that it was as if "David had guillotined Boucher," David had done this without the help of the guillotine a decade earlier in *The Oath of the Horatii* of 1784–85.

Hugo was of course right in one sense. Year II was dominated by the style adopted by David in painting and by many architects: a stern, stripped, almost abstracted form of neo-classicism—the simple geometries of the Roman theater adopted as the symbol of Roman virtue. But while this might well have been the *architecture messidor,* it was certainly not invented in Messidor year II; indeed, for David, as for many artists and architects, this style belonged rather to 1785. It was the style of the backdrop to *The Oath of the Horatii,* of Boullée's Temple to Newton, and of Ledoux's prison for Aix, where Ledoux, so to speak, might be said to have guillotined Delafosse with a severity that was well established by the time of David's *Brutus* of 1788–89.

THE POETICS OF PROGRAM

If there were to be a single candidate for an architect who best represented the ideals, if not the political debates, of the Revolution, it would perhaps be Boullée rather than Ledoux. His grand series of designs for public monuments between 1789 and 1799 certainly bears comparison to those developed by Ledoux during the same years; Pérouse de Montclos has drawn the parallel in detail. Yet the difference in monumental approach is marked. For Ledoux, architecture was ever a practical and social art, one immersed necessarily in the business of reforming and restructuring an already existing order; thence his relations, intellectual and administrative, with the foremost reformers of the last decades of the *ancien régime.* Boullée, on the other hand, produced his designs as the most idealized exemplars, the highest forms to which architecture might aspire; his politics were neither reformist nor revolutionary but academic and imaginary, fed by dreams of a majestic and perfect antiquity. Ledoux drawings responded to actual projects; Boullée's were deliberately prepared as answers to academic programs. Ledoux's list of building types assembled on the frontispiece of *L'architecture* was entirely based on real or proposed commissions; Boullée's, as described in his *Architecture,* was developed for intending students as a demonstration of the poetics of the art.

Thus Boullée preferred those programs that "tend to confirm how architecture demands the study of nature." But for Boullée, in contrast with Ledoux, the sublime resided more in painting than in architecture; or rather, it was better expressed in painting, which might join a representation of a building with the natural phenomena—storms, lightning, dawn, or nightfall—that would enhance the prescribed effect. Boullée's painterly designs, all in near monochrome and grandiose in scale, seem textbook illustrations of Burkean aesthetics: their emphasis on the repetition of similar elements, the nakedness of walls, dimensions of infinite height and depth; their introduction of the powers of nature, from the "starry heavens" of the Newton cenotaph to the cloudy reaches of the heaven in the dome of the Metropolitan Temple; their depiction as subject to all the dark and light moods of the seasons, lashing storms and rays of sunlight; finally, their absolute simplification, their reduction to a minimum of forms endlessly recombined. Certainly Boullée spoke of the sublime often in his treatise, proposing it as fundamental to architectural character: "Architecture being the only art in which nature can be brought into play, this unique advantage establishes its sublimity," he wrote, stressing the specific effects, analogous to nature's, that a building might emulate.[86] Here he rewrote the theory of character as entirely dependent on sensation and, applying the maxim to all public programs, suppressed any hierarchy of genre and convention in favor of a universal search for elevated sensation:

Do you hear the spectators cry out in admiration? What a sublime image is presented to us by this temple dedicated to piety! What touching simplicity reigns in this house of charity! With what radiance are these monuments raised to the glory of the nation! What imposing nobility characterizes the Temple of Themis! How these pleasant retreats allow us to taste the sweetness of life! Ah! into what profound reflections are we thrown by the appearance of these funerary monuments![87]

Architecture, no longer confined by classical codes, is transformed into a spectator sport for the emotions, at one with the sublime landscapes of the explorer or the poet. Ledoux, while he certainly shared such aesthetic enthusiasm, remained unconvinced by Boullée's gigantism, which massed buildings and populace alike in a vision of unity that, in retrospect at least, can only be interpreted as having totalizing

Etienne-Louis Boullée, Interior of a Military City. From the Bibliothèque Nationale, Cabinet des Estampes, Ha 55, pl. 31.

Boullée, Palace of Justice, detail of perspective view. From the Bibliothèque Nationale, Cabinet des Estampes, Ha 56, pl. 25.

overtones. The meticulous attention to individuality, to the smallest *métier* as to the highest office of state, was lost in Boullée's slightly chilly dreams, as was the context. Boullée's settings were "natural" enough, but of a nature defined by its seasonal and pictorial aspect, distinctly apart from the productive and tamed agrarian sites of Ledoux's Franche-Comté.

But if Ledoux should be distinguished from Boullée, his relationship to the following generation was perhaps closer than has normally been admitted. Thus the often-drawn contrast between Ledoux's poetic projects and those apparently more prosaic and pedantic typologies published by Boullée's student Durand as teaching aids, between 1801 and 1821, deserves reexamination. Reduced, even more simplified, disassembled into their component parts, abstracted into lines, points, and planes in a combinatorial geometry that paralleled that of Gaspard Monge, laid out for ready reference and efficient use by students with only a short time to learn the rudiments of design, Durand's projects have seemed to bear little affinity with those of his mentors or teachers. Indeed, they have been interpreted as drawn in direct opposition or implied criticism by a student who was generous in his castigation of eighteenth-century theory and practice from Laugier to Soufflot. Durand's explicit rejection of the theory of character has seemed to give the coup de grace to any idealized visions of sublime style, resting his case on a pragmatism of means and ends, with economy serving as the main criteria of judgment:

Without doubt the grandeur, magnificence, variety, the effect and character that one notices in buildings are so many beauties, so many causes of pleasure that we feel at the sight of them. But where is the need to run after all of that? If one disposes a building in a way that is suitable for its use, will it not be obviously different from another building intended for another use? Will it not naturally have a character, and, what is more, its own character?[88]

The end of representation, thus announced, was reinforced by the thin-line plans and stripped elevations of the plates devoted to the method of design and exemplary projects in the *Précis des leçons* and the *Partie graphique* of 1821. A former student, H. Rohault, remembered that Durand would repeat in-

cessantly "that the source of beauty in architecture was economy joined to fitness."[89] In this ascription Durand seems to herald an engineer's architecture, where, as Louis Bruyère, Inspector-general of Public Works for Paris from 1815, remarked, "architecture can doubtless seek to please the eye, but the embellishments to which it is susceptible should be compared to the draperies of antique figures which reveal their nudity."[90]

Yet closer inspection of Durand's career and work indicates that his aesthetic was, in fact, not so distant from that of Boullée or Ledoux, either in form or in theory. Werner Szambien has, for example, discovered a remarkable series of examples of the effects of buildings and of nature, a catalogue of sublime scenes, drawn to small and comparative scales, no doubt under Boullée's supervision.[91] He has also systematically compared the original designs of Durand and Thibault, demonstrating their affinities with other monumental projects around 1800; and he has shown that the apparent change in aesthetic occurred less in the designs themselves than in their reduced reproduction for the publications of 1801–21. When Durand's elevations and sections of prisons, libraries, fairs, barracks, palaces of justice, stock exchanges, and museums are compared to those of Ledoux or Boullée, the difference is primarily one of an increasing rationalization, repetition, reduction, and abstraction, rather than of any complete loss of "characterization." In this sense, Durand's dismissive attitude to "searching after characters" might be explained by the increasing standardization of character by the 1800s; what Ledoux's generation had had to invent had become a commonplace for their students. The poetic sublime had become an academic sublime. Thus Durand's Museum project, an amalgam of three different projects conceived for the Grand Prix competition of 1799, despite its simplification and typification, resembles Boullée's more atmospheric design in its plan and domed central area, as well as in its repeated rows of columns on the four sides of entry.[92]

This complementarity might explain Ledoux's prominent position in Durand's assessment of eighteenth-century architecture. Indeed, the first indications of the older architect's rehabilitation had come in the late 1790s with the pub-

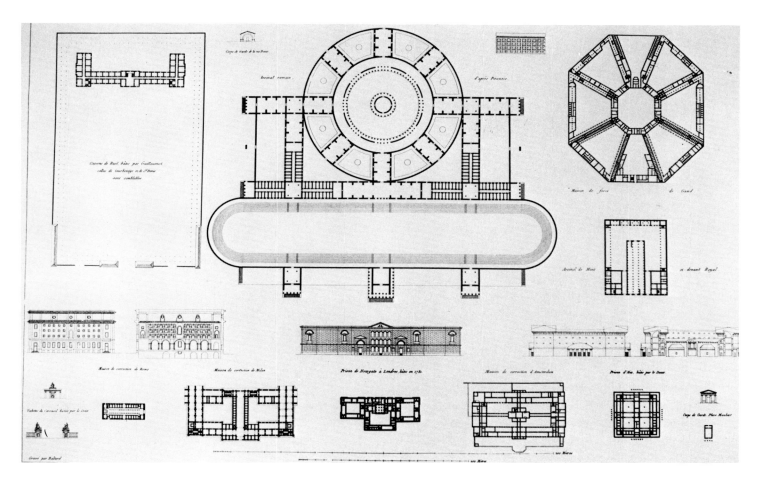

Jean-Nicolas-Louis Durand, Barracks, Arsenals, Prisons, etc., comparative plans, elevations, and sections, including Ledoux's project for the prisons of Aix-en-Provence. Engraving from Jean-Nicolas-Louis Durand, *Recueil et parallèle des édifices de tout genre* (Paris, 1799–1801), pl. 28.

lication of Durand's *Recueil et parallèle des édifices de tout genre, anciens et modernes* between 1799 and 1801. Durand, who included only fifteen contemporary projects by French architects in his comparative collection of hundreds of historical examples of different building types, affirmed Ledoux's position as the principal public architect of his day by selecting four of his designs to illustrate in plan, elevation, and section: the Theater of Besançon as an example of the "théâtres modernes" of plate 38; the project for the library of Hesse-Cassel as an example of the "palestres, collèges, bibliothèques, portiques, bourses, etc." of plate 18; the Hôtel de Ville of Neuchâtel and the Palais de Justice of Aix as paradigmatic examples of the "maisons de ville, palais de justice, etc." of plate 17; and the prisons of Aix among the "casernes, arsenaux, prisons" of plate 28.

Durand's implied praise is only one indication that Ledoux's reputation among the younger generation of architects between the turn of the century and the Restoration was by no means negligible. The opinion of Jacques-Guillaume Legrand, who had contributed the historical introduction to Durand's plates, was, as we have seen, even more positive as he reviewed the *barrières* in successive numbers of the *Annales du musée.*

If we look at the work of Ledoux's students and followers who were more sympathetic with revolutionary premises and who were employed by the state during this period, it is easy to see his influence. To take only one example, Legrand's own Amphitheater for Chemistry and Anatomical Demonstrations, his restoration of the auditorium in the Jardin des Plantes or Jardin National after 1795—which remains, as Szambien has noted, the sole surviving example of a revolutionary *salle*—would certainly have pleased the architect of the Theater of Besançon.[93] The stone seating, in the form of a U, was stepped *à l'antique* within a semicircular auditorium covered by a plain half dome, top-lit from a circular glazed oculus. The demonstration area was sheltered beneath a large coffered arch, a pure semicircle reminiscent of Ledoux's proscenium at Besançon, supported on baseless Doric columns. The chemical furnace was set to the rear, carved with hieroglyphic symbols; its stepped, semicircular hood projected dramatically from the back wall, framed beneath a decorative "Egyptian" stepped pyramid topped by the figure of Justice.

Ledoux's influence on his student Jean-Nicolas Sobre, in, for example, the speculative development of the Cour Batave in the rue Saint Denis of 1790, is equally striking. Here, the courtyard was entered through a long barrel-vaulted passage lined with Ionic columns, an axis that ended to the rear in a coffered niche and fountain. In the domain of the private house, the typical plans for the Country Houses of Chaux were developed and standardized even further by another student, Louis-Ambroise Dubut. His *Architecture civile: Maisons de ville et de campagne de toutes formes et de tous genres,* published in 1803, borrowed freely from Ledoux's nine-square inventions, while confirming their usefulness as models for the new bourgeois house. Dubut advertized his plans as "useful for builders and contractors and all who, with some knowledge of building, want to direct their buildings themselves."[94] Louis-Emmanuel-Aimé Damesne, another former student, who had worked on the *barrières,* proposed a project for a monumental arch, before 1805, that freely emulated Ledoux in its combination of temple and triumphal arch. Szambien has also noted the influence of Ledoux's project for the Market of Chaux on a number of Durand's contemporaries, notably C.-W. Coudray. Finally, as late as 1830, Charles Rohault de Fleury built a stable in the Jardin des Plantes that in its cruciform plan and cylindrical central hall directly reflected the pheasantry at Mauperthuis.[95] From these examples alone it is clear that, despite Ledoux's official and unofficial pro-

scription during the Revolutionary years, his architecture, if not his ideology, was a powerful influence on a younger generation forced to improvize a new, "republican" style out of the shards of pre-Revolutionary neoclassicism. The judgment of an anonymous reviewer of *L'architecture* some ten years after Ledoux's death was, in this respect, more accurate than those of later critics:

Ledoux, they said, departed from good taste in returning the art to forms that most often strayed from the severe simplicity of the ancients. We agree with this, which in any case is strikingly obvious to all those who have studied the monuments of Greece and Rome. But it must also be agreed that Ledoux, who principally looked for effect with regard to the ordering of buildings and for solidity in their construction, was nevertheless obliged to depart from the received principles of the ancients. Firstly, because they did not offer the necessary resources for an imagination as ardent as his own, which was particularly attached to variety. Secondly, because our land produces no materials of a grandeur and strength equal to those of the marbles from the quarries of Greece and Italy, he was obliged to search for forms, lines, and new sections in order to obtain, with stones of small dimension, and without the use of iron, the solidity that the ancients achieved with enormous masses. Hence Ledoux searched for curves of different kinds that he succeeded in uniting, often with much taste, with the vertical and perpendicular line of the column. To render justice to Ledoux, one could say that he endowed his very forms with the imprint of a creative genius.[96]

INTRODUCTION

1. Antoine-Chrysostôme Quatremère de Quincy, "Barrière," *Encyclopédie méthodique: Architecture*, 3 vols. (Paris, 1788–1825), 1:216.

2. Victor Hugo, "Guerre aux démolisseurs!" (1825–32), from *Littérature et philosophie mêlées*, in *Oeuvres complètes: Critique*, presentation by Jean-Pierre Reynaud (Paris, 1985), 187.

3. [Léon Vaudoyer], *Magasin pittoresque* 20 (1852): 388ff.

4. Emil Kaufmann, *Von Ledoux bis Le Corbusier: Ursprung und Entwicklung der Autonomen Architecktur* (Vienna and Leipzig, 1933). The thesis of this book was advanced in his article "Die Stadt des Architekten Ledoux zur Erkenntniss der Autonomen Architektur," *Kunstwissenschaftliche Forschungen* 2 (1933): 131–60. For full references to Kaufmann's writings see the bibliography to the present work. His early approach is summarized in Georges Teyssot, "Neoclassic and 'Autonomous' Architecture: The Formalism of Emil Kaufmann," *Architectural Design* 51, no. 6–7 (1981): 24–29, and in the introduction and notes to Emil Kaufmann, *Trois architectes révolutionnaires: Boullée, Ledoux, Lequeu*, ed. Gilbert Erouart and Georges Teyssot (Paris, 1978).

5. See Hans Sedlmayr, *Art in Crisis: The Lost Centre* (London, 1956).

6. Meyer Schapiro, "The New Viennese School," *The Art Bulletin* 18, no. 2 (June 1936): 258–66.

7. Ibid., 265.

8. Ibid.

9. Ibid.

10. See bibliography.

11. See bibliography.

1 THE ENCYCLOPEDIC DISCOURSE

1. Claude-Nicholas Ledoux, *L'architecture considérée sous le rapport de l'art, des moeurs et de la législation* (Paris, 1804), 148. Subsequent citations to this work are enclosed in parentheses within the body of the text. All translations, unless otherwise noted, are by the author.

2. Quatremère de Quincy, writing in the *Encyclopédie méthodique* in 1788, listed three classes of architect: "Architects, members of the Académie Royale d'Architecture; the *architectes experts bourgeois*, who have the title of experts by the purchase of an office that gives them the right, exclusive of all others, to draw up the reported minutes on the subject of buildings that are the object of juridical disputes between individuals or between individuals and building-workers. The third class is that of architects who are neither of the Académie nor of the community of experts, but who practice architecture freely as a liberal art" (Quatremère de Quincy, "Architecte," *Encyclopédie méthodique: Architecture*, 1:108–9).

3. See Michel Gallet, *Demeures parisiennes: L'époque de Louis XVI* (Paris, 1964), 29.

4. The history of architectural education in the eighteenth century has not yet been written. The clearest summary is Gallet, *Demeures parisiennes*, 27–38.

5. See the comprehensive catalogue published by the Académie de France in Rome, *Piranèse et les français, 1740–1790* (Rome, 1976), and the equally informative collection of papers from the international conference on the same subject published in *Piranèse et les français: Colloque tenu à la Villa Médicis, 12–14 Mai 1976* (Rome, 1978).

6. Among numerous *mémoires* published in the 1760s and 1770s, see, for example, Ferrand de Monthelon, *Projet pour l'établissement d'écoles gratuites de dessin* (Paris, n.d.), a project for the children of poor artisans, and the report prepared for the National Assembly after the Revolution, *Mémoire sur l'origine, les progrès et la situation de l'école Royale gratuite de Dessin* (Paris, 1790), which described the foundation of the Royal Free School of Drawing, with Letters Patent of 1767 and 1776, followed by a second school in the Faubourg Saint Antoine in 1785. These schools were modeled on the project conceived by Bachelier in 1762 and itself opened in 1766.

7. For the education of Jean-Jacques Lequeu and its basis in drawing, see Philippe Duboy, *Lequeu: An Architectural Enigma* (Cambridge, Mass., 1987), 20–30.

8. Arthur Birembaut, "L'enseignement de la minérologie et les techniques minières," in René Taton, ed., *Enseignement et diffusion des sciences en France au XVIIIe siècle* (Paris, 1964), 379.

9. The early life of Ledoux is only scantily documented. A certificate of baptism and an extract from the Registers of Parliament for September 1749 (certifying Ledoux's scholarship to the Collège de Dormans-Beauvais) are cited by Michel Gallet, *Claude-Nicolas Ledoux, 1736–1806* (Paris, 1980), 259.

10. Claude-Nicolas Ledoux, *Prospectus* to *L'architecture* (Paris, 1802), 26. Hereafter cited as *Prospectus* within the text.

11. For a history of the Collège de Dormans-Beauvais, see Jean-Baptiste Crevier, *Histoire de l'Université de Paris, depuis son origine jusqu'en l'année 1600*, 7 vols. (Paris, 1761), 2:464ff. Crevier takes the

history of the college to 1760, the year when he retired from the Professorship of Rhetoric. See also Auguste Silvy, *Les collèges en France avant la Révolution* (Paris, 1885), and idem, *Essai d'une bibliographie de l'enseignement sécondaire et supérieure en France avant la Révolution* (Paris, 1894).

12. Jean le Rond d'Alembert, "Collège," in Denis Diderot and Jean le Rond d'Alembert, *Encyclopédie ou Dictionnaire raisonné des sciences, des arts et des métiers, par une société des gens de lettres,* 33 vols. (Neuchâtel, 1751–80); this article is discussed in Jean-Claude Chevalier and P. Kuentz, "Autour de l'article *Collège,*" in *Langue et langages de Leibniz à l'"Encyclopédie,"* ed. Michèle Duchet and M. Jalley (Paris, 1977), 226.

13. Chevalier and Kuentz, "Autour l'article *Collège,*" 226.

14. Charles Rollin (1661–1741), a pupil of the Jansenist school of Port Royal, elaborated his teaching method under the influence of Antoine Arnauld, coauthor with Pierre Nicole of the celebrated *Logique, ou l'art de penser* (1667) and with C. Lancelot of the equally influential *Grammaire générale et raisonnée* (1660). Rollin's treatise, *De la manière d'enseigner et d'étudier les belles-lettres, par rapport à l'esprit et au coeur,* 4 vols. (Paris, 1726–28), became a standard textbook for the rest of the eighteenth century; see H. Ferté, *Rollin, sa vie, ses oeuvres et l'université de son temps* (Paris, 1902).

15. See Charles-M. Jourdain, *Histoire de l'Université de Paris au XVIIe et XVIIIe siècle,* 2 vols. (Paris, 1888), 2:167ff.

16. The traditional schema of the *trivium* and the *quadrivium* is discussed in Taton, ed., *Enseignement et diffusion.* The history of this distinction among the *artes liberales* is well treated in Ernst Robert Curtius, *European Literature and the Latin Middle Ages* (Princeton, 1953), especially chap. 3.

17. See Augustin Sicard, *Les études classiques avant la révolution* (Paris, 1887).

18. These texts, of course, together with others that Ledoux does not explicitly mention but obviously paraphrases, were the required reading of the eighteenth-century schoolboy.

19. The best treatment of eighteenth-century rhetorical education is in George Snyders, *La pédagogie en France au XVIIe et XVIIIe siècles* (Paris, 1965); he characterizes the typical student as placed in "a kind of unreal and ideal setting, where men were no more than emblematic figures of virtues, vices, and passions" (p. 97).

20. Charles Rollin, *The Method of Teaching and Studying the Belles-Lettres,* 4 vols. (London, 1734), 1:25.

21. Rollin, "Discours préliminaire" to *De la manière d'enseigner;* quoted in Snyders, *La pédagogie,* 74.

22. Rollin, *De la manière d'enseigner,* vol. 4, pt. 3, art. 5.

23. Pierre Goubert, *The Ancien Régime* (New York, 1973), 270.

24. For a historical study of the influence and legitimizing role of the classics during the Revolution, see H. T. Parker, *The Cult of Antiquity and the French Revolutionaries* (Chicago, 1937).

25. Virgil, *Georgics,* II, 13.

26. Nicolas-Edme Rétif de la Bretonne, *Le pornographe, ou idées d'un honnête homme sur un projet de règlement pour les prostituées propre à prévenir les malheurs qu'occasionne le publicisme des femmes* (1769), reprinted, with a preface by Béatrice Didier (Paris, 1977).

27. Cf. Snyders, *La pédagogie,* 110ff. Roland Barthes in "L'ancienne rhétorique: Aide mémoire," *Communications* 16 (1970), traces the history of the rhetorical tradition, thematically and critically, and supplies a useful bibliography. See also Curtius, *European Literature,* chaps. 4–5.

28. P. de Jouvency, *L'élève de rhétorique,* pt. 4, chap. 1; quoted in Snyders, *Le pédagogie,* 115.

29. Snyders, *La pédagogie,* 51. See also Michel Legagneux, "Rollin et le 'mirage spartiate' de l'éducation publique," in *Recherches nouvelles sur quelques écrivains des lumières,* ed. Jacques Proust (Geneva, 1972).

30. See George Snyders, "Rhétorique et culture au XVIIe siècle," in *XVIIe siècle* (Paris, 1968), vols. 80–81, 81ff., who gives the example of an exercise in describing a "promenade aux environs de Troyes," which, in *transposition* becomes an evocation of the Elysian Fields.

31. See Taton, *Enseignement et diffusion.*

32. Dominique-François Rivard (1697–1778), *Eléments de géométrie* (Paris, 1732); idem, *Traité de la sphère,* 2d. ed. (Paris, 1743). With the latter volume was bound Rivard's *Traité du calendrier,* perhaps an early source for Ledoux's fascination with almanacs.

33. "J. C." [Jacques Cellérier] *Notice rapide sur la vie et les ouvrages de Claude-Nicolas Ledoux* (Paris, 1806), 3. The ascription of this brief account of Ledoux's life to Cellérier is confirmed by the copy in the Marquand Library, Princeton University, which carries the inscription: "Monsieur Cellérier, architecte du gouvernement, Membre du Conseil des Bâtiments Civils et Inspecteur-générale des travaux, auteur de ce petit ouvrage, m'en à fait présent à Paris ce 1er Décembre 1810. Caumont."

34. Etienne-Louis Boullée, *Architecture: Essai sur l'art (1789–99),* ed. *Jean-Marie Pérouse de Montclos* (Paris, 1968), 45.

35. François-Joseph Bélanger, "Notice nécrologique," *Journal de Paris* (Paris, 1 Frimaire year VII [1798]), 260; quoted in Monique Mosser and Daniel Rabreau, eds., *Charles De Wailly: Peintre architecte dans l'Europe des lumières,* exhibition catalogue (Paris, 1979), 18.

36. For a preliminary discussion of the relation between engraving, painting, and architecture in the milieu of the Piranesians, see Gilbert Erouart, *L'architecture au pinceau: Jean-Laurent Legeay. Un Piranésian français dans l'Europe des Lumières* (Paris, 1982).

37. For a brilliant analysis of the system of representation in the plates of the *Encyclopédie,* see Roland Barthes, "Les planches de l'*Encyclopédie,*" in *Le degré zéro de l'écriture suivi de nouveaux essais critiques* (Paris, 1972), 89–105. See also Anthony Vidler, "Spaces of Production: Factories and Workshops in the *Encyclopédie,*" chap. 2 of *The Writing of the Walls: Architectural Theory in the Late Enlightenment* (Princeton, 1987).

38. Jacques-François Blondel, *Cours d'architecture, ou traité de la décoration, distribution et construction des bâtiments; contenant les leçons données en 1750, et les années suivantes,* 9 vols. (Paris, 1771–77), 5:v. This was the first volume to be published under the editorship of Pierre Patte, after Blondel's death in 1774.

39. Blondel stated (*Cours d'architecture,* 3:lxxxii) that the Ecole des Arts received its approval from the Académie Royale d'Architecture on 6 May 1743. Blondel delivered four series of public lectures through 1747, when he reformulated the curriculum, as outlined in his *Discours sur la manière d'étudier l'architecture et les arts qui sont relatifs à celui de bâtir* (Paris, 1747), delivered 3 May. In 1754 Blondel recognized the deficiency of a purely theoretical treatment of architecture and presented a broader curriculum that responded to the needs of the Ecole des Ponts et Chaussées and the interested public. A new series of public lectures was begun that year. In November 1755 Blondel was elected to the Académie and in October 1762 he was appointed professor of the Académie school and closed his own (*Cours d'architecture,* 3:lxxxi–ii). For Blondel, see Auguste Prost, *J.-F. Blondel et son oeuvre* (Metz, 1860), and W. Knight-Sturges, "Jacques-François Blondel," *Journal of the Society of Architectural Historians,* 11, no. 1–4 (1952): 16–19; his influence is traced in Donald Drew Egbert, *The Beaux-Arts Tradition in French Architecture* (Princeton, 1980), 25–31; the course of instruction is examined in Robin Middleton, "Jacques-François Blondel and the *Cours d'architecture,*" *Journal of the Society of Architectural Historians* 17 (December 1959).

40. Diderot recited Blondel's qualities as a contributor to the *Encyclopédie* in the "Prospectus" to the *Encyclopédie* (Paris, 1750). See d'Alembert, *Discours préliminaire de l' "Encyclopédie"* (1751; rpt. Paris, 1965), 147–48: "Love of the public welfare and the desire to contribute to the development of the arts in France has led him to establish, in 1741 [sic], a school of architecture that has quickly become very popular. Besides architecture, which he teaches to his students, M. Blondel employs talented men to teach the elements of mathematics, fortification, perspective, stone cutting, painting, sculpture, etc., related to the art of building."

41. See Gaston Serbos, "L'Ecole royale des Ponts et Chaussées," in Taton, *Enseignement et diffusion,* 345–63; Bruno Fortier, "La nascità dell'Ecole des Ponts et Chaussées: 1. Lo spazio," *Casabella* 495 (October 1983): 40–47; and idem, "La nascità dell'Ecole des Ponts et Chaussées: 2. Il projetto," *Casabella* 496 (November 1983): 36–45. Fortier's articles demonstrate the intimate relations between Trudaine's measures for economic and technical reform and the control of the French territory through mapping and engineering works. See also A. Léon, *La Révolution française et l'éducation technique* (Paris, 1968), 57ff., and the classic work by Mortimer d'Ocagne, *Les grandes écoles de France;* pt. 1, *Service d'état* (Paris, 1879).

42. Jacques-François Blondel, *Discours sur la nécessité de l'étude de l'architecture* (Paris, 1754), 10. This lecture was delivered on the occasion of the reopening of public courses after their five-year suspension. See n. 39 above.

43. Blondel, *Discours sur la manière,* 11.

44. Ibid.

45. Jacques-François Blondel and Jean-François Bastide, *Les amours rivaux ou l'homme du monde éclairé par des arts,* 2 vols. (Paris and Amsterdam, 1774).

46. Blondel, *Discours sur la manière,* 11

47. Ibid.

48. For a complete list of these articles see R. N. Schwab and W. E. Rex, "Inventory of Diderot's *Encyclopédie,*" *Studies in Voltaire and the Eighteenth Century,* vols. 80, 83, 85, 91, 92, 93 (Geneva, 1971–72), which attributes most of Blondel's contributions through volume 8 of the *Encyclopédie.* Many of his definitions were later included in the text of his *Architecture française,* 4 vols. (Paris, 1752–56).

49. Blondel, *Cours d'architecture,* 1:374.

50. For Boullée's library, see Jean-Marie Pérouse de Montclos,

Etienne-Louis Boullée, 1728–1799: De l'architecture classique à l'architecture révolutionnaire (Paris, 1969), 253–57; for Ledoux's library, see the inventory of Ledoux's possessions made after his death, 26 November 1806, Archives Nationales, Minutier Central des Notaires, Etude XXXIII, 841; first cited in Geneviève Levallet-Haug, *Claude-Nicolas Ledoux, 1736–1806* (Paris and Strasbourg, 1934). These lists are discussed in detail in chap. 6 below.

51. For an excellent introduction to the transformation of the classical vocabulaty in the early eighteenth century, see Werner Szambien, *Symétrie, goût, caractère: Théorie et terminologie de l'architecture à l'âge classique, 1550–1800* (Paris, 1986).

52. Blondel, *Cours d'architecture*, 2:229.

53. Pierre Patte, *Discours sur l'architecture* (Paris, 1754), 32; Jacques Gondouin, *Description des écoles de Chirurgie* (Paris, 1780), 6; Nicolas Le Camus de Mézières [Wolf d'orfeuil, pseud.], *Le génie de l'architecture ou l'analogie de cet art avec nos sensations* (Paris, 1780), 3; Boullée, *Architecture*, 73–79; and Quatremère de Quincy, "Caractère," *Encyclopédie méthodique: Architecture*, 1:477–571.

54. Blondel, *Cours d'architecture*, 4:lxxxiv.

55. Ibid.

56. Michel Gallet, *Stately Mansions: Eighteenth-Century Paris Architecture* (London, 1972), 59 and pl. 111–12.

57. See Michel Gallet, "Louis-François Trouard et l'architecture religieuse dans la région de Versailles au temps de Louis XVI," *Gazette des Beaux-Arts* (1976): 201–18.

58. For comparison of these three designs, see Allan Braham, *The Architecture of the French Enlightenment* (Berkeley and Los Angeles, 1980), 123–36.

59. These works were first documented by Michel Gallet in "La jeunesse de Ledoux," *Gazette des Beaux-Arts* (February 1970): 65–72.

60. For a complete list, see Gallet, "La jeunesse," 88 n. 31. Gallet notes that Ledoux's appointment was perhaps a result of his marriage to Marie Bureau on 24 August 1764. The marriage certificate records as a witness Joseph Marin Masson de Courcelles, a friend of the bride's parents and former Grand Maître des Eaux et Forêts for the Département of Soissons, who no doubt introduced Ledoux to Du Vaucel. Ledoux is already named as Architecte des Eaux et Forêts in this document, quoted in Gallet, *Ledoux*, 251. See also J.-Cl. Waquet, *Les grands maîtres des Eaux et Forêts de France, de 1689 à la Révolution* (Geneva and Paris, 1978).

61. See Gallet, *Ledoux,* 40. Ledoux's description is in his letter of application to the Académie in 1767, Archives de l'Institut, B21; first quoted by H. Ottomeyer, "Autobiographies d'architectes parisiens, 1759–1811," *Bulletin de la Société de l'histoire de Paris et del'Ile de France* (Paris, 1974): 178–79.

62. Ibid., 179.

63. Jean-Rodolphe Perronet, *Description des projets et de la construction des ponts de Neuilly, de Mantes, d'Orléans et autres; du projet du canal de Bourgogne pour communication des deux mers par Dijon; et celui de la conduite des eaux de l'Yvette et de Bièvre à Paris,* 2 vols. and supplement (Paris, 1782–89). In this work, published at the end of his career, Perronet summarized his principles of design and construction. At Neuilly, designed and built between 1766 and 1771, he had pioneered what became known as "cow horns," champfering the edges of the arches and their supports to ease the flow of flood water and lessen the danger of collapse by erosion. See Fortier, "La nascità dell-'Ecole," pt. 2, 36–43.

64. See Yves Durand, *Les fermiers-généraux au XVIIIe siècle* (Paris, 1971), especially 231, 242.

65. Their first daughter, Adélaïde-Constance, was born in 1771, their second, Alexandrine-Euphrasie, in 1775.

66. Cellérier, *Notice rapide,* 4.

67. Ibid., 15.

2 THE LANGUAGES OF CHARACTER

1. Blondel, *Cours d'architecture*, 2:256.

2. For a detailed discussion of the changing idea of character in the late eighteenth century, see Szambien, *Symétrie, goût, caractère*, especially 174–99.

3. Blondel, *Cours d'architecture*, 2:230.

4. Ibid., 231.

5. German Boffrand, *Livre d'architecture* (Paris, 1745), 16.

6. Blondel, *Cours d'architecture*, 1:373–446.

7. Ibid., 2:229–468.

8. Quatremère de Quincy, "Caractère," *Encyclopédie méthodique: Architecture*, vol. 1.

9. Blondel and Bastide, *Les amours rivaux*, 1:255.

10. Gallet, *Ledoux,* 47–49.

11. Elie Fréron, *L'Année littéraire* (1762): 282.

12. Daniel Rabreau, presentation at the Fondation Claude-Nicolas Ledoux, Arc-et-Senans, 2 May 1986.

13. For a full treatment of the Abbé Laugier's contribution to eighteenth-century French theory and design, see Wolfgang Herrmann, *Laugier and Eighteenth-Century French Theory* (London, 1962), and Anthony Vidler, "Rebuilding the Primitive Hut: The Return to Origins From LaFitau to Laugier," chap. 1 of *The Writing of the Walls.*

14. Fréron, *L'Année littéraire* 6:282.

15. See Michel Gallet, "Ledoux et sa clientèle parisienne," *Bulletin de la Société de l'histoire de Paris et de l'Ile de France,* 101–2 (1976): 131–73.

16. See François Furet and Denis Richet, *La Révolution français,* rev. ed. (Paris, 1973), 15–47.

17. On the ideologies of the nobility at the end of the *ancien régime,* see G. Chaussinand-Nogaret, *La noblesse au XVIIIème siècle* (Paris, 1976).

18. Cited in Furet and Richet, *La Révolution française,* 28.

19. See Gabriel-Henri Gaillard, *Généalogie de la maison de Montesquiou* (Paris, 1784); and Joseph-Ripault Désormeaux, *Histoire de la maison Montmorenci,* 5 vols. (Paris, 1764). Gaillard was a professional historian specializing in the history of the French kings from Charlemagne to François I; Désormeaux was a member of the Académie des Inscriptions, librarian to the Prince de Condé, and author of a long history of the house of Bourbon. Both were linked to the circle of Jean-Baptiste de La Curne de Sainte-Palaye, the medievalist whose work has been treated at length by L. Gossman, *Medievalism and the Ideologies of the Enlightenment* (Baltimore, 1968). For the attempt by the families of newly enriched Fermiers Généraux to to support their claims to noble descent, see Durand, *Les fermiers généraux,* 240–46.

20. President Jean-Hyacinthe-Louis-Emmanuel Hocquart (1727–78) was the son of Jean-Hyacinthe Hocquart II, also a Fermier Général (and himself the son of a Fermier Général) and Intendant de la Marine under Colbert after 1681; see Durand, *Les fermiers généraux.*

21. Anne-Pierre, marquis de Montesquiou, playwright, essayist, poet, and soldier, married to the sister of Président Hocquart, Jeanne-Marie, inherited the domain of Maupertuis and began rebuilding the old *château* in 1763; Ledoux started work there no more than two years later. According to a survey of 1776, the *château* was by then complete. In a summary of his work prepared in 1767 for submission of his candidacy to the Académie d'Architecture, Ledoux described it as finished in November of that year. See Gallet, *Ledoux,* 261, and C. Rivière, *Un village de Brie au XVIIIe siècle: Mauperthuis* (Paris, 1939).

22. François-Emmanuel de Crussol, ninth duc d'Uzès, commissioned Ledoux to reconstruct the old Hôtel de l'Hôpital in 1768; see Michel Gallet, "Le salon de l'Hôtel d'Uzès," *Bulletin du Musée Carnavalet* (1969): 2.

23. For this legal struggle see Gallet, "Ledoux et sa clientèle parisienne."

24. Hippolyte-François Sanguin, marquis de Livry, was married to the heiress of the Marquis de Bénouville, near Caen, Normandy. Ledoux was employed from 1769; work was still in progress in 1778.

25. See Th. Lhuillier, "Le château de Cramayel en Brie et son théâtre au XVIIIe siècle," in *Réunion des Sociétés des Beaux-Arts des départements* (1882), 268ff.

26. Louis-François-Joseph, prince de Montmorency, and his wife, Anne de Montmorency-Luxembourg, commissioned Joseph-Florent de Mézières, a landowner at Eaubonne, seat of the Montmorency-Luxembourgs and Rousseau's last home, to act as agent for the building of their Parisian *hôtel* in 1769.

27. Ledoux, Memorandum, Archives Nationales, Z1J 944; transcribed in Gallet, *Ledoux,* 263.

28. In Blondel, *Cours d'architecture,* 5:85–89.

29. Ibid.

30. A good general treatment of these publications can be found in Dora Wiebenson, *Sources of Greek Revival Architecture* (London, 1969).

31. Blondel, *Cours d'architecture,* 1:110, and Blondel and Bastide, *Les amours rivaux,* 1:255ff. and 2:109.

32. Ledoux, Report to the Académie d'Architecture, 1767; cited in Gallet, *Ledoux,* 263.

33. Ibid.

34. Jean-Louis Viel de Saint-Maux, *Lettres sur l'architecture des anciens et celles des modernes* (Paris, 1787), "Septième lettre," 58 n. 29.

35. Blondel and Bastide, *Les amours rivaux,* 1:255ff.

36. Gallet, *Ledoux,* 50.

37. Blondel and Bastide, *Les amours rivaux,* 264.

38. See Alain Le Bihan, *Francs-Maçons parisiens du Grand Orient de France (fin du XVIIIe siècle)* (Paris, 1966), 144; Marie-François-Emmanuel Crussol d'Uzès, duc de Crussol (1756–1843), was a member of Les Amis Réunis in 1788 and an officer of the Grand Orient.

39. Cellérier, *Notice rapide*, 6: "He drew up projects for palaces, country houses, and other buildings for the first lords [of England], notably for Lord Cliwes [*sic*], that rich governor of India, who built some of them." Robert, Lord Clive, returned from a second tour of duty in India as Governor of Bengal in 1767; he traveled in France from January to September 1768, buying tapestries from the Gobelins and, according to his biographer, "a great quantity of velvets, rich silks, silver and gold tissues etc., designed for his use or presents to some of his correspondents in India" (Sir George Forrest, *The Life of Lord Clive* [London, 1918], 2:365). Gallet (*Ledoux*, 10) has surmised that Ledoux referred to this splendid consumption when he spoke in *L'architecture* of goods being sent to Monopotapa (127); but Ledoux was there speaking of the activities of the new financial association he imagined operating in the Stock Exchange of the ideal city of Chaux, and in any event he would not have addressed Lord Clive in the "tu" form ("Déjà tu envoies au Monopotapa . . . nos tableaux, nos sculptures, nos étoffes de Lyon, chefs-d'oeuvre des arts"). Finally, Monopotapa was in central Africa, not in India. Elsewhere in *L'architecture* Ledoux spoke of the humane treatment of horses by "les Insulaires" (59) who used only a simple bit without harness, and recorded his impressions of "the single balustrade of London Bridge" (47).

40. The English writer William Beckford, who met Ledoux in Paris in the late 1770s, mentioned in a draft of a letter to his sister-in-law, Louisa Pitt-Rivers, that Ledoux had once been considered as architect to Louisa's mother for a villa in Lyons. Louisa's father, George Pitt, first Baron Rivers, was appointed envoy-extraordinary to Turin in 1761 and may well have thought of residing in Lyons after the peace of 1763. The family did possess a house outside Lyons in the 1780s. See J. W. Oliver, *The Life of William Beckford* (London, 1932), 171ff.

41. The revival of interest in Palladio in France after the 1760s, fueled by the recent peace with England, is summarized in Michel Gallet, "Palladio et l'architecture française dans la seconde moitié du XVIIIe siècle," *Monuments historiques de la France* no. 2 (1975): 43–55.

42. Gallet, *Ledoux*, 71–73.

43. Madame Vigée-Lebrun, *Souvenirs*, 1:106; quoted in Jacques Silvestre de Sacy, *Alexandre-Théodore Brongniart (1739–1813), sa vie et son oeuvre* (Paris, 1940), 55.

44. Ledoux, Report to the Académie d'Architecture, cited in Gallet, *Ledoux*, 263.

45. Villiers, *Manuel du voyageur aux environs de Paris* (Paris, 1806), 58–62.

46. Anne-Pierre Montesquiou-Fezensac, *Discours prononcé dans l'Académie française, 15 Juin 1784* (Paris, 1784). For a general history of the family, see Philippe-Joseph de Montesquiou-Fezensac, *Histoire de la maison de Montesquiou* (Paris, 1837).

47. Abbé Jacques Delille, *L'Imagination, poëme en huit chants, accompagné de notes historiques et littéraires par J. Esménard*, chant 5 (1806), in *Oeuvres* (Paris, 1833), 145.

48. Gallet, *Ledoux*, 74.

49. See Wolfgang Herrmann, "The Problem of Chronology in Claude-Nicolas Ledoux's Engraved Work," *Art Bulletin* 41 (September 1960): 191–210; Johannes Langner, "Ledoux' Redaktion der eigenen Werke für die Veröffentlichung," *Zeitschrift für Kunstgeschichte* 23 (1960): 133–66; and Gallet, *Ledoux*, 78–80.

50. Still the best account of the career of Marie-Madeleine Guimard is the gossip-filled *La Guimard* of Edmond de Goncourt (Paris, 1893).

51. See Edmond de Goncourt, *La Dubarry* (Paris, 1878).

52. Le Camus de Mézières, *Le génie de l'architecture*, 85.

53. Jean-François de Bastide, *La petite maison* (Paris, 1879), first published in *Le journal économique* in 1753, seems to have formed the basis of Le Camus's detailed descriptions of interiors. Pérouse de Montclos has pointed out the close similarity between interiors described by Bastide and built by Boullée in *Boullée*, 117ff.

54. De Bastide, *La petite maison*, 11.

55. Ibid., 14.

56. Le Camus de Mézières, *Le génie de l'architecture*, 97ff.

57. Choderlos de Laclos, *Les liaisons dangereuses* (Paris, 1782), and the Marquis de Sade, *Philosophie dans le boudoir* (Paris, 1795).

58. Pérouse de Montclos, *Boullée*, 113–22.

59. Ibid., 118.

60. Blondel and Bastide, *Les amours rivaux*, 2:109.

61. See Gallet, *Ledoux*, 86.

62. See Pierre Verlet, *Le château de Versailles* (Paris, 1985), 485ff.

63. Fragonard's suite is now in the Frick Collection, New York; see Franklin M. Biebel, "Fragonard et Madame du Barry," *Gazette des Beaux-Arts* 1101 (1960): 207–25.

64. See Geneviève Levallet-Haug, "Les écuries de Madame du Barry," *Revue d'histoire de Versailles et de Seine-et-Oise* 35, no. 1 (January-March 1933): 6–12.

65. Jean-Jacques Menuret de Chambaud, *Essais sur l'histoire médico-topographique de Paris,* new ed. (Paris, 1804), 283.

66. Pierre Pinon, "Lotissements spéculatifs, formes urbaines et architecture à la fin de l'Ancien Régime," in *Soufflot et l'architecture des lumières: Actes du colloque* (Paris, 1980), 178–92.

67. See Monique Moser et al., *Alexandre-Théodore Brongniart, 1739–1813* (Paris, 1986), 27–95.

68. For the building of the Hôtel Thélusson, see Archives Nationales AB XIX 213–15, including the estimates and accounts of Ledoux; letters of Haudry de Soucy; memoranda on the carpentry, masonry, ironwork, painting, marble sculpture, bronzework, glazing, etc; documents of sale (1785 and 1802); and plans and views of the *hôtel,* signed by Ledoux. Madame Thélusson, widowed from Georges-Tobie de Thélusson in 1776, engaged Haudry de Soucy to find a site and select an architect. Work on the foundations was started in September 1778. The contractor Géry was forced to build the *hôtel* on a raft of wooden piles bound by iron clamps that rested on the water and sand of the subsoil. See Archives Nationales AB XIX 213. The hôtel was sold in 1785 to the Comte and Comtesse de Pons and in 1802 to Joachim Murat; it was demolished in 1824.

69. Pinon, "Lotissements spéculatifs," 188.

70. See, for example, the late design for the Rural School of Meillant, 1795.

71. Gallet, *Ledoux,* 202.

72. See, for a discussion of the movement to introduce the *jardin anglais* into the new quarters of Paris, Monique Mosser, "The Picturesque in the City: Private Gardens in Paris in the 18th century," *Lotus International* 30 (1982): 29–35.

73. Madame Vigée-Lebrun, *Souvenirs,* 1:67–70; quoted with commentary in Jean Starobinski, *1789: Les emblèmes de la raison* (Paris, 1979), 196–97.

74. Following a youth of dissipation, Saint Hubert (d. 727), a descendent of Clovis, had been converted to the priesthood while hunting in the Ardennes by a vision of a stag carrying a radiant crucifix; thereafter he was adopted as the protector of hunters.

75. See Françoise Vignier, *Dictionnaire des châteaux de france: Franche-Comté, Pays de l'Ain* (Paris, 1979), 173.

76. Jean-Baptiste de La Curne de Sainte-Palaye, *Mémoires sur l'ancienne chevalerie considérée comme un établissement politique et militaire,* 2 vols. (Paris, 1759), 1:92. In a *mémoire* added to the edition of 1781, the author stressed the nobility of hunting as a necessary attribute of aristocratic prowess, also descended from Clovis; "Mémoires historiques sur le chasse dans les différents âges de la monarchie," in *Mémoires sur l'ancienne chevalerie,* (Paris, 1781), 3:165.

77. J.-M. Léquinio de Kerblay, *Voyage pittoresque et physico-économique dans le Jura,* 2 vols. (Paris, year IX [1801]), 2:102–3.

---

3 THE ARCHITECTURE OF PRODUCTION

1. For a description of these *salines* in the eighteenth century, see C.-I. Brelot and R. Locatelli, *Les salines de salins: Un millénaire d'exploitation du sel en Franche-Comté* (Besançon, 1981), 7–23.

2. Arrêt du Conseil, signed by de Maupeau and the Abbé Terray, addressed to Trudaine de Montigny, 20 September 1771, Archives Nationales, E2474.

3. A monopoly of the royal domain, the production and trade of salt was supervised by the office of the Contrôleur Général through the Intendance du Commerce. In Franche-Comté from 1674 and in Lorraine from 1737, the mangement of salt production had been subcontracted to the Ferme Générale, which also held the contract for collection of the taxes on its sale. See Durand, *Les fermiers-généraux,* 50–59, and G. Chaussinand-Nogarat, *Gens de finance au XVIIIe siècle* (Paris, 1972), 40ff.

4. Jean-Charles-Philibert Trudaine de Montigny (1733–77), named Maître des Requêtes in 1755, joined his father as adjunct to the Directeur du Commerce in November 1759, succeeding him as Intendant in 1769. A chemist, in whose laboratory at Montigny-en-Brie Antione-Laurent de Lavoisier worked, Trudaine de Montigny was also an expert in navigation, engineering, agriculture, and commercial and industrial organization. From 1754 on, he undertook many tours of inspection to ports and mines. See Ernest Choullier, *Les Trudaine* (Arcis-sur-Aube, 1884).

5. André Haudry de Soucy served as an administrator of the Ferme from 1768 and was a Fermier Général from 1768 to 1781. A close friend of Trudaine, Thélusson, and the Princesse de Conti (for whom Ledoux later designed a palace), Haudry supported Ledoux

until ruined financially in 1781 by his passion for the dancer Mlle La Guerre. Alexandre-Parseval Deschênes, a member of Monclar's financial association, was Directeur des Fermes for Franche-Comté and an entrepreneur at Montmorot, licensed to produce epsom, glauber, and ammoniac salts in his laboratory as by-products of the *saline*. He had apparently loaned Ledoux money in November 1772; see Gallet, *Ledoux*, 252.

6. The Ferme Générale administered the collection of the *gabelles* (salt taxes), the *traités* (customs duties), the *aides* (sales taxes and excises), and the *domaines* (the revenue of the old *finances ordinaires*). The *gabelles* were one of the most important sources of royal revenue, rising throughout the eighteenth century from 26,500,000 livres in 1726 to 45,602,583 livres in 1774. Collected in different amounts and according to different systems of measurement in six regions of France, their imposition was unequal and brutally enforced.

7. Furet and Richet, *La Révolution française*, 32.

8. For a general survey of the doctrines of Physiocracy and their transformation in the 1770s, see Georges Weulersse, *Le mouvement physiocratique en France (de 1756 à 1770)* (Paris, 1910), and idem, *La physiocratie sous les ministères de Turgot et de Necker (1774–1781)* (Paris, 1950).

9. For an account of salt manufacture in the east of France during the eighteenth century, the article "Salines" in the *Encyclopédie,* by the Fermier Général Dupin and the administrator of commerce Charles-Georges Fenouillot de Falbaire de Quingey, remains the most informative (14:544–69). See, too, *Encyclopédie méthodique: Arts et métiers mécaniques,* 8 vols. (Paris, 1790), 7:130–60; de Falbaire also wrote a "Supplément à l'article des salines de Franche-Comté, Saline de Chaux" (1787), published in the *Oeuvres* de M. de Falbaire de Quingey (Paris, 1787), 352–58. For modern studies, see Pierre Boyé, *Les salines et le sel en Lorraine au XVIIIe siècle* (Nancy, 1901); Etienne-A. Ancelon, "Historique de l'exploitation du sel en Lorraine" (1871); republished in *Mémoires de l'académie de Metz* 58–59 (1877–78): 145–222; idem, "Recherches historiques et archéologiques sur les salines d'Amelécourt et de Château-Salins," *Mémoires de la Société d'archéologie Lorraine et du musée historique Lorraine,* 3d ser., 7 (Nancy, 1880): 98–134; E. Gréau, *Le sel en Lorraine* (Paris and Nancy, 1908); and, especially, Max Prinet, *L'industrie du sel en Franche-Comté avant la conquête française* (Besançon, 1900). The best contemporary accounts are Pierre-François Nicolas, *Mémoire sur les salines de la République* (Nancy, year II [1794]), reprinted in *Annales de chimie* 20 (Paris, year V [1797]): 78–188, and Piroux (architect), *Mémoire sur le sel et les salines de Lorraine* (Nancy, 1791).

10. The *type primitif* of a *saline* was, as Max Prinet put it, little more than a large, flat iron pan, or *chaudière,* suspended over a wood-burning furnace, drawing its brine from adjacent wells by pumps turned by man or horse power (Prinet, *L'industrie du sel,* 156–57). The best descriptions of this process are in Brelot and Locatelli, *Les salines de salins.*

11. Contemporary descriptions of the process abounded; some, like that of Trudaine de Montigny, were scientific, others less so. The most detailed can be found in the *Encyclopédie,* 14:544–69, and in Nicolas's comprehensive *Mémoire sur les salines de la République.*

12. For an account of the traditional management structure, see H. Dubois, "L'activité de la saunerie de Salins au XVe siècle d'après le compte de 1459," *Le Moyen Age* (1964): 419–71.

13. The glass factory of Saint Louis in Lorraine was typical: as well as apartments for its officials and visitors' rooms, it provided two workers' dwellings, each housing some twelve families and containing a communal kitchen, wine cellar, and grain storage. See Warren Scoville, *Capitalism and French Glass-Making, 1640–1789* (Berkeley, 1950), 45.

14. Prinet, *L'industrie du sel,* 156.

15. Léquinio de Kerblay, *Voyage pittoresque,* 2:81.

16. Cf. Jean-Charles-Philibert Trudaine de Montigny, "Mémoire sur les salines de Franche-Comté" (21 April 1762), *Mémoires de l'Académie royale des sciences* (1764): 102–30. See also Jean Cousin "L'Académie des sciences, belles-lettres et arts de Besançon au XVIIIe siècle et son oeuvre scientifique," *Revue d'histoire des sciences* 12, no. 4 (October–December 1959): 327–44, which summarizes previous experiments in the design of furnaces for Montmorot in 1756.

17. See L. Mazoyer, "Exploitation forestière et conflits sociaux en Franche-Comté à la fin de l'Ancien Régime," *Annales E.S.C.* 4 (1932): 339ff.; S. Monniot, "Le rôle de la forêt dans la vie des populations Franc-comtoises de la conquête française à la Révolution, 1674–1789," *Revue d'histoire moderne* (September–December 1937): 449ff; François Vion-Delphin, "Salines et administration forestière en Franche-Comté à la fin du XVIIIe siècle: Exemple des salines de Chaux," *99ᵉ congrès national des sociétés savantes (Besançon 1974) Section d'histoire moderne* (Besançon, 1976), 2:181–190.

18. The graduation building was lyrically described by the Chevalier d'Éon de Beaumont (1728–1810) in *Les loisirs du chevalier d'Éon,* 9 vols. (Amsterdam, 1775), vol. 9, *Considérations sur la gabelle,* 237ff.

19. The Arrêt Royal of 1743 called for the construction of a new *saline* between Montmorot and Lons-le-Saunier; on 17 September a contract was signed with Jean Lallemand for the production of 60,000 quintaux of salt per year. Lallemand was given twenty-four years of exploitation and a 300,000 livre, interest-free advance for the construction of the *saline,* reimbursable in six years; the salt was to be exported to Yverdun in Switzerland. The contract specified the works in detail. (Arrêt Royal, 17 September 1743, Archives Départementales du Jura [hereafter AD Jura], C375). See also, André Bouvard, *La Saline de Montmorot au XVIIIe siècle* (Besançon, 1967), for a complete history of the *saline;* Paul Baud, "Une industrie d'état sous l'Ancien Régime: L'exploitation des salines de Tarantaise," *R.H.E.S.* (Paris, 1936): 149ff., for a comprehensive account of the *salines* of Savoy and of the introduction of graduation buildings.

20. De Falbaire de Quingey "Salines," *Encyclopédie,* 14:565.

21. Arrêt du Conseil, 29 April 1773, AD Jura, C 406, folio 4.

22. The royal contract with the Ferme was normally renewed every six years; see Durand, *Les fermiers-généraux.*

23. The *bail* (or lease) David succeeded the *bail* Alaterre, taking effect from October 1774.

24. *Traité pour la construction d'une saline en Franche-Comté, son exploitation et celle des autres salines de la même province, et les salines de Lorraine et des Trois Evêchés, pendant quatre-vingt-quatre années* (Paris, 1774), Archives Nationales, G1 93.

25. For a detailed description of the circumstances leading to the appointment of Turgot, see Edgar Faure, *La disgrâce de Turgot* (Paris, 1961), 369 ff.

26. Ibid.

27. Archives Nationales, G1 93.

28. Rendue, 1 April 1782, AD Jura, 8J 502. This account, drawn up by the director of the *saline,* Jean-François Dorval, not only details the state of the buildings and machinery eight years after the start of construction, but also elaborates the chronology of the building campaign itself.

29. Levallet-Haug, *Ledoux,* 67.

30. From the Archives de la Commune d'Arc-et-Senans, I, i; cited in Levallet-Haug, *Ledoux,* 66. François-Marie Maréschal, seigneur de Longeville et de Vuillafans, was a Commissaire Général du Conseil pour la Réformation des Bois, the agency responsible for policing the Forest of Chaux and thus its *saline.* An admirer of Ledoux, he

later recommended him for the Cordon de Saint-Michel in 1785. See Gallet, *Ledoux,* 151.

31. Levallet-Haug, *Ledoux,* 66.

32. See Abbé Lédontal, *Arc-et-Senans à travers les âges* (Besançon, 1927).

33. Rendue, 1 April 1782.

34. The following chronology is drawn from the Rendue of 1 April 1782.

35. Throughout the construction of the Saline de Chaux, Monclar's association had called for capital advances from the administration on eight occasions, from 29 March 1775, when they asked for 210,000 livres, to the final call for funds on 30 August 1780. In all 1,766,815 livres was spent on the building of the *saline;* although this amount included interest payments, clearly more than twice the estimated sum of 600,000 livres was disbursed. There is no record of Ledoux receiving his claimed 200,000 livres for architectural services; Archives Nationales, G 93.

36. *Traité pour la construction d'une saline,* 2. Monclar was instructed to undertake "major repairs, restorations, and new constructions," together with "all the repairs and maintenance needed by the *salines,"* while at the same time overseeing the condition of roads and *canaux de flottage* in the region.

37. Ibid., 3.

38. The most comprehensive and detailed study of these works is in Pierre Lacroix, *La saline d'Arc-et-Senans et les techniques de canalisation en bois: Notes d'histoire comtoise* (Lons-le-Saunier, 1970). Lacroix was the first to utilize the newly catalogued archives of the Saline de Montmorot in the Archives Départementales du Jura.

39. Plans of the canalization from Salins to the Saline de Chaux, 1775–80, surveyed by Denis-François Dez, "géomètre et arpenteur en la réformation des Salines de Salins," AD Jura, 8J 581 to 8J 589.

40. Illustrated in Lacroix, *La Saline d'Arc-et-Senans,* pl. IV; a similar boring mill is described by Lequinio, *Voyage pittoresque,* 1:36–37, 2:440.

41. See Wolfgang Herrmann, "The Problem of Chronology," 191–210.

42. Chevalier d'Éon, *Les loisirs,* 237.

43. Despite the comparatively recent buildings of Montmorot, completed in 1749, and its rational "engineering" plan, Ledoux, who in

all probability had not visited Lons-le-Saunier, included these works in his list of "constructions built haphazardly" (35).

44. Blondel, in his course, simply noted that "each kind of factory requires an individual treatment that determines its appearance, its siting, and the distribution of its different buildings . . . their architectural ordering should be simple, without in any way presenting a martial character (*Cours d'architecture*, 2:398–99).

45. The plan alone offended traditional hierarchies of distribution, with the chapel symbolically compared to the bakery and displaced to the corner of the scheme; Ledoux redressed this undervaluation in the final project.

46. Ledoux's report, drawn up with the collaboration of Jean-François Chalgrin, is summarized in E. Chambardel, "Une solution inédite des problèmes de gestion hospitalière: C.-N. Ledoux (1736–1806)," *L'hôpital et l'aide sociale* (September–October 1963): 559–63. The debate over the hospitals is set out with full documentation in Michel Foucault et al., *Les machines à guérir: Aux origines de l'hôpital moderne* (Brussels, 1979), and in Anthony Vidler, "Confinement and Cure: Reforming the Hospital, 1770–1789," chap. 4 of *The Writing of the Walls*.

47. Antoine Petit, *Mémoire sur la meilleure manière de construire un hôpital des malades* (Paris, 1774), 5. This report systematically outlined the functional criteria that should guide the architect in selecting a suitable plan.

48. The evident reference to this city of the winds was given practical substance by the needs of the graduation building: planned along one of the radical axes of the *saline,* this wind-dependent structure seems to anticipate a battery of similar sheds, radiating from the center of the *saline.*

49. Claude Perrault, *Les dix livres d'architecture de Vitruve* (Paris, 1673), XLII, XLIV, XLV.

50. For the best general discussion of the debates and projects concerning the proper form for the theater, see Monika Steinhauser and Daniel Rabreau, "Le théâtre de l'Odéon de Charles De Wailly et Marie-Joseph Peyre, 1767–1782," *Revue de l'art* 19 (1973): 9–49.

51. This motif is to be found, according to Guy Nicot, "Les salines d'Arc-et-Senans," *Monuments historiques de la France* no. 2 (1978): 33–48, in the old *salines* of Salins as well as in those at Montmorot, and in many contemporary engravings of salt working. See Gréau, *Le sel en Lorraine,* 9, "Médaillon allégorique d'après la pompe funèbre de Charles III (1608)."

52. Rendue, 1 April 1782.

53. Julien-David Le Roy, *Les ruines des plus beaux monuments de la Grèce considérées du côté de l'histoire et du côté de l'architecture,* 2d ed., 2 vols in 1 (Paris, 1770), pl. XIII, "Reconstruction of the Propylea of Athens."

54. *Encyclopédie méthodique: Arts et métiers mécaniques,* 6:123.

55. These insulating walls not only prevented the heat from escaping but also protected the exterior walls of the *bernes* from fire:

Has [the architect] important furnaces to construct? He will understand the need to use the fuel economically, to isolate the furnaces by galleries that are ventilated by the cooling air from the outside in order to preserve their enclosing walls from the dangers of contact. As they are constructed in brick, their thickness will retain an intense heat: the economic artist will distribute this through the first and second stoves, over the long drying racks for the salt; he will block its effects by a damper that will accumulate new heat to distribute through the upper drying rooms. (122)

His English experience also led Ledoux to favor the use of coal to supplement diminishing supplies of wood—an innovation in the event not effected until well into the nineteenth century. Thus he was concerned to design, in his words, "less expensive forms, that will encourage the use of coal so that the earth will be able to lend a helping hand to the forests" (122).

56. Here was the link between the saline and its immense and extended external economy. "This tiny hut," wrote Ledoux, "precedes the entry gate of the *saline;* it is occupied by the overseer charged with distributing the bulletins, with sending the wood to the place closest to its use in order to avoid uncertain movements and costly displacements" (120).

57. Boyé, *Les salines,* 10.

58. Dubois, "L'activité de la saunerie de Salins," 421. The Register of the Saline de Chaux differed little from this traditional model. See *Saline de Chaux, Service Intérieure,* 1787–89, AD Jura, 8J 503.

59. *Saline de Chaux, Service Intérieure.*

60. *Ordre donné par Monsieur Haudry pour le service de la porte de la Saline de Montmorot,* 2 January 1775, AD Jura, 8J 323.

61. *Encyclopédie méthodique: Arts et métiers mécaniques,* 6:123.

62. Ibid., 6:134, 157.

63. Dubois, "L'activité de la saunerie de Salins."

64. Bertrand Gille, *Les origines de la grande industrie métallurgique en France* (Paris, 1947), and Scoville, *Capitalism and French Glass-Making.*

65. Scoville, *Capitalism and French Glass-Making,* 77–78.

66. Baud, "Une industrie d'état," 271–73, "Organisation du travail aux salines de moutiers."

67. Ibid., 271.

68. *Ouvriers de la saline de Montmorot,* 26 February–26 June 1776, AD Jura, 8J 440. The oldest worker, Benoît de Vidan Kuerby, had in 1762 fallen into a boiling pan, leading to the amputation of one hand. As *chef de cuites* he was noted as "still having much zeal, but his great age slows down his activity."

69. Michel Foucault, *Surveiller et punir: Naissance de la prison* (Paris, 1975), 176.

70. Petit defined the purpose of his radial plan in terms of visual access for the patients in the ward blocks to participate in the central religious services, as well as in terms of continuous supervision: "A single glance from the sisters and others designated to maintain good order will encompass everything that goes on in the wards" (*Mémoire,* 15). Similar arguments for their circular plan were put forward by Claude-Philibert Coquéau and Bernard Poyet in their *Mémoire sur la nécessité de transférer et reconstruire l'Hôtel-Dieu de Paris* (Paris, 1785); this radial plan also situated its chapel, in the form of a freestanding *tempietto,* at the center. For a discussion of the radial shipyard plans of the late eighteenth century, see Alain Demangeon and Bruno Fortier, *Les vaisseaux et les villes* (Brussels, 1978).

71. See Sidney Pollard, *The Genesis of Modern Management* (London, 1969), chap. 5, "The Adaptation of the Labour Force."

72. The complexities embedded in Bentham's deceptively simple diagram have been revealed by the excellent analysis of Robin Evans, *The Fabrication of Virtue: English Prison Architecture, 1750–1840* (Cambridge, 1982). For a more balanced historical account of the juridical and social context of these "geometrical reforms," perhaps oversimplified by Foucault in the interests of clarity, see Michael Ignatieff, *A Just Measure of Pain: The Penitentiary in the Industrial Revolution, 1750–1850* (New York, 1978), and especially Michelle Perrot, ed., *L'impossible prison: Recherches sur le système pénitentiaire au XIXe siècle* (Paris, 1980), which includes an important "débat avec Michel Foucault."

73. The *source de la Loüe* was a favorite subject for lyrical guidebook descriptions, engravings, and paintings; Gustave Courbet was only the most celebrated of many painters fascinated by the combination of secret grotto and dramatic waterfalls. Ledoux's engraving for the House of the surveyors of the Loüe River was based, with exaggeration, on topographical reality. For a comparison of Ledoux's grotto with those of his contemporaries, see Monique Mosser, "Le rocher et la colonne: Un thème d'iconographie architecturale au XVIIIe siècle," *Revue de l'art* 58–59 (1983): 53–74.

74. See H. and E. H. Mueller von Asow, *The Collected Correspondence and Papers of Christoph Willibald Gluck* (New York, 1962); Ledoux, married to the daughter of a highly placed musician, was a supporter of Gluck, despite the du Barry faction's preference for Nicola Piccini, who was brought to Paris in 1776. Gluck was sustained by the patronage of Louis XVI and of Marie Antoinette, who for a short period had been his pupil in Vienna (p. 48).

75. *La descente d'Enée aux enfers: Représentation donnée sur le théâtre des Thuilleries par le sieur Servandoni, le cinquième avril, 1740* (Paris, 1740); the *Observations sur l'art du comédien par D . . . d'Hannetaire, ancien comédien,* published in 1774, still remembered this mise-en-scène with admiration (p. 283).

76. See, for comparison, the "reconstruction" of Solomon's Temple by Claude Perrault, published in Maimonedes, *De Culto Divino* (Paris, 1678), and discussed in Wolfgang Herrmann, "Unknown Designs for the 'Temple of Jerusalem' by Claude Perrault," in *Essays in the History of Architecture presented to Rudolph Wittkower,* ed. D. Fraser, H. Hibbard, and M. J. Levine, 2 vols. (London, 1967), 1:143ff.

77. See Anthony Vidler, "The Architecture of the Lodges: Rituals and symbols of Freemasonry," chap. 6 of *The Writings of the Wall,* for a summary of the Freemasonic movement and its architectural representation.

78. In his later descriptions of the religious "sublime" embodied in the artifical mountain of the director's chapel, Ledoux drew on Antoine Court de Gébelin, *Monde primitif* (Paris, 1773–84), and Charles-François Dupuis, *Origine de tous les cultes* (Paris, 1795). Ledoux searched for an "original sublime," already intimated in Longinus, and elaborated by Burke, that transcended iconography and operated by means of light and dark alone.

79. In this sense, these architectural motifs are treated like so many "hieroglyphs" of the kind investigated by theorists of the origins of writing, from Condillac to the Chevalier de Jaucourt; see the republication of William Warburton, *Essai sur les hiéroglyphes des Égyptiens, traduit par Léonard des Malpeines (Paris, 1744),* ed. Patrick Tort (Paris, 1977), with its comprehensive bibliography of eighteenth-century enquiries into the hieroglyphs, and Madeleine V.-David, *Le débat sur les écritures et l'hiéroglyphe aux XVIIe et XVIIIe siècles* (Paris, 1965), for its excellent analysis of the parameters of the debate.

80. Despite Ledoux's idealization of the *berne* as a sublime evocation of production, its windows belching thick "Egyptian" smoke as if

from some primitive funeral pyre, the working conditions inside were virtually insufferable. The thick steam, mixed with acidic vapors and smoke from the furnaces, together with the intense heat, made breathing difficult; ventilation was more or less nonexistent. The workers, afflicted by chronic bronchial and mucous illnesses, often partially disabled from accidents—the loss of limbs from falling into the boiling brine or of eyes from the furnaces was common—worked for twelve-hour shifts, day and night, for the pitiful sum of six sous per day. See Rendue, 1 April 1782.

81. The most comprehensive summary of late-eighteenth-century, pre-Revolutionary knowledge of Egyptian architecture was provided by Quatremère de Quincy in his study, written in 1785 but not published until 1803, *De l'architecture égyptienne considérée dans son origine, ses principes et son goût* (Paris, 1803). An "Egyptian" crematorium was presented in detail by Pierre Giraud in his *Essai sur les sépultures*, in a style that unmistakably echoes that of Ledoux. This was designed in year IV (1796) and published three years later.

82. Jean-Jacques Rousseau, *Discours sur l'origine et les fondements de l'inégalité parmi les hommes* (1754) (Paris, 1980), 208.

83. "Manufacture," *Encyclopédie*, 10:60, and *Encyclopédie méthodique: Arts et métiers mécaniques*, 20:1003ff.

84. Rendue, 1 April 1782. A second Rendue of 1793 confirmed this design fault.

85. Ibid.

86. See Monniot, "Le rôle de la forêt"; Mazoyer, "Exploitation forestière"; and, especially, Lacroix, *La Saline d'Arc-et-Senans*, 76–78.

87. Lacroix, *La Saline d'Arc-et-Senans*, 22.

88. Monniot, "Le rôle de la forêt," and Mazoyer, "Exploitation forestière."

89. Monniot, "Le rôle de la forêt," 457.

90. See G. Plaisance, "La Révolte des demoiselles, "*Barbizier* (1951): 483–86, and Mazoyer, "Exploitation forestière," 351.

91. Lacroix, *La Saline d'Arc-et-Senans*, and François Vion-Delphin, "Salines et administration forestière en Franche-Comté à la fin du XVIIIe siècle.

92. Lacroix, *La Saline d'Arc-et-Senans* 69.

93. Ibid.

94. Bertrand Gille, ed., *Les forges françaises en 1772* (Paris, 1960), 52.

95. Lacroix, *La Saline d'Arc-et-Senans*, 69.

96. Mazoyer, "Exploitation forestière," 355.

97. Lacroix, *La Saline d'Arc-et-Senans*, 58.

98. Gille, *Les origines de la grande industrie*, 148.

99. Ibid.

100. *Encyclopédie méthodique: Arts et métiers mécaniques*, 6:138.

101. Ibid., 6:125.

102. Lacroix, *La Saline d'Arc-et-Senans*, 77.

103. The first published description of the Saline de Chaux was written by Charles-George Fenouillot de Falbaire de Quingey (1727–1800), the son of the Regisseur de Salins, Jean-Baptiste Fenouillot. A successful playwright (his *L'honnête criminal ou l'amour filial* of 1767 was a popular favorite) and a protegé of Trudaine, he entered the Department of Finances; he also undertook contracts with his brother for the upkeep of the *salines* of Franche-Comté, canceled in 1771 in favor of the new contracts with the Ferme Général (Arrêt du Conseil, 8 March 1771, AD Jura, 764, folio 70v). In 1774 he replaced his father at Salins and settled at Quingey. In May 1782 he was appointed Inspecteur Général des Salines (AD Jura, A765, folio 14), an office suppressed in 1787. In 1789 he wrote a *Mémoire adressé au roi et à l'assemblée nationale* on the reorganization of the Salines de l'Est. The Revolution destroyed his fortune, and his forges at Quingey and Champagnolle were closed. See his *Oeuvres*, "Description des Salines: Sur les salines de Franche-Comté (1761)," 294–351, and the "Supplément," 352–58. Embittered by his treatment by the Ferme, de Falbaire launched a protest against Ledoux in 1789, attempting to defame the architect for embezzlement; Ledoux was defended by Le Fevre d'Ormesson, who pleaded that the architect had already been punished for any oversight by the loss of work following the Revolution. See Gallet, *Ledoux*, 277, "Défense de Ledoux contre une accusation de Fenouillot de Falbaire. . . ."

104. François-Marie de Longeville, "Rapport à M. de Lessart," 19 July 1780, AD Jura, 8J 502; first noted by Lacroix, *La Saline d'Arc-et-Senans*, 28. Submitted to Claude-Antoine Valdée de Lessart, Maître des Requêtes, it was followed by a letter written directly by de Longeville to Jacques Necker, 23 July 1780, AD Jura, 8J 502.

105. Maréchal de Longeville to Jacques Necker, quoted in Lacroix, *La Saline d'Arc-et-Senans*, 33.

106. Claude-Joseph-Alexandre Bertrand (1734–97) worked on the reconstruction of Besançon, on the town's theater designed by Ledoux. See R. Tournier, "L'Architecte . . . Bertrand," *Académie Besançon* 169 (1944): 13–302.

107. Jean-Rodolphe Perronet to Claude-Joseph-Alexandre Bertrand, 12 December 1780; quoted in Lacroix, *La Saline d'Arc-et-Senans*, 44–45.

108. Ibid., 45.

109. Lacroix, *La Saline d'Arc-et-Senans*, 20–21, n. 31.

110. Rendue, 1 April 1782.

111. Two of these registers survive, for the years 1787 and 1789; see *Saline de Chaux, Service Intérieur*, 1787–89.

112. De Falbaire de Quingey, *Mémoire*, 356–57.

113. Léquinio de Kerblay, *Voyage pittoresque*, 1:478.

114. Ibid., 480–82.

115. See Otto Karmin, *La question du sel pendant la Révolution* (Paris, 1912), and G. Hottenger, *Les anciennes salines domaniales de l'est: Histoire monopole (1790–1840)* (Nancy, 1929).

116. In response to the anonymous *Mémoire sur les salines de Lorraine, Trois Evêchés et Franche-Comté* (1790), Simon Willier, a pseudonym for Simon Vuillier, Deputy to the Convention for the Jura) wrote a series of impassioned attacks on the Ferme: *Réponse au mémoire sur les salines de Lorraine, des Trois-Evêchés et de Franche-Comté* (Dôle, 1790); *Ma profession de foi sur les salines* (Dôle, 1790); and *Ultimatum sur les salines locales* (Dôle, 1790).

117. Willier, *Ultimatum*, 13.

118. Jean Debry, "Sur le commerce et l'industrie du département du Doubs," *Annales des arts et manufactures* 22 (Paris, year XIII [1805]): 8–10.

119. Ibid., 8.

120. Pierre-François Nicolas, *Mémoire sur les salines*. Nicolas, the "chemist of Nancy," was presented to the Comité de Salut Public by the Commission d'Agriculture et des Arts, 26 Prairial, year II (1794). See Baud, "Une industrie d'état," 238.

121. Baud, "Une industrie d'état," 31. Others were less enthusiastic: the architect-engineer François-Michel Lecreulx, whose *Discours sur le goût* had been published by the Académie de Nancy in 1778, complained in a report of 1799 of "the uselessness of sumptuous buildings for the housing of directors, receivers, inspectors, controllers, . . . of these large sites taken up with *parterres* of flowers, icehouses, etc." (*Examen de la propriété des salines nationales et sources salées des départements de l'Est, et des avantages que l'etat peut en tirer* [Nancy, year VII (1799)], 19–20).

122. Ibid., 27.

123. See Hottenger, *Les anciennes salines*.

124. On Grimaldi (1796–1872), see Lacroix, *La saline d'Arc-et-senans*, 20.

125. Ibid., 13.

---

4 URBAN TYPOLOGIES

1. For a comparison of Ledoux's professional career with those of his contemporaries, see Braham, *French Enlightenment*.

2. For a description of the brief encounter between Ledoux and Frederick, see Pierre Colombier, *L'architecture française en Allemagne au XVIIIe siècle*, 2 vols. (Paris, 1956), 1:232ff.

3. See the detailed article by Geneviève Levallet-Haug, "L'Hôtel de Ville de Neuchâtel," *Bulletin de la Société de l'histoire de l'art français* (1933): 88–99.

4. See the study by J.-M. Dudot et al., eds., "Le devoir d'embellir" (Nancy, 1977), an unpublished report for CORDA, no. 76.73.021.00.202.75.01.

5. Pierre Patte, *Mémoires sur les objets les plus importants de l'architecture* (Paris, 1769); for a short description of this movement, see Anthony Vidler, "The Scenes of the Street," in *On Streets*, ed. Stanford Anderson (Cambridge, Mass., 1978), 28–111.

6. On Calonne, see R. Lacour-Gayet, *Calonne* (Paris, 1963).

7. Ledoux's application is quoted in full in Gallet, *Ledoux*, 261.

8. See Henri Lemonnier, ed., *Procès-verbaux de l'Académie royale d'architecture, 1671–1793*, 10 vols. (Paris, 1911–26), vol. 4, introduction.

9. J.-B.-L. Coquereau, *Mémoires de l'abbé Terray*, 2 vols. (Paris, 1776), 1:271. I am indebted for this reference to Thomas E. Crow, whose own study of the political rivalry between the party of Lenormand (Madame de Pompadour) and that of du Barry for the control of artistic patronage is illuminating for that of architecture. See Thomas E. Crow, *Painters and Public Life in Eighteenth Century Paris* (London and New Haven, 1985).

10. Lemonnier, *Procès-verbaux de l'Académie*, 8:167–70.

11. Ledoux was present in July 1774 for Soufflot's reading of a report by Raimond on the aqueducts and water supply, palaces and private houses of ancient Rome; in November 1774 for the discussion of David Le Roy's course in the history of architecture; in December 1774

for the examination of Jean-François de Neufforge's *Recueil élémentaire d'architecture;* in July 1777 for the reading of a *mémoire* by the Abbé Camus on good taste; in March 1779 for the study of Antoine Desgodets's treatise on the antiquities of Rome and discussion of its possible reprinting; in March 1780 for Gondouin's presentation of his work on the Ecoles de Chirurgie; in August 1780 for the reading of Montesquieu's essay on taste in the *Encyclopédie* and a poem by Mailler on architecture as well as the presentation of Jean-Louis Viel de Saint-Maux's second *Lettre sur l'architecture;* in September 1781 for the discussion of the concept of *caractère,* followed by Peyre's report on the *Jardins d'Ermenonville;* in January 1782 for the reading of the Abbé Brotier's essay on circuses, later to be quoted by Boullée; in June 1782 for the revision of all the *Encyclopédie* articles relating to architecture; in June, July, and August 1784 for Lussault's reading of his work on architecture; in March 1785 for the examination of Jean Martin's *Vitruve;* for the discussion of Diderot's article "Génie" from the *Encyclopédie* and its relation to architecture; in June 1788 for the reading of the article "Architecture" in the *Encyclopédie.* See Lemonnier, *Procès-verbaux de l'Académie,* vol. 8.

12. Jean-Marie Pérouse de Montclos, *"Les prix de Rome": Concours de l'Académie royale d'architecture au XVIIIe siècle* (Paris, 1984), and Helen Rosenau, "The Engravings of the *Grands Prix* of the French Academy of Architecture," *Architectural History* (1960).

13. Such was the case of the cenotaph to Newton, probably set as a *prix d'émulation* subject in January 1785 on the basis of Boullée's design of the previous year; see Pérouse de Montclos, *"Les Prix de Rome",* 17.

14. See Lemonnier, *Procès-verbaux de l'Académie,* vol. 8, and Pérouse de Montclos, *"Les Prix de Rome."*

15. Ledoux to Frederick II of Hesse-Cassel, 16 January 1776, Archives of the State of Marburg; quoted in Gallet, *Ledoux,* 267.

16. Boullée, Architecture, 73.

17. Ibid., 73–74.

18. Jean-Jacques Rousseau, *Discours sur les sciences et les arts* (1750; Paris, 1971), 40.

19. Jean-Jacques Rousseau, *Essai sur l'origine des langues,* ed. C. Porset (Bordeaux, 1968), chap. 1.

20. Edmund Burke, *A Philosophical Enquiry into the Origin of Our Ideas of the Sublime and Beautiful,* edited with an introduction and notes by James T. Boulton (London, 1958). It was translated into French by the Abbé L.-A. Des François (Paris, 1765).

21. Nicolas Boileau-Déspreaux, *Traité du sublime ou du merveilleux dans le discours: Traduit du Grec de Longin,* in *Oeuvres diverses* (Paris, 1685), preface, x.

22. Blondel, *Cours d'architecture,* 2:377ff.

23. Burke, *A Philosophical Enquiry,* pt. 1, sec. 7, 39.

24. Ibid., pt. 2, sec. 3, 59.

25. Ibid., pt. 2, sec. 9, 74–76.

26. Ibid., pt. 4, sec. 13, 141–42.

27. Ibid., pt. 2, sec. 12–16, 77–82.

28. Abbé Marc-Antoine Laugier, *Essai sur l'architecture* (Paris, 1755), 110–11.

29. Laugier, *Essai sur l'architecture,* 170.

30. For full details of the planning and construction of the Hôtel de Ville of Neuchâtel, see Levallet-Haug, "L'Hôtel de Ville de Neuchâtel."

31. Ledoux, who immediately claimed fees of one hundred louis, was not finally paid until 1790, when he received three-quarters of the sum due.

32. See Durand, *Les fermiers-généraux,* 54.

33. Bruno Fortier, "Introduction. Histoire et planification urbaine: Les années 1800," in Demangeon and Fortier, *Les vaisseaux et les villes,* 15.

34. Viel de Saint-Maux, *Lettres sur l'architecture,* "Septième lettre," 59. In a long footnote Viel attacked Ledoux's decorative program as confusing to the observer: "A stranger considered this building and wished to decide what it might be without the help of passersby. He looked alternately at the setback in the form of a stair above the halfporch, and at the torso of Mercury represented on the door; then he raised his eyes to guess from the cornice what had been intended; finally, he found no help in the royal coat of arms since it is placed indiscriminately on the doors of Churches, Hospitals, Theaters, Colleges, and over chimneypieces, tobacco shops etc. The Mercury gave him no clearer message, since it might be considered as the Sun God or Hermes, who by his influence over the human organism produced the sciences and the arts, or as the Globe, or a carrier of cupids, a surgical remedy, or finally as the God of Thieves or Merchants. Suddenly he imagined that this was the stockexchange they had begun to construct. . . . From passersby he learned that these were the offices of the clerks of the Ferme."

35. In Jean-Charles Krafft, *Traité théorique et pratique sur l'art de la charpente* (Paris, 1819), 2d pt., 18.

36. Ramée, *L'architecture,* pls. 101–5, follows this hypothesis; Gallet, *Ledoux,* without explaining his reasoning reverses the schemes. Stylistically as well as programmatically, it would seem that Ramée is correct: the rustication of the pavilions of the first scheme belongs to the period of Ledoux's design for the Hôtel d'Artagnan de Fézensac (de Montesquiou), that is, around 1779; the grand plan and monumental isolation of the second scheme, together with the regularization of the surrounding square, seem to place this scheme in the 1780s, and it is perhaps Ledoux's attempt to compete for Calonne's competition in 1785.

37. See Mosser et al., *Alexandre-Théodore Brongniart,* 125–29.

38. Ibid., 131ff.

39. The best and most comprehensive account of Ledoux's theater architecture is Jacques Rittaud-Hutinet, *La vision d'un future: Ledoux et ses théâtres* (Lyons, 1982). Rittaud-Hutinet, as a sociologist, is interested in the implied reformulation of the "audience" by Ledoux's redistribution of the *salles,* but he also provides a complete documentation of the building campaign of Besançon, the scenographic designs by Guillaume Dard de Bosco, together with a documentary appendix covering Ledoux's correspondence in the *Journal de Paris,* as well as reports relating to Besançon and Marseilles. I have drawn liberally from this study in the following interpretation of Ledoux's designs. The informative article by Ernest de Ganay, "La salle de spectacle de l'architecte Ledoux à Besançon," *Revue de l'art ancien et moderne* 52 (June–December 1927): 2–21, is still useful in its attempt carefully to reconstruct the original appearance of the theater before its nineteenth-century restoration and the destruction of the interior by fire in 1958.

40. Charles-André de Lacoré, 24 August 1775 Archives du Doubs, C 40; the full text of this letter is transcribed in Rittaud-Hutinet, *La vision d'un futur,* 132–33, and in Gallet, *Ledoux,* 267. Charles-André de Lacoré was Intendant of Franche-Comté from 1761 to 1784. His reputation as an enlightened administrator and reformer was second only to Turgot's.

41. Ibid.

42. "Réflexions du Magistrat de Besançon sur le projet de construire une salle de spectacle dans l'emplacement du magasin de Transmarchement et du Jardin des plantes," 24 July 1776, Archives Municipales de Besançon, DD 35, piece 36 (i).

43. See Rittaud-Hutinet, *La vision d'un futur,* 38–40.

44. "Réflexions du Magistrat."

45. Ibid.

46. Ibid.

47. Charles-André de Lacoré to the Magistrature, Paris, 30 June 1776, Archives Municipales de Besançon, DD 35, piece 37 (i). It was possible, he admitted, that the site proposed by the municipality would offer advantages.

48. Charles-André de Lacoré to the Magistrature, Paris, 6 August 1776, Archives Municipales de Besançon, DD 35, piece 38 (2).

49. Ibid.

50. Charles-André de Lacoré to the Magistrature, Paris, 18 October 1777, Archives Municipales de Besançon, DD 35.

51. Registre des Déliberations de la Ville de Besançon, 3 January 1778; quoted in Rittaud-Hutinet, *La vision d'un futur;* 39.

52. Ibid.

53. Registre des Déliberations, 16 February 1778; quoted in Rittaud-Hutinet, *La vision d'un futur,* 39.

54. "Eloge à Lacoré, 14 Juin 1771," composed by Talbert, Prédicateur de Roi, Archives Municipales de Besançon, DD 35.

55. This gradual transformation is examined in detail in Henri Lagrave, *Le théâtre et le public à Paris de 1715–1750* (Paris 1972); see also Max Fuchs, *La vie théâtrale en province au XVIIIe siècle* (Geneva, 1933).

56. For a summary of the most important polemical and critical writings, see Marian Hobson, *The Object of Art: The Theory of Illusion in Eighteenth-Century France* (Cambridge, 1982), especially pt. 3, "Illusion and the Theatre," 139–95.

57. Denis Diderot, "Entretiens sur *Le fils naturel*" (1757), and "De la poésie dramatique" (1758), in *Oeuvres esthétiques,* ed. Paul Vernière (Paris, 1959); Yvon Belaval, in *L'esthétique sans paradoxe de Diderot* (Paris, 1950), summarizes Diderot's complex and sometimes ambiguous positions.

58. Jean-Claude Bonnet, Introduction to Denis Diderot, *Le neveu de Rameau* (Paris, 1983), 35.

59. This journey is recounted and analyzed in Daniel Rabreau, "Autour du voyage d'Italie (1750): Soufflot, Cochin et M. de Marigny réformateurs de l'architecture théâtrale française," *Bollettino del centro internazionale di studi di architettura Andrea Palladio* 17 (1975): 213–25.

60. Jacques-Germain Soufflot, Report read to the Académie de Lyon, December 1753, "Introduction à l'explication des dessins de la salle de spectacle de Lyon," manuscript, Académie de Lyon, no. 121, fol. 29–30; quoted in Rabreau, "Autour du voyage d'Italie," 217. Also see Gilles Chomer, "Le théâtre," in L'oeuvre de Soufflot à Lyon, ed. Alain Charre et al. (Lyons, 1982), 99–113.

61. Charles-Nicolas Cochin, Projet d'une salle de spectacle pour un théâtre de comédie (Paris, 1765); he termed his elliptical auditorium, cut on the long axis, "the theater of Palladio, applied to our own uses." The pure semicircle that he had seen at Herculaneum was too deep at the center for the audience to see with any ease (Projet, 14). For his report on the theater at Herculaneum, see Charles-Nicolas Cochin and Jérôme-Charles Bellicard, Observations sur les antiquités de la ville d'Herculanum (Paris, 1754), 10.

62. On Charles De Wailly and the Odéon, see Steinhauser and Rabreau, "Le théâtre de l'Odéon," 9–49; see also Mosser and Rabreau, Charles De Wailly, 49ff.

63. Jean Damun, Prospectus du nouveau théâtre trace sur les principes des Grecs et des Romains (Paris, 1776).

64. André-Jacques Roubo, Traité de la construction des théâtres et des machines théâtrales (Paris, 1777).

65. Pierre Patte, Essai sur l'architecture théâtrale (Paris, 1782), 126.

66. See John Lough, Paris Theatre Audiences in the Seventeenth and Eighteenth Centuries (London, 1957), especially chap. 3.

67. Denis Diderot, "Lettre à Mme Riccoboni," in Oeuvres complètes, ed. J. Assézat and M. Tourneaux, 20 vols. (Paris, 1875–77), 7:401, not dated, but probably written after 1758.

68. For a good summary of the discourse on air, see Richard Etlin, "L'air dans l'urbanisme des Lumières," Dix-huitième siècle 9 (1977): 123–34.

69. Ledoux to de Lacoré, 24 August 1775.

70. The section preserved in the Fonds Pierre-Adrien Pâris, Etudes d'architecture, vol. 5, pl. 304, is perhaps of this first project, showing the auditorium without the upper row of columns separating the parterre from the final two rows of the theater. The elevation of the first project and what seems to be a plan, in pencil and partially sketched, are in the Archives Municipales de Besançon, Yc B2, pieces 20 and 21, respectively.

71. Ledoux to de Lacoré, 24 August 1775.

72. Fonds Pierre-Adrien Pâris, Architecture, vol. 5, 299–303, 305, and Archives Municipales de Besançon, Yc B2, pieces 21 and 22.

73. See the sociological analysis of this layout by Rittaud-Hutinet, La vision d'un futur, 60ff.

74. Ledoux, L'architecture, pl. 114–22, and description, 218–34.

75. "Observations relatives aux ancienne et nouvelle salles" (1784), Archives Municipales de Besançon, DD 35.

76. Ibid. During the first weeks of the Revolution, the director of the then nearly deserted theater petitioned the architect Claude-Joseph-Alexandre Bertrand to reestablish the parterre in the traditional position as a way of opening the performances to a more popular audience; see Rittaud-Hutinet, La vision d'un futur, 141–42.

77. Ledoux to de Lacoré, 24 August 1775.

78. Ibid.

79. Jean-Jacques Rousseau, Lettre à M. d'Alembert sur son article "Genève" (Lettre sur les spectacles) (Paris, 1758), and idem, Julie, ou la Nouvelle Héloïse (Paris, 1761).

80. Charles De Wailly developed a geometrical formula, based on two intersecting circles, to join the auditorium to the stage in a "natural" bond; see Monique Mosser and Daniel Rabreau, "Nature et architecture parlante: Soufflot, De Wailly et Ledoux touches par les lumières," in Soufflot et l'architecture des lumières, 222–39, where they compare Ledoux's semicircle to that of De Wailly, published in the Supplément to the Encyclopédie (Paris, 1777), article "Theatre," and pl. 1–9.

81. For this reason, Ledoux has often been compared to Richard Wagner, anticipating by nearly a century the latter's attempts to relate audience to performance through a "mystic gap." See Helen Leclerc, "Au théâtre de Besançon (1775–1784): Claude-Nicolas Ledoux, réformateur et précurseur de Richard Wagner," Revue d'histoire du théâtre 10 (1958): 103–27. The claim is repeated by Rittaud-Hutinet, La vision d'un futur, 89–93. A more illuminating inquiry would be to relate Ledoux's illusionism with the shift in ideas of dramatic representation in the latter half of the eighteenth century, as noted by Marian Hobson, The Object of Art.

82. Journal politique de Bruxelles, supplément du Mercure, 36 (4 September 1784): 36–37; quoted in Rittaud-Hutinet, La vision d'un futur, 137.

83. See the description in Ganay, "La salle de spectacle."

84. Boullée, Architecture, 121.

85. Claude-Nicolas Ledoux, "Dernière réponse à M. Poyet," Journal

de Paris 97 (7 April 1783): 403.

86. See Belavel, L'esthétique sans paradoxe, chap. 3.

87. See the excellent article by Peter Szondi, "Tableau et coup de théâtre: Pour une sociologie de le tragédie domestique et bourgeoise chez Diderot et Lessing," Poétique 9 (1972): 1–14. For an analysis of Le neveu de Rameau, see Herbert Josephs, Diderot's Dialogue of Language and Gesture (Columbus, Ohio, 1969); for the theatrical implications of this highly gestural technique, reaching toward the melodrama, see Peter Brooks, The Melodramatic Imagination: Balzac, Henry James and the Mode of Excess (New Haven, 1976).

88. Archives Nationales, 0¹ 846, 8; quoted in Fuchs, La vie théâtrale, 74.

89. Guillaume Dard de Bosco to the municipality of Besançon, 9 July 1784, Archives Municipales de Besançon, DD 35.

90. Guillaume Dard de Bosco, "Observations sur le service du théâtre," February 1785, Archives Municipales de Besançon, DD 35 (123).

91. Report of L. Breton, professor of the Académie de Sculpture et Peinture of Besançon, and D. Lapret, professor of the Académie d'Architecture, 20 December 1784, Archives Municipales de Besançon, DD 35, 86 (1).

92. Ganay, "La salle de spectacle," 17, quoting from the account of the lawyer, Grimont, whose manuscript journal is conserved in the Bibliothèque de Besançon.

93. Ibid., quoting from the journal of the Hôtel de Ville, 14 July 1784.

94. Ibid.

95. Daniel Rabreau, "Des scènes figurées à la mise en scène du monument urbain," in Piranèse et les français: Colloque, studies architecture in the scenography of the late eighteenth century, noting the peculiar "reflection" of the auditorium in Ledoux's backdrop for Besançon.

96. Kurt W. Forster, "Schinkel's Panoramic Planning of Central Berlin," Modulus 16 (1983): 65.

97. Carmontelle [Louis Carrogis], Jardin de Monceau, près de Paris, appartenant à . . . monseigneur le duc de Chartres (Paris, 1779).

98. Le Camus de Mézières, Le génie de l'architecture. The family of Le Camus were noted for their interest in the theater.

99. See Louis-Sébastien Mercier, Du théâtre, ou nouvel essai sur l'art dramatique (Amsterdam, 1773).

100. Nicolas-Edme Rétif de la Bretonne, Le mimographe, ou idées d'une honnête femme pour la réformation du théâtre national (Amsterdam, 1770).

101. Le Camus de Mézières, Le génie de l'architecture, 7.

102. Charles De Wailly, "Vue perspective de la place de l'Odéon, des gradins et du velum," and "Plan d'amenagement de la place du Théâtre français, transformée en aire de rassemblement public, avec gradins et tribune d'orateur," project of 1794, Paris, Bibliothèque de la Comédie-Française. See Steinhauser and Rabreau, "Le théâtre de l'Odéon," 21.

103. For Soufflot's theater at Lyons, see Charre et al., L'oeuvre de Soufflot à Lyon; for the theater at Bordeaux designed by Victor Louis between 1767 and 1771, see Daniel Rabreau, "Le grand théâtre de Victor Louis: Des vérités, des impressions," in Victor Louis et le théâtre: Scénographie, mise-en-scène et architecture théâtrale aux XVIIIᵉ et XIXᵉ siècles (Paris, 1982).

104. The commission was occasioned by the destruction of Moreau-Desproux's Opéra at the Palais-Royal, which burned down in 1781. Boullée, Architecture, 97–107, described his project, designed for the Place du Carroussel between the Louvre and the Tuileries, isolated to prevent a recurrence of fire. Not only did it contain a semicircular salle, but the entire theater itself was conceived within a circle drawn from the same center, and domed like the Pantheon. In this sense, Boullée's scheme was the most "theoretical" and uncompromising of all the proposals based on circular geometries. See Pérouse de Montclos, Boullée.

105. "Projet d'une nouvelle salle d'Opéra proposée par le sieur Poyet, architecte," Journal de Paris 80 (21 March 1783). This correspondance is reprinted in full by Rittaud-Hutinet, La vision d'un futur, 146–52.

106. [C.-A. de Lacoré], letter to Journal de Paris 81 (22 March 1783): 345.

107. Bernard Poyet, letter to Journal de Paris 88 (29 March 1783): 367.

108. Ledoux, "Dernière réponse à M. Poyet," 403.

109. Bernard Poyet, "Dernière réponse de M. Poyet à M. Ledoux," Journal de Paris 105 (15 April 1783): 440.

110. The rancor continued to grow however. Seemingly Poyet became well known for such "plagiarism," for an intimate of Ledoux, or very probably Ledoux himself, published a pamphlet in December 1788, attacking Poyet on all fronts for having built his practice on architectural thievery. See [Ledoux?], Un bon-homme aux Etats-

Généraux, sur quelques objets relatifs aux arts; sur M. Poyet et les pla-giaires, etc., etc., etc. ("Londres," December 1788).

111. For a full account of the building of the theater in Marseilles, see Max Fuchs, "Le théâtre de Marseille au XVIIIe siècle," *Mémoires de l'Institut historique de Provence* 3 (1926): 180–202; also Rittaud-Hutinet, *La vision d'un futur,* 111ff.

112. Ledoux, Memorandum on the Theater of Marseilles, Archives Nationales, H. 1359. This is the justificatory account of his design, submitted following the decision of the Compagnie de l'Arsenal of Marseilles, 2 February 1785.

113. Memorandum of the Maréchal de Beauvau, Intendant de Prov-ence, Archives Départmentales de Marseille, Fonds de l'Intendance de Provence, C 3811; published in full in Rittaud-Hutinet, *La vision d'un futur,* 144–46.

114. Ledoux, Memorandum on the Theater of Marseilles.

115. Ledoux, Rendering of the Theater of Marseilles, water color, Germany, collection L. H. Houthakker; reproduced in Gallet, *Le-doux,* 133.

116. Ledoux, Memorandum on the Theater of Marseilles.

117. Ibid.

118. Memorandum of the Maréchal de Beauvau; cited in Rittaud-Hutinet, *La vision d'un futur,* 145.

119. See the excellent and evocative study by Serge Conard, "Aux sources de l'architecture parlante, l'archéologie mystique de C.-N. Ledoux," in *Colloque Piranesi e la cultura antiquaria* (Rome, 1979), 231–46.

120. Charles-Louis Clérisseau, *Les monuments de Nîmes,* with *Texte historique et descriptif* by Jacques-Guillaume Legrand (Paris, 1778–1804). Ledoux mentioned Calonne's support of the excavations of the amphitheater at Nîmes in his *éloge, Architecture,* 177. Conard, "Aux sources de l'architecture parlante," draws a convincing picture of an antiquarian revival in the south of France in the last years of the century.

121. The fundamental study of Ledoux's work at Aix-en-Provence is Jean-Jacques Gloton and Serge Conard, "Aix-en-Provence dans l'oeuvre de Claude-Nicolas Ledoux," in *Monuments et mémoires pub-liés par l'Académie des inscriptions et belles-lettres* (Vendôme, 1983), 55–150, which outlines the stages of the building campaigns, deduces a chronology for Ledoux's designs, and provides a catalogue of the

drawings for the Palais de Justice and prisons in the collection of the Bibliothèque Méjanes.

122. The clearest description of the old Palais de Justice is in J.-P. Coste, *Aix en 1765: Structure urbaine et société* (Aix-en-Provence, 1970), 195ff., 230ff. The structures and functions of the Parlement are analyzed in Sharon Kettering, *Judicial Politics and Urban Revolt in Seventeenth-Century France: The Parlement of Aix, 1629–1659* (Prince-ton, 1978), and Louis Wolff, *Le parlement de Provence au XVIIIe siècle* (Aix-en-Provence, 1920). See also Prosper Cabasse, *Essais historiques sur le Parlement de Provence,* 3 vols. (Paris, 1826). Marcel Bernos et al., eds., *Histoire d'Aix-en-Provence* (Aix-en-Provence, 1977), is a useful introduction and has a good bibliography.

123. See Michel Clerc, *Aquae Sextiae: Histoire d'Aix-en-Provence dans l'antiquité* (Paris, 1910), chap. 5, 379ff., for a discussion of these tow-ers and their presumed functions; also Albert Grenier, *Manuel d'ar-chéologie gallo-romaine, pt. 3, L'architecture,* 2 vols. (Paris, 1958), 1:115–27, which gives a plan and description of the Roman town.

124. Bernos et al., *Histoire d'Aix-en-Provence,* 163.

125. See Kettering, *Judicial Politics,* 22–23.

126. See the excellent study of parliamentarians in Aix by Monique Cubells, *La Provence des Lumières: Les parlementaires d'Aix au 18ème siècle* (Paris, 1984).

127. See Bernos et al., *Histoire d'Aix-en-Provence,* 224ff.

128. See Wolff, *Le parlement de Provence au XVIIIe siècle.*

129. Jules-François-Paul de Fauris de Saint-Vincens, *Mémoire pour re-mettre à Monseigneur l'archevêque d'Aix pour presser la reconstruction du palais,* 6 February 1784, Bibliothèque Méjanes, MS 929, piece 18; quoted in Gloton and Conard, "Aix-en-Provence," 60.

130. In a later report, Ledoux noted, "On 15 May 1776, M. de La Tour [Des Gallois de La Tour] Premier Président of Parlement and Intendant of Provence, wishing to inform himself on the state of the constructions of the Palais de Justice of Aix, asked M. de Beaumont [an official in the Intendance du Commerce under Trudaine] for an architect, who noticed me and sent me. Having found the founda-tions in no state to support any useful restorations, I proposed a new building at the entry to the Cours. It is useless to go into details here on the reasons that made me propose a change in the site of the pal-ace. It will suffice to say for my justification that the speculation (in which I nevertheless think I was wrong) had as its sole object the economy and embellishment of the town of Aix." Ledoux, Report of October–November 1784, Archives Nationales H^1 1359, tran-

scribed in full by Serge Conard, in Gloton and Conard, "Aix-en-Provence," 125–26.

131. Ibid.

132. Plan, Bibliothèque Méjanes, 1059, 10.

133. Of Ledoux's two alternative schemes, one was sited behind the Place des Prêcheurs, just outside the old ramparts, and joined to the old palace by a short axial street (Bibliothèque Méjanes 1059, 9); the other, also sited at the end of the Cours, but without an extension of the promenade to the east, separated for the first time the palace and the prisons into different blocks (Bibliothèque Méjanes 1059, 8).

134. Claude-François Achard, *Description historique, géographique et topographique des villes . . . de la Provence ancienne et moderne,* 2 vols (Aix-en-Provence, 1787), 1:185, specified the dress and order of procession for the important entries and fêtes of Aix; the historian and antiquarian Abbé Paul de Grégoire wrote a detailed description of the rites of All Saints' Day, comparing their quasi-carnivalesque ceremonies with those of chivalric jousts in *Explication des cérémonies de la Fête-Dieu d'Aix-en-Provence* (Aix, 1777), dedicated to the Parisian medievalist Jean-Baptiste de La Curne de Sainte-Palaye. The ceremonies moved constantly between the Cathedral of Saint Sauveur and the Palais de Parlement; the carnival, or *bazoche,* proper took place in the courtyards and *grande salle* of the Parlement.

135. Michel Vovelle, "Apogée ou declin d'une capitale provinciale; le XVIIIe siècle," in Bernos et al., *Histoire d'Aix-en-Provence,* 181–228, recounts these rumors (p. 220). Certainly any demolition in the quarter of the Place des Prêcheurs was bound to enrich the local property owners, including the rich entrepreneur Joseph Saveur Mignard, with whom Ledoux had formed a financial association and who was already a close friend in 1784.

136. Calonne increased the royal subvention from Necker's one-third to two-thirds of the cost of construction late in 1784; a last-minute attempt by the Archbishop of Aix, Jean de Boisgelin, to exclude Ledoux in favor of his own architect Jean-Arnaud Raymond was blocked by Calonne, who confirmed Ledoux as his choice in a letter to des Gallois de La Tour, 23 December 1784. De Boisgelin then tried the tactic of asking the Académie d'Architecture in Paris to review the plans; in June 1785, a group of Ledoux's fellow academicians wrote in his support to de la Tour (including Chalgrin, Gondouin, and Jardin), and in August the committee appointed by the Académie also ruled in his favor. See Lemonnier, *Procès-verbaux de l'Académie,* 9:163, and Gloton and Conard, "Aix-en-Provence," 127 for a publication of the letter to de la Tour.

137. The historical culture of the *parlementaires* is discussed in Cubells, *La Provence des lumières,* and by Michel Vovelle, in Bernos et al., *Histoire d'Aix-en-Provence,* 115, where he addresses the use by the Abbé Grégoire of "history as a means of the struggle against privileges." Fauris de Saint-Vincens's *Mémoire sur la tour du Mausolée autrefois incorporée dans le Palais démoli en 1786,* conserved in the Bibliothèque Méjanes, MS 1010, 86–102, was communicated to the Académie des Inscriptions by the Abbé Barthélemy, 12 September 1786. Esprit Gibelin, "history painter," described the demolition-excavation in detail, in *Lettre sur les tours antiques qu'on a démolies à Aix-en-Provence et sur les antiquités qu'elles renfermoient* (Aix-en-Provence 1787), dedicated to the art collector and local antiquarian J.-B. Boyer de Fonscolombe.

138. Fauris de Saint-Vincent, *Mémoire;* quoted in Clerc, *Aquae Sextiae,* 400.

139. Gibelin, *Lettre,* 1.

140. Bouche, *Essai sur l'histoire,* 1:132: "The Greeks had a way of conserving fine buildings that one could have made use of on this occasion, it seems to me. . . . They numbered each piece and thereby transported the whole in parts to the site they had set aside for the monument they wished to conserve."

141. Charles-François Bouche, "Discours sur l'état actuel de la Provence," Introduction to Achard, *Description historique,* 1:41–45.

142. Ledoux to Joseph Saveur Mignard, 14 November 1786; published in Léon de Berluc-Pérussis, "L'architecte Ledoux et le sculpteur Chardigny à Aix: Documents inédits (1776–1803)," *Réunion des Sociétés des Beaux-Arts des départements* 26–27 (1902): 189–225. Berluc-Pérussis was the first to publish Ledoux's correspondence on Aix, republished in Gallet, *Ledoux,* 274ff.

143. "Plan de l'ancien palais," Bibliothèque Méjanes, 1059, 11; analyzed in Coste, *Aix en 1695,* 195ff.

144. Ledoux, Memorandum on the Theater of Marseilles, and Rittaud-Hutinet, *La vision d'un futur,* 143.

145. See Conard, "Aux sources de l'architecture parlante."

146. Sangallo's journey through the south of France in 1496 was recorded in a sketchbook, now in the Vatican Library, Codex Vat. Barb. Lat. 4424, with the "restoration" of the palace of Aix on fascicule IV, f. 40 verso; see J. de Laurière and E. Müntz, "G. da Sangallo et les monuments antiques du midi de la France au XVe siècle," *Mémoires de la Société nationale des antiquaires de France* 45 (1884): 207ff., and Clerc, *Aquae Sextiae,* 430–31.

147. "Les tours de palais d'Aix," in *Antiquités de la ville d'Aix . . . dédiées à Messire Louis Henry de Gaillard* (Aix, 1760), a collection of seventeen engravings; noted by Conrad, "Aux sources de l'architecture parlante."

148. "Temple du soleil," in *Antiquités de la ville d'Aix*.

149. Daniel Ramée, ed., *L'architecture de C. N. Ledoux*, pls. 44–59; the original drawings, conserved in the Bibliothèque Méjanes, 1059, are listed in full in Gloton and Conard, "Aix-en-Provence."

150. Blondel, *Cours d'architecture*, 2:626–27. See Anthony Vidler, "The Design of Punishment: Concepts of the Prison before the Revolution," chap. 5 of *The Writing of the Walls*, for a summary of the reform movement before the Revolution in France.

151. See in particular the extraordinary tour de force by Jean-Charles Delafosse, "Project for a Prison," watercolor drawing in the Cooper-Hewitt Museum, New York.

152. See Vidler, "The Design of Punishment," in *The Writing of the Walls*. For Tenon, see Bibliothèque nationale, Nouv. Acquis. 22137, Papiers de Tenon, 284–387. For Boullée at the Hôtel de la Force, see Pérouse de Montclos, *Boullée*, 136–40.

153. Jacques-Pierre Brissot de Warville, *Théorie des lois criminelles*, 2 vols. (Paris, 1781).

154. See Jeremy Bentham, *A View of the Hard Labour Bill* (London, 1778), in *Works*, ed. John Bowring (London, 1843), 4:5ff.

155. Brissot de Warville, *Théorie des lois criminelles*, 1:183–85.

156. Ibid., 184.

157. Michel Foucault, *Histoire de la folie à l'âge classique*, rev. ed. (Paris, 1972), 448–49: "In this marvelous economy, labor acquires a double efficacy: it produces by destroying—the necessary work of society being born from the very death of the worker who is undesirable for it. The disturbing and dangerous life of man disappears in the docility of the object. All the irregularities of insane lives are finally equalized in this polished surface of marble."

158. Brissot de Warville, *Théorie des lois criminelles*, 1:185.

159. Ledoux to Charles-Jean-Baptiste des Gallois de La Tour, 25 July 1785, Archives des Bouches-du-Rhône, C. 4084–10; transcribed in Gallet, *Ledoux*, 273.

160. The *Physiognomische Fragmente* of Johann Caspar Lavater (1775) were translated into French as *Essai sur la physionomie destiné à faire connoistre l'homme et à le faire aimer*, 4 vols. (Paris and The Hague,

1781–1803). For a concise outline of Lavater's theories and their influence in Europe, see Graeme Tytler, *Physiognomy in the European Novel* (Princeton, 1982), pt. 1. The physiognomical tradition in painting, from Charles Le Brun to Jean-Baptiste Greuze, is treated in Norman Bryson, *Word and Image* (Cambridge, 1981).

161. Jacques Pernetti, *Lettres philosophiques sur les physionomies* (Paris, 1746).

162. Le Camus de Mézières, *Le génie de l'architecture*, 3–4.

163. Ibid., 4.

164. Pierre-Claude-Jean Tournatoris (born in Aix in 1730; died after 1794) practiced as a doctor from 1753. His interest in anatomical studies and talent for dissection were noted with displeasure in Aix. His landlord prosecuted him for the odors that came from his room, where, as Ledoux later confirmed, "were found two or three human heads," in the words of the legal account of the *procès* of 1758. He amassed a private collection of bones and pathological curiosities that was celebrated in the region. He helped to fight a series of epidemics in Provence after 1772, and in 1776 was accorded the stipend of the Chair of Anatomy at the Faculty of Medecine of Aix; he became Professor in 1783. His reputation, reinforced by his continual difficulties in obtaining cadavers for his work, was consistently attacked; in 1787 the city architect, Vallon, even condemned his house as dangerous to the public. See Félix Chavernac, *Le docteur Tournatoris, sa vie et ses manuscrits* (Marseilles, 1871).

165. Elevation of the prison at Aix, Bibliothèque Méjanes, 1059, 21.

166. The best discussion of the building of the *barrières*, and the intricate political and fiscal battles between 1784 and 1791, is still E. Frémy, "L'enceinte de Paris, construite par les fermiers-généraux et la perception des droits d'octroi de la ville (1784–1791)," *Bulletin de l'histoire de Paris et de l'Ile de France* 39 (1912): 115–48. Where not otherwise noted, my account is drawn largely from this source.

167. See Roger Dion, *Histoire de la vigne et du vin en France des origines au XIXe siècle* (Paris, 1959), especially 505–31.

168. Frémy, "L'enceinte de Paris," 117–18.

169. "Comte rendu," 7 May 1784; quoted Frémy, "L'enceinte de Paris," 118.

170. François-Nicolas, comte de Mollien, *Mémoires d'un ministre du trésor public, 1780–1815* (Paris, 1845) 1:95.

171. Jacques-Antoine Dulaure, *Réclamation d'un citoyen contre la nouvelle enceinte de Paris élevée par les fermiers généraux* (Paris, 1787).

172. Lucien Lambeau, *Vaugirard,* vol. 1 of *Histoire des communes annexées à Paris en 1859,* 5 vols. (Paris, 1910–23), 287.

173. Fortier, "Introduction. Histoire et planification urbaine: Les années 1800," 14.

174. See the full listing and iconography for the *barrières* in Gallet, *Ledoux,* 155–61.

175. Report of 21 October 1784, Bibliothèque Nationale, fr 6685, 18; quoted in Frémy, "L'enceinte de Paris," 119.

176. Frémy, "L'enceinte de Paris," 120.

177. L.-P. de Bachaumont, et al., *Mémoires secrets pour servir à l'histoire de la République des lettres en France de 1762 jusqu'à nos jours* (London, 1777–89), 16 November 1787.

178. Ibid. Another favorite pun played on the names of the three major officials involved in the Bureau des Finances: "Thus they continue the *Colonnades,* the *Calonnades,* or *Coloniades*" (ibid., 6 November 1787).

179. Report of 24 January 1787, Archives Nationales, X¹ᵇ 8984; quoted in Frémy, "L'enceinte de Paris," 121.

180. Dulaure, *Réclamation d'un citoyen,* 6.

181. Ibid., 16.

182. Quoted in Frémy, "L'enceinte de Paris," 128, and transcribed in Gallet, *Ledoux,* 277–78.

183. See Victor le Clercq, "L'incendie des barrières de Paris en juillet 1789 et les procès des incendiaries," *Bulletin de la Société de l'histoire de Paris et de l'Ile de France* 65 (1938):31–48.

184. Laugier, *Essai sur l'architecture,* 214.

185. Ibid., 219.

186. The most complete record, and that in the spirit of Ledoux's designs, was provided by a young architect-engraver who worked in Ledoux's office in the 1790s, Gaitte, whose *Recueil des plus belles maisons et des plus belles édifices de Paris* (Paris, c. 1792) included nine plates of the *barrières* in perspective vignettes.

187. Report of 6 August 1786, Archives Nationales, T 705 Colonia; see also Report of 3 August 1785.

188. Report of 6 August 1786.

189. Ibid.

190. Report of 10 November 1785, Archives Nationales, T 705 Colonia.

191. Ibid.

192. Report of 3 August 1785.

193. Report of 10 November 1785.

194. For an interesting discussion of the political uses of historical subjects and styles in the late eighteenth century, see Crow, *Painters and Public Life,* especially 211ff. for David and his patrons.

195. "Village de Maupertuis, vue perspective," Archives Nationales, N II Seine-et-Marne, 35; first published in Rivière, *Un village de Brie.*

196. Here, Ledoux seems to anticipate, at full scale, the museum of architectural models assembled in the 1790s by Louis-François Cassas as examplary types selected from the (mainly classical) history of architecture. See Dominique Poulot, "Modelli d'architettura," *Lotus International* 35 (1982): 32–35.

197. See Dion, *Histoire de la vigne.*

198. Luc-Vincent Thiéry, *Almanach du voyageur à Paris* (Paris, 1784). For a good analysis of the social life in the *guinguettes* in eighteenth-century Paris, see Thomas Brennan, "Beyond the Barriers: Popular Culture and Parisian *Guinguettes,*" *Eighteenth-Century Studies* 18, no. 2 (Winter 1984–85): 153–69. Brennan compares the *guinguettes,* relatively new in formation, to the old taverns and cabarets in the center of the city, tracing the shift in leisure habits toward the increasing use of the outskirts and country on holidays and Sundays by a mass public of artisans and laborers. The rural site of the *guinguette* provided amenities unobtainable in the city: gardens, bowling greens, dance halls, gambling rooms, restaurants.

199. Edme Verniquet (1727–1804) began the mapping of Paris in 1774 and completed the seventy-two plates of the great atlas between 1789 and 1791, *Plan de la ville de Paris avec sa nouvelle enceinte levé géométriquement sur la méridienne de l'observatoire.* Callone gave him official encouragement in 1783 and again in 1785 on the submission of his *Mémoire sur l'utilité des Plans de la Ville de Paris,* November 1785.

200. Mosser and Rabreau, *Charles De Wailly,* 71.

201. Ibid., 72.

202. Dulaure, *Réclamation d'un citoyen,* 25.

203. Ibid., 27.

204. Louis-Sebastien Mercier, *Tableau de Paris,* 12 vols. (Amsterdam, 1782–88), 9:214–17.

205. See especially, Quatremère de Quincy, *Encyclopédie méthodique: Architecture,* "Abus," 1:3–4, "Barrière," 1:214–16; "Bizarrerie," 1:282–86; "Bossage," 1:304–311.

206. Quatremère de Quincy, "Barrière," 1:214.

207. For this and the following quotations from Quatremère, see ibid., 216.

208. The most incisive treatment of Quatremère's aesthetics is the brief essay by Jean-Claude Lebensztejn, "De l'imitation dans les beaux-arts," *Critique* (January 1982): 3–21.

209. Hugo, "Guerre aux démolisseurs!" 187.

210. Jacques-Guillaume Legrand, *Annales de Musée* (1804), 6:79. The *barrières* continued to provoke comment and scorn throughout the nineteenth century. The anonymous author in the *Magasin pittoresque* 18 (1848): 196ff., writing on "Les barrières de Ledoux," was scornful of these "caprices of a disordered imagination" and repeated all the commonplaces of late-eighteenth-century criticism. No doubt the writer was Léon Vaudoyer, who in a later article characterized the *barrières* as recognizing neither "principles nor rules" (*Magasin pittoresque* 20 [1852]: 388ff.).

211. Alain-Charles Gruber, *Les grandes fêtes et leurs décors à l'époque de Louis XVI* (Geneva, 1972), 1.

212. Illustrated in Marie-Louise Biver, *Fêtes révolutionnaires à Paris* (Paris, 1979), pl. 57.

213. See the useful catalogue, *Les fêtes de la Révolution* Musée Bargoin, Clermont-Ferrand, 1974), 33, "Fête de la Liberté, 9 et 10 thermidor an IV." Also see Monique Mosser and Daniel Rabreau, "Il circo, l'amfiteatro, il colosseo: La Parigi della Rivoluzione come nuova Roma," *Lotus International* 39 (1983): 108–18.

214. The fundamental work on the Revolutionary festivals is Mona Ozouf, *Le fête révolutionnaire, 1789–1799* (Paris, 1976).

---

5   UTOPIA IN THE COUNTRYSIDE

1. Franche-Comté was definitively brought under French rule in 1674. For the early history of the region, see L. Febvre, *Philippe II et Franche-Comté* (Paris, 1912). For Franche-Comté in the eighteenth century, see the contemporary survey by Abbé Jean-Joseph d'Expilly, *Dictionnaire géographique, historique et politique des Gaules et de la France* (Paris, 1762), 1:307, "Besançon" and 3:508, "Franche-Comté"; also, F.-I. Dunod de Charnage, *Histoire . . . du Comté de Bourgogne* (Dijon, 1737), vol. 2. The industry of the region is treated

in Jean-Marie Suchet, "L'industrie en Franche-Comté avant et après la conquête," in *Bulletin de l'Académie de Besançon* (1876–77), 62; and A. Lieffroy, "L'industrie métallurgique en Franche-Comté," in ibid (1892), 220. Mazoyer, "Exploitation forestière," notes the existence in 1771 of five glassworks, forty-four furnaces, thirty-six forges, eighteen foundries, eleven martinets, as well as innumerable cheese, brick, and saltpeter factories.

2. "Mémoire de Jean Querret, ingénieur en chef des Ponts et Chaussées pour le Roy au Comté de Bourgogne" (1760); quoted in the detailed study by Léon Four, *Le long des routes.* Appointed 17 May 1744, Querret employed a corps of young engineers from the Ponts et Chaussées, including his nephew, Querret du Bois, and the architect-engineer Philippe Bertrand (who eventually succeeded him) to map and develop the province's roads and canals.

3. Querret, "Mémoire"; quoted in Four, *Le long des routes,* 69.

4. Four, *Le long des routes,* 101.

5. Claude-Joseph Vernet (1714–89), *La construction d'un grand chemin.* Exhibited in the salon of 1775, this work depicts (according to L. de Bachaumont) the engineer Perronet visiting the site of a new road in Franche-Comté. In the context of the commission for the Saline de Chaux, it is significant that this picture was commissioned by the Abbé Terray, together with its pendant, *Les abords d'une foire,* during the period of Terray's joint administration of finances and royal buildings (1773–74). See L. Lagrange, *Les Vernet: Joseph Vernet et la peinture au XVIIIe siècle* (Paris, 1864), and F. Ingersoll-Smousse, *Joseph Vernet peintre de marine, 1714–1789,* 2 vols., (Paris, 1926). The landscape details were utilized in different combinations by Ledoux in his "fictitious" portrayal of Franche-Comté as the site of an ideal city. A close comparison of Vernet's landscapes and Ledoux's engravings reveals that both artists utilized a combination of idealized scenes, real fragments, and historical evocations to produce an image of a reformed reality.

6. Philippe Bertrand (1730–1811), an engineer of the Ponts et Chaussées, was appointed engineer of Franche-Comté in 1771, where he built major bridges and roads, constructed the canal from the Doubs to the Saône, and studied the joining of the Rhône and the Rhine. He is sometimes confused with his brother, Claude-Joseph-Alexandre Bertrand (1734–97), "architecte et ingénieur en chef des ponts et chaussées pour la Comte," collaborator with Ledoux at the Theater of Besançon. See Pierre Pinon et al., *Un canal, des canaux* (Paris, 1986), 343.

7. Quoted in Four, *Le long des routes,* 107. Bertrand's project was published in his mémoire, *Projet d'un canal de navigation pour joindre le*

Doubs à La Saône dressé par ordre du Conseil et de M. de Lacoré, intendant de Franche-Comté (Besançon, 1777).

8. See Ronald Meek, *Turgot On Progress, Sociology and Economics* (London, 1973), Introduction, and especially, Weulersse, *La physiocratie*.

9. Pierre-Samuel Dupont de Nemours, *Physiocratie, ou constitution naturelle du gouvernement le plus avantageux au genre humain*, 2 vols. (Leyden and Paris, 1767–68).

10. Ibid., 19.

11. Quoted in Four, *Le long des routes*, 11.

12. François du Quesnay (1694–1774), "Fermier," *Encyclopédie*, 6:527–40; quoted in Eugène Daire, *Economistes français* (Paris, 1843), 246.

13. François du Quesnay, "Hommes," *Encyclopédie*, 7:278–81; quoted in Ronald Meek, *The Economics of Physiocracy* (London, 1962), 100–101.

14. Meek, *Turgot*, and Jacques Turgot, *Oeuvres*, ed. G. Schelle, 5 vols. (Paris, 1913–23), 1:214–35. Turgot's *Discours sur les progrès successifs de l'esprit humain*, presented on 11 December 1750 at the Sorbonne, was the second of two discourses delivered there; the first, on 3 July, addressed the advantages of Christianity.

15. Jacques Turgot, *Réflexions sur la formation et la distribution des richesses* (Paris, 1766, 1788); see Meek, *Turgot*.

16. See the still good review of Turgot's career, Douglas Dakin, *Turgot and the Ancien Régime in France* (London, 1939), and, for a more detailed study of the failure of the financial measures of 1774–76, Faure, *La disgrâce de Turgot*.

17. Ledoux, *L'architecture*, 234: "This house [pl. 123] was among those approved in 1773." In the Introduction Ledoux stated, "I presented the projects of the town together with the extensions that were suitable for it" (40). Later he noted, perhaps hopefully, "The government, wishing to give models to the less fortunate classes, had built many houses, which brought together all the conveniences of utility and solidity" (78).

18. See Ira O. Wade, "The Search for a New Voltaire," *Transactions of the American Philosophical Society*, new ser., 48 (1958): 94–105.

19. Report by Duplieux to Trudaine de Montigny, "Sur l'état de la construction"; notes communicated to the author by Ira O. Wade.

20. See Sylvia Pressouyre, "Un ensemble néoclassique à Port-Vendres," *Monuments historiques de la France*, new ser., 19, no. 4

(1963): 199–222, and Mosser and Rabreau, *Charles De Wailly*, 72–73. De Wailly's projects were engraved and published in Alexandre de Laborde et al., *Voyage pittoresque de la France avec la description de toutes les provinces*, vol. 5 (Paris, 1787), 17–19.

21. B. N. Cartes et Plans, Ge C 9779. The first to attempt to date these projects on the basis of a close examination of the engravings was Wolfgang Herrmann in "The Problem of Chronology." Although he dismisses the map in the Bibliothèque Nationale as too small in scale to have served for Ledoux's later engravings, it nevertheless traces the same geographical elements to the same detail and indicates that Ledoux, if not the administrators of the *saline*, had reserved the land for expansion early on. Little can be gained from a study of the different engravers, or, as Herrmann has shown, from the dates on the engravings themselves. Both Herrmann and Langner, "Ledoux' Redaktion," have tried to reconstruct the stages of each engraving and its reworking over time as Ledoux "improved" or idealized his designs. Gallet has summarized the available documentation (*Ledoux*, 222–23).

22. Helen Rosenau, "Boullée and Ledoux as Town-Planners: A Reassessment," *Gazette des Beaux-Arts*, ser. 6, 63 (March 1964): 173–90.

23. Bruno Fortier and Bruno Vayssière, "L'architecture des villes: Espaces, cartes et territoires," *Urbi* 3 (March 1980).

24. See Jacques Delille, *Les jardins ou l'art d'embellir les paysages* (1782; new ed., Paris, 1804). Ledoux's "landscapes" of Franche-Comté are assembled out of his own recollections, fragments from paintings by artists like Vernet and Robert, and set pieces from classical landscape painters like Poussin, Rosa and Lorrain. Each engraving, while not strictly inaccurate, heightens the dramatic effect of contrasts between mountains, waterfalls, grottoes, plains, and peaceful rivers by abrupt juxtaposition. Thus in Bovinet's perspective of the Bridge over the Loüe River, the medieval fortress that overlooks Salins together with its crags and cliffs are transported to the banks of the Loüe, in fact a flat flood plain.

25. Meek, *The Economics of Physiocracy*, 375.

26. Geometry for Ledoux was both instrumental and symbolic, the latter because of the former—this was the attitude of an architect trained in the milieu of the Ponts et Chaussées; geometry for Boullée was natural, therefore symbolically meaningful—this was the position of an architect-painter clinging to the last vestiges of imitation theory.

27. For an account of the canal and road network from a technological viewpoint, see A. Wolf, *A History of Science, Technology and Phi-*

losophy in the Eighteenth Century, 2 vols. (New York, 1961), 2:553ff., and Pinon et al., Un canal, des canaux.

28. See Michael Petzet, "Soufflot et l'ordonnance de Sainte-Geneviève," in Soufflot et l'architecture des lumières, 13–25, and Richard Etlin, "Grandeur et décadence d'un modèle: L'église Sainte-Geneviève et les changements de valeur esthétique au XVIIIe siècle," ibid., 27–37.

29. Boullée, Architecture, 84.

30. See Pérouse de Montclos, Boullée, 155–61.

31. See the excellent study of cemeteries by Richard Etlin, The Architecture of Death: The Transformation of the Cemetery in Eighteenth-Century Paris (Cambridge, Mass., 1984), and [Villedieu], Projet de catacombes pour le ville de Paris, en adaptant à cet usage les carrières qui se trouvent tant dans sons enceinte que dans ses environs (London and Paris, 1782); see also Michel-Augustin Thouret, Rapport sur les exhumations du Cimetière et de l'Eglise des Saints-Innocents (Paris, 1789).

32. See, for example, Quatremère de Quincy, "Catacombes," Encyclopédie méthodique: Architecture, 1:546.

33. Quatremère de Quincy, Encyclopédie méthodique: Architecture, 1:680.

34. See, among the numerous works that have taken the late-eighteenth-century fashion for the sphere as their subject, Helen Rosenau, "The Sphere as an Element in the Mongolfier Monuments," Art Bulletin (March 1968); Adolf Max Vogt, Boullée's Newton-Denkmal (Basel and Stuttgart, 1969); Klaus Lankheit, Der Temple der Vernunft: Unveröffentlichte Zeichnungen von Boullée (Basel and Stuttgart, 1968); Barbara Maria Stafford, "Science as Fine Art: Another Look at Boullée's 'Cenotaph for Newton,'" Studies in Eighteenth-Century Culture 11 (Madison, 1982).

35. For a discussion of Boullée's sources for the Cenotaph to Newton, see Stafford, "Science as Fine Art," 241–78.

36. See Jean-Marie Pérouse de Montclos, "De nova stella anni 1784," Revue de l'art 58–59 (1983): 75–84.

37. Ibid., 69–137.

38. Ibid., 133.

39. Abbé Nicolas Baudeau, Idées d'un citoyen sur les devoirs et les droits d'un vrai pauvre (Paris, 1765), and Pierre-Samuel Dupont de Nemours, Idées sur les secours à donner aux pauvres malades dans une grande ville (Paris, 1786).

40. See Foucault et al., Les machines à guérir.

41. See Dupont de Nemours, Idées sur les secours.

42. For a brief summary of this debate and a full bibliography, see Vidler, "Confinement and Cure," in The Writing of the Walls.

43. As recorded in 1787 by the continuator of Bachaumont's Mémoires secrets, Pidansat de Mairobert, noting the Duc de Praslin as a subscriber to a new hospital: "He has added the condition that M. Ledoux will not be charged with any of these buildings. One does not know whether through horror of his architecture or from the belief that there should not be too much luxury in hospitals where simplicity should create the character—this is not the case with the buildings of S. Le Doux" (Mémoires secrets, 7 March 1787).

44. See Henry Ronot, "Les établissements thermaux du XVIe au XVIIIe siècle," Monuments historiques de la France no. 1 (1978): 17–20, and idem., "Bourbonne-les-Bains et les établissements thermaux en France au XVIIIe siècle," Bulletin de la Société de l'histoire de l'art français (1960).

45. Lemonnier, Procès-verbaux de l'Académie, 8:153.

46. Daniel Rabreau, "Les thermes, exercice de style," Monuments historiques de la France, no. 1 (1978): 14.

47. Jean-Jacques Gloton, "Aix-en-Provence, deux mille ans de thermalisme," Monuments historiques de la France no. 1 (1978): 54.

48. Ibid., 56–57.

49. Serge Conard, "Notes pour une herméneutique de L'architecture . . . de C.-N. Ledoux," in Soufflot et l'architecture des lumières, 288.

50. Ledoux seems to have been following the program set by the Académie in 1784 for "Une Halle composée des principaux marchés nécessaires à une très grande ville du Royaume." This consisted of "a meat market, a grain market, one for poultry and game, one for fish, and other, smaller ones for vegetables, flowers, and fruits; each of these markets will be separated from the next. They will all be enclosed in a space 720 feet square." The medal went to a project by Le Clothe, who presented a scheme that, except for the semicircular exedrae, was subdivided in the same way as Ledoux's Market. Ledoux similarly enclosed his markets within a square of 720 feet on each side.

51. The Guerre des Farines of 1775, which contributed to the fall of Turgot, was still very present in the mind of the administration. See Jacques Godechot, La prise de la Bastille (Paris, 1965); for a more detailed study, see M. Baulant, "Le prix des Grains à Paris," Annales 3 (1968).

52. Here Ledoux anticipates, or rather provides a model for, Brogniart's Stock Exchange of 1808.

53. Ledoux, *L'architecture*, 240: "When I conceived the project of this building I was far from believing the ills that it would enclose."

54. For the origins of Le Creusot, see the excellent study by Christian Devillers and Bernard Huet, *Le Creusot: Naissance et développement d'une ville industrielle, 1782–1914* (Seyssel, 1981). For Calonne, see Lacour-Gayet, *Calonne*.

55. Louis Daubenton, *Détails de la manufacture royale de Montcenis* (Paris, 1788), 380–86.

56. The most comprehensive survey of this movement for agricultural reform is André J. Bourde, *Agronomie et Agronomes en France au XVIIIe siècle*, 3 vols. (Paris, 1967); also see idem, *The Influence of England on the French Agronomes, 1750–1789* (Cambridge, 1953). It should be emphasized that these two works are almost solely preoccupied with a reading of the texts of agricultural theory and not with the results in practice, or with local and regional studies of social and technical change. For the difference between Physiocratic and agronomic thought see Bourde, *Agronomie*, 2:981–83, 1072.

57. Butet-Dumont, *Recherches historiques sur l'administration des serres* (Paris, 1779): quoted in Bourde, *Influence*, 5.

58. Henri-Louis Duhamel du Monceau, *Eléments d'agriculture* (Paris, 1779).

59. The Trudaines, father and son, studied the physiology of sheep on their farm at Courtagny, publishing the results in the *Mémoires* of the Académie des Sciences (1767–69). On Buffon, see H. Dargentolle, "Buffon et Montbard," *Bulletin de la Société archéologique et biographique du canton de Montbard* (July 1930), and Bourde, *Agronomie*, 1:258ff; on Turgot, see Dakin, *Turgot;* on Malesherbes, see Bourde, *Agronomie*, 3:1574. Malesherbes was a member of the Société Royale d'Agriculture. In 1790, arguing for a reconciliation between Physiocrats and agronomes, he proposed a Bureau de Correspondance for agricultural research, a partnership between "les agriculteurs sédentaires" and urban scientists (*Mémoire sur les moyens d'accélérer les progrès de l'économie rurale en France* [Paris, 1790]).

60. The theme of rural happiness is comprehensively developed in the definitive study by Robert Mauzi, *L'idée du bonheur au XVIIIe* (Paris, 1965); however, this work remains in the domain of literary analysis, not distinguishing clearly among the different political and social genres and interests. The eighteenth-century writings on this theme were for the most part sentimental, concerned with the individual's state of mind in natural surroundings and with landscape aesthetics. Or they were clearly utopian, depicting the site of a regenerated social order, such as the Abbé Morelly's *Naufrage des isles flottantes, ou Basiliade du célèbre Pilpai* (Paris, 1753), and his *Code de la nature, ou Le véritable esprit de ses lois* (Paris, 1755). Where they took into account existing rural institutions, as in the nostalgic narratives of Rétif de la Bretonne, it was to confirm the cooperative ethical "good" village of rural tradition. See, for example, Rétif de la Bretonne's "Les statuts du bourg d'Oudun," a project for the ordered social and economic life of an ideal village, based on a settlement in the department of Yonne, and added as a postscript to his *Paysan perverti* (Paris, 1775); reproduced in the valuable, annotated edition of *La vie de mon père* (Paris, 1970). For the intersection between rural utopia and rural reality, see the excellent essay on Rétif de la Bretonne by Emmanuel Le Roy Ladurie in *Le territoire de l'historien*, vol. 2 (Paris, 1978).

61. See Bourde, *Agronomie*, 2:1051ff, Andrew Young was scornful of the actual effect of these initiatives, as of the numerous agricultural societies that were formed in the last half of the century. Speaking of the Société d'Agriculture de Limoges, supported by Turgot, he noted, "This society acts like other societies—they meet, converse, offer premiums, and publish nonsense. This is not of much consequence, for the people, instead of reading their reports, are not able to read at all" (*Travels during the Years 1787, 1788 and 1789* [Bury St. Edmund's, 1792], 6 June 1787).

62. Bourde, *Agronomie*, 2:981.

63. "The use of reins that restrains the movement while eating . . . is subject to many inconveniences; if the tether is too short it tires and worries the horse, if too long, it presents incalculable dangers; it should allow irregular movements according to the horse's caprice, by means of underground slots" (146). *Le parfait maréchal* (Solleysel, 1706), while referring to the care of horses in general, and written especially for the use of military officers and nobility in war, the hunt, or travel, did not, as Bourde notes, consider the horse as an integral part of agricultural economy (Bourde, *Agronomie*, 1:73).

64. For a detailed discussion of the experiments of Stephen Hales into the ventilation of ships, prisons, and granaries, see Evans, *The Fabrication of Virtue*, 98–103. Hales was in correspondence with the Duc de Noialles regarding the ventilation of the Hôtel-Dieu, and his work was popularized in France by Duhamel du Monceau.

65. The widely distributed and many times reprinted *Praedium Rusticum* (1707–30) of Jacques Vannière took the form of a classical poem based loosely on Virgil's *Georgics*. Ledoux himself recommended this work, which described in detail the ideal site for a rural house, its plan and surroundings, the different tasks of laborer and shepherd,

the care of animals, trees, and crops, as well as outlining calendars for each season's work. The Abbé Rozier (1734–93), more concerned with practical agrarian reform, published his *Cours complet d'agriculture* between 1781 and 1805 in twelve volumes containing articles on every aspect of agricultural practice including building.

66. Contemporary reformers stressed that *bergeries* should be built out of fireproof materials, like ashlar, and well ventilated and drained to prevent illness among the sheep (see Rozier, "Bergerie," in *Cours complet*). The arguments over whether it was better practice to allow the flocks to range free, *sans règle*, in a *parc* overlooked by a shepherd or to enclose them in a more regulated interior *bergerie* were assessed by the Abbé Carlier in *Traité des bêtes à laine ou méthode d'élever et de gouverner les troupeaux*, 2 vols. (Paris, 1770): he concluded in favor of the *parc*. See also Rozier, "Parc," in *Cours complet*, and Antoine-Laurent Lavoisier, "Instruction sur le parcage des bêtes à laine" (1785), in *Oeuvres*, 6 vols (Paris, 1864–93), 6:195–202. The *Nouvelle maison rustique* showed a model *parc* and a shepherd's house on wheels (Bourde, *Agronomie*, 2:812). P.-M. Bondois, "La protection du troupeau français au XVIIIe siècle: L'épizootie de 1763," *Revue d'histoire économique et sociale* (1932), summarizes the medical problems faced by sheep owners in the eighteenth century.

67. Gallet (*Ledoux*, 216) argues that Ledoux prepared this design for the Marquis de Montesquiou, whose estate at Maupertuis included the lands of Meilhan. But the orthography of the title given to Piquenot and Ransonnette's engraving—"Meilliand"—could equally well refer to the rural school projected by the reformer-*agronome* the Duc de Béthune-Charost for his domain in Berry at Meillant; this is reinforced by the spelling of the name in the engraving of Beutrois, "Meilliant." Béthune-Charost (1738–1800) was an agricultural reformer, suppressing feudal rights on his lands in 1769 and introducing merino sheep, artificial meadows, and new ploughs. Imprisoned during the Terror, he established, or projected, a rural school at Meillant in 1794 and published his *Vues generales sur l'organisation de l'instruction rurale* in 1795. He was a member of the Société d'Agriculture of Paris in 1785 and thus of Ledoux's circle from early on. In 1784 he offered a prize to the Académie at Amiens for "a study on ways to improve rural buildings." A. de Calonne noted that "the Duc de Béthune-Charost dreams of organizing a vast system of agricultural instruction with model plantings, rural schools, rural museums, libraries . . ." (*La vie agricole sous l'ancien régime dans le nord de la France* [Paris, 1885]).

68. Compare the slanted profile of this bridge with that built by Ledoux over the Suize at Marac (1765) and with that designed by the engineer Chézy for Trilport (1775); see Fortier, "La nascità dell-

'Ecole," pt. 2, 40. The flattened rusticated arch also gives the aspect of a theatrical scene, as seen through the proscenium of Besançon.

69. Descriptions of the *chaumières*, the squalid thatched cottages of the poor, abounded in sentimental and reformist literature; Arthur Young notes appalling conditions throughout the regions he visited. Inspired by the example of English landowners and architects, from John Wood, Jr., to John Soane, the picturesque cottage was invested with utilitarian functions, an an instrument of rural improvement and aesthetic embellishment. On this movement, see Georges Teyssot, "Cottages et pittoresque: Les origines du logement ouvrier en Angleterre, 1781–1818," *Architecture, Mouvement, Continuité* 34 (1974): 26–37.

70. The investigation of building methods that would avoid the use of thatched and other highly combustible materials was spasmodically undertaken from the 1760s; Bourde, *Agronomie*, 2:947ff., summarizes these initiatives. François Cointeraux (1740–1830) became an indefatigable proponent of his own method, following a prize essay for the Académie d'Amiens in 1784, on the topic, "What is the simplest and least expensive way of preventing and avoiding . . . fires in the countryside?" In 1788 he submitted a report on rural dwellings to the Société Royale d'Agriculture of Paris, which was published as *La ferme* (Paris, 1789). After 1790 both the French and English governments reviewed the construction technique in *pisé*. In *Les erreurs de mon siècle sur l'agriculture et les arts* (Paris, year II [1794]), Cointeraux himself claimed that his long interest in housing the rural poor demonstrated his Revolutionary ideals. The durability of Cointeraux's method was, however, put to the test in the newly built Napoléon-Vendée (1804), where, during the heavy rains of 1811–12, houses constructed in *pisé* dissolved; see Paolo Morachielle and Georges Teyssot, "La colonizzazione del territorio nel primo impero," *Lotus International* 24 (1979): 24–39.

71. This seems to be echoed in the propositions of Jacques-Guillaume Legrand (1753–1807), a supporter of Ledoux, who argued in his *Essai sur l'histoire générale de l'architecture*, published in conjunction with Jean-Nicolas-Louis Durand's *Recueil et parallèle des édifices de tous genre* (Paris, year IX [1801]), that simple dwellings might become architecture by means of their formal combination. The passage is of interest as tracing the transition between forms of need and those of art; his description seems drawn with Ledoux's project for Maupertuis in view.

72. For a history of Maupertuis and the de Montesquiou family, see Rivière, *Mauperthuis*. The new village was demanded by the expansion of the park during the reconstruction after 1761 and by the demolition of some older houses in the village. Each individual house

was designed in detail, as is demonstrated by a drawing in the Musée des Arts Décoratifs, CL 12917, discovered by Werner Szambien and communicated to the author by the kind offices of Bruno Fortier.

73. Rousseau, *Lettre à M. d'Alembert sur les Spectacles*, 80–81.

74. See the useful appendices to Lacroix, *La saline d'Arc-et-Senans*, 66–78. The forest was the home of a large and extremely diverse working population, temporary and permanent: hunters, herdsmen, gleaners, poachers, mingling with and doubling for a host of small *métiers: charbonniers, cendriers, tourneurs, boisseliers, sabotiers, vanniers, cercliers, tonneliers, charpentiers, menuisiers, charronniers, scieurs de bois, marchands de bois*. These craftsmen were found side by side with the workers of the small industries that relied, like the *saline*, on the forest for fuel: *briquettiers, tuiliers, forgerons, potiers, verriers, mégissiers*, etc. For a detailed description of this forest population, see M. Devèze, *La vie de la forêt française au XVIe siècle* (Paris, 1961), and Bourde, *Agronomie*, 1:143ff.

75. For a comparison of Ledoux's rural architecture with the ornamental garden architecture and the fashion for the *fabrique*, see Johannes Langner, "Cl.-N. Ledoux und die Fabrike," *Zeitschrift für Kunstgeschichte* 26 (1963): 1–36.

76. "Les charbonniers dans le bois comme le loup hurle sans cesse," a proverb from the Basse-Auvergne; quoted in Paul Sebillot, *Légendes et curiosités des métiers* (Paris, 1894–95).

77. The plates illustrating "Economie rustique" published in the first volume of illustrations for the *Encyclopédie*, 1762, include several "pyramidal" rural constructions. See, for example, plate 44, "Manière de faire les sabots," which shows a section of the *atelier de sabotiers* that corresponds to the typical form of Ledoux's *ateliers*; and plates 56 and 57, "Charbon de Bois."

78. Emile Souvestre, *Les derniers paysans* (Brussels, 1851), 257; quoted in Devèze, *La vie de la forêt*.

79. Desiré Monnier, *Souvenirs d'un octogénaire de province, 1867–69* (Lons-le-Saunier, 1871), 369.

80. Perrault, *Les dix livres d'architecture de Vitruve*, pl. V.

81. See *Actes du colloque sur la forêt (Besançon 1966)* (Paris, 1967), especially the article by Annie Kriegel, "Les syndicats de bûcherons au XIXe siècle." For other accounts of the life of these rural voluntary guilds, see Monnier, *Souvenirs*, 219, 370, where the author describes the confraternities of the charcoal burners—the Bons Cousins or Charbonniers—as a mutual help society "on behalf of travelers and woodcutters lost in the labyrinths of the forest" (181). Monnier's other books are also useful: *Les jurassiens* (1888), *Moeurs et usages sin-*

guliers du peuple dans le Jura (1823), and *Traditions populaires comparées* (1854), all published in Lons-le-Saunier. E Coornaert, *Les Compagnonnages en France, du moyen âge à nos jours* (Paris, 1966), is a good summary.

82. The Bishop of Nevers in 1673; cited in Kriegel, "Les syndicats de bûcherons."

83. Bourgeois and aristocratic societies, generally linked to the Masonic lodges, delighted in the conceits of rural *émulation*, a fashion advanced by Marie Antoinette in her rustic picnics at Versailles. The Fendeurs were said to have been founded by a Chevalier Beauchaine, a Master of the Grand Lodge in 1747; its members dressed in rustic clothes and adopted the rituals of the forest worker lodges. See *O.: ou Histoire de la Fondation du Grand Orient de France* (Paris, 1812), 361. The context for these societies is developed in Vidler, "The Architecture of the Lodges."

84. Monnier, *Souvenirs*, 219.

85. Drinking, storytelling, and singing often accompanied long nights of domestic labor. In the article "Chanvre" in his *Cours complet*, the Abbé Rozier described the making of hemp: "All the women and children of the village gather in the evening in one or another house, grouped in a circle around the hearth."

86. The pyramidal form of this design responds entirely to the neat pyres illustrated in the *Encyclopédie*.

87. Ledoux's spherical design was probably drawn around 1785. Boullée's Cenotaph to Newton (1784), Ledoux's own Cemetery of Chaux (c. 1785), Nicolas Sobre's "Temple de l'Immortalité," and Antoine Vaudoyer's "Maison d'un cosmopolite" (1785) were only a few examples of the fashion that might be seen to end with the Masonic designs of Jean-Jacques Lequeu, such as the "Temple de la Terre," dedicated to "la sagesse suprême" and exhibited in 1793–94. For a sketch of this geometrical tradition, see Werner Oechslin, "Pyramide et sphère: Notes sur l'architecture révolutionnaire du XVIIIe siècle et ses sources italiennes," *Gazette des Beaux-Arts* 77 (April 1971): 201–38.

88. See the *Encyclopédie*, pl. I, "Charpente, Pont militaire," which affords a direct comparison with Ledoux's fantasy. The bridge of boats in stone was a common motif of the 1780s; see Fortier's recent study of the bridges of the Ponts et Chaussées, "La nascità dell'Ecole."

89. Emiliand Gauthey (1732–1806), an almost exact contemporary of Ledoux, studied architecture with Dumont and engineering with Perronet. He became engineer-in-chief of Burgundy in 1782, after

having built a series of bridges in the region of Auxerre, each as idio-syncratic as the next, both in experimental engineering and in architectural expression. The Greek ornamentations, obelisks, and rigorously simplified stereotomy of the bridge at Auxerre itself, entry to the region; the similarly geometrical obelisks at Gueugnon, Navilly, and Saint-Laurent de Chalon (1766); the ubiquitous use of deeply carved dentils, rustication, and coffered arches, all testified to Gauthey's almost Piranesian imagination in the scale and detailing of his stoneworking. His buildings, which included the Hôtel de Ville at Tournus (1771), the Theater at Chalon (1778), the Château de Chagny (1777), together with the churches of Saint-Germain-au-Plain and Barizey (1778), seemed likewise to anticipate Ledoux's dramatic handling of stereotomy and ornament, with their mingling of abstracted classical motifs and pure geometries. The celebrated group of structures at Givry—the Hôtel de Ville in the form of a triumphal arch, the fountain in the shape of an obelisk, and the church (1772–91) with its complex combination of primary forms—reinforce this impression and suggest that Ledoux had more than slight aquaintance with his work. The church, in particular, with its bell tower in the form of a giant obelisk over a simple cubic porch, its circular, domed, central rotunda surrounded by columns, and its oval presbytery at the rear, presents an object lesson in the massing of linked and juxtaposed primary forms.

90. Boullée, *Architecture*, 146. The coincidence of language used by both architects would indicate a mutual influence, either through the Académie meetings or the dissemination of Boullée's text in his last years.

91. See Frank E. Manuel, *The Eighteenth Century Confronts the Gods* (Cambridge, Mass., 1959), 210–27, for an excellent summary of the ideas of this neglected author (1722–59), whose writings were so influential on the *philosophes* from D'Holbach to Diderot and Rousseau.

92. Delille, *Les jardins*, Preface.

93. René-L. de Girardin, *De la composition des paysages ou des moyens d'embellir la nature autour des habitations, en joignant l'agréable à l'utile* (Geneva and Paris, 1777), v.

94. Ibid., xi.

95. Ibid., 147.

96. Ibid., 137.

97. Ibid., 159.

98. See the Abbé L. Paulet, *Eyguières, son histoire féodale, communale et religieuse* (Marseille, 1901), 160–61, and, for a detailed survey of the life of de Boisgelin, Abbé E. Lavaquery, *Le cardinal de Boisgelin, 1732–1804* (Paris, 1921).

99. Lavaquery, *Le cardinal de Boisgelin*, 13–14, 75.

100. For an excellent discussion of Ledoux's relationship to these utopian thinkers, his differences and similarities, see Mona Ozouf, *L'école de la France: Essais sur la Révolution, l'utopie et l'enseignement* (Paris, 1984), 286–320, and idem, "Architecture et urbanisme: L'image de la ville chez Claude-Nicolas Ledoux," *Annales E.S.C.* 21, no. 6 (November-December 1966).

101. Abbé Marquet, *Discours sur l'esprit de société (1735); quoted in Mauzi, L'idée du bonheur*, 593.

102. Diderot, "Société," *Encyclopédie*, vol. 16; quoted in Mauzi, *L'idée du bonheur*, 595.

103. Abbé Pluquet, *De la sociabilité* (Paris, 1767), "Avant-propos."

104. See Vidler, "The Architecture of the Lodges," in *The Writing of the Walls,* and for a good summary history of Freemasonry in France, Pierre Chevalier, *Histoire de la franc-maçonnerie française*, 3 vols. (Paris, 1974). The Lodges of Adoption, separate lodges for women, were fashionable counterparts of the male enclaves from the 1750s on; see Chevalier, ibid., 1:200–10.

105. See Oliver, *The Life of William Beckford*. While some later biographers have disputed the authenticity of this account, attributing it to Beckford's wayward imagination, it contains enough circumstantial details—about Ledoux's *atelier* and designs for the *barrières* then in progress—to be regarded as historical. The following quotations of Beckford are all taken from Oliver's transcription of Beckford's "letter" (Oliver, *William Beckford*, 172–81).

106. William Beckford wrote the oriental tale *Vathek* in French in 1782; a translated version was published in London in 1786, and a revised French version in Paris in 1787. In the letter to Louisa Pitt-Rivers, Beckford claims to have been intimate in the society of Hubert Robert and Ledoux. Ledoux would undoubtedly have read this strange preromantic piece that became immediately fashionable. See William Beckford, *Vathek*, ed. Roger Lonsdale (Oxford, 1970); André Parreaux, *William Beckford, Auteur de Vathek (1760–1844)*, is both exhaustive and exhausting; Stephane Mallarmé's "Preface" to *Vathek* (Paris, 1876), is still brilliant.

107. Oliver, *William Beckford*, 166–70.

108. By far the most illuminating and elegant analysis of Ledoux's social utopia of Chaux is Ozouf, "Architecture et urbanisme," which situates Ledoux's ideals in the context of the discourse of *bonheur;* see

also B. Baczko, "Lumières et utopia," *Annales E.S.C.* (March–April 1971), and idem, *Les Lumières de l'utopie* (Paris, 1979), which links Ledoux's designs to universal language schemes of the later eighteenth century.

109. See Roland Barthes, *Sade, Fourier, Loyola* (Paris, 1971): "On voyage beaucoup dans certains romans de Sade. . . . Le voyage est un thème facilement initiatique" (p. 21).

110. Abbé Jean Terrasson, *Séthos, ou vie tirée des monuments anecdotes de l'ancienne Egypte* (Paris, 1731), became widely read, cited, and even used as a source of ritual forms in the eighteenth century; its most celebrated incarnation was, of course, in the libretto by Schikaneder for Mozart's *Magic Flute*. Architects in particular were drawn to its graphic descriptions of the Egyptian underworld—witness the fantasies of Jean-Jacques Lequeu.

111. For the narrative summarized below, see Ledoux, *L'architecture*, 43–64.

112. Beckford, *Vathek*, 54.

113. The late-eighteenth-century interest in neologisms here intersects with the demand to invent new institutions: new worlds will lead to new things. This spirit of linguistic combination also parallels the permutations of geometry in architectural planning characteristic of Ledoux's generation.

114. These three arches are equally reminiscent of the three "Etruscan" arches that form the backdrop of David's painting *The Oath of the Horatii*, itself a legal and moral scene.

115. Viel de Saint-Maux in his *Lettres sur l'architecture* described the emblematic and hieroglyphic architecture of ancient agricultural cults in detail; he was followed by Antoine Vaudoyer, whose Maison d'un Cosmopolite, emulated the Temple of the Sun mentioned by Viel ("Deuxième lettre").

116. See Payne, *The Philosophes and the People*, 94–116.

117. This monument, the plan of which echoes the phallic-shaped atrium of Piranesi's imaginary temple dedicated to Augustus on the Campo Marzio, takes its place beside other priapic *capricci* in the late eighteenth century, including Ledoux's own House of Pleasure designed for Paris. See Oscar Reutersvärd, "The Neo-classic Temple of Virility and the Buildings with a Phallic-shaped Ground Plan." *Formae* (Studies from the Institute of Art History at the University of Lund, Sweden, 1971).

118. Rétif gave elaborate "etymologies" for his choice of Greek names: for "Pornographe" he noted that "pornognomonie" signified the "rule for places of debauchery," and thus "pornographe" would refer to a writer who treated of places of prostitution. "Parthénion," similarly, taken from the Greek meaning a "conclave of sacred virgins," was chosen, noted Rétif, with an (ironical) sensitivity to "French delicacy." See Rétif de la Bretonne, *Le pornographe*, 39, 56.

119. Rétif de la Bretonne, *Le pornographe*. 80–82.

120. For a detailed examination on Rétif's Parthénion project in the context of eighteenth-century prostitution, see the excellent study by Erica-Marie Benabou, *La prostitution et la police des moeurs au XVIIIe siècle* (Paris, 1987), 482–99.

121. *Mercure de France,* 19 August 1786, 104, review of Claude-François-Adrien, marquis de Lezay-Marnésia, *Le bonheur dans les campagnes* (Paris and Neuchâtel, 1785). Lezay-Marnésia was born at Metz in 1735, served in the army, and retired to his estate near Lons-le-Saunier to devote himself to writing on garden design and rural philanthropy. His essay on rural happiness was followed in 1787 by *Essai sur la nature champêtre, poème,* in which he argued for a transformation of poetic sensibility toward the countryside by means of practical reforms. In 1790 he left France for Pennsylvania in the United States to establish a utopian community; returning in 1792, he was imprisoned by Robespierre. See Mauzi, *L'idée du bonheur,* 362–68.

122. *Mercure de France,* 19 August 1786, 109.

123. Ibid.

124. For the careful organization, generally by the church, of games and fêtes in the countryside, see Abel Poitrineau, "La fête traditionnelle," *Annales historiques de la Révolution française* 221 (July–September 1975): 11–26. See also idem, *La vie rurale en Basse-Auvergne au XVIIIe siècle, 1726–1789* (Paris, 1966).

125. Ledoux's careful attention to all the kinds of rural games suggests an extension of the encyclopedic approach toward a primitive rural anthropology. The *Encyclopédie* itself only illustrated aristocratic games such as tennis and fencing. That Ledoux based his designs on close observation of traditional practice is demonstrated by the meticulous study of rural life in Franche-Comté by Michel Vernus, *La vie comtoise au temps de l'ancien régime,* 2 vols. (Lons-le-Saunier, 1983–85), especially 2:39–56.

126. See Rousseau, *Lettre à M. d'Alembert,* 181–82, for Rousseau's description of the spectacles of Geneva, carefully supervised by the adult citizens.

127. Ibid., 181.

6 FRAGMENTS OF AN ARCHITECTURAL DISCOURSE

1. Gallet, *Ledoux*, 255.

2. François-Joseph Bélanger to Royer, 28 March 1789, Bibliothèque Historique de la Ville de Paris, N.A. MS. 181, fol. 150; cited in Jean Stern, *A l'ombre de Sophie Arnould, François-Joseph Bélanger*, 2 vols. (Paris, 1930), 1:224–25.

3. Ledoux, Memorandum, in papers seized by the Comité Révolutionnaire, Section de Faubourg du Nord, 29 November 1794, Archives Nationales, F7.4774.11.

4. As reported by the police inquiry of 1794; see Archives Nationales, F7.4774.11.

5. Ledoux to Joseph Saveur Mignard, 2 November 1789; first published in Berluc-Pérussis, "L'architecte Ledoux," 206–7.

6. Ibid., 207.

7. Furet and Richet, *Le Révolution française*, 66.

8. Police report on Ledoux's arrest, 9 Frimaire year II [1793], Archives Nationales, F7.4774.11.

9. Ledoux to Mignard, 2 November 1789.

10. Ledoux to the Procureurs du Pays de Provence, 13 December 1789; published in Berluc-Pérussis, "L'architecte Ledoux," 210.

11. Gloton and Conard, "Aix-en-Provence," 66.

12. Berluc-Pérussis, "L'architecte Ledoux," 212–19.

13. Lemonnier, *Procès-verbaux de l'Académie*, 9:316–17.

14. Ibid., 9:317, and Werner Szambien, *Les projets de l'an II, concours d'architecture de la période révolutionnaire* (Paris, 1986), 27. Lemonnier cites the date of 8 August 1793 for the suppression of the academies.

15. Hosten had bought the land on the corner of the rue Saint-Georges and the rue Saint-Lazare early in 1792; Ledoux started construction in June and the complex was largely completed by 1795. See Gallet, *Ledoux*, 209, and A. de Champeaux, *L'art décoratif dans le vieux Paris* (Paris, 1898), 319, for a description of the interior of Hosten's house. Hosten, in exile in London, was reportedly dissatisfied with the high cost of the work. The painter Henri-Pierre Danloux noted in his journal for 15 June 1795: "M. Hostein [*sic*] spoke to me about his house in Paris that he had had built by Ledoux and that Ledoux had robbed him! That man [Ledoux] was an unmitigated knave. His salon cost him more than sixty thousand francs, for mirrors, bronzes, and furniture. He had employed the best artists. The one he praised most was Robert" (Baron R. Portalis, *Henri-Pierre Danloux et son journal durant l'Emigration* [Paris, 1910], 267).

16. This journey was mentioned in the *Mémoires secrets* of 1787.

17. Gallet, *Ledoux*, 256.

18. De Champeaux, *L'art décoratif*, 319.

19. Gallet, *Ledoux*, 255–56.

20. Comité Révolutionnaire, Section de Faubourg du Nord, "Tableau des détenus . . . ," Archives Nationales, F7. 4774.11.

21. Ibid.

22. Ibid.

23. "Demandes en liberté," Archives Nationales, F7. 4774.11.

24. Of these three letters, one written on 18 Thermidor year II stated that their father "was not complaining, attributing his detention solely to a misunderstanding of his true principles," and concluded, "You love Justice, return my father to me . . . render it to a desolate family, deprived of the society of a tender father, the dearest in the world." See Archives Nationales, F7. 4774.11.

25. Ledoux, Letter of 1 Thermidor year II, Archives Nationales, F17. 1047.1.

26. Ibid.

27. Ibid.

28. Ibid.

29. Dossier 11, Archives Nationales, F. 17. 1047; quoted in full by Szambien, *Les projets de l'an II*, 185–86. Only a few changes in orthography were made from his first draft.

30. Archives Nationales, F.17.1047.1.

31. Quoted in C.-A. Dauban, *Les prisons de Paris sous la Révolution d'après les relations des contemporains* (Paris, 1870), 457.

32. Copied by Jean-Jacques Lequeu in his *Architecture civile*, 4 vols., unpublished, Bibliothèque Nationale, Estampes, Ha80a–Ha80c, 1:73, verso. The text of this placard was first transcribed by François Benoît, *L'art français sous la Révolution et l'Empire: Les doctrines, les idées, les genres* (Paris, 1897), 252. Lequeu dates the notice 19 Germinal year II (8 April 1794), but Pérouse de Montclos has pointed out that the content of the poster refers to the second jury of the arts

and must therefore date from after the publication of the names of this jury, 24 Frimaire year III (14 December 1794); see Pérouse de Montclos, *Boullée*, 35 n. 4.

33. Lequeu, *Architecture civile*.

34. Pérouse de Montclos, *Boullée*, 35.

35. *Journal des bâtiments civils et des arts* 64 (Floréal year VI): 11. The letter was apparently written at the request of Détournelle. The reporter called this list of signatories "a peculiar mixture: Ledoux with Moitte, Sobre with Poyet, Bienaimé with Fontaine and Percier."

36. Police reports, year VII, Archives Nationales, F7. 6217–3885, 3983; cited in Gallet, *Ledoux*, 280.

37. Cellérier, *Notice rapide*, 13.

38. The commission for the Desaix monument was established in 1801 and the prize awarded to Percier and Fontaine the next year. See Werner Szambien, *Jean-Nicolas-Louis Durand, 1760–1834: De l'imitation à la norme* (Paris, 1984), 38.

39. Pérouse de Montclos, *Boullée*, 36–37.

40. Cellérier, *Notice rapide*, 12.

41. Charles-François Viel, *Décadence de l'architecture à la fin du dix-huitième siècle* (Paris, year VIII), 8.

42. Ibid., 9.

43. Ledoux, *Prospectus*, 27.

44. Ledoux to Joseph Saveur Mignard, 28 March 1803; published in Berluc-Pérussis, "L'architecte Ledoux," 219.

45. Ibid.

46. Ibid.

47. Cellérier, *Notice rapide*, 13.

48. Antoine-Laurent-Thomas Vaudoyer, "Société académique d'architecture," 1806. MS. in the Marquand Library, Princeton University, NA1. S68q. My attention was drawn to this document by the late Donald Egbert, 8 October 1972. Vaudoyer and Le Roy had already developed the idea of a new school of architecture in 1801; see Antoine-Laurent-Thomas Vaudoyer, *Projet d'organisation d'une école nationale d'architecture* (Paris, 24 Pluviôse year IX).

49. See Archives Nationales, Minutier Central des Notaires, Etude XXXIII, 841.

50. Gallet, *Ledoux*, 256.

51. Ledoux, "Testament de Ledoux," 12 November 1806, Archives Nationales, Minutier Centrale des Notaires, Etude XXXIII, 841.

52. Cellérier, *Notice rapide*, 15.

53. "Un ami des arts," "Nécrologie de C.-N. Ledoux, ancien Architecte du Roi," *Annales de l'architecture et des arts* 41 (20 November 1806): 667. This "friend of the arts" was probably Cellérier.

54. Ibid.

55. Inventory of Ledoux's house, starting 26 November 1806, Archives Nationales, Minutier Central des Notaires, Etude XXXIII, 841; first cited in Levallet-Haug. *Ledoux*.

56. Cellérier, *Notice rapide*, 14.

57. Luc-Vincent Thiéry, *Guide des amateurs et des étrangers voyageurs à Paris*, 2 vols. (Paris, 1787), 1:177. The work had already been noticed in Thiéry's *Almanach du voyageur* of 1784.

58. "Précis de l'ouvrage de Ledoux," accompanied by a letter dated 20 Fructidor year IX; transcribed in Ottomeyer, "Autobiographies d'architectes parisiens, 1759–1811," 180–81.

59. For a brief history of the idea of the museum in the Revolutionary period, see Anthony Vidler, "Architecture in the Museum: Didactic Narratives from Boullée to Lenoir," chap. 11 of *The Writing of the Walls*.

60. "Précis de l'ouvrage de Ledoux."

61. Ibid.

62. Ibid.

63. Ottomeyer, "Autobiographies d'architectes parisiens," 18–21.

64. See the excellent article by A. M. Wilson, "The Concept of *Moeurs* in Diderot's Social and Political Thought," in *The Age of the Enlightenment: Studies Presented to Theodore Besterman*, ed. W. H. Barber et al. (St. Andrews, 1967).

65. Diderot, *Oeuvres complètes*, 6:390.

66. See Jean Starobinski, "André Chénier and the Allegory of Poetry," in Karl Kroeber and William Walling, eds., *Images of Romanticism* (New Haven, 1978), 39–60.

67. Constantin-François de Chasseboeuf, Comte de Volney, *Les ruines* (Paris, 1790).

68. *Journal des bâtiments, des monuments et des arts* 246 (8 January 1803): 94.

69. Ibid.

70. *Annales de l'architecture et des arts* 36 (1 November 1806): 591ff.

71. Ibid.

72. Pierre-Athanase Détournelle, *Journal des arts, des sciences et de littérature* 340 (20 Germinal year XII): 73–79; 341 (25 Germinal year XII): 97–101; 342 (30 Germinal year XII): 121–125; 343 (5 Floréal year XII): 145–51; and 344 (10 Floréal year XII): 169–73.

73. Ibid., 330 (30 Pluviôse year XII): 265–68.

74. Ibid., 340:73.

75. Ibid., 75.

76. Ibid., 327 (15 Pluviôse year XII): 194.

77. Ibid.

78. Ibid., 341:100.

79. Ibid., 340:77–78.

80. Ibid., 78.

81. Ibid., 344:172–73.

82. Anonymous [Maurice-François-Camille Le Bars?], *Journal des monuments et des arts* 4 (14 Vendémiaire year XIII). Helen Lipstadt, in "Soufflot, De Wailly, Ledoux: La fortune critique dans la presse architecturale (1800–1825)," in *Soufflot et l'architecture de lumières*, 302, argues for an attribution to the editor of the journal, Le Bars, against Gallet who cites from the review in *Ledoux*, 280–81, and who attributes the piece to Détournelle. Lipstadt points out that elsewhere Détournelle was critical of the *Prospectus*.

83. J.-M. Quérard, "Ledoux," in *La France littéraire, ou Dictionnaire bibliographique* (Paris, 1833), 5:68.

84. Emil Kaufmann, "Three Revolutionary Architects: Boullée, Ledoux, and Lequeu," *Transactions of the American Philosophical Society*, new ser., 42, 3 (1953): 431–564.

85. Pierre Giraud, *Les tombeaux, ou essai sur les sépultures par P. Giraud, composé en l'an IV et déposé au département de la Seine, le 11 nivôse an VII, avec les plans, coupes et élévations du monument projeté* (Paris, 1801).

86. Boullée, *Architecture*, 34.

87. Ibid., 37.

88. Jean-Nicolas-Louis Durand, *Précis des leçons d'architecture données à l'Ecole polytechnique*, 2 vols. (Paris, 1802–5), 1:19.

89. H. Rohault, *Projet d'hôpital pour 1500 malades* (Paris, 1810), 4.

90. Louis Bruyère, *Etudes relatives à l'art des constructions*, 2 vols. (Paris, 1823–28), 1:4.

91. Szambien, *Durand*, 35 and pl. 45–46; this "Rudimenta Operis Magni et Disciplinae" of around 1790 is discussed more fully in Szambien, "Aux origines de l'enseignement de Durand: Les cent soixante-huit croquis des Rudimenta Operis Magni et Disciplinae," *Etudes de la revue de Louvre* 1(1980): 122–30.

92. Szambien, *Durand*, 222–25.

93. For a discussion of Revolutionary projects, see Szambien, *Les projets de l'an II*.

94. Louis-Ambroise Dubut, *Architecture civile: Maisons de ville et de campagne de toutes formes et de tous genres* (Paris, 1803), title page.

95. Szambien, *Durand*, 90 and pl. 225.

96. "M." [J.-J.-L. Monnin?], Review of Ledoux's *L'architecture* in *Annales des bâtiments* 3(1818): 283–84.

A full bibliography and list of archival sources is given in Gallet, *Ledoux*, 283–85. The following list includes only a selection of those works consulted that were of especial use in the preparation of this study.

MANUSCRIPT SOURCES

1. Archives de l'Institut de France. B 21 [Ledoux, Letter of candidacy to the Académie Royale d'architecture, November 1767]

2. Archives Nationales
G1 92–96 [Salines and Saline de Chaux]
E 2474 [Salines]
E 2508 fol. 458, 459, 460, 476 [Salines]
144 AP 132 [Fenouillot and the salines]
G1 24 [Grenier de sel, Compiègne]
AB XIX 213–215 [Hôtel Thélusson]
265 AP 421–422, 161–162 [Hôtel d'Uzès]
N III Seine, 1265 [Hôtel d'Uzès]
N III Seine et Marne, 35 [Maupertuis]
H 1259 [Aix-en-Provence]
O1 1932, 7–8 [Aix-en-Provence]
H 1349, 1350, 1359 [Marseilles Theater]
N III Seine, 1054. [Hosten Houses]
T 705 [*Barrières*]
Q1 1100–1101 [*Barrières*]
F7 4774–11 [Dossier of police reports on Ledoux's arrest, 1793]
F7 6217–3883 [Police report on Ledoux, year VII]
Minutier Centrale des Notaires, Etude XXXIII, liasse 841 [Ledoux's will and inventory of house]

3. Archives Départementales du Jura
C 276, 349, 372, 375,406
8J 323, 435 [Enquiry into aqueduct]; 440 [Saline de Montmorot]; 494–501 [Saline de Chaux 1806–1910]; 502 [*Rendue,* 1782]; 503 [Saline de Chaux, daily registers]; 581–89 [Survey of aqueduct, D.-F. Dez, 1775–80]

4. Archives Municipales de Besançon
DD35.36–140 [Theater of Besançon]
Yc B2.20–22 [Elevations and plans, Theater of Besançon]
Fonds Pierre-Adrien Pâris, *Etudes d'architecture,* vol. 5
[Theatrical designs, including Ledoux's drawings for the Theater of Besançon]

5. Bibliothèque Méjanes, Aix-en-Provence
Ms. 929; Ms.1059 [Studies for the Palais de Justice and prisons]

PUBLISHED WORKS

1. Works by Ledoux

Ledoux, Claude-Nicolas. "Dernière réponse à M. Poyet." *Journal de Paris* 97 (7 April 1783): 403.

————. *Prospectus: L'architecture considérée sous le rapport de l'art, des moeurs et de la législation.* Paris: C.-F. Patris, Imprimerie de l'Académie de Législation, 1802.

————. *L'architecture considérée sous le rapport de l'art, des moeurs et de la législation.* vol. 1. Paris: L'imprimerie de H.-L. Perroneau [chez l'auteur, rue Neuve d'Orléans], 1804.

————. *L'architecture considérée sous le rapport de l'art, des moeurs et de la législation.* vol. 2. Edited with a memoir of the author by Daniel Ramée, London, 1846.

————. *Architecture de C.N. Ledoux: Premier volume contenant des plans, élévations, coupes, vues perspectives, des palais, hôtels de ville, temples, bibliothèques publiques, bourses, théâtres, usines, greniers à sel, bâtiments de graduation, bains publics, marchés, églises, cimetières, propylées de Paris, etc., etc., etc. Collection qui rassemble tous les genres de bâtiments employés dans l'ordre social. Second volume contenant des plans, élévations, coupes, vues perspectives d'hôtels, châteaux, maisons de ville et de campagne, édifices destinés aux récréations publiques. Pavillons, parcs, fermes parées, bergeries, écuries, etc., etc.* Edited with an introduction by Daniel Ramée. 2 vols. Paris: Lenoir éditeur, 5 quai Malaquais, 1847.

[Ledoux, Claude-Nicolas?]. *Un bon-homme aux Etats Généraux, sur quelques objets relatifs aux arts; sur M. Poyet et les plagiaires, etc., etc., etc.* "Londres," December 1788. [Anonymous pamphlet, almost certainly by Ledoux, B.N. Imprimés Lb39 6750.]

2. Collections of Engravings and Works Planned by Ledoux

[Ledoux, Claude-Nicolas]. *Recueil d'Etampes "Joly de Fleury."* Paris, private collection. Inscribed as given to the nephew of Joly de Fleury, 28 April 1791.

————. *Ornements et Architecture.* Paris: Bibliothèque d'Art et d'Archéologie, Fol. Rés. 169.

Ledoux, Claude-Nicolas. *L'architecture de C.N. Le Doux: Premier volume, contenant des plans, élévations, coupes, vues perspectives de villes, usines, greniers à sel, bâtiments de graduation, bains publics, marchés, églises, cimetières, théâtres, ponts, hôtelleries, maisons de ville et de campagne en tout genre, maisons de commerce, de négociants, d'employés, d'édifices destinés aux récréations publiques, etc., etc. Construits ou commencés depuis 1768 jusques en 1789. Collection qui rassemble tous les genres de bâtiments employés dans l'ordre social.* Paris: chez l'auteur, rue Neuve d'Orléans, no. 16, près la Porte St. Martin, 1789. [First title page to *L'architecture*, 1804].

————. *Architecture sentimentale contenant tous les genres d'édifices connus dans l'ordre social. La maison du pauvre, du charbonnier, du bûcheron, du commis, de l'employé, du berger, du garde agricole ou garde de forêt, d'ouvrier, d'artisan, d'artiste. Communs, portiques, hôtelleries, maisons de négociants, de ville, de campagne variées à l'infini, maisons de plaisance, de plaisir, fermes, parcs, grange parées, atteliers, ville, village, bains publiques, usines, forges, salines, greniers à sel, pacifer, calendrier des honnêtes gens, école de morale, prétoires, temples églises, théâtres, maisons de vente, de jeux, de commerce, des cénobies, palais, temple de justice, palais de gouverneur, prisons, marchés publics, magazins de graines de toute espèce. Bâtiments de graduation; succursalle, écoles publiques, maison d'éducation, d'union, fontaines publiques, lavoir, abreuvoir, écuries, pont, cimetières, arcs de triomphe, places publiques, cazernes, palais sacerdotal, bibliothèque, salle d'antiques, de models, châteaux, restaurations de palais, palais, commices ruralles, maisons destinées aux récréations publiques, maison pour deux amis, maison pour une famille considérable dont les besoins de chacun sont isolés et se communiquent etc. C'est une Encyclopédie ou Muséum architectural.* 6 vols., each with one hundred plates, including thirty-four perspective views, and one hundred pages of text. [Summary of the work, 20 Fructidor year IX (1801)]

3. Primary Sources

Achard, Claude-François. *Description historique, géographique et topographique des villes . . . de la Provence ancienne et moderne.* 2 vols. Aix-en-Provence, 1787.

D'Alembert, Jean le Rond. *Discours préliminaire de l'"Encyclopédie."* Paris, 1751. Reprint. Paris, 1965.

Bachaumont, L.-P. de, et al. *Mémoires secrets pour servir à l'histoire de la République des lettres en France de 1762 jusqu'à nos jours.* London, 1777–89.

Barthélemy, Abbé Jean-Jacques. *Voyage du jeune Anacharsis en grèce dans le milieu du quatrième siècle avant l'ère vulgaire.* 4 vols. Paris, 1788.

Bastide, Jean-François de. *La petite maison.* Paris, 1753. Reprint. Paris, 1879.

Blondel, Jacques-François. *Discours sur la nécessité de l'étude de l'architecture.* Paris, 1754.

————. *Discours sur la manière d'étudier l'architecture et les arts qui sont relatifs à celui de bâtir.* Paris, 1747.

————. *Cours d'architecture, ou traité de la décoration, distribution et construction des bâtiments; contenant les leçons données en 1750, et les années suivantes.* 9 vols. Vols. 5–9 edited by Pierre Patte. Paris, 1771–77.

Blondel, Jacques-François, and Jean-François de Bastide. *Les amours rivaux ou l'homme du monde éclairé par les arts.* 2 vols. Amsterdam and Paris, 1774.

Boffrand, Germain. *Livre d'architecture.* Paris, 1745.

Bouche, Charles-François. *Essai sur l'histoire de Provence.* 2 vols. Marseilles, 1785.

Boulanger, Nicolas-Antoine. *L'antiquité dévoilée par ses usages, ou Examen critique des principales opinions, cérémonies et institutions religieuses et politiques des différents peuples de la terre.* Amsterdam, 1766.

Boullée, Etienne-Louis. *Architecture: Essai sur l'art.* Paris, 1789–99. Reprint. Edited by Jean-Marie Pérouse de Montclos. Paris, 1968.

Brissot de Warville, Jacques-Pierre. *Théorie de lois criminelles.* 2 vols. Paris, 1781.

Burke, Edmund. *A Philosophical Enquiry into the Origins of Our Ideas of the Sublime and Beautiful.* London, 1757. Reprint. Edited by James T. Boulton, London, 1958.

Carmontelle [Louis Carrogis]. *Jardin de Monceau, près de Paris, appartenant à . . . Monseigneur le duc de Chartres.* Paris, 1779.

[Cellérier, Jacques]. *Notice rapide sur la vie et les ouvrages de Claude-Nicolas Ledoux.* By "J. C." Paris, 1806.

Clérisseau, Charles-Louis. *Les monuments de Nîmes.* Paris, 1788.

————. *Les monuments de Nîmes, texte historique et descriptif par J.-G. Legrand.* Paris, 1808.

Cochin, Charles-Nicolas. *Projet d'une salle de spectacle pour un théâtre de comédie.* Paris, 1765.

Cochin, Charles-Nicolas, and Jérôme-Charles Bellicard. *Observations sur les antiquités de la ville de Herculanum.* Paris, 1754.

Contant d'Ivry, Pierre. *Oeuvres d'architecture.* Paris, 1765.

Coquéau, Claude-Philibert. *Mémoire sur la nécessité de transférer et reconstruire l'Hôtel-Dieu, suivi d'un projet de translation de cet hôpital, proposé par le Monsieur Poyet.* [Paris], 1785.

Damun, Jean. *Prospectus du nouveau théâtre tracé sur les principes des Grecs et des Romains.* Paris, 1772.

Delafosse, Jean-Charles. *Nouvelle iconologie historique.* Paris, 1768.

Delagardette, C.-M. *Règles des cinq ordres d'architecture, de Vignole.* Paris, 1786.

Delille, Abbé Jacques. *Les Géorgiques de Virgile.* Paris, 1770.

————. *Les jardins, ou l'art d'embellir les paysages.* Paris, 1782. New ed. Paris, 1804.

————. *L'imagination, poëme en huit chants, accompagné de notes historiques et littéraires par J. Esménard.* Paris, 1806.

————. *Oeuvres.* Paris, 1833.

Détournelle, Pierre-Athanase. Review of *L'architecture* by Claude-Nicolas Ledoux. *Journal des arts, des sciences et de littérature* (1804–5).

Détournelle, Pierre-Athanase, Antoine-Laurent-Thomas Vaudoyer, and G.-E. Allais. *Projets d'architecture . . . qui ont mérité les grands prix accordés par l'Académie, l'Institut national de France et par les jurys du choix des artistes et du gouvernement (1791–1803).* Paris, 1806.

Diderot, Denis. *Oeuvres complètes.* 20 vols. Edited by J. Assézat and M. Tourneux. Paris, 1875–77.

Diderot, Denis, and Jean Le Rond d'Alembert. *Encyclopédie ou Dictionnaire raisonné des sciences, des arts et des métiers, par une société de gens de lettres,* 17 vols. Neuchâtel, 1751–65; *Supplément.* 4 vols. Neuchâtel, 1776–77; *Recueil des planches.* 11 vols. Neuchâtel, 1762–72; *Suite du Recueil des planches.* 1 vol. Neuchâtel, 1777.

Dubut, Louis-Ambroise. *Architecture civile: Maisons de ville et de campagne de toutes formes et de tous genres, projetées pour être construites sur des terrains de différentes grandeurs; ouvrage utile à tous constructeurs et entrepreneurs, et à toutes personnes qui, ayant quelques connaissances en construction, veulent elles-mêmes diriger leurs bâtimens.* Paris, 1803.

Dulaure, Jacques-Antoine. *Nouvelle description des curiosités de Paris.* Paris, 1785.

————. *Description des environs de Paris.* Paris, 1786.

————. *Réclamation d'un citoyen contre la nouvelle enceinte de Paris élevée par les fermiers généraux.* Paris, 1787.

Dumont, G.-P.-M. *Les vues, plans, coupes, élévations de trois temples antiques faisant partie de l'ancienne ville de Paestum.* Paris, 1764.

Dupuis, Charles-François. *Origine de tous les cultes.* Paris, 1795.

Durand, Jean-Nicolas-Louis. *Recueil et parallèle des édifices de tout genre, anciens et modernes, remarquables par leur beauté, avec un texte extrait de l'Histoire général de l'architecture par J.-G. Legrand.* Paris, 1801.

————. *Précis des leçons d'architecture données à l'Ecole polytechnique.* 2 vols. Paris, 1802–5.

Gaitte. *Receuil des plus belles maisons et des plus beaux édifices de Paris.* Paris, n.d. [c. 1792].

Gibelin, Esprit. *Lettre sur les tours antiques qu'on a démolies à Aix-en-Provence et sur les antiquités qu'elles renfermoient.* Aix-en-Provence, 1787.

Girardin, René. *De la composition des paysages ou des moyens d'embellir la nature autour des habitations, en joignant l'agréable à l'utile.* Geneva and Paris, 1777.

Giraud, Pierre. *Les tombeaux, ou essai sur les sépultures par P. Giraud, composé en l'an IV et déposé au département de la Seine, le 11 nivôse an VII, avec les plans, coupes et élévations du monument projeté.* Paris, 1801.

Gondouin, Jacques. *Description des Ecoles de Chirurgie.* Paris, 1780.

Hancarville, Pierre-François, dit d'Hugues. *Recherches sur l'origine et les progrès des arts de la Grèce.* 3 vols. London, 1785.

Krafft, Jean-Charles. *Traité théorique et pratique sur l'art de la charpente.* Paris, 1819.

Krafft, Jean-Charles, and Nicolas Ransonnette. *Plans, coupes et élévations des plus belles maisons et des hôtels construites à Paris et dans les environs.* Paris, 1802.

Laborde, Alexandre de. *Description des nouveaux jardins de la France et de ses anciens châteaux.* Paris, 1808.

Laborde, Jean-Benjamin de. *Description générale et particulière de la France.* 12 vols. Paris, 1781–96.

Landon, Charles-Paul, ed. *Annales du Musée.* 8 vols. Paris, 1801–5.

Laugier, Marc-Antoine. *Essai sur l'architecture.* Paris, 1753. 2d ed. Paris, 1755.

————. *Observations sur l'architecture.* The Hague and Paris, 1765.

Le Camus de Mézières, Nicolas [Wolf d'Orfeuil, pseud.]. *L'esprit des almanachs, analyse critique et raisonnée de tous les almanachs tant anciens que modernes.* Paris, 1783.

————. *Le génie de l'architecture ou l'analogie de cet art avec nos sensations.* Paris, 1780.

Lecreulx, François-Michel. *Discours sur le goût appliqué aux arts et particulièrement à l'architecture.* Nancy, 1778.

Legrand, Jacques-Guillaume. *Collection des chefs-d'oeuvre de l'architecture des différens peuples, exécutés en modèles sous la direction de L.-F. Cassas.* Paris, 1806.

————. *Essai sur l'histoire générale de l'architecture.* Paris, 1809.

Legrand, Jacques-Guillaume, et al. *Description de Paris.* 2 vols. Paris, 1808.

Lenoir, Alexandre. *La Franche-maçonnerie rendue à sa véritable origine, ou l'Antiquité de la franche-maçonnerie prouvée par l'explication des mystères anciens et modernes.* Paris, 1814.

Lequeu, Jean-Jacques. *Architecture civile.* Ms. Estampes, Ha.80a. Fo, Bibliothèque Nationale, Paris.

Le Roy, Julien-David. *Histoire de la disposition et des formes différentes que les chrétiens ont données à leurs temples.* Paris, 1764.

————. *Observations sur les édifices des anciens peuples.* Paris, 1767.

————. *Les ruines des plus beaux monuments de la Grèce considérées du côté de l'histoire et du côté de l'architecture.* 2d ed. 2 vols. in 1. Paris, 1770.

————. *Les navires des anciens, considérés par rapport à leurs voiles et à l'usage qu'on en pourroit faire dans notre marine.* Paris, 1783.

Lubersac, Abbé Charles-François de. *Discours sur les monuments publics de tous les âges.* Paris, 1775.

Maire, N.-M. *La topographie de Paris, ou plan détaillé de la ville de Paris et de ses faubourgs.* Paris, 1808.

Menuret de Chambaud, Jean-Jacques. *Essais sur l'histoire médico-topographique de Paris.* New ed. Paris, 1804.

Mercier, Louis-Sébastien. *Du théâtre, ou nouvel essai sur l'art dramatique.* Amsterdam, 1773.

Morel, J.-M. *Théorie des jardins ou l'Art des jardins de la nature.* Paris, 1776.

Neufforge, Jean-François de. *Traité élémentaire de l'architecture.* Paris, 1757.

Patte, Pierre. *Discours sur l'architecture.* Paris, 1754.

————. *Monuments érigés en France à la gloire de Louis XV.* Paris, 1765.

————. *Mémoires sur les objets les plus importants de l'architecture.* Paris, 1769.

————. *Essai sur l'architecture théâtrale.* Paris, 1782.

Perrault, Claude. *Les dix livres d'architecture de Vitruve.* Paris, 1673.

Perronet, Jean-Rodolphe. *Description des projets et de la construction des ponts de Neuilly, de Mantes, d'Orléans et autres; du projet du canal de Bourgogne pour la communication des deux mers par Dijon; et celui de la conduite des eaux de l'Yvette et de Bièvre à Paris.* 2 vols. and supplement. Paris, 1782–89.

Petit, Antoine. *Mémoire sur la meilleure manière de construire un hôpital des malades.* Paris, 1774.

Poyet, Bernard, and Claude-Philibert Coqueau. *Mémoire sur la nécessité de transférer et reconstruire l'Hôtel-Dieu de Paris.* Paris, 1785.

Prieur, Armand-Parfait, and Pierre-Louis Van Cléemputte. *Collection des prix qui la ci-devant Académie d'architecture proposait et couronnait tous les ans: Tome premier 1773–1789.* Paris, n.d.

Quatremère de Quincy, Antoine-Chrysostôme. *De l'architecture Egyptienne considérée dans son origine, ses principes et son goût.* Paris, 1803.

———. *Encyclopédie méthodique: Architecture.* 3 vols. Paris, 1788–1825.

Rétif de la Bretonne, Nicolas-Edme. *La mimographe, ou idées d'un honnête femme pour la réformation du théâtre national.* Amsterdam, 1770.

———. *Le pornographe, ou idées d'un honnête homme sur un projet de règlement pour les prostituées propre à prévenir les malheurs qu'occasionne le publicisme des femmes.* Paris, 1769. Reprint. With a preface by Béatrice Didier. Paris, 1977.

Rondelet, Jean. *Traité théorique et pratique de l'art de bâtir.* Paris, 1802.

Roubo, André-Jacques. *Traité de la construction des théâtres et des machines théâtrales.* Paris, 1777.

Taillefer, Wilgrin. *L'architecture soumise aux principes de la nature et de l'art.* Périgueux, 1804.

Thiéry, Luc-Vincent. *Almanach du voyageur à Paris.* Paris, 1784.

———. *Guide des amateurs et des étrangers voyageurs à Paris ou Description raisonnée de cette ville, de sa banlieu et de tout ce qu'elles contiennent de remarquable.* 2 vols. Paris, 1787.

Toussaint, Claude-Jacques. *Traité de géométrie et d'architecture, théorique et pratique.* 2 vols. Paris, 1811.

Vaudoyer, Antoine-Laurent-Thomas, "Société académique d'architecture" [1806]. Ms. NA1. S68q, Marquand Library, Princeton University.

Verniquet, Edme. *Plan de la ville de Paris avec sa nouvelle enceinte levé géométriquement sur la méridienne de l'Observatoire.* Paris, 1791.

Viel, Charles-François. *Décadence de l'architecture à la fin du dix-huitième siècle.* Paris, 1800.

Viel de Saint-Maux, Jean-Louis. *Lettres sur l'architecture des anciens et celles des modernes.* Paris, 1787.

Warburton, Bishop William. *Essai sur les hiéroglyphes des Egyptiens.* Translated by Léonard des Malpeines. Paris, 1744.

Watelet, C.-H. *Essai sur les jardins.* Paris, 1774.

4. Secondary Sources

The Age of Neo-Classicism. Exhibition Catalogue. London, 1972.

Antal, F. *Classicism and Romanticism with other Studies in Art History.* London, 1970.

Belavel, Yvon. *L'esthétique sans paradoxe de Diderot.* Paris, 1950.

Benabou, Erica-Marie, *La prostitution et la police des moeurs au XVIIIe siècle.* Paris, 1987.

Benoît, François. *L'art français sous la Révolution et l'Empire: Les doctrines, les idées, les genres.* Paris, 1897.

Berluc-Pérussis, Léon de. "L'architecte Ledoux et le sculpteur Chardigny à Aix: Documents inédits (1776–1803)." *Réunion des Sociétés des Beaux-Arts des départements* 26–27 (1902): 189–225.

Bernos, Marcel, et al., eds. *Histoire d'Aix-en-Provence.* Aix-en-Provence, 1977.

Biver, Marie-Louise. *Fêtes révolutionnaires à Paris.* Paris, 1979.

Blanc, Charles. *Grammaire des arts du dessin.* Paris, 1862.

Bonnel, E. "L'architecte Ledoux et le Théâtre de Marseille." *Marseille,* 3d ser. (1958): 30.

Bouleau-Rabaud, Wanda. "L'Académie d'architecture à la fin du XVIIIe siècle." *Gazette des Beaux-Arts,* ser. 6, 68 (December 1966): 355–64.

Braham, Allan. *The Architecture of the French Enlightenment.* Berkeley and Los Angeles, 1980.

Brennan, Thomas. "Beyond the Barriers: Popular Culture and Parisian *Guinguettes.*" *Eighteenth-Century Studies* 18, no. 2 (Winter 1984–85): 153–69.

Brion, Marcel. "Un précurseur de l'architecture moderne: Claude-Nicolas Ledoux." *Beaux-Arts* (January 1937):3

Cailleux, J. de. "Le pavillon de Mme du Barry à Louveciennes." *Revue de l'art ancien et moderne* 67 (1935): 213–24; 68 (1935): 35–48.

Caire, G. "Bertin, Ministre physiocrate." *Revue d'histoire économique et sociale* 38, no. 3 (1960): 257–84.

Campardon, Emile. *Les comédiens du roi de la troupe française.* Paris, 1879.

Un canal . . . des canaux. Exhibition catalogue. Paris, 1986.

Cassirer, Ernst. *The Philosophy of the Enlightenment.* Translated by Fritz C. A. Koellin and James P. Pettegrove. Princeton, 1951.

Cassirer, Kurt. *Die ästhetischen Hauptbergriffe der französischen Architekturtheoretiker von 1650–1780.* Berlin, 1909.

Cavaillès, Henri, *La route française, son histoire, sa function.* Paris, 1946.

Chambardel, E. "Une solution inédite des problèmes de gestion hospitalière: C.-N. Ledoux (1736–1806)." *L'hôpital et l'aide sociale* 23 (September–October 1963): 559–63.

Champeaux, A. de. "L'art décoratif dans le vieux Paris." *Gazette des Beaux-Arts* 70 (1892): 249–52.

———. *L'art décoratif dans le vieux Paris.* Paris, 1898.

Chaussinand-Nogaret, G. *Gens de finance au XVIIIe siècle.* Paris, 1972.

Chevalier, Pierre. *Histoire de la franc-maçonnerie française.* 3 vols. Paris, 1974.

Choppin de Janvry, O. "Le désert de Retz." *Bulletin de la Société d'histoire de l'art français* (1970): 125–48.

Choullier, Ernest. *Les Trudaine.* Arcis-sur-Aube, 1884.

Chouillet, Jacques. *L'esthétique des Lumières.* Paris, 1974.

Clerc, Michel, *Aquae Sextiae: Histoire d'Aix-en-Provence dans l'antiquité.* Paris, 1910.

Colombier, Pierre. *L'architecture française en Allemagne au XVIIIe siècle.* 2 vols. Paris, 1956.

Combarnous, Victor. *Histoire du théâtre de Marseille.* Marseille, 1927.

Conard, Serge. "Aux sources de l'architecture parlante, l'archéologie mystique de C.-N. Ledoux." In *Colloque Piranesi e la cultura antiquaria.* Rome, 1979.

Cornon, F. *Elie Fréron.* Paris, 1922.

Coste, J.-P. *Aix en 1765: Structure urbaine et société.* Aix-en-Provence, 1970.

Crow, Thomas E. *Painters and Public Life in Eighteenth Century Paris.* London and New Haven, 1985.

Crozet, René. "David et l'architecture néo-classique." *Gazette des Beaux-Arts,* ser. 6, 45 (April 1955): 211–20.

Cubells, Monique. *La Provence des Lumières: Les parlementaires d'Aix au 18ème siècle.* Paris, 1984.

Dakin, Douglas. *Turgot and the Ancien Régime in France.* London, 1939.

David, Madeleine V.-. *Le débat sur les écritures et l'hiéroglyphe aux XVIIe et XVIIIe siècles.* Paris, 1965.

Demangeon, Alain, and Bruno Fortier. *Les vaissaux et les villes.* Brussels, 1978.

Dion, Roger. *Histoire de la vigne et du vin en France des origines au XIXe siècle.* Paris, 1959.

Dockès, P. *Lo spazio nel pensiero economico dal XVI al XVIII secolo.* Milan, 1971.

Duboy, Philippe. *Lequeu: An Architectural Enigma.* Cambridge, Mass., 1987.

Duchet, Michèle. *Diderot et l'histoire des deux Indes, ou l'écriture fragmentaire.* Paris, 1978.

Duchet, Michèle, and M. Jalley, eds. *Langue et langages de Leibniz à l' "Encyclopédie."* Paris, 1977.

Dudot, J.-M., et al., eds. *Le devoir d'embellir.* Nancy, 1977.

Durand, Yves. *Les fermiers généraux au XVIIIe siècle.* Paris, 1971.

Eriksen, Svend. *Early Neo-Classicism in France.* London, 1974.

Erouart, Gilbert. *L'architecture au pinceau: Jean-Laurent Legeay. Un Piranésian français dans l'Europe des Lumières.* Paris, 1982.

Etlin, Richard. "L'air dans l'urbanisme des Lumières." *Dix-huitième siècle* 9 (1977): 123–34.

———. *The Architecture of Death: The Transformation of the Cemetery in Eighteenth-Century Paris.* Cambridge, Mass., 1984.

Evans, Robin. *The Fabrication of Virtue: English Prison Architecture, 1750–1840.* Cambridge, 1982.

Faure, Edgar. *La disgrâce de Turgot*. Paris, 1961.

Les Fêtes de la Révolution. Exhibition catalogue. Clermont-Ferrand, 1974.

Fortier, Bruno. "L'invention de la maison." *Architecture, Mouvement, Continuité* 51 (1980): 29–35.

———. "La nascità dell'Ecole des Ponts et Chaussées: 1. Lo spazio." *Casabella* 495 (October 1983): 40–47.

———. "La nascità dell'Ecole des Ponts et Chaussées: 2. Il projetto." *Casabella* 496 (November 1983): 36–45.

Foucault, Michel. *Naissance de la clinique: Une archéologie du regard médical*. Paris, 1963.

———. *Les mots et les choses*. Paris, 1966.

———. *Histoire de la folie à l'âge classique*. Rev. ed. Paris, 1972.

———. *Surveiller et punir: Naissance de la prison*. Paris, 1975.

Foucault, Michel, et al. *Les machines à guérir: Aux origines de l'hôpital moderne*. Brussels, 1979.

Four, Léon. *Le long des routes de Franche-Comté au XVIIIe siècle*. Besançon, 1935.

Fournier, Edward. "Notice sur la famille et l'Hôtel Thélusson." *Chroniques et légendes des rues de Paris*. Paris, 1864.

Frémy, E. "L'enceinte de Paris, construite par les fermiers-généraux et la perception des droits d'octroi de la ville (1784–1791)." *Bulletin de la Société de l'histoire de Paris et de l'Ile de France* 39 (1912): 115–48.

Fuchs, Max. "Le théâtre de Marseille au XVIIIe siècle." *Mémoires de l'Institut historique de Provence* 3 (1926): 180–202.

———. *La vie théâtrale en province au XVIIIe siècle*. Geneva, 1933.

Furet, François, and Denis Richet. *La Révolution française*. Rev. ed. Paris, 1973.

Gallet, Michel. *Demeures parisiennes: L'époque de Louis XVI*. Paris, 1964.

———. "Le salon de l'Hôtel d'Uzès." *Bulletin du Musée Carnavalet* 2 (1969): 3–22.

———. "La jeunesse de Ledoux." *Gazette des Beaux-Arts* (February 1970): 1–92.

———. *Stately Mansions: Eighteenth-Century Paris Architecture,* London, 1972.

———. "Palladio et l'architecture française dans la seconde moitié du XVIIIe siècle." *Monuments historiques de la France* no. 2 (1975): 43–55.

———. "Louis-François Trouard et l'architecture religieuse dans la région de Versailles au temps de Louis XVI," *Gazette des Beaux-Arts* (1976): 201–18.

———. "Ledoux et sa clientèle parisienne." *Bulletin de la Société de l'histoire de Paris et de l'Ile de France* (1976): 131–73.

———. *Claude-Nicolas Ledoux, 1736–1806*. Paris, 1980.

Ganay, Ernest de. "La salle de spectacle de l'architecte Ledoux à Besançon." *Revue de l'art ancien et moderne* 52 (June–December 1927): 2–21.

———. "La salle de spectacle de Besançon," *Bulletin de l'Académie des sciences, belles-lettres et arts de Besançon* (May 1927).

———. *Les jardins de France et leur décor*. Paris, 1949.

———. "Fabriques aux jardins du XVIIIe siècle." *Gazette des Beaux-Arts* (March–June 1955): 287–98.

Giedion, Sigfried. *Spätbarocker und Romantischer Klassizismus*. Monaco, 1922.

Gloton, Jean-Jacques, and Serge Conard. "Aix-en-Provence dans l'oeuvre de Claude-Nicolas Ledoux." In *Monuments et mémoires publiés par l'Académie des inscriptions et belles-lettres*. Vendôme, 1983.

Godechot, Jacques. *La prise de la Bastille*. Paris, 1965.

Goncourt, Edmond de. *La Dubarry,* Paris, 1878.

———. *La Guimard*. Paris, 1893.

Gossman, Lionel. *Medievalism and the Ideologies of the Enlightenment*. Baltimore, 1968.

Goubert, Pierre. *The Ancien Régime*. New York, 1973.

Gruber, Alain-Charles. *Les grandes fêtes et leurs décors à l'époque de Louis XVI*. Geneva, 1972.

Guillerme, Jacques, "Lequeu et l'invention du mauvais goût," *Gazette des Beaux-Arts* (September 1965): 153–66.

———. "Themes, partis et formes chez l'architecte Lequeu." *La vie médicale* no. 47 (1966): 67–82.

———. "Notes pour l'histoire de la régularité." *Revue d'esthétique* 3 (1971): 383–94.

———. "Lequeu, entre l'irrégulier et l'éclectique." *Dix-Huitième Siècle* 1 (1974): 127–40.

Harris, John. "Sir William Chambers and his Parisian Album." *Architectural History* 6 (1963).

———. "Le Geay, Piranesi and International Neoclassicism in Rome." In vol. 1 of *Essays in the History of Architecture Presented to Rudolph Wittkower.* Edited by D. Fraser, H. Hibbard, and M. J. Levine. 2 vols. London, 1967.

———. *Sir William Chambers, Knight of the Polar Star.* London, 1970.

Hautecoeur, Louis. *Rome et la renaissance de l'antiquité à la fin du XVIIIe siècle.* Paris, 1912.

———. *Histoire de l'architecture classique en France.* 11 vols. Paris, 1943–57.

Herrmann, Wolfgang. "The Problem of Chronology in Claude-Nicolas Ledoux's Engraved Work." *Art Bulletin* 41 (September 1960): 191–210.

———. *Laugier and Eighteenth-Century French Theory.* London, 1962.

———. "Unknown Designs for the 'Temple of Jerusalem' by Claude Perrault." In vol. 1 of *Essays in the History of Architecture Presented to Rudolph Wittkower.* Edited by D. Fraser, H. Hibbard, and M. J. Levine. 2 vols. London, 1967.

Hobson, Marian. *The Object of Art: The Theory of Illusion in Eighteenth-Century France.* Cambridge, 1982.

Honour, Hugh. *Neo-Classicism.* Harmondsworth, 1968.

Ignatieff, Michael. *A Just Measure of Pain: The Penitentiary in the Industrial Revolution, 1750–1850.* New York, 1978.

Kalnein, W., and M. Levey. *Art and Architecture of the Eighteenth Century in France.* Harmondsworth, 1972.

Kaufmann, Emil. "Die Architekturtheorie der französischen Klassik und des Klassizismus." *Repertorium für Kunstwissenschaft* 64 (1924): 197–237.

———. "Architektonische Entwürfe aus der französischen Revolution." *Zeitschrift für bildende Kunst* 63 (1929–30): 38–46.

———. *Von Ledoux bis Le Corbusier: Ursprung und Entwicklung der Autonomen Architektur.* Vienna and Leipzig, 1933.

———. "Die Stadt des Architekten Ledoux zur Erkenntniss der Autonomen Architektur." *Kunstwissenschaftliche Forschungen* 2 (1933): 131–60.

———. "Klassizismus als Tendenz und als Epoche." *Kritische Berichte* (1933): 204–14.

———. "Claude-Nicolas Ledoux, Inaugurator of a New Architectural System." *Journal of the Society of Architectural Historians* 3 (July 1943): 15.

———. "Jean-Jacques Lequeu." *Art Bulletin* 21 (June 1949): 130–35.

———. "Three Revolutionary Architects: Boullée, Ledoux and Lequeu." *Transactions of the American Philosophical Society,* n.s., 42, pt. 3 (1953): 431–564.

———. *Architecture in the Age of Reason: Baroque and Post-Baroque in England, Italy and France.* Cambridge, Mass., 1955.

Kettering, Sharon. *Judicial Politics and Urban Revolt in Seventeenth-Century France: The Parlement of Aix, 1629–1659.* Princeton, 1978.

Kimball, Fisk, "Les influences anglaises dans la formation du style Louis XVI." *Gazette des Beaux-Arts* (January 1931): 36–39.

———. "Romantic Classicism in Architecture." *Gazette des Beaux-Arts* 25 (February 1944): 95–111.

Lagrave, Henri. *Le théâtre et le public à Paris de 1715–1750.* Paris, 1972.

Lagrave, H., et al. *La vie théâtrale à Bordeaux des origines à nos jours.* 2 vols. Paris, 1985.

Lambeau, Lucien. *Histoire des communes annexées à Paris en 1859.* 5 vols. Paris, 1910–23.

Langner, Johannes. *Claude-Nicolas Ledoux: Die erste Schaffenzeit, 1762–1774.* Thesis. Dusseldorf, 1959.

———. "Ledoux' Redaktion der eigenen Werke für die Veröffentlichung." *Zeitschrift für Kunstgeschichte* 23 (1960): 136–66.

———. "Cl.-N. Ledoux und die Fabrike," *Zeitschrifte für Kunstgeschichte* 26 (1963): 1–36.

———. "Architecture pastorale sous Louis XVI." *Art de France* (1963).

Lavaquery, Abbé E. *Le cardinal de Boisgelin.* Paris, 1921.

Leclerc, Helen. "Au théâtre de Besançon (1775–1784): Claude-Nicolas Ledoux, réformateur et précurseur de Richard Wagner." *Revue d'histoire du théâtre* 10 (1958): 103–27.

Le Clercq, Victor. "L'incendie des barrières de Paris en juillet 1789 et les procès des incendaires." *Bulletin de la Société de l'histoire de Paris et de l'Ile de France* 65 (1938): 31–48.

Lemagny, J.-C., *Visionary Architects: Boullée, Ledoux, Lequeu.* Houston, 1968.

Lemonnier, Henri, ed. *Procès-verbaux de l'Académie royale d'architecture, 1671–1793.* 10 vols. Paris, 1911–26.

Léon, A. *La Révolution française et l'éducation technique.* Paris, 1968.

Levallet-Haug, Geneviève. "L'Hôtel de Ville de Neuchâtel." *Bulletin de la Société de l'histoire de l'art français* (1933): 88–89.

———. "Les écuries de Madame du Barry." *Revue de l'histoire de Versailles et de Seine-et-Oise* 35, no. 1 (January–March 1933): 6–12.

———. *Claude-Nicolas Ledoux, 1736–1806.* Paris and Strasbourg, 1934.

Levy, Michael, and Wend Graf Kalnein. *Art and Architecture of the 18th Century in France.* London, 1972.

Lhuillier, Th. "Le château de Cramayel en Bois." *Réunion des Sociétés des Beaux-Arts des départements* (1882): 268–84.

Lough, John. *Paris Theatre Audiences in the Seventeenth and Eighteenth Centuries.* London, 1957.

May, Gita. "Diderot et Burke." *Publications of the Modern Language Association* (1960): 527–39.

Middleton, Robin. "Revolutionary Urge." *Architectural Design* 7 (1970): 359.

———. "Jacques-François Blondel and the *Cours d'architecture.*" *Journal of the Society of Architectural Historians* 17 (December 1979).

Metken, Gunther. "Jean-Jacques Lequeu ou l'architecture rêvée." *Gazette des Beaux-Arts* (April 1965): 213–30.

Mollien, François-Nicolas, Comte de. *Mémoires d'un ministre du trésor public, 1780–1815.* 2 vols. Paris, 1845.

Mosser, Monique. "Monsieur de Marigny et les jardins: Projets inédits de fabriques pour Menars." *Bulletin de la Société de l'histoire de l'art français* (1973): 269–93.

———. "The Picturesque in the City: Private Gardens in Paris in the 18th century." *Lotus International* 30 (1981): 29–38.

———. "Le rocher et la colonne: Une thème d'iconographie architecturale au XVIIIe siècle." *Revue de l'art* 58–59 (1983): 53–74.

Mosser, Monique, and Daniel Rabreau, eds. *Charles De Wailly: Peintre architecte dans l'Europe des lumières.* Exhibition catalogue. Paris, 1979.

Mosser, Monique, et al. *Alexandre-Théodore Brongniart, 1739–1813.* Paris, 1986.

Oliver, J. W. *The Life of William Beckford,* London, 1932.

Ottomeyer, H. "Autobiographies d'architectes parisiens, 1759–1811." *Bulletin de la Société de l'histoire de Paris et de l'Ile de France* (1974): 178–79.

Ozouf, Mona. "Architecture et urbanisme: L'image de la ville chez Claude-Nicolas Ledoux." *Annales E.S.C.* 21, no. 6 (November–December 1966).

———. *La fête révolutionnaire 1789–1799.* Paris, 1976.

———. *L'école de la France: Essais sur la Révolution, l'utopie et l'enseignement.* Paris, 1984.

Parker, H. T. *The Cult of Antiquity and the French Revolutionaries.* Chicago, 1937.

Perrot, Michelle, ed. *L'impossible prison: Recherches sur le système pénitentiare au XIXe siècle.* Paris, 1980.

Pérouse de Montclos, Jean-Marie. *Etienne-Louis Boullée, 1728–1799: De l'architecture classique à l'architecture révolutionnaire.* Paris, 1969.

———. "De nova stella anni 1784." *Revue de l'art* 58–59 (1983): 75–84.

———. *"Les prix de Rome": Concours de l'Académie royale d'architecture au XVIIIe siècle.* Paris, 1984.

Petzet, Michael. *Soufflot's Sainte Geneviève und der französiche Kirchenbau des 18: Jahrhunderts.* Berlin, 1961.

Pevsner, Nikolaus. *Studies in Art, Architecture and Design.* 2 vols. London, 1968.

Piranèse et les français, 1740–1790. Exhibition catalogue. Rome, 1976.

Piranèse et les français: Colloque tenu à la Villa Médicis, 12–14 Mai 1976. Rome, 1978.

Pressouyre, Sylvia. "Un ensemble néoclassique à Port-Vendres." *Monuments historiques de la France,* n.s., 19 (1963): 199–222.

Prost, Auguste. *Jacques-François Blondel et son oeuvre.* Paris, 1860.

Quérard, J.-M. "Ledoux." In *La France littéraire ou Dictionnaire bibliographique,* 5:68. Paris, 1833.

Rabreau, Daniel. "L'architecture néoclassique en France et la caution de Palladio." *Bollettino del centro internazionale di studi d'architettura Andrea Palladio* (1970): 206–17.

———. "Autour du voyage d'Italie (1750): Soufflot, Cochin et M. de Marigny réformateurs de l'architecture théâtrale française." *Bollettino del centro internazionale di studi di architettura Andrea Palladio* 17 (1975): 213–25.

———. "Le grand théâtre de Victor Louis: Des vérités, des impressions." In *Victor Louis et le théâtre: Scénographie, mise-en-scène et architecture théâtrale aux XVIIIe et XIXe siècles.* Paris, 1982.

Rabreau, Daniel, and Monique Mosser. "Paris en 1778: L'architecture en question." *Dix-Huitième Siècle* 11 (1979): 141–64.

Ravel, Marcel, and J.-Ch. Moreux. *Claude-Nicolas Ledoux, 1736–1806.* Paris, 1945.

Renouvier, J. *Histoire de l'art pendant la Révolution.* Paris, 1863.

Reutersvärd, Oscar. "The Neoclassic Temple of Virility and the Buildings with a Phallic-shaped Ground Plan." *Formae.* Studies from the Institute of Art History at the University of Lund, Sweden, 1971.

Rittaud-Hutinet, Jacques. *La vision d'un futur: Ledoux et ses théâtres.* Lyons, 1982.

Rivière, C. *Un village de Brie au XVIIIe siècle: Mauperthuis.* Paris, 1939.

Rosenau, Helen. "Claude-Nicolas Ledoux." *The Burlington Magazine* 88 (July 1946): 162–68.

———. "Stylistic Changes and their Social Background." *Town Planning Review* 22 (1952): 311–19.

———. *Boullée's Treatise on Architecture.* London, 1953.

———. "French Academic Architecture, c. 1774–1790." *Journal of the Royal Institute of British Architects,* 3d ser., 67 (December 1959): 56–61.

———. "The Engravings of the *Grands Prix* of the French Academy of Architecture." *Architectural History* (1960).

———. "Boullée and Ledoux as Town-Planners: A Reassessment." *Gazette des Beaux-Arts,* ser. 6, 63 (March 1964): 173–90.

———. "The Functional and the Ideal in Late-Eighteenth-Century French Architecture." *Architectural Review* 140, no. 836 (October 1966): 253–58.

Rosenblum, Robert. *Transformations in Late-Eighteenth-Century Art,* Princeton, 1967.

Schapiro, Meyer. "The New Viennese School." *The Art Bulletin* 18, no. 2 (June 1936): 258–66.

Schiefenbusch, Erna. "L'influence de Jean-Jacques Rousseau sur les Beaux-Arts en France." *Annales de la Société Jean-Jacques Rousseau* 19 (1929–30).

Schoy, Auguste. *L'art architectural, décoratif, industriel et somptuaire de l'époque Louis XVI.* Liège and Paris, 1868.

Sedlmayr, Hans. *Art in Crisis: The Lost Center.* London, 1956.

Sicard, Augustin. *Les études classiques avant la Révolution.* Paris, 1887.

Silvestre de Sacy, Jacques. *Alexandre-Théodore Brongniart (1739–1813), sa vie et son oeuvre.* Paris, 1940.

Sirén, O. "Le désert de Retz." *The Architectural Review* 106 (November 1949): 327ff.

Snyders, George. *La pédagogie en France au XVIIe et XVIIIe siècles.* Paris, 1965.

Soufflot et l'architecture des lumières: Actes du colloque. Paris, 1980.

Soufflot et son temps, 1780–1980. Exhibition catalogue. Paris, 1980.

Starobinski, Jean. *L'invention de la liberté.* Geneva, 1961.

———. *1789: Les emblèmes de la Raison.* Paris, 1973.

Steinhauser, Monika, and Daniel Rabreau. "Le théâtre de l'Odéon de Charles De Wailly et Marie-Joseph Peyre, 1767–1782." *Revue de l'art* 19 (1973): 9–49.

Stern, Jean. *A l'ombre de Sophie Arnould, François Bélanger.* 2 vols. Paris, 1930.

Szambien, Werner. "Aux origines de l'enseignement de Durand: Les cent soixante-huit croquis des Rudimenta Operis Magni et Disciplinae." *Etudes de la revue de Louvre* 1 (1980): 122–30.

———. *Jean-Nicolas-Louis Durand, 1760–1834: De l'imitation à la norme.* Paris, 1984.

———. *Symétrie, goût, caractère: Théorie et teminologie de l'architecture à l'âge classique, 1550–1800.* Paris, 1986.

———. *Les projets de l'an II, concours d'architecture de la période révolutionnaire.* Paris, 1986.

Tafuri, Manfredo. "Simbolo e ideologia nell'architettura dell'illuminismo." *Communità* 124–25 (November-December 1964).

———. "*Architettura artificialis:* Claude Perrault, Sir Christopher Wren e il dibatto sul linguaggio architettonico." In *Barocco europeo, barocco italiano, barocco salentino: Atti di Congresso Internazionale sul Barocco* (Lecce, 1969): 375–98.

Taton, René, ed., *Enseignement et diffusion des sciences en France au XVIIIe siècle.* Paris, 1964.

Teyssot, Georges. *George Dance il giovane: Architettura e utopia nell-'Illuminismo inglese.* Rome, 1974.

————. "Neoclassic and 'Autonomous' Architecture: The Formalism of Emil Kaufmann." *Architectural Design* 51, no. 6–7 (1981): 24–29.

Tournier, René. *Les église Comtoises: Leur architecture des origines au XVIIIe siècle*. Paris, 1954.

[Vaudoyer, Léon]. *Magasin pittoresque* 20 (1852): 388ff.

Vernus, Michel. *La vie comtoise au temps de l'ancien régime*. 2 vols. Lons-le-Saunier, 1983–85.

Vidler, Anthony. "The Architecture of the Lodges: Ritual Form and Associational Life in the Late Enlightenment." *Oppositions* 5 (Summer 1976): 76–97.

————. *Ledoux,* Paris, 1987.

————. *The Writing of the Walls: Architectural Theory in the Late Enlightenment*. Princeton, 1987.

Vovelle, Michel. *L'irrésistible ascension de Joseph Sec, bourgeois d'Aix*. Aix-en-Provence, 1975.

Wade, Ira O. "The Search for a New Voltaire." *Transactions of the American Philosophical Society,* n.s. 48 (1958): 94–105.

Weulersse, Georges. *Le mouvement physiocratique en France (de 1756 à 1770)*. Paris, 1910.

————. *La physiocratie sous les ministères de Turgot et de Necker (1774–1781)*. Paris, 1950.

Wiebenson, Dora. *Sources of Greek Revival Architecture,* London, 1969.

————. *The Picturesque Garden in France*. Princeton, 1978.

Wolff, Louis. *Le parlement de Provence au XVIIIe siècle*. Aix-en-Provence, 1920.

Waquet, J. C. *Les grands maîtres des eaux et forêts*. Paris, 1978.

Wittkower, Rudolph. "English Neo-palladianism: The landscape garden, China and the Enlightenment." *L'arte* (6 June 1969): 18–35.

5. Salines and Salt in the *Ancien Régime*

Actes du colloque sur la forêt (Besançon, 1966). Paris, 1967.

Ancelon, Etienne-A. "Historique de l'exploitation du sel en Lorraine" [1871]. *Mémoires de l'académie de Metz* 58–59 (1876–78): 145–222.

————. "Recherches historiques et archéologiques sur les salines d'Amelécourt et de Château-Salins." *Mémoires de la Société d'archéologie Lorraine et du musée historique Lorraine*. 3d ser., 7 (Nancy, 1880): 98–134.

Bacquié, F. *Les inspecteurs des manufactures sous l'ancien régime, 1669–1791*. Toulouse, 1927.

Baud, Paul. "Une industrie d'état sous l'ancien régime: L'exploitation des salines de Tarentaise." *R.H.E.S.* (Paris, 1936): 149ff.

Blanchard, M. "Le sel de France en Savoie (XVIIe et XVIIIe siècles)." *Annales d'histoire économique et sociale* 9 (1937): 417–28.

Bouvard, André. *La saline de Montmorot au XVIIIe siècle*. Mémoire de Diplôme d'études supérieures. Besançon, 1967.

Boyé, Pierre, *Les salines et le sel en Lorraine au XVIIIe siècle*. Nancy, 1901.

Brelot, C.-I., and R. Locatelli. *Les salines de Salins: Un millénaire d'exploitation du sel en Franche-Comté*. Besançon, 1981.

Cousin, Jean. "L'Académie des sciences, belles-lettres et arts de Besançon au XVIIIe siècle et son oeuvre scientifique." *Revue d'histoire des sciences* 12, no. 4 (October–December 1959): 327–44.

Debry, Jean. "Sur le commerce et l'industrie du département du Doubs." *Annales des arts et manufactures* 22 (1805):8–10.

Dubois, H. "L'activité de la saunerie de Salins au XVe siècle d'après le comte de 1459." *Le Moyen Age* (1964): 419–71.

Eon de Beaumont, Chevalier d'. *Les loisirs du chevalier d'Eon*. 9 vols. Amsterdam, 1775.

Fenouillot de Falbaire de Quingey, Charles-Georges. "Supplément à l'article des salines de Franche-Comté, Saline de Chaux." In *Oeuvres de M. de Falbaire de Quingey,* 352–58, Paris, 1787.

————. "Salines." In *Encyclopédie méthodique: Arts et métiers mécaniques,* 7:130–60. 8 vols. Paris, 1790.

Gille, Bertrand. *Les origines de la grande industrie métallurgique en France*. Paris, 1947.

Gréau, E. *Le sel en Lorraine*. Paris and Nancy, 1908.

Hauser, H. "Le sel dans l'histoire." *Revue économique internationale* 3 (1927): 270–87.

Hottenger, G. *Les anciennes salines domaniales de l'est: Histoire monopole (1790–1840)*. Nancy, 1929.

Jars, Gabriel. *Voyages métallurgiques*. Lyons, 1774.

Karmin, Otto. *La question du sel pendant la Révolution*. Paris, 1912.

Lacroix, Pierre. *La saline d'Arc-et-Senans et les techniques de canalisation en bois: Notes d'histoire comtoise*. Lons-le-Saunier, 1970.

Lecreulx, François-Michel. *Examen de la propriété des salines nationales et sources salées des départements de l'Est et des avantages que l'état peut en tirer*. Nancy, 1799.

Lédontal, Abbé. *Arc-et-Senans à travers les âges*. Besançon, 1927.

Lefebvre, Eugène. *Le sel*. Paris, 1882.

Léquinio de Kerblay, J.-M. *Voyage pittoresque et physico-économique dans le Jura*. 2 vols. Paris, 1801.

Mazoyer, L. "Exploitation forestière et conflits sociaux en Franche-Comté à la fin de l'Ancien Régime." *Annales E.S.C.* 4 (1932): 339ff.

Mollat, Michel, ed. *Le rôle du sel dans l'histoire*. Paris, 1968.

Monniot, S. "Le rôle de la forêt dans la vie des populations Franc-comtoises de la conquête française à la Révolution, 1674–1789." *Revue d'histoire moderne* (September–December 1937): 449ff.

Nicolas, Pierre-François. *Mémoire sur les salines de la République*. Nancy, 179. Reprinted as "D'un mémoire sur les salines nationales des départements de la Meurthe, du Jura, du Doubs et du Mont-Blanc." *Annales de chimie* 20 (1797): 78–188.

Nicot, Guy. "Les salines d'Arc-et-Senans." *Monuments historiques de la France* no. 2 (1978): 33–48.

Pingeron, J.-P. "Lettre sur la saline de Dieuze." *Journal Encyclopédique* 8 (1771): 275–83.

Piroux [architect]. *Mémoire sur le sel et les salines de Lorraine*. Nancy, 1791.

Polti, Julien. "Les salines d'Arc et Senans." *Monuments historiques de la France* (1938):17–27.

Prinet, Max. *L'industrie du sel en Franche-Comté avant la conquête française*. Besançon, 1900.

Scoville, Warren. *Capitalism and French Glass-Making, 1640–1789*. Berkeley, 1950.

Tournier, René. "L'ancienne saline royale d'Arc." *Revue Franche-Comté, Monts-Jura et Haute-Alsace* (March 1930): 36–39.

Traité pour la construction d'une saline en Franche-Comté, son exploitation et celle des autres salines de la même province, et les salines de Lorraine et des Trois Evêchés, pendant quatre-vingt-quatre années. Paris, 1774.

Trudaine de Montigny, Jean-Charles-Philibert. "Mémoire sur les salines de Franche-Comté, sur les défauts des sels en pain qu'on y dé-bite, et sur les moyens de les corriger" 21 April 1762. *Mémoires de l'Académie royale des sciences* (1764): 102–30.

Vion-Delphin, François. "Salines et administration forestière en Franche-Comté à la fin du XVIIIe siècle: Exemple des salines de Chaux." In *99e congrès national des sociétés savantes, Besançon, 1974. Section d'histoire moderne*, 2:181–90. 2 vols. Besançon, 1976.

Willier, Simon [Simon Vuillier]. *Réponse au mémoire sur les salines de Lorraine, des Trois-Evêchés et de Franche-Comté*. Dôle, 1790.

———. *Ma profession de foi sur les salines*. Dôle, 1790.

———. *Ultimatum sur les salines locales*. Dôle, 1790.

6. Rural Life in Franche-Comté

Bourde, Andre-J. *Agronomie et agronomes en France au XVIIIe siècle*. 3 vols. Paris, 1967.

Cointereaux, François. *Ecole d'architecture rurale ou leçons par lesquelles on apprendra soi-même à bâtir solidement les maisons . . . avec la terre seule*. Paris, 1790.

Girardin, René-L de. *De la composition des paysages ou des moyens d'embellir la nature autour des habitations, en joignant l'agréable à l'utile*. Geneva and Paris, 1777.

Lezay-Marnésia, Claude-François-Adrien. *Essai sur la nature champêtre, poème*. Paris, 1787.

Mandrou, Robert. *De la culture populaire aux 17e et 18e siècles*. Paris, 1964.

Monnier, Desiré. *Les jurassiens recommandables*. Lons-le-Saunier, 1828.

Perthuis, M. *Traité d'architecture rurale, contenant les principes généraux de cet art*. Paris, 1810.

Poitrineau, Abel. *La vie rurale en Basse-Auvergne au XVIIIe siècle, 1726–1789*. Paris, 1966.

———. "La fête traditionnelle." *Annales historiques de la Révolution française* 221 (July–September 1975).

Proust, Jacques. "La fête chez Rousseau et chez Diderot." *Annales de la Société Jean-Jacques Rousseau* 37 (1966–68): 175–96.

Rigoley de Juvigny, Jean-Antoine. *Art du charbonnier*. Paris, 1775.

Teyssot, Georges. "Cottages et pittoresque: Les origines du logement ouvrier en Angleterre, 1781–1818." *Architecture, Mouvement, Continuité* 34 (1974): 26–37.